Praise for *At Day's C*

A *Discover* Magazine Top Science Boo

An *Observer* Book of the Year, 2005

"Professor Ekirch has produced a book of exceptional range and originality. His investigation of *nocturnes* in pre-modern civilization spans literature and social history, psychology and the history of thought. This is a pioneering achievement of a rare order. It truly casts light on absolutely vital spheres of darkness." —George Steiner

"What happened at night in times past? Who did what at night? How did people cope with darkness and the perils of violence and fire? What were the rhythms of sleep and the forms of nighttime sociability and intimacy? Ekirch illuminates the world of darkness in early modern Europe and America with clarity and rich documentation. *At Day's Close* is the result of years of study, and it's a revelation."

—Bernard Bailyn, Harvard University,
Adams University Professor Emeritus

"For Ekirch, the night has been a hubbub of activity, a sequence of comings and goings, a bustling fiefdom with its own distinct customs and rituals. . . . To a remarkable degree, he has reclaimed that portion of the circadian cycle which historians have traditionally neglected. Ekirch has emptied night's pockets, and laid the contents out before us. . . . *At Day's Close* serves to remind us of night's ancient mystery."

—Arthur Krystal, *The New Yorker*

"An enthralling anthropology of the shadow realms of Western Europe from the late Middle Ages to the Industrial Revolution. . . . [Ekirch] weaves his own Bayeux tapestry, but instead of stories of warrior bishops and court dwarfs, he wants to tell us about privacy and police power, torture and summary courts, the physiology of sleep, the sociology of prostitution, and political and religious heresies. . . . An informed and passionate case against too much artificial light." —John Leonard, *Harper's*

"A book that anybody with any imagination will find fascinating, but one that is the mirror image of conventional popular history. . . . Wonderful, for Ekirch spares no pains to rediscover the lost world of the dark. . . . [It is] a book that can't be summarized but must be experienced."

—David Wootton, *London Review of Books*

"Absorbing . . . fascinating. . . . [Ekirch] has plundered an extraordinary range of cross-cultural sources for his material, and he tells us about everything from witches to firefighting, architecture to domestic violence. . . . [A] monumental study."

—Terry Eagleton, *The Nation*

"Engrossing, leisurely paced, and richly researched. . . . He provides fascinating insight into nocturnal labor. . . . A rich weave of citation and archival evidence, Ekirch's narrative is rooted in the material realities of the past, evoking a bygone world of extreme physicality and pre-industrial survival stratagems."

—*Publishers Weekly*

"A tour de force. Throwing shafts of light onto nocturnal life—its dangers, intimacies, rituals, rhythms, laboring patterns, class affiliations, and gradual transformation—reveals a whole new world only dimly seen before. Thanks to this pathbreaking and compelling work, pre-industrial nighttime now has a history."

—Philip Morgan, Harry C. Black Professor of History,
Johns Hopkins University

"Delightful details fill Ekirch's narrative of the night."

—*Discover*

"To us today, nightfall is a time to turn on the lights. But of course it was not always so. Ekirch's richly researched and entertaining study, *At Day's Close*, reclaims for history the half of past lives that was lived at night: in partial or total darkness, at work and at play, in stillness and in motion, in solitude or in shared reflection. Perfect reading for insomniacs and stargazers alike."

—Jonathan Spence, Sterling Professor of History, Yale University

"Night and day Ekirch's history of darkness is the one—massive, original, and completely enlightening."

—Steven Ozment, McLean Professor of Ancient and Modern History, Harvard University

"A fresh and thought-provoking cultural inquiry. . . . Maintaining throughout an infectious sense of wonder, Ekirch ignites the reader's imagination. . . . [He] vividly evokes the old magic of true night."

—Donna Seaman, *Booklist*, starred review

"A wonderfully monomaniacal undertaking: a study of how night affected (mainly) European societies before the advent of street and, in certain instances, domestic lighting. Ekirch is folklorist, criminologist, psychologist. The mass of graphic detail is gripping."

—Jonathan Meades, *The Observer*

"*At Day's Close* is uncommonly welcome, for it covers ground that just about all others have ignored. . . . [Ekirch] writes exceptionally well. . . . The range of his research is both broad and deep."

—Jonathan Yardley, *Washington Post*

"*At Day's Close* is the best sort of bottom-up history, taking nighttime—half of existence—and rendering it new and strange and full of marvels."

—Fritz Lanham, *Houston Chronicle*

"Wise and compendious. . . . Ekirch's command of the material is impressive. . . . It truly is a labor of love." —Ian Pindar, *The Guardian*

"A triumph of social history. Almost every page contains something to surprise the reader. . . . The great achievement of *At Day's Close* is precisely its invasion of privacy: it shines a torch through the curtains of our ancestors and gives us a glimpse of them at their most vulnerable. Watching them blink back is one of the most enjoyable literary experiences of the year."

—Damian Thompson, *Mail on Sunday*

"A magisterial history of nighttime." —Jay Walljasper, *Ode Magazine*

"Night-time has been curiously ignored by social historians. This fine book, the fruit of 20 years' diurnal and nocturnal work by an American professor of history, corrects that lack. . . . Entertaining and informative."

—Ross Leckie, *Sunday Times*

"A glorious book. . . . Captivating." —*De Morgen* (Brussels)

"A fascinating panorama of social history." —*Wirtschaftsblatt* (Vienna)

"In his fascinating survey of the dark hours of the pre-industrial era, A. Roger Ekirch takes us deep into an age when the very lack of light threw life into confusion. . . . Ekirch's profound understanding of the period provides such enlightening details. . . . This engrossing book illuminates the darker recesses of the past." —Philip Hoare, *Sunday Telegraph*

"Meticulously researched. . . . *At Day's Close* is a splendid book. . . . [It is] great entertainment, and to social historians it will be of immense value."

—Sir Patrick Moore, *Times Higher Education Supplement*

"A vivid panorama of nighttime customs in city and country, among peasants and courtiers. . . . *At Day's Close* relentlessly makes clear how much our comforts separate us from previous generations—and how much our conquest of night has cost us in fellowship and imagination. . . . Stands with other pioneering scholarship on natural phenomena . . . that has taught us how much culture needs nature, perhaps more than the other way around." —William Howarth, *Preservation*

"*At Day's Close* . . . has been getting some of the most enthusiastic reviews of the year. This is the sort of life's work that you wish every book could be. . . . The result is a vivid account, rich in surprising anecdote. . . . [It is] the sort of book that, paradoxically, brings the past closer by showing how radically different it was from our own time. You'll never look at nighttime the same way once you've read it."

—Tom Nissley, senior editor, Amazon.com

"This innovative, scholarly book offers a fresh perspective on early modern Europe. . . . Gracefully written and richly illustrated." —S. Bailey, *Choice*

"A can't-put-down volume. . . . Ekirch succeeds marvelously."
—Jackie Loohauis, *Milwaukee Journal Sentinel*

"[Ekirch] carries us into the night, both literally and metaphorically. . . . A truly valuable book."
—Jane Davis, *Decatur Daily*

"*At Day's Close* is not only distinct (one is hard-pressed to think of another book like it) but also consistently entertaining. . . . An elegy for times past."
—Bill Eichenberger, *Columbus Dispatch*

"Rigorously researched. . . . An impressively original book. Ekirch's primary achievement here is in giving the distinct culture of night its first real history, and cataloging what strange creatures we become after dark."
—Brad Quinn, *Daily Yomiuri* (Tokyo)

"Rhythmic and often poetic prose. . . . A fascinating book. . . . We have forgotten what that dark reign was like, but *At Day's Close* does a marvelous job of bringing it back to life for us."
—Andrew Hudgins, *Raleigh News & Observer*

"Now and then a book can be called amazing. Here is such a book."
—Ron Kirbyson, *Winnipeg Free Press Review*

At DAY'S CLOSE

NIGHT IN TIMES PAST

A. Roger Ekirch

W. W. NORTON & COMPANY
New York London

Frontispiece: Peter Paul Rubens, *Return from the Fields*, seventeenth century.

Printed in the United States of America
First published as a Norton paperback 2006

Manufacturing by LSC Harrisonburg
Book design by Rhea Braunstein
Production manager: Andrew Marasia

Library of Congress Cataloging-in-Publication Data

Ekirch, A. Roger, 1950–
At day's close : night in times past / A. Roger Ekirch.—1st ed.
p. cm.
Includes bibliographical references and index.
ISBN 0-393-05089-0 (hardcover)
1. Social history. 2. Night—History. 3. Night—Social aspects. I. Title.
HN8.E48 2005
306.4—dc22

2005002784

ISBN-13: 978-0-393-32901-8 pbk.
ISBN-10: 0-393-32901-1 pbk.

W. W. Norton & Company, Inc., 500 Fifth Avenue, New York, N.Y. 10110
www.wwnorton.com

W. W. Norton & Company Ltd., 15 Carlisle Street, London W1D 3BS

0

FOR ALEXANDRA, SHELDON, AND CHRISTIAN

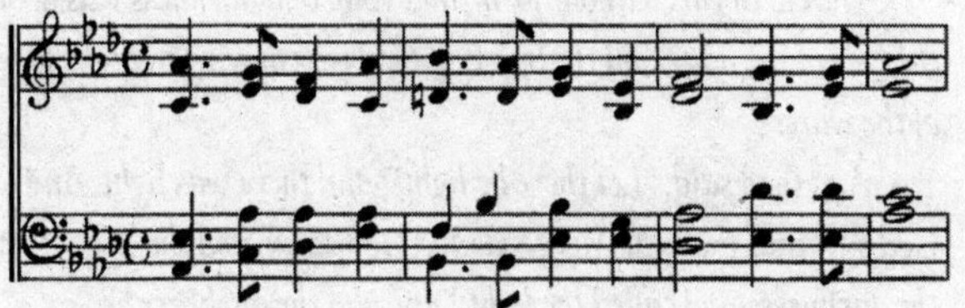

In the beginning God created the heavens and the earth.

The earth was without form, and void, and darkness was upon the face of the deep; and the Spirit of God was moving over the face of the waters.

And God said, "Let there be light"; and there was light. And God saw that the light was good; and God separated the light from the darkness. God called the light Day, and the darkness he called Night.

GENESIS 1:1–5

CONTENTS

PART FOUR: PRIVATE WORLDS

ILLUSTRATIONS

COLOR ILLUSTRATIONS

(appear between pages 192 and 193)

ACKNOWLEDGMENTS

"YOU JUST GO too slow," my smiling ten-year-old daughter, Sheldon, teased recently about the pace of my writing. If only the words had come more easily! That I have not taken longer is owing to the help of friends and family coupled with the kindness of institutions on both sides of the Atlantic Ocean. The inspiration for this book came many years ago from André-Philippe Katz, a close friend in graduate school. Despite our plans to collaborate, other responsibilities prevented his participation. The book would have benefited enormously from his remarkable intellect and imagination.

Financial assistance for research and writing originated from a variety of sources. I am profoundly grateful to the National Endowment for the Humanities; the John Simon Guggenheim Memorial Foundation; the American Council of Learned Societies; the American Philosophical Society; the Virginia Center for the Humanities; and the American Historical Association. Virginia Tech generously provided research assistance and leaves from teaching.

Over the past two decades, I relied upon the staffs and resources of many splendid institutions. I am indebted to the Public Record Office (formerly at Chancery Lane as well as Kew); the British Library; the Guildhall Records Office in London; the British Library of Political & Economic Science at the London School of Economics; the Bodleian Library of Oxford University; the Cambridge University Library; St. John's College, Cambridge; Chetham's Library in Manchester; the record offices of Dorset and Hertfordshire; the Hereford City Library; the District Central Library in Rawtensall; the Somerset Archaeological and Natural History Society; the Bristol Central Library; the Department of Irish Folklore at University College Dublin; the National Library of Scotland and the Scottish Record Office, both in Edinburgh; the University of Wales, Bangor; the National Library of Wales in Aberystwyth; and the Archives Geneve. In the United States, I am grateful to the Library of Congress; Alderman Library at the University of Virginia; the Earl Gregg Swem Library at the College of William and Mary; the New York Public Library; the Beinecke Library at Yale University; the Lewis Walpole Library; the North Haven (Connecticut) Historical Society; the Bennington (Vermont) Historical Society; the Harvard University Law School Library; Houghton Library at Harvard; and the Suffolk County Court House in Boston. At the Library of Virginia in Richmond, I owe a special debt of gratitude to Sandra G. Treadway and her colleagues. Still other institutions, identified elsewhere, supplied the book's artwork. They have my deep appreciation.

Closer to home, I benefited from the diligence and generosity of the staff of Newman Library at Virginia Tech, including the late Dorothy F. McCombs, Bruce Pencek, and, most of all, Sharon Gotkiewicz, Lucy Cox, Janet R. Bland, Nancy Weaver, Michele Canterbury, Robert Kelley, and others in the interlibrary loan office headed by Harry M. Kriz. They worked tirelessly on my behalf and always with good cheer. Thanks also to Annette Burr for her expertise in art history. Ruth Lipnik Johnson and Becky Woodhouse at the Roanoke County Public Library were tremendous assets. I am grateful to the Church of Jesus Christ of Latter-Day Saints for the use of their genealogical facilities in Salem. I wish to thank Rabbi Manes Kogan for letting me consult the fine library at Beth Israel Synagogue in Roanoke.

A small legion of translators enabled me to canvass a broad range of non-English sources, far beyond my own limited command of French and Latin. Of vital help were Cornelia Bade, Trudy Harrington Becker, Maebhe Ní Bhroin, Blanton Brown, Michel Dammron, Doreen Ebert, Christopher J. Eustis, Dinia Fatine, Jennifer Hayek, Christine Huzil, Berwyn Prys Jones, Andy Klatt, Rabbi Manes Kogan, Keun Pal Lee, Francesca Lorusso-Caputi, William L. McKone, Michele McNabb, Annick Mikailoff, Violaine Morand, Luciano Nardone, Sera Oner, Lida Ouwehand, Joseph Pierro,

Shannon Prince, Haingonirina Ramaroson, Alexander Shaffer, Carey Smith, Giuliana E. Taylor, and Naomi de Wolf.

Colleagues at Virginia Tech who assisted my research and writing included Linda Arnold, Mark V. Barrow, Jr., Glenn R. Bugh, David Burr, the late Albert E. Moyer, Steven Soper, Robert Stephens, Peter Wallenstein, Joseph L. Wieczynski, and Young-tsu Wong. Most of all, Frederic J. Baumgartner lent a helping hand, answering repeated questions and drawing my attention to useful sources. He and Richard F. Hirsh both took the time, at any early stage, to read the manuscript. Linda Fountaine, Janet Francis, and Rhonda Pennington all made this project easier, as did a number of students, whether in sharing their insights, scanning illustrations, or volunteering references. I thank especially Sarah Taylor, Jamie Rife, Anne Elizabeth Wohlcke, David Ferro, Estare Alston, Bridgett Dehart, Nicole Evans, Doris Johnson, Eric Robertson, Al Harrison, Larry McCall, and Carlton Spinner. Soo Kang logged countless hours helping me to wade through eighteenth-century newspapers on microfilm, and Lindsay Metts chased down loose ends in Charlottesville. Jason Cruff kindly assisted in organizing my sources. Keith Wilder provided expert help in Edinburgh.

Many friends and professional acquaintances shared references or research of one sort or another. I am grateful to James Axtell, Jonathan Barry, Sharon Block, Mark J. Bouman, Amy Turner Bushnell, Cary Carson, John E. Crowley, David Dauer, Cornelia Dayton, Carl B. Estabrook, Paul Finkelman, Jan Garnert, Karla Girona, David D. Hall, Barbara Hanawalt, Ruth Wallis Herndon, William Lee Holladay, Marja Holmila, Steven C. Hughes, Craig Koslofsky, Allan Kugel, Michael Meranze, Kathryn Mary Olesko, David Smolen, John M. Staudenmaier, SJ, Keith Thomas, and Marc Weissbluth. Robert Gifford and Jennifer Veitch addressed my questions about interior lighting. The clinical insights of Thomas A. Wehr were immensely helpful as I tried to unravel the complexities of preindustrial sleep.

As always, Jack P. Greene was a welcome voice of encouragement, as was George Steiner. Timothy H. Breen, Richard S. Dunn, and Joanna Innes lent their aid early on. Bernard Bailyn, from the book's inception, helped mightily. I greatly appreciate the references he shared but, even more, his expressions of support and enthusiasm, which were instrumental to the completion of my research. Numerous friends in the profession devoted their time to reading the manuscript, either the full text or selected chapters. For their advice and criticism, I owe much to Thomas Brennan, Robert J. Brugger, Peter Clark, Thomas V. Cohen, Rudolph Dekker, Paul Griffiths, Gilbert Kelly, A. Lynn Martin, Philip D. Morgan, Sara Tilghman Nalle, Paul F. Paskoff, Bruce R. Smith, and Daniel J. Wilson. They helped me tremendously. Joyce and Richard Wolkomir provided intellectual stimulus with their probing questions. In addition, I am grateful for the comments I received when presenting portions of my research at Johns Hopkins University, Louisiana State University, Ohio State University, the State University of New York at Albany, and the University of Sydney. I also gave a talk at the (now) Omohundro Institute of Early American History and Culture during the year that I served as visiting editor of publications. I am indebted to the staff of the Institute and, most particularly, to Thad W. Tate for the many kindnesses I received during my stay. A small portion of my research previously appeared as an article, "Sleep We Lost: Pre-industrial Slumber in the British Isles," in the April 2001 issue of the *American Historical Review*. I am grateful to members of the *AHR* staff, especially Allyn Roberts and Michael Grossberg.

For their valuable aid, I express my warm appreciation to my exceptional editor, Alane Salierno Mason, along with Alessandra Bastagli, Mary Helen Willett, Janet Byrne, Eleen Cheung, Neil Hoos, Evan Carver, and so many others at Norton. I am indebted to Ede Rothaus for her knowledgeable help with the artwork. Georges and Valerie Borchardt were critical to the book's progress. I am deeply appreciative to Georges for his wisdom and good will. I would also like to pay tribute to several old friends: Clyde and Vickie Perdue, John and Mary Carlin, Mary Jane Elkins and her late husband, Bill, and Carolyn and Eddie Hornick. Tobie Cruff was a bulwark for both my wife, Alice, and me.

In 1697, the French expatriate Thomas D'Urfey wrote that "night, love and fate rule the world's grand affairs." Certainly, for the better part of two decades, "night" and family have ruled mine. My late parents, Arthur and Dorothy Ekirch, were enormously supportive, as were my sisters, Cheryl and Caryl, and their husbands, Frank and George. My parents-in-law, Keun Pal and Soon Lee, opened their home—and their hearts—during my frequent forays to the Library of Congress. I should also like to thank Anna, Don, Annette, David, and their families. I relied shamelessly upon Don and David for their medical insights. Alice, who does so much good in her own work, repeatedly came to my rescue in the course of this book. For that and so much more, I am profoundly blessed.

Shortly after my arrival in Blacksburg nearly thirty years ago, a wise senior colleague reflected that most academics, as they advance in age, think not of their books but of their children. This book is dedicated with love to Alexandra, Sheldon, and Christian, ever in my thoughts, past, present, and for all tomorrows to come.

PREFACE

Let the night teach us what we are, and the day what we should be.

THOMAS TRYON, 1691[1]

THIS BOOK sets out to explore the history of nighttime in Western society before the advent of the Industrial Revolution. My chief interest lies in the way of life people fashioned after dark in the face of both real and supernatural perils. Notwithstanding major studies on crime and witchcraft, night, in its own right, has received scant attention, principally due to the longstanding presumption that little else of consequence transpired. "No occupation but sleepe, feed, and fart," to quote the Jacobean poet Thomas Middleton, might best express this traditional mindset. With the exception of enterprising scholars in Europe, historians have neglected the primeval passage from daylight to darkness, especially before the modern era. Nighttime has remained a *terra incognita* of peripheral concern, the forgotten half of the human experience, even though families spent long hours in obscurity. "We are blind half of our lives," observed Jean-Jacques Rousseau in *Emile* (1762).[2]

Rather than a backdrop to daily existence, or a natural hiatus, nighttime in the early modern age instead embodied a distinct culture, with many of its own customs and rituals. As a mark of its special nature, darkness in Britain and America was frequently known as the "night season." Night and day, of course, shared qualities in common, and many differences were a matter of degree and intensity. But along with alterations in diet and health, dress, travel and communication, significant changes arose in social encounters, work rhythms, and popular mores, including attitudes toward magic, sexuality, law, and hierarchical authority. Not only, then, does this book challenge longstanding assumptions about the past scale of nocturnal activity, but it also seeks to resurrect a rich and vibrant culture very different from daily reality, an "alternate reign," as an English poet put it. More than that, darkness, for the greater part of humankind, afforded a sanctuary from ordinary existence, the chance, as shadows lengthened, for men and women to express inner impulses and realize repressed desires both in their waking hours and in their dreams, however innocent or sinister in nature. A time, fundamentally, of liberation and renewal, night gave free rein to the goodhearted as well as the wicked, forces both salutary and malignant in ordinary existence. "Night knows no shame," affirmed a proverb. Despite widespread dangers, multitudes drew fresh strength from the setting sun.[3]

At Day's Close consists of twelve chapters, divided into four parts. Part One, "In the Shadow of Death," focuses on night's perils. Threats to body and soul expanded and intensified after dark. Probably never before in Western history had evening appeared more menacing. Part Two, "Laws of Nature," is devoted to both official and popular responses to nighttime. I begin by examining a variety of repressive measures, from curfews to watchmen, designed by church and state to curb nocturnal activity. Only toward the eighteenth century did cities and towns take half-steps to render public spaces accessible at night. By necessity, ordinary folk, at home and abroad, relied upon magic, Christianity, and natural lore to counter the darkness in urban and rural areas. This complex matrix of popular conventions and beliefs sets the stage for the remarkable undercurrent of activity in communities after sunset. Part Three, "Benighted Realms," probes the haunts of men and women at work and play. Shrouded interiors weakened social constraints, creating spheres of intimacy among family, friends, and lovers. If evening, for most, was a time of personal freedom, it exerted special appeal for classes at opposite ends of the social spectrum. Successive chapters examine night's multi-faceted importance for both patricians and plebeians. After dark, power shifted from the mighty to the meek. Sleep, the farthest refuge from the throes of daily life, forms the basis of Part Four. "Private Worlds" analyzes bedtime rituals and sleep disturbances, as well as a pattern of slumber, dominant since time immemorial, whereby preindustrial households awakened in the dead of night. Families rose to urinate, smoke tobacco, and even visit close neighbors. Many others made love, prayed, and, most important historically, reflected on their dreams, a significant source of solace and self-awareness. Finally, the book's epilogue, "Cock-Crow," analyzes the demystification of darkness under way in cities and large towns by the mid-eighteenth century. The foundation, even then, was laid for our modern "twenty-four/seven" society, with profound consequences for personal security and freedom.

This narrative of nocturnal life covers Western Europe from Scandinavia to the Mediterranean. The British Isles form the heart of my inquiry, but extensive material is included from across the Continent. In addition, I have incorporated relevant information from early America and Eastern Europe. The book's time period is equally broad, stretching from the late Middle Ages to the early nineteenth century, though the principal focus is the early modern era (ca. 1500–1750). That said, I make occasional reference to both the medieval and ancient worlds, drawing comparisons as well as contrasts to earlier practices and beliefs. Although many developments explored in this book were unique to the early modern era, some clearly were not. Seen from that perspective, this study represents a more extended exploration of nocturnal life in preindustrial times than ever I anticipated.

By the same token, my research has occasionally benefited from the ground-level insights of Humphrey O'Sullivan, Émile Guillaumin, and other close observers of rural life in the nineteenth century. I strongly subscribe to the historical viewpoint that the values and traditions of many agrarian regions in Europe and America did not significantly change until the late 1800s, with the expansion of transportation and commerce. As Thomas Hardy wrote in *Tess of the d'Urbervilles* (1891), "a gap of two hundred years" separated the worldviews of Tess and her mother—"when they were together the Jacobean and the Victorian ages were juxtaposed."[4]

Uniformities in nocturnal life, across time and space, often outweighed variations during the early modern period. Nocturnal culture was by no means monolithic, but people were more alike in their attitudes and conventions than they were different. Just as preindustrial folk, after dark, shared common fears, so did many act in similar ways. Besides persuading me to structure the book thematically, this realization reinforced my view of night's fundamental importance. Such was the impact of this natural cycle that it frequently transcended differences in culture and time. When significant deviations did arise, such as in forms of courtship or artificial lighting, I have explored these in the text. But not until the eighteenth century would nocturnal life anywhere be markedly transformed, and then only in cities and towns. In fact, often more influential in preceding years than temporal or regional differences were differences rooted in social position and gender, in addition to divisions between town and country.

My research draws from a broad range of sources, as one might suspect for such a ubiquitous subject. Most valuable have been personal documents—letters, memoirs, travel accounts, and diaries. Despite its breadth, the book, in large measure, is constructed around the lives of individual men and women. Diaries, especially, have permitted this for members of the middle and upper classes. For information regarding the lower orders, I have mined rich veins of legal depositions along with a small number of diaries and autobiographies. An unparalleled source for urban street life has been the *Old Bailey Session Papers*, eighteenth-century pamphlets that chronicled trials at London's chief criminal court. For traditional beliefs and values, wide use has been made of glossaries, dictionaries, and, most of all, collections of proverbs. "There's the peasant's creed," observed a French priest of proverbs—"the learning he has ripened and assimilated to the innermost recesses of his soul."[5] To help explore different strata of thought, I have examined a wealth of both "high" literature and "low," not just poetry, plays, and novels but also ballads, fables, and chapbooks. All of these I have tried to employ with caution, pointing out instances when imaginative works diverged from social reality. Didactic writings have been useful, primarily sermons, religious tracts, and handbooks of advice. Revealing, too, are eighteenth-century newspapers and magazines, medical, legal, and philosophical treatises, and agricultural tracts. And, for illustrative and explanatory purposes, I have drawn upon studies from medicine, psychology, and anthropology. Other recent works, on topics ranging from popular culture to blindness, have been instructive, as have monographs focusing on selected aspects of nocturnal life (for thematic unity, I have not examined sources relating to warfare at night).

A last point deserves special emphasis. While I take up, on several occasions, the question of night's impact upon daily life, including whether darkness in the main was a source of social stability or disorder, that issue has not been my foremost concern. Hopefully, the material contained in these pages will afford justification enough for studying nighttime on its own terms.

ROGER EKIRCH
Sugarloaf Mountain
Roanoke, Virginia
November 2004

All dates are rendered in new style, with the new year beginning on January 1. Quotations, for the most part, are in the original spelling, though capitalization has been modernized and punctuation added when necessary.

SHUTTING-IN

Shepherds all, and maidens fair, fold your flocks up, for the air gins to thicken, and the sun already his great course hath run.

JOHN FLETCHER, ca. 1610[1]

RATHER THAN FALLING, night, to the watchful eye, rises. Emerging first in the valleys, shadows slowly ascend sloping hillsides. Fading rays known as "sunsuckers" dart upward behind clouds as if being inhaled for another day. While pastures and woodlands are lost to gloom, the western sky remains aglow even as the sun draws low beneath the horizon. Were he guided by the firmament, the husbandman might keep to his plough, but the deepening shadows hasten his retreat. Amid reappearing rooks and lowing cattle, rabbits scamper for shelter. Screech owls take wing over a heath. Whistling like conspiring assassins, they inspire equal alarm in mice and men, both taught at an early age to fear this high-pitched harbinger of death. As daylight recedes, color drains from the landscape. Thickets grow larger and less distinct, blending into mongrel shades of gray. It is eventide, when, say the Irish, a man and a bush look alike, or, more ominously, warns an Italian adage, hounds and wolves.[2]

The darkness of night appears palpable. Evening does not arrive, it "thickens." Wayfarers are "overtaken" as if enveloped by a black mist, not only seen but felt as the Old Testament recounts of the darkness that befell Pharaoh's Egypt. With the sun's flight, noxious fumes are widely thought to descend from the sky—"night fogges" and "noysom vapours"—cold, raw, and dank. In the popular imagination night *has* fallen. No longer is the day's atmosphere transparent, odorless, and temperate—washed by welcome beams of light. What Shakespeare describes as "the daylight sick" spreads contagion and pestilence, laden with malignant damps that infect the prostrate countryside. "Make haste," warns Duke Vincentio in *Measure for Measure* (1604), "the vaporous night approaches."[3]

Gloaming, cock-shut, grosping, crow-time, daylight's gate, owl-leet. The English tongue contains a vast corpus of evocative idioms for day's descent into obscurity, with Irish Gaelic possessing four terms just to chart successive intervals of time from late afternoon to nightfall. No other phase of the day or night has inspired a richer terminology. Before the advent of industrialization, certainly none mattered more to the lives of ordinary men and women. For most persons, the customary name for nightfall was "shutting-in," a time to bar doors and bolt shutters once watchdogs had been loosed abroad. For night—its foul and fetid air, its preternatural darkness—spawned uncertain perils, both real and imaginary. And, oddly, no age in Western history other than that bounded by the Renaissance and the Enlightenment has ever had more reason to dread its offspring.

PART ONE

IN THE SHADOW OF DEATH

PRELUDE

Never greet a stranger in the night, for he may be a demon.

THE TALMUD[1]

NIGHT WAS man's first necessary evil, our oldest and most haunting terror. Amid the gathering darkness and cold, our prehistoric forbears must have felt profound fear, not least over the prospect that one morning the sun might fail to return.

No environs more distant from the Paleolithic age might be imagined than the Georgian chambers of Edmund Burke in London. Concerned with the relationship between obscurity and aesthetics, Burke, a young Irish émigré, took a keen interest in mankind's age-old fear of darkness, to which even London's enlightened citizenry still succumbed. It was a topic last visited in England with any clarity by John Locke in his famous philosophical treatise *An Essay Concerning Human Understanding* (1690). To Locke's explanation for childhood fears of the dark, Burke, however, gave short shrift. Whereas Locke had blamed nurses for spinning ghost stories among impressionable infants, Burke, in *A Philosophical Enquiry into the Origins of Our Ideas of the Sublime and Beautiful* (1757), insisted that darkness remained, as always, "terrible in its own nature." "It is very hard to imagine," he concluded, "that the effect of an idea so universally terrible in all times, and in all countries, as darkness, could possibly have been owing to a set of idle stories."[2] In short, terror of the dark was timeless.

One can only speculate about when an inherent fear of darkness might first have taken root in the human psyche. In view of the terror that must have struck our earliest ancestors, very likely this most ancient of human anxieties has existed from time immemorial, much as Burke contended.

Some psychologists, however, have surmised that prehistoric peoples, rather than naturally fearing darkness in its own right, may have first feared specific perils arising in the dark. Only then, as night grew increasingly synonymous with danger, might early populations, across a span of many generations, have acquired an instinctive terror.[3]

Whatever its exact source, whether this fear originated at the outset or over time, certainly later cultures stood to inherit a pronounced aversion to nocturnal darkness. Everywhere one looks in the ancient world, demons filled the night air. Nyx, born of Chaos in Greek mythology, was the goddess of "all-subduing" night who, in the *Iliad*, makes even Zeus tremble. Among her fierce brood numbered Disease, Strife, and Doom. In Babylon, desert denizens suffered from the depredations of the night-hag Lilith. Ancient Romans feared the nocturnal flights of the strix, a witch that transformed itself into a screeching bird preying upon the entrails of infants, while to the east of Jerusalem, an "Angel of Darkness" terrorized Essene villagers in the arid environment of Qumran.[4] So, too, many early civilizations, including Egypt and Mesopotamia, equated darkness with death, as would Christian Europe. The Twenty-third Psalm speaks famously of the "valley of the shadow of death." Christianity, from its birth, revered God as the source of eternal light. His first act of creation, the gift of light, rescued the world from the domain of chaos. "And the light shineth in darkness," declares the Book of John, "and the darkness comprehended it not." The Bible recounts a succession of sinister deeds—"works of darkness"—perpetrated in the dead of night, including the betrayal of Christ in the Garden of Gethsemane. Following his crucifixion, "there was darkness over all the land."[5]

In more recent times, in lands far removed in longitude and age from the ancient world, nighttime has continued to inspire intense apprehension. Paul Gauguin discovered in Tahiti, for example, that Kanaka women never slept in the dark. As late as the twentieth century, the Navaho recoiled from nocturnal demons, as did the Pacific natives of Mailu. In African cultures like the Yoruba and Ibo peoples of Nigeria and the Ewe of Dahomey and Togoland, spirits assumed the form of witches at night, sowing misfortune and death in their wake. Significantly, where day-witches were believed to exist, such as among the Dinka, their conduct was thought less threatening.[6]

Not that every society since the dawn of time has viewed night with similar revulsion. To underscore man's instinctive fear of the dark, originating somewhere in the primordial past, does not preclude the fact that night has aroused greater dread in some cultures than in others. Ancient Greek cults staged all-night religious festivals called *pannchídes*. And while, according to Juvenal, pedestrians prowling the streets of early Rome after sunset risked life and limb, the city, at the inception of the second century A.D., enjoyed a rich night life. In Antioch, wrote Libanius, residents "shook off the tyranny of sleep" with the aid of oil lamps—as did societies like the Sumerians and Egyptians, similarly blessed with this early source of artificial illumination that permitted greater freedom after dark. Nor were they the first. In France, the remains of some one hundred lamps from the late Paleolithic period have been unearthed in the vicinity of the Lascaux cave paintings.[7]

All forms of artificial illumination—not just lamps but torches and candles—helped early on to alleviate nocturnal anxieties. "Evil spirits love not the smell of lamps," declared Plato. Still, technological innovations only played a partial role. Cultural differences no doubt help to explain, for example, why some peoples avoided military engagements at night, while others did not. The Vikings appear to have relished nocturnal assaults, as European coastal communities sadly learned. Rather than access to lighting, perhaps habitual exposure every winter to Scandinavian darkness steeled Norsemen to its terrors. Equally stark were the contrasting reactions of Indian tribes along the eastern seaboard of North America that English settlers encountered centuries later. In New England, William Wood advised fellow colonists not to fear Indian assaults at night: "They will not budge from their own dwellings for fear of their Abbamocho (Devil), whom they fear especially in evil enterprises." Still, a visitor to North Carolina, John Lawson, reported that the members of a local tribe "are never fearful in the night, nor do the thoughts of spirits ever trouble them, such as the many hobgoblins and bugbears that we suck in with our milk"—for which, like Locke, he blamed the "foolery of our nurses and servants" who "by their idle tales of fairies and witches makes such impressions on our tender years."[8]

Sundry influences have shaped the reactions of past cultures to nighttime, including, for that matter, the ways in which children have been acclimated at an early age to the dangers of darkness. These, the genuine hazards that night has posed across time, have in their own right colored perceptions, often more profoundly than other circumstances. Equally apparent, the past does not reveal a chronological pattern to our fears. Instead of any simple linear evolution, the tides of human adrenaline have ebbed and flowed over the course of many years. With the modern age, man's aversion to darkness has, of course, progressively diminished, particularly in industrialized societies owing to electric lighting, professional police, and the spread of scientific rationalism. Yet in the centuries preceding the Industrial Revolution, evening appeared fraught with menace. Darkness in the early modern world summoned the worst elements in man, nature, and the cosmos. Murderers and thieves, terrible calamities, and satanic spirits lurked everywhere.

CHAPTER ONE

TERRORS OF THE NIGHT: HEAVENS AND EARTH

I

So when night in her rustie dungeon hath imprisoned our ey-sight, and that we are shut seperatly in our chambers from resort, the divell keepeth his audit in our sin-guilty consciences.

THOMAS NASHE, 1594[1]

IT WAS AN era of dire apocalyptic visions. "This abominable age, where of the Scripture so clearly speaks," bewailed Jean-Nicholas de Parival, a French writer in the 1600s. Dearth, disease, death, and damnation. As European paintings and literature beginning in the late fifteenth century grimly suggest, the natural world seemed as merciless as it did cruelly unpredictable—a perpetual struggle, to paraphrase a later writer, between the whims of the heavens and the wants of the earth. "A man's destiny is alwayes dark," rued a seventeenth-century proverb. Only salvation—the Kingdom of God, not of man—offered mortals certain sanctuary from fear. These were not faint tremors born of timidity but tangible anxieties rooted in danger and uncertainty, as subsequent generations appreciated. "Our ancestors," recalled a London newspaper in 1767, "spent one half of their life in guarding against death . . . they dreaded fire, thieves, famine, hoarded up their gains for their wives and children, and were some of them under terrible apprehensions about their fate in the next world."[2]

It would be difficult to exaggerate the suspicion and insecurity bred by darkness. "We lie in the shadow of death at *night*, our dangers are so great," remarked the author of *The Husbandmans Calling* in 1670. Numerous Shakespearean characters plumbed the depths of night's "foul womb." "O comfort-killing night," Lucrece exclaims after her rape, "image of hell! / Dim register and notary of shame! / Black stage for tragedies and murders fell! / Vast sin-concealing chaos! / Nurse of blame!"[3] Just as heaven glowed with celestial light, darkness foreshadowed the agonies awaiting transgressors after death. Often likened to hell ("eternal night"), nighttime anticipated a netherworld of chaos and despair, black as pitch, swarming with imps and demons. Declares the King of Navarre in *Love's Labour's Lost* (1598), "Black is the badge of hell, / The hue of dungeons, and the suit of night." Indeed, it was the conviction of some divines that God created night as proof of hell's existence. "Like the face of hell," was how a seventeenth-century Venetian described the advance of evening.[4]

Night brutally robbed men and women of their vision, the most treasured of human senses. None of sight's sister senses, not even hearing or touch, permitted individuals such mastery over their environs.[5] Were early modern communities not so dependent upon personal interaction, the power of sight would have been less critical. But these were small-scale, traditional societies in which face-to-face encounters predominated, in urban as well as rural settings. Vision allowed people to gauge character and demeanor, vital aspects of identity in the preindustrial world. Carriage and posture revealed inner qualities, as could the expressiveness of a person's eyes. Claimed a seventeenth-century Polish aristocrat, "When a rustic or cowardly person wants to say something seriously, what do you see? He squirms, picks his fingers, strokes his beard, pulls faces, makes eyes and splits every word in three. A noble man, on the contrary, has a clear mind and a gentle posture; he has nothing to be ashamed of."[6] Dress sharpened social contrasts. Some cities, by virtue of sumptuary legislation, permitted just the gentle classes to wear silk or satin. Fashion and color, whether clothing appeared plain or extravagant, bespoke age and occupation as well as rank.[7]

But at night, lamented the Scottish poet James Thomson, "order confounded lies; all beauty void; distinction lost; and gay variety one universal blot."[8] Friends were taken for foes, and shadows for phantoms. Natural landmarks—hedges, coppices, and trees—acquired new life. "When men in darknesse goe, /" Humphrey Mill wrote in 1639, "They see a bush, but take it for a theefe." Hearing, too, played tricks. Passing noises during the day demanded to be heard in the darkness. "The night is more quiet than the day," observed the Jacobean writer George Herbert, "and yet we feare in it what we doe not regard by day. A mouse running, a board cracking, a dog howling, an owle scritching put us often in a cold sweat."[9]

By day, safety was found in numbers. In large towns and cities, the "multitude effectually guard and protect individuals," a London newspaper correspondent noted. After dark, with families forced to fend for themselves, yet deprived of the protection of sight, threats to body and soul multiplied. When else but in the black of night might evil thrive unmolested—unbridled by the customary restraints of the visible world? "Here never shines the sunne of discipline," moaned Thomas Middleton. "At night," allowed Dame Sarah Cowper, "I pray Almighty God to keep me from ye power of evil spirits, and of evil men; from fearfull dreams and terrifying imaginations; from fire, and all sad accidents . . . so many mischiefs, I know of, doubtless more that I know not of."[10]

II

> *There is no doute, but that almost all those things which the common people judge to be wonderfull sightes, are nothing lesse than so. But in the meane season it can not be denied, but that straunge sightes, and many other suche lyke things, are sometymes hearde and also seene.*
>
> LEWES LAVATER, 1572[11]

At night, bizarre sights and queer sounds came and vanished, leaving widespread anxiety in their train. On some evenings, deafening bangs and strange music broke the silence. In the English village of Wakefield, a tenant reported hearing "a great noyse of musicke and dancinge about him," followed another night by the "ringinge of small bells." The sound of "deepe groneing" could also be heard. The evening before a woman at Ealand died, servants grew terrified by "a great knocking and variety of music." Common omens of ill-fortune included loud thunder and the cries of screech owls.[12]

For people steeped in biblical wonders and supernatural lore, alterations in the night sky, including the aurora borealis in northern latitudes, carried even greater portent. "Terrible sights were in the sky all night," George Booth of Chester recorded in 1727. "All my family were up and in tears, or there prayers, the heavens flashing in a perpetual flame." As in the Middle Ages, comets, meteors, and lunar eclipses inspired awe and trepidation, as either omens of God's will or marks of his wrath. Known as "blazing stars," comets, it was said, foretold "destruction & corruption of earthly things," whether from tempests, earthquakes, wars, plagues, or famine. In 1618, an entry in the parish register of Nantwich noted, "Many times there appeared eastward a blazing star, betokenninge godds judgements towards us for sine." "Gods preaching visibly from the heavens by a late astonishing comet," the Yorkshire minister Oliver Heywood wrote of a marvel—most of which were vastly more visible than celestial phenomena today owing to "light pollution" from the glare of modern street lamps.[13]

Frequent outbursts of hysteria followed these sensations, with reverberations felt for days afterward. Early modern woodcuts bear witness to their impact. In England, the descent on a March night in 1719 of a great "globe of fire" reportedly "struck all that saw it into a strange terror." According to the Wiltshire vicar John Lewis, "Many who were in the open air fell to ye ground, & some swooned away; & the children & some of ye common people imagin'd the moon was dropt from its orb, & fallen to ye earth." A colonist in Connecticut, viewing a bright light in the sky, reportedly sacrificed his wife to "glorify God."[14] Such exclamations as "dreadful," "remarkable," and, most commonly, "strange" colored the testimony of eyewitnesses; even more when fantastic apparitions flooded the sky, whether images of coffins, crosses, or bloody swords. These, by all accounts, were horrifying to behold. On a summer night in Prague, residents saw a horrendous scene that included a marching column of headless men. Elsewhere, sightings occurred of shimmering clouds and streams of blood. Shortly after the Great Fire of 1666, terror seized the people of London upon viewing gleams of light one evening—"their apprehensions," observed Samuel Pepys, being that "the rest of the city" was "to be burned, and the papists to cut our throats." These marvels never grew commonplace. No less ghastly than wondrous, they constituted the most spectacular of night's mysteries.[15]

Anon., *The Influence of the Moon on the Heads of Women*, seventeenth century.

"nightfall is a certain rheumatic quality in the evening and night air that falls from the sky." "There is no evil quality in nightfall air," he insisted, with night itself being "nothing more than the obscurity or darkness of the air as a result of the absence of the sun."[18] All the same, the traditional wisdom about nightfall persisted for many years. The night "demitting unwholesome *vapours*, upon all that rest beneath," wrote the seventeenth-century moralist Owen Feltham.[19]

Fevers and colds were only a few of the contagious maladies ascribed to the raw fumes of night. By entering the skin's pores, dank evening air was believed to imperil healthy organs. In *Ricordi Overo Ammaestramenti* (1554), the Italian priest Sabba da Castiglione warned of the "numerous illnesses that night air is wont to generate in human bodies." Thomas

Dekker wrote of "that thick tobacco-breath which the rheumaticke night throws abroad." Men and women appeared more likely, after dusk, to fall sick and even die. Thus popular opinion in 1706 attributed the overnight deaths of five men in Hertfordshire to "some pestilential blast of the air." Particularly dangerous were sultry climates, where malarial fevers, born by mosquitoes, were ascribed to night vapors. A visitor to southern Italy pronounced the air "particularly fatal at night." But fear of noxious air pervaded most of Europe and, for that matter, colonial America well into the eighteenth century. The sun's impact on human illness, conversely, was thought salutary, in large measure for dispersing harmful damps. "At her sight," rhapsodized the Elizabethan Robert Greene of the sun, "the night's foul vapours fled."[20]

Fears of contagion were intensified by the common perception that illnesses worsened at night. "All sickness," wrote the Minorite friar Bartholomaeus Anglicus, "generally is stronger by night than by day." Observed Thomas Amory, "There is never a night passes wherein sickness and death do not afflict and lay waste many."[21] In truth, symptoms associated with many illnesses almost certainly grew worse at nighttime, much as they do today. Deaths themselves, we know, are most likely to occur during the early morning hours, often due to circadian rhythms peculiar to such maladies as asthma, acute heart attacks, and strokes brought on by blood clots, accentuated perhaps by reduced blood flow to the brain owing to the position of the body while asleep. In general, we become most vulnerable when the body's "circadian cycle is at its lowest ebb." There is no reason to suspect that physiological cycles were significantly different four hundred years ago. A related problem is that immune systems weaken while we sleep, thereby releasing fewer "killer cells" to ward off infection.[22] Premodern families typically blamed the dangerous properties of the atmosphere for contributing to respiratory tract illnesses. Two of the most common early modern diseases, influenza and pulmonary tuberculosis (consumption), worsened after dark, whether from constricted airways, heightened sensitivity to allergens, or added stress inflicted upon the lungs while bodies lay prone. Tragically, many persons might have been saved had their chambers been better ventilated at night, especially when occupied by multiple members of a family. A single window, perched slightly open, might have countered the deadly microorganisms spread by coughing and sneezing. The late eighteenth-century reformer

Jonas Hanway wrote that the poor, in particular, when sick "imagine that warmth is so necessary to their cure." As a consequence, "they frequently poison themselves with their own confined air."[23]

III

The twilight is approaching,
The night is approaching,
Let us ask God for help
and for protection
From evil spirits,
Who in darkness practise
Their cunning most.

ANDRZEJ TRZECIESKI,
ca. 1558[24]

"Night," cautioned a proverb, "belongs to the spirits." The uninviting climes of evening—their horrible sights and foreign sounds, their noysome vapors—beckoned a host of demons and spirits, which the Stuart playwright John Fletcher called the "blacke spawne of darknesse." The sky was their empire, the night air their earthly domain.[25] None, of course, was more feared than Satan, the "Prince of Darkness," whose misdeeds were legion, spread far and wide with the growth of printing by popular tracts and scholarly texts. "One hears daily," a German clergyman wrote in 1532, "of the hideous deeds effected by the Devil. There many thousands are struck dead; there a ship goes down with many people beneath the sea; there a land perishes, a city, a village." Because of the millenarian cast of Christian beliefs and prophecies of Armageddon, Satan, now more than ever, was thought on the attack. He was just as feared for scourging sinners as for robbing mortals of their souls—"God's hangman," in the words of James I (1566–1625). Naturally dark in color, Satan assumed a range of clever disguises, often adopting the likeness of a black dog or crow. Although rumored to appear at all hours, he was believed to favor the darkness of night. Some writers, like the Elizabethan Thomas Nashe and the Anglican bishop Jeremy Taylor, supposed that God had forbidden his presence during daylight. Of nighttime, Nashe wrote, "Our creator for our punishment hath allotted it him as his peculiar segniorie and kingdome." "The night, the ways of hell, the time of Satan's reign," warned a German evening devotion.[26]

Plainly, night best suited his designs. The darkness of evening closely resembled hell, Satan's eternal home, where fire gave no light and the "foulest of fumes" blinded the eyes "with a choking smoke." By rejecting the light of God's word, the devil embraced darkness, literally as well as metaphorically. Night alone magnified his powers and emboldened his spirit. Conversely, at no other time was man more vulnerable, blinded as well as isolated, and likely to be taken by surprise.[27] Indeed, darkness had become Satan's unholy realm on earth, a shadow government from which to wage perpetual warfare against the kingdom of Christ. His armies included a hierarchy of demons, imps, hobgoblins, and witches, all as real to contemporaries as their leader. "The Dark World," warned the jurist Sir Matthew Hale in 1693, "sometimes afflicting us with dreadful shapes, abominable smells, loathsome tastes, with other operations of the evil angels." The malevolent powers of demons were formidable. Appearing before men "in divers shapes," commented the Calvinist leader James Calfhill, they "disquiet them when they are awake; trouble them in their sleeps, distort their members; take away their health; afflict them with diseases."[28]

As elsewhere in Europe, the topography of nearly every British hamlet was freighted with supernatural importance. Local lore cautioned village natives and unwary strangers alike, with numerous sites named after the Prince of Darkness himself. So at the "Devil's Hollows" in the Scottish parish of Tannadice, it was well-known that Satan had once "given some remarkable displays of his presence and power." Such was his reputed boldness in an Essex village that he tore down at night a church steeple that parishioners had raised during the day. Despite a local gentleman's offer to purchase fresh materials, none dared to reconstruct the spire. Other than haunted houses, demonic sites included ponds, woods, and churchyards. "Those places are so frightful in the night time," the French lawyer Pierre Le Loyer wrote in 1605, particularly among the "vulgar sort." A century later, a writer in the *Spectator* opined, "There was not a village in *England* that had not a ghost in it, the churchyards were all haunted, every

Matthias Grunewald, *The Devil Attacking the Window* (detail from *St. Anthony the Hermit* from the Isenheim Altarpiece), ca. 1512–1516.

large common had a circle of fairies belonging to it, and there was scarce a shepherd to be met with who had not seen a spirit."[29]

Where learned authorities spoke in generalities, demons bore distinct identities in the popular mind. Especially in rural areas, residents were painfully familiar with the wickedness of local spirits, known in England by such names as the "Barguest of York," "Long Margery," and "Jinny

Green-Teeth." Among the most common tormentors were fairies. In England, their so-called king was Robin Good-fellow, a trickster whose alleged pranks included leading wanderers astray at night through bogs and forests. In *A Midsummer Night's Dream* (ca. 1595), he was Shakespeare's inspiration for the pixie Puck.[30] Closely allied were will-o'-the-wisps, mischievous imps that glowed at night above marshlands, which persons mistook, at their peril, for the light of a lantern. "The Devil's lontun," they were called in parts of England. "An *ignis fatuus*, that bewitches," Samuel Butler wrote in 1663, "and leads men into pools and ditches."[31]

Variously defined as ghosts or fallen angels, some fairies were believed benign, but others absconded with livestock, crops, and even young children. "The honest people," if we may believe a visitor to Wales, "are terrified about these little fellows," and in Ireland Thomas Campbell reported in 1777, "The fairy mythology is swallowed with the wide throat of credulity." No part of the British Isles was thought safe from their kindred—brownies, sprites, colts, or pixies, as they were called. Dobbies, who dwelt near towers and bridges, reportedly attacked on horseback. An extremely malicious order of fairies, the duergars, haunted parts of Northumberland in northern England, while a band in Scotland, the kelpies, bedeviled rivers and ferries. Elsewhere, the peoples of nearly every European culture believed in a similar race of small beings notorious for nocturnal malevolence. Whether foliots, trolls, or elves, their powers far outweighed their Lilliputian size. "When ill treated," wrote a traveler to Westphalia, "these powerful little spirits are cruelly vindictive, and will hide, mangle, and destroy everything before them."[32]

Equally prevalent were disembodied spirits of the dead. Known as boggles, boggarts, and wafts, ghosts reportedly resumed their mortal likenesses at night. On other evenings, they were known to dress in white or take on the shapes of animals. Denied entry to the light of God, according to Christian tradition, they almost always appeared after dark. "The Lord gave day to the living," observed Thietmar of Merseburg, "and night to the dead." Some restless souls bore news of an impending death. Others were suicides condemned to wander indefinitely. Occasionally, specters returned to old neighborhoods seeking to right prior wrongs. In 1718, James Withey of Trowbridge was said to have twice witnessed, by his bedside, the ghost of a deceased girlfriend that he had deserted. "He visibly saw at 2 several times," a neighbor recounted, "the apparition of his old sweetheart in ye dress that she ware at ye time of his courtship of her, & that after looking with a stern visage upon him, she disppear'd, & his candle was extinguished."[33]

Ghosts afflicted numerous communities, often repeatedly, like the Bagbury ghost in Shropshire or Wiltshire's Wilton dog. Apparitions grew so common in the Durham village of Blackburn, complained Bishop Francis Pilkington in 1564, that none in authority dared to dispute their authenticity. Common abodes included crossroads fouled by daily traffic, which were also a customary burial site for suicides. After the self-inflicted death in 1726 of an Exeter weaver, his apparition appeared to many by a crossroads. "'Tis certain," reported a newspaper, "that a young woman of his neighbourhood was so scared and affrighted by his pretended shadow" that she died within two days. Sometimes no spot seemed safe. Even the urbane Pepys feared that his London home might be haunted. The eighteenth-century folklorist John Brand recalled hearing many stories as a boy of a nightly specter in the form of a fierce mastiff that roamed the streets of Newcastle-upon-Tyne.[34]

Other denizens of the nocturnal world included banshees in Ireland, whose dismal cries warned of impending death; the *ar cannerez*, French washwomen known to drown passersby who refused to assist them; and vampires in Hungary, Silesia, and other parts of Eastern Europe who sucked their victims' blood. Night, a sixteenth-century poet remarked, by reviving the dead, threatened the living with death. As late as 1755, authorities in a small town in Moravia exhumed the bodies of suspected vampires in order to pierce their hearts and sever their heads before setting the corpses ablaze. During the sixteenth and seventeenth centuries, reports of werewolves pervaded much of Central Europe and sections of France along the Swiss border, notably the Jura and the Franche-Comté. The surgeon Johann Dietz witnessed a crowd of villagers in the northern German town of Itzehoe chase a werewolf with spears and stakes. Even Paris suffered sporadic attacks. In 1683, a werewolf on the Notre-Dame-de-Grâce road supposedly savaged a party that included several priests.[35]

But, of course, witches in much of Christendom were thought to pose the gravest threat during the early modern era, as hunts bent on their annihilation tragically reflected. Following an initial spasm of panics in the

1400s, few parts of Western Europe, mostly Italy, Spain, and Portugal, escaped the waves of trials and executions that erupted during the sixteenth and seventeenth centuries. Hunts grew most feverish in southwestern Germany, Switzerland, France, and Scotland. Within England, where witchcraft became a capital crime in 1542, the county of Essex experienced abnormally high levels of prosecution during the second half of the sixteenth century, though the greatest single outbreak occurred in East Anglia in the mid-1640s, culminating in nearly two hundred executions. There is no way of telling the total number of Europeans put to death. Upward of thirty thousand from the fifteenth to the seventeenth centuries might have lost their lives. To judge from contemporary reports, the most common defendant seems to have been a single woman of small means and mature years eking out a marginal existence. Besides being needy, she was also considered spiteful. "These miserable wretches," Reginald Scot wrote in 1584, "are so odious unto all their neighbors, and so feared, as few dare offend them or denie them anie thing they ask." Crops, livestock, not even the weather was immune to their malevolence. In Amsterdam, a maid reported being attacked with bricks one night by four oddly clad women. "Your face shall catch flies," they repeatedly exclaimed.[36]

There was nothing new, of course, about the idea of witches and other nocturnal demons. Repeated references in early Christian texts to the "outer darkness" and the "shadow of death" only served to reinforce ancient stereotypes about nighttime. In the fourth century, St. Basil the Great wrote of those who viewed "the darkness as an evil power, or rather, as evil itself." Little wonder that so much of *Beowulf* (eighth century), one of the most violent works in Old English literature, transpires at night or that its principal villain, Grendel, is a fierce monster that waits until darkness to scour the countryside looking for fresh victims to devour—"this hugest of night-horrors, that on his people came."[37] And yet, however disturbing, most supernatural beings did not incite widespread anxiety in Western Europe until the late Middle Ages, when nighttime became profoundly demonized—*la nuit diabolisée*, in the words of the French historian Robert Muchembled. The modern author of a study of early revenants flatly states: "We must be careful not to dramatize too greatly the medieval fear of the night. In the Middle Ages one could savor the calm of a beautiful night without fear." Medieval witches and ghosts remained relatively innocuous. Within England, according to a leading authority, known crimes attributed to witches before 1500 consisted only of "two or three deaths, a broken leg, a withered arm, several destructive tempests and some bewitched genitals." *Macbeth*, probably first performed in 1605 or 1606, was among the earliest English plays to portray sinister deeds of witchcraft.[38]

By then, however, Satan had assumed a more menacing persona. No longer just an annoyance, the devil was viewed by Christian theologians as a powerful adversary in the struggle between good and evil. Enlisted in Satan's service were vast hordes of witches, having each entered into a solemn covenant with the Prince of Darkness. Armed with fresh powers, they reputedly congregated to worship the devil at nocturnal festivals initially called "synagogues" and, later, "sabbaths." Besides engaging in sexual perversions and diabolical rites, they devoured young children, whose flesh enabled them to fly. At Aix in 1610, a defendant charged with witchcraft recounted a sabbath: "Sometimes they ate the tender flesh of little children, who had been slain and roasted at some synagogue, and sometimes babes were brought there, yet alive, whom the witches had kidnapped from their homes." Not only guilty of magic to harm their neighbors (*maleficium*), witches were condemned as dangerous heretics, especially by the upper classes—enemies of God as well as man.[39]

In England, the Netherlands, and parts of Scandinavia, anxiety over nocturnal sabbaths never grew widespread. For myriad reasons, ranging from the aftershocks of the Reformation to the peculiarities of the English legal system, witches continued to be blamed for acts of personal malice, not for demonic assemblies. But, in English eyes, witches were still agents of Satan, and, as such, widely feared. One historian has quipped, "In England witches hanged, while on the Continent they were burned"—usually, it seems, at the behest of legal authorities and clerics, whereas popular fears more often propelled English prosecutions. Charges of heresy rarely arose in English trials, but apprehensions became so rife that several thousand deaths might have been ascribed to witchcraft by courts during the sixteenth and seventeenth centuries, with many more victims allegedly blinded, crippled, or rendered sterile. In Cumberland, of fifty-five deaths arising from causes other than "old age" reported in the parish register of Lamplugh during a five-year period from 1658 to 1662, as many as seven persons had been "bewitched." Four more were "frighted to death by fairies," one was "led into a horse pond by a will of the wisp," and three "old women" were "drownd" after being convicted of witchcraft.[40]

How can the European witch craze be explained? Although studies have stressed conditions peculiar to the settings where witch hunts erupted, several sweeping trends have received attention, including religious conflicts, legal changes, and the birth of printing. In many respects, these societies were in the throes of rapid change, much of it naturally alarming as the feudal order gave way around them. Especially after the fifteenth century, war, famine, natural disasters, and plague only intensified feelings of distress as families struggled with their misfortunes. More helpless than ever, less able to chart their own fate, men and women increasingly personified their woes by blaming Satan and his minions, many of whom were discovered among the destitute poor roaming the countryside. Caught in the grips of despair, early modern communities projected their anxieties onto society's most vulnerable members. Of widespread starvation in Poland, a person observed in 1737, "This calamity has sunk the spirits of the people so low, that at Kaminiech, they imagine they see spectres and apparitions of the dead, in the streets at night, who kill all persons they touch or speak to." And, of course, it *was* at night,

Claude Gillot, *The Witches' Sabbath*, eighteenth century.

when persons felt acutely vulnerable, that evil spirits most frequently appeared.[41]

A handful of skeptics openly derided the existence of demonic beings. Creaking doors and ill-fitted windows, critics insisted, lay behind most supernatural reports, with hobgoblins representing nothing more than the distant glow of marsh gas. In England, both Reginald Scot in *The Discoverie of Witchcraft* (1584) and John Webster, author of *The Displaying of Supposed Witchcraft* (1677), scoffed at witches and evil spirits; like Johann Weyer in Germany, author of *De Praestigiis Daemonum* (1563), they consigned their depredations to biblical times.[42] Some critics were really agnostics at heart, ready to believe in phantoms, just not the legions claimed by proponents. Apostates, as skeptics themselves recognized, were genuinely few. "The fables of witchcraft have taken so fast hold and deepe root in the heart of man," despaired Scot. The staunchest critics, in fact, conceded that rational persons frequently fell prey to supernatural visions. If women, children, and the "stolid and stupid vulgar" remained susceptible, so, too, were travelers and shepherds—"folk," acknowledged the French priest Noel Taillepied in 1588, "who are brought face to face with unspoiled nature."[43]

IV

Drink less and go home by daylight.

ENGLISH PROVERB[44]

What persons in their fright took for evil spirits often sprang instead from mishaps in the dark. In the countryside, near drownings, overturned carriages, and nasty falls likely lay behind many supernatural encounters. "Pixy led" was a term reserved in western England, for instance, for nocturnal misadventures attributed to will-o'-the-wisps. "When fear, weak sight, and man's senses all combine to deceive him," Taillepied wrote, "he may encounter any apparition, however strange."[45]

Although claimed from the wilderness as early as the eleventh century, much of the preindustrial landscape remained treacherous, even in daylight. Whereas forests cover 21 percent of modern Italy, they comprised 50 percent in 1500, though the peninsula was among the most densely settled parts of continental Europe. Steep hillsides, turbulent streams, and thick underbrush cut across pastures, fields, and villages. Even where lands had been cleared in Europe by agriculture, tree stumps and trenches scarred the rock-strewn terrain. Thick slabs of peat, cut for fuel, left deep ditches. In parts of England, Wales, and Scotland with active or abandoned collieries, quarries and coal-pits pocked the ground—"a publick nuisance, by which the lives of men are often exposed to real danger," deplored a Scottish minister.[46] Little better were many roads. As late as the mid-1700s, Sir John Parnell complained: "There is scarce any journey can be undertaken without some remarkably inconvenient not to say dangerous spots of roads intervening even in the flattest parts of England."[47]

Poor visibility at night coupled with dangerous terrain was a formula for disaster. Numerous were the times, remarked the seventeenth-century writer Isaac Watts, when "travellers have been betrayed by the thick shadows of the night." Making matters worse, human beings are least able to tackle physical and mental tasks late at night, not only for want of sleep but also because of changes in body chemistry. Alertness and reflexes typically deteriorate. By ignoring nature's "commands" to sleep, the Florentine philosopher Marsilio Ficino observed, "man without doubt fights both with the order of the universe and especially with himself."[48] Even sure-footed natives on a dark night could misjudge the lay of the land, stumbling into a ditch or off a precipice. In Aberdeenshire, a fifteen-year-old girl died in 1739 after straying from her customary path through a churchyard and tumbling into a newly dug grave. The Yorkshireman Arthur Jessop, returning from a neighbor's home on a cold December evening, fell into a stone pit after losing his bearings. "So extremely dark" was the night that others, too, "were lost and could not hit their way," Jessop noted in his diary. With a bruised leg and back, he avoided any of the injuries normally crowding the pages of coroners' reports, such as crushed skulls and broken limbs. After rambles spanning several decades, William Coe escaped with nary a fracture, he boasted in 1721. Yet the Suffolk farmer was no stranger to close scrapes at night, including not only slips and spills but also falls from his horse—once down a deep bank. Sometimes, the natural landscape swallowed up its victims without a clue, such as in the mysterious disappearance of a Wakefield man, James Wilkinson, who tarried on his way home in 1682. Anxious to drink several pots of ale, he ignored the advice of a friend to "get over the moor before it is dark." Wilkinson never reached his destination. Weeks of searching "all along the moor and in colepits and in the river," recorded Reverend Heywood, were "all in vain."[49]

There can be little doubt that alcohol, the lubricant of early modern life, often contributed to accidents. Available at all hours, during work as well as leisure, ale, beer, and wine flowed freely in drinking houses and private dwellings. Despite the expense, the daily consumption of ale was particularly high in England among the lower and middle classes, children as well as adults. Based upon a partial survey in 1577, there were an estimated 24,000 alehouses in the country, approximately one for every 140 inhabitants. Moreover, beer on both sides of the Atlantic became progressively cheaper and more powerful. A New England newspaper in 1736 printed a list of more than two hundred synonyms for drunkenness. Included were "Knows not the way home" and "He sees two moons" to describe people winding their way in the late evening.[50]

Then as now, persons at that hour likely grew more susceptible to intoxication. From 10:00 P.M. until 8:00 A.M., according to clinical research, the stomach and liver typically metabolize alcohol less rapidly than at any other time, thereby keeping it longer within the body.[51] Not surprisingly, with vision and alertness impaired, accidents followed close on the heels of nighttime revels. A man named Kerry, on his way to Manchester in 1635, paused at an alehouse to drink with friends. Finally refused pints by the hostess, he "swore he would drink 10 dozens that night" and left for another alehouse "far into the night," only to fall into a pit and drown. Of the "squadrons of drunkards staggering" into Paris late at night from the suburbs, Louis-Sébastien Mercier observed, "In vain the semi-blind leads the blind, each step is perilous, the ditch waits for them both, or rather the wheels." Besides broken necks, some victims perished from exposure after passing out. In Derby an inebriated laborer snored so loudly after falling by the side of a road that he was mistaken for a mad dog and shot.[52]

Drownings of all sorts were unavoidable. Overturned boats and treacherous docks contributed their share of mishaps, by day as well as night. But often in the darkness persons miscalculated the turbulence of a swollen creek or failed to spy debris before it struck their craft. Sometimes, too, they simply found it impossible to follow a well-traveled road. The Duke of Northumberland, for example, nearly died when a servant ran his coach and horses down a steep bank into a nearby river. On a rainy evening in 1733, a young woman near Horsham, Pennsylvania, had an infant swept from her arms while crossing a swift stream on a log. By one report, the horse she was leading pulled mother and child into the water.[53] Often, at night, horses were dangerous. Not only were riders tired and roads bad, but mounts spooked. Of a treacherous road along the Italian coast, Johann Wolfgang Goethe commented, "It has been the scene of many accidents, especially at night when the horses shy easily."[54]

No less hazardous than the countryside were the streets of preindustrial towns and cities. By 1700, urban areas with five thousand or more persons comprised some 15 percent of England's population of five million inhabitants, a proportion slightly above the norm for Western Europe as a whole. The country's metropolis, London, boasted a citizenry of 575,000, dwarfing provincial centers with between twelve and thirty thousand inhabitants apiece. By then, large-scale urbanization had already transformed much of continental Europe, from the Italian peninsula to southern Scandinavia.[55] Most cities and towns resembled a rabbit warren of narrow streets and alleys—cramped, crooked, and dark. Upper façades, by projecting over streets below, obstructed light from both the sun and moon. Already by the 1600s, buildings in Amsterdam towered four stories high. Not until the eighteenth century would linear thoroughfares of ample breadth set the standard in urban design.[56]

In the absence of adequate street lamps, darkness reestablished the supremacy of the natural world. On most streets before the late 1600s, the light from households and pedestrians' lanterns afforded the sole sources of artificial illumination. Thus the Thames and the Seine claimed numerous lives, owing to falls from wharves and bridges, as did canals like the Leidsegracht in Amsterdam and Venice's Grand Canal. Men and women dodged fast-moving coaches and carts, whose drivers, railed a visitor to Paris, often failed to shout a warning. Keeping to the wall, on the other hand, surprised pedestrians with open cellars and coal vaults, while shop signs menaced strollers from overhead. Only the flash from a sudden bolt of lightning, one "very dark" August night in 1693, kept the merchant Samuel Jeake from tumbling over a pile of wood in the middle of a road near his Sussex home. Dirt and pebble streets contained a labyrinth of ditches for channeling sewage and rainwater to "kennels" running down the center, or, with wider thoroughfares, gutters on either side. The Duchess of Orleans expressed amazement in 1720 that Paris did not have "entire rivers of piss" from the men who urinated in streets, already littered with dung from horses and livestock. Ditches, a foot or more deep, grew clogged with ashes, oyster shells, and animal carcasses. "All my concern is to keep clear of the kennel," wrote a town resident of his midnight rambles. Poor drainage transformed some streets into swamps.[57]

Only in the eighteenth century did most town fathers take responsibility for street paving, with mixed results. Stone pavements, favored for the protection they offered from dust and filth, became broken and uneven. In continual repair, they were patched, as one Londoner pointed out, by different workmen with different stones at different times. Most cities fared no better. "There is no flat pavement to walk on," complained a person of Geneva in 1766. Worse, streets and footpaths furnished dumping grounds for rubbish through which pedestrians were forced to wade. A critic wrote of the "dismal accidents" caused by "rough, unequal or broken pavements; especially when these are covered with filth, as to make them scarcely visible to the most cautious passenger by day, and much less so by night." The nuisance of garbage-strewn streets was pervasive in European towns, with the notable exception of those in the Netherlands, where the Dutch enjoyed a well-earned reputation for cleanliness. In the English town of Prescot, one in every four households in 1693 were fined for not removing piles of rubbish from the front of their homes.[58]

Most notorious were the showers of urine and excrement that bombarded streets at night from open windows and doors. The emptying of "piss-pots" was a common hazard. Suffering from crowded populations and inadequate sewage facilities, many cities and towns, some well into the 1700s, appear to have tolerated the practice, at least tacitly. A French saying declared, "It stains like the dirt of Paris"; and of Madrid, a resident remarked in the seventeenth century, "It has been calculated that the streets are perfumed every day with more than 10,000 turds." Lisbon, Florence, and Venice enjoyed ill reputations, but the residents of Edinburgh achieved the greatest infamy for converting their streets into sewers. Daniel Defoe defended their practice by noting the city's tall buildings and congested citizenry, who were only permitted to empty their waste after 10:00 P.M., upon the sound of a drum, and only once they had shouted a warning of "Gardy-loo!" ("Mind the water!") to passersby. In Marseilles, residents were required to give three warnings, though in nearby Avignon the onus was heaped upon pedestrians, "so that," a visitor grumbled, "you are obliged to cry Gare, Gare [Attention, Attention], when you walk the streets at night."[59]

In the evening, not even one's home guaranteed safety from accidents. In the absence of adequate light, open doors, stairwells, and hearths became traps for the unwary, especially if prone to drink. In 1675 a Lancashire physician, being "full of drink," was badly burned after falling backwards into a fireplace, a common mishap, to gauge from contemporary reports. After a similar instance in Boston, Massachusetts, Reverend Samuel Sewall remarked of the victim, "His face so burnt away, that what remain'd resembled a fire-brand"; while a Coventry woman, "her veins" filled "with pure spirits," became as flammable "as a lamp" after falling from her bed onto a candle. Others tumbled down steps, badly bruising themselves if not breaking their backs. Pepys's new maid Luce, not yet familiar with the household, nearly cracked her skull one night falling down a flight of stairs. Yards contained not only fences and gates to avoid in the dark but also ponds and open pits. Many people fell into wells, often left unguarded with no wall or railing. If deep enough, it made little difference whether dry. On a winter night in 1725, a drunken man stumbled into a London well, only to die from his injuries after a neighbor ignored his cries for help, fearing instead a demon. As reflected in coroners' reports, women and servants were particularly vulnerable to falls at night when fetching water. More unusual was the sad fate in 1649 of a five-year-old girl in New England. With her parents visiting a neighbor one evening, she arose from her bed only to plummet through an opening into the cellar. There, she rolled into an interior well and drowned. Her father, having broken the Sabbath the day before, attributed the death to the righteous hand of God.[60]

"The night is no man's friend," warned a well-known adage. At least in England, ordinary folk each evening no longer worried about one traditional nemesis, as their ancestors often had. For all of night's hazards, wild

William Hogarth, *Night* (pl. 4 of *The Four Times of the Day*), 1738. A pair of besotted pedestrians, armed with a sword and cane, brave a London lane amid an overturned coach and a shower of human waste. Illuminated windows and a bonfire mark the anniversary of the restoration of Charles II. In the distance, a larger fire burns out of control. The cast of characters includes a crouching "linkboy" and several "bulkers," fast asleep beneath the shop of a barber. From within the coach, a passenger fires his pistol.

animals, except for an occasional fox, no longer bedeviled rural households and their livestock. What bears and wolves once roamed the countryside had been hunted down by the late Middle Ages and destroyed. In contrast, much of continental Europe, while increasingly agricultural, still contained expanses of wilderness, such as the Ardennes Forest, inhabited by a variety of wild predators, as did, of course, the eastern seaboard of North America, where wolves for English colonists caused widespread concern. Cotton Mather warned of "the *evening wolves*, the rabid and howling *wolves of the wilderness*." Residents of Cambridge, Massachusetts, awoke one morning in 1691 to discover the carcasses of more than fifty sheep, with the blood drained from their throats.[61]

Yet even the tame English countryside still housed nocturnal pests. Owls, bats, and toads all bred varying degrees of apprehension and were linked, inevitably, with Satan. But, as most people understood, the direct menace these vermin posed paled in comparison to that of other nocturnal predators, including not just vicious beasts but also man himself, who on most nights represented the greatest threat of all to life and limb. Preindustrial England might have been devoid of wolves, but as a proverb declared, "One man is oftentimes a wolf to another." Of that breed, there was no dearth.[62]

CHAPTER TWO

MORTAL PERILS: PLUNDER, VIOLENCE, AND FIRE

I

The good people love the day and the bad the night.

FRENCH ADAGE[1]

"ONE CAN BEWARE of the devil but not of man," declared the Danish writer Ludvig Baron Holberg. *Homo Homini Demon*, as an Englishman in 1675 defined mankind. As if the nocturnal landscape was not already perilous enough, still greater suffering issued from mortal hands. Neither evil spirits nor natural misfortune gave rise to the chronic fear bred by human malevolence. Thomas Hobbes, who dreaded lying alone at night, claimed not to be "afrayd of *sprights*, but afrayd of being knockt on the head for five or ten pounds."[2] It was at night, according to common thought, that crime posed the greatest menace. After sunset, rogues and miscreants, like wild beasts, emerged from their lairs seeking fresh quarry. *Gatos de noche* (cats out of the night) was a Spanish colloquialism for thieves. "With fox and wolfe, by night doe prey," wrote Samuel Rowlands of malefactors in 1620. Noted another, "Night affords the most convenient shade for works of darkness," a term employed, literally as well as metaphorically, to describe criminal acts.[3]

In England, as early as the reign of Edward I (1239–1307), the Statute of Winchester in 1285 authorized the arrest at night of suspicious persons. In Northamptonshire, John Key of Brigstock, for example, was charged with "wandering at night through the streets and common areas, to the harm of all his neighbors and a dangerous example to others." *Noctivagator*, a Latin term coined for such villains during the Middle Ages, gave way by 1500 to "nightwalker" in England, where for centuries the expression continued to enjoy wide currency. *Rôdeurs de nuit*, they were called in Paris, and *andatores di notte* in Italy. A London author in 1659 wrote of nightwalkers as "idle *fellows* who use to sleep by day and walk abroad by night and are suspected to live by dishonest courses."[4]

By then, no longer was it axiomatic that only rogues at night roamed the countryside, and, at least in the environs of London, the appellation of "nightwalker" fell increasingly to describing prostitutes, as it would elsewhere in time. Still, "lying-out" overnight, as opposed to enjoying a few late hours of merriment, continued to invite condemnation. The small hours past midnight, attested a watchman in 1748, were the "time for all honest people to be in bed." "In my early part of life," a later writer remarked, "when it was said of any man, he keeps BAD HOURS, it was in effect stamping on him a mark of disgrace." Moreover, the public's belief that darkness afforded fertile fields for criminals of all stripes remained deep-seated. "Our time is in the deep, and silent night," wrote John Crowne in 1681—"The time when cities oft are set on fire; / When robberies and murders are committed."[5] In fact, crimes only seemed to multiply in response to the rising numbers of urban pedestrians at night, who were plentiful enough to make tempting targets though not so numerous to deter armed brigands. Most nights, malefactors enjoyed opportunities for illicit gain at minimal risk.

II

> *The first person I meet shall stand or die, or deliver, for it is now dark nights, and I am resolved to make use of that advantage.*
>
> PHILIP THOMAS, 1727[6]

Crime in early modern times varied greatly in type, frequency, and location. A single shire, province, or region could experience levels of lawlessness markedly divergent from those of its neighbors, depending upon differences in urban growth, cultural norms, and social stratification.

Within heterogeneous jurisdictions like the county of Surrey, bordering London, the incidence of crime sometimes varied enormously between rural and urban locales, just as rates fluctuated from one generation to the next. Two conclusions, nonetheless, are inescapable. Fueled by chronic poverty and social dislocation, crime posed a worrisome concern in most of the Western world, with the exception of America's fledgling provinces, where for much of the colonial era travelers marveled at the safety of personal property. In Europe, infractions typically included not only such property offenses as shoplifting and pickpocketing but also assaults, homicides, and other acts of violence.[7] Moreover, as with many perils, crime appeared to increase in magnitude and ferocity during the hours of darkness. For the Elizabethan dramatist Thomas Kyd, night was the "coverer of accursed crimes." "In the night," affirmed Isaac Watts, "we are exposed here on earth to the violence and plunder of wicked men, whether we are abroad or at home."[8]

These fears, though prone to hyperbole, were by no means unfounded. To be sure, most nocturnal crime was relatively minor, consisting of nonviolent thefts. Such was the reputed fondness of thieves for darkness that a dictionary in 1585 defined them as felons "that sleepeth by daye" that they "may steale by night." Pilfering from lumberyards and docks were common offenses in urban areas. All types of property, in the eyes of thieves, were fair game. At London's chief criminal court, the Old Bailey, Francis Marlborough faced prosecution for ripping lead from the roofs of dwellings in the early morning. Meanwhile, in the countryside, with the growing impoverishment of England's rural population by the late sixteenth century, larcenies included poaching, robbing orchards, and filching firewood. In December 1681, the Yorkshire nonconformist Oliver Heywood observed in his diary, "Multitudes come a begging, theres also much stealing," including his own loss of three hens one evening, followed two nights later by the theft of money and a "fat goose" from two neighboring homes. In the eighteenth century, nearly three-quarters of thefts in rural Somerset occurred after dark, as did 60 percent in the Libournais region of France.[9]

A pervasive problem, these crimes did not arouse the fear reserved for thefts that threatened violence. Burglary and armed robbery, although less frequent, gave rise to widespread dread among the public. During a night in 1666, Samuel Pepys, for example, initially felt "much frighted" upon being awakened by noise outside his bedchamber. After learning, however, that the clamor originated from the outdoor theft of a neighbor's wine, he returned to sleep much relieved. More alarming was the threat of armed robbery, as when Pepys, fearful of "rogues," was forced to walk the whole distance one evening from Greenwich Palace to Woolwich. Central to the act of robbery was the explicit threat of physical force. Although deaths seldom resulted, at least in England, that foot-pads were prepared to employ violence was hardly to be doubted. Often, in fact, for intimidation, victims were brutally knocked off their feet before being ordered to "stand and deliver." Weapons included pistols, staves, and short swords called hangers; and while large gangs were uncommon, few robbers acted alone. Rarely did they exhibit the courteous demeanor for which a handful of mounted highwaymen, like Dick Turpin and Jack Sheppard, became renowned in the 1700s. "Damn your bloods you are all dead, if you don't deliver your watches and money this minute," an armed foot-pad warned the inhabitants of a coach in London's Princess Square. Reported the City Marshal in 1718, "It is the general complaint of the taverns, the coffee-houses, the shopkeepers and others, that their customers are afraid when it is dark to come to their houses and shops for fear that their hats and wigs should be snitched from their heads or their swords taken from their sides, or that they may be blinded, knocked down, cut or stabbed."[10]

Urban robberies, with few exceptions, were common throughout Europe. In some cities, thieves tripped their victims by stretching ropes across narrow streets. During the late sixteenth century, pedestrians in Vienna or Madrid rarely felt safe after dark. Foot-pads rendered Paris streets menacing, a visitor discovered in 1620; one hundred years later, a resident wrote that "seldom not a night passes but some body is found murdered."[11] Less often did robberies occur in broad daylight. In sixteenth-century Ireland, some brigands, as a matter of personal honor, reportedly refrained from robbing victims at night, but such magnanimity was exceptional. Within London, robberies were "seldom heard of" in "the *open street*, in the *day-time*." Instead, less violent thieves predominated, particularly pickpockets whose trade was tailored to noisy and congested streets.[12]

Nor was the countryside free from the blight of robbers. Often on foot rather than horseback, they prowled highways linking towns and cities to

William Hogarth, *A Night Encounter*, ca. 1740.

the hinterland, whistling to one another in the dark from behind hedges. Outside London, "low-pads" grew notorious for knocking riders flat with long poles. In 1773, two soldiers, Thomas Evans and John Earley, armed with pistols, took to a highway one night near the West Yorkshire community of Doncaster—because it had been "markett day, and there would be many farmers going home from markett, who would have money." Even in colonial America, travelers were sometimes forced to follow treacherous routes. On the outskirts of Philadelphia in northern Delaware, one fearful party, taking refuge in a private home, sat up all night on their guard. "This part of the country is hardly inhabited," observed John Fontaine, "and the few people who are here make it their business to rob all passengers."[13] More dangerous, still, were roads on the European continent, where a fear of nocturnal assault runs through the journals of travelers. The countryside, with its dense forests and thick vegetation, was infested with bandits, many of them hardened veterans of military clashes. Notorious for killing their victims, brigands also included vagrants and deserters. "Men-slayers," a traveler called them, ranging from *Strassenräubers* in Germany to *briganti* in Italy. In France, claimed a visitor, "If you are robbed on the highway, you lose both your money and your life."[14]

Everywhere malefactors eagerly exploited night's advantages. "At night I shall get more money," Dennes Brannam declared to a London accomplice in 1750, which meant knocking people down with a hammer before stripping their purses. Conversely, another fellow, charged with a daytime assault netting nearly five guineas, insisted in his defense, "It is very improbable I should put a man in bodily fear in the middle of the day." For some thieves, who avoided specializing in a single variety of crime, there was a rough rhythm to most days. Crime kept its own timetable. Charles Mascall, a former carter in London who had "met with losses," described a typical day: "We met that morning as usual about nine o'clock, at the *King's Arms*, and there we staid 'till between 6 and 7 at night; and that's the time we commonly go out to pick pockets, and what handkerchiefs we meet with we bring to the woman at the *King's Arms*; then we get our suppers, and afterwards *turn-out*, upon street-robberies." That evening at nine, Mascall and three armed accomplices attacked a servant on Albemarle Street, striking him in the face with a pistol, covering his eyes, and putting another pistol to his throat, which earned them just under twenty shillings. "Witnesse the dayly begarries, and nightly robberies throughout the land," a person declared in 1650.[15]

Had that menace, each night, been the worst of it, urban families would have slept more soundly. But what always they feared most was the invasion of their dwellings by burglars. Every evening, men retired with their families to the shelter of their homes, whose sanctity they were charged with preserving. Besides protection from the elements, the home provided a refuge from the dangers and disorder of daily existence. Asserted a sixteenth-century prayer, "Houses are builded for us to repair into, from the annoyances of the weather, from the cruelty of beasts, and from the waves and turmoils of this troublous world." Critical to the offense of burglary was its occurrence at night, which the jurist Sir Edward Coke defined to be "when darknesse comes and day-light is past, so as . . . you cannot discerne the countenance of a man." The commission of a theft was not necessary but rather the forceful entry of a "dwelling house" with "an intent to do felony." Along with arson, burglary in English law ranked as a crime against not only property but also one's "habitation."[16]

Many burglars, because of the planning their craft demanded, operated as professional gangs, and, worse, they struck when persons were defenseless, disarmed by sleep. Some ruffians, known as "smudges" or "night-sneaks," gained entry during the day and hid beneath beds until families retired. "The cull is at snoos" was street slang for a sleeping target. Every portal at night offered potential access for a thief. Large homes made tempting targets, as much for their entrances as for their possessions. "My house is mighty dangerous," Pepys bemoaned, "having so many ways to come to."[17]

There was never any guarantee violence would not erupt, particularly when families awakened to confront intruders. Not all housebreakers gained easy entry, failing either to pick door locks, a skill labeled the "black art," or to prop open windows with iron rods. As suggested by the term "housebreaking," doors might be forced and shutters broken. Rare was the sort of burglary reported in County Cork where thieves removed a window and its frame from a wall without the slightest sound. After two men broke into a London house in 1734, one recounted, "I wrenched open the lock of the cellar-door with a chissel; but it making a noise, we look'd up and saw a light in the window, and being afraid the people were alarm'd, we went off a little." The thieves returned once the candle was out and the family asleep.[18] Unusual noises proved terrifying to households. Like "all rich men that are covetous," Pepys grew anxious whenever his home contained large sums of money. Possessing £1,000 one evening, he "fell into a most mighty sweat in the night," only, upon hearing a noise, "to sweat worse and worse" until he "melted almost to water." Of burglars, the "dread of them is greater than can well be express'd," affirmed the author in 1701 of *Hanging, Not Punishment Enough.*[19]

Despite the risk of execution if caught, housebreaking attracted large numbers eager to reap quick rewards. Homes contained items easily resaleable to receivers of stolen goods, such as silver and jewelry. Whereas fewer than 10 percent of robberies in the London suburb of Surrey netted property worth more than ten pounds apiece, a quarter of Surrey burglaries yielded that amount or more. Princely sums of several hundred pounds were not unknown. "We have made a pretty good hand on't too night," a

London burglar assured an accomplice in 1707, to which his friend expressed the hope that they should yet "make a better hand on't tomorrow night." To the pickpocket Richard Oakey, a band of burglars bragged, "We slum a ken when all's boman [i.e., break into a house when it's safe], and get more in one night, than you do in a month." In Geneva, a housebreaker's greed led him to steal items from a bedroom where two persons slept, not once but twice after an interval of just two hours—even though the victims had awakened to pursue him after the first theft.[20]

Owing to the larger threat burglary posed, it became a separate offense in England, apart from housebreaking in the daytime, early in the sixteenth century. Among persons indicted by courts between 1660 and 1800, burglars exceeded housebreakers by four to one in urban Surrey. In his poem "Of Darknesse," Humphrey Mill opined that when thieves "breake houses, 'tis not in the day, / 'Tis in thy presence, when men are asleepe." In seventeenth-century Avignon, the inhabitants were said to "fear every night that rogues should creep in at their windows." A visitor to Orleans in 1715 reported frequent burglaries, as did Henry Swinburne while traveling in Spain.[21]

Less frequent in the countryside, burglaries were scarcely unknown. In eastern Sussex from 1592 to 1640, sixty-seven instances were reported to courts (9 percent of all thefts). And rural crimes more often assumed a brutal cast. Bands of a half-dozen or more members were typical, as were violent break-ins, sometimes called "faggot and storm." Wooden doors were smashed open with battering rams and shutters bashed apart by staves. Gaping holes were cut through walls of wattle and daub. Nine thieves in 1674 stormed into the Yorkshire home of Samuel Sunderland. After binding every member of the household, they escaped with £2,500. At full strength, the Hales-Burley gang in the Midlands comprised upward of forty men armed with bows and guns.[22]

On the Continent, some bands boasted several hundred members. French gangs, known as *chauffeurs*, grew notorious for torturing families with fire. Even villages, if isolated, were not safe from raiders. In the country, distance as well as darkness aided a band's flight. "What would it avail there to cry help! Murder!" asserted a writer. "Murder might be perpetrated a dozen times before help could come!" Typically, in the urban province of Holland, burglars tunneled under doors and cut holes in roofs,

Essaias van de Velde, *A Village Looted at Night*, 1620.

but in the rural stretches of Brabant, bands ransacked homes and assaulted families with impunity. Burglaries were more serious in the open countryside, declared a Dutch court in 1620, "where people are less able to defend themselves against thieves and violence than in enclosed towns." A German innkeeper on the outskirts of Oberau welcomed the construction of a nearby forge, since being "all alone every night he had to fear being plundered by evil folk."[23]

Thefts occurred with greatest frequency from late fall to early spring, when dearth was greatest and nights longest. A Venetian official in the thirteenth century wrote anxiously of "this time of long nights," a concern that prevailed throughout the early modern era. "The season chiefly for breaking into houses is during the winter, and long nights," noted Daniel Defoe. Pedestrians, too, made tempting targets, forced in the first hours of evening to run errands or make their way home in darkness. "It is then that most murders, robberies, and other brushes with danger occur," observed a Parisian in 1643.[24]

Whatever the season, thieves prized nights with little or no natural light. In the *cant* pidgin of habitual criminals, "a good darky" meant "a fit night for stealing." Least desirable were nights when the "tattler" (moon) was up. Invited to rob a night coach near Nottingham, Charles Dorrington refused because "it was too light." On several occasions, the London thief Joseph Davis and his partner hesitated to break into a home owing to the "moon shining so bright." Only after becoming intoxicated in a brandy shop one night did they summon the courage. Even on moonlit evenings, towns offered thieves alleys, courts, and alcoves for shelter. "It was indeed a moonlight night," testified the victim of an assault in 1732, "but I was robb'd on the dark side of the way." On the Hampstead Road from London, a notorious spot for robberies, a band grabbed a man off his horse to assault behind a haycock, "because it was then a moon-light night."[25]

Criminals took added steps to conceal their identities. Besides blacking their faces, some wore hats and heavy cloaks, even on warm summer nights. His bedchamber invaded in August 1738 by two burglars, the Penrith yeoman John Nelson described one as "pretty tall in a dark coulered coat with his hat pulled over his face & the other of lesser size with a white horseman's coat with the cape buttoned under his chin & his hat pulled also over his face." Thieves masked their voices and, at most, carried "dark lanterns," which emitted light from just one side.[26] When clashes erupted, in burglaries or robberies, they immediately extinguished their victims' lights. "Linkboys," lighting pedestrians through city streets, were the first knocked off their feet. Lamps and lanterns were smashed, candles blown out, and torches snatched. "D——n your Eyes, . . . put out the light, or we will blow your brains out," was an oft-repeated command,[27] as was the demand to keep silent, lest cries for help breech the darkness. Robbed at knifepoint by a man and a woman, William Carter had his candle doused and an apron pressed against his mouth. Handkerchiefs made handy gags and even dung mixed with straw. When Humphrey Collinson was confronted by three young robbers one October evening, his jaw was pried open and his tongue held to enforce silence. One band of London robbers, anxious to drown out cries for help, shouted for a coach.[28]

Criminals guilty of like offenses in the daytime were occasionally thought deranged. At a minimum, they ran the risk of witnesses. After viewing a thief steal a pair of shoes "one by one" from a shop display, an employee testified at the Old Bailey, "I think he did not look like a man in his senses, to take the shoes in the day-time and come by the door [where I stood] with them." This poor soul was found guilty of a reduced charge of petit larceny. A highway robber in 1727 was ruled *non compos mentis* after halting a coach one Sunday near Hackney. Besides being "on the back of a horse that was thought not worth 20 shillings," he was found to have stopped the coach "at noon day, when people were coming from church."[29]

Secrecy was not the only dividend darkness paid. Thieves readily exploited fears of evil spirits; to avoid pursuit, some rogues masqueraded as demons. According to the Zürich pastor Lewes Lavater in 1572, criminals "under this colour have many times robbed their neighboures in the night time, who supposing they heard the noyse of walking spirites, never went about to drive the theeves away." In Dijon during the fifteenth century, it was common for burglars to impersonate the devil, to the terror of both households and their neighbors. Sheep-stealers in England frightened villagers by masquerading as ghosts. Of German burglars who wore white shirts and coated their faces with flour, Johanna Elenore Peterson recalled, "They would carry lights around the house, break open closets and cupboards, and take what they wanted. We were so scared that we would crawl behind the stove, trembling." Members of the Nickel List gang, on the other hand, in central and northern Germany, were thought blessed with supernatural powers, due to their ingenuity and skill.[30]

In fact, rogues routinely resorted to magic of all sorts, which at night was thought especially potent. "Experience shows that very often famous thieves are also wizards," observed the German legal scholar Jacobus Andreas Crusius in 1660. By the late Middle Ages, charms exerted a broad appeal among criminals. Moonwort, for instance, was reputed to open locks when placed within keyholes, as did mandrake, a narcotic plant that supposedly flourished in the pools of urine and excrement beneath a gallows. In Denmark, burglars felt they could elude detection by leaving at the scene a small quantity of coins. Often for the same reason, there and elsewhere in Europe, they left behind their feces. Some murderers hoped to escape capture by consuming a meal from atop their victim's corpse. In 1574, a man was executed for slaying a miller one night and forcing his wife, whom he first assaulted, to join him in eating fried eggs from the body. "Miller, how do you like this morsel," he taunted.[31]

The most notorious charm, the "thief's candle," found ready acceptance in most parts of Europe. The candle was fashioned from either an amputated finger or the fat of a human corpse, leading to the frequent mutilation of executed criminals. Favored, too, were fingers severed from the remains of stillborn infants. Because they had not been baptized, their magical properties were considered more powerful. To enhance the candle's potency, the hands of dead criminals, known as Hands of Glory, were sometimes employed as candlesticks. Not unknown were savage attacks on pregnant women whose wombs were cut open to extract their young. In 1574, Nicklauss Stüller of Aydtsfeld was convicted of this on three occasions, for which he was "torn thrice with red-hot tongs" and executed upon the wheel. (In Germany, a thief's candle was called a *Diebeskerze.*) Burglars used these gruesome amulets to make certain that families remained asleep while homes were plundered. Imitating a magician, the seventeenth-century French satirist Cyrano de Bergerac declared, "I cause the thieves to burn candles of dead men's grease to lay the hoasts asleep, while they rob their houses." "Let those who are asleep, be asleep" began a typical spell employed by English thieves. Before entering a home in 1586, a German vagabond ignited the entire hand of a dead infant, believing that the unburned fingers signified the number of persons still awake. Even in the late eighteenth century, four men were charged in Castlelyons, Ireland, with unearthing the recently interred corpse of a woman and removing her fat for a thief's candle. Her husband had grown suspicious after fishermen, looking for bait, found an amputated hand along the seashore.[32]

III

In the night, every cat is a leopard.

ITALIAN PROVERB[33]

In preindustrial societies, violence left few realms of daily life unscathed. Wives, children, and servants were flogged, bears baited, cats massacred, and dogs hanged like thieves. Swordsmen dueled, peasants brawled, and witches burned. Quarrels rose swiftly to the surface. "Their anger seems to overpower their utterance, and can vent only by coming to blows," a traveler observed of the English. Short tempers and long draughts made for a fiery mix, especially when stoked by the monotony and despair of unremitting poverty. The incidence of murder during the early modern era was anywhere from five to ten times higher than the rate of homicides in England today. Even recent murder rates in the United States fall dramatically below those for European communities during the sixteenth century. While no social rank was spared, the lower orders bore the brunt of brutality, often from the blows of kith and kin. "Animals who live on the same feed," sneered a Venetian magistrate, "naturally detest each other."[34]

Night witnessed the worst bloodletting. All hours of the day occasioned outbursts of violence, but the threat of physical harm increased markedly after dark—not only from armed robbers but, more often, from street fracases and personal assaults. An Italian proverb warned, "Who goes out at night looks for a beating." Personal animosities repressed during the day were more likely to erupt in the evening. Thus, in 1497, a foreign visitor, describing the "uncontrolled hatred" of Londoners, remarked, "They look askance at us by day, and at night they sometimes drives us off with kicks and blows of the truncheon." In sixteenth-century Douai, three in four homicides happened between dusk and midnight, a ratio exceeded slightly in Artois for the period from 1386 to 1660. During the same hours, two in three murders occurred in seventeenth-century Castille.[35]

Contemporary accounts, penned by fearful travelers, amplify the hard statistics culled from coroners' reports and court records. Evening homicides were thought commonplace. Because of a paucity of firearms, assailants delivered their blows at close quarters. All manner of weapons, including crossbows and pikes, were reputedly used in southern Germany, where murders were judged "numerous" in the early sixteenth century by Antonio De Beatis. Daggers and stilettos in Italy were the order of the night and in Spain and Portugal swords and knives. "As soon as night falls, you cannot go out without a buckler and a coat of mail," a visitor to Valencia declared in 1603; whereas Fynes Moryson discovered, "In all partes of Italy it is unsafe to walke the streetes by night." Or travel by water. On a night in Venice, a young English lady suddenly heard a scream followed by a "curse, a splash and a gurgle," as a body was dumped from a gondola into the Grand Canal. "Such midnight assassinations," her escort explained, "are not uncommon here." First light in Denmark revealed corpses floating in rivers and canals from the night before, just as bloated bodies littered the Tagus and the Seine. Parisian officials strung nets across the water just to retrieve corpses. According to the glazier Jacques-Louis Ménétra, one gang of thieves struck its victims over the head with eelskins filled with lead and then threw "them into the river by night." In Moscow, so numerous were street murders that authorities dragged corpses each morning to the *Zemskii Dvor* for families to claim. In London, where murders were less frequent than in most metropolises, Samuel Johnson warned in 1739, "Prepare for death, if here at night you roam, and sign your will before you sup from home." "The *sons of violence*," echoed the Northampton rector James Hervey, "make choice of this season, to perpetrate the most outrageous acts of wrong and robbery."[36]

Some murders, usually premeditated, arose from jealously, revenge, or just the need to repair male honor. In 1494, the father of a young Florentine stabbed in the face could only conclude that the attack had been a mistake—"he has never offended anyone or suspected anyone of having a grudge against him." On moonless nights in many Italian cities, young men called "Bravos" prowled as paid assassins. Of a conspiracy that went awry, a visitor to Italy recounted:

> A fellow having a quarrell with his brother in law for some words said to his sister, hired a Bravo to kill him, who told him he must be sure not to miss him and loaded a blunder buss soe high with powder and ball that as he was fireing it at him, it did noe harm to the man but burst and struck the Bravo such a stroke on the shoulder that it knocked him down. Upon which the man that had soe narrowly escaped death pulled out his stilleto and stuck the Bravo to the heart.[37]

Personal vendettas were not as common in England and colonial America, where the male cult of personal honor was less entrenched. Moreover, social competition within the upper ranks found other outlets, such as gambling, horseracing, and hunting. When attacks did occur, victims might be bruised and battered, but lives were normally spared. At Oxford, for example, several Fellows of New College in 1692, believing that Anthony Wood had "abused their relations," vowed "they would beat" him when "dark nights" arrived. In London, according to John Gay, "No *Spanish* jealousies thy lanes infest, nor *Roman* vengeance stabs th' unwary breast."[38]

More prevalent, everywhere at night, were acts of impulsive violence, unplanned and sudden, due to the insecurity bred by darkness. Not only was the likelihood of danger greater, but natural defenses were weaker, in marked contrast to daily life. By the sixteenth century, there arose within most social ranks a protocol of public decorum, first discernible among the nobility toward the end of the Middle Ages. Courtiers took the place of knights, satin and silk replaced chain mail. The growing power of nation states, marked by their monopolization of military force, only broadened the scope of this transformation. Well-understood rules of civility governed social exchanges among friends and strangers. Hence, it was thought inappropriate, if walking on a street, to ask questions of a stranger or to touch, much less jostle, other pedestrians. Above all, persons of quality required respect, lest their dignity be affronted. Besides curtsying or doffing one's hat, commoners kept their distance along with their place. Deference demanded "giving the wall" by walking next to the street, where, naturally, lay the greatest danger of stepping in dung or being struck by a coach. Declared *The Rules of Civility*, published in 1685, "If occasion offers to walk with a nobleman in the street, we must give him the wall and remember not to keep up directly by his side, but a little behind."[39]

Yet at night the boundaries of proper conduct grew dangerously blurred. "All shapes, all colours, are alike in night," observed the early seventeenth-century writer Sir Thomas Overbury. In the absence of clear frontiers, opportunities for altercations expanded, and petty affronts gave way to violence. Not only was offense more easily given, but it was also more easily taken. Being bumped or shoved in a narrow alley unleashed, at a minimum, a volley of sharp words. "In Fleetstreet, received a great jostle from a man that had a mind to take the wall," fumed Pepys in his diary. Worse, innocent pedestrians risked being stabbed or clubbed amid the confusion. Clashes of all sorts became likely when tempers were shortest, fears greatest, and eyesight weakest. Thus, in Siegsdorf, a Bavarian market town, in 1616, a servant named Wolf crossed paths with another servant, Adam, whom he stabbed in the armpit "without provocation." The two men, reported the court record, had not known one another. On a Sunday evening in London, two pedestrians, a journeyman and a merchant, jostled one another in the dark near St. Paul's churchyard. They quarrelled and raised their canes; then one struck the other with his sword, killing him instantly. Even in the sparsely populated countryside, confusion could end in violence. In 1666 near the northern town of Birdsall, Edward Ruddocke, walking through a wood one night, shot at several young men trying to find a Maypole, probably suspecting poachers or thieves. Fatally wounding one, Ruddocke shouted, "Ho rogues! Ho rogues! Have we mett with you. Ile make rogues on you. It's more fitt you were in your bedds then here at this tyme of night."[40]

Very likely, violent deeds were committed more easily against an anonymous foe, whose humanity, let alone identity, was at best obscured. "Faceless people are more likely to harm each other," psychological research has shown.[41] Further, the vicissitudes of human physiology must have soured late-night tempers. Along with losses in alertness and motor skills, persons suffered heightened feelings of irritability from fatigue. From 9:00 P.M. to midnight, humans typically experience the greatest impulse to sleep; and often during that time, moods grow increasingly quarrelsome. Of the typical gallant, Francis Lenton wrote in 1631, "Cursing, swearing, and quarrellings are his nocturnall attendants, which arise from choller, and the losse of coyne, mixed with want of sleepe." Especially when compounded by tension and anxiety, physical exhaustion exacerbated social interactions.[42]

As did alcohol, which figured as prominently in preindustrial violence as it did in nocturnal accidents. Drink made many individuals, including close friends, all the more belligerent. In early seventeenth-century Stockholm, approximately 60 percent of all homicides were committed under the influence of alcohol. "In drunkenness and late hours are bred quarrels," warned the *Domostroi*, a sixteenth-century guide for Russian households.[43] Squabbles typically broke out on the premises of drinking houses, where large numbers of males gathered at the close of the workday, whether in rural hamlets or cities and towns. During the seventeenth century, Amsterdam alone contained more than five hundred alehouses. A keeper in West Donyland was faulted in 1602 for "such disorder in the nights that there is like to be manslaughter in their company." The Danish theologian Peder Palladius urged individuals to drink at home to prevent "anyone from killing you in a beer house and you from killing anyone else." Indeed, in Artois, over one-half of all violent acts took place within cabarets.[44]

In the overwhelmingly male atmosphere of drinking houses, violence could follow quickly on the heels of political disputes, ill-chosen words, or cheating at cards. Access to a hearth precipitated a brawl in a South Gosford alehouse. "Booger your eyes, give us one side of the fire," a newcomer demanded of other patrons. At an Amsterdam establishment, a fatal dispute occurred among four drunken friends over which tavern to visit next. In addition, a host of conventions governed the consumption of drink; to ignore any of them invited derision and contempt. But plainly the intoxicating effects of alcohol, by transforming petty disputes into major altercations, constituted the principal catalyst in this already combustible atmosphere. As a "country clergyman" described:

> Men inflamed with strong drink are not in a capacity to weigh well what they say, or to bear patiently what is said to them. Arguments arise, passion on both sides is stirred up, the whole soul is in commotion, abusive language ensues, oaths and curses are reciprocally hurled at each other, defiance and menaces irritate still farther, a blow takes place, with all the fury of the wildest animal it is returned; and one of the party drops under the hand (not of an enemy but) of a companion, a near neighbour, friend, perhaps a relative.[45]

No one was safe in such fights, neither tavern-keepers nor bystanders. Some combatants, of course, wisely resorted to their heels rather than their fists. Then, also, staves and blades usually took the place of pistols. If calmed by an anxious keeper, frays might be halted, at least until smoldering resentments flared anew outdoors. Following a tavern brawl in Alt-Scheitnig, Johann Dietz and his companions were beset in the dark by laborers with swords and cudgels. "No one knew pot from kettle," as each struggled in the blackness "to look after his own skin." Prospects for violence remained alive long into the evening. Drunkards on their way home might cross paths or, worse, cross swords with strangers on guard for trouble. After eluding rogues and robbers, innocent pedestrians could suddenly fall victim to random violence, arising not from greed or revenge but from the delirium of intoxication. Wrote Samuel Johnson, "Some frolick drunkard, reeling from a feast, / Provokes a broil, and stabs you for a jest."[46]

IV

Father, Son, and Holy Ghost, that these houses may not turn to toast.
INSCRIPTION ON A RESIDENCE IN ODENSE, DENMARK[47]

Fire, a persistent threat after dark, terrified preindustrial populations even more than crime and violence. Not only were precautions weaker at night, but the need for heat and light was greater. A source of anxiety since time immemorial, the peril of fire—"that most terrible and ruthless tyrant"—acquired new urgency in tightly packed urban areas, where for cheapness and ease wood and thatch still dominated new construction, especially in northern and central Europe. Only the plague, which offered greater warning, instilled as much fear. As late as 1769, "Palladio," writing in the *Middlesex Journal*, complained, "The English dwell and sleep, as it were, surrounded with their funeral piles." Congested rows of homes and shops created a maze of narrow lanes and winding alleys highly vulnerable to conflagrations. Iago in *Othello* (ca. 1604) speaks of fires "spied in populous citties" by night, and Sir William Davenant in 1636 wrote of the horrible dangers "which mid-night fires beget, in citties overgrowne."[48]

A strong breeze could make matters worse. During a fire in 1652 that consumed much of Glasgow, the wind changed direction five or six times. "The fire on the one syde of the street fyred the other syde," reported the minister of New Kilpatrick parish. A visitor to Moscow found, "Not a month, nor even a week, goes by without some homes—or if the wind is strong, whole streets—going up in smoke." The sacred suffered with the profane, the rich with the poor. Innocent lives might be lost to flames normally reserved by towns for heretics and witches. Fire, unlike other predators, noted the writer Nicolas de Lamare, "devours all and respects neither churches nor royal palaces." Within minutes, one's home and property, the labor of a lifetime, could be destroyed, as could future opportunities for subsistence.[49] Among other ill consequences was the damaging impact large fires had on local economies. Beset by as many as four fires from 1594 to 1641, Stratford-upon-Avon was already described in 1614 as "an ancient but a very poore market towne."[50]

Little wonder that just the alarm of fire at night could strike a person dead with fright, or that a mob in 1680, upon learning that a woman had threatened to burn the town of Wakefield, carried her off to a dung heap, where she lay all night after first being whipped. A worse fate befell a Danish boatman and his wife, upon trying to set the town of Randers ablaze. After being dragged through every street and repeatedly "pinched" with "glowing tongs," they were burned alive.[51]

Despite the introduction of fire engines in cities by the mid-seventeenth century, most firefighting tools were primitive, limited largely to leather buckets, ladders, and "great hooks" to tear down timbers and thatch before sparks could spread. Often, barely a year passed before some town or city in England experienced disaster. From 1500 to 1800, at least 421 fires in provincial towns consumed ten or more houses apiece, with as many as 46 fires during that period destroying one hundred or more houses each. "In some great town a fire breaks out by night, /" wrote Sir Richard Blackmore in 1695, "And fills with crackling flames, and dismal light, / With sparks, and pitchy smoak th' astonish'd sky."[52] Of course, London's Great Fire, originating in a bakehouse in the early morning hours of September 2, 1666, still ranks among the worst in human history. At first, the flames appeared manageable, prompting the Lord Mayor to opine that "a woman might piss it out." But fanned by an east wind, the fire consumed four-fifths of the city over the course of four days. Reduced to ashes were Old St. Paul's Cathedral, 87 churches, more than 13,000 houses, and such public buildings as the Guildhall, Custom House, and the Royal Exchange. The diarist John Evelyn wrote, "The stones of *Paules* flew like grenados, the lead mealting downe the streetes in a streame, & the very pavements of them glowing with fiery rednesse, so as nor horse nor man was able to tread on them." In its wake, the city would endure forty more serious fires in the years before 1800.[53]

No other metropolis suffered London's ordeal, but fires spread terror from Amsterdam to Moscow, where an early morning blaze in 1737 took several thousand lives. Few cities escaped at least one massive disaster. Paris was unusually fortunate, with a writer in the eighteenth century estimating that at least fifty houses ordinarily burned in London for every five lost in the French capital. But Toulouse was all but consumed in 1463, as was Bourges in 1487, and practically a quarter of Troyes in 1534. The better part of Rennes was destroyed in 1720 during a conflagration that raged for seven days.[54] In colonial America, as cities grew, so did fire's threat.

Jan Beerstraten, *The Great Fire in the Old Town Hall, Amsterdam, 1652*, seventeenth century.

Boston lost 150 buildings in 1679 after a smaller blaze just three years before. Major fires again broke out in Boston in 1711 and in 1760 when flames devoured nearly 400 homes and commercial buildings—the "most amazing fire ever known in this age in this part of the world," recorded a diarist. While New York and Philadelphia each suffered minor calamities, a fire gutted much of Charleston in 1740.[55]

Rural localities experienced less crowding, but fire still posed a serious menace. Most hamlets, however ordered or haphazard, were sufficiently compact for flames to spread among houses, barns, and other buildings; open fields, both private and common lands, lay outside the village center. Once ignited, a thatch roof, made from reeds or straw, was nearly impossible to save, as is evident from the dramatic paintings of the seventeenth-century Dutch artist Egbert van der Poel. In Denmark, noted Ludvig Baron Holberg, "Villages were laid out with the houses so close together that, when one house burned down, the entire village had to follow suit." Crops, livestock, and stables strewn with straw all stood at risk, particularly when seasons remained dry. One of the most horrific rural disasters occurred on a night in 1727 in the Cambridgeshire hamlet of Burwell. A barn caught fire with more than 70 persons trapped inside watching a puppet show. Because the doors had been bolted, nearly everyone perished. So indistinguishable were the remains that they were interred in a common grave denoted by a tombstone still standing in the Burwell churchyard.[56]

With good reason, fears mounted after nightfall. The Restoration playwright John Bancroft wrote of "old kingdom night, / Where the fierce element of fire ne'r fades."[57] Even before being rendered defenseless by sleep, households became vulnerable when families lit hearths to escape the cold and the dark. As Benjamin Franklin observed, "Accidental fires in houses are most frequent in the winter and in the night time," and a London newspaper one January spoke of "the frequency of fires at this time of the year." Open hearths threw sparks onto wood floors, or worse, onto thatch roofs, when belched from chimneystacks. Clothing and flax hung dangerously next to fireplaces in order to dry. Chimneys themselves were a persistent hazard. Not only did they blaze out when clogged with soot, but cracks within chimneys and hearths permitted flames to reach a house's joists. Some homes lacked chimneys altogether, to the consternation of anxious neighbors. Complaining that John Taylor, both a brewer and a baker, had twice nearly set his Wiltshire community ablaze from not having a chimney, petitioners in 1624 pleaded that his license be revoked. Of their absence in an Irish village, John Dunton observed, "When the fire is lighted, the smoke will come through the thatch, so that you would think the cabin were on fire."[58]

Candles, oil lamps, and other sources of artificial illumination posed perils of their own. Fire, to paraphrase an English proverb, could change quickly from being a good servant to an ill master. Clothing was highly combustible: the neckcloth of Reverend Ralph Josselin's daughter, Mary, suddenly burst into flames from a candle in 1669, as did, another evening, the head cloth of Elizabeth Freke of County Cork while she was reading in her chamber. Just to carry a naked brand outdoors courted disaster. Newmarket's Great Fire of 1683 began on a March night when someone's torch accidentally set a rick of straw ablaze. In New York City, a cartman lost his home as well as his stable after his children's candle ignited a fire when they were putting horses up. "Feare candle in hayloft, in barne, and in shed," instructed Thomas Tusser.[59]

Most blazes began less dramatically, with untended candles causing the greatest devastation. Untrimmed wicks dropped cinders onto tables and floors. "A snuffe of a candle will set a whole house on fire," warned an Elizabethan writer.[60] Lit candles also made tempting targets for hungry rats and mice. Samuel Sewall of Boston attributed a fire within his closet to a mouse's taste for tallow. "If sickness or any other cause should oblige you to leave a candle burning all night," advised *The Old Farmer's Almanack*, "place it in such a situation as to be out of the way of rats."[61] Another refrain faulted the mishandling of candles by servants. In the Netherlands, the *Ervarene Huyshoudster* lectured, "Darning hose, done by the maids in their bedrooms by candlelight, is very dangerous, for when such a maid, being fatigued, falls from her chair, thus fire can start from the candle." Domestics were condemned for using candles in bed, always a perilous risk. "It is a dangerous fire begins in the bed straw," asserted a proverb.[62] In truth, there was ample blame to go around in view of people's late-night predilections for reading in bed and consuming alcohol, sometimes simultaneously. Several homes on London's Albermarle Street burned to the ground in 1734 after a gentleman fell asleep reading.[63]

Also vulnerable at night were workplaces. Along with candles for lighting, many tradesmen, including brewers, bakers, and tallow-chandlers, employed "constant large and violent fires," with wood, coal, or other fuels stockpiled nearby. Too costly to extinguish, fires in ovens and furnaces often burned through the night. "No sensible person ought to live in an house contiguous to those trades," exhorted a contemporary. Judging from the numbers of reported blazes, bakeries and malthouses seem to have been peculiarly vulnerable to accidents. Of brewers, *Piers Plowman* complained in the fourteenth century, "We've all seen sometime through some brewer / Many tenements burnt down with bodies inside."[64]

If most nighttime fires arose from human negligence, and lightning caused sundry more, an alarming number were intentional. Certainly no more frightening crime existed—the "most pernicious to society," declared a Scottish pastor in 1734. In English criminal law, nearly all forms of arson, directed against a home or a haystack, were punishable by death.

Gerard Vlack, *Sleeping Servant*, n.d.

In Denmark, whether or not lives were lost, beheading was the penalty for a *mordbroender*, meaning literally a murderer by fire. The crime endangered lives and property on a horrific scale, as both innocents and incendiaries understood.[65] Some persons, seeking to exploit public fears, extorted money from property owners in anonymous letters threatening arson. You will be "woken up by the red cock" was a favorite taunt. Named *le capitaine des boutefeu*, a twenty-four-year-old student at the University of Paris was convicted of both arson and extortion in 1557, for which he was burned alive. Years later, several residents of Bristol received letters threatening fire, including a merchant, whose defiance resulted in the destruction of his brick home shortly past midnight. Warned a letter in 1738 to a London ironmonger in Holborn, "We are all resolutely determined to kill you and yours by consuming your house to ashes."[66]

Burglars employed arson, hoping to disguise their crimes. In old regime France, this was a known ruse among thieves. Even in a small Scottish village late one night, a woman set a cottage afire after first combing its belongings. A full-scale blaze was averted only when a passerby alerted the community. Less fortunate was the owner of a London home consumed by a fire set to hide a theft of nearly £1,000 in banknotes. In Piccadilly on a Sunday night in 1761, the servant of a grocer stole clothing and linen before setting lit pieces of coal in three different spots of his master's home. Alerted by smoke, family members barely escaped.[67] A variation on this ploy occurred when thieves pillaged homes amid the confusion accompanying fires that they themselves set. Observed the seventeenth-century jurist Roger North, "It is believed that houses are often fired by thieves for opportunities of stealing." In Muzzle-Hill, outside London, a gang ignited a barn containing a large quantity of hay. As the frantic farmer and his family worked to extinguish the flames, the incendiaries stole money and goods from their home.[68]

Often, however, arson arose from other hands. Across Western Europe, fire was used against landowners by bands of peasants and vagabonds. Arson was a "weapon of the weak"—inexpensive and accessible, with small chance of prevention at night. Used during the Middle Ages, "fireraising" first reached epidemic proportions in the sixteenth century. Within Germany, for example, during the *Bundschuh* disturbances in

1513 and 1517, homes were fired, as were many more following the Peasants' War of 1524–1526. In the Black Forest, an abbey was torched to avenge the death of a peasant leader. From Austria to the Low Countries, bands of incendiaries terrorized country villages. A gang near Salzburg in 1577 supposedly contained eight hundred members. That appears unlikely, but such exaggerations reflected the depth of rural fears. In the Netherlands, the Estates General in 1695 imposed new penalties against "the large bands of gypsies travelling in these areas, carrying arms and threatening arson."[69] And though fireraising was less prevalent in the British Isles, agrarian rioters in eighteenth-century Ireland routinely employed arson at night. In 1733, rumors circulated of a band of incendiaries in western England, whereas in Sussex, residents of Horsham, disgruntled over a ban on bonfires, posted a notice on the town hall vowing to fire the homes of local officials. "We should desire no better diversion than to stand at a distance and see your houses all in flames," they declared. In the American provinces, some fires were attributed to discontented slaves, for example in Boston in the early 1720s and in New York City twenty years later.[70]

In most instances of arson, personal, not social or political, grudges were responsible, although these impulses occasionally dovetailed when servants or slaves were involved. In Germany, the community of Dutz burned in 1538 after a former prisoner in the town gaol set his own house ablaze. "Tonight I have to pay back the Dutz people's friendship," he first informed his family. The late-night burning of a Gloucestershire barn in 1769 resulted in the arrest of a servant girl, whose apron was used to hide a fire-stick. Upon confessing, she admitted that she disliked her "place," from which she wished to be discharged.[71]

Yet the final agony attending blazes came in their waning hours. After managing in the dead of night to escape both smoke and flames, survivors faced the pilfering of what few goods they could salvage. Fireside thefts were endemic, committed less often by arsonists than by onlookers nicknamed fire-priggers, notorious for stealing valuables on the pretense of helping distraught victims retrieve their belongings. So routine was this form of larceny that Parliament legislated in 1707 against "ill-disposed persons" found "stealing and pilfering from the inhabitants" of burning homes. A generation later nothing had changed, with thefts common on both sides of the Atlantic. "There was much thieving at the fire," reported the *Pennsylvania Gazette* in 1730 of a nighttime blaze that destroyed stores and homes along the Philadelphia waterfront.[72]

Such was the early modern nightscape, a forbidding place plagued by pestilential vapors, diabolical spirits, natural calamity, and human depravity, the four horsemen of the nocturnal apocalypse. Of these were the darkest nightmares composed. Unlike such recurrent perils as war, famine, and plague, these dangers were a pervasive source of anxiety for most households.

Not that violence, fire, and other nightly terrors spared daily life, for plainly lives and property stood at risk during all hours in such a precarious age. There need be no doubt, however, that nightfall occasioned the gravest threats to personal safety. Darkness gave free rein to the most threatening elements in the natural and supernatural worlds. Dangers that by day remained sporadic multiplied both in number and in severity. "The terrors of the night," explained Thomas Nashe, are "more than of the day, because the sinnes of the night surmount the sinnes of the day."[73] Never before in Western history, at least since the time of Christ, had night appeared more menacing. With crime a persistent threat, both evil spirits and the terror of fire posed heightened dangers in the centuries following the Middle Ages.

It is a wonder that with the initial shades of darkness men and women did not flee to their beds, warily banking their fires first. And yet, for all of night's terrors, for all the dangers from demons, rogues, and poisonous damps, many persons retreated neither to their chambers nor even to their homes. Instead, they worked and played into the night. Complained a Swiss pastor in 1696, "In the evening, when the sun is setting, the cattle returning from the field home to the stall, and the birds in the wood are falling silent, man alone in his foolishness acts against nature and the general order."[74]

PART TWO

LAWS OF NATURE

PRELUDE

If there was no obscurity, man would not sense his own corrupt state.

BLAISE PASCAL, 1660[1]

FOR MOST OF THE early modern era, night's perilous domain escaped the normal vigilance of church and state. Much of the scaffolding of civic and religious institutions so vital within European communities to the preservation of social order fell dormant each evening—courts, councils, and churches to which ordinary men and women looked to settle local disputes and help protect life and property. Magistrates, aldermen, and churchwardens returned home, shedding robes and responsibilities. "The still village lies dissolv'd in sleep," wrote the poet Thomas Foxton.[2]

Nightfall, in the view of secular and ecclesiastical officials, commanded a close to hours of daily toil. On a practical level, to avoid the risks of both fire and poor craftsmanship, most tradesmen were required to snuff candles and bank hearths. But there was also a heavenly imperative to obey. Darkness mandated that the profane demands of the visible world be forsaken. In their stead, authorities expected men and women to embrace their deity through prayer and meditation. Such early Church Fathers as Ignatius, Jerome, and Cyril of Jerusalem all stressed the value of prayer at night, as did, in the sixteenth century, the Spanish mystic St. John of the Cross. In the poem "On a Dark Night," he proclaimed, "O you my guide, the night, / O night more welcome than dawn." By closing eyes and ears, darkness and solitude opened hearts and minds to the word of God. In the evening, related Bishop James Pilkington, "the senses are not drawn away with fantasies, and the mind is quiet." And no time made prayer more essential than night, the time of Satan's reign, when persons retired to their beds, entrusting themselves to their creator's care.[3]

Most of all, darkness was intended for rest. "The day sees work and labor; the night sees rest and peace," wrote the seventeenth-century Jesuit Daniello Bartoli in *La Ricreazione del Savio* (1656). Nocturnal slumber strengthened the faithful for their daily duties. Admonished a Puritan minister, sleep should never be taken "out of season" so "that we may the better serve God and our neighbours." To spurn rest defied divine providence, but it also endangered personal health. By turning night into day, stated Reverend John Clayton, men imperiled both their "principles" and their "constitutions."[4] Equally alarming, venturing abroad put persons at needless risk, exposing them to all the "troubles and dangers that continually ensue." "Except in extreme necessity," warned Monsignor Sabba da Castiglione, "take care not to go out at night."[5]

Nighttime's final importance for authorities lay in drawing heightened attention to the glory of God's earthly paradise. How better to appreciate the wonder of daily life than by contemplating the black obscurity of night? For the people of this age, there was no more useful way, in fact, to understand any subject than by studying its antithesis. By providential design, observed writers, the horrors of darkness set life's blessings in sharper relief. "Safe from the dangers" of "the night season," men and women awakened each morning to the "beauty and order of the creation." Asserted *Piers Plowman*, "If there were no night, I believe no man / Should really know what day means," a sentiment routinely echoed by later generations. A New England clergyman declared, "God sends our *night* upon us, to make us *children of the day*."[6]

Fundamentally, then, night's paramount value, apart from encouraging devotion and rest, lay in its negation of the waking world. It should not surprise us that the established order viewed "nightwalkers" with trepidation or took few steps after dark to make common thoroughfares safer and more accessible. Not that its attitude was one of indifference or inaction, for night remained a source of profound concern. But rather than seeking to render darkness more habitable, authorities resorted instead to restraint and repression. The fewer persons abroad the better. Night was a no-man's-land, or so, at least, civic and religious officials prayed.

CHAPTER THREE

THE FRAGILITY OF AUTHORITY: CHURCH AND STATE

I

The gates of the citty were shutt, and the streetes chayned at dinner tyme, as if it were in tyme of warr.

FYNES MORYSON, 1617[1]

ACROSS THE preindustrial countryside, fortified cities and towns announced the advance of darkness by ringing bells, beating drums, or blowing horns from atop watchtowers, ramparts, and church steeples. In Catholic lands, the hum of daily life slowed to a soft murmur as men and women of faith recited the *Ave Maria*, a prayer of thanks for divine mercies. With the return of peasants and peddlers to the countryside, townspeople hurried home before massive wooden gates, reinforced by heavy beams, shut for the evening and guards hoisted drawbridges wherever moats and trenches formed natural perimeters. "When Ave Maria you hear, see that your house be near," advised a customary saying. The daily intercourse between town and country abruptly halted at nightfall, as households took shelter behind walls of earth, brick, and stone, some more than fifty feet in height and ten feet in width. During the summer, gates might not be barred until eight or nine o'clock, but in winter, when darkness came on quickly, they could shut as early as four o'clock. At no other time was the contrast more evident between urban and rural life. Town folk eagerly abandoned the surrounding countryside to frightening perils, as armed sentinels with torches patrolled the ramparts. In Italian towns, guards were obliged to ring a small bell every five minutes to signal that none had fallen asleep.[2] For anyone caught and convicted of either defacing or scaling urban walls, penalties were harsh, including, in Stockholm, the loss of one's head. Just to approach ramparts without warning at night constituted a crime. After all, a Milanese scholar pointed out in 1602, it was for the offense of vaulting the walls of Rome that Romulus slew his brother Remus. "So perish all who cross my walls," Romulus had allegedly exclaimed.[3]

Predominantly medieval in origin, urban fortifications dominated the surrounding terrain for centuries afterward. For every city or town cursed by crumbling battlements, there stood another with freshly strengthened façades. In spite of the expenditure of time, labor, and money, more than a few small towns received protection. The Netherlands, according to an estimate in the sixteenth century, contained over two hundred walled towns. Even rural villages occasionally took refuge behind crude bastions. A visitor to Germany reported, "Every village has a wall or ditch around it; few country farmhouses; all are huddled together in towns." Fearing an attack by water, authorities in Amiens forbade all boat traffic at night on the Somme where the river passed the city's ramparts. Boatmen were required to bring their skiffs within the walls before sunset "on pain of being punished as enemies of the town."[4]

England's comparative freedom from foreign invasion by the end of the Middle Ages largely explains its dwindling number of fortified communities, from just over one hundred earlier in the era. Several of the more enduring structures encircled the Great Towns of Norwich, Exeter, and York. Some English towns, in the absence of walls, enjoyed the protection of ditches and earthen banks. In London, despite the ancient city's decaying bastions, numerous gates separated one neighborhood from another, even in the years following the Great Fire. Along with gates that survived the conflagration, others, such as Ludgate and Newgate, were rebuilt with "great solidity and magnificence." All the city's portals, testified William Chamberlayne in 1669, "are kept in good repair, and all are shut up every night with great diligence."[5]

For the sake of social order, communities barred gates in peace as well as war. Long after walls lost their military value, they guarded townspeople against rogues of all stripes, including vagrants and gypsies. Brigands whipped out of a town by day might return by night bent on vengeance, hoping to set homes ablaze. As early as the thirteenth century, Bartholomaeus Anglicus wrote of the dangers posed by both "enemies" and "thieves." Without walls, magistrates in one French city dreaded "entry by every sort of person."[6]

Often, benighted travelers, caught abroad once gates closed, were forced to lie outdoors if lodging could not be had in a *faubourg*. Three times, Jean-Jacques Rousseau, to his great anxiety, found himself outside the barred gates of Geneva, a city without suburbs. Of one instance, he wrote, "About half a league from the city, I hear the retreat sounding; I hurry up; I hear the drum being beaten, so I run at full speed: I get there all out of breath, and perspiring; my heart is beating; from far away, I see the soldiers from their lookouts; I run, I scream with a choked voice. It was too late." Elsewhere, entry occasionally followed the payment of a toll, known in Germany as *Sperrgeld*, or entrance-money. The city of Augsburg featured a special night-gate, *Der Einlasse* (the wicket-gate), which required passage through a series of locked chambers and across a drawbridge. In a French community, the sergeant of the guard, hoping to reap a small fortune from the throngs of citizens attending a distant fair, ordered the town's bell rung a half-hour early, with tardy souls forced either to pay a penny or remain abroad all evening. Such was the mad crush of panicked crowds as they neared the gate that more than one hundred persons perished, most trampled in the stampede, others pushed from the drawbridge, including a coach and six horses. For his rapacity, the guardsman was broken upon the wheel.[7]

To curb nocturnal traffic within town walls, municipal authorities imposed curfews. Only hours after gates closed (or sooner, in the summer), bells warned families to repair to bed once fires were covered. The term "curfew" reportedly originated from the French word *couvre-feu*, meaning "cover-fire." In 1068, William the Conqueror (ca. 1028–1087) allegedly set a national curfew in England of eight o'clock. Whether his intention was to prevent fires or, as critics later alleged, to avert midnight conspiracies against his reign, similar restrictions found favor throughout medieval Europe. Not only were streets swept of pedestrians, but homes still aglow after the curfew bell ran afoul of authorities. Besides incurring fines, offenders faced the risk of incarceration, especially if caught outdoors.[8] Few exemptions were allowed, mostly for persons on missions of life or death—priests, doctors, and midwives—also scavengers (garbage collectors) and veterinarians, for the loss of domestic stock could be devastating to a struggling family. Night laid bare society's most pressing priorities. In England at least, mourners were permitted to keep watch all night over bodies of the dead (fearing the Church's retribution for invoking magic, one guild mandated that none of its members at such vigils "calls up ghosts" or "makes any mockeries of the body or its good name").[9]

Lending weight to curfews, massive iron chains, fastened by heavy padlocks, blocked thoroughfares in cities from Copenhagen to Parma. On moonless nights, these barriers posed a formidable challenge to riders and pedestrians alike. Nuremberg alone maintained more than four hundred sets. Unwound each evening from large drums, they were strung at waist height, sometimes in two or three bands, from one side of a street to the other. In Moscow, instead of chains, logs were laid across lanes to discourage nightwalkers. Paris officials in 1405 set all of the city's farriers to forging chains to cordon off not just streets but also the Seine. In Lyons, chains blocked the Saône, while in Amsterdam, iron barriers spanned canals.[10]

Not until the close of the Middle Ages did urban curfews grow less repressive, with 9:00 or 10:00 P.M., rather than eight o'clock, becoming the standard hour for withdrawing indoors. More significant, public rather than private conduct increasingly prompted officials' concern—wayfarers loitering abroad, not citizens burning late hours at home. An "Acte for Nyghtwalkers," adopted for the town of Leicester in 1553, condemned "dyvers ryottous and evyll disposed persons" who spent nights "walkying in the strettes" causing "moche truble to the well dyssposyd people that wold take ther naturall rest." This more liberal policy owed much, not to any diminished sense of nocturnal peril, but to the impracticality of earlier restrictions. In the face of law enforcement's frailty, the unavoidable fact was that work and sociability occupied many families past the curfew hour. Often, for another hour or more, household windows stayed lit. To be sure, late-night merriment, whether at home or abroad, still provoked officials' ire. In the words of a London regulation in 1595, "No man shall after the houre of nine at the night, keep any rule whereby any such suddaine out-cry be made in the still of the night." Apart from revelry, common sources of disturbance, according to the ordinance, included brawling and beating one's wife or servants—any instance of which could result in a fine of three shillings four pence.[11]

In time, curfews also grew less restrictive for pedestrians. Step by step, more persons enjoyed greater freedom of movement, particularly if they bore honest reputations and sound reasons for travel, unlike nightwalkers, who, by definition, lacked "reasonable cause." Besides those whose demeanor, looks, or location made authorities wary, several groups were enjoined from circulating at night because of the perceptible threat they posed to public order. These included foreigners, beggars, and prostitutes. In Paris, beginning in 1516, vagrants found themselves at night tethered together in pairs, whereas in Geneva, they were expelled at sunset. No stranger could remain inside Venice for more than a single evening without a magistrate's approval. According to the medical student Thomas Platter in 1599, Barcelona confined prostitutes to a narrow street, closed each evening by chains. In many communities, they faced sporadic harassment from the nightwatch. The Common Council of London in 1638, for example, instructed constables "to do their best endeavour" to arrest "lewd and loose women wandring in the streetes" at night.[12]

Of all marginal groups, Jews, where their numbers were greatest, endured the most systematic segregation, forced either to remain in urban ghettos, with their gates bolted at dusk, or to take refuge in the surrounding countryside. Among the "many detestable and abominable things" for which Jews were blamed at night was consorting with Christian women. Of Jews in Vienna, a seventeenth-century visitor discovered, "They must all depart at night beyond the river into the suburbs." In Venice, where the late sixteenth-century population numbered a few thousand, ghetto gates, guarded by four Christian sentries, were shut from sunset to sunrise. Notably, an exception was made for doctors, of whom a large number resided in the *Ghetto Nuovo* after its completion in 1516. Because many of these possessed patients outside the ghetto, they were permitted to remain abroad on condition of supplying guards with written reports.[13]

Not just prostitutes, but women in general were not to stray at night. Besides compromising their own virtue, they might sully, through low intrigues, the reputations of honorable men. By force of custom if not statute, women of all ranks and ages, save for midwives, risked public disgrace if they did not keep to their homes. They might be mistaken for adulteresses or prostitutes, only to be accosted by strange men or arrested. In Thomas Dekker's pamphlet *Lanthorne and Candle-Light* (1608), a constable demands of a woman, "Where have you bin so late? . . . Are you married? . . . What's your husband? . . . Where lie you?" Years later, a band of law clerks in Grenoble justified their assault upon two maidservants by claiming that the girls "had no candles and prostitutes are the only women out of doors at night."[14]

Even males of good repute still faced constraints after dark. In Catalonia, for instance, no more than four men could walk together in a group. Unless licensed by permits, carrying weapons was frequently forbidden—arquebuses, pistols, or other firearms along with swords and knives, despite the prevalence of private arms within early modern households. Beginning in the late thirteenth century, English law prohibited pedestrians at night from wearing "sword or buckler, or other arms for doing mischief." Italian towns forbade "secret weapons" such as daggers and pocket pistols, easily concealed under a cloak. If caught with a pistol in Rome, an offender might be sent to the galleys. Where nobles first claimed special privileges, laws repealed most of these by the late 1600s, in keeping with efforts by authorities throughout the nation states of Europe to wean subjects from their weaponry. In Paris, by virtue of an ordinance in 1702, not only were men of quality forbidden to carry firearms, but their servants were stripped of canes and staffs. The necessity to maintain order grew all the more urgent after nightfall, when opportunities multiplied for both personal and political violence. By day, armed travelers to Italian cities were instructed, "*Liga la spada*" (tie the hilt to the sheath), but at night swords were confiscated. "They who have license to cary swordes in the cittyes," noted a visitor to Florence, "yet must not weare them when the evening beginns to be dark." "The carrying of arms fosters violence," a Spanish decree explained in 1525, and "many persons take advantage of the cover of darkness to commit all kinds of crimes and misdemeanors."[15]

Along with restrictions on weaponry, towns prohibited nocturnal disguises, including the use of visors and masks—employing a "false face," in the words of an English law. Banned from time to time were hooded cloaks worn by women and oversized hats by men.[16] Urban ordinances mandated that citizens, when abroad, bear a lantern, torch, or other "light" (not permitted were dark lanterns, possession of which in Rome could send one to prison). The main design was not to avert accidents. In Venice, in fact, members of the powerful governing body the Council of Ten were exempt from such restrictions. The purpose of these regulations, widespread throughout Europe, was, instead, to allow authorities to monitor citizens when the need for oversight was greatest. Seen from a short distance, the light from a lantern or flambeau might reveal an individual's clothing and rank, if not their identity. Penalties for noncompliance were harsh. In Paris, not to carry a light risked a fine of ten *sous*, equivalent in the late fourteenth century to the price of sixty eighteen-ounce loaves of bread.[17]

Otherwise, artificial lighting was scarce on city streets, not to mention in rural villages. Apart from the moon and stars, lanterns outside private homes afforded the principal illumination. Containing a lit candle, these were metal cylinders with narrow slits for protection from the wind or transparent sheets made from animal horn (the sawn horns of slaughtered cattle were first soaked in water, then heated, flattened, and thinly sliced)—hence the vernacular spelling "lanthorn." At the beginning of the fifteenth century, London officials required households on main streets to hang one lantern apiece on designated evenings, always at private expense. Included were saints' days as well as sessions of Parliament for the benefit of members forced to return late to their lodgings. In 1415, the first of many London regulations extended this mandate to all evenings falling between All Hallows' Eve (October 31) and Candlemas (February 2). Paris, at the behest of Louis XI (1423–1483), adopted a measure in 1461 ordering lanterns to hang in the windows of dwellings fronting major streets, thereafter known as *rues de la lanterne*; and in 1595 Amsterdam established a similar decree, though meant to apply to only one house out of every twelve.[18] Outside metropolitan centers, municipal improvements proceeded more slowly. In England, it would be another hundred years before provincial towns took halting steps in the wake of London's lead. In the early 1500s, for example, lanterns were required to be hung in York by aldermen and in

Chester by the mayor, sheriff, and innkeepers. Bristol and Oxford, on the other hand, made no provisions for street lighting before the seventeenth century.[19]

Never were these maiden measures calculated to provide cities and towns with illumination each and every night. Most ordinances decreed that lanterns be displayed a few months a year, when winter nights grew longest, and only on evenings when the moon was "dark." In London, lights were deemed unnecessary from the seventh night following each new moon until the second night after a full moon. More important, candles were not meant to burn overnight, but just to remain lit for several hours. Declared a watchman's song:

A light here, maids, hang out your light,
And see your horns be clear and bright,
That so your candle clear may shine,
Continuing from six to nine;
That honest men may walk along
And see to pass safe without wrong.

Intended to guide families homeward, candlelight failed to provide consistent security for either pedestrians or households. Owing to the expense of lanterns and tallow candles, coupled with persistent threats of vandalism and theft, the compliance of homeowners was erratic. Wind and rain made even more difficult the maintenance of lanterns, whose light, at best, cast a faint glow.[20]

For the most part, streets remained dark. There were a few exceptions. In sudden emergencies, municipalities required families to furnish lighting, either by illuminating windows, setting bonfires, or placing candles outside doors. Residents of Danish towns, by law, had to repair outside, with candles and weapons in hand, to aid victims of violent crime. Fires mobilized households, as did military hostilities. In contrast to the use of urban blackouts in modern warfare, preindustrial cities required more, not less, lighting to mount defenses. One night in the early fifteenth century, the threat of a treasonous conspiracy in Paris caused an uproar "as if the city were full of Saracens," with lanterns ordered lit by homeowners. Residents of Leeds, upon rumored fighting in a nearby town during the height of the Glorious Revolution of 1688–1689, placed "thousands of lighted candles" in windows, as men prepared to march to their neighbors' aid.[21]

Public celebrations also occasioned displays of light at night. Government authorities organized massive illuminations, including fireworks, in observance of royal births, marriages, and coronations, as well as in honor of military victories during wartime. When the King of France in 1499 captured the citadel of Milan, joyous residents of Florence lit bonfires and illuminated the city's towers to the accompaniment of pealing bells. In 1654, at the urging of officials, citizens of Barcelona lit their homes for three straight nights to celebrate the end of the plague. "Even though this was a time when there was little wealth and much hardship," noted a contemporary, "everyone made an effort to do what they could." On ceremonial occasions in England, typically the windows of urban homes glowed with candlelight, normally in unison with bonfires and fireworks. In 1666, on the night of the king's birthday, Samuel Pepys barely reached home because of numerous fires in London's streets. At patriotic celebrations, dazzling illuminations, set against the blackness of night, inspired widespread awe. "The people," averred the "Sun King" Louis XIV (1638–1715), "enjoy spectacles, at which we, in any event, endeavor always to please." A later observer shrewdly remarked that their purpose was to "keep the people in the dark."[22]

The Church, too, relied upon the power of pageantry. The centrality of light to Christian theology lent added force to sacred occasions, drawing attention to the presence of Christ and the Church's continual struggle against darkness—a conflict as real as it was symbolic. After all, light, as John Milton wrote in *Paradise Lost*, was the "prime work of God." To celebrate Christ, Pope Gelasius (d. 496) in the late fifth century established Candlemas, on which candles would thereafter be blessed every February 2. Illuminating the dark reaffirmed in dramatic fashion God's dominion over the invisible world. Before the Reformation, all churches felt this imperative; but with the "stripping of the altars" in Protestant lands across Europe, the ornate use of candles and tapers invariably smacked of papist idolatry—"burning lampes, & lightes that alwaies flame / Before the Virgins image fayre," ridiculed an English diatribe in 1553. Catholic sacraments continued to make extensive use of giant beeswax candles to

Jean Le Pautre, *The 1674 Festival at Versailles Organized by Louis XIV to Celebrate the Re-conquest of the Franche-Comté*, seventeenth century.

illuminate church altars. White in color, the wax emitted little smoke and burned with a clear flame. Years later, James Boswell thought the candles, even unlit, gave "a clearer idea of heaven than any of the rites of the Church of England ever did."[23]

It was at night that Catholics staged their most magnificent spectacles. More than any of the Protestant faiths, the Church of the Counter Reformation publicly proclaimed its nocturnal domain. Periodically, church bells assisted in this task, rung on both somber and festive occasions as well as during thunderstorms to frighten evil spirits. In the archdiocese of Salzburg, for example, church bells tolled all night during the summer solstice in 1623 because of fears of "devilish activities."[24] But light was the Catholic Church's foremost weapon against darkness. Streets were strewn from one end to another with candles and paper lanterns to illuminate festivals. In seventeenth-century Germany, passion plays, organized every Good Friday by the Jesuits and the Capuchins, animated Catholic communities. In Spain on the Wednesday evening of Holy Week, processions, lit by candles with four wicks, passed in the streets as penitents were lashed before onlookers. Of a festival in the Sicilian town of Messina, a visitor noted in the early 1670s, "The streets are as lightsome

in the dark nights" about which authorities increasingly complained. "Most theft," warned a Paris official in 1667, "has been done as a result of the darkness in districts and streets where there are no lanterns." The following year, a proposal to light Amsterdam's streets cited the perils of crime, fire, and accidental drownings.[27]

Whereas not one leading European city before 1650 employed some form of public lighting, increasing numbers of municipalities did by 1700, beginning with Paris (1667), Amsterdam (1669), Berlin (1682), London (1683), and Vienna (1688). National capitals, in particular, felt some urgency not to be outdone by rival metropolises. Funded by tax revenues, street lights included both oil lamps and, as in prior years, lanterns lit by candles. In Paris, hundreds of lanterns were hung from ropes strung high across major streets at approximate intervals of sixty feet. "Archimedes himself, if he were still alive, could not add anything more agreeable or useful," a Sicilian visitor rhapsodized. The original impetus came from the city's first lieutenant general of police, Nicholas de La Reynie, who successfully touted the project's merits to Louis XIV. By century's end, the annual expense of maintaining more than six thousand lanterns, according to an English estimate, totaled nearly fifty thousand pounds sterling. In addition to lamplighters' wages, heavy costs arose from employing metalworkers, ropemakers, glassmakers, and tallow chandlers. A traveler to Paris, noting that the lanterns stayed lit at all hours of the evening, thought the expense warranted. Less charitable was his opinion of London officials, who restricted use of the city's new oil lamps to the darkest winter nights—"as though," on other evenings, "the moon was certain to shine and light the streets." Even so, in the half-century after their installation in London, more than fifteen provincial towns followed suit, from Coventry and York in 1687 to Birmingham and Sheffield in 1735.[28]

Yet it is important to keep these improvements in perspective. On most nights, cities and towns remained predominantly dark. In spite of public funding, urban lighting early in the eighteenth century was poor. With the exception of major thoroughfares, most streets stayed unlit. Rare were those neighborhoods that enjoyed adequate illumination by which one pedestrian could easily identify another. And, as in London, streets in a majority of cities and towns were illuminated just on the darkest nights of winter, and then only until midnight. Some major cities, such as Stockholm, Lisbon, and Florence, continued to make no provisions for public lighting. Lamps in Dublin, as late as 1783, were spaced one hundred yards apart—just enough, complained a visitor, to show the "danger of falling into a cellar."[29] Even in Paris, where lanterns burned all night, myriad problems arose, from a shortage of lighters to an epidemic of vandalism and theft. Lantern lighters themselves pilfered candles. Critics groused about not only the high cost but also the poor quality of light, especially for pedestrians shunted to the sides of streets. Claiming that lighting in Paris and other French cities was designed for the "interests of the higher classes" in coaches, a traveler testified, "The pedestrian must stumble on his way as he can, through darkness and dirt, by the sides of the road or street." Moreover, lanterns in Paris burned just during the winter months, as had lanterns in European cities ever since the late Middle Ages. Not surprisingly, as late as 1775 a visitor to Paris noted, "This town is large, stinking, & ill lighted." Louis Sébastien Mercier thought the city's lanterns valuable only for "making darkness visible."[30]

Old habits of mind persisted. Within the conclaves of church and state, there lingered the conviction that darkness represented an inviolable period of time, an interval as sacred as it was dangerous. Manifested in its purest form in Rome, this mentality resonated among Protestant as well as Catholic functionaries. Notwithstanding its embrace of public lighting, the Leipzig city council in 1702 instructed residents to "keep their own [family] at home in the evening." Of the mindset in Geneva, Rousseau wrote, "God does not agree with the use of lanterns." Except for urgent circumstances or special ceremonies, reputable citizens, in theory, were expected to confine themselves to home, devoting evening hours to prayer and rest. Equally, there would be less chance of a fire being ignited by some besotted pedestrian carrying a lit torch. Illuminated streets were designed to aid people on essential errands, not mischievous souls bent on revelry. "We ought not to turn day into night, nor night into day," wrote a London pastor in 1662, "without some very special and urgent occasion." Otherwise, from the vantage of established authorities, the chief contribution of artificial lighting lay in assisting members of the nightwatch, lone guardians of law and order in communities large and small.[31] The protection of life and property rested squarely on their shoulders, however faint their silhouettes invariably appeared amid the shadows.

II

I start every hour from my sleep, at the horrid noise of the watchmen, bawling the hour through every street, and thundering at every door; a set of useless fellows, who serve no other purpose but that of disturbing the repose of the inhabitants.

TOBIAS SMOLLETT, 1771[32]

In all likelihood, the nightwatch, not prostitution, is the world's most ancient profession, originating as soon as men and women first feared the darkness. In early cultures, sentries remained vigilant at all hours, as soldiers on foot and horse patrolled urban streets. But it was at nighttime that cities and towns most relied upon watchmen's eyes and ears. "Rulers that are watchful by night in cities," observed Plato, "are a terror to evildoers, be they citizens or enemies." Of the nightwatch, the Roman prefect Cassiodorous wrote in the fifth century, "You will be the security of those who are sleeping, the protection of houses, guardian of gates, an unseen examiner and a silent judge."[33] Medieval communities, too, employed guardians of the peace. As early as 595, the Frankish king Chlotar II (584–628) required towns to post *gardes de nuit*. Centuries later, guilds occasionally assumed this responsibility. By 1150, merchants and artisans supplied men each night to keep watch in Paris. Within England, the Statute of Winchester in 1285 created the framework for regular watches in every city, town, and borough. The law decreed that officers patrol at night around the clock. Watchmen had the power to arrest suspicious wayfarers and, if necessary, to raise the community by "hue and cry."[34]

The Tuscan city of Siena, by the early 1300s, also maintained a small force, but not until the sixteenth century did many European cities do so, relying instead upon sentries and fixed barriers. The *Famile de Guet*, a citizens' guard, emerged during these years in France, where it remained an urban institution throughout the years of the ancien régime. Across Switzerland, Moryson discovered "armed citizens keepinge the watch in divers streetes." Typical, perhaps, of large towns and cities in England, York in the mid-1500s relied upon a force of six men for each of its wards, with patrols scheduled from 8:00 P.M. until 5:00 A.M. Of London, Thomas Platter reported, "Since the city is very large, open, and populous, watch is kept every night in the streets."[35] In colonial America, the largest towns, from Boston to Charleston, instituted watches during the first decades of settlement. The earliest was Boston's, created in 1636 to patrol after sunset during summer months, but New York's was the most imposing. By the mid-1680s, it numbered forty men, divided into companies of eight apiece, each assigned to patrol one of New York's five wards.[36]

Not all communities relied upon watchmen. In Berlin, regular patrols did not commence until the seventeenth century. Dublin waited until 1677 to employ a guard, modeled after the Statute of Winchester's blueprint. Frankfurt offered private citizens cash bounties to apprehend criminals.[37] Many small localities, with at most a constable or two, refrained from utilizing watchmen unless roused by a sudden crisis. In the Essex village of Maldon, only a spate of burglaries during the eighteenth century persuaded residents to appoint a modest force of three men. Conversely, urban sites of strategic importance instituted stronger defenses. Whereas Venice by the fifteenth century used professional guards known as *sbirri* to protect its streets, the city's famed Arsenal, with its vital shipbuilding industry, formed companies of men from its own workforce. The largest of these, the *guardiani di notte*, patrolled the shipyards regularly. More unusual was the pack of mastiffs set loose each evening within the walls of Saint-Malo, a garrison town on the northern coast of France with valuable quantities of naval stores. The lineage of this practice dated to the thirteenth century, when the Dominican monk Albertus Magnus commented that the dogs "patrolled well and trustily." In the early 1600s, a passing observer recorded,

> In the dusk of the evening a bell is rung to warn all that are without the walls to retire into the town: then ye gates are shut, and eight or ten couple of hungry mastiffs turn'd out to range about the town all night, to secure their naval stores etc. from being stollen: and some that have had the misfortune to be drunk, & lie abroad have been found next morning as Jezabel was at Jesreel.[38]

Notwithstanding these anomalies, watchmen became a common feature of the urban nightscape. Variations existed in their numbers, appearance, and cost, but their essential duties almost everywhere were the same. Ordinarily, members patrolled circuits on foot—alone or in pairs—within the borders of a single ward or parish, though some forces, like the *Guet* in Paris, also operated on horseback. Most hours of the night, all nights of the year. "This," asserted a writer in 1719, "is practis'd, in all countries, in well-governed cities." Within England, each set of watchmen answered to a constable at a local watch-house. London introduced these structures by the 1640s. Each watch-house served as a guard room in which to assemble by a warm hearth before and after one's shift.[39] Most officers were lightly armed, limited to a lantern and either a staff or a watch-bill, which featured a concave blade at the end of a pole. In Norway and Denmark, watchmen equipped themselves with a spiked mace called a *morgenstern* (morning-star). Officers in Stockholm wielded a staff with a set of pincers to seize ruffians by the neck or leg. Along with a hand-rattle for sounding alarms, members of the Amsterdam "rattle-watch" each bore a pike or halberd. Only in American towns, near the Indian frontier, were firearms standard before the eighteenth century. In the fledgling settlement of New Haven, watchmen were instructed to report "within an hower after the setting of the sun, with their armes compleate, and their guns ready charged."[40]

Preindustrial towns also posted watchmen in church towers, ready to blow a horn or sound a bell upon the first glimpse of trouble. In the event of fire, a lantern might be hung on the side facing the blaze. Outside the British Isles and the Mediterranean, lookouts were a standard precaution by the sixteenth century. From Bergen to Gdansk, they assisted ground patrols. Typically, the highest steeple, with the best view, was selected for the site, though in a large city like Amsterdam as many as four towers were manned. The Tower of St. Bertin in St. Omer, France, contained more than three hundred steps. In contrast, the skyline of early American towns hugged the horizon, though New England settlers occasionally kept watch from the roofs of meetinghouses. New Haven officials ordered watchmen to scan the town several times a night for fire or Indians. Apart from monotony, frigid temperatures and high winds posed the greatest challenge for lookouts. Danes kept bottles of spirits by their sides. To ward off sleep, watchmen beneath Nuremberg's towers routinely blew horns.[41]

Along with announcing the weather, officers on foot cried the time. This was done every hour on the hour, in contrast to church bells that traditionally tolled at curfew and again at dawn. Verses, sung at the top of their lungs, accompanied watchmen's reports. Some of these adopted a playful tone. Declared an English verse, "Men and children, maides and wives, / 'Tis not late to mend your lives. / Lock your doors, lie warm in bed— / Much loss is in a maidenhead." Even so, this verse, like most, imparted a practical message. "Looke well to your locke, / Your fier and your light," was standard advice. Some cries were meant to be comforting—"Sleep in peace, I am watching" was the chant in Marseilles. Many bore a strong religious character, interspersing calls for prayer with reports of the time. "Rise up, faithful soul, and go down on your knees," intoned a Slovakian verse. A watchman's song from northern England implored:

Ho, watchman, ho!
Twelve is the clock!
God keep our town
From fire and brand,
And hostile hand;
Twelve is the clock![42]

The calls of the watch, chanted methodically throughout the night, beg an interesting question. To whom did officers address their cries? Who possibly could have been listening in the late hours of the evening? Perhaps the calls were designed to verify that watchmen had not themselves drifted asleep, slumped in some alley, as critics occasionally charged? But certainly horns or bells could have served that purpose. In Leipzig, where watchmen blew horns to announce the hour, they still recited pious homilies. It seems obvious, there and elsewhere, that communication was a goal of municipal authorities, no matter how late the hour—hence the didactic content of the watch's verse for everyone within earshot to hear. As an ordinance explained in the Danish port of Helsingør, residents needed to know "how the night was passing."[43]

The watch's cries might have served an additional purpose, directed instead at families asleep. If the frequent complaints of urban denizens are any indication, slumber in towns and cities was light and fitful, due, at least in part, to loudmouthed watchmen. The irony of this was not lost upon contemporaries, accustomed to being awakened by paeans to sound slumber. "For though you lay you downe to sleepe, /" fumed an early seventeenth-century poet, "The Belman wakes your peace to keepe." In the Danish play *Masquerades* (ca. 1723), by Ludvig Baron Holberg, the servant Henrich complains, "Every hour of the night they waken people out of their sleep by shouting to them that they hope they are sleeping well." (A London newspaper correspondent named "Insomnius" attributed the watch's racket to envy.) Still, in the eyes of local officials, broken slumber heightened people's vigilance to perils of all sorts, including enemy attacks, criminal violence, and fire. The cries of sentries guarding Irish castles reportedly served the same purpose. The late sixteenth-century historian Richard Stainhurst noted, "They shout repeatedly as a warning to the head of the household against nocturnal thieves and vagrants lest he sleep so soundly that he be unprepared to repel his enemies bravely from his hearth." Whether, in the case of urban watchmen, theirs represented a deliberate policy or an unintended consequence, town fathers rarely heeded complaints about their clamor.[44]

Fire prevention, for the nightwatch, was a critical responsibility. Not only were fires more prevalent at night, but they were also more dangerous, with fewer people abroad to sound a warning. It was the watch's duty to investigate unusual sources of light or smoke. Officers in colonial Philadelphia had orders to arrest anyone found smoking outdoors, while in Boston, members of the watch were themselves forbidden to "take tobacco" next to any home. More important, if a blaze flared, watchmen were expected to raise an alarm. Only streetwalkers, in cities where prostitution was legal, shared a like charge. Church bells typically contributed to the alarm. After a Stockholm fire in 1504, a bellringer, for his negligence, was ordered to be broken on the rack, until pleas for mercy resulted instead in his beheading. In France, members of the watch had the power to enlist passersby for fire-fighting "without respect," complained Mercier, "for age or function or insignia." Any who refused to help were subject to arrest and, if convicted, having their ears cut off.[45]

Additional tasks occupied watchmen on their rounds, including checking that homeowners locked their doors. "As they pass," noted a visitor to London, "they give the hours of the night, and with their staves strike at the door of every house." The sound of knocking awakened Pepys early one morning: "It was the constable and his watch, who had found our backyard door open."[46] So, too, it was the watch's duty to remain vigilant against potential wrongdoers. In England, watchmen were empowered to arrest nightwalkers on the strength of their own suspicions. That meant the right to apprehend—with at most a general warrant—drunkards, prostitutes, vagrants, and other disorderly persons. A contemporary noted, "If they meet with any persons they suspect of ill designs, quarrelsome people, or lewd women in the streets, they are empowered to carry them before the constable at his watch-house." There, suspects could either be interrogated by a justice of the peace, if one was available, or jailed overnight until examined the following morning, when often they would be committed to a house of correction. There was ample opportunity for abuse. Respectable pedestrians resented the authority of watchmen, who could sieze "better men than themselves," as a seventeenth-century writer complained. Worse, at times, was the watch's treatment of the poor. One night in 1742, drunken constables in London threw twenty-six women, whom they had collected, into a "roundhouse," with the windows and doors shut. By morning, four had died from asphyxiation. Exclaims the fictional constable in a play by Ned Ward, "I'm monarch of the night, can stop, command, examine, loll in ease, and, like a king, imprison whom I please."[47]

In view of the lawlessness afflicting urban centers, one might wonder why authorities did not deploy larger, more professional forces. Besides the heavy cost, within England and America, traditional fears of monarchical power hindered the creation of trained police, lest like a standing army they fall under despotic control. As late as 1790, a Russian visitor reflected, "The English have a dread of a strict constabulary, and prefer to be robbed rather than see sentries and pickets."[48] Among some officials, there also may have been a grudging recognition that night afforded a safety-valve for criminal violence. Better to conceal human vices in darkness than run the risk of daily disorders. Just how shortsighted this belief was would become increasingly clear in many cities and towns; but, for the time being, it may have helped to discourage tougher responses to crime. Most important, the goals of officials in preindustrial towns were confined to curbing misbehavior and preventing fires, mostly by discouraging nocturnal activity. Across Europe, the duty of the watch was "to keep the streets clear of people, that had no real business in them." Their purpose was not to render nighttime more habitable to pedestrians, other, perhaps, than offering to see them home. And even that service was erratic. Abroad in the dark and "rather afraid," the Londoner Sylas Neville failed to enlist any of the watchmen whose aid he repeatedly requested. "They declining," he wrote, "I ventured & got to the inn safe, thank God!"[49]

All the same, watchmen bore a heavy burden of responsibility. For eight or more hours each night, they alone embodied legal authority in contrast to the network of municipal institutions in daily operation. Except for constables to whom they reported, no other public officials were entrusted with keeping the peace or protecting households from sudden conflagration. "The watch," declared a Boston resident, "are the greatest safeguard to the town in the night." If that charge were not burden enough, fatigue, icy weather, and streets strewn with refuse made rounds all the more onerous.[50]

Initially, within many communities, it was the civic duty of all able-bodied townsmen, from time to time, to donate their services, with little or no compensation. Already in the sixteenth century, however, men of property paid money to local officials with which to hire substitutes instead. Almost everywhere—on both sides of the Atlantic—this pattern seems to have rapidly taken hold. Nonetheless, the wages of watchmen remained meager. Many, by necessity, held daytime jobs. Numerous others, aged or infirm, depended upon alms for alternate income. "Decrepit," "feeble," and "worn-out" were among common descriptions. A Norwich court in 1676 attributed frequent fires to a shortage of "sober and substantial inhabitants" among the watch; whereas a London jury acquitted a burglar, for "the matter depending purely upon the watchman's evidence," he was thought "old and his sight dark." At least a few members were adolescents. New York authorities warned against enlisting boys, apprentices, and servants; and Boston selectmen observed in 1662 that "the towne hath beene many times betrusted with a watche consistinge of youths." Although constables occasionally came from the middling ranks of their communities, most members of the watch belonged to the lower orders—the "very dregs" of the "human race," claimed a commentator. In Slovakian villages, widows are known to have served.[51]

It would be difficult to exaggerate the extent of popular contempt for nightwatchmen. Neither their credentials nor their appearance inspired public confidence. These men were not the swashbuckling guards, resplendent in ruffles and silk, portrayed in Rembrandt's famous painting of Captain Frans Banning Cocq's militia company, later misnamed *The Nightwatch*. In the absence of uniforms, watchmen donned tattered hats and either cloaks or heavy coats to guard against the chill night air. Of a London watchman, a writer described, "He was covered with a long sooty garment, that descended to his ankles, and his waste was clasp'd close within a broad leathern girdle." Sometimes, rags were wrapped like scarves about their heads. English officers were ridiculed for eating onions. These, wrote Thomas Dekker, "they account a medicine against the cold." Most of all, it was the watch's conduct that invited derision. They were frequently the butt of playwrights and poets. In *Much Ado About Nothing* (1600), Shakespeare reflected prevailing prejudices in his portrait of the constable Dogberry. Under his merry command, parish officers turned a willing backside to benches but a blind eye to thieves. "The most peaceable way for you," instructs Dogberry, "if you do take a thief, is to let him show himself what he is and steal out of your company."[52]

Some officers wisely desisted from enforcing unpopular laws at their neighbors' expense, especially when infractions were minor. Thus the watch in Paris refrained from dispersing late-night revelers at a cabaret for they were "*honnêtes gens*." Allegations of corruption were common—not just consorting with prostitutes but taking bribes and colluding with thieves. Citizens of the Swedish market town of Borgerne complained in 1483 that a constable routinely extorted coins at night from small boys and adolescents. A London author wrote of "constables going around their parishes and precincts to the several bawdy-houses to receive sufferance-money." More often, members of the watch were faulted for negligence—napping, tippling, and shirking their rounds. As proof of their diligence in Geneva, officers were required to drop chestnuts into boxes along the route of their patrols. In England, the "Watch-mens Song" from the mid-seventeenth century lampooned:

Sing and rejoyce, the day is gone,
and the wholsome night appears,
In which the constable on throne
of trusty bench, doth with his peeres,

Anon., *The Midnight Magistrate*, eighteenth century. Watchmen as monkeys delivering their charges to the constable at the watch-house.

> *The comely watch-men sound of health,*
> *sleep for the good ot'h Commonwealth.*[53]

Small wonder that watchmen, during rounds, suffered verbal and physical abuse. "Fowle words" and "ill language" some nights flowed freely. In Paris, derisory nicknames included *savetiers* (bunglers) and *tristes-à-pattes* (flatfeet). Told to return home late one evening, Joseph Phillpot retorted that the "constables of Portsmouth should kiss his arse." Abuse of parish officers comprised a significant portion of assaults in seventeenth-century Essex, whereas in the Dalmatian port of Dubrovnik, even armed patrols fell prey to violence. In the Danish town of Naestved in 1635, two watchmen fled to the door of the mayor one night, rousing him in his nightshirt, after a troop of journeymen shoemakers, crying "Kill them, kill them," attacked with knives. Fumed an English critic, "So little terror do our watchmen carry with them, that hardy thieves make a mere jest of 'em."[54]

III

The law is not the same at morning and at night.

GEORGE HERBERT, 1651[55]

Night, the French legal scholar Jean Carbonnier mused, probably gave birth to the rule of law. Deeds of darkness, not daylight, spurred early communities to fix sanctions for personal misconduct. All the more ironic, declared Carbonnier, that by the late Middle Ages law at best exerted a faint influence at night. Edicts and ordinances became little more than dead letters. Indeed, until the advent of the Industrial Revolution, evening hours escaped legal oversight in both urban and rural areas—"*vide de droit*," in Carbonnier's elegant words. So frail were institutions and so immense were night's dangers that authorities abdicated their civic responsibilities.[56]

Certainly, most courts and tribunals fell silent each evening. Proceedings were barred not just by fatigue and hazardous travel but also by a belief among officials in night's inviolability. As early as the *Twelve Tables*, the ancient foundation of Roman law, judges were instructed to render decisions by "the setting of the sun." And, too, darkness connoted deceit and secrecy. The famous Roman advocate Quintilian observed, "'With bad intention, then, means something done in treachery, at night, in solitude." As a guiding precept of Roman law, which experienced a resurgence in the late Middle Ages, the conviction that nighttime fostered duplicity exerted an enduring influence across continental Europe. Some localities prohibited civil transactions after dark; and even when permitted, their validity remained suspect. Contracts, covenants, and codicils all aroused suspicion when executed at night. Beginning in the sixteenth century, pawned goods in sections of Switzerland, according to a regional code, could not be appraised after the "sunshine disappears behind the mountain top." In some places, the selection of beneficiaries by testators was forbidden, whereas wills themselves could be read only in the presence of "three lights."[57]

One suspects that similar attitudes informed English courts, though the common law contained few explicit restrictions. A noteworthy exception concerned the right of landlords to seize the property of tenants for nonpayment of rent. After dark, common law expressly forbade this practice, permitting only the overnight confinement of livestock that strayed from a neighbor's fields. In addition to customary prejudices against nocturnal transactions, personal dwellings, in the eyes of English courts, constituted protected sanctuaries at night. "Every man by the law hath a special protection in reference to his house and dwelling," observed Sir Matthew Hale in the *History of the Pleas of the Crown* (1736). "Every English," John Adams of Massachusetts proclaimed, "glories justly in that strong protection, that sweet security, that delightful tranquility which the laws have thus secured to him in his own house, especially in the night."[58]

Still, Carbonnier's skepticism about the law's reach is only partially merited. How greater, by comparison, the compass of criminal justice at night became. Just as evening announced the cessation of civil society, it signaled the increased danger of crime. True, the response of authorities could have been more energetic—employing trained police rather than constables and watchmen with the added responsibility of fire prevention. On the other hand, no officers at all regularly patrolled urban streets by day. Their presence at night represented a singular assertion of government power. Then, too, these "midnight magistrates," as a critic called constables, possessed considerable legal authority. In England, unlike daytime officers with restricted powers of arrest, watchmen and constables enjoyed wide latitude. In the absence of police, inflating their powers offerred a way to compensate for the weaknesses of an amateur constabulary.[59]

Other steps, too, were taken to stem nocturnal crime. In places that permitted the limited use of torture in criminal interrogations, judges relaxed restrictions for offenses after dark. Within Italy, summary courts arose in the late Middle Ages for the investigation and prosecution of nighttime offenses. Foremost among these tribunals were the *Signori di Notte* (Guardians of the Night Watch) in Venice and the *Ufficiali di Notte* (Officials of the Night) in Florence. Towns in Denmark occasionally granted citizens the right to convene their own courts in order to try offenders at night. Nor were evening executions unknown, sometimes fol-

Pierre-Paul Prud'hon, *Justice and Divine Vengeance Pursuing Crime*, 1808.

lowing immediately after convictions in order to quell popular discontent or to underscore the importance of swift justice. In August 1497, for example, five prisoners in Florence were quickly executed after a trial lasting from morning until midnight. Noted the Milanese law professor Polydorus Ripa in 1602, "A punishment is able to be performed even at nighttime if there is danger in delay." Darkness also magnified the horror of the death penalty. When Dublin fell prey in 1745 to a rash of street robberies, officials hanged seven criminals by torchlight. "The unusual solemnity of such an execution," a contemporary remarked, "struck such a terror in the minds of the populace" that the number of robberies fell.[60]

More commonly, courts everywhere exacted stiffer punishments for nighttime offenses. If not stipulated by law, this calculation usually occurred in the normal course of deliberations by judges and juries. During the late Middle Ages, numerous nocturnal offenses were punished with added severity. A woman in Siena in 1342, found guilty of an assault, first had her punishment halved because her victim was male, then doubled "because she struck him in his house," and doubled yet again because the crime took place at night. Such, too, was the predominant pattern in early modern courts, where thefts routinely crammed dockets. "A nighttime thief must be punished more than a daytime one," wrote Ripa. For thefts committed after the curfew bell, towns in Sweden decreed the death penalty, while in the Sénéchaussée courts of eighteenth-century France, darkness was the most common aggravating circumstance in the sentencing of thieves. Just as bills of indictment in English courts, as a matter of course, specified whether a crime occurred at night, Scottish proceedings pointedly noted offenses committed "under cloud and silence of night."[61]

Especially serious was burglary. Under the Tudors, it became one of the first crimes in England removed from the list of those which allowed a felon to escape the death penalty by claiming literacy. In the county of Middlesex during the second half of the 1500s, over four-fifths of convicted burglars were sentenced to hang. Death by hanging or the galleys for life was standard punishment in France. Colonial American assemblies left English law intact, with only slight changes. In Massachusetts, where the Puritans initially proved reluctant to execute property offenders, the government in 1715 declared burglary a capital crime, even for first-time offenders.[62]

In the view of courts, only one deed, if committed at night, merited lenience: the slaying of a domestic intruder. Early legal codes from the *Twelve Tables* to *Rothair's Edict* in the mid-seventh century to the *Coutumes de Beauvaisis* in 1283 recognized this basic principle, as did St. Augustine and English law. What by day constituted homicide, even if the victim were a housebreaker, by night became a justifiable act of self-defense. So in 1743, a Geneva prosecutor declined to charge a peasant for shooting a burglar. Besides citing Mosaic law, the *procureur général* explained that it had been impossible for the peasant to know at nighttime whether the intruder had theft or murder in mind. "In the day time," a correspondent to the *London Magazine* reflected in 1766, "it might possibly be discovered who he [the thief] was, and it might be presumed he intended only to steal not to kill." "In this case," the writer explained, "a man should not avenge himself, but have the thief before the magistrate." But at night, everything was different. The "master of the house could *then* neither know *who* he was, nor expect, or have the help of others to secure him."[63]

It should not surprise us that procedures and penalties, indeed basic rights and privileges, changed from day to night. The arrival of darkness placed heightened emphasis upon the preservation of public order. A French prosecutor in 1668 bemoaned that two thieves from Lieges were merely sentenced to hang. "Public safety during the night is so important that one would think they would be condemned to the wheel." Not only did nighttime afford criminals a cloak of secrecy, but it hindered the ability of persons to defend themselves, particularly when home asleep—or to come to the assistance of their neighbors. "Stealing in the night time is certainly ane aggravation of theft," observed a Scottish prosecutor, "because then people are most unguarded." In the case of burglary, the availability of moonlight, unlike daylight, did not obviate the terrible nature of the crime, even when an offender's identity was known. Sir William Blackstone declared in 1769, "The malignity of the offence does not so properly arise from its being done in the dark as at the dead of night, when all creation except beasts of prey are at rest, when sleep has disarmed the owner and rendered his castle defenceless."[64]

So it was. At that late date, most persons at night still remained on their own, confronting crime and other dangers with, at best, the aid of family and close neighbors. Despite the steadily rising powers of the state, nighttime defied the imposition of government authority. Acknowledging this reality, early modern laws vainly sought to deter criminals from exploiting night's natural advantages. Without the support of daily institutions and controls, authorities relied upon repressive penalties and procedures to keep the worst excesses of criminal violence at bay.

All to little effect. As late as the mid-eighteenth century, a Londoner complained of the "armies of Hell" that "ravage our streets" and "keep possession of the town every night." So, too, in Paris, observed a lawyer in 1742, "no one was out past 10 P.M.," even though a professional *garde* by then supplemented the city's watch. Instead, criminals with clubs, *assommeurs*, roved the main streets. The best that can be said is that, in the absence of watchmen and rudimentary lighting, urban conditions would have been worse. Ultimately, night lay beyond government control, a natural law that neither courts nor constables could change. A tenacious fatalism, grounded in an awareness of God's omnipotence and man's frailty, undergirded the official mindset. Hence the well-known psalm, inscribed on an ancient building in the Danish town of Aalborg, "Unless the Lord watches over the city, in vain the watchman stands on guard."[65]

CHAPTER FOUR

A MAN'S HOUSE IS HIS CASTLE: DOMESTIC FORTIFICATIONS

I

Thro God's great mercy we were safe at my house before the day light was gone.

EBENEZER PARKMAN, 1745[1]

WELL BEFORE TOWNS barred their gates, nature signaled day's retreat. For many families, the rural environment, not watches or clocks, kept life's daily pulse. Only parish church bells, periodically rung during the day, rivaled nature's precision. Innumerable omens foretold evening's advance, many of them routinely decipherable, others intuited by the received wisdom of bygone generations. Toward sunset, marigold petals began to close. Flocks of crows returned to their nests, and rabbits grew more animated. The pupils of goats and sheep, normally oval in shape, appeared round. "The goats' eyes were my clock," recalled Ulrich Bräker of his labors as a young Swiss shepherd.[2]

No time of the day aroused greater anticipation than the onset of darkness. Nor did any interval merit more careful calibration. On clear days, guidance came from the heavens—the sinking course of the sun, leaving streaks of light across the sky. Wrote a seventeenth-century Neapolitan, "The sky was darkening to the colour of a wolf's snout." Still, nature's most reliable timetable lay in shadows cast by the sun's descent. As daylight dimmed, darkness to the human eye advanced in stages. Day in, day out, fields fell to the shadows in unerring succession. *Brune*, a French term for dusk, testified to the altered hue of the evening landscape. In contrast to Mediterranean latitudes, twilight in northwestern Europe was prolonged. The typical countryman, Thomas Hardy remarked in *The Woodlanders* (1887), "sees a thousand successive tints and traits in the landscape which are never discerned by him who hears the regular chime of a clock."[3]

Rarely did preindustrial folk pause to ponder the beauty of day's departure. In contrast to the praises sung of dawn, neither in literature nor in letters and diaries did contemporaries marvel at the sun's decline. Feelings of insecurity more often than awe swept the terrain. "Begins the night, and warns us home repair," wrote a Stuart poet. Eager to avoid nightfall, numerous men and women hastened homeward, hoping to return in "good season." Some, tarrying too long, lodged at the house of a relation or friend rather than brave the night. Detained by a court hearing, Matthew Patten, a farmer in colonial New Hampshire, observed, "It was so near night when it was done that we could not come home."[4] As evening blanketed the countryside, tardy travelers wrote of being "covered" or "overtaken." "Night overtook us, and made the remainder of the journey disagreeable and dangerous," recounted one. Sometimes night's miasmic atmosphere seemed impenetrable to sight. "Come, thick night," implores Lady Macbeth, "And pall thee in the dunnest smoke of hell."[5]

II

Theeves, wolves, and foxes now fall to their prey, but a strong locke, and a good wit, will aware much mischiefe.

NICHOLAS BRETON, 1626[6]

Easily, the most common idiom in English for nightfall was "shutting-in." More than other expressions, it captured popular apprehensions. After a short trip, the Puritan minister Samuel Sewall jotted in his diary, "Got well home before shutting in. Praised be God." In part, this oft-repeated term signified the metaphorical "shutting-in" of daylight—"I returned home on foot, just as day light shut in," recounted a London resident. But on a practical level, "shutting-in" emphasized the need for households to bolt portals against the advancing darkness. The fifteenth-century poet

François Villon instructed, "The house is safe but be sure it is shut tight." Attested an English proverb, "Men shut their doors against a setting sun."[7]

The saying that "a man's house is his castle" assumed profound importance at night. This timeworn expression, at least as old as the 1500s, applied alike to turf huts and brick manor homes. According to Sir Edward Coke, the home served as much for man's "defense against injury and violence as for his repose." A sacred boundary, the domestic threshold was demarcated by a door and a sill of stone or wood. However exposed during the day, thresholds represented frontiers at night that unexpected visitors were not to cross. The reaction of a rural household in Scotland when approached by a rider would have been a common one: "Upon the trampling of my horses before the house," discovered Edward Burt, "the lights went out . . . and deafness, at once, seized the whole family."[8]

Despite prevailing fears, families at night were far from powerless. Without the protection afforded by institutions, they relied heavily upon their own resources. Everyone assisted, but care and protection of the family lay with the *paterfamilias*, the male head of the household. First and foremost, evening saw quarters made fast once laundry and tools were brought inside. Doors, shutters, and windows were closed tight and latched. A London wine merchant observed, "I never keep the door open after 'tis dark." "Barricaded," "bolted," and "barred," as an English playwright described a Georgian home—"backside and foreside, top and bottom." Of his Bavarian childhood, the writer Jean Paul reflected, "Our living room would be lit up and fortified simultaneously, viz, the shutters were closed and bolted." A child, he noted, "felt snugly preserved" behind "these window embrasures and parapets." The working poor also took precautions, for even the most mundane items—food, clothing, and household goods—attracted thieves. Richard Ginn, who worked for a coachmaker, testified, "My house is constantly locked up half an hour past 8, when I return from my business, for I may be killed as well as another man." As one who earned her bread from washing, Anne Towers had a "great charge of linen" besides personal belongings in her London home on Artichoke Lane—"I always go round every night to see that all is fast."[9]

In well-to-do homes, large wooden doors, set in frames of stone or wood, guarded the front entrance. Iron hinges and latches gave added strength to the thick wood. All the same, many locks provided scant security. The standard mechanism, common since medieval times, permitted a key to push a bolt into a groove in the frame, thereby fastening the door. Not until the introduction of the "tumbler" lock in the eighteenth century would keyholes better withstand the prowess of experienced thieves. In the meantime, families resorted to double locks on exterior doors, bolstered from within by padlocks and iron bars.[10]

More vulnerable were windows. Despite their small size by modern standards, at night windows represented the weakest points in a home's perimeter. Whereas the lower orders covered openings with oilcloth, canvas, or paper, aristocratic housing began to boast glazed windows by the late Middle Ages. Only in the sixteenth century, however, did glass panes spread to middle-class dwellings. Besides confining heat, windows lent protection from the wind and rain, and also from the night air. Wooden shutters afforded a safeguard against both intruders and the elements, especially if caulked during the winter with soil or moss.[11] Often, in preindustrial homes, iron grates and bars protected windows on the ground floor, prompting frequent comparisons with convents and gaols—"more like prisons," observed a visitor to Madrid, "than the habitations of people at their liberty." Even where living conditions were meager, iron bars, in the absence of glass windows, were thought a necessity. A traveler in northern France remarked, "The people are very poor, and live in most dreadful huts, . . . no glass in the windows but iron bars, and wooden shutters." Although barred windows were most common on the Continent, visitors noted their presence in parts of England and the Scottish lowlands. In London, the magistrate Sir John Fielding endorsed the practice of securing windows with bars in the shape of a cross; he also recommended that each door have double bolts along with a bar and chain.[12]

Naturally, families took extra pains to protect such valuables as money, plate, and jewelry. Within propertied households, oak chests, fitted with locks and iron bands, were common. Counseled Paolo da Certaldo in the late fourteenth century, "Close up all your day-time things always, whenever you go to sleep at night." Samuel Pepys concealed valuables throughout the rooms of his house, including his dressing room, study, and cellar, where he stored sundry chests constructed of iron. "I am in great pain to think how to dispose of my money," he fretted, "it being wholly unsafe to keep it all in coin in one place." Blessed with one hundred and fifty pounds, Anne Feddon of Cumberland always locked her fortune in a drawer during the day but "took it to bed with her at night." John Cooper in Yorkshire hid ten pounds beneath a large stone in a corner of his home. As reflected in fairy-tales, hiding places were not restricted to dwellings. In addition to closets, chests, and beds, they included dry wells and hollow tree trunks. Among villagers in eighteenth-century Languedoc, burying the family treasure in a nearby field was a favorite tactic.[13]

All these steps constituted a family's preliminary line of defense. There were also precautions designed to alert slumbering households, such as equipping shutters with bells. Servants, too, knew to sound an alarm. Late one evening in 1672 when three maids, washing dishes in a Northamptonshire home, heard a noise in the yard, they promptly awakened the household—"one beat the bell, another blew a horn, a third put candles in every room." Wealthy estates occasionally employed guards and, by the late seventeenth century, spring-traps. The author of *Systema Agriculturae* in 1675 advised placing sharp iron spikes in the ground, surrounded by brass trip-wires, "which wire and spikes are not visible by night." In 1694, an English inventor even devised a "night engine" to be stationed "in a convenient place of any house, to prevent thieves from breaking in." The exact nature of the device remains a mystery, but it likely anticipated another "machine," advertised a century later by William Hamlet of London. A spider's web of bells and rope stretched across a broad frame, Hamlet's design promised to sound an alarm against both thieves and fire.[14]

Most households were armed, often more heavily than members of the nightwatch. Domestic arsenals contained swords, pikes, and firearms, or in less affluent homes cudgels and sticks, both capable of delivering mortal blows. In the country, sickles, axes, and other farm tools made convenient weapons. Having passed through a cornfield, the Oxfordshire adolescent Thomas Ellwood was attacked at night by husbandmen wielding staves "big enough to have knockt down an ox." Once a family retired for the night, weapons were kept close. A Middlesex squire, his house invaded by five masked burglars in 1704, immediately snatched a sword "that always lay at his beds-head"—only to be stabbed from behind. Valued as a club was the common bed-staff, a short, sturdy stick used in sets of two on each side of a bed to hold its covers in place. The staff enjoyed a widespread reputation as a handy weapon—hence, in all likelihood, the expression "in the twinkling of a bed-staff." When a Hampshire apprentice in 1625 attacked his sleeping master with a hatchet, he was quickly beaten off with one.[15]

Firearms, owing to advances in accuracy and other technological breakthroughs, grew more prevalent among homeowners after the mid-seventeenth century. Whereas in Kent, guns figured in fewer than 3 percent of all violent deaths between 1560 and 1660, shootings claimed more than one-quarter of such fatalities by the 1720s. Many of these, arising from the protection of home and family, ended at court in acquittals. Anxious to light his candle late one evening, James Boswell desisted from searching for a tinderbox for fear that his landlord—"who always keeps a pair of loaded pistols by him"—would mistake him for a thief. Few London households were as well armed as that of Charlotte Charke, who as a young girl grew fearful that her home would be burglarized. Stashing her parents' silverware by her bedside, she assembled a personal armory, containing "my own little carbine," a "heavy blunderbuss, a muscatoon, and two brace of pistols"—"all which I loaded with a couple of bullets each before I went to bed."[16]

Accidental fatalities at night were a common hazard. Any strange noise or unfamiliar light put households on edge. In a Cumberland village, the son of a blacksmith was shot for a burglar after he whistled outside a home to signal a servant maid. When an aged man suffering from senility entered an unfamiliar house in Pontrefract, a maid shouted "thieves," causing her master to "cut him in pieces" with a sword. Colonists in early New England were occasionally mistaken at night for Indians and shot.[17]

Watchdogs prowled inside and out. In the countryside, they did double duty, guarding against thieves as well as predators. "Bandogs," for their ferocity, were chained during the day. According to William Harrison, the mastiff, or "master-thief," received its name for its prowess against intruders. Dogs everywhere were prized for their vigilance, from the feared Kalmuk dogs in southern Russia to rural France, where the nineteenth-century author George Sand observed that even the meanest peasant possessed one. It was the rare night that early modern villages did not echo with sporadic barking. Failing to find shelter late one evening, a traveler in rural Scotland lamented, "None made reply but their dogs, the chief of their family." In towns and cities, dogs guarded shops as well as homes. In

Thomas Rowlandson, *Housebreakers*, 1788.

Harp-Alley, a London brazier kept "a crass, crabbed" mutt that barely tolerated customers in the day, "much less in the evening," according to a wary neighbor.[18]

Of the proper qualities for a watchdog, a sixteenth-century writer recommended an animal that was "big, hairy, with a big head, big legs, big loins, and a lot of courage"—"big," of course, being the cardinal qualification. Harrison suggested a "huge dog, stubborn, ugly, eager, burdenous of body (and therefore of but little swiftness), terrible and fearful to behold." All the better, commentators agreed, if the dog was black, so that it could surprise a thief in the dark. A watchdog's worth lay in its bark as much as its bite. Owners, just from the pitch and intensity of their dog's bark, could determine the presence of an intruder. In England, these dogs were called "warners" or "watchers." Equally important was their value as a deterrent. "Whenever I went upon any such expedition, we immediately desisted upon the barking of a dog, as judging the house was alarm'd," one burglar claimed. The Florentine Leon Battista Alberti urged in the mid-1400s that not just dogs but also geese patrol inside homes—"one wakes the other and calls out the whole crowd, and so the household is always safe."

Experienced thieves poisoned watchdogs, but such efforts were fraught with risk. In London, an impatient burglar, after throwing poisoned food over a wall, entered the property too quickly and was badly mauled.[19]

III

To whom but night belong enchantments?

THOMAS CAMPION, 1607[20]

Thus the array of common-sense measures families adopted to protect their homes from intruders: locks, dogs, and weapons. Across the social spectrum, defenses varied more in degree than in kind, with most households, however modest, taking steps to safeguard lives and property. In addition to these rudimentary precautions, a family's religious faith provided an important sense of security. While many households remained ignorant of basic tenets of Christian theology, God to most believers was not a lifeless abstraction confined, in word and deed, to the impersonal pages of scripture. For Protestants and Catholics alike, his presence affected every sphere of daily existence, including one's physical and mental well-being. "Were it not for the providence of God," asked Sarah Cowper, "what security have we?"[21]

Seldom was God's protection more valued than at night. Dangers were greater and less predictable. The venerable salutation "good night" derived from "God give you good night." "By night," affirmed the poet Edward Young, "an atheist half-believes a God." Locks and latches, by themselves, afforded little protection from Satan's minions. Special prayers existed not only for bedtime but also for sunset and evening. Of his Lutheran childhood in Germany, Jean Paul recalled that his family, "at the toll of the evening bell," joined hands in a circle to sing the hymn, "The Gloom of Night with Might Descends." With hosts of angels at his command, God, in his infinite mercy, kept night's terrors at bay. A seventeenth-century meditation "for the night season" implored "that thy guardian angel may both guide and protect thee." A French priest advised, "Upon hearing any strange noise or crack in a house let us fervently recommend ourselves to God."[22]

Preindustrial families also embraced the occult. Beliefs and practices that religious authorities increasingly condemned as superstition, much of the laity viewed more benignly. Rather than rivaling God's word, folk magic equipped ordinary men and women with an additional means of combating Satan's wiles. On a practical level, there was no contradiction in most eyes between faith and the occult. Amulets rested side-by-side with crucifixes, both prized for their protective powers. In one Irish household, an early eighteenth-century poem described:

St. Bridget's cross hung over door,
Which did the house from fire secure . . .
And tho' the dogs and servants slept,
By Bridget's care the house was kept.
Directly under Bridget's cross
Was firmly nail'd the shoe of horse
On threshold, that the house might be
From witches, thieves, and devils free.[23]

Popular magic lay rooted in centuries of rural tradition. Every generation inherited from its forbears an ancient faith in the importance of supernatural beliefs and practices. "Transmitted down from one generation to another," a minister in Scotland observed. Specialized knowledge of magical spells came from conjurers who inhabited premodern communities—"white witches" and "cunning" men and women, including *kloka gubbarna* and *visa käringarna* in Sweden, *saludadores* in Spain, and *giravoli* in Sicily. Often, it was their intimate mastery of magic that enabled neighbors to manipulate supernatural forces. In 1575, a German clergyman reported from Neudrossenfeld, "Magic and recourse to soothsayers have become very common on account of theft, and it follows from this that many use magic in times of illness, and bring those soothsayers to themselves." Unlike "black witchcraft," practiced to inflict harm, "white witchcraft" was beneficent—"mischievously good" in the words of John Dryden. Within England, much to the annoyance of church authorities, conjurers likely equaled parish clergy in number. Of his Lutheran parishioners, a German pastor despaired, "They hold such people in their hearts as a God."[24]

Foremost in a household's battery were "night-spells." Containing both Christian and occult elements, these guarded homes, livestock, and crops from thieves, fire, and evil spirits. An English verse implored, "From elves, hobs, and fairies, / That trouble our dairies, / From fire-drakes and fiends, / And such as the devil sends, / Defend us, good Heaven!"[25] Similar in purpose were amulets, ranging from horse skulls to jugs known as "witch-bottles," which typically held an assortment of magical items. Contents salvaged from excavated jugs have included pins, nails, human hair, and dried urine. Highly valued everywhere were amulets fashioned from iron, long preferred for its magical properties over bronze or stone. Hung to ward off evil spirits, horseshoes were common throughout Europe and early America. "Naile a horse shoo at the inside of the outmost threshold of your house," instructed Reginald Scot in 1584, "and so you shall be sure no witch shall have power to enter."[26] Among slaves in the British West Indies, the use of amulets, or possets and fetishes, was routine. Of West African origin, they included an assortment of broken glass, blood, alligators' teeth, and rum, hung by a hut or garden to frighten evil spirits and thieves, who, according to a traveler, "tremble at the very sight." An estate manager on St. Kitts wrote in 1764, "Their sable country daemons they defy, / Who fearful haunt them at the midnight hour."[27]

Just as families fortified doors and windows against burglars, so too were objects with supernatural powers placed by household entrances. Small crosses, holy water, and consecrated candles, ashes, and incense all offered spiritual protection. "I put the cross on the windows, on the doors, on the chimney," declared a Slavic verse. Although Protestant clerics in the wake of the Reformation disdained sacramentals, many households continued to employ them. Common, too, in parts of Europe was the practice of placing on doors religious icons and inscriptions beseeching God's care. "O Lord," began a verse in the Danish town of Kolding, "if you will preserve our house and keep it from all danger and fear. . . ." Remarked a traveler to Switzerland, "Here as in Germany they have verses or texts of Scripture on the front of their homes." Customary outside Jewish homes were *mezuzas*, encased scrolls of biblical verse affixed to doorposts.[28]

Other objects were less orthodox but no less popular. Even the gateposts fronting the home of Reverend Samuel Sewall bore the traditional safeguard of two "cherubims heads." Besides horseshoes, doors bore wolves' heads and olive branches. To keep demons from descending chimneys, suspending the heart of a bullock or pig over the hearth, preferably stuck with pins and thorns, was a ritual precaution in western England. In

Somerset, the shriveled hearts of more than fifty pigs were discovered in a single fireplace. Favored along the Holderness coast of East Yorkshire were flat oolite stones known as "witch-steeans" that inhabitants tied to the door-keys of their cottages; whereas in Swabia, for protection from fire, families were urged to bury beneath their thresholds the stomach of a black hen, an egg laid on Maundy Thursday, and a shirt soaked in the menstrual blood of a virgin, all bound with wax.[29]

For ordinary folk confronting an uncertain cosmos, the occult formed a potent part of their lives. If nothing else, the existence of supernatural forces provided another way to understand life's misfortunes—to render more comprehensible the frightening uncertainties of everyday existence. Confessed John Trenchard, author in 1709 of *The Natural History of Superstition*, "Nature in many circumstances seems to work by a sort of secret magick, and by ways unaccountable to us." While religion furnished, in the words of Keith Thomas, "a comprehensive view of the world," magic's role was more circumscribed. Despite a grassroots belief in fairies, there is no evidence, at least in England, to suggest the actual worship of pagan deities or spirits. Instead, magic was confined largely to concrete problems and their resolution. If the occult did not address life's greatest mysteries, it nonetheless made ordinary life more susceptible to human control—especially in the hours after sunset when the world seemed most threatening.[30]

IV

> *When the absence of the moon, or the thickness of the air, takes from us the light we stand in need of, we are always masters of procuring it to ourselves.*
>
> "OF THE NIGHT," 1751[31]

"All would be horror without candles," stated a sixteenth-century religious meditation.[32] Each evening, darkness itself, not merely the perils it unleashed, was pushed back within homes. With fire and fuel, men and women created for themselves small patches of light amid the blackness. Light, of course, had immense supernatural importance. Endowed with religious symbolism, it also possessed magical properties dating to pagan times. Sparks from a candle's flame could bear enormous portent for the future. Peasants in Upper Languedoc punctuated their conversation by swearing oaths "by the fire" or "by the flame of the candle." At night, such was light's prophylactic appeal that in Germany a large house candle was lit to fend off evil spirits and storms, just as candles in Poland reputedly prevented the devil from frightening livestock. In parts of the British Isles, to guard against demons, persons "clipped," or encircled, buildings and fields with lit tapers.[33]

Also common, naturally, for those who could afford the expense, was the practical use of candlelight to ward off thieves. Besides denying anonymity to burglars, artificial lighting signified human activity. With the windows of his parlor under repair, William Dyer of Bristol burned a candle all evening to deter "nightly depradators," while Pepys, "to scare away thiefs," ordered a candle lit in his dining room. In the Auvergne of France, so alarmed by crime were peasants in the mid-1700s that an official reported, "These men keep watch with a lamp burning all night, afraid of the approach of thieves."[34]

Still, light's principal value lay in expanding the borders of domestic space for work and sociability. During long winter evenings, the hearth furnished the greatest glow. Even in dwellings with more than a single room, it became the focus for evening life, combating the cold darkness with both heat and light. In Normandy, as late as the nineteenth century, the room containing a fireplace, even in large homes, was called "the room" or "the heated room." Because of the hearth's importance to domestic life, tax assessments were sometimes based on their number within a home. Chimney fireplaces first appeared in English dwellings in the thirteenth century, but not until the 1600s in many households did they eclipse the

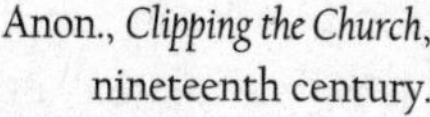
Anon., *Clipping the Church*, nineteenth century.

open central hearth, ringed either by stones or hardened clay. Despite the gradual spread of fireplaces to private chambers, the large majority of homes in England and France in the seventeenth century still contained just a single hearth. Most were constructed from stone or brick, though some rural chimneys were fashioned from timber and wattle and daub. Besides their cost, fireplaces were messy and dangerous. "It is easier to build two chimneys," declared a proverb, "than to maintain one." Fireplaces were also inefficient, with most of their heat escaping up the chimney until the eighteenth-century introduction of flues. Stoves offered a common alternative to the hearth in Germany, Eastern Europe, and parts of Scandinavia; beginning in the sixteenth century upper-class homes in England occasionally used them to burn coal. But, as a source of light, stoves were a dismal substitute for fireplaces.[35]

Mending or "beating" a fire required patience and skill. Just igniting a small pile of kindling could be time-consuming. Before the nineteenth-century invention of "lucifer" or friction matches, the easiest solution was to borrow a burning brand or hot coal from a neighbor, taking care not to start a fire in transit. Otherwise, the alternative was to strike a piece of steel against flint to ignite a small quantity of tinder, typically linen, cotton, or soft paper wet by a solution of saltpeter. "No easy matter," recollected a West Yorkshire native of the difficulty, especially when attempted in the dark. Iron or ceramic firedogs (andirons) helped to assure enough oxygen. Once lit, fires burned best at a slow and steady pace, unless cooking required a "high" blaze. "The French readily say that fire keeps company," noted a German, "because they spend much time making it."[36]

Fuels varied widely depending upon local resources. Throughout Europe and early America, wood was a popular source of heat, particularly hardwoods like oak, beech, and ash that gave off the most warmth. A typical household required from one to two tons of wood per year. Brush provided faggots for kindling, as did, each fall, cuttings from vineyards in winemaking regions of the Continent.[37] Another popular fuel in England was bituminous or "pit" coal, which boasted a higher caloric value (6.9) than wood (3.5) and required less maintenance. Most prized, from northern England and Wales, was "candle coal," a form of bituminous coal that burned with a brilliant flame and emitted little smoke. Such was its radiance, commented a visitor, that "in winter time poor people buy it to serve instead of candles." Owing to their expanding size and distance from woodland areas, London and other large cities grew ever dependent upon supplies of coal.[38]

For heat, the preindustrial poor relied upon anything and everything, ranging from such shrubs as heather, furze, and gorse to dried seaweed in coastal areas (its use on the Scottish island of Eriskay imparted a pungent flavor to baked bread). Along England's Dorset coast, popular were pieces of shale impregnated with enough oil for a good blaze.[39] Widely used in West Country moorlands and other woodless regions was peat or turf, cut in slabs from the ground with spades and stacked in large piles to dry and harden. Easily kindled, peat fires required less care than wood but burned more quickly than coal. They emitted a very strong smell along with abundant smoke. On the other hand, extensive deposits existed not only in England but also in Ireland, Scotland, and the Netherlands. In Ireland, where all classes employed this fossil fuel, fully one-seventh of the land area reputedly consisted of peat bogs. According to a minister in the Scottish community of Tongue, peat afforded "a strong, though not a clear light" used "instead of candles." A traveler to Scotland in 1699 claimed, "In some parts where turf is p[l]entiful, they build up little cabbins thereof ... without a stick of timber in it; when the house is dry enough to burn, it serves them for fuel and they remove to another."[40]

Finally, in place of costlier alternatives, the lower orders burned cow, oxen, and horse dung. Demand, naturally, increased in the winter when temperatures plummeted and peat fell in short supply. Widely available, dung was kneaded with straw or sawdust, patted into cakes, and piled next to homes to dry. "Dithes," they were called in Lincolnshire, where, a resident reported, "The cows shit fire." Despite a sharp odor when burned, dung generated more heat than did wood. In the Cambridgeshire town of Peterborough in 1698, Celia Fiennes noted, "The country people use little else in these parts." A century later, a set of travelers—in Cornwall and Devon—was followed by "an old woman hobbling after" their "horses in hopes of a little fuel."[41]

Whatever the source of domestic heat, hearths gave off limited light, confined to a radius of several feet. Usually, just the meanest hovels depended entirely for light upon a fire, located in the center of the dwelling. Forced to take shelter with a poor family, the Birmingham traveler William Hutton recounted, "I was now in a room ten feet square, dignified with the name of *house*, totally dark, except a glow of fire, which would barely have roasted a potato." The absence of subsidiary lighting inside a home invited derision and contempt, as jokes contained in chapbooks reflected—thus, the story of Leper the Tailor, who boarded overnight in the farmhouse of a penurious Scotswoman. Denied a decent bed, he was forced to sleep on the floor, only to discover that she had mistakenly placed his pile of straw atop a slumbering calf, so dim was the light. Leper had his revenge when, to the shame of his hostess, the "bed" moved next to the hearth.[42]

A broad spectrum of illuminants in early modern communities afforded light. All, in spite of their diversity, relied upon the common medium of fire; not until the twentieth century would most Western households turn to a radically different technology in the form of electricity. Apart from the hearth, there were really just three basic types of preindustrial lighting, none of which had essentially changed in over a thousand years. Most widespread were candles, a form of solid fuel whereby a wick was encased in wax or animal fat; and lamps, in which oil was drawn through a wick from a small receptacle. In fact, the top of a candle really functioned as a small lamp, with the wick mounted in a pool of oil. Cruder in form than either candles or lamps were resinous splinters of wood called candlewood, which burned with a steady flame.[43]

Candles predominated in the English-speaking world and throughout much of northern Europe, especially among the propertied classes. Common sayings reflected their ubiquity, such as "burning a candle at both ends" and "holding a candle to the devil."[44] Introduced by the Phoenicians, the beeswax candle first became popular among European aristocrats during the late Middle Ages. Renowned for its pleasant odor and clear flame, it was long favored by genteel households. According to the *Boke of Curtasye* (ca. 1477–1478), it was the chandler's duty to see that "in the chamber no light there shall be burned but of wax." Such was the extravagance of the court of Louis XIV that used candles were never relit. Of comparable quality, with the rise of whale hunting in the North Atlantic during the early eighteenth century, were spermaceti candles, fashioned from a rose-colored liquid wax found in the head of sperm whales—thus the mission of Captain Ahab's vessel, the *Pequod*, in *Moby-Dick* (1851). Such illuminants

Thomas Frye, *Young Man Holding a Candle*, eighteenth century.

were costly. Prices fluctuated over time, but never did wax or spermaceti candles become widely accessible. To light and heat the palatial home of the Marquis de la Borde, a wealthy Parisian financier, Horace Walpole in 1765 estimated an annual expense of more than 28,000 livres.[45]

Tallow candles, by contrast, offered a less expensive alternative. The mainstay of many families, their shaft consisted of animal fat, preferably rendered from mutton that was sometimes mixed with beef tallow. (Hog fat, which emitted a thick black smoke, did not burn nearly as well, though early Americans were known to employ bear and deer fat.) Among other rural chores reserved for fall, Thomas Tusser advised, "Provide for thy tallow, ere frost cometh in, and make thine wone candle, ere winter begin." Unlike wax or spermaceti candles, however, those made from tallow gave off a rancid smell from impurities in the fat. Describes Shakespeare in *Cymbeline* (ca. 1609), "Base and unlustrous as the smoky light that's fed with stinking tallow." As tallow candles burned, the quality of their light deteriorated. They also required continual attention to avoid wasting the fat. Unless "snuffed" (trimmed) every fifteen minutes, the fallen remains of the cloth wick could create a "gutter" of molten fat down one side of the candle. Charred bits of wick, known as "snot," posed a fire hazard, depending upon where they landed. And tallow candles required careful storage so that they would neither melt nor fall prey to hungry rodents. Still, despite such drawbacks, even aristocratic households depended upon them for rudimentary needs. At the country estate of Castletown, home to Ireland's richest man, Thomas Connolly, some 2,127 pounds of tallow supplied candles in the single year 1787, compared to the family's consumption of 250 pounds of beeswax candles, reserved for such formal spaces as the parlor and dining room.[46] Only on special occasions did wax candles light bourgeois homes. Of a friend's festive dinner, the Norfolk parson James Woodforde recorded, "Mr. Mellish treated very handsomely indeed. Wax candles in the evening." Similarly, Woodforde noted, one Christmas, briefly burning his "old wax-candle." "It is almost finished, it might last for once more."[47] Further complicating the use of both wax and tallow candles in England were the taxes levied on each, at least during the eighteenth century. At the same time, making one's own candles became illegal.[48]

For families farther down the social ladder, rushlights (rushes coated in fat) provided a crude substitute. Although similar in design to candles, they were exempted from taxation. Homemade, rushlights were fashioned from meadow rushes for which Britain's moist climate was well suited—both the soft rush, *Juncus effusus*, and the common rush, *Juncus conglomeratus.* Dried and peeled, except for a single strip of bark for support, the pith was repeatedly dipped in hot kitchen tallow and allowed to harden. "The careful wife of an industrious *Hampshire* labourer," noted the eighteenth-century naturalist Gilbert White, "obtains all her fat for nothing; for she saves the scummings of her bacon-pot for this use." Suspended horizontally in an iron holder at a slight angle, the typical rush, measuring over two feet, burned for nearly an hour, about half the time of a tallow candle. The reformer William Cobbett later wrote of his childhood, "I was bred and brought up mostly by rush-light." His grandmother, married to a day laborer, "never," to Cobbett's recollection, "burnt a candle in her house in her life." Reported the minister of a Highlands parish, "When the goodman of the house made family worship, they lighted a rushy, to enable him to read the psalm, and the portion of scripture." Middle-class homes, to varying degrees, utilized rushlights to save the expense of candles. Observed White, "Little farmers use rushes much in the short days [winter], both morning and evening, in the dairy and kitchen."[49]

In large parts of continental Europe, families relied upon oil lamps. Outside the British Isles, there were fewer flocks of sheep to supply tallow but abundant sources of oil. Moreover, warmer temperatures, at least in Mediterranean countries, made the use of tallow candles problematic, with their low melting point; conversely, in Britain and other northern climes some varieties of oil ran the risk of congealing during winter months. Oil lamps ranged from scallop and conch shells to the common *cruisie* or *cresset* lamp, an elongated iron vessel of French origin with a handle at one end. At the opposite end lay a wick of soft cord partially submerged in the oil. Wicks required trimming, but just one pint of oil could sustain a flame for many hours. Plants and trees afforded sources of oil for lamps, including flax and rapeseeds, olives, and walnuts. In coastal areas, fish livers were treasured for their oil, as was fat from seals in Scandinavia. An especially unctuous sea bird, the fulmar, made its home on the outer islands of St. Kilda, Borrea, and Soa in the North Atlantic. When disturbed, it regurgitated a liquid from its beak suitable for lamps. So oily was

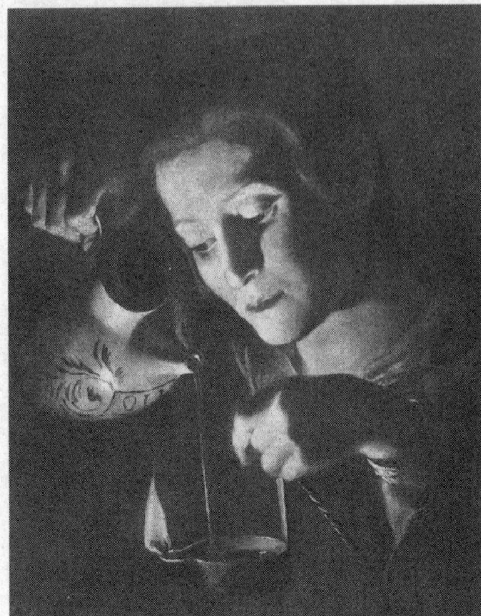

Trophîme Bigot, *A Boy Pouring Oil into a Lamp*, 1620.

the stormy petrel in the Shetland Islands off northern Scotland that residents used its carcass for a lamp by sticking a wick down its throat.[50]

In France, a rushlight made from kitchen fat was known as *a meche de jonc* and in Germany as a *Bisenlicht*. Indigent families had an alternative in candlewood wherever there was an abundance of pine and fir trees. Often trunks were stripped bare of their bark and allowed to die standing upright. Once felled, splinters of the dead wood, full of a dark, tarry resin, burned as small torches in iron holders. The lit end of a splinter pointed downward in order to preserve its flame. Pine knots, too, were burned as both kindling and a source of light. There was widespread use of candlewood from Sweden to the Canary Islands. Russian archaeologists researching medieval sites in Novgorod uncovered pine chips and splinters, bound together to make torches. A variation of candlewood, known as bogwood, was available in northern England and Scotland. Along with branches pulled from dead fir trees, residents unearthed decaying trunks from bogs—not just firs but also elm and oak trees, all packed with resin. "Instead of candle," noted a visitor to the Scottish Highlands, "the common people here, and thro' most of the highlands, use chips of fir dug out of the mosses. These chips being full of resin, burn generalie with a bright flame." Tenants sometimes paid part of their rent by supplying cartloads of "candle fir."[51]

Perhaps nowhere was candlewood more widely used than in early America, where thick pine forests blanketed much of the eastern seaboard. No doubt, English colonists, in their adoption of this technology, profited from the experience of Indian tribes. An early description of New England proclaimed, "Here is good living for those that love good fires. And although New-England have no tallow to make candles of, yet by the abundance of fish thereof it can afford oil for lamps. Yea, our pine trees that are the most plentiful of all wood doth allow us plenty of candles, which are very useful in the house, and they are such candles as the Indians commonly use, having no other."[52]

Myriad conventions governed the use of artificial lighting. Preindustrial families were constrained by concerns for both safety and frugality. Rules controlled not only access to candles and lamps but also the time and location of their use. Not all persons, hours, and places were equal. High on the list of iniquities was "burning daylight," resorting to artificial light unnecessarily during the day. Wasting candlelight was synonymous with extravagance and dissipation. Individuals thought naturally profligate, such as children, servants, and slaves, received special scrutiny. Such was the outrage of the Virginia planter William Byrd II upon discovering his slave Prue with "a candle by daylight" that he "gave her a salute" with his foot.[53] Normally, not even twilight brought the first glimmer of household lights. The interval between sunset and nightfall in Iceland and most of Scandinavia was called the "twilight rest," a hiatus during which it was too dim to ply one's trade and too light to warrant candles or lamps. Persons instead reserved this hour before the evening's tasks for rest, prayer, and quiet conversation. In Britain and colonial America, only once darkness descended did the time widely known as "candle-lighting" arrive. Jonathan Swift advised cost-conscious servants "to save your master's candles, never bring them up until half an hour after it be dark, although they be called for ever so often."[54]

Most dependents were not permitted their own lighting, even to guide one's way to bed. In Joseph Addison's comedy *The Drummer* (1715), the mistress of a household explodes with indignation over her servants' use of night-lights in their chamber. "Are the rogues afraid of sleeping in the dark?" she demands of her steward. Of the mathematician William Oughtred, John Aubrey wrote that his wife, "a penurious woman," would "not allow him to burne candle after supper, by which means many a good notion is lost." Compounding the expense, transporting an open flame burned fuel more rapidly. And there was always a risk of fire, en route to bed and then afterwards.[55]

At all hours of the evening, families often had to navigate their homes in the dark, carefully feeling their way through familiar rooms and halls. "Man's best candle is discretion," declared a Welsh proverb. The sense of touch was critical. Individuals long committed to memory the internal topography of their dwellings, including the exact number of steps in every flight of stairs. Others, finding themselves in an unfamiliar setting, had to cope as best they could. In *Emile*, Rousseau advised, in a strange room, clapping one's hands. "You will perceive by the resonance of the place whether the area is large or small, whether you are in the middle or in a corner." Forced to take "miserable" lodgings one evening along the Italian coast, a nineteenth-century traveler "took a very accurate survey" of his chamber in order "to pilot" himself "out of it" before daybreak. The absence of lighting in homes spawned a number of ingenious techniques, most no doubt passed from one generation to another. Within the elegant two-story house that once dominated Sotterley Plantation in colonial Maryland, there remains to this day a handmade notch in the wood railing leading to the second floor, located at an abrupt right turn up the stairs. Furniture in Scandinavian homes was placed at night against walls in order to avert collisions. And everywhere it was important to maintain a tidy home, lest a tool or weapon needed to be located in the dark. The saying "everything has its place" took on added importance at night. Of servants, Robert Cleaver wrote in *A Godly Forme of Houshold Government* (1621), "If it be in the night season, and that without a light, they then not only can say, in such a place it lyeth, but also, if they be required, they can presently fetch the same."[56]

Too much should not be made of domestic lighting before the Industrial Revolution. An immense gulf separates modern lamps from their precursors. Light from a single electric bulb is one hundred times stronger than was light from a candle or oil lamp. Premodern observers spoke sarcastically of candles that made "darkness visible." "A constant dimnes" was another's description. Stated a French adage, "By candle-light a goat is lady-like." Feebler was the faint glow cast by rushlights. In homes at night, small islands of light pulsed amid the shadows. Wicks not only flickered but often spat, smoked, and smelled. "Always ready to disappear," an essayist in 1751 lamented of artificial or "borrow'd" light. Rather than flooding every nook and corner of a room, as it does today, light cast a faint presence in the blackness. Unlike overhead fixtures in modern homes and offices, candles and lamps sat at lower heights, allowing convenient access to wicks. Familiar faces and furniture, as a consequence, took on an altered appearance. Visibility was limited to an object's façade, not its top and sides. Ceilings remained preponderantly dark, and often one could barely see from one end of a room to the other. According to Fynes Moryson in the early 1600s, Irish peasants, due to an absence of tables, set rushlights on the floor.[57] On the other hand, domestic needs were far simpler then. So long as families could eat, socialize, perform basic chores, and negotiate the interiors of their homes—so long, in short, as they could tend to nightly necessities—conditions were far from intolerable.

V

The solitary man becomes wolves meat.

FRENCH PROVERB[58]

During the day, a complex web of intersecting ties bound citizens together. Networks of mutual assistance typified not only organized institutions such as guilds and religious fraternities but also less formal bodies. Family connections and neighborhood loyalties formed the most important support systems. Most Europeans resided either in tightly knit villages or in compact urban neighborhoods. Until the mid-eighteenth century, provincial towns and even large cities like London and Paris contained a patchwork of well-defined wards and parishes in which residents knew one another by sight if not by name. Italian cities were frequently divided into sections with their own insignia and patron saints. Parisians lived "in one another's almost constant presence," remarked the lieutenant general of police. And in one another's debt. Being a trusted neighbor entailed working together, worshiping together, and attending one another's weddings, baptisms, and funerals. "We are all brothers in this parish. We must all watch over what belongs to others," urged the priest of a small French village. This is not to deny the daily existence of backbiting gossip, violent assaults, and other eruptions of interpersonal discord. Some individuals relied solely upon their extended families, believing neighbors to be "foreigners," as the Amsterdam resident Hermanus Verbeecq called them in his autobiography. But if men and women occasionally neglected their civic responsibilities, the large majority placed their faith in the imperatives of good neighborliness.[59]

Nor were social obligations suspended by darkness, notwithstanding the absence of organized institutions. Although duties were fewer and families more isolated, people continued to help one another at all hours. Some performed small acts of kindness, such as lending a candle to a neighbor. Late one spring night in 1645, the Essex household of Reverend Ralph Josselin received two pounds of fresh butter. "Here was a providence suited to our necessitys," Josselin delighted.[60] Unlike the reception given strangers after dark, friends and relatives were normally welcome, all the more when visits were expected. On particularly foreboding nights, neighbors occasionally gathered together, sleeping under the same roof if not the same covers to allay their fears. With James Gregory, a Yorkshire staymaker, absent from home, his wife requested a friend to "lodge with her that night." Of a solitary evening in Philadelphia, Elizabeth Drinker noted, "I was favour'd with a good night, void of fears, 'tho that is not the case with all of us, when alone as we call it—*donnez cet maten*." Alternatively, Reverend William Cole despaired of remaining alone at his Bletcheley home with just his servant Tom, whose courage he very much doubted. If Tom's father could not join them, Cole resolved to enlist the company of a neighbor for "these dark & long nights."[61]

Often in the evening, reciprocal obligations acquired special urgency. Not only was sickness common, but darkness contributed its share of injuries. Families possessed a passing knowledge of remedies and cures, combined with a small inventory of potions, plasters, and possets, some acquired from local cunning-men. "Use any remedy that may help during the night," advised Paolo da Certaldo. Castile-soap pills and rhubarb were among the medications ingested by Parson Woodforde. Tormented one evening by a throbbing earache, he placed a roasted onion in his ear.

When, shortly before midnight, the Virginia squire Landon Carter thought his slave Daniel near death, he prescribed twenty to thirty drops of liquid laudanum in mint water, followed an hour later by a "vomit of Ipecacuana."[62]

Upon serious illness or injury, a servant or neighbor ran to fetch the nearest doctor or surgeon, assuming one was available. It was not unusual for physicians to visit one or more homes at night, even after a day's work. True, some practitioners, as a visitor to London complained, were notoriously lazy: "Those that are men of figure amongst them, will not rise out of their beds, or break their rest, on every call." Physicians' journals, however, suggest that most were remarkably conscientious. "Lodged at home at night, think it [rare?] enough to mention after four nights absence," a New England doctor scribbled in his diary. Scarcely had the Lancashire physician Richard Kay returned home one June evening in 1745 than he "was sent for to visit one that was bad, being a considerable distance from home that it made me out late." "Lord," he declared, "let me always live in thy fear and service."[63]

No less resolute were midwives. If death was a constant presence at night, so too was life, with the number of births rising dramatically after 3:00 A.M., to judge from modern deliveries. For midwives, often that meant being called at the first pangs of labor and staying after the delivery for postpartum care. During a single year, the Maine midwife Martha Ballard, by her own reckoning, lost more than forty nights of sleep. "It is now near the middle of the night," she wrote in 1795, "and Mr. Densmore calls me to his house." The city of Glasgow, by the eighteenth century, employed "sedan-chairs" at night for midwives, but most traveled in less comfort. Ballard arrived by foot, canoe, and horse—one evening she was thrown en route to a patient. Of a midnight trip she described, "The river dangerous, but arrived safe, through divine protection." Frequently, she stayed overnight at the homes of patients. A London newspaper in 1765 described the "hardship" of midwives who, "being roused from" a "warm bed," went "through frost, rain, hail, or snow, at all hours of the night."[64]

Other neighbors, too, mobilized in emergencies. Village ministers lent comfort to the sick and their families. One April, just past midnight, Josselin traveled to the home of a friend "who earnestly desired mee to bee with her at her death," whereas Woodforde visited a poor home in order to baptize a newborn "very dangerously ill in convulsions."[65] Often, comfort

Gerrit van Honthorst, *Dentist*, 1622.

came from closer quarters. Common acts of compassion happened nightly as persons sat up with an ill neighbor or relation. The sick were rarely left alone, surrounded by one or more "watchers" from the ranks of friends and family. *Veiller un malade* was the French expression for this age-old practice. Many attendants were women with long hours of experience. Besides monitoring changes in appearance and temperament, they eased patients' suffering by replacing dressings, administering medicine, and feeding broth. "We sat with him far into the night," Glückel of Hameln recalled of the hours preceding her father's death. If some watchers were apt to nap, probably most withstood the temptation. Nor, upon a death, did duties for family and friends always end. Protestants and Catholics alike felt a customary obligation to maintain a vigil at night before the burial. Protection from evil spirits alone made that necessary. In 1765, following the death of his master's son, the New England apprentice John Fitch "sat up with the child all night alone" in "keeping off spirits."[66]

The menace of fire at night forged broader bonds of cooperation. Self-preservation reinforced one's sense of community. "When thy neighbours house is on fire, by its light thou mayest see thine own danger," stated an English proverb, no doubt meant to be taken literally as well as metaphorically. When a chimney beam in 1669 caught fire at 3:00 A.M. in the East Anglian home of Isaac Archer, neighbors were immediately alerted as Archer, in nightshirt and bare feet, ran outside for water. Villagers "came in abundance," he reported with relief. In urban areas, strangers and neighbors alike joined forces. If a handful of bystanders had larceny in their hearts, most folk willingly lent their aid. In his essay "Brave Men at Fires," Benjamin Franklin observed, "Neither cold nor darkness will deter good people, who are able, from hastening to the dreadful place, and giving their best assistance to quench the flames." Summoned by a London alarm in 1677, the scholar Ralph Thoresby, visiting from Leeds, dashed off with a friend to "give the best assistance we could."[67]

At first glance, it would seem that residents responded in the same spirit to acts of crime. In England, each citizen possessed the authority to raise a hue and cry in pursuit of dangerous offenders. According to Sir Thomas Smith in *De Republica Anglorum* (1583), "He that is robbed, or he that seeth or perceiveth that any man is robbed doe levie hue and crie, that is to say, doe call and crie for aide." Certainly, victims, when attacked at night, either at home or abroad, knew to shout for aid, loudly and repeatedly. Dire cries of "Murder, murder" constituted the customary alarm, no matter the assault's severity. In *My Father's Life* (1779), Restif de la Bretonne recounted a childhood incident in which villagers, upon the cry of "murder" late one evening, wrongly feared that his father, a well-to-do peasant, had been attacked. Immediately, "everyone left their supper, picked up whatever they could find near at hand, and rushed along the main road," only to find the man unharmed. Victims of crime often addressed calls for help to "neighbors," rather than to members of the nightwatch. Mortally wounded in the head, John Eckles in the Yorkshire hamlet of Brighton lived long enough to appeal, "Help neighbours for Christ's sake!" Exclaimed a naked woman from her window in Rome, "Neighbors, help. Help me. I'm being attacked."[68]

At a minimum, urgent pleas drew families to their windows. Some of stouter heart rushed outside. In response to a midnight alarm in a Northamptonshire home, a small mob poured into the street with "forks, sticks and spits," demanding "the cause of the uproar." In 1684, the entire village of Harleton, "excepting one," pledged their aid to Henry Preston, a yeoman who feared a nocturnal attack by robbers. If heard from outside a dwelling, cries of murder gave neighbors the right to enter private premises at night. In 1745, for example, a husband and wife lured a mulatto girl into their Clerkenwell home late one evening. Sexually assaulted, the girl cried out "Murder," whereupon a fearless friend, Betty Forbes, forced her release, shouting from the street, "You black dog, what are you doing with the girl, turn her out of doors, or I'll make you, for upon the cry of murder we can break open the door."[69]

All the same, there were practical limits to neighborly support. For one thing, darkness magnified mayhem, making it difficult to identify victims from assailants. Some urban neighborhoods, home to brothels and alehouses, rarely escaped a night without screams and curses breaking the silence. In testimony at the Old Bailey, the neighbors of a prostitute calmly deposed, "She was a very civil neighbour, and they knew no harm of her, only that she kept a bawdy house, and now and then some of her lodgers and visitors used to cry out Rogues! Whores! Thieves! Murder!" From another brothel, "an outcry of murder was so frequently heard" that the loud "disturbance" surrounding the stabbing of a prostitute "was little regarded by the neighbours."[70] Interference risked injury or death. In Salem, Massachusetts, Thomas Smith, hearing cries of "Murder! Murder!" entered a home, believing, as he later attested, that "it was a shame to let neighbors kill one another." They nearly killed *him* instead when Smith was brutally beaten for his heroics. In 1728, hearing shouts for help, a Londoner vainly sought a watchman's aid. Rebuffed, the pedestrian seized the street robber himself only after other onlookers refused—"one saying he was a dangerous fellow, and they would not seize him for twenty pounds." Further, there was always the danger that screams for help were a ruse to lure unwitting pedestrians into an alley or street. Passing through Smithfield at midnight, Audley Harvey ran with sword drawn to a man's aid, only to be clubbed by the "victim" and his gang. "There are so many traps laid to draw people in," deplored a contemporary.[71]

Many families, having shut their doors and windows for the evening, were loath to leave the safety of their homes. "Don't go out," one of several rapists warned a resident in Villy le Maréchal. "We don't want to do any harm, we only want to take a bitch." Spying a man and a woman pull a corpse from a home, Robert Sanderson recorded in his diary, "I did not thinke it proper to draw nearer to them, because I really apprehended that the people were ill folkes." Most often, citizens turned a deaf ear when strangers were at risk. Unlike friends and family, outsiders enjoyed no claim to the support and protection of a neighborhood. Nor did their lives warrant endangering other innocents. Grabbed at dusk in 1745 outside the White Lion Tavern in London's Strand, Mary Barber boldly informed her assailants that "she was in a Christian country, and did not fear getting assistance." Later, battered and bruised, she was kicked into the street, only to lie sprawling on the ground. "No body knew me there, nor nobody came to my assistance," Barber recounted. Least civic-minded, according to travelers, were residents of Moscow, where violence at night was endemic. Olearius in the seventeenth century reported, "The Burghers showed no pity. If they heard someone suffering at the hands of robbers and murderers beneath their window, they would not even look out, much less come to his assistance."[72]

Single acts of crime, unlike fires, rarely imperiled an entire village or neighborhood. Nor, when fighting the flames from a nighttime blaze, did volunteers ordinarily face life-threatening dangers; duties instead extended to bailing water and raising buildings. Whereas fire meant catastrophe to a village if left unchecked, crime posed a sharp risk to civic-minded samaritans who ran to the aid of victims. Small wonder, then, that many citizens remained behind closed doors. Small wonder, too, that street-savvy victims of crime knew at night to shout, "Fire! Fire!" when assaulted in public. Attested Bonaventure Des Périers in *Cymbalum Mundi* (1539), "This routs the people out of their homes, some in nightshirts, others entirely naked."[73] If murder or robbery failed to animate their sense of community, the threat of being burned alive almost always did.

CHAPTER FIVE

DARKNESS VISIBLE: NAVIGATING THE NIGHTSCAPE

I

We'le live as others doe, as much i'th practises of night, as day.

SIR WILLIAM DAVENANT, 1636[1]

FOR ALL OF night's dangers, surprising numbers of men and women, either by necessity or by choice, forsook the safety of the family hearth. In moonlit paintings by Aert van der Neer and Adriaen Brouwer, we catch glimpses of their silhouettes—shrouded figures walking and conversing with one another in the still night. The Dutch schoolmaster David Beck, on a summer evening in 1624, "walked back and forth through The Hague," finding "under the full moon . . . many people in the street." When, late on a November night in 1683, the nonconformist Oliver Heywood preached in rural Yorkshire, "God sent abundance of people many miles, tho it was in the night and very dark and slippery." By the same token, in New England, a contemporary wrote of children who routinely attended prayer meetings, trudging on dark nights "two and some three miles thro' a thick wood."[2]

True, some persons, after dark, pointedly refrained from venturing outside. Long after towns and cities abandoned curfews, learned wisdom discouraged nocturnal excursions. "The night is the time to remain at home," warned a Portuguese saying.[3] The Yorkshire yeoman Adam Eyre vowed "never hereafter to stay out in the night." Afraid of robbers and the "bad" night air, James Boswell resigned himself "always to be at home early, in spite of every temptation." But such pledges seldom lasted, often springing from momentary mishaps, not from deep-seated aversions to nocturnal travel. In Derbyshire, the physician James Clegg, violently thrown by his horse one evening, resolved "to return home in better time or stay all night" with his patients. Within weeks, having resumed his evening housecalls, he was following neither prescription.[4]

Preindustrial folk, in facing the natural world, drew on a deep reservoir of rural culture, one fed by many wellsprings, including both pagan and Christian traditions. The critical role at night of customary beliefs and practices cannot be stressed enough. A poet wrote contemptuously in 1730 of "vain notions by traditions bred, among the vulgar." Some conventions were transmitted from one place to another by peddlers, preachers, and minstrels, though many, in turn, were homegrown. Households profited from the inherited wisdom of earlier generations, mastering the arcane skills by which to range over menacing terrain at all hours, occasionally for long distances. Differences naturally existed in local conventions, as did dissimilarities between ethnic and religious groups. But more remarkable than these sometimes subtle variations was the collective body of values, skills, and customs found in early modern communities. Nearly everywhere at nighttime, persons embraced a way of doing things distinct from the rhythms and rituals of the visible world. "Times and places demand different behavior," observed Sarah Cowper, and nighttime was no exception.[5]

II

They must . . . early get habituated to darkness.

JEAN-JACQUES ROUSSEAU, 1762[6]

Observers as early as Aristotle and Lucretius have commented upon the timidity of young children at night. According to psychologists, around two years of age the young first exhibit an instinctive fear of the dark. Anxieties, dormant since birth, are awakened by a rising awareness of the outside world. There is no reason to think that this standard pattern of childhood development was any different in premodern communities. The ancient Spartans reputedly made their sons spend entire evenings among the tombs to conquer their fears. "Men feare death as children feare to goe in the dark," observed Francis Bacon.[7]

In early modern times, youthful fears, in parents' eyes, often served a salutary purpose. Rather than soothe children's anxieties, adults routinely reinforced them through tales of the supernatural, in part bearing testimony to their own apprehensions. "That natural fear in children is increased with tales," Bacon noted. Of "our mothers maids," the Elizabethan author Reginald Scot described, "they have so fraied us with bull beggers, spirits, witches, urchens, elves, hags, fairies . . . that we are afraid of our owne shadowes." There were also narratives involving kidnappers, murderers, and thieves. As a girl in seventeenth-century Ghent, Isabella de Moerloose was frightened by the story of "the man with the long coat, of whom it was said that he looked for firstborn children" to kill. The specter of a one-eyed soldier in the royal guard was used to discipline Louis XIII of France (1601–1643) as a child. By warning of bogeymen that preyed on naughty youngsters, parents and servants, critics alleged, played upon children's worst fears to compel obedience. "As soon as one tries to still a child," complained the Dutch author Jacob Cats, "one introduces a variety of bizarre features: a ghost, a bogeyman, a lifeless spirit." Some parents, as punishment, confined children to dark closets or impersonated evil spirits. A Dutch father, Constantijn Huygens, used a doll dressed in black to threaten his infant daughter. The father of Philippe de Strozzi in sixteenth-century France knocked on his chamber door one night. "Disguising his voice in a horrible manner," the father hoped to test his son's courage. Philippe passed the test. Struck on the forehead, his father was forced to retreat, "swearing to never again frighten him in this way at night."[8]

Examples like these offer ample fodder for those historians who have depicted the early modern family in a harsh light, as a repressive institution devoid of human affection. To draw that connection here, however, would be to miss a larger point. Although used as an occasional tool of discipline, storytelling and bogeymen served an important educational function. At night, most of all, young children needed to be put on guard. Tales, along with ballads and proverbs, afforded a customary means in this largely illiterate age of imparting cautionary advice. Thus in *Traitè de l'Education des Filles* (1687), the French churchman Fénelon described nurses

Vincent van der Vinne, *The Safe Refuge*, 1714.

who gave "children stupid fears of ghosts and spirits," thereby exercising their own judgment "as to the things" infants "should seek after or avoid." Similarly, a visitor to Sicily wrote of "superstitious parents, nurses, and others such like teachers" who spread tales of witchcraft. There was nothing impersonal or abstract about most stories. Many recounted the terrible deeds of neighborhood ghosts and witches, taking care to identify spots that children at night should avoid. According to Jean Paul, his father, a schoolmaster, "did not spare us a single apparition or foolery, which he had ever heard of or believed to have met with, himself." In contrast to most adults, however, his father "combined with a firm belief in them the equally firm courage to face them."[9]

Central, also, to children's education was their progressive exposure to darkness. Collecting firewood, gathering berries, and tending livestock all took youths outdoors in the evening. The engraver Thomas Bewick, growing up in Northumberland, was sent by his father on "any errand in the night." "Perhaps," he reflected as an adult, "my being frequently exposed to being alone in the dark" helped to lessen the terror.[10] Some tasks were contrived. In 1748, the author of *Dialogues on the Passions, Habits, and Affections Peculiar to Children* advised parents: "You must create little errands, as if by accident, to send him in the dark, but such as can take up but little time; and encrease the length of time by degrees, as you find his courage encrease." The son of a shoemaker, young Thomas Holcroft was sent one night to a distant farm. "Now and then making a false step," he remembered later of the route. With his father and a companion secretly following at a distance, the lad completed his journey unscathed. "At last I got safely home, glad to be rid of my fears, and inwardly not a little elated with my success."[11]

Games served the same purpose. Rousseau urged reliance on "night games" for children, including a complex labyrinth formed by tables and chairs. "Accustomed to having a good footing in darkness, practiced at handling with ease all surrounding bodies," he observed, "his feet and hands will lead him without difficulty in the deepest darkness." Outdoor contests, such as "Fox and Hounds," were designed for the obscurity of night. Restif de la Bretonne, as a boy, enjoyed the contest of "Wolf," which in his French village "was always played in the dark," as in parts of Britain was "Bogle about the Stacks," a game that allowed children to act out their fears of ghosts. A favorite throughout the British Isles was "Can I Get There by Candle Light?" Dating to the sixteenth century, if not earlier, one version of the game pitted a coven of "witches" against a larger band of "travelers." Although not intended for the dark, the game conveyed two practical lessons: the importance of returning home, when possible, before "candle-lighting"; and the need to beware of sinister forces once night fell. "Watch out!" chanted the players, "mighty bad witches on the road tonight."[12]

Some youngsters, like Jonathan Martin, were impatient learners. The son of a Northumberland forester, he routinely absconded from bed on summer nights to ramble alone in the woods. One morning, finally, he was returned home by men who had first taken the six-year-old for a ghost. His father, alert to the dangers of such rash behavior, immediately forbade Jonathan's solitary excursions.[13] Both at home and abroad, prudence after nightfall was essential. It was one thing to invade night's dominion; it was quite another to flout its laws.

III

The leagues are longer by night, than by day.
ITALIAN PROVERB[14]

Despite fears of evil spirits and foot-pads, more common still were natural hazards concealed by night's obscurity—fallen trees, thick underbrush, steep hillsides, and open trenches. Just a short jaunt to a neighbor's dwelling could be fraught with difficulty, as could returning to one's residence. Coming home at 10:00 P.M. after assisting a patient, a New England doctor recorded, "Rather disagreeable time riding, bad night, cloudy, dark; difficult time keeping the path which was very narrow." For Cowper, darkness, a source of incalculable peril, was "a state that robbs us of our noblest sense, disables or confounds all our powers of motion." To it, she observed, "wee seem to have ye most naturall, the most just, the most unconquerable aversion."[15]

For guidance, ordinary folk drew upon local lore and an intimate awareness of nature acquired from childhood. While adjoining counties sometimes seemed like foreign lands, most persons claimed a detailed knowledge of the parishes in which they had been reared, having committed to memory a mental map of every ditch, pasture, and hedge row. Games like "Round and Round the Village," popular in much of England, familiarized children at any early age to their physical surroundings, as did fishing, collecting herbs, and running errands. Schooled by adults in night's perils, children learned to negotiate the landscape "as a rabbit knows his burrow"—careful after dark to skirt ponds, wells, and other hazardous terrain. In towns and cities, shop signs, doorways, and back alleys afforded fixed landmarks for neighborhood youths. As a child, Jacques-Louis Ménétra claimed a first-hand knowledge of the Parisian waterfront, where he played games like hide-and-seek and slept nights when banished from home by an abusive father. Lessons could be painful. Fleeing his stepfather, the peasant Valentin Jamerey-Duval, as a boy, tumbled into the muck of an empty wolf pit, where he lay trapped overnight. The goat-boy Ulrich Bräker, at four years of age, ran off on a "pitch-dark rainy night" across a meadow, nearly somersaulting down a muddy slope into a swift brook. Rescued by his father, they returned to the site the next morning. "Here, lad," his father declared, "only a few steps more, and the brook rushes over the cliff. If the water had managed to sweep you away, you'd be lying dead down there."[16]

Certainly by adolescence, most youths had learned to master the footpaths crisscrossing rural fields, or, in towns, the narrow lanes intersecting serpentine streets. "Be not fearful," a Berliner counseled his friend at night, "I know by heart the streets of home." Even in the shadows, asserted Leon Battista Alberti, "those who knew the country by experience and had seen all the places in the light of day would recognize them and could say what they were and who lived there."[17] Only during the winter, in the event of a heavy snowfall, could surroundings lose their familiarity, despite the advantage to travelers of a lighter, more visible landscape. So in 1789, a pair of Pennsylvanians drowned in the Susquehanna River. The "night being dark, and the path covered by the snow, they mistook the road" and fell through the ice.[18]

Human eyesight, in less than an hour's time, gradually improves in the dark as the iris expands to permit sufficient light. Despite losses in color recognition and depth perception, peripheral vision may actually sharpen. Humans see better at night than most animals, many of which are virtually blind. Quite possibly, the nocturnal sight of preindustrial populations benefited from consumption of leafy green vegetables and fresh fruit, rich in vitamin A, though availability was largely limited to late spring and summer. In addition, consumption of alcohol, a staple of early diets, improves night vision, unless imbibed to excess. Plainly, some individuals, said to have "cat's eyes," exhibited a superior ability to see after dark. A correspondent to the *Gentleman's Magazine* described "men" whose sight nearly approached that of "the cat, the owl, or the bat."[19]

Then, too, lanterns and torches afforded portable sources of light. Made from thick, half-twisted wicks of hemp, dipped in pitch, resin, or tallow, a single torch weighed up to three pounds. Lighter by contrast, lanterns were also dimmer. Featuring a handle attached to a metal frame, either cylindrical or rectangular in shape, the typical lantern contained a single candle protected by sheets of animal horn, though animal skin, talc (mica), and glass were also employed. Some lanterns, made entirely of metal, emitted light through perforated holes. Beginning in the late seventeenth century, with the steady growth of British glassmaking, "bull's-eye lanterns," with their central glass lens, bodies of thin sheet brass, and magnified light, gradually gained favor.[20]

Among propertied families, it was common on black nights for a single servant to light the way. Gracious hosts instructed footmen to escort departing guests safely home. And when a master was late in returning after dark, diligent servants knew where to fetch him. "Met Sam at ye head of St. Clements' Lane coming for me with a lanthorn," noted Robert Sanderson in 1729. In the Danish town of Roskilde, a blacksmith's guild ordered servants to meet their masters with lanterns, candles, and staffs. Wealthy households traveled in grander style. Footmen accompanied coaches through city streets, carrying flambeaux aloft as they trotted alongside. Ahead of the coach, a "moon-man" sometimes served as a guide, holding a globular lantern—the "moon"—atop a long pole.[21]

In most towns and cities, one could hire a linkboy for a small sum. These, for the most part, were orphans or other impoverished adolescents who, for a pedestrian's benefit, carried links (torches) or, less often, lanterns. In some English communities, they were nicknamed mooncursers, for the harm done their trade by moonlight. Within London, they congregated in such well-known spots as Temple-Bar, London-Bridge, and Lincoln Inn-Fields. Samuel Pepys occasionally relied upon linkboys when trudging home to Tower Hill. In Venice, they were termed *codeghe*, and in France *porte-flambeaux* or, for lantern-carriers, *falots*. "Here's your light," they cried in Paris streets. Louis-Sébastien Mercier exulted, "The lantern-man's light is a convenience, and a precaution well worth while for those whose business or pleasure keep them late from home."[22] At least in London, however, linkboys bore a checkered reputation for consorting with street ruffians. "Thieves with lights," Daniel Defoe charged. It was a common complaint that they conveyed besotted customers into the waiting grasp of robbers, extinguishing their links at the critical moment. Warned John Gay, "Though thou art tempted by the link-man's call, / Yet trust him not along the lonely wall; / In the mid-way he'll quench the flaming brand, / And share the booty with the pilf'ring band." Defoe favored strict regulation by licensing linkboys, akin to the prevailing system in Paris during most of the 1700s. There, in sharp contrast, *falots* became infa-

Thomas Rowlandson, *A Linkboy*, 1786.

mous toward the end of the ancien régime for acting as spies. "Hand in glove with the police," described Mercier, who applauded their contribution to public safety. Customers kept their money if not their secrets.[23]

Although lighting was commonly a function of wealth, from a distance it probably offered onlookers few clues of social rank. Apart from the retinues of footmen accompanying individuals of privilege, a lone torch or lantern, at most, remained customary for pedestrians, whether borne by a servant, linkboy, or just oneself. A London victualer of modest purse taught his dog to carry a lantern in its mouth.[24] Scrounging small nubs of tallow, the poor fashioned makeshift lanterns, using paper or hollowed-out turnips for protection from the wind and rain. In the French city of Poitiers, a Scottish visitor during the seventeenth century was impressed by the resourcefulness of "the poor folk" at night. "They take a piece [of] wood that's brunt only at one end, and goes thorow the toune waging it from one syde to the other, it casting a little light." Rarely did authorities restrict artificial light by social class. On the British Channel Island of Guernsey, a law granted persons of "first rank" the sole privilege of burning three lights in their lanterns, in contrast to one or two lights accorded lesser ranks. "Differently from all other places in the world, it is on a dark night that one can best distinguish the rank of persons passing through the streets," a bemused visitor remarked in the early 1800s.[25]

Even the brightest torch illuminated but a small radius, permitting one, on a dark night, to see little more than what lay just ahead. By all accounts, its glow, though superior to that of a lantern, was a dismal substitute for the light of day. "In comparison of the sun," affirmed an adage, "a torch is but a spark." Additionally, there was always the risk, with any type of lighting, that strong winds or rain could douse a flame, even when shielded inside a lantern. In his poem *Venus and Adonis* (1593), Shakespeare described the frequent surprise of "night wand'rers," their "light blown out in some mistrustful wood."[26]

Despite access to artificial light, many relied upon the heavens for illumination. The darkness of the night sky, for travelers of all ranks, was their single greatest concern. As contemporaries knew firsthand, nighttime took on many different shades, sometimes over the course of a single evening. From the black gloom known as "pit-mirk" to the bright glow of a full moon, there existed a variety of possibilities, some too subtle for our modern eyes to appreciate. For half of each month, 50 percent or more of

Adriaen Brouwer, *Dune Landscape by Moonlight*, seventeenth century.

the lunar face on clear evenings provides a significant source of reflected light. In spite of the reputed menace its beams posed to human health, residents in many parts of Britain referred to the moon as the "parish lantern." During evenings when full or nearly full, it was sometimes likened, half in jest, to a second sun.[27] Persons even awakened, on occasion, in the middle of the night, thinking that it was daybreak, only to be fooled by a "false dawn." "The moon shining bright mistook it for day light," wrote a Pennsylvanian in 1762. "Arrose & drest but after rousing the family & getting a light found it was not 2 o'clock." In Yorkshire, the apprentice clothier Mary Yates arose at 3:00 A.M., thinking "it was day," though "it being then moonlight" instead.[28]

A full moon rises at dusk and sets at dawn. Unlike most lunar phases, its glow lasts the entire night. In parts of northern England, the inhabitants referred to this as "throo leet." Full moonlight revealed the contours of preindustrial landscapes in welcome detail—"obliging me with as much light as was necessary to discover a thousand pleasing objects," noted a writer in 1712. Wayfarers could discern a small spectrum of colors, including red from yellow and green from blue. According to modern-day lighting engineers, direct sunlight ranges in strength from 5,000 to 10,000 foot-candles, with moonlight roughly equal to 0.02 foot-candles. Despite the dramatic difference, only when lighting declines in strength to 0.003 foot-candles does the human eye fail altogether to detect either colors or detailed features. On a practical level, this meant on moonlit evenings that objects could be sighted from afar. Testifying at the Old Bailey about a robbery, the constable Samuel Clay vouched, "It was a very fine moon-shining night. I could distinguish a person at the distance of one hundred yards, and could swear to a person's face at the distance of ten yards, or more." Similarly, a bricklayer in 1676 observed the perpetrator of a burglary in the city of York, "it being then very moonlight." Even when the moon was hazy, the outline of a human figure could be discerned at a distance. It is not surprising that thieves hid in the shadows or avoided plying their trade on such evenings.[29]

Among rural folk, the phases of the moon, their sequence and duration, were common knowledge, part of the essential lore conveyed to youngsters at an early age. So, in a simple English verse, "The Honest Ploughman," children learned that the husbandman "finds his way home by the light of the moon." Urban households were less tutored in such matters, but almanacs were readily accessible by the seventeenth century. Published across Europe, these charted the moon's progress in monthly tables. In England, upward of four hundred thousand almanacs were published annually by the 1660s, with an estimated one family in every three a consumer; in early America, almanacs represented the most popular publication after the Bible. Although lunar phases had reputed ramifications for the weather and personal health, nothing was more critical than learning what future nights held for being abroad. In 1764, noting the absence of tables in recent almanacs, an Eton resident asserted, "People may know by looking into the almanack, how long they shall have the moon's light every night it shines; which is of use to so many purposes."[30]

Certainly, travel after dark, apart from brief excursions, often hinged upon moonlight. In the view of Henry David Thoreau, who ruminated upon the "infinite" varieties of moonlight, even a "faint diffused light" supplied "light enough to travel." Time and again, persons wrote of visiting friends, performing errands, or returning home by the moon. "Rather late with us before we got home as we waited some time for moonlight," commented Parson James Woodforde of dinner at a friend's. In Paris, a pair of physicians in 1664 consented to visit a feverish patient, "it being about full moon." Many cities and towns that had once required pedestrians to carry lanterns or torches no longer did so by the seventeenth century. Elsewhere, restrictions went unenforced. Londoners, including men of property, routinely traveled by "brave mooneshine," as Pepys called it. Of a coach ride to the Lord Treasurer's home for dinner, Jonathan Swift related, "The moon shone, and so we were not in much danger of overturning." Conversely, a night's entertainment, in the moon's absence, might be canceled or postponed. "He would not dine with us on account of there being no moon," wrote Nancy Woodforde in 1792 of a Norfolk neighbor.[31]

Even then, there was often the natural light of the stars, whose glow, though fainter, was more reliable. "It was neither dark nor light; it was a starlight night," observed a man in 1742. In some parts of England, the first "star" after sunset, Vesper (actually the planet Venus), was called the "Shepherds-Lamp" because of its bright glow above the western horizon. "The shepherd's lamp, which even children know," penned John Clare in the early nineteenth century. Besides seeming brighter than today, stars appeared vastly more plentiful, likely totaling on a clear night in excess of two thousand. Like the moon, their light was capable of casting shadows. Wrote the poet Robert Herrick, "Let not the dark thee cumber: / What though the moon does slumber? / The stars of the night will lend thee their light." A Londoner recounted in the mid-eighteenth century, "Between 11 and 12 it being a fine star-light night, I put my sword and cane under my arm and walked."[32]

Unless haze interfered, the Milky Way, a broad swath of white light, stretched from one horizon to another, dividing the sky in two: "The region seems to be all on a blaze with their blended rays," described a writer in the *Universal Magazine of Knowedge and Pleasure* in 1753. Although Chaucer and others early on employed the expression Milky Way, it was used interchangeably with the names of different highways, whose routes, depending upon the season, ran in the galaxy's general direction. Early pilgrims kept to such roads as the "Walsingham Way" in East Anglia and the "Strada di Roma" in Italy by eyeing the sky. "By us," wrote the astronomer Thomas Hood in 1590, "it is called the Milke way: some in sporting manner doie call it Watling streete," the ancient Roman road that ran from the outskirts of London to Wroxeter near the Welsh border.[33]

In the end, neither moon nor stars but clouds regulated the flow of celestial light. Thus Thoreau wrote of the moon's "continual war with the clouds" on the traveler's behalf.[34] The density and velocity of cloud formations were vital considerations. "Moon shines, tho' clouds are flying," noted Elizabeth Drinker on a June evening. The Irish draper Humphrey O'Sullivan referred regularly to nights that were either "thin" or "heavy" clouded. Only on clear evenings could one be confident of protracted light, for within minutes the sky might dramatically change. Observed a passing visitor to Scotland in the late eighteenth century, "During some part of this ride the moon was so much obscured I could scarcely see if I was upon the road, at other times it shone so bright as to give me a distinct view of the country."[35]

The blackest nights, when clouds blanketed the sky, inspired numerous expressions—"pit-mirk," "lowry," "darkling," and, of course, "pitch-dark" in reference to the tarry resin of pine trees. "As dark as pitch," Pepys remarked upon returning home at 2:00 A.M. on a January evening in 1666. *Nóche ciéga*, Spaniards called "blind nights." Winter temperatures, due to

Thomas Bewick, *Benighted Traveler*, n.d.

cloud cover, might be warmer, but vision on such evenings was severely impaired. The sky, let alone distant objects or their colors, was barely visible. "It was such a dark night I could hardly see my finger," described a London resident in 1754.[36] Options for travel were few, with most people all the more inclined to remain safely at home. Some, if possible, employed torches or lanterns, for which they were said to be "belanter'd." "We were obliged to have a lantern," wrote Parson Woodforde in 1786, "being very dark." But, invariably, occasions arose when overcast skies caught individuals off-guard or winds extinguished a candle or torch. Passing through Palaiseau in France, a group of men, finding their lamp broken, canvassed the occupants of an inn for a lantern, for which they exchanged a bottle of wine. "We got a lantern with a rushlight in it, but the wind soon blew it out, and we went on our way darkling."[37]

To make the most of black nights, wayfarers displayed a rough-hewn resourcefulness. In 1661, overtaken by darkness in mountainous countryside, a mounted party placed a rider on a white horse in front to lead the way. "We followed his trace," described the servant Robert Moody. The member of another body of travelers recounted a "pit dark" night near Durham: "We was forced to ride close on one another, otherwise we should have losed one another." And whenever darkness descended on a Georgia plantation, Aunt Sook wore "a white cloth 'round her shoulders" to lead fellow slaves from the fields.[38] Just as trees blazed by axes charted paths at night through dense woodlands, so, too, did seasoned travelers get their bearings by viewing the dark silhouettes of coppices and trees against the skyline.[39] By contrast, where soil contained large quantities of sand or chalk, men and women scanned the ground around them. In the Down-country of southern England, villagers heaped mounds of chalky soil, known as "down-lanterns," to mark routes through open fields. Heading south from Edinburgh in 1745, Alexander Carlyle and his brother traveled along the shoreline "as there was no moonlight . . . and the sands always lightsome when the sea is in ebb."[40]

On the worst nights, ordinary folk relied heavily upon secondary senses, including their powers of hearing, touch, and smell. Although today the large bulk of our sensory input is visual, sight's sister senses, for much of the early modern era, remained critical to everyday existence, particularly at nighttime. On overcast evenings, individuals often were forced to navigate, not with their eyes, but with their ears. The nocturnal experience was heavily aural. "The day has eyes, the night has ears," affirmed a Scottish proverb. After sunset, reliance on hearing was so pronounced that in East Yorkshire the verb "dark" meant "to listen."[41] Nighttime, as contemporaries understoood, was well suited to communicating sound. Although the moist air could have a damping effect, impairment of sight naturally sharpened one's hearing. Observes Hermia in *A Midsummer Night's Dream*, "Dark night, that from the eye his function takes, / The ear more quick of apprehension makes. / Wherein it doth impair the seeing sense, / It pays the hearing double recompense." In addition, nocturnal silence gave heightened resonance to isolated noises. With a less complex soundscape, it was easier for a cocked ear to detect the source and direction of separate sounds.[42]

Unfortunately, hearing, unlike sight, is a passive sense, and sound can be intermittent at best. "Sounds come and go in a way that sights do not," John M. Hull, the blind author of *Touching the Rock*, has recently noted. At night, noises become more sporadic. On the other hand, hearing is a more pervasive sense than sight, not limited to a single direction; nor is it as easily blocked by an intervening obstacle such as a building or a tree. And with the range of earshot extended at night, preindustrial sounds represented the aural equivalent of landmarks.[43] Overtaken by darkness on an unfamiliar road outside the Scottish town of Paisley, a set of travelers "proceeded with great caution and deliberation, frequently stopping to *look* forward and listen." Where wind and rain, by their sounds, could help to reveal the contours of a landscape, familiar noises afforded welcome wayposts. The "clattering" of their horses' hooves told visitors to Freiburg that they were entering "a large pavd town." Bleating ewes and bellowing bulls provided bearings, as did tolling church bells. In 1664, Richard Palmer of Berkshire bequeathed funds for the village sexton to ring the great bell at eight o'clock each night as well as in the morning, not only to encourage "a timely going to rest" but also that persons "might be informed of the time of night, and receive some guidance into their right way." Most helpful were dogs, whose barks pierced the air. Like a homing signal, the noise increased in volume and intensity the closer that one approached. "We lost our road," wrote a traveler in France, "and about midnight, directed by the sound of village dogs, dropt upon Fontinelle." Noted a colonist in seventeenth-century Maryland, "It was a remarkable circumstance, as dogs are used to keep men away from dwellings, but served to bring us to them."[44]

Even smells could help to orient persons to their locations, all the more at night when noses grew more sensitive and odors lingered in the damp air. "The whole air of the village of an evening is perfumed by effluvia from the hops drying in the kilns," commented Gilbert White on a late summer night in 1791. For individuals intimately familiar with their environs, the fragrance of a honeysuckle bush or a bakery on a warm evening or, conversely, the stench of a dunghill afforded invisible signposts, as did smells associated with horses, cattle, and other farm animals.[45]

Touch, on the other hand, enabled individuals to navigate at close quarters, warily shuffling their feet as they advanced with outstretched arms. "Better walk leisurely than lie abroad all night," advised a familiar saying. Deprived of their sight, pedestrians grew intensely conscious of their limbs and extremities. "We groped about, like a couple of thieves, in a cole hole," described a London resident. Few persons, admittedly, navigated on all fours as the agricultural writer Arthur Young did one night in Italy. With his lantern extinguished by wind, Young was forced to crawl to avert falling over a cliff. It was not unusual for drivers to halt their coaches in order to gauge the road. "Mr. Taylor," described a passenger in Scotland, "was oft obliged to descend from the carriage to *feel* whether we were upon the road or not."[46] Fingers and feet were employed to best effect on well-marked paths, whereas, on a "blind road," the surface differed little from the shoulders. Smooth, open spaces, such as a pasture or commons, also provided few orienting clues, in contrast to rough, uneven surfaces, despite the threat of tripping. Visiting a patient without the aid of a lantern, the New England midwife Martha Ballard removed her shoes to feel the path in her stockings. "Steerd as strait a coars as I could," she recorded of her safe arrival.[47]

In cities, differences in pavement could alert pedestrians to their location, as they struggled to keep to the beaten track. Of navigating London's streets, Gay wrote, "Has not wise nature strung the legs and feet / With finest nerves, design'd to walk the street? / Has she not given us hands to groap aright, / Amidst the frequent dangers of the night?"[48] Canes and staffs gave a feel of the road by extending one's reach. Among all social classes, these appear to have been commonplace, intended as much for navigation as for self-defense. "No doubt you have had the experience of walking at night over rough ground without a light, and finding it necessary to use a stick in order to guide yourself," wrote Descartes. "You may have been able to notice that by means of this stick you could feel the various objects situated around you, and that you could even tell whether they were trees or stones or sand or water or grass or mud."[49] With or without a cane or staff, the experience of traveling by foot on dark evenings could be daunting, particularly for the upper classes, accustomed to horseback or coach. Fanny Boscawen in 1756 wrote her husband Edward, the admiral, "I have made such profession of my aversion to *groping* that at length I seem to have obtained a dispensation never to visit in the dark." A traveler to the Swiss city of Lausanne, to his great dismay, was forced "to walk gropingly like a blind man."[50]

IV

There is a proper time and season for every thing; and nothing can be more ridiculous than the doing of things without a due regard to the circumstances of persons, proportion, time and place.

SIR ROGER L'ESTRANGE, 1699[51]

Embodying the distilled wisdom of past generations, popular conventions governed nearly every aspect of night journeys, both long and short—from treading ancient sheep-tracks to traversing unfamiliar woodlands and meadows. In spite of the critical role that human senses played in surmounting night's obscurity, there were still other challenges to mind, body, and soul. Custom governed not only people's mode of lighting but also their dress and form of travel, their companions, what they did or did not carry, and when and where they went. So, too, did unwritten protocols exist for encountering fellow travelers as well as for seeking help when lost. As Thoreau later reflected, "What a man does abroad by night requires and implies more deliberate energy than what he is encouraged to do in the sunshine."[52]

Before embarking outside, travelers usually dressed with care. During the day, neat clothing suitable to class and calling was customary, as was cleanliness, regardless of station. Many working men and women took pride in their garments. "The people of England, from the highest to the lowest," wrote Tobias Smollett, "are remarkably neat in their attire." The *London-Spy* spoke of the "abundance of rubbing, scrubbing, washing and combing" men performed to make "tolerable figures to appear by day light."[53] But at night, appearance mattered less, and standards changed. For some persons, darkness disguised garments too dirty or torn to be worn by day. A drunken squire returned home from a London alehouse at night because he "was too dirty to go home by day-light." "In the night," affirmed an Italian saying, "any cap will serve."[54]

Outer clothing, in general, became less varied and more functional. Colors were plainer. Because manure and mud lay everywhere, leather boots and shoes were favored by those who could afford them, along with leggings by the end of the seventeenth century. For protection from wet and cold weather, men and women wore buttoned capes or cloaks made from felt. "Great cloaks," predominantly used by men, were thick, heavy garments that hung loosely—to mid-calf for pedestrians, whereas riders required a shorter design. In Rome, a visitor discovered that the "great cloak" was "worn by all when walking the streets." By the late 1600s, "great coats" or "watch coats" also grew popular, featuring a turned-up collar for foul weather. In *The Life and Adventures of Sir Launcelot Greaves* (1762), Smollet wrote of a man "muffled in a great coat." Defoe's Robinson Crusoe saves from his shipwreck "a great watch-coat to cover" him. For added comfort, Dutch women affixed small pots of hot embers or smoldering turf beneath their petticoats. Sicilians, when the "night air was sharp," tied similar devices to their wrists. Among the poor, with neither cloaks nor coats, multiple layers of clothing lent a measure of warmth.[55]

Heads, too, required protection. Of the "damps of the night air," a traveler wrote that the English "take more precautions here against a cold, than they do in the Eastern countrys against the plague." Pepys attributed a bad cold to not wearing his periwig more often. Shawls, hoods, and scarves among women were customary. Others placed atop their heads linen "night-mobs" with lappets on the sides tied beneath the chin. Indifferent to fashion, some men wrapped scarves around their heads and "uncocked" (turned down) the brims of their three-cornered hats. "Cover your head by day as much as you will, by night as much as you can," advised a proverb. Fearful of the night air, Romans drew cloaks close to their mouths "as to enclose a space for breathing." "This they do in order that they may respire the air of the chamber in walking the streets, and not be exposed to the natural element."[56]

Plain apparel at night served to conceal wealth and rank, an advantage when traveling alone. Samuel Johnson claimed never to have been robbed, "for the rogues knew he had little money, nor had the appearance of having much." Donning tattered garments, gentlemen might even masquerade as laborers. A Scottish saying declared, "A raggit coat is armour against the robber." Other precautions included carrying little money or jewelry. Asked why she walked late one night through London's suburbs—"for it was very dangerous"—Mary Hicks replied "that she fear'd nothing, having left her money and rings" at the home of a friend. Some persons, when traveling, secreted money in the fabric of their cloaks or the soles of their shoes or hose. A Polish gentleman in 1595, crossing the Italian countryside, was attacked at nightfall by two bandits from behind a clump of bushes. Not only had he covered his shoes in rags, but he had also sewn eighty Hungarian florins into his stockings. "It was difficult to guess by looking at me, because of my bad shoes and because I was traveling on foot," he noted. One robber, taking pity on the Pole, gave him two coins before absconding![57]

Apart from disguising one's gentility, there was another advantage to journeying on foot. Because horses in the dark could be skittish, mishaps were fewer. "How can the best horse be sure of his foot-steps," queried John Byng, a seasoned rider by day.[58] Families occasionally shunned riding in coaches, despite their greater refinement. "Too dark for a carriage," Parson Woodforde concluded before returning home from playing cards at the estate of a local squire. "Myself and nephews put on our great coats and walked home to supper." What's more, it was easier, thought some, to protect oneself on foot. With robberies rising, London's hackney-coach drivers complained in 1729 about their declining trade. "People, especially in an evening, choose rather to walk than ride in a coach, on account that they are in a readier posture to defend themselves."[59]

Any mode of travel by land was preferable to water. Amid shoals and sandbanks, restricted visibility rendered river navigation perilous. Moreover, if a boat capsized, there was less likelihood of rescue. All these dangers of travel combined near Leeds on an August evening in 1785 when the young driver of a carriage paused by a riverbank to water his horses. Due to the river's swift current from recent flooding, the horses lost their footing, dragging the carriage and its doomed driver into the water. According to a report in the *London Chronicle*, "The night being very dark, it was impossible to render him any effectual service."[60]

Time, too, mattered to travelers. Preindustrial societies divided evenings as well as days into well-defined intervals. Ancient Romans partitioned their nights into as many as ten different periods, which, unlike modern hours, varied in length. Extending from dusk (*crepusculum*) to the break of day (*conticinium*), each was identified with either a natural event or a human activity, such as bedtime (*concubium*). So, also, did the medieval Church institute canonical hours for prayer.[61] For households in early modern Britain, sundry intervals at night were commonplace. The most familiar chronology consisted of sunset, shutting-in, candle-lighting, bedtime, midnight, the dead of night, cock-crow, and dawn. Despite the growing regimentation of time by the seventeenth century into hours and minutes, traditional intervals afforded members of all social ranks a frame of reference for calibrating the darkness. Even men and women able to afford clocks or other timepieces found these temporal categories convenient. Natural transitions marked some intervals, making nights easier to chart. Roosters, for the regularity of their habits, were hailed as the "peasant's clock."[62]

For other nocturnal times, such as midnight, rural families often depended upon the stars and the moon. Asked the time in the play *Rhodon and Iris* (1631), the shepherd Acanthus replies that it is the eleventh hour, for "Orion hath advanced very high." Famed for their accuracy were the Pleiades, a cluster of stars in the constellation of Taurus—"called by the vulgar, the hen and chickens," wrote Samuel Purchas in 1613. Claimed a Boston writer in 1786, "The poor peasant, who never saw a watch, will tell the time to a fraction, by the rising and setting of the moon, and some particular stars." In contrast, many urban residents relied upon clock towers and the cries of the nightwatch. Despite their erratic performance, church clocks could be found by the sixteenth century in a growing number of cities and towns. On a dark winter morning in 1529, the Cologne student Herman Weinsberg wakened and left home for school, unaware that it was barely past midnight. When the clock tower struck one o'clock, he "thought the clock was not working right." Finally realizing his error, yet locked outside, he "wandered up and down the streets to stay warm," nearly dying from the cold.[63]

All hours after sunset were perilous, but some were thought particularly threatening. A visitor to Scotland commented that travelers, "so 'fraid of riding in the dark at nights, should be so courageous in the mornings, when it is equally dark." Most feared of all was the "dead of night." Also called the "dead time" or the "dead hour," reputedly it was the darkest time of the evening, falling between midnight and cock-crow (around 3:00 A.M.). At no other juncture were roads and fields so deserted, or dangers so great. Ancient Romans called this interval *intempesta* (without time). "The dead vast and middle of the night," Shakespeare wrote. In *The Rape of Lucrece* (1594), he related:

Anon., *The Labourer's Clock, or a Very Easy Method of Telling the Time at Night by the Stars*, eighteenth century.

Now stole upon the time the dead of night,
When heavy sleep had closed up mortal eyes:
No comfortable star did lend his light,
No noise but owls' and wolves' death-boding cries;
Now serves the season that they may surprise
The silly lambs: pure thoughts are dead and still,
While lust and murder wake to stain and kill.[64]

In most localities, though crimes were more numerous in the hours preceding midnight, pedestrians likely faced a higher risk of robbery and assault afterwards. Clearly that was the conventional perception. Thus, a London gentleman, between the hours of 1:00 and 2:00 A.M., counseled a drinking companion "how dangerous it would be" to return home "at that time o'night"; and a newcomer to London wrote, "If one does not travel either very early or very late, there is no fear of being attacked." Following an assault on a Paris street just before midnight, the glazier Ménétra steadfastly "refrained from coming home so late."[65]

Then, also, evil spirits, according to common lore, were more likely to prowl during those hours. It was "aboute the dead of the night" that John Louder of Massachusetts imagined in his bed "a great weight" from a demon straddling his stomach. Not just boggarts and witches but the devil himself freely roamed, his reign on earth lasting until cock-crow, when, warned of day's approach, demons took flight, much as the ghost in *Hamlet* (ca. 1601). "Then, they say, no spirit dare stir abroad," observes the character Marcellus. This belief was at least as old as the fourth-century writings of the Spanish poet Prudentius. According to the Newcastle antiquary Henry Bourne, centuries later, "Hence, it is, that in country places, where the way of life requires more early labour, they always go chearfully to work at that time; whereas if they are called abroad sooner, they are apt to imagine every thing they see or hear, to be a wandring ghost." Worse was to frequent those hours on certain nights of the year. All Hallows' Eve and the Eve of St. John (Midsummer Eve) in the British Isles, for example, reportedly endowed spirits with heightened powers. "The risk is never so great as on St. John's Eve," observed an early nineteenth-century visitor to Ireland.[66]

Along with time, place mattered. Night dramatically transformed the communal landscape, investing innocuous landmarks with sinister portent. In a Yorkshire valley, for example, the decayed ruins of a small chapel were a "perfect paradise for boys" by day, but "not to be approached for the world by night, being haunted by a variety of strange ghosts," as William Howitt noted. Bourne wrote, "Stories of this kind are infinite, and there are few *villages*, which have not either had such an house in it, or near it." Indeed, he observed, "The common people say now and then, such a place is dangerous to be passed through at night." Often, such spots were thought impassable, and pedestrians took alternate paths. The late eighteenth-century folklorist Francis Grose estimated that the typical churchyard contained nearly as many ghosts at night as the village had parishioners. "To pass them at night, was an achievement not to be attempted by any one in the parish, the sextons excepted."[67]

The streets of large towns and cities generated fewer apprehensions of this sort. Certainly, a well-defined "ghostly topography," as an Ulster child later described his rural environs, did not exist in most urban neighborhoods. Notwithstanding churchyards and heaths, natural landmarks were too sparse, populations too transient, and public spaces too animated for traditions to take root. Only haunted houses from time to time created a stir, such as when a home in Cambridge in the 1690s occasioned "strange noises" for two weeks.[68] There, as in most urban areas, the threat of crime, not supernatural forces, redefined neighborhoods at night. London contained more than its share of hazardous thoroughfares, including the notorious Cut-throat Lane. In the Danish town of Roskilde, Thieve's Alley had a fearful reputation. Always perilous at night were roads leading to cities. "Afraid of being robbed," Sylas Neville found it "very disagreeable to travel all night alone" by coach, "especially so near London." To travel by night on the roads east and northeast of Paris put both one's life and purse at risk, as did crossing The Hague's "Wood." Even the small Somerset community of Wellington lay near a spot, Rogue's Green, infamous for robbers.[69]

Ignorance was no excuse. Gibbets with human corpses littered the early modern countryside. These were tall wooden posts with one or more arms from which hung the decomposing remains of executed felons, though trees provided handy substitutes. Often corpses would remain suspended in an iron cage or chains for months, warning prey and predator alike. In the village of Brusselton Common, a skeleton finally fell to the ground after nearly four years when lightning split the gibbet into "a thousand splinters." Sighting two corpses outside Coventry, a person remarked, "They serve as double warnings, to him that follow the same occupation, & to him who travels to guard against the attacks of such villains." No vague warning this, for gibbets ordinarily stood at the site of the original crime. Crossing a section of Flanders, the Englishman John Leake encountered so many "unhappy wretches upon gibbets" that he lamented not being armed—"however, under the conduct of God's good providence we found ourselves all safe" within town walls "before sunset." Invariably, more than one traveler brushed past a dead body in the dark. "It made me shudder with fright," wrote Felix Platter after nearly bumping into a corpse along a "dangerous road" in France.[70] If nothing else, gibbets supplied wayfarers with a terrifying roadmap of perilous sites. Small wooden crosses and, in Danish towns, lit candles served a similar function, but they failed to convey the same sense of horror. The widespread belief that gibbets were haunted by the ghosts of executed malefactors only enhanced their terror. "Those places are so frightfull in the night time to some fearefull and timorous persons," wrote Noel Taillepied in 1588, "that if they heare the voyce of any person neere the place where any be hanging, they will thinke it is their spirites or ghosts."[71]

In areas ridden with crime, pedestrians often traveled in groups. Servants accompanied men and women of property, but other persons, too, avoided walking alone, especially in deserted locations. In the Scottish Highlands, custom discouraged solitary journeys at night. Thomas Platter, on his way to the Kent town of Rochester in 1599, journeyed an entire night by wagon "through many very dangerous localities." But since "there was a whole wagon-load of us," he "suffered no anxiety." Joined by several guards, Pepys walked from Woolwich to Redriffe on the south bank of the Thames. "I hear this walk is dangerous to walk alone at night," he acknowledged. Paolo da Certaldo advised, "Do not go unless you have a faithful friend and a big light." Or a large dog. Tending his cows at 3:00 A.M., Richard Mitchel in 1749 took both his "man" and "a great dog" with him to the pasture.[72]

Weapons, naturally, strengthened frail spirits. In large parts of continental Europe, where thieves bore a fearsome reputation for violence, most people left home armed—not just gentlemen but peasants too, for whom bearing a dagger or quarterstaff was second nature. Country folk in France typically carried a "double-ended stick" reinforced top and bottom by iron caps. "From Verona to Brescia," noted an English traveler to Italy in the early 1700s, "all the peasants carryed arms, there had been robberys on the road." In the British Isles, pedestrians in towns and cities took similar precautions. Where laws restricted personal weapons, enforcement seems to have been ignored by a weak and indifferent nightwatch. Even in London's affluent western suburbs, a newcomer, John Knyveton, was urged in 1750 to carry a cudgel or a small sword, particularly after dark.[73] Crime represented less of a problem in the countryside, although coaches bore armed guards and often, too, armed passengers. Boswell kept a loaded pistol in his hand on a journey from Scotland to London. "During our two last stages this night, which we travelled in the dark, I was a good deal afraid of robbers."[74]

Spells and amulets offered additional protection. Candles and lanterns, prayers, and rosaries, all were employed to deter sinister forces when venturing abroad. A variety of charms were laden with sacred meaning. For security in Sicily, coaches bore religious paintings on their sides. Images of "the virgin and child, and the souls in purgatory, are seldom omitted," remarked a passing observer. Women in the Hautes Pyrenees, to guard against evil spirits, sprinkled their shifts with holy water. In Cologne, papers were hawked that reportedly had touched the faces of the three Magi. "Being carried in one's pockett will protect one from all dangers and robberies," reported Twisden Bradbourn in 1693.[75] Other charms bore no discernible imprint of Christianity. Carrying a strap or apron in parts of France, for example, was thought to deter werewolves. In the fens of East Anglia, holly branches protected against witches; and among Breton peasants, it was common wisdom never to whistle in the dark lest the noise summon demons. In northern England, the same blunder, according to an early modern manuscript, required that the offender walk three times around his house "by way of penance." Children in Yorkshire learned to "cruck" their thumbs as a defense, placing them within their balled hands. To ward off spirits, midwives in Liège wore articles of clothing inside out, as did slaves in different regions of America.[76]

Night set its own rules of engagement. Darkness precluded the normal courtesies that facilitated the give and take of daily life, the salutations and gestures of respect routinely exchanged on public lanes. Instead, advised Gay, "Let constant vigilance thy footsteps guide." Unable to discern an approaching pedestrian's clothing or demeanor, much less their identity or intentions, individuals relied upon other clues. Travelers proclaimed their identities as well as their proximity by their footsteps and voices. The mere act of coughing or spitting could give an inkling. "It is important for us to have an alert ear," Rousseau wrote in *Emile*, "to be able to judge . . . whether the body causing it is big or little, far or near, whether its motion is violent or weak." A miner in the Yorkshire village of Grasington, John Burnap, knew the doctor's horse "by its foot."[77]

Among strangers, distance was important to forestalling conflict—avoiding the paths of other passersby and ensuring that they avoided yours. Counseled a writer, "I would advise all strangers not to let any body come too near them particularly in the night-time." Hence the narrow escape of the American Elkanah Watson when lost one evening on a rural road in France. Seeing an oncoming coach, he ran into its path, crying "*postillon, arrête! arrête!*" only to discover that the driver thought him a bandit.

"Expecting he would send a ball at me, I made the best of my way down the hill, and the postillon made the best of his over it; being mutually afraid of each other."[78]

When paths crossed, silence only heightened suspicions. Alarmed by a passing figure in the market square of Traunstein, the clerk Andre Pichler declared, "If you do not speak, I shall stab you." Exchanges were terse and to the point: "Who is there?" or "Who is that?" were common questions. "A friend and a neighbor," William Mowfitt replied in 1647 during his way home. As important as one's words was tone of voice, which needed to be strong but inoffensive. Timidity, no less than hostility, invited clashes. Most wayfarers projected a brave front, often by brandishing their weapons. Fearful of being robbed in the Spanish countryside, Thomas Platter and his companions shook swords above their heads "to make them gleam in the light of the moon." Scraping one's sword against the ground, on the other hand, was an unmistakable "declaration of war." Against bands of brigands in rural Scandinavia, a traveler in 1681 instructed the unarmed drivers of a convoy of carriages to equip themselves with white sticks of wood, "which appeared by the light of the moon, as if they had been muskets." Thomas Ellwood crossed paths with a ruffian upon returning home from a court session in Watlington. "The suddain and unexpected sight of my bright blade, glittering in the dark night," Ellwood marveled, "did so amaze and terrify the man." Less fortunate, by contrast, was Michael Crosby as he made his way on a Sunday night from the alehouse Black Mary's Hole. Jostled in a nearby field by a thief, Crosby declared that he "wanted nothing but civility," only to be assaulted and robbed. Any bump in the night, cautioned Rousseau, required force. "Boldly grab the one who surprises you at night, man or beast—it makes no difference. Hold on and squeeze him with all your might. If he struggles, hit him."[79]

Supernatural encounters called for different defenses. Evil spirits were identified by their dark color and threatening sounds. Many appeared as serpents, toads, or other creatures. Other than flight, one's natural response was to recite a prayer while making the sign of the cross. "Here is the Cross, adverse forces disperse" was a customary verse in Poland. Local lore in France counseled boldness. In Basse-Bretagne, the admonition was direct: "If you are coming from the Devil, go on your way as I go on mine." Before fainting, a young Spanish woman invoked the Holy Trinity upon sighting a "demon" on a moonlit evening, whereas the German father of Jean Paul faced them with "God or the cross" as his "buckler and shield." A few stout souls responded more aggressively, with Satan himself on rare occasions reportedly put to flight. Felix Platter, during a visit to Marseilles, no doubt took comfort from knowing that his Swiss guide was nicknamed the "devil-chaser," after one such encounter.[80]

Only in desperation did persons sleep abroad in the open countryside. "Who goeth abroad must look about him, and sleep in the night, as a hare," warned an Italian proverb. So anxious was the German surgeon Johann Dietz when lost outside Lübeck that after trying to sleep in the woods he found strength enough to make his way to a granary (only to happen upon a band of robbers asleep in the cribs). And Thomas Platter, arriving too late to enter the city gate at Munich, sought overnight shelter at a "leper-house."[81] Besides listening for familiar sounds, stray souls "hallooed" into the dark, hoping to rouse a nearby family. Returning from Birmingham to Nottingham, the bookbinder William Hutton found himself lost in Charnwood Forest. "I wandered slowly, though in the wet, for fear of destruction, and hallooed with all my powers, but no returns." Lost as a child, Ulrich Bräker called to two men across a meadow. "No answer was forthcoming; maybe they took me for some monster." To extend their range, persons fired guns as a signal of distress. Plymouth Colony in 1636 forbade firing weapons at night, with just two exceptions: to kill a wolf and "for the finding of some one lost." Benighted during a trip to Italy, Boswell "groped" his way to a town after hearing several gunshots. Not having fired any himself, he likely profited from someone else's distress.[82]

V

I came ploughing home in the night, yet gott no harm thanks be to God who suffers not men nor devils to do all the mischief they would.

DAME SARAH COWPER, 1704[83]

No other time of the day so challenged the ingenuity and wit of ordinary mortals. Darkness tested their knowledge of local customs and magic as well as their understanding of the natural world. And, of course, night tried their souls or, at least, the mettle of their religious convictions. More than a few folk, upon safely returning from an evening abroad, thanked God for his protection. Even short jaunts merited occasional expressions of gratitude. To judge from early modern diaries, these were not formulaic phrases recited by rote but earnest expressions of relief. "Set out for home but had dark and dangerous travelling," noted a Derbyshire vicar, "yet thro the mercy of God I came safe and found all well." Thomas Turner recorded, "I came home about 9.10, thank GOD very safe and sober."[84]

With good reason, men and women gave thanks. Misfortune might strike even seasoned travelers. Nighttime could be cruelly unpredictable. Some scrapes defy understanding, at least by modern minds. John Pressy of Amsbury, Massachusetts, around the year 1668 embarked upon a three-mile trip to his home "near about the shutting in of day light." Taking a familiar path, he "steered by the moone w'ch shone bright" but repeatedly became "wildered." Encountering a series of odd lights, one of which he struck with his staff, Pressy fell into a pit. Finally, after finding a woman "standing on his left hand," he reached home "seazed with fear"—as, from his appearance, was his family. Other misadventures, despite travelers' well-laid plans, were more foreseeable. In the Irish village of Dereen, probably few residents were as cautious as John "of the moon" O'Donoghue when picking times to tread abroad. He was well known for going home after nightfall by moonlight—"I'll go home with the light of the moon," he frequently declared. But returning from a tavern on an October night, he stumbled into a ditch and drowned. For earlier that evening John had indulged another habit, drinking large quantities of whiskey and beer. And to human frailty, nighttime often proved unforgiving. "Though the moon was full, and he had the benefit of its light," grieved an acquaintance, "there was no light in his eyes."[85]

PART THREE

BENIGHTED REALMS

PRELUDE

I curse the night, yet doth from day me hide.
WILLIAM DRUMMOND OF
HAWTHORNDEN, 1616[1]

IN THE SHARP glare of daylight, privacy was scarce in early modern communities. Face-to-face relationships predominated in urban as well as rural settings, with most inhabitants intimately familiar with their neighbors' affairs. Affording persons moral and material assistance, communities also upheld common standards of public and private behavior. In theory, vigilance in the spirit of combating sin was every good neighbor's duty. "If any in the neighbourhood, are taking to bad courses, lovingly and faithfully admonish them," urged New England's Cotton Mather. "The neighborhood," as the historians David Levine and Keith Wrightson have written, "was not only a support network, but also a reference group and a moral community."[2]

For reasons rooted in self-interest as well as public morality, personal misbehavior courted exposure—more often from prying eyes and loose tongues than from constables and churchwardens. The transgressions of a single household, feared residents, could harm the wider community by its corrupting influence. Had neighbors been less dependent upon one another, this danger would have mattered less. In cases of sexual misconduct, burdening the local parish with an illegitimate child threatened financial hardship and invited punishment from the Almighty. In 1606, a set of petitioners in Castle Combe, Wiltshire, condemned a woman's "filthy act of whoredom" for, among other reasons, provoking "God's wrath" upon "us the inhabitants of the town."[3] In short, social oversight was essential. "In England," a German visitor commented in 1602, "every citizen is bound by oath to keep a sharp eye at his neighbour's house."[4]

Close quarters, whether at home or the workplace, lessened the likelihood of misbehavior. In most dwellings, rooms were few and cramped. During their trip to the Hebrides, James Boswell and Dr. Johnson, whose tastes ran to plusher quarters, often conversed with one another in Latin "for fear of being overheard in the small Highland houses." Secrets large and small fell victim to servants, who ranked among the most notorious rumormongers.[5] Making matters worse were the narrow lanes separating early modern dwellings, with their thin walls, revealing cracks, and naked windows. Not until the eighteenth century did curtains adorn many urban portals, while in the countryside they remained a rarity. In towns, closing them invariably aroused suspicion in daytime. A New England colonist called them "whore curtains" when he detected a pair drawn at a neighbor's home.[6] And while forests and fields afforded natural refuges, they, too, were vulnerable to surveillance. A writer in the *Westminster Magazine* averred in 1780, "A person in a country place cannot easily commit an immoral act without being detected or reproved by his neighbours."[7]

The good opinion of neighbors was not a trifling concern, especially in small, close-knit communities. "A man that hath an ill name is halfe hangd," stated an English proverb. Bonds, personal as well as financial, depended upon one's honor and reputation, which any number of misdeeds, from domestic quarrels and drunkenness to promiscuity and theft, could imperil. "Bad fame" often constituted the basis of presentments at court, and trials frequently invoked "the report of the neighborhood." A damaged reputation was usually irreparable, an indelible stain reviled by the community. "He is not look'd upon to be an honest man in the neighborhood, for they say he buys stolen goods," Ann Parfit noted of a London neighbor in 1742. Of his Inveresk parishioners, a Scottish minister commented, "There is no censorial power half so effectual as the opinion of equals."[8]

Men and women on the lower rungs of society attracted the greatest scrutiny. Common laborers, servants, vagabonds, and slaves all bred deep suspicion among social superiors. The truly indigent were not even subject to the authority of a master—"nobody to govern them," observed John

Aubrey. "The lower class of people," spewed the *British Magazine*, "are in England the meanest, dirtiest, wickedest and most insolent creatures of all the human species." The mobility of vagrants, possessing neither "fire nor place," fueled apprehension. Of the typical beggar, the Elizabethan Nicholas Breton wrote, "Hee is commonly begot in a bush, borne in a barne, lives in a highway and dyes in a ditch."[9] In some regions, social pariahs such as Jews, prostitutes, and heretics had to wear badges of shame tagged to their clothing. In Augsburg, beggars bore the *Stadtpir*, a civic symbol, on their garments. Prostitutes wore a green stripe and Jews, a yellow ring. An English statute in 1572 required that vagrants be "grievously whipped and burned through the gristle of the right ear with a hot iron."[10] Marked already by their tattered garments and physical infirmities, the lower orders reputedly exhibited a roguish demeanor, the product of years of hardship and insecurity. Of thieves like himself, an Irishman remarked, "If we go abroad in the day, a wise man would easily find us to be rogues by our faces, we have such a suspicious, fearful and constrained countenance, often turning back and slinking thro' narrow lanes and alleys." Not surprisingly, vagrants fantasized about magical hats that could render them invisible to their tormentors. One German adolescent spoke of a white powder that, with the devil's assistance, shielded him from human sight.[11]

It would be wrong to conclude that privacy is a modern priority neither known nor valued by earlier generations. While its importance has varied by period and place, the appeal of privacy has been an enduring characteristic of Western culture. Common throughout the classical world, concern for privacy seems to have intensified during the late Middle Ages with the increasing accumulation of personal possessions and greater interest in their safekeeping. First used in the 1400s, the words "privacy" and "private" became part of popular parlance by the time of Shakespeare, as his plays reflect. Clearly, for early modern folk, the close scrutiny of communities did not diminish privacy's appeal. Quite the contrary. Local oversight coupled with the threat of sanctions only fostered a heightened appreciation for seclusion. Especially at nighttime. "Be private as the night is," counsels one character to another in the play *The Bastard* in 1652. "Night makes me bold," wrote George Herbert, "and I dare doe that in the dark and in privat, which in companie I forbeare."[12]

There were, of course, institutionalized occasions for personal gratification and social license. Catholic lands had a variety of outlets for festive behavior, such as Carnival, the Feast of Fools, and other annual holidays. Popular diversions were marked by large quantities of food and drink and ample opportunities for sports and rough play. On the occasion of Carnival in the days approaching the observance of Lent, townspeople teased, tricked, and tormented friends and animals alike. By donning disguises, revelers delighted, too, in the ritual of role reversal, parading as clerics and civic officials. "It is sometimes expedient," a sixteenth-century French lawyer wrote, "to allow the people to play the fool and make merry, lest by holding them in too great a rigor, we put them in despair."[13]

In Protestant countries like England, the number of saints' days and other religious holidays steadily decreased in the wake of the Reformation. Condemned for their intemperance and frivolity, some festivals gave way to secular or Protestant substitutes, but on a more modest scale. "Our holy and festival days are very well reduced," reported the Elizabethan William Harrison.[14] Even in Catholic communities, cathartic interludes among the common people were of limited duration, confined, as holidays, to special times of the year. And over time, carnal excess declined, with mounting efforts by clergy and town councils to impose greater order. Significantly, only after darkness fell did opportunities for merriment occasionally enter a more violent, at times anarchic stage. So in the Auvergne, weddings typically climaxed in evening violence, and May Day festivities, in parts of Italy, grew more disorderly at night. During Carnival season, anxious authorities in much of Europe forbade masks after dark, lest they incite rioting and bloodshed. "None are suffered to carry swords or arms, while they go masked thus; nor to enter into any house; nor to be abroad masked after it grows dark," reported a foreign visitor to Rome.[15]

Routinely, the darkness of night loosened the tethers of the visible world. Despite night's dangers, no other realm of preindustrial existence promised so much autonomy to so many people. Light was not an unalloyed blessing, nor darkness inevitably a source of misery. "In the *day*," observed the Restoration satirist Tom Brown, "'tis *constraint*, 'tis *ceremony*, 'tis *dissimulation*, that speaks." Appearances were often deceiving, because they were meant to be. "All's restraint," echoed a contemporary. It was after sunset that opportunities expanded and intensified for behavior otherwise forbidden. Night alone permitted the expression of man's inner character. "Night is conscious of all your desires," stated a writer. A London song described how "many a face, and many a heart, / Will then pull off the mask" to sin "openly at night."[16]

Nighttime had deep symbolic value, its appeal owing much to its traditional association with licentiousness and disorder. In the popular mind, nocturnal darkness lay beyond the pale of the civilized realm. "'Tis only daylight that makes sin," wrote John Milton. Dusk represented a borderland between civility and freedom—freedom in both its benign and malignant qualities. "Metaphors matter," as Bernard Bailyn has reminded us, for "they shape the way we think"—all the more when they make sense in the light of actual experience.

On a practical level, the sources of night's allure were considerable, including the natural mask it afforded persons in lieu of the façades often adopted during the day. "Dark enough," affirmed a London writer in 1683, "to come back to one's house without being taken notice of by the neighbours." Even on clear nights, danger of public exposure receded owing to fewer pedestrians. With most persons confined to their dwellings, public behavior invariably became more private—all the more, observed the playwright Aphra Behn, once "mortal eyes are safely lockt in sleep." Then, too, personal associations at night were the product of choice, not circumstance—trusted friends and family rather than workmates or inquisitive superiors. Darkness, as a late eighteenth-century writer noted, created "little separate communities" quite apart from one's diurnal relationships.[17]

The immensity of night, for some, conferred a pronounced sense of personal sovereignty. "Everything belongs to me in the night," declared Restif de la Bretonne. In his famed poem *The Complaint; or Night Thoughts on Life, Death, and Immortality* (1742–1745), Edward Young echoed, "What awful joy! What mental liberty! / I am not pent in darkness; / . . . in darkness I'm embower'd." For all of the fear engendered by pestilential damps and celestial spectacles, the outdoors invited mortals' grandest visions. "We can fix our eyes more comfortably on the heavens," observed Bernard le Bovier de Fontenelle—"our thoughts are freer because we're so foolish as to imagine ourselves the only ones abroad to dream." Night knew no bounds. Goethe, on a moonlit evening in Naples, was "overwhelmed by a feeling of infinite space." And not just poets and philosophers. Exclaimed an English grazier treading home from an evening's merriment, "Would I had but as many fat bullocks as there are stars." To which, replied his companion, "With all my heart, if I had but a meadow as large as the sky."[18]

CHAPTER SIX

WORKS OF DARKNESS: LABOR

I

What use of thee can any creature make? For any good? What profit dost thou bring?

HUMPHREY MILL, "OF DARKNESSE," 1639[1]

AND, TOO, NIGHT often declared a welcome truce from daily toil. For countless laborers, darkness brought freedom not only from social oversight but also from punishing hours of work. "The night cometh, when no man can work," affirmed the Book of John. In sections of Britain, the expression "blindman's holiday" customarily signified the arrival of evening, when it became too dark for most labor. "The sun set, the workman freed," declared a Spanish saying.[2]

During the Middle Ages, nocturnal labor in many trades was illegal. In a variety of crafts, municipal regulations forbade work, even during the early hours of winter darkness preceding the curfew bell. In 1375, Hamburg required farriers to stop their labors in the autumn when "the sun turns golden" and each winter "when day gives way to night." Not that the physical well-being of workers weighed heavily on the minds of medieval authorities. Along with religious objections to night's desecration, there existed the heightened risk of fire. Moreover, by limiting trades to daylight, towns imposed greater order upon economic activity, whether for setting taxes or instituting price controls. Tradesmen themselves, to ensure the quality of their goods, often restricted hours. As much for pride as for profit, master craftsmen found candlelight deficient for their chisels, files, and other fine tools. "The night work is a daies confusion," went a familiar adage. Beginning in the twelfth century, English guilds typically prohibited work at night. In the forefront were skilled crafts that required keen wits, sharp eyesight, and ample illumination. A French *Book of Trades* in the thirteenth century forbade gold and silversmiths to work, for "light at night is insufficient for them to ply their trade well and truly." During a street riot in Dijon, a cutler was stabbed for keeping late hours. Magnifying such concerns was a deep-rooted suspicion of nocturnal commerce of any sort. Not only was nighttime associated with the devil's work, but unwitting customers placed themselves at the mercy of unscrupulous tradesmen—eager to "practice deception in their work," condemned the Spurmakers Guild of London in 1345. "Choose not a woman, nor linen clothe by the candle," warned a saying.[3]

Even so, not all labor in medieval towns and villages subsided at dusk. There existed a variety of exceptions, including some rural tasks and unskilled trades. Within the fourteenth-century account books of a large Florentine cloth company, the term *notte*, or night, indicated workers who toiled until midnight. In St. Omer, sailors and weavers were among those exempted in 1358 from heeding the night bell to cease labor. Of a neighborhood smith reluctant to extinguish his forge, a medieval poet protested, "Such noise on nights ne heard men never, / What [with] knaven cry and clattering knocks!" Even tailors and cobblers occasionally performed rudimentary tasks by candlelight. Filling orders for noble families, they were given exemptions—as were workers on the eve of markets and fairs. Louis XI permitted Parisian glovemakers, one winter, to labor until 10:00 P.M. Not only had their orders mounted, but masters complained of the need to keep apprentices and servants at night from gaming. Work, among other things, was a form of social control.[4]

Not until the early modern era, however, was there a marked rise in nocturnal labor. With the emergence of new markets and manufacturers, regional economies expanded in all directions, temporally as well as spatially. Despite persistent fears of fire, guilds and municipal authorities adopted less stringent regulations. In Sweden, for example, such was the importance of beer production that breweries remained in operation overnight. The same was true in Amsterdam. When the monk Woulter Jacobszoon in 1573 abruptly awoke at 2:00 A.M. from a noise, he suspected a nearby brewery "where beer was put into vats." For most callings, to be sure, the day's work still ended with darkness, as it normally did for the urban middle classes. Strictly speaking, the English Statute of Artificers of 1563 required that artisans and other laborers work during spring and summer from five in the morning to between seven and eight in the evening and during fall and winter from daybreak to dusk (two and a half hours were allotted for rest and meals). In seventeenth-century France, the common expression "day-laborer" meant a laborer who worked from sunrise to sunset. Louis-Sébastien Mercier, in his evocative description of pre-Revolutionary Paris, described the exodus home each sunset of carpenters and masons, leaving trails of white plaster from their shoes.[5]

All the same, a wealth of evidence indicates that nocturnal labor became surprisingly widespread in preindustrial communities, especially when days grew shortest from autumn to spring. Notwithstanding the loss of daylight, numerous people toiled past nightfall, both in towns and in the country. "In this age, tradesmen, and those that have any toiling employment in the world," complained an English writer in 1680, "have brought themselves to an ill custom of sitting up at their trade." Where many extended their labors by several hours, some persons worked past midnight. "In the day-time as much as thou wilt, in the night as much as thou canst," affirmed a seventeenth-century adage. Counseled a Scottish saying, "Stabel the steed and put your wife to bed when there's night wark to do."[6]

II

As touching intemperance and excess in sleep, necessity cures most of you that are poor of this evil.

WILLIAM BURKITT, 1694[7]

Who labored at night, and why? Was the decision to work more a matter of choice or necessity? One answer to these questions lies in the irregular hours that marked some laborers' travail. Not all times of the day or days of the week for these workers were alike in intensity. The Sabbath naturally brought a respite from labor. But even on other days, rather than adhering to fixed hours, laborers set their own pace by performing piecework inside cottages and small shops or selected tasks on farms. According to E. P. Thompson, "The work pattern was one of alternate bouts of intense labour and of idleness, wherever men were in control of their working lives." What portion of the premodern workforce they represented is impossible to say; but plainly more than a few men and women deferred to evening tasks that might have been completed earlier, albeit at a less leisurely tempo. Days were devoted not just to labor but also to gossip and drink.[8] Then, too, such trades as baking, due to their unique demands, operated overnight, whereas still other trades grew busy at times from the sudden press of fresh orders. Goods were produced on demand. In Hertford, the apprentice tailor John Dane "sat up three nights to work" because his master "had manie sargants cotes to make." And the glazier Jacques-Louis Ménétra devoted a night to completing a set of windows for a church in Vendôme, having pledged to deliver them the following day. A London shoemaker in 1722, "being oblig'd to get a pair of shoos made," worked in his stall close to midnight.[9]

Most often, however, pressures of subsistence—not personal preference, the pace of business, or a "preindustrial work ethic"—drove workers to toil late hours. "The day is short, the work is much," affirmed an English proverb. Evenings let individuals of small means complete the day's drudgery and, in some cases, find gainful employment. The Elizabethan writer Thomas Dekker, in an essay on candlelight, asked rhetorically, "How many poore *handy-craftes* men by *thee* have earned the best part of their living?" A resident of London, the laborer Thomas Long, worked two nights straight just to get "the money up" to pay his rent. "The hardest part of the day's service," declared Reverend James Clayton, "often falls upon our poor, at that time which God and nature have allotted to rest." So, also, in a fourteenth-century tale by Franco Sacchetti, the character Bonamico asks a neighbor, "Art thou then in such great poverty that thou canst not do without working at night?"[10]

In urban areas, a broad spectrum of laborers comprised the working poor at night. Servants, found in a quarter or more of all English families, remained subject to a master's summons. Some domestics, like chamberlains and maidservants, bore assigned duties after dark, from locking

Pehr Hilleström, *The Testing of an Egg*, 1785.

doors and windows to preparing bedchambers and snuffing candles. In the wake of company, complained a Dutch writer, a family's maidservants might not retire until two or three o'clock. Outside the home, manual laborers such as porters and carmen occasionally toiled late hours. At two in the morning, the London workman John Thomson was called to heave ballast aboard a vessel on the Thames, where the tides, not daylight, determined shipping schedules, as they did for commercial fishermen. Urban peddlers at night peopled streets, like the young *oublieurs* who sold waffles each evening in Paris. In the Venetian engravings of Gaetano Zompini may be found men and boys hawking such perishables as calves' blood and fresh shellfish by moonlight. "Come, buy my mussels," shouts a youth, "there's no fish will keep." In Rome, vendors sold brandy to combat night's "bad air."[11] And everywhere, "bunters" foraged lanes for rags and other articles dropped by crowds that could be sold for making paper. Returning home one evening, Samuel Pepys encountered a boy with a lantern "that was picking up of rags"—"he could get sometimes three or four bushels of rags in a day, and gat *3d* a bushel for them," Pepys marveled. Dunghills, rummaged, yielded small treasures of their own. Persons scavenged deserted market stalls, hunting for bread, vegetables, and scraps of meat to sell. Others collected excrement from lanes to peddle in the country for fertilizer. There was money in manure. In Naples, Goethe discovered boys and farmhands "reluctant to leave the streets at nightfall," such was the "gold mine" to be had from the "droppings of mules and horses."[12]

Ordinary folk followed various trades requiring rudimentary skills. English weavers, in response to a burgeoning cloth industry, sometimes sat at looms until 10:00 P.M., even in wintertime. On the Continent, conditions were little different. Male weavers in Lyons, for example, labored from 5:00 A.M. to 9:00 P.M., as did women in silk mills. Tailors, shoemakers, feltmakers, and dyers endured long days. "Burgess bedtyme," stated a Scottish proverb, "is surtois [shoemaker's] suppertyme." In The Hague, when David Beck, one January evening in 1624, returned to his dwelling after nine o'clock, he found "Abraham the tailor who was still working at our home." Of tallow chandlers, an eighteenth-century guide to London trades noted that their "time of working must be as the season permits, or goods are wanting, by night or by day." The youth Tom Poundall, nearly blind from smallpox, cut candlewicks evenings for a chandler.[13]

Late hours typified the regimen of masons, carpenters, and other members of the building trades. Scattered workmen labored at night inside Pepys's home on Seething Lane. On Christmas Eve in 1660, painters did not finish until 10:00 P.M.—"this night I was rid of their and all other work," a relieved Pepys recorded in his diary. According to the Northampton squire Daniel Eaton in 1726, joiners frequently worked by candlelight when autumn days grew short.[14] Bakers labored much of the night in order to provide morning customers with warm bread. "He burns the midnight oil for me," wrote Mercier of Paris's bakers.[15] To produce ale or beer, commercial brewers began after midnight the laborious process of grinding the malt, boiling it in water to produce mash, drawing off the wort, furnishing hops (for beer), and adding yeast.[16]

Shifts of glassmakers and iron smelters kept vigil beside blazing furnaces. To sustain the intense temperatures, furnaces burned around the clock, as did lime kilns and mounds of wood, covered by peat, to produce charcoal. In the coastal town of Lymington, Celia Fiennes found workers boiling large pans of sea water to make salt. "They constantly attend night and day all the while the fire is in the furnace . . . they leave off Satterday night and let out the fire and so begin and kindle their fire Monday morning, it's a pretty charge to light the fire." Except for cities like London with noise restrictions, blacksmiths worked late many evenings.[17] Mills ran overnight in order to take advantage of the natural power, whether wind or water, propelling their wheels. Just as olive oil mills in southern France operated "day and night," so did gristmills in England. "They keep theire mills goinge all night, if they have but whearewithall to keepe her doinge," observed a Yorkshire farmer in 1642. (Millers, because of their nocturnal labors, were sometimes rumored to dabble in magic.)[18] Mines, too, functioned through the night, for the time of day mattered little in shafts lit by miners' lamps. Such was the regimen within copper mines in central Sweden and silver mines outside Freiburg. In Cornwall, according to a writer, "poore men" earned "their living hardly by mininge and digging tinne and metall oute of the grounde bothe daye and night." Already, in these nascent enterprises—the mills, forges, and mines of early modern Europe—we can glimpse the profound contribution that nighttime would one day make to industrial productivity.[19]

For most tasks, semi-skilled workers found crude illuminants suffi-

Joseph Wright of Derby, *The Blacksmith's Shop*, eighteenth century.

cient. Oil lamps and candles were preferred. On the Isle of Man, the word *arnane* in the Manx language signified "work done at night by candlelight." In Sweden, masters each fall invited apprentices and journeymen to their homes for a *ljusinbrinning*, or "burning-in," a frolic designed to inaugurate the season for laboring by artificial light. Conversely, German artisans celebrated the end of winter darkness with a meal called a *lichtbraten* (light roast), as did English shoemakers each March in a ritual known as "wetting the block." Preindustrial workers also resorted to rushlights, candlewood, and even, on occasion, moonlight. The costs incurred by artificial illumination were another matter. An Elizabethan writer condemned the high price of tallow candles "to the great hindrance of the poor workeman that watcheth [remains awake] in the night." The common expression, "not worth the candle," denoted work too minor to warrant the expense. Still, for many tradesmen, profits outweighed the costs. In a popular song entitled "The Clothier's Delight," an employer declares, "We have soap and candles whereby we have light, / That you may work by them so long as you have sight." Indeed, the *London Evening Post* reported in 1760, "For several months in the winter season, many working businesses are prosecuted by seven or eight hours of candle-light work in the morning and evening"—even though, the paper added, they "require a great deal of it."[20]

Among the hardest workers—night in, night out—were women. Unlike men of middling or plebeian rank, who mostly worked outside the home, many urban wives and daughters confined their days to the domestic realm, except for running errands, performing outdoor chores, or visiting a close neighbor. By the late sixteenth century, women were increasingly discouraged from traveling "fro hous to hous, to heere sundry talys," as does the Wife of Bath in *The Canterbury Tales* (ca. 1387). Rather than a "wanderer abroad," the virtuous woman was expected to be "a worker at home." Her moral character was thought essential to the good repute of the household, where, after all, her conduct remained under tighter control. If not the master of her home, the wife, nonetheless, was its keeper, with all the obligations that burden entailed. A full day's labor included cooking, cleaning, and childcare. Although most women rose earlier than their husbands, they had less opportunity during the day to rest. "Some respit to husbands the weather may send," wrote Thomas Tusser in the sixteenth century, "but huswives affaires have never an ende."[21]

Nights brought little seeming relief. Often, to paraphrase a contemporary, work was exchanged for work. Domestic tasks invariably extended the day's toil. "The good huswive's candle never goeth out," remarked William Baldwin in *Beware the Cat* (1584). A late July evening in 1650 found Jane Bond of Massachusetts making a cake and collecting firewood. Jane Morris of London mended linen from the early afternoon to nearly midnight. So well known was the seventeenth-century ballad "A Woman's Work is Never Done" that the Maine midwife Martha Ballard invoked it, late one evening, when scribbling in her diary–"happy shee," reflected Ballard, "whos strength holds out to the end of the rais." Indeed, when the Wiltshire laborer Stephen Duck published his celebrated poem "The Thresher's Labour" in 1739, it brought a stinging response from the poet Mary Collier. "When night comes on, and we quite weary are, / We scarce can count what falls unto our share." Unlike the toil of men, protested Collier, "Our labours never know an end."[22]

Certainly not when laundry needed washing. This task was unpleasant and laborious. Tubs of water had to be carted inside and heated, and garments scrubbed, starched, and ironed. Cleansers, in the absence of soap, included lye, urine, and even dung mixed with cold water. In propertied households, women servants bore the brunt of the labor. So time-consuming was washing that they typically began late at night to minimize domestic disruption. "A washing pickle," Pepys called the confusion upon returning home one November night. Indigent women earned a living by washing clothes at home or, more commonly, by traveling to dwellings as laundresses. The widow Mary Stower, on "a very moon light" evening, visited a house in Leeds at 2:00 A.M. Stated Ann Timms of London, "I wash for a living, being late at work between eleven and twelve o'clock."[23]

Women augmented the family income in other ways—brewing ale and making cheese, to name two evening enterprises. Of beermaking, Collier complained, "Our wort boils over if we dare to sleep." Above all, women devoted nights to spinning and knitting, carding wool, and weaving. Starting in the fourteenth century, the putting-out system emerged in many sections of Europe, whereby urban merchants provided households with wool, flax, and other raw materials. Making textiles was a major activity in both rural and urban households. On long winter evenings, from Sweden to the Italian peninsula, mothers, daughters, and servants turned their hands to spinning wheels or looms. Instructed the steward of a Scottish laird, "Keep the maids closs at their spinning till 9 at night when they are not washing or at other necessary work." Of his childhood home in Bavaria, Jean Paul recalled the cattle maid "at her distaff in the servants' room, which was lit by what little light the pinewood torches afforded." None of these tasks required much light. Of knitting, an Aberdeen minister noted that many of his parishioners performed "their work throughout the winter evening, with the faintest light issuing from a few turfs." So important a source of income was spinning in parts of Germany that widows were allowed to keep their wheels after selling other possessions for debt. In the East Anglian city of Norwich, according to a census in the early 1570s, 94 percent of poor women performed textile work of some sort. At times of economic crisis, spinning afforded families vital support. In 1782 during crop failures in Scotland, women, reported a local resident, contributed "more to the welfare of their families than the men" by "sitting up at their work every other night."[24]

Finally, in urban communities a handful of occupations were nocturnal, limited largely to the hours of darkness. For the most part, they were jobs staffed by persons of small means who could not compete successfully in the daytime economy. Instead of rest, night offered these souls a livelihood. Together with the nightwatch, paid at public expense, scattered numbers, for example, found employment as private "watchers." Enlisted by manufacturers and tradesmen, they guarded merchandise from vandalism, theft, and fire. Watchers protected mills, counting houses, and stables. In Florence, private guards patrolled warehouses. Having "frequently lost coals," the proprietor of a London coalyard in 1729 hired a force of four watchmen. Servants served their masters in twin capacities. At mills near Edinburgh, for instance, it was the "custom of the miller's servants to watch the mills nightly by turns." In Newcastle, a butcher's maidservant, Catherine Parker, "watch'd his stall" at night in the city's fleshmarket. A few persons were watchers by calling. "I am watchman at the steel-yard," declared John Stubley, testifying at the Old Bailey against a thief.[25]

"Nightmen," for their part, emptied underground cesspools, or "vaults." Over each pit stood a privy, known as a "jake" or "house of easement," located in a cellar or garden. Advised Tusser, "Foule privies are now to be clensed and fide, / let night be appointed such baggage to hide." With the rapid growth of cities and towns, nightmen played an essential role in urban sanitation. Already by the sixteenth century, the city of Nuremberg employed *Nachtmeister* to empty some fifty public pits. Of course, many municipalities permitted the evening disposal of human waste in streets, which, in theory, workmen called scavengers swept clean in the hours before daybreak. Cities like London, however, discouraged this practice as a danger to public health, and civic-minded households increasingly relied upon private latrines. "Night-soil" was the euphemism coined for the ordure that professional nightmen hauled in buckets to waiting carts. Some families, like the Pepys household, benefited from sharing their cellar with a neighbor. "So to bed," Samuel wrote in July 1663, "leaving the men below in the cellar emptying the turds up through Mr. Turner's own house; and so, with more content, to bed late." Besides mandating the emptying of cesspools at night, Parisian officials in 1729 required that *gadouards*, or nightmen, proceed directly to dumps rather than pause at taverns for refreshment. In England, whereas the countryside initially

Anon., *John Hunt, Nightman and Rubbish Carter, near the Wagon and Horses in Goswell Street, near Mount Mill, London*, eighteenth century.

received most urban waste, transportation costs became prohibitively high once cities increased in size and density. And, unlike other premodern peoples, such as the Japanese, who relied heavily upon human waste for fertilizer, Western households generally preferred animal excrement. In the case of London, much of its waste was dumped into the Thames.[26]

The objectionable nature of the work is suggested by the sarcastic nickname "goldfinder," given to nightmen. In Augsburg, senior latrine cleaners were known as "night kings." If a vault had gone long unemptied, the undertaking could be arduous. At the Philadelphia home of Elizabeth Drinker, forty-four years of "depositing" elapsed before a cesspool in the yard was cleaned in 1799. The ordeal required two carts and five men laboring for two consecutive nights until four or five each morning. Wondered Drinker afterward, "If liberty and equality which some talk much about, could take place, who would they get for those, and many other hard and disagreeable undertakings?" The dangers were considerable, including asphyxiation whenever workmen entered a vault, equipped at most with lanterns for light. At a Southwark tavern called the Tumbledown Dick, the *Gentleman's Magazine* reported in July 1753:

> The first man that went down, overcome by the stench, call'd out for help, and immediately fell down on his face; a second went to help him, and fell down also; then a third, fourth went down, when these two were obliged to come up again directly: and the stench of the place being by this time greatly abated, they got the two that went down first; but the second was dead, and the first had so little life in him, that he died in the afternoon.[27]

As with human excreta, so with bodies of the dead. Cities and towns reserved their worst tasks for night. Thus, during epidemics, municipal officials waited for darkness to dispose of their dead. With fewer citizens abroad, there was less risk, according to common thought, of spreading infection. And there was less likelihood then of public panic. During London's Great Plague of 1665, which killed some fifty-six thousand people, "dead-carts" were stationed evenings at the entrance of streets and alleys for families to deposit bodies. Municipal officials in Bavaria muffled their wheels with rags. "All the needful works, that carried terror with them, that were both dismal and dangerous, were done in the night," noted Daniel Defoe in his *Journal of the Plague Year* (1722). In the event of plague, night also brought the burning of victims' clothes and bedding. Of an outbreak in Barcelona during the mid-1600s, a contemporary reported:

> If anyone died of the plague they took the body at night to be buried in the graveyard of Nazareth along with the mattresses and sheets. The following night they would come to burn the wooden bed frame and curtains and the clothing and everything the sick person might have touched.

Charged with all these tasks were gravediggers known in England as *vespillons* for their evening duties (that is, at the time of vespers). In Italy, they were named *beccamòrti*, or corpse-carriers. Sometimes clad in white, gravediggers carried torches as a warning. When smallpox afflicted Boston in 1764, they were ordered to place each body in a tarred sheet and a coffin "in the dead of night," with a man to proceed before the corpse "to give notice to anyone that may be passing." Pepys restricted his nocturnal peregrinations in 1665 during London's plague. On one such outing—"in great fear of meeting of dead corpses carrying to be burned"—he periodically spied "a linke (which is the mark of them) at a distance." "Blessed be God, met none," he confided to his diary.[28]

III

Many things even go best in the raw night-hours.

VIRGIL, 1ST CENTURY B.C.[29]

"My business drives me dreadfully," complained the New England farmer Hiram Harwood. "Go to bed late and rise early." From the early American piedmont to the steppes of western Russia, more than three-quarters of the population worked the soil as tenants, laborers, servants, serfs, and slaves, in addition to smaller numbers of landowning peasants, yeoman farmers, and planters. Fields produced flax and grains like oats, rye, and wheat, along with hay and other sources of animal fodder. Common were vegetable gardens and orchards. On colonial plantations, tobacco, rice, indigo, and sugar dominated. Rather than a hiatus, evenings for rural folk frequently represented a continuation of the working day. More than a few vainly struggled to eke out an existence, toiling, like one farmer, "night and day" to stave off debt and the loss of their meager plots (more often rented than owned). The London writer "Mus Rusticus" in the 1770s lamented the typical laborer's plight, who "in order to support himself and his family" was forced to work for a larger landholder "from four A.M. 'til eight at night, if he can get any glimmering of light." Always pressing were the demands of farming and planting, regardless of one's economic independence. "You will find no diligent overseer who does not stay up for the greater part of the night," claimed the German Jacobus Andreas Crusius in 1660. For the early Roman writer Columella, an aversion to sleep in addition to wine and "sexual indulgence" was a prerequisite for good husbandry.[30]

Often there were jobs at night to do, from butchering stock to chopping wood to picking apples, all labor-intensive tasks able to be performed in poor light. Having in May 1665 gathered furze all day, the Norfolk laborer Thomas Rust carted it home later that evening. Farm workers near

Francesco Bassano the Younger, *Autumn Harvest (Grape-picking)*, 1585–1590.

Aberdeen, on summer nights, cut slabs of peat for fuel. Nighttime found Abner Sanger of New Hampshire mending fences, building hogpens, and hauling lumber. "I work until daylight," he recorded in 1771 after digging a garden the entire evening. From late spring to fall, it was not unknown for fieldwork to be completed after nightfall, whether that meant breaking ground, sowing seed, haymaking, or harvesting a crop. "They finished my haycock at night," noted a country vicar in his diary.[31] In late summer and early autumn, harvests consumed long hours, as workers scrambled to gather mature crops. "This night we cut down all our corn," recorded a Yorkshireman with satisfaction in late August 1691. In parts of the Continent, the vintage beckoned. Of southern France, a seventeenth-century observer wrote, "In the vintage time the people are very busy early and late." A sudden thunderstorm could destroy a harvest left lying overnight. And there were easier pickings then for thieves. A visitor to Scotland reported, "No part is left in the field but carried home every night as it is cut down & deposited in barns." A manorial official instructed Prussian villagers in 1728, "In the harvest, there can be no fixed hours for service with horse-teams, which must be regulated according to the work that needs doing."[32]

Domestic animals also required close attention. Returning from pasture, cows were foddered, watered, and milked, nighttime as well as morning. Once cleaned, stalls needed fresh straw. Horses, hogs, and poultry, all had to be fed and put to bed. Not until eleven o'clock did the Cumberland servant John Brown on a March evening "get some straw to clean and bed up" his master's horse. Animals occasionally fell sick, while the birth of a foal or calf could mean long hours waiting by the stall. In early spring, newborn lambs necessitated constant care.[33] Stock sometimes broke loose, trampling crops and gardens. In Dorset, on a spring evening in 1698, John Richards's dairy cow, Bexington Red, fell into a ditch. Unable to rise, it had to be watched through the night.[34]

Some rural tasks were specially suited to evening, from destroying slugs to shifting beehives. Wasps' nests, too, were best burned after dark. Starlings, sparrows, and other "nuisance" birds were easiest then to catch with a combination of lanterns and nets. Although thought harmful to humans, the damp, cool night air had a variety of salutary effects, according to agricultural writers and farmers. Just as the author Di Giacomo Agostinetti in 1707 advised sowing millet "in the evening when the air is cool" to "benefit from the dew of the night," so, too, on an April night in 1648, did Adam Eyre of Yorkshire plant mustard seed and turnips in his garden. Evening was the preferred time to water crops in order to avoid evaporation. On the Virginia plantation of Landon Carter, slaves scrupulously irrigated young tobacco plants at night to speed their maturation. "We have gangs enough to dispatch a field in a hurry," the wealthy planter boasted in his diary. The farming book of Henry Best of Elmswell advised that straw be watered at night in preparation for thatching roofs.[35]

Also important, each evening, were clues that the night sky furnished of the day ahead. Displayed across the heavens were meteorological signs thought capable of forecasting everything from thunderstorms to hard frosts. As the authors of *Maison Rustique* explained in 1616, a good farmer, "although he need not to be booke-wise," must "have knowledge of the things foretelling raine, wind, faire weather, and other alterations of the seasons." Sundry omens existed, but most people seem to have put their faith in the night sky. Declared the London author of *A Prognostication Everlasting* (1605), "Behold the stars whose magnitude you know best. If they appeare of much light, in bignesse great, more blazing then they are commonly, it betokeneth great wind or moysture in that part where they shew."[36]

Moonlight assisted many labors. When possible, men hoed, planted, and mowed by natural light. Of thatchers, Best remarked, "They leave not worke att night soe longe as they can see to doe anythinge." Sanger in wintertime transported wood by sled, the white snow reflecting the lunar light. By contrast, when on another night Sanger carried a bushel of rye to a mill, the moon was new. "I come home in the evening through mud and mire," he moaned. It was at harvest time, when fieldwork was most grueling, that moonlight became especially critical. For several nights every September, light from the full moon nearest to the autumnal equinox is more prolonged than usual because of the small angle of the moon's orbit. Well known in England as the "harvest moon," it bore the name in Scotland of the "Michaelmas moon." Farmers on both sides of the Atlantic benefited from the moonlight to gather crops. "Sometimes," Jasper Charlton wrote in 1735, "the harvest people work all night at their hay or corn." Nearly as useful was the "hunter's moon" in October, when a full moon next appeared. "The moon of September," declared a writer, "shortens the night. The moon of October is hunter's delight."[37]

Fishing, too, drew rural folk abroad. Besides supplying food, a night's catch might be bartered or sold to supplement meager livings. Certain types of fish, like trout, were easier after dark to catch, especially when torchlights doubled as lures. Italian peasants in small boats speared fish in the Mediterranean. In Scottish lochs, vast quantities of herring were caught with nets from late summer to early spring. "They are always caught in the night-time," observed a resident of Lochbroom; and "the darker the night is, the better for fishers."[38]

In much of the countryside, predators at night posed a worrisome threat. Accompanied by watchdogs, men guarded orchards, fields, and stock. Throughout Saxony, peasants feared deer and wild boar for their damage to cornfields. Villagers took turns "all night long" ringing bells to ward off intruders. Peasants in southern Norway guarded cattle and cornfields against bears. Worst were wolves. In France, to protect flocks of sheep, peasants were known to invoke magical charms. Armed with guns and crooks, shepherds, for protection as well as warmth, burned fires through the night, crying warnings to compatriots should a pack be seen or heard. (In the *campagna* of Italy, shepherds also lit small fires to "banish" the night air.) Dogs, too, were essential for guarding flocks—preferably ones with white coats so that they would not be taken for wolves. Some dogs wore spiked collars. According to the agricultural writer Augustin Gallo, the wise shepherd, "in order to preserve his herd from the wolf & other nasty beasts, must set up ramparts [a sheep-fold] & put a good & strong sentinel of brave & scary dogs." New England farmers, to deter wolves, were reputed to smear a concoction of gunpowder and tar on their sheeps' heads.[39]

Just as threatening were thieves. A visitor to France found that peasants, to protect their corn from theft, stood watch overnight until crops could be gathered and carted home. Hired to watch a small flock of sheep one winter night, Peter Butler, from behind a hedge in a London field, witnessed four thieves grab one of the animals. With the moon just rising—"it was as light as day"—Butler's gun misfired. Badly beaten, he was tied up and left to die. Not unusual for two Italian brothers was their tedious regimen on an October night in 1555. Rising from bed after midnight, Lorenzo and Giacobo Boccardi of Fara spent the remainder of the evening patrolling an oak grove and several fields. Rather than taking separate paths, the pair, for safety's sake, remained together. Normally armed with a battle-axe and sword, this night they took a gun instead. Among other escapades, the two had to frighten off a set of threshers that had freed their horses in the family vineyard to feed.[40]

Among a farmer's final labors was taking his crops or stock to market, arriving hours before daybreak to haggle with vendors. Along with carts laden with vegetables and fruit, small herds of cattle passed in the darkness, their collars strung with bells lest any stray. At night, the countryside moved to the city. In Venice, beginning at 3:00 A.M., peasants arrived in boats "loaded with every produce of nature," while a visitor to Lyons was awakened at four o'clock "by the braying of asses, and a busy hum of people" loaded with baskets. The timing of such trips depended upon market days and the availability of moonlight. Fortified towns needed to open their gates well before dawn. The largest urban centers had an insatiable appetite for foodstuffs, with public markets open daily from early morning until dusk, if not later. In a single week, farm animals alone brought to London, according to an estimate in 1750, included one thousand bullocks, two thousand calves, six thousand sheep, three thousand lambs, thirty-five hundred hogs and pigs, and nearly twenty thousand fowl. "How many labour all day, and travell, nay wake att night to bring provisions to this town," wondered Sarah Cowper. Peasants traveled to Paris from distant towns like Gisors and Aumale. "At one in the morning six thousand peasants arrive, bringing the town's provisions of vegetables and fruits and flowers," Mercier wrote. At the central market of *Les Halles*, he noted:

> The noise of voices never stops, there is hardly a light to be seen; most of the deals are done in the dark, as though these were people of a different race, hiding in their caverns from the light of the sun. The fish salesmen, who are the first comers, apparently never see daylight, and go home as the street lamps start to flicker, just before dawn; but if eyes are no use, ears take their place; everyone bawls his loudest.[41]

Once temperatures began to fall, frequent evenings found rural families working inside their homes. The French saying "To the fire in winter, to the fields and woods in summer" applied to night as well as day. As early as the first century, Columella wrote in *Res Rustica* of the "many things which can be properly done by artificial light." As in urban households, there was weaving or spinning. A visitor to Sweden thought nearly every peasant at night a weaver, some so poor that they relied upon moonlight to card wool. Often, too, rural women produced cloth for regional textile markets once commercial links penetrated the hinterlands. "In many parts of *Yorkshire*," Josiah Tucker wrote in 1757, "the woolen manufacture is carried on by small farmers and freeholders. These people buy some wool, and grow some; their wives, daughters, and servants spin it in the long winter nights."[42]

Families used evenings to mend shoes and clothing or to repair and sharpen tools. There could be flax to beat or grain to thresh. Apples might be stamped for cider, or malt ground for ale and beer. One February, Parson Woodforde rose at 3:00 A.M. "to brew a hogshead of strong beer." Three nights later, he was up again, this time before 1:00 A.M. to brew two batches. In the short story "The Ploughman's Wife," Restif de la Bretonne recounted winter evenings when "lads prepared stakes for the vines whilst they talked, and the girls stripped flax or spun." Sanger, in addition to tasks at his own farm, performed odd jobs at night for friends and neighbors, from husking corn to splitting wood, standing by an open door to catch the moonlight. "I help Tilly boil sap all night," he wrote one early April.[43] In the Chesapeake colonies, planters occasionally kept slaves at work stripping tobacco and husking corn by moon- or candlelight; on South Carolina plantations, slaves often spent winter evenings pounding rice, prompting more than a few, evidently, to flee despite the season.[44] No doubt, other rural laborers at night, even some farmers, thought of doing the same.

IV

Night-worke and day-worke is not all one.

JOHN TAYLOR, 1643[45]

For after a full day's labor, night work could be grueling. Prolonged toil exhausted both body and spirit. In medieval France, clothworkers declared that late hours were "dangerous for them and greatly to the peril of their bodies." Of the typical rural laborer, a London writer, much later, claimed, "Although he wants rest and subsistence, he perseveres, whereby he is much hurt; it wears him out, and brings on sickness and untimely old age." Each fall in the Auvergne during threshing, peasants barely got "even a few hours of sleep" at night. Given such rigors, accidents inevitably followed, resulting in the loss of limbs and lives. Standard equipment at a Jamaican sugar works toured by Lady Nugent was a hatchet used to sever the forearms of slaves who, from falling asleep, caught their fingers in the mill—the sole means, she noted, of saving their lives.[46]

Nearly as bad was the lot of laborers for whom nighttime comprised their "working day." Among modern workers on night shifts, research has found high levels of insomnia, fatigue, and gastrointestinal disorders. During the small hours of the night, the human body is not intended to remain awake or to consume significant quantities of food. To do either defies circadian rhythms and countless years of human evolution. None better understood this than night workers themselves. In 1715, an anonymous pamphlet by journeymen bakers in Paris complained, "We start our days in the evenings, we kneed the dough at night; we have to spend all night in captivity," with no chance to nap. "Night, the time of rest," the pamphlet declared, "is for us a time of torture." Indeed, night work was one of the reasons that contemporaries offered to explain the irascibility of bakers and their proclivity for violence on and off the job.[47]

And yet, despite severe hardships, the rigorous labor and physical exhaustion, nighttime did offer workers advantages. For one thing, during hot summer months, evenings were less oppressive for fieldwork. Laborers gladly slept during the midday heat in order to toil after dark. Smiths and ironworkers benefited from cooler evening temperatures.[48] In certain callings, there was less supervision at night, making hours less regimented and discipline more lax. In 1728, the servant Francis Biddle, instructed "to sit up every other night" to protect the goods of his London master, seized the chance to steal three barrels of beer, two bushels of malt, and three firkins of ale. Darkness routinely made it easier for laborers to pilfer from worksites. Favorite targets in towns and cities included lumberyards and wharves. Vulnerable to watermen were ships anchored in London and other ports. The Navy Board in the early eighteenth century sought to restrict work at royal dockyards to daylight in order to curb "the roguery and villainy" laborers "commit when it is beginning to grow dark." At the Venetian Arsenal, not only at night did guards defy regulations against fraternizing but they also carried away large quantities of goods, passing them to conspirators in boats.[49]

Opportunities for sexual misconduct were also greater. In Nuremberg, where laundresses relied upon a small number of wash-houses bordering a stream, these in 1552 had to be locked at sunset so that "the laundresses have no place for their indecent behavior." Similarly, the apprentice John Dane was alone in his master's shop in Berkhamsted, "when most folke was a bead," when a "mayd" visited for a sexual tryst. Though they "jested togetther," he reluctantly declined her entreaties. The Massachusetts colonist Esay Wood, on a moonlit evening in 1662, lay outside with Mary Powell, after she had been sent by her mother to help husk his corn.[50]

At the same time, night often meant working for oneself rather than a master. With the day's tasks complete, many hired laborers turned instead to tilling their own fields, typically small leaseholds. Tenants and cottagers, who worked the lands of substantial landowners by day, cultivated private plots by moonlight. Discontented with tending goats, the Swiss shepherd Ulrich Bräker purchased a small tract to clear by himself. "During the day," he noted, "I worked for my father; as soon as I was free, for myself; even by moonlight there I was, making up the timber and brushwood I'd chopped down while it was still light." Many no doubt looked forward to the day when they could work just their own land. A writer in an English agricultural magazine complained in 1800, "When a labourer becomes possessed of more land than he and his family can cultivate in the evenings . . . the farmer can no longer depend on him for constant work." Household dependents, too, labored at night for personal gain. Thomas Platter's future wife, the Swiss servant Anna, "frequently spun late in the night," producing cotton yarn for her mistress but also making "quite good clothing" for herself. When Bräker was still a child living at his grandparents' home, his mother, "to earn a secret penny behind" his "grandparents' backs" at night, "would surreptitiously spin by lamplight."[51]

Equally industrious were African-American slaves who occasionally received provision grounds on which to plant gardens or raise hogs and poultry. Nights when plantation regimens did not interfere were a favored time. In size, plots could range from small patches of dirt to extensive tracts of wasteland. In 1732, an observer in the Chesapeake remarked that gardens enabled slaves to plant potatoes, peas, and squash, either on Sundays or at night. Besides adding variety to otherwise bland diets, these enterprises provided slaves with goods to sell in public markets, which in the Carolina Lowcountry and much of the West Indies they regularly supplied. A market in Antigua, according to one report, drew "an assemblage of many hundred negroes and mulattoes," selling "poultry, pigs, kids, vegetables, fruit and other things." Hunting and fishing also occupied slaves' evenings, notwithstanding the need to cross miles of difficult terrain. In South Carolina, the naturalist William Bartram witnessed slaves returning "home with horse loads of wild pigeons" caught "by torch light" in a swamp. In Jamaica, land crabs, captured at night, furnished a source of income for workers whose provision grounds were poor. "Crowds of

Jan Asselijn, *Crab Catching in the Night*, seventeenth century.

negroes from the neighbouring plantations pass my house every evening with their torches and baskets, going to a crab wood on the other side, and return before midnight fully laden," a white resident recorded.[52]

Above all, nighttime commonly blurred the boundaries between labor and sociability. More than any time during the day, work and play intersected. Many tasks became collective undertakings, marked by a spirit of conviviality and companionship. Social superiors in Italy faulted peasants for attending "licentious threshings and prohibited games." Women joined one another in clothes washing. At the Drinker household in Philadelphia, Elizabeth and other women had "a washing frolick" one summer night in 1760. In southern Scotland, herring fishing, despite winter darkness, drew "men and women of all ages, and in different companies . . . carrying lamps of flaming charcoal . . . accompanied with the mixed cries of emulation, merriment, and hope." No different in spirit were early American corn "huskings," which, like "shuckings" on southern plantations, customarily took place after dark. As a servant in colonial New Jersey described, "The neighbours assist one another in stripping the corn from the husks, and are treated with rum and punch." In Massachusetts, due to their festive nature, the Puritan patriarch Cotton Mather condemned "the riots that have too often accustomed our *huskings*." Vainly, he admonished local farmers, "Let the *night of your pleasure* be turned into *fear*."[53]

No doubt, many people derived satisfaction from sharing tedious tasks with neighbors and family—their feelings of camaraderie occasionally intensified by alcohol. More important still, nighttime, by its very nature, connoted freedom from the constraints of daily life, the innumerable rules and obligations that repressed gaiety and playfulness. Night, on top of everything else, was a state of mind. Amid familiar countenances and helping hands, formalities fell by the wayside, along with feelings of fear and degradation. Inhibitions receded in the darkness, as friends laughed and toiled together. Affirmed a Welsh adage, "John" in the morning became "Jack" at night. Among other benefits, communal labor allowed families to conserve precious fuel, sharing the light from a lone torch or lamp. Indoors, men and women, hoping to escape the biting cold, assembled around the soothing glow of a hearth. Just to catch the warmth, let alone complete one's tasks, made it necessary to close ranks. Under such ill-lit, cramped conditions, night could be a time of profound intimacy and companionship. "Evening words are not like to morning," attested an English proverb.[54]

One is struck by the prevalence of such gatherings. The predominant type of social work, especially during winter months, was the spinning or knitting bee, of which there were numerous variations—for example, *veillées* in France, *Spinnstuben*, *Rockenstuben*, and *Lichstuben* in Germany, Russian *posidelki*, and *veglia* in Tuscany. On Guernsey, spinning parties known as *vueilles* assembled, as did, dating to the thirteenth century, *kvöldvaka* in Iceland. In the British Isles, almost everywhere there were similar occasions, from *céilidhe* or *áirneán* in Ireland and *rockings* in Scotland to the Welsh *y noswaith weu*, or "knitting night."[55] As early as the mid-fifteenth century, Enea Silvio Piccolomini, the future Pope Pius II (1405–1464), while traveling in northern England, observed a large company of women sitting all night by a fire, conversing and cleaning hemp. Less common elsewhere in England, spinning sessions, even in the nineteenth century, remained widespread in the north. Of villagers in Yorkshire and Lancashire, William Howitt remarked, "As soon as it becomes dark, and the usual business of the day is over, and the young children are put to bed, they rake or put out the fire; take their cloaks and lanterns, and set out with their knitting to the house of the neighbour where the sitting falls in rotation."[56]

Assembling one or more nights a week, work parties could last until one or two o'clock in the morning. Most, however, began after the evening meal and concluded well before midnight. Up to a dozen or more close neighbors customarily attended, though some were known to travel several miles, following beaten paths with lanterns on dark nights. Peasants in the Irish countryside, wrote an observer, "would often go a distance of three or four miles, through swamps and bogs." Stables and barns afforded shelter along with homes and workshops. On frigid nights, the presence of farm animals generated warmth, as did steaming manure. Often, a cottage hearth supplied small quantities of both light and heat. There was no shortage of tasks. In addition to beating hemp and stripping corn, men turned their hands to shelling nuts or weaving baskets. Requiring the sharpest sight, women normally sat up front, spinning, knitting, weaving, and carding wool either for themselves or for one another. At night, hands and forearms replaced shoulders, legs, and backs.[57]

Along with the normal run of gossip, there were jokes at the expense of local officials, especially religious leaders. Seethed a critic of the *Spinnstuben* in German villages, "Nothing else happens but exposing people and destroying their honour." Popular were tales of magic. As a youth in the Swiss town of Hittnau, the writer Jakob Stutz listened by the hearth to the folk wisdom of a "spinner" named Barbara Ott, who claimed she had once been able to fly. As voices softened, storytelling often afforded the night's principal entertainment—legends, fables, and tales of evil spirits—eternal stories recounted again and again by seasoned narrators with well-trained memories. "So pass the tales of old, along my soul, by night," declared the Scottish poet James Macpherson. So attentively did Irish audiences in Dungiven listen to ancient poems that errors in narration were queried on the spot. "The dispute," remarked an observer, "is then referred to a vote of the meeting."[58]

For preindustrial peoples, obscurity suited storytelling. In both Western and non-Western cultures, the recitation of myths and folktales long enjoyed the aura of a sacred ritual, traditionally reserved for night's depths. Darkness insulated hearts and minds from the profane demands of ordinary life. Any "sacred function," averred Daniello Bartoli in *La Recreazione del Savio*, "requires darkness and silence." Within early modern households, ill-lit rooms gave added force to the resonant talents of storytellers. These men in much of Ireland bore the title of *seanchaidhthe*, and in Wales, *cyfarwydd*. The spoken word, in the absence of competing distractions, acquired unique clarity at night. Darkness encouraged listening as well as flights of fancy. Words, not gestures, shaped the mind's dominant images. What's more, sound tends to unify any disparate body of listeners. Not only is sound difficult to ignore, but it promotes cohesion by drawing persons closer together, literally as well as metaphorically. Coupled with the dim light of a lamp or hearth, the act of storytelling created an unusually intimate milieu.[59] And, too, nighttime lent a dramatic backdrop to local tales, many of which dwelled on fears of the supernatural. Of childhood stories in Lancashire, Moses Heap recalled, "No wonder the awful tales told in the wide-open firegrate on a cold winter's night with the wind from the moors howling round the house had its affect on the young ones." There and elsewhere, witches, spirits, and apparitions were standard fare, as were perilous encounters with robbers and thieves. "Nothing is commoner in *country places*," observed Henry Bourne in 1725, "than for a whole family in a *winter's evening*, to sit round the fire, and tell stories of apparitions and ghosts."[60]

Violence, poverty, and natural disasters were persistent motifs. But there were also proverbs, moral precepts, and clever tricks one could master—useful lessons for confronting life's dangers, including magical beliefs and practices. In *My Father's Life*, Restif described hearing instructive tales on long winter evenings that contained "the loftiest maxims of the ancients." Probably more typical was a laborer's story recounting a "nighted traveller's" encounter with a will-o'-the-wisp. Drawn to its light, the traveler narrowly escapes drowning "by knowing well the brook that wimpered down the vale." While everyday events could be, at best, capricious, there were inspirational stories to "gild the horrors of the winter night," as a Scottish pastor remarked. If, in some legends, rich and powerful men fell from glory, so in others the poor triumphed over adversity. During evening gatherings at his home, the French laborer Robin Chevet drew from a trove of tales, designed both to educate and amuse. As related in the *Propos Rustiques de Maistre Léon Ladulfi* (1548) by Noël du Fail:

Jean Jacques de Boisseau, *Evening in the Village*, 1800.

> Goodman Robin, after imposing silence, would begin a fine story about the time when the animals talked (it was just two hours before); of how Renard the fox stole a fish from the fishmongers; of how he got the washer-women to beat the wolf when he was learning how to fish; of how the dog and the cat went on a voyage; about Asnette's hide; about fairies and how he often spoke with them familiarly, even at vespers as he passed through the hedgerows and saw them dancing near the Cormier fountain to the sound of a red leather bagpipe.[61]

Many stories, rooted in generations of past strife, recounted the familiar deeds of heroic warriors. Everywhere, it seems, listeners took epic legends to heart, from Icelandic sagas to *bylini* in Russia. Noted Howitt of knitting-nights in Yorkshire, "Here all the old stories and traditions of the dale come up." Amid the darkness, superior storytellers spirited suggestible minds to realms of wonder, far removed from daily hardships. In Brittany, according to Pierre-Jakez Hélias, his grandfather, a sabot-maker, was well known for his ability to "transform a gathering of peasants in a farmhouse into so many knights and ladies." Only then, reflected Hélias, might rural folk have stopped worrying about "the price of suckling pigs, or daily bread, or Sunday meat soup." Such a story is recounted in *The Old Wive's Tale* (1595), a comedy by George Peele. Urged one winter evening to share a fireside tale, Madge, the blacksmith's wife, begins:

> Once upon a time there was a King or a Lord, or a Duke that had a faire daughter, the fairest that ever was; as white as snowe, and as redd as bloud; and once uppon a time his daughter was stollen away, and hee sent all his men to seeke out his daughter. . . . There was a conjurer, and this conjurer could doo anything, and hee turned himselfe into a great dragon, and carried the King's daughter away in his mouth to a castle that hee made of stone. . . . [62]

It was not uncommon in some regions for small clusters of women to assemble, bringing their spinning wheels or distaffs to a neighbor's home. In parts of France, makeshift huts called *écreignes* (little shelters) were constructed each winter for this purpose. Some, such as those in Burgundy described by Etienne Tabourot during the sixteenth century, were little more than tents. Too poor to afford their daughters fires by which to spin, winemakers used poles to construct outdoor enclosures overlaid with manure and dirt, "so well mixed that it was impenetrable." By contrast, *écreignes* in Champagne, according to a later observer, were "houses dug out below ground-level," though these too were covered with dung. A lamp, supplied by one of the women, hung in the middle. "Each one arrives, carrying her distaff, with the spindle in the distaff, with her two hands on her sewing-kit, and her apron over her hands, enters hurriedly and takes her seat."[63]

These occasions offered women an opportunity to work and socialize apart from the presence of men. During the day, such encounters were limited—women's paths might cross at markets and wells, or at communal events like births and wakes. Spinning bees gave rise to prolonged, often intense conversations. Amid animated banter, the jests and ballads, women gave and gathered news. "The winter's night is for the gossips cup," opined Nicholas Breton. According to another contemporary, "One talked intimately of one's babies, of a cousin, of a neighbour, of flax, spinning; of geese, ducks, chickens, and eggs; of making cheese and butter, and probably had a word about blue milk, a dried up cow, caused by a wicked neighbour." Gossip shaped local perceptions of people and events. Through the spoken word, ordinary women exercised extensive influence within their communities, independent of the institutionalized power of males. "Words are women, deeds are men," stated an Italian proverb.[64]

Often, too, women drew emotional support from workmates whose empathy provided a welcome counterweight to the patriarchal household. "Many a stone," we are told, "which lay heavy and long on the heart, would be lifted" as a result of the "experience, interpretation, explanation, and expertise of the many women present." Where inspiring stories recounted the deeds of biblical heroines like Judith and Esther, more mundane information included magical charms for domestic happiness. Among the revelations contained in *Les Évangiles des Quenouilles*, drawn from the fifteenth century, was a spell to soften the temperaments of abusive husbands. Wives bent on vengeance, on the other hand, could resort to another formula in the collection: "When a woman gets up in the night to piss before the cock has crowed for the third time, and she straddles her husband, be it known that, if any of his limbs are stiff, they will never relax if she does not return to her place by way of the same place." In addition, women learned ways to deter demons and to encourage conception—at night, should one wish to have a baby girl (in the morning for a boy).[65]

These seedbeds of subversion made men uneasy. In the sixteenth century, an Italian moralist railed against women for "telling dirty stories all evening," and a German writer noted "the jealousy of the men when their faithful partners leave the four walls." Worse, spinning sessions by their very nature kindled fears of witches' sabbaths. Some communities, in vain, tried to forbid such "scandalous" gatherings. Still, male intruders risked being sternly reproached or even assaulted. In 1759, upon visiting a *Spinnstuben*, the journeyman Conrad Hügel suffered a severe beating at the hands of women armed with distaffs. For three weeks, he lay close to death. Claiming the punishment was their "good right" because of Hügel's indecent flirtations, the women later declared that "they should have injured him even more."[66]

Night saved the day. As neighborhood forums, work parties gave vent to a day's most pressing events. News and gossip were brooded over and discussed before becoming disseminated on public streets. To a large degree, *veillées* and like gatherings not only reflected the communal consciousness, they also shaped and refined it, apart from the opinions and tastes of social elites. More broadly, these occasions provided a vital conduit for age-old traditions, preserving and protecting the oral legacy of preindustrial communities. "Round every fire-side, the entertainment of the evening was rehearsing tales of former times," observed a Highlands minister. Most obviously, winter gatherings helped to soften the rigors of nocturnal tasks, permitting neighbors to share past glories and present privations. "Labor ceased to be a toil," wrote a visitor to Ireland. As fires burned low, lucky listeners might be transported by a storyteller's wizardry to some distant time or place. For a few precious hours, in a dim and drafty cottage, peasants too might become rich, or even lords and ladies. Of the common sort, remarked a contemporary, "Popular tales, the stories heard during the *veillées*, make a greater impression on them than the lessons of their pastors."[67]

CHAPTER SEVEN

THE COMMON BENEFACTRESS: SOCIABILITY, SEX, AND SOLITUDE

I

Night is the common benefactress of every thing that breathes; it is during her reign the greatest share of happiness is spread over the earth.

LOUIS-SÉBASTIEN MERCIER, 1788[1]

NOT EVERY EVENING, of course, fell prey to work, even for the toiling classes. Along with more affluent families, ordinary folk embraced idle hours as a time to do as they pleased. 'Twas a worker's reward, declared a sixteenth-century ballad, "to spend at the night, in joy and delight, now after his labours all day." The better part of many evenings, especially for males, was devoted to recreation and leisure. "The gods have established a respite from heavy labor," affirmed a Dutch writer.[2]

If our modern concept of leisure had yet to evolve in the preindustrial age, traditional notions of "ease," "pleasure," and "play" were common among all social ranks. In his diary, the Suffolk farmer William Coe routinely recorded nights spent at "play." "Set up 'till midnight att play," he entered on four different occasions in January 1694. While, in the course of a day, urban and rural workers suspended their tasks for meals and rest, these respites were generally brief, particularly for laborers who answered to a master or employer. Along with Sundays and holidays, nighttime, by contrast, afforded a prolonged period of relaxation for personal enjoyment. Hence the gleeful refrain in a seventeenth-century masque staged by the Grocers' Company of London, "We labour all day, but we frollick at night / With smoaking and joking, and tricks of delight."[3]

Of course, some laborers must have collapsed after returning home, barely able from numbing fatigue to consume an evening meal, especially in rural regions during the summer when fieldwork grew most strenuous. In southern Wiltshire, complained John Aubrey, workers, "being weary after hard labour" lacked "leisure to read and contemplate of religion, but goe to bed to their rest." A doctor in the Haute-Loire in 1777 described peasants "returning home in the evening, harassed by weariness and misery."[4] Still, for most persons, nighttime represented more than a dormant interlude between working hours. In spite of myriad perils, it was night, not morning, not afternoon, that was valued most.

Popular among middle-class families were cards, dice, and other games of chance. In Sussex, Thomas Turner and his wife favored whist, brag, and cribbage, whereas Parson Woodforde frequently played backgammon. Of winning two shillings at quadrille, he vouched, "We were very merry tonight & kept it up late." Drink was common. "Not one of us went to bed sober," Turner remarked after a night's frolic with friends. Of another evening, he observed, "We continued drinking like horses (as the vulgar phrase is) and singing till many of us was very drunk, and then we went to dancing and pulling off wigs, caps, and hats. And there we continued in this frantic manner (behaving more like mad people than they that profess the name of Christians)." In early New England, where local officials took particular offense at such behavior, court records are strewn with prosecutions for tippling at "unseasonable times of night."[5]

The detailed diary of the Dutch teacher David Beck throws light upon middle-class sociability in The Hague during the early seventeenth century. To judge from his observations, urban families and friends frequently visited one another on moonlit evenings. Recently widowed, Beck may have been unusually peripatetic, but he was far from unique among his married acquaintances. The web of his nocturnal relationships was extensive. In addition to his brother Hendrick, an uncle, and both his mother and mother-in-law, Beck socialized with numerous friends, including a swordmaker who invited him one January evening to "a festive dinner on the occasion of slaughtering time." In spite of the occasional street stabbing or fire, nights brimmed with late meals, humorous tales, music, and fireside conversations "about a thousand things." Wine and beer flowed freely. "Talking and warming ourselves together," he wrote of a November evening filled with "good cheer" at his brother's home. A few nights later, Beck joined a small company at his tailor's, "singing, dancing, playing the lute, and jumping like the unruly children in The Hague." Not until 2:00 A.M. did he leave, "very drunk."[6]

Comparable in many respects was the social world of Samuel Pepys in Restoration London. Intimates were more genteel, and Pepys was more cosmopolitan than Beck in his tastes. Otherwise, many of their pastimes were similar. When not working late in the Naval Office or engaging in a tryst, Pepys devoted nights to cardplay, drinking, meals, and music, both at home and abroad. "Sat playing at cards after supper, till 12 at night; and so by moonshine home and to bed," he wrote in January 1662. Another evening found him in his garden with Sir William Penn, the Navy Commissioner, both indifferent to the night air. "There we stayed talking and singing and drinking of great draughts of clarret and eating botargo and bread and butter till 12 at night, it being moonshine. And so to bed—very near fuddled."[7]

Scores of preindustrial folk flocked to alehouses. In communities large and small, they represented important hubs of social activity for men. Patrons gathered in the evening to tell jokes, play games, and swap news, most seeking a warm sanctuary from work, family, and everyday cares. Unlike inns, which supplied tired travelers overnight accommodation with food and wine, alehouses offered men a meeting place with material comforts often superior to those at home. Continental drinking houses included the French cabaret, the *Wirthaus* in Germany, and the Spanish *venta.* Although spare, alehouse furnishings included chairs and tables along with an oversized hearth. Some interiors contained wood partitions for a measure of privacy. In England, during the decades following the Reformation, the popularity of drinking houses grew as traditional sources of popular entertainment declined, both sporting contests and religious festivals. "I have never seen more taverns and ale-houses in my whole life than in London," marveled Thomas Platter. Writing of the late sixteenth century, Richard Rawlidge remarked in 1628:

> When what the people generally were forbidden their old and ancient familiar meetings and sportings, what then followed? Why, sure ale-house haunting: . . . so that the people would have meetings, either publicely with pastimes abroad, or else privately in drunken alehouses. . . . The preachers did then reprove dalliance, and dancings of maides and young men together; but now they have more cause to reprove drunkennesse and whoring, that is done privately in ale-houses.[8]

For the most part, alehouses catered to the lower orders, whereas inns and taverns attracted a wealthier clientele. Merchants, yeomen, and substantial craftsmen graced alehouse doors, but most patrons hailed from the ranks of husbandmen, journeymen, servants, and other members of the laboring poor. Customers were single as well as married, both young and middle-aged. According to detailed studies of drinking houses in London, Paris, and Augsburg, evenings drew the largest numbers. And where visits during the day, between one's working hours, were usually brief, those at night could last several hours or more. A French visitor to London noted during the early 1660s, "A taylor and a shoemaker, let his business be never so urgent, will leave his work, and go to drink in the evening," "oftentimes" coming "home late." In the *London Chronicle*, a correspondent condemned the "stupid amusement of guzzling at an alehouse three or four hours in an evening." Immediate gratification came from imbibing ale and hopped beer, or wine across much of continental Europe. Declared a seventeenth-century Polish poet: "Our lords are a great woe to us, / They fleece us almost like sheep. / You can never sit in peace, / unless you forget the bad things / over a mug of beer." Important, too, for peasants was the nutritional value of these beverages, "without which they cannot well subsist, their food being for the most part of such things as afford little or bad nourishment," claimed a writer. Safer to drink than either water or milk, beer and ale were also a source of warmth—"the warmest lining of a naked man's coat," professed John Taylor the Water-Poet.[9]

Jan Steen, *The Ace of Hearts*, seventeenth century.

Equally inviting was the opportunity for good fellowship among one's peers—rubbing elbows and sharing draughts with men of the "right kidney." "Good drunken company is their delight; what they get by day, they spend by night," opined Daniel Defoe. In colonial Massachusetts, John Adams attributed the prevalence of taverns to "poor country people, who are tired with labour and hanker after company." Toasting one another's health, playing dominoes and cards, or passing a pipe of tobacco in a crowded tippling-house reinforced male companionship. As did ballads and drinking contests. As the song "Good Ale for My Money" had it, "A good coal fire is their desire, / whereby to sit and parley; / They'll drink their ale, and tell a tale, / and go home in the morning early." Common were mutual laments over domestic squabbles—"railing at matrimony," one observer recounted. Once tongues loosened, masters, clerics, and landlords, all were fair game. "Rant and carouse, damn and drink all in a breath," remarked a contemporary. There were also displays of fortitude and strength, critical to masculine standing and self-worth. Hence the nickname *Frappe-d'abord* (First-strike) earned by a French journeyman. In England, a person described a group of regulars addicted to the "noble art of boxing"—"shewing their own skill," he related, "by clenching their fists, putting themselves in a posture of defence, with *here* I could have you, and *there* I could have you."[10]

Alehouses also spawned sexual encounters. Although fewer, female patrons represented a mix of maidservants, aging "wenches," and prostitutes. "A little Sodom," pronounced a writer. (In provincial Massachusetts, taverns bore a similar reputation. Adams complained in 1761, "Here diseases, vicious habits, bastards and legislators are frequently begotten.") Within these cramped, ill-lit environs, men and women drank, flirted, and fondled, as depicted by Jan Steen, Adriaen van Ostade, and other northern European artists. An English critic in 1628 urged the removal of partitions to prevent sexual play. And, too, court records divulge that couples copulated in nearby lofts and privies. In temperate weather, adjacent yards supplied convenient spots in the dark. Even neighboring churchyards were used for sexual intercourse. Sarah Badrett of Chester, for example, was allegedly "caught whoring" in the yard of St. John's Church, having just left "the inn of Widow Kirk." Less discreet was an amorous pair, John Wilkinson and Ellen Laithwaite, inside a Wigan alehouse in 1694. After three hours of caressing one another (she "handling his prick and he had his hand on her placket"), John "had carnal knowledge" of Ellen against a wall. Usually such encounters were fleeting, with little prospect of courtship, much less matrimony. Alehouses, after all, were meant to be an alternative to domesticity. More than a few male suitors earned reputations for whispering false promises to young women. As a late seventeenth-century ballad described:

Sometimes to the tavern with Betty I go,
And like a true lover much kindness I show;
I kiss, nay I hug, and I cuddle her then,
And vow I will marry, but I know not when.[11]

II

Nothing is more tempting or contagious to the life of a young man, than the opportunity of night, the operation of wine, & the blandishments of a woman.

BACCHYLIDES, 5TH CENTURY B.C.[12]

Night was a fertile time for romantic liaisons of all sorts, notwithstanding rigorous restrictions against sexual activity. Church and state both prohibited relations outside the confines of married life, premarital sex as well as adultery. Laws loosely enforced at the end of the medieval era received heightened attention in the wake of the Reformation by Catholic and Protestant authorities. Even public displays of affection, including petting and kissing, were thought sinful according to Christian teachings. The Genoese Ansaldo Ceba warned, "There is no passion by which the citizen is more impeded in acquiring and exercising the virtues needed to render happy his republic, than the storms of sensual love."[13]

Local variations in sexual attitudes invariably existed, often between town and country. Class mattered as well. In much of Europe, propertied families adopted unusually restrictive controls for the courting of young women. "Persons of rank and figure even in this province, are desirous that their daughters should be married to men who never saw them," remarked a Massachusetts colonist. Beliefs tended to be most conservative in Mediterranean cultures, unlike a more tolerant disposition toward sexual relations in northern and central Europe. But these were differences of degree, not substance. Nowhere was it possible for unmarried individuals to indulge their affections in public. And only once couples entered a formal courtship, by declaring their feelings openly, were regular meetings condoned. Sexual intercourse remained forbidden except, occasionally, when matrimony lay near at hand. So when Agnes Bennet of Devonshire was teased about a night's lovemaking with her fiancé George Pearse, she replied "that it was nothing between those that were in love . . . that they were assured together meaning in marriage."[14]

Flouting these conventions was risky, especially for women, for whom penalties could be severe. During the day, social oversight and the requirements of work, among the lower and middle orders, sharply curtailed opportunities for sexual transgressions. "Light and lust are deadly enemies," observed Shakespeare. Apart from alehouses, safe havens were few, even in the country. In woods outside Tours, Jacques-Louis Ménétra and a companion "spotted a little shepherd and a young shepherd girl in action." Panicked, the naked boy fled, leaving his lover to be raped by Ménétra—"I amused myself with the girl half willingly the rest by force." On another occasion, Ménétra and a married woman were themselves assaulted while copulating, seemingly "out of sight" on a slope near Belleville. "That taught me a lesson," he later acknowledged.[15]

In sharp contrast, night to lovers appeared vastly more inviting. "The pleasures light deny, thy shades for ever yield," rhapsodized the poet Thomas Yalden. Put more bluntly, according to a Cambrian saying, "The lewd and naught love long nights." Not only did nighttime give "love *that* leysure that the day cannott allow," but darkness afforded lovers a natural refuge. "Night blinds all jealous eyes," noted the anonymous author of *Lusts Dominion* (1657). Fields, churchyards, cellars, and stables fell prey to sexual desires. In Massachusetts, Thomas Waite and Sarah Gowing in 1682 resorted to a deserted brewhouse. In cities, parks and walks drew lovers. Of men and women along the Palle-Malle in Orleans, Peter Heylyn wrote in 1656, "At all hours of the night, be it warm and dry, you shall be sure to finde them there, thus coupled." Ill-lit streets, too, found favor. Recorded a visitor to Rome in the eighteenth century, "In the midst of this darkness, amorous assignations in the street are not unfrequent among the inferior people." In fact, Roman couples of all ranks, when approached by pedestrians with lanterns, routinely instructed, "*Volti la luce*" (turn the light) in order to protect their privacy.[16]

On top of everything else, darkness generated an intimate atmosphere in which words of affection flowed more freely. Low levels of light, whether from a candle or lamp, brought couples closer together, physically and emotionally. Declared an Italian writer, "Darkness made it easy to tell all." With sight impaired, hearing, touch, and smell, with their greater power to arouse emotions, all acquired heightened importance. "How silver-sweet sound lovers' tongues by night," Romeo proclaims to Juliet. By the same token, extinguishing a candle or lamp among mixed company was an act charged with sexuality. When Hester Jackson, within a Massachusetts tavern, doused a candle, another woman exclaimed that

Paul Bril, *Fantastic Landscape*, n.d.

Philip James de Loutherbourg, *Attack by Robbers at Night*, ca. 1770

Hieronymous Francken, *Witches' Kitchen*, 1610

Egbert van der Poel, *Fire in a Village at Night*, 1655

Jacopo Bassano, *Workshop of Weavers*, sixteenth century

Anon., *Ferry by Moonlight*, n.d.

Gerrit van Honthorst, *The Matchmaker*, 1625

Cornelis Troost, *Those Who Could Walk Did; the Others Fell*, 1739

Leandro Bassano, *Camp at Night*, n.d.

Thomas Luny, *Teignmouth by Moonlight*, eighteenth century

David Teniers the Younger, *The Invocation*, seventeenth century

Giulio Carponi, *The Kingdom of Hypnos*, seventeenth century "she was a bold slutt, or a bold housewife." Although married, Hester quickly departed outdoors hand-in-hand with a seaman.[17]

Adulterous liaisons, in spite of conventional morality, were common enough. In England, "Dark Cully" referred to a married man who consorted with his mistress "only at night, for fear of discovery." "The *adulterer* watcheth for his twilight," warned a writer in paraphrasing a verse from the Book of Job. According to diaries, more than a few couples violated their vows. Married with two children, Batt Haler of Basle courted a young woman, dancing in her home on Catalan carpets "so that the neighbours should not be disturbed in the night." Acts of infidelity, at night, were a persistent source of literary humor, from the comic narratives of Chaucer to the rampaging epics of Defoe and Fielding. Nocturnal liasions, with confused identities and mistaken beds, fill the pages of novels, plays, and poems. Some misadventures, naturally, were intentional. Wrote the author of "Mistaking in the Darke" in 1620, "We have divers night men now a daies, / That in the darke become such wilfull straies, / When they should goe unto their wives chast bed, / Doe get unto the maids, in mistris stead." Rife with nocturnal trysts are tales by Boccaccio, Sacchetti, and other Italian writers. Unfaithful wives were popular protagonists, receiving lovers at home in the absence of unwitting husbands. Standard rules for clever adulteresses ranged from bribing servants to bolting chamber doors. And always lovers were instructed to arrive in the dark to evade nosy neighbors.[18]

The marital infidelities of Samuel Pepys were legion, for he seldom missed an opportunity to fondle a willing wife or widow. Easy prey included maidservants like Deb Willett, who at bedtime combed his hair for lice. "This night yo did hazer Deb tocar mi thing with her hand after yo was in lecto—with great pleasure," he wrote in a mix of several languages in August 1668. Even by the relatively carefree standards of the Restoration era, many of Pepys's adventures were impulsive and reckless. During the years of his diary (1660–1669), he had sexual contact with more than fifty women, some on repeated occasions, and intercourse with more than ten. As a man of affairs with frequent cause to visit different London neighborhoods, he was peculiarly advantaged to avail himself of secluded locations; some of Pepys's assignations were conducted in transit behind the drawn curtains of hackney coaches. Still, Pepys often reserved his most passionate liaisons for the cover of darkness. Visits to the Deptford home of "Mrs. Bagwell," the wife of a ship's carpenter, were made at night, the darker the better. Of one June evening, Pepys wrote, "It being dark, I did by agreement andar a la house de Bagwell; and there, after a little playing and besando, we did go up in the dark a su cama and there fasero la grand cosa upon the bed." On another visit, he first "walked up and down in the fields till it was dark night." Less successful was an evening stop at another port of call—the Old Swan on Fish Street Hill—where he found his beloved Betty Mitchell sitting at the door. "It being darkish, I stayd and talked a little with her, but no oasis bezar la."[19]

More troubling to elders than their own moral lapses was sexual activity among the young. Adolescent conduct after dark prompted widespread concern, less the risk of midnight elopements and clandestine marriages than opportunities for carnal license. No age group was thought more susceptible to sensual passions. Outside the routine of work, single youths socialized on festive and ceremonial occasions. Adult supervision at night was erratic. Of the traditional gathering of flowers on the eve of May Day, the Puritan Philip Stubbes complained in 1583, "I have heard it credibly reported . . . by men of great gravitie and reputation, that of fortie, threescore, or a hundred maides going to the wood over night, there have scarcely the third part of them returned home againe undefiled." In addition to fairs and festivals, wedding celebrations attracted young persons, with dancing and singing lasting into the night. "Look how much shameless and drunken the evening is more than in the morning, so much the more vice, excess, and misnurture," railed the sixteenth-century cleric Miles Coverdale. In the Netherlands, a passing visitor found couples "dancing all night" after "theire fathers, mothers, and all other were gone to bedd."[20] No less raucous were funeral wakes, designed by the High Middle Ages to console the dead (and presumably the living) with food, drink, and good cheer. Prevalent throughout early modern society, those in Ireland and Scotland grew notorious for drinking bouts, dancing, and "mock marriages." In 1618, the Catholic Synod of Armagh in Ireland condemned the frequency of "improper songs and gesticulations" that "would even be unlawful in festive rejoicings." "Works of darkness," it declared, "are united with darkness."[21]

Spinning bees, in much of Europe, afforded a more regular setting during long winters for conviviality and courtship. In homes and stables, male adolescents joined female companions to work, listen to stories, and perhaps find suitable marriage partners. Of unmarried women on Guernsey, a visitor wrote in 1677, "In these watches they have a further design, and that is either to meet with or draw in gallants, who are never wanting to make up the consort, and from these meetings many marriages are contracted." Even at single-sex gatherings in France, young men occasionally received permission to attend. Remarked Etienne Tabourot during the sixteenth century, "In these assemblies of girls, one finds a great number of young striplings and lovers." As the hours advanced, knitting and spinning gave way to games like "blindman's buff," and talk laden with "dirty *double entendres*." Singing was popular, though not so loud as to frighten the livestock. To the unease of adults, some songs were openly erotic. A favorite ritual called for a girl to drop her distaff to see which suitor picked it up. More seriously, one or more boys might suddenly extinguish the lights, "shewing thereby that their only aim is to accomplish works of darkness," claimed a French curé in the late seventeenth century. Authorities spoke anxiously of the potential for "sowing" circles.[22]

Hans Sebald Beham, *A Spinnstube*, 1524. A carricature, from an urban perspective, of peasants at a spinning party, with both adults and adolescents cavorting with unbounded license.

Still, most spinning parties enjoyed some degree of parental supervision. In contrast, informal dances among the young, in stables and barns, escaped such scrutiny. "Come let's drink the night away, let the married sleep it out," declared a seventeenth-century ballad. Couples in the Spanish city of Cuenca spent entire nights dancing and feasting inside shrines. In Cambridge, Massachusetts, twenty youths, mostly white and black servants, frolicked at night over a period of four months, dancing and consuming kegs of cider and rum. (During the day, stated a contemporary, "Ere long the young men must pass by the mayds like quakers and take no notice of them.") Religious and civic officials criticized youth dances as secret and illicit. Just as a Berne edict in 1627 condemned "indecent songs and dances, in the evening and at night," so an English writer demanded, "What kissing and bussing, what smouching and slabbering one of another, what filthie groping and uncleane handling is not practised everywhere in these dancings?" Varying shades of obscurity magnified opportunities for mischief. "Never dance in the dark," cautioned a seventeenth-century proverb. It is not surprising that village authorities occasionally tried to restrict adolescent meetings to daytime, believing, like a German pastor, that "girls and boys" at "the right time of the day" should "go home again to their masters, lords and mistresses." In the early 1600s, the Swiss town of Wil attempted to limit to five the number of visits girls could annually receive at home from suitors, with all respects to be paid before nightfall.[23]

One may marvel at the willingness of young couples to brave the darkness. Of her son, Elizabeth Drinker fretted, "When young men go a courting so far from home, they should make their visits shorter, and not walk two miles in a dark night alone; the resk of meeting with mischievous persons, or of taken cold this season of the year, should have some weight with 'em." But such dangers seldom did. Dark nights afforded little deterrence to the young. According to an eighteenth-century ballad, "The Roving Maids of Aberdeen's Garland," maidens wore white aprons to signal suitors. "There's lasses bright, turns out at night," declared a verse. In the Gloucestershire community of Dursley, men "pulled out the tails of their shirts." These so-called Dursley Lanterns reportedly helped to guide female companions.[24]

Male adolescents on dark nights may have relished the chance to prove their fortitude. A poem written by John Dobson celebrated the courage of a country swain named Robin. "Nor dogs, nor darkness, guns or ghosts could fright, / When Robin ventured for his Sue's delight." Late at night, there was greater opportunity for intimacy once social gatherings ended—the chance to escort "one's chosen sweetheart home in the dark." Thus, the seventeenth-century yeoman Leonard Wheatcroft, following a dance, eagerly accompanied his Derbyshire girlfriend several miles to her family's dwelling. "At night coming home together, there were no small discourse of love betwixt us, neither any scarcity of loving situations." In *The Life of a Simple Man* (1904), the laborer Tiennon warmly kisses his amour Thérèse after attending a *veillée* together and trudging home in a cold drizzle—displaying his gallantry along the way. "On that dark winter night of wind and rain my heart was full of blue sky," he reflects.[25] Such, for the young, was the power of blind love on raw evenings in the French countryside.

III

The bed is a far better place to go courting.

BARDUS LOCHWD,
EARLY 19TH CENTURY[26]

In part, it was in response to such passion—and the adult desire to control it—that the preindustrial custom of bundling emerged among the young. Broadly speaking, couples were permitted to remain together overnight at the home of the girl's parents without engaging in intercourse. An intermediate stage of courtship, bundling followed a period of wooing, marked by private walks and public encounters. Only once flirtations yielded to mutual affection were young men and women allowed to bundle. That notwithstanding, there was no formal expectation of marriage, though hopes for such a union usually ran high.

Contrary to popular thought, bundling was not an early American innovation, despite its prevalence in New England. Its origins, though obscure, were deeply rooted in the European countryside. Within the British Isles, the custom was most common in Wales. Even in the late eighteenth century, a resident claimed that "bundling very much abounds, in many parts in country towns." On the Orkney Islands in the North Sea, young men and maidens typically kept company on a layer of sheaves known as a "lang bed"; while in the Lowlands, despite opposition from the Church of Scotland, bundling was said to be the "custom of the place." Brought before a kirk court in 1721 for sharing a bed with Isobel Midy, the laborer Duncan McCurrie protested "that there were many others who lay together as they did." So, too, in Ireland, a traveler discovered a traditional pattern of night visiting "among the common people."[27]

The evidence for England is more checkered. That bundling, or "sitting up," was popular in the north is not in doubt. In 1663, for example, Roger Lowe, a young Lancashire mercer, arranged to "sit up awhile" with Mary Naylor. "This was the first night that ever I stayd up a wooing ere in my life," he jotted in his diary. Much later, a town clerk in Yorkshire noted the "practice in this county, of young men and women sitting up alone at nights, with the permission of their masters or mistresses." For other sections of the country, information is more scattered. In the village of Dullingham, for instance, Walter Appleyard regularly visited his Cambridgeshire girlfriend at her mother's home. By one report, he "manie times stayed there all night and manie time a great part of the nighte, and would not suffer her to goe to bed and sometimes a maide sate up with them and sometimes no bodie at all." Thomas Turner in Sussex twice remained overnight with his future bride, whereas Wheatcroft did so on several occasions with his Derbyshire love. "I stayd all night again with my dear and chief delight, using unto her many sweet expressions of my love."[28]

Elsewhere in Europe, various forms of bundling were practiced among the common sort, though not in the Mediterranean, where serenades by young males were a customary method of courting. Bundling was prevalent both in Scandinavia and in parts of the Netherlands, where it was known as *queesting* (chatting). Nightcourting was no less accepted in Germany and Switzerland; in fact, a rural minister observed in a visitation report that *zu Licht gehen*, or "going to the light" of a girl's chamber, was "considered a right and a freedom" at night among the young. And in seventeenth-century Savoy, a contemporary wrote of the custom of *albergement*: "It is usual for young peasants to stay up until late at night in the company of marriageable girls, and pleading that their homes are far away, they ask for hospitality, and seek to share the girls' beds," which usually "the girls do not refuse."[29]

Almost everywhere, nightcourting seems to have followed a common pattern, a testament to the diffusion of European popular culture. Saturday and Sunday evenings were favorite times for boys to visit. At least some entered through unlocked windows lit by candles. According to a Cambridgeshire song, "So when the moon is waxing bright, across the fen you make for a light." A German tract claimed that youthful pride required a lad to scale the home of his beloved in order prove his merit. All the same, nearly always bundling enjoyed parental permission. Indeed, among other benefits, it afforded a way for parents to supervise a daughter's courtship.[30] To be certain, some couples met illicitly while parents slept, but the dangers were great, including being mistaken for a thief. Awakened from bed, a Somerset minister in 1717 spied two men crossing his yard in the moonlight. He shot both, one fatally, only to learn that they had come to court his maidservants—"it being their practice," recounted a contemporary, "to visit them when their master & mistress was in bed & they, to accommodate their sparks, used to stock beer, ale, & cyder & bread & cheese for their night adventures."[31]

As a consequence of parental control, rules for nightcourting governed both attire and conduct. Undergirding these strictures was a strong injunction against sexual intercourse, which, at the least, imperiled a maiden's eligibility for marriage. Boys in Savoy were required to take an oath against violating a girl's virginity, which New England suitors reputedly "regarded as a sacred trust." In some locales, both parties were expected to remain seated, but, more often, they lay next to one another on the girl's bed. Modesty necessitated that males remove just their waistcoats and shoes, if any garments at all. In Norway, a young lady, unaccustomed to the rituals of her suitor's village, vociferously objected when he shed his jacket. "If you're taking off your jacket," she exclaimed, "you'll be taking off your trousers." Females remained in shifts or petticoats, which in Wales were occasionally tied at the bottom. In Scotland, by contrast, a maiden's thighs were bound in order to underscore the symbolic importance of chastity. And in early America, a German traveler reported, "If the anxious mother has any doubt of the strict virtue of her daughter, it is said she takes the precaution of placing both the daughter's feet in one large stocking." So, too, in New England were "bundling boards" reportedly employed to separate youths in bed.[32]

Few couples opted to sleep. In the Netherlands, according to Fynes Moryson, they devoted the night to "banqueting and talking together." Besides conversation, a modicum of physical contact was assumed, during subsequent visits if not at first. This included warm embraces and kissing. "Coupling and cheeking," described a Welsh poem. Noncoital forms of sexual play often followed, "stopping short of those reserved for marriage alone," found a French visitor to America. Scandinavians were quite explicit about which parts of the body might be caressed, as were Russian households, which in some nineteenth-century provinces restricted suitors to fondling their girlfriends' breasts. (On the other hand, in the Melnki district of Novgorod province, touching a maiden's genitals was permitted.) Gentle caresses sometimes gave way to hard blows among peasant populations that equated rough play with expressions of passion. Moreover, slapping one another on the back tested a lover's strength and physical health, important considerations for potential mates in rural communities. Should sexual play get out of hand, despite precautions, families lay nearby—some parents stayed awake in the same room as chaperones. Most trusted their daughters' probity, ready to intervene, however, if called. "Woe to him," related a contemporary, "if the least cry escapes her, for then everybody in the house enters the room and beats the lover for his too great impetuousity."[33]

Even so, the most honorable intentions could be swept away by sudden paroxysms of passion. "In a cosy bed much mischief can occur," warned a Welsh song, while a Connecticut ballad in 1786 affirmed, "Breeches nor smocks, nor scarce padlocks / The rage of lust can bind." On both sides of the Atlantic, moralists forecast the worst whenever "the fire" lay "much too near the tinder," as a French storyteller cautioned. Though scanty, surviving statistics appear to confirm prevailing fears. For whatever combination of reasons, illegitimacy rates climbed appreciably in eighteenth-century New England, roughly the time when bundling grew in popularity. "This cursed course," wrote an opponent, "is one great source / Of matches undersigned, / Quarrels and strife twixt man and wife, / And bastards of their kind." In rural New England after American independence, almost one-third of brides were pregnant at the time of marriage. As were, it would seem, many European maidens. "It is a very common thing," concluded a visitor to Wales, "for the consequence" of bundling "to make its appearance in the world within two or three months after the marrage ceremony." How many unions were compelled by premature pregnancies is impossible to say. It seems just as likely, as some historians have posited, that couples only elected to have intercourse once marriage was in the offing. According to this view, pregnancy was less often a cause for marriage than were marital plans a precondition of copulation. Noting the popularity of "bundelage" in America, a European visitor observed that once "the swain promises marriage" his partner "gives herself without reserve."[34]

Despite periodic opposition from religious authorities, bundling survived in parts of Europe well into the nineteenth century. Doubtless, some of its popularity derived from the ingrained belief, shared by countless generations, that adolescent courtships belonged at home under parental surveillance. Remarked a German in the sixteenth century, "When their parents are questioned about these familiarities, they answer 'caste dormiunt' [sleeping chastely]; it is a game devoid of villainy, where good and happy marriages are prepared and begin."[35] In addition, some persons have claimed that bundling was designed to save families the costs of "fire and candle" for courting couples. That, however, fails to explain why the young retreated to beds on warm summer nights. Or why candlelight had anything to do with whether one sat upright when courting or lay prone. Then, too, at least one observer speculated whether bundling was not just "a cunning trick to know whether the wives would be fruitful."[36]

A more compelling explanation for the enduring popularity of this convention lies in the twin functions that night visits served. For one thing, they permitted young couples a measure of privacy for courting, shielded from the scrutiny of friends and neighbors. Bundling could not always protect couples from snoops and eavesdroppers. The New Hampshire farmer Abner Sanger spied on the home of his cherished Nab Washburn whenever his arch-rival, Unction, was calling. "I spy Unction before sunrise coming from Old Mr. Washburn's very gaily dressed," Sanger sulked one morning. But in most cases, darkness and domestic seclusion granted couples an uncommon degree of privacy, particularly for that age. "Let's blow the candle out" was the standard refrain in "The London Prentice," a song describing how one pair of lovers escaped the prying eyes of "peeping" pedestrians.[37]

Still more important, bundling provided a trial period enabling the young to probe a potential mate's suitability for marriage—"hugging and fooling and talking till dawn," described the Swiss shepherd Ulrich Bräker. Of courting his beloved "Annie," he fondly recalled, "We had thousands and thousands of different kinds of lovers' conversations." Amid all the soft entreaties and passionate embraces, amid the still darkness was a rare chance to become deeply acquainted with a lover's character and temperament. Reported a contemporary in New England, "The girls seek only to please and to use their freedom in associating with men to make a good choice, on which their future happiness depends." Of some bearing, as well, was a couple's sexual compatibility. As a Cambridgeshire youth bluntly informed his skeptical parson, "But vicar, you wouldn't buy a horse without getting astride it to see how it trotted." In fact, in parts of Germany, after several nights of courting (known as "welcome nights"), couples embarked upon a more telling sequence of "trial nights" that could eventually lead to marriage. Should matters turn out differently, no embarrassment or dishonor, barring a pregnancy, attached to either party, with each free to commence a future relationship.[38]

IV

This grand volume of epistles, for which the final draft is now being copied out, bears witness, letter by letter, to whatever muses I have managed to muster in the dead of night.

LAURA CERETA, 1486[39]

"What is more conducive to wisdom than the night?" asked St. Cyril of Jerusalem. For all of the opportunities that nighttime afforded for courting and companionship, it also permitted preindustrial folk unprecedented freedom to explore their own individuality. On myriad evenings, growing numbers of men and women devoted an hour or more to solitude and mental reflection, resulting ultimately in an enhanced self-awareness. Individuals found evenings particularly well suited to contemplation, as religious sages had for centuries. Competing obligations were fewer, while the silence created an ideal environment for self-scrutiny. "Much more fit for any employment of the mind, than any other part of the day," opined a

French writer in the seventeenth century. The author of *La Ricreazione del Savio* observed, "The day counts on labor; the night counts on thinking. Clamor is useful for the first; silence for the second."[40]

Naturally, members of the middle and upper classes, by retiring to their bedchambers, enjoyed the greatest opportunity for personal reflection. Farther down the social ladder, inadequate time and space invariably made solitude harder. Still, as early as the mid-1600s, many laboring families resided in homes with more than just a single room; plus there were occasions, on pleasant evenings, to retreat to a barn or shed. In the late fifteenth century, the Parisian servant Jean Standonck labored by day at a convent only to ascend a bell tower at night to read books by moonlight. Thomas Platter, as a rope-maker's apprentice, regularly defied his master by rising silently at night to learn Greek by the faint glow of a candle. To avoid falling asleep, he put pieces of raw turnip, pebbles, or cold water in his mouth. (Other individuals were known to wrap their heads in wet towels to stay awake.) Plainly, the well-traveled saying "The night brings counsel" held meaning for people of varying social backgrounds.[41]

Reading was an increasingly common pastime, despite the multitudes that remained unlettered. For the poor, exposure to printed materials was predominantly communal, limited to oral readings at spinning bees and other intimate gatherings. Early modern literacy, nevertheless, was more prevalent than one might suspect. During the late Middle Ages, a few persons outside the clergy could read and write, a trend greatly accelerated by both the Reformation and the growth of printing. Already by the seventeenth century, a large majority of yeomen and skilled artisans in the English countryside were literate, as were many urban males. Enjoying fewer educational opportunities, women were less fortunate, though there were numerous exceptions. The Stuart playwright Sir William Davenant wrote of "those mourning histories of love, which in / The dreadful winter nights, our innocent maids / Are us'd to read." In general, literacy rates were highest in northern and northwestern Europe, though many regions witnessed a marked rise during the 1700s, caused in part by the spread of Pietism, a Protestant movement that stressed personal study of the Bible.[42]

Within well-educated households, the critical transition from reading aloud to silent reading occurred during the fifteenth century. In time, other readers would master this liberating technique. Revolutionary in

Gerrit Dou, *Scholar with a Globe*, seventeenth century.

scope, silent reading let individuals scrutinize books with ease and speed. No less important, it allowed them to explore texts in isolation, apart from friends and family, or masters. Reading became vastly more personal, as more people pondered books and formed ideas on their own. As Machiavelli related in a letter in 1513:

> When evening comes, I return home and go into my study. On the threshold I strip off the muddy, sweaty clothes of every day, and put on the robes of court and palace, and in this graver dress I enter the antique courts of the ancients where, being welcomed by them, I taste the food that alone is mine, for which I was born. And there I make bold and speak to them and ask the motives of their actions. And they, in their humanity, reply to me. And for the space of four hours I forget the world, remember no vexation, fear poverty no more, tremble no more at death: I am wholly absorbed in them.[43]

Besides other times of the day, an hour or two before bedtime was set aside by many for reading. According to estate inventories, personal libraries were frequently located in chambers where persons slept. Pepys, for one, often read at night. "I to my book again, and made an end of Mr. Hooker's Life, and so to bed," he recorded on May 19, 1667. On scattered evenings, he requested a servant to read aloud to him. During the nine years covered by his diary, Pepys read an estimated 125 books, most in their entirety. His tastes were far-flung. Along with traditional works of history and theology, he read widely in science and literature. Books sometimes occupied David Beck past midnight. "Came home at 11:00, read the entire Gospel of St. John," he noted one November evening in 1624. Favorite fare for this budding Dutch poet included the verse of Jakob Cats and Pierre de Ronsard. In Somerset, John Cannon's adolescent tastes ran to the occult as well as to Aristotle and the Bible. At age sixteen, he explored a book about midwifery in order to learn the "forbidden secrets of nature." A hardworking husbandman, he read avidly despite the disapproval of the uncle who employed him. "For all these my hard & laborious employments," noted Cannon in 1705, "I never slighted or disregarded my

Joseph Wright of Derby, *Girl Reading a Letter by Candlelight, with a Young Man Peering over Her Shoulder*, ca. 1760–1762.

books, ye study of which augmented my understanding, stealing an opportunitie by day, but more by night and that when all was safe in bed, sitting up late."[44]

Most of all, in this religious age, nocturnal solitude was reserved for expressions of personal piety. In the wake of the Reformation, growing numbers of theologians emphasized the importance of private acts of spirituality. Despite differences in doctrinal beliefs, Protestant and Catholic leaders alike sought to strengthen an individual's relationship with God through private prayer. That occurred with greatest regularity at bedtime when individuals prepared for sleep. But even earlier, men and women were expected to perform devotional readings as well as to reflect on the day's events. "Meditation and retired thoughts fit us for prayer," noted Sarah Cowper.[45] Jewish theologians encouraged nocturnal exercises, believing in the Maimonidean precept that "man acquires most of his wisdom by study at night." According to the eighteenth-century rabbi Jonathan Eibeschütz, God, in punishing the "first man" for his "sin," reserved daylight for labor. Long winter nights, by contrast, were meant for study of the Torah. "God darkened his world so man could study" and "focus and concentrate his mind and thoughts on God," explained Eibeschütz.[46]

All this, despite the dangers and expense of artificial lighting by which to read. Of his eighteenth-century childhood in Yorkshire, Thomas Wright recalled poring over the Bible in bed by candlelight. "On this I used to read till twelve, one, or two o'clock in the morning, till I fell asleep, a dangerous practice." Some youths had to fend for themselves, scavenging rushlights, pine knots, or small nubs of tallow. Although born to an aristocratic family, even François-René, Vicomte de Chateaubriand, was forced as a student to steal candle-ends from chapel to read the sermons of Jean Baptiste Massillon, the renowned Bishop of Clermont. More fortunate was the sixteenth-century German student Friederich Behaim. Residing in the town of Altdorf, he received supplies of large candles from his mother in Nuremberg. "Buy yourself a few small candles," she instructed in 1578, "and use them when you are not reading and writing so that the large candles may be saved for studying."[47] Whatever its source, the poor quality of artificial light proved difficult for readers. Pepys grew plagued by "sore eyes" and discontinued writing his diary at the age of thirty-six, fearing that he might go blind. Late hours spent working in his office were the principal cause, though books were an aggravation. "My eyes, with overworking them, are sore as soon as candlelight comes to them," he lamented in 1666. A Lancashire physician complained of failing sight due to "reading and writing so much by candle light," notwithstanding his efforts to use a "thick candle" and "to keep a steady light."[48]

For small numbers of people, writing filled late hours. "It smells of the candle" was a saying reserved for midnight compositions. Not surprisingly, these hours were coveted by the author of *Night Thoughts*, poet Edward Young. At Oxford, to stimulate his creativity at midday, Young even drew his curtains and lit a lamp. John Milton, completely blind later in life (due, he believed, to a childhood penchant for reading at bedtime), composed verse at night in his head, which he dictated each morning to a scribe. Journals provided an increasingly popular outlet for self-reflection. Rarely were they intended for one's family, much less the educated public—some diarists, like Pepys, wrote entries in cipher. Apart from reading books and keeping a diary, Beck poured his emotions at night into writing poetry. As a widower, he spent hours composing elegies to his deceased wife, Roeltje. "At night, until 1:00, I wrote the 2nd elegy upon the death of my dear departed wife," he scribbled on January 2, 1624. Letters, too, addressed to intimate acquaintances, afforded a vehicle for personal thoughts. This was one of the joys of Laura Cereta, the young wife of an Italian merchant in the late fifteenth century. Responsible for helping to maintain her parents' household as well as her own, she found rare freedom at night, especially from males in her family, to cultivate her many talents. Hours were lavished both on books ("my sweet night vigils of reading") and needlework. The artistry involved in embroidering an intricate silk shawl, adorned with images of savage beasts, gave her special pleasure. To a close friend, she confided, "My firm rule, of saving the night for forbidden work, has allowed me to design a canvas that contains a harmonious composition of colors. The work has taken three months of sleepless nights." Above all, Cereta composed long, highly introspective epistles, filled with classical allusions. As she described in one letter:

> I have no leisure time for my own writing and studies unless I use the nights as productively as I can. I sleep very little. Time is a terribly scarce commodity for those of us who spend our skills and labor equally on our families and our own work. But by staying up all night, I become a thief of time, sequestering a space from the rest of the day.[49]

Such were the principal diversions of preindustrial folk when nights were free. Rather than retire with the sun, most people instead chose to prolong their evenings with like-minded souls of good cheer, whether families, friends, or lovers. Notwithstanding a small literate minority, intensely devoted like Laura Cereta to solitary study, large numbers delighted in hours of idle play and conviviality. Nights inside cramped dwellings and alehouses were as vibrant as they were ill lit. "Easier flows a song at night," went a saying, "than a song by morning light." Moderation, proclaimed a Polish song, "is for the day, eve and night to be gay." That said, darkness brought the greatest freedom of all, not to the middle-class likes of David Beck and Samuel Pepys, but to men and women at opposite ends of the social spectrum. If night, the common benefactress, was a time of autonomy and license for most, it bore heightened significance for patricians and plebeians. It was the mean and the mighty, paradoxically, for whom darkness had the most profound bearing. Declared a sixteenth-century ballad, "Welcome the nights, / That double delights as well as [for] the poore as the peere."[50]

CHAPTER EIGHT

KNIGHTWALKERS: PRINCES AND PEERS

I

. . . Come,
Let's have one other gaudy night. Call to me
All my sad captains. Fill our bowls once more.
Let's mock the midnight bell.
WILLIAM SHAKESPEARE, 1606–1607[1]

DURING THE LATE Middle Ages, princes and knights laid claim to night's domain. Across the darkened countryside, distant fortresses stood as lonely outposts of light, their turrets and parapets aglow with blazing torches. Nocturnal displays of princely power were grand spectacles of self-indulgence, festive evenings when nobles reveled within the great halls of their castles. Amid open fires, candles, and flambeaux, enormous banquets, larded with game, testified to feudal extravagance. So it was that Charles VI of France (1368–1422) and his entourage, over four days in 1389, celebrated the Feast of Saint-Denis. Days of jousting ended each night with dance and drink. On the fourth evening, reported a chronicler, "The lords, making night into day, indulging in all the excesses of the table, were led by drunkenness into such disorders that, with no respect for the presence of the king, several of them profaned the holiness of the religious edifice and gave themselves up to libertinage and adultery."[2]

In due course, with the appearance of court aristocracies by the sixteenth century, more refined entertainments arose within noble households. As military competition among lords diminished amid the emergence of strong nation-states, aristocratic life revolved around civil amusements at court, coupled with intellectual and artistic pursuits. At the same time, the growth of cities afforded less isolated settings for nocturnal merriment. Just as the upper classes proclaimed their power and wealth at night through public illuminations, so they appropriated evenings for private amusements, "lengthening out" their "pleasures," to paraphrase a commentator. And whereas, initially, daytime, too, proved a popular venue for court diversions, night increasingly appealed to royal sensibilities. Noted a German writer, "They stay awake in order to indulge in their entertainments, though other people sleep." Diversions distinguished elites from social subordinates, consigned by necessity to their beds. "Instead of roaring, / We waste the night / In love and snoaring," a commoner jests in *The Two Queens of Brentford* (1721). By contrast, wrote an observer in the mid-1600s, "Courtiers of both sexes turn night to day, and day to night."[3]

Across Europe, from London to Vienna, noble courts staged lavish entertainments against the blackness of night. At a Florentine opera in 1661 entitled *The Horse Dance*, performed in a garden behind the palace of the Grand Duke, more than one thousand torches lined the arena as a "troope of horse" paraded to the music of over two hundred violas and violins. "Beyond all expression," an English visitor marveled. Spectacular fireworks displays enjoyed immense popularity, as did theatrical performances utilizing new techniques of stage lighting. No paean more passionately proclaimed the aristocratic affinity for night than Isaac de Benserade's *Le Ballet de la Nuit* (1653). Staged in honor of Louis XIV, it was the most lavish of Benserade's early ballets. The young king himself appeared in several roles during the baroque spectacle, which featured lush costumes and opulent sets. Appropriately, the king in the final act donned a plumed headdress in the image of the rising sun. Although populated by beggars and thieves, *Le Ballet de la Nuit* offered a transcendent vision of nocturnal life, one replete with deities against the ornate backdrop of the heavens. Performed on several occasions, the ballet was a great favorite at court.[4]

Wolfgang Heimbach, *Nocturnal Banquet*, 1640.

Balls, concerts, and opera were among the principal nocturnal diversions of urban patricians, escorted in the comfort of coaches by armed servants with links. "Show, equipage, pomp, feasts," and "balls," described a writer. Toward the late seventeenth century, promenades of carriages along public walks captured aristocratic fancies. Renowned sites included the Prado in Madrid and St. James's Park in London. Of the Voorhout in The Hague, a visitor remarked in 1697, "Everyone endeavoured to be the most admired for richnesse of liverie and number of footmen."[5] In the early eighteenth century, elegant amusements only proliferated, including illuminated pleasure gardens like Ranelagh and Vauxhall in London. "Ranelagh," exclaims a wide-eyed admirer in Smollett's *Humphry Clinker*, "looks like the inchanted palace of a genie, adorned with the most exquisite performances of painting, carving, and gilding, enlightened with a thousand golden lamps." Elegance was paramount. Invited to an evening party in Palermo known as a *conversazione*, the Englishman William Beckford and a companion found themselves bereft of a coach. Alarmed by the public disgrace of arriving on foot, their Sicilian guide Philip went to heroic lengths en route, leading the pair without flambeaux through a maze of back lanes "only known to himself" in order to conceal their shame. Meanwhile, assemblies, or parties, among persons of quality acquired immense popularity from London to Moscow. In Paris, a traveler in 1717 found assemblies "every night," as did a visitor to Prague. A London writer declared, "Masquerades, ridottos, operas, balls, assemblies, plays, the gardens, and every other big-swoln child of luxury, in the height of excess, becomes the proof of a taste for the elegancies of life."[6]

Indeed, even nocturnal funerals, favored by some aristocratic families during the seventeenth century for their solemnity, became for others ostentatious exhibitions of wealth and privilege—"as much pomp as the vanity of man could wish," derided a London resident in 1730. Upon the death of Cardinal Richelieu in 1642, more than two thousand candles and torches illuminated his çortège. Among Lutheran elites in Germany, the *Beisetzung*, or nocturnal burial, became a coveted honor for members of court society. In 1686, the Saxon Consistory complained to Elector John George III (1647–1691) that the "increasingly common nocturnal interments . . . are transforming Christian burial into a base carnal display."[7]

II

Now is the wisht for time to crowne delight
Turne night to day and day into the night,
Prepare for stirring, masque, midnight revells,
All rare varietie to provoke desire.

NATHANIEL RICHARDS, 1640[8]

The preeminent entertainment during much of the early modern era was the masquerade. Long popular in European capitals, it provided a source of genteel amusement in England from the reign of Henry VIII (1491–1547). The Elizabethan poet Thomas Campion wrote of "youthful revels, masques, and courtly sights." Confined to courts and estates of the nobility, early masquerades were dramatic spectacles in which guests danced and performed in costume. Soon enough, dancing and conversation became their principal attractions, always, however, in some manner of disguise. For central to a masque's mystique was anonymity, achieved by a vizard covering one's face. In the same spirit, introductions were suspended between revelers, in sharp contrast to the requirements of formal etiquette.[9]

To understand a masquerade's broad appeal, it is important to note the constraints of aristocratic life. Gentility and good manners defined the existence of courtiers, with elaborate canons to guide their words, gestures, and deeds. Success at court rested upon reserve and self-control, especially in the presence of superiors. No realm of personal behavior went unregulated, not even coughing and spitting. Ceremonious conduct, however feigned, was critical to preferment. Among the precepts in an early seventeenth-century conduct book, "A courtier must be serviceable to ladies & women of honour, dutiful to high officers, gracefull amongst councellers, pleasant among equalls, affable to inferiors, and curteous to all." Margaret Cavendish, the Duchess of Newcastle, contrasted aristocratic manners with the "natural behavior" of the lower classes: "Whereas the countrey peasants meet with such kind hearts and unconcerned freedom as they unite in friendly jollity, and depart with neighbourly love, the greater sort of persons meet with constrain'd ceremony, converse with formality, and for the most part depart with enmity." In short, preferment and status rested upon theatrical "self-fashioning," with courtiers playing contrived roles.[10]

Masquerades, by contrast, afforded a hiatus from the repressive milieu of early modern courts. Baroque spectacles, they featured lavish costumes of silk and satin bathed in the brilliance of beeswax candles. But on several levels, masquerades represented dramatic departures from courtly etiquette. By stripping persons of their identity, they undermined distinctions between social ranks, with all revelers recreated equal. Within the privileged universe of aristocrats, this ramification was significant enough, but time would bring yet more sweeping changes. By the early eighteenth century, London was hosting midnight masques open, by ticket, to the general public so long as one arrived masked and unarmed. During one gathering, the ballroom was lit by five hundred candles, with women adorned in a "vast variety of dresses (many of them very rich)." Clearly, these remained grand entertainments, but with unprecedented opportunities for leveling. "A country of liberty," pronounced a contemporary of the typical masque. Indeed, subscription masquerades arose in other cities, too. A writer in a Manchester newspaper predicted in 1755 the direst consequences:

Giuseppe Grisoni, *Masquerade at King's Opera House*, 1724.

> The masquerade houses may, with propriety enough, be called shops, where opportunities for immorality, prophaneness, obscenity, and almost every kind of vice, are retailed to any one who will become a customer; and at the low rate of seven and twenty shillings, the most abandon'd courtezan, the most profligate rake or common sharper, purchases the privilege of mingling with the first peers and peeresses of the realm.[11]

Most important of all was the freedom conferred by a masque's anonymity. Candor and spontaneity replaced artifice and inhibition, exposing the inner self while concealing one's public identity. To "masque the face" was to "unmasque the mind," Henry Fielding wrote in "The Masquerade" (1728). Conversations were bolder and more impulsive. "Absolute freedom of speech" was the protocol, according to *Mist's Weekly Journal*. Flirtations became more daring and jests less subtle. Polite manners, stiffened by courtly etiquette, yielded to gestures of physical intimacy.

Rued a writer in the *Gentleman's Magazine*, "Whatever lewdness may be concerted; whatever luxury, immodesty, or extravagance may be committed in word or deed, no one's reputation is at stake." Critics of masquerades complained loudly of the liberties taken by men and women, though the latter received the greatest blame for their defiance of traditional stereotypes—shedding, as a person put it, one's "daily mask of innocence and modesty." More than that, alcoves and gardens permitted sexual liaisons, often, one presumes, with vizards still intact. "Immodesty and leudness propagate, and with promiscuous congress in disguise, practise obscene and flagrant villanies," condemned a poet.[12]

And then there were the costumes. These, often worn in place of a black silk gown, or "domino," added to one's sense of liberation. No doubt some disguises were donned in a spirit of derision, yet a further annoyance to critics, particularly when government and religious authorities were targets. But often, guests chose instead to indulge personal fantasies, and to some degree wearers were transformed by the experience of such close identification. For a single night, one could become a pauper or a prince, or, for that matter, a demon or a god. For Joseph Addison, commenting in the *Spectator*, masquerades permitted persons to dress as they "had a mind to be." In addition to impersonating such historical figures as Henry VIII or Mary Queen of Scots, guests appeared in abstract guises, attired, for instance, as Day or Night. Common were costumes modeled after proletarian clothing. Dairymaids, shepherds, prostitutes, and soldiers were all popular characters. Cross-dressing was prevalent. Henry III of France (1551–1589) usually appeared in a low-cut gown that "showed his throat hung with pearls." Horace Walpole arrived one evening dressed as an elderly woman. A writer railed in 1722, "Women, lewd women, dress in mens habits, that they may vent their obscenity more freely, and that to their own sex; and where men dress in the female habit, to give and receive a flood of unclean, and, to them, luscious conversation."[13]

Masquerades, then, occasioned evenings of striking license. Still, genteel entertainments represented, at most, momentary reprieves from reality—passing fancies staged sporadically over the course of a year. Nor in their lavish displays of pomp and privilege, their sumptuous buffets and beeswax candles, did masquerades embody a genuine spirit of egalitarianism. Despite critics' fears, any commitment to social leveling was at best ephemeral. Lords and ladies invariably departed from masquerades as they arrived, in coaches squired by squads of footmen. A Danish writer remarked, "A servant is as good as his master," but only, he noted, "for as long as the masquerade lasts."[14]

III

O thou the silent darkenesse of the night,
Arme me with desperate courage and contempt,
Of gods—lou'd men, now I applaud the guile,
Of our brave roarers which select this time
To drink and swagger, and spurne at all the powers
Of either world.

THOMAS GOFFE, 1631[15]

What did directly affect the tenor of upper-class society, if not masquerades, was the opportunity evening granted for rowdier escapades. Bloods, bucks, and blades, roarers and gallants—upper-class libertines went by a variety of titles. For them, the natural mask of darkness, not vizards of brocade, afforded a refuge from the regimen of courtly life. They embraced night as a time of boundless freedom. In train were assorted youths of gentle breeding, equally disdainful of polite society. No one city claimed a monopoly, for nearly every European capital, and many a large town, had its share of delinquent aristocrats. By the mid-eighteenth century, early American cities even spawned small bands of "bucks." In New York, Dr. Alexander Hamilton, during a visit in 1744, encountered "three young rakes" bent on "whoreing"; in Philadelphia, six youths "in the dress of gentlemen" brutalized a woman, first throwing her to the ground. And though certain eras, such as the Restoration in late seventeenth-century England, saw their numbers grow, few periods were free of gallants.[16]

Their behavior bespoke a fierce individualism, contemptuous of hypocrisy and social conformity in the pursuit of wealth and riches. Guilty on both scores were courtiers, clerics, and men of trade, all wedded to lives of artifice and false propriety. To gallants, the chivalric ideal of personal honor had long given way to servility, good manners, and fealty to king and country. In *Night*, his ode to libertinism published in 1761, the dissolute poet Charles Churchill affirmed,

Let slaves to business, bodies without soul,
Important blanks in nature's mighty roll,
Solemnize nonsense in the day's broad glare,
We NIGHT prefer, which heals or hides our care.

Such men, "unpractis'd in deceit," were "too resolute" to "brook affronts," "too proud to flatter, too sincere to lie, too plain to please"—at least, that is, during the hours of darkness, when repressive forces were weakest. More important, instead, was the unbridled pursuit of pleasure that nighttime encouraged. Gratification, free of social obligations and constraints. Stated the author of *The Libertine* (1683), "Long tales of heav'n to fools are given, / But we put in pleasure to make the scale even." Appalled by such libertinism, Henry Peacham warned in *The Compleat Gentleman* (1622) that "to be drunke, sweare, wench, follow the fashion and to do just nothing are the attributes and markes nowadayes of a great part of our gentry."[7]

In cities and towns, blades typically slept much of the day, drinking and roaring after sunset. Some cavorted openly at aristocratic gatherings, to the shock of less debauched company. At a concert in 1706, the Duke of Richmond proposed extinguishing all the candles so that guests "might do as they list [choose]," prompting more sober heads to object "while so many of their wives and relations were present." More often, young males shunned polite entertainments in favor of coarser fare, relishing the low life of brothels and alehouses. "To drink away their brains, and piss away their estates," according to a critic. "Lords of the street," they were christened by Samuel Johnson, "flushed as they are with folly, youth and wine." Emphasized a London newspaper in 1730, "There is a certain pleasure in sometimes descending."[18]

In fact, one suspects that social elites in general, notwithstanding their professed distaste for the poor, often envied their "vulgar pleasures." This was a theme of Richard Steele's comedy *The Gentleman* (17??), to judge from a surviving portion. "I think you are happier than we masters," Sir Harry Severn tells his servant Tom Dimple, before joining him and the "lower world" for a night's merriment. In 1718, the Duchess of Orleans confided to a friend, "The peasant-folk of Schwetzingen and Oftersheim used to gather around and talk to me, and they were more entertaining than the

William Hogarth, *A Rake's Progress* (pl. 3), 1735. Note in this riotous scene of a tavern chamber the broken lantern and staff at the young gallant's feet, spoils from scouring the nightwatch. Meanwhile, his own watch is lost to a pair of prostitutes.

duchesses in the *cercle*." No less a figure than the Holy Roman Emperor, Charles V (1500–1558), tradition has it, delighted in the vulgar manners of a peasant with whom, one night, he was forced to shelter outside Brussels. Reportedly, Charles laughed heartily at the peasant's coarse speech as he urinated, unaware of his sovereign's identity. "You are farting," reprimanded Charles, upon which the peasant retorted, "There is no good horse that does not fart while pissing!"[19]

James Boswell, the future Laird of Auchinleck, derived periodic pleasure from consorting at night with streetwalkers. On a visit to Germany, he recorded in his journal, "In the evening I must needs go and look at the Dresden streetwalkers, and amuse myself as I used to do in London. Low. Low." Besides supplying carnal gratification, "low debauchery" held great interest for Boswell, who donned a disguise for some outings. In June 1763, to celebrate "the King's birthnight" in London, he wore a ragged dark suit along with "dirty buckskin breeches and black stockings." Determined "to be a blackguard and to see all that was to be seen," he wenched his way across the city, alternately calling himself a barber, a soldier, and finally, to a young prostitute in Whitehall, a highwayman! "I came home about two o'clock, much fatigued," he wrote. Even ecclesiastics forsook their vows by cavorting in drinking houses and brothels. In seventeenth-century Flanders, two officials, Dean Henri Wiggers and Canon Arnold Cryters, during their "night games" not only drank and gambled in taverns but also danced and brawled. "Run him through," shouted the canon to his embattled friend one tumultuous evening at the Corona tavern. Travelers in Italian cities attributed their want of street lamps to prelates anxious to conduct sexual affairs in the dark. Volunteered a visitor to Rome, "The darkness of the streets has been in itself alledged, as having an object not strictly spiritual."[20]

Genteel women were not immune to night's appeal. Besides the burdens of courtly civility, they faced domestic constraints. Even more than other women, their lives revolved around the home, with fewer opportunities for personal fulfillment or independence. Of forced marriages suffered by young maidens, the heroine of the ballad "Loves Downfall" bemoans, "Would I had been a scullian-maid / Or a servant of low degree, / Then need not I have been afraid, / To ha' loved him that would love me." Once married, complained Margaret Cavendish, women had "to live in constant masquerade," hiding their true selves. Remarked a woman in Cavendish's *Orations* (1662), men "would fain bury us in their houses or beds, as in a grave." As a result, she remonstrated, "We are as ignorant of our selves, as men are of us."[21]

Consigned by day to the domestic sphere, upper-class wives and daughters occasionally took flight at night, notwithstanding traditional injunctions against unescorted travel. As one woman advised another in a seventeenth-century tale, "Since he barreth you of your libertie in the day, take it your selfe in the night." A character in *The Corbaccio* (ca. 1365), by Boccaccio, marvels at the ability of women to cross great distances at night for illicit meetings, despite their normal fears of "ghosts, spirits, and phantoms." Some wives reportedly assumed dual identities. The London playwright George Chapman wrote in 1599 of a "hundred ladies in this

William Hogarth, *The Bagnio* (pl. 5 of *Marriage à la Mode*), 1745. Following a masquerade, the lawyer Silvertongue and the Countess have repaired to a bathhouse of ill repute, only to be pursued by her husband, the Earl, who is mortally wounded in the ensuing confrontation.

towne that wil dance, revill all night amongst gallants, and in the morning goe to bed to her husband as cleere a woman as if she were new christned." Besides frequenting genteel diversions like masquerades, aristocratic wives were said to game, riot, and whore. Hence, for example, the promiscuous likes of Barbara Palmer, Countess of Castlemaine in the Restoration court, after whom Samuel Pepys lusted. Such was her love of gaming that she allegedly "won £15,000 in one night and lost £25,000 in another night at play." An April evening in 1683 found three "gentelwomen of Cambridge," attired in male gowns, breaking windows and assaulting female pedestrians. Madame de Murant, the estranged wife of the Count de Rousillon, was reported to sing "lewd songs during the night, and at all hours" with her lesbian lover, even "pissing out the window" of her Paris home after "prolonged debauchery." Plainly, while literary depictions reflected misogynist fears of infidelity, night afforded scattered numbers of women a measure of personal autonomy, not just at home but also, in some cases, abroad. Of mornings, Montesquieu claimed, "Often the husband's day began where his wife's ended."[22]

Descending the social ladder for persons of property was not always easy. Nocturnal frolics, especially in unfamiliar neighborhoods, posed myriad risks, not least negotiating one's way through the muck of ill-lit streets. In the play *Squire Oldsapp: or, the Night Adventures* (1679), the character Henry laments, "Ah, plague'o these night-rambles; the trouble a man gets in finding his way home after 'em, is more by half than the pleasure he gets by 'em." Boswell, after one of his drunken expeditions, returned home "all dirty and bruised." Unescorted women ran the risks of taunts and jeers, or worse, even at polite entertainments. In 1748, Lady Charlotte Johnston and two friends ventured into the "dark walks" of London's Vauxhall Gardens, a notorious spot for midnight assignations. Whatever their reasons (prurient curiosity perhaps), they were mistaken for prostitutes, chased by a half-dozen drunken apprentices, and assaulted. Moreover, it was one thing to dress as a ruffian, and quite another to behave as one. The London law student Dudley Ryder became tongue-tied whenever approaching a prostitute. "I am under a strange confusion and hurry when I attack a whore and cannot tell how to talk to them freely," he confessed in his diary. Boswell, despite his shabby costume, found it difficult to hide his true identity when consorting with prostitutes. "Notwithstanding of my dress," he later noted with thinly veiled pride, "I was always taken for a gentleman in disguise."[23]

Some social friction was unavoidable. An Irishman wrote of the mannered gentleman who, having spent the "whole day in company he hates," turns at night to vice "among company that as heartily hate him." Claiming to be a "gentleman and a scholar," Francis Woodmash, while drunk, antagonized a table of tradesmen at a London alehouse by speaking Latin. A flurry of heated insults followed—"Blockhead," "Brandy-Face," "*Irish* Rogue"—before Woodmash killed one of them with his sword. Other gallants, however, appear to have frolicked freely with the lower orders, at least until tempers warmed. Of an evening in a Covent Garden alehouse, a "watchman" reported in a newspaper:

> Bullies, whores, bawds, pimps, lords, rakes, beaux, fops, players, fiddlers, singers, dancers, &c. who are strangely mixed together. You will sometimes find a Lord in deep conversation with a pimp, a Member of P—— explaining his privilege to a whore; a bawd, with a great deal of prudency, exclaiming to a rake against riots, a whore with a fribble, a beau with a butcher, and yet all hail fellow well met, as the saying is; till the gentleman get quite drunk, and then the bullies, sharpers, whores, bawds, pimps, &c. get to their trade of kicking up a dust, as they call it, and begin to fleece those who have any money. Now begins the high scene; swords, sticks, hats, wiggs, any thing, away they go; bloody noses, black eyes, broken heads, broken glasses, bottles, &c.[24]

For drunken gallants, no jest at the expense of polite behavior or human decency seemed too outrageous. In Leeds, "young gentlemen," for their late-night amusement, summoned persons from bed, falsely notifying them of some dying friend or relation. In June 1676, John Wilmont, the rakish second Earl of Rochester, together with three comrades, severely beat a constable in Epson after vainly searching for "a whore." At a nearby tavern, they had already terrorized several fiddlers by "tossing" them "in a blanket for refusing to play." Before the night ended, Rochester drew his sword, prompting one of his party to be slain by the nightwatch. Even Pepys, no prude, occasionally found his middle-class sensibilities shocked, such as when two blades, Sir Charles Sedley and Lord Buckhurst, reportedly ran "all the night with their arses bare through" London streets, "at last fighting and being beat by the watch." On another evening, Pepys spied "two gallants and their footmen" drag off "a pretty wench" by "some force." ("God forgive me," he confessed, "what thought and wishes I had of being in their place.") More unfortunate still was the fate of a provincial innkeeper who objected to noise made by "a party of Bucks." Taking the path of her furniture, she was tossed out an upstairs window to her death.[25]

Violent confrontations were inevitable among gallants who eschewed both the protections and the constraints of civil society. Swordplay and drunken brawls fueled youthful exuberance, making nocturnal escapades seem more heroic. Wrote the Earl of Rochester, "I'll tell of whores attack'd, their Lords at home, / Bawds quarters beaten up, and fortress won: / Windows demolish'd, watches overcome." A visitor to Lisbon complained of the late-night "squabbles of bullying rake-hells, who scour the streets in search of adventures." Most violence was gratuitous and unprovoked. On a December night in 1693, three swordsmen paraded through London's Salisbury Court, declaring "damn them they would kill the next man they met, making responses I will, I will, I will." Vandalism was customary, with windows, doors, and street lamps broken and smashed. Young women, beaten and kicked, bore the brunt of their aggression. Some were pulled into dark streets from their beds. Targets included members of the nightwatch, lone symbols of royal authority whose advanced years made them objects of greater contempt. James Shirley's play *The Gamester* (1633) spoke of "blades, that roar, / In brothels, and break windows, fright the streets, / At midnight worse that constables, and sometimes, / Set upon innocent bell-men." Following a masquerade, a band of gallants that included the dukes of Monmouth and Richmond mortally wounded a watchman, a crime also imputed to the Duke of York before ascending the throne as James II (1633–1701). In turn, a small crowd led by two French noblemen, on an April night in 1741, attacked the front door of the mayor of Libourne, first with an axe, then with a battering ram.[26]

Some cities saw the rise of nocturnal gangs composed of blades with servants and retainers in tow. Loosely organized at best, they acquired notorious reputations for violence. In Amsterdam, members of the Damned Crue routinely assailed innocent pedestrians at night, as did Chalkers in Dublin. Italian cities were beset by bands of young nobles and gentlemen. In Florence toward the late sixteenth century, a traveler discovered:

> The gentlemen in companies walked by nights in the streets, with rapyers, and close lanthornes, I meane halfe light, halfe darke, carrying the light syde towardes them, to see the way, and the darke syde from them, to be unseene of others, and if one company happened to meete with another, they turned their light syde of their lanthorns towardes the faces of those they mett, to knowe them, . . . and except they were acquainted frendes they seldome mett without some braule, or tumult at the least.

Anon., *Drunken Rakes and Watchmen in Covent Garden*, 1735.

In Rome, the painter Caravaggio belonged to a group of gallants that preyed on prostitutes and rival swordsmen. "*Nec spe, nec metu*" ("without hope or fear") was their credo. In 1606, after killing a member of another gang in a brawl, Caravaggio was forced to flee to Naples.[27] In London, members of the Bugles, formed in 1623, allegedly contained the scourings of "taverns and other debauched places," led by "diverse knights, some young noblemen, and gentlemen." In later years, London suffered such bands as the Scowrers and the Hectors, who cut their veins in order to "quaff their own blood." Of Rochester's Ballers, Pepys described an evening in which "young blades" danced naked with prostitutes. Most feared were the Mohocks, who acquired their name shortly after the well-publicized visit to London of four Iroquois chiefs from America. For several months in 1712, the city was terrorized by the gang's brutality. Besides knifing pedestrians in the face, they stood women on their heads, "misusing them in barbarous manner." Mohock numbers were such, taunted a handbill, that watchmen feared to make arrests. Jonathan Swift, concerned for his safety, resorted to riding in coaches at night and coming home early. "They shan't cut mine [face]," he wrote, "I like it better as it is, the dogs will cost me at least a crown a week in chairs." Lamented Sarah

Cowper, "The manners of Indian savages are no[w] becoming accomplishments to English Earls, Lords, and gentlemen."[28]

In English literature, no pair of peers cavorted more famously than Prince Hal and his stout companion, Falstaff. In Part 1 of *Henry IV* (1598), we discover them conspiring with other rowdies, for the sake of a "jest," to waylay wealthy travelers in the dark. Declares Falstaff to the prince, "There's neither honesty, manhood, nor good fellowship in thee, nor thou camest not of the blood royal, if thou darest not stand for ten shillings." Real-life sovereigns of this sort reportedly included the peasant king Matthias of Hungary (1440–1490), France's Francis I (1494–1547), and Francis Duke of Milan, who disguised himself at night as a peddler. Equally, it was said that though the Duke of Orleans, brother to Charles VI, "showed himself to be so pious during the day," he "secretly" led "a very dissolute life at night," which included heavy drinking and frolics with prostitutes. The Scandinavian monarch Christian II (1481–1559), as prince, quitted his hall to drink wine in Copenhagen taverns, having first bribed the nightwatch to open the castle gate. Another Danish king, Christian IV (1577–1648), was known to rampage through streets, breaking windows like other young aristocrats. Such, too, was said of England's Henry VIII, whose "rambles" as a youth inspired the well-known tale of *The King and the Cobbler*, published in the seventeenth century. Charles II (1630–1685), during one of his "nocturnal rambles" with Rochester, reputedly visited a Newmarket brothel in "his usual disguise," only to have his pocket picked by a prostitute. Perhaps most notorious were the escapades of Henry III of France, a devout Catholic by day who caroused on Paris streets at night, usually with faithful courtiers called *mignons*. Of these, a contemporary complained, "Their occupations are gambling, blaspheming, jumping, dancing, quarreling, fornicating, and following the King around."[29]

CHAPTER NINE

MASTERS BY NIGHT: PLEBEIANS

I

Who dares not stir by day must walk by night.
WILLIAM SHAKESPEARE, 1596[1]

NIGHT REVOLUTIONIZED the social landcape. If darkness rendered members of the mighty more plebeian, it made legions of the weak more powerful—walking "the streetes," moaned a writer, "as uprightly, & with as proud a gate as if they meant to knock against the starres with the crownes of their heads." Freed from hours of toil and degradation, multitudes in Europe and America drew renewed purpose from the setting sun. Night's widespread appeal—freedom from both labor and social scrutiny—resounded among the lower orders. Personal associations were by choice, confined to family and friends, social peers rather than superiors. "No eyes break undistinguish night / To watch us or reprove," wrote John Clare, the former Northamptonshire hedge-setter. The attraction of darkness takes on richer significance if we consider night's ability to obscure vestiges of the visible world. Veiled on black evenings were common reminders of institutional power and privilege, designed to instill fear along with veneration and respect. Crests and crucifixes receded from sight; guildhalls and gaols loomed less large; and church steeples no longer dominated the terrain. "All real ills in dark oblivion lye," wrote Charles Churchill, "and joys, by fancy form'd, their place supply."[2]

Night, to be sure, afforded asylum to diverse sorts. Forced to conceal their identities by day, dissident minorities found fresh resolve after dark, successfully eluding the constraints of church, state, and popular prejudice. In England not only did political outsiders like the Jacobites cabal at night, but rival factions during times of heightened unrest used the cover of darkness to circulate incendiary broadsheets. In the tense period surrounding the Glorious Revolution of 1688–1689, mornings brought the discovery of handbills strewn about the streets of London. Years later, during the Hanover Succession Crisis, Mary, Countess Cowper remarked, "Not a night passing but some scandalous pamphlet or other was cried about."[3]

Religious dissenters congregated at night much in the tradition of early Christians during the Roman persecution. In the Middle Ages, Cathars, Waldensians, and other heretical sects assembled secretly. Their enemies circulated rumors of midnight orgies. Of a sect in 1427, the Sienese friar Bernadino wrote, "Deep in the night they all get together, men and women in the same room, and they stir up quite a broth among themselves." Crypto-Jews, like the *marranos* in Spain, worshipped in private and committed isolated acts of defiance. So in early seventeenth-century Seville, for two nights in a row, signs appeared on the door of the Church of San Isidro proclaiming, "Long live the laws of Moses. They are the best." Late one evening in 1551, a small band of Italian Jews, during the Jewish festival week of Purim, roamed freely through the empty streets of Rome, even at one point masquerading as the nightwatch.[4]

On the heels of the Reformation, Protestant minorities, fearing arrest, held nocturnal services, including weddings and burials. Reportedly, French Protestants (*Huguenots*) acquired their name from meetings at night in the city of Tours, where once the spirit of a medieval monarch, King Hugo, was said to haunt the streets. Whether true or not, secret assemblies for reading and discussion were customary in French cities. Persecuted Anabaptists in Strasbourg congregated in nearby forests. According to an eyewitness in 1576, two hundred men and women prayed and listened to sermons, having first taken secret "paths and by-ways" pro-

François Morellon la Cave, *Night Meeting of the Adamites*, eighteenth century. An antiauthoritarian religious sect active at different times in England and other parts of Europe. Seeking to regain the innocence of the Garden of Eden, they worshipped in the nude.

tected by guards. "The many lighted candles looked like wolves' eyes shining among the trees and bushes on a dark night." Some may have been.[5]

In Britain, Catholic recusants occasionally met at night for services and sacraments. Of a widow in 1640, a Monmouth gentleman noted, "She was unlawfully buried by night in the church, she being a papist." In the wake of the Clarendon Code re-establishing the primacy of the Church of England after the Civil War, numerous nonconformists met covertly. The diary of Oliver Heywood in Yorkshire is filled with evening excursions to preach in private homes, some nearly too crowded with followers to enter. Years later, during another spasm of Anglican persecution, the Manchester dissenter Thomas Jolly wrote, "Our danger of being deprived of our priviledges wholly made us meet in the evening and the night-time mostly according to the example of the primitive christians."[6]

Refugees from daylight also included victims of disease, lepers and other sufferers whose physical disfigurements exposed them to daily scorn. During outbreaks of plague, urban officials frequently restricted victims and their families to home, with doors barred from the outside, and, in London beginning in 1519, marked with a red cross and the plaintive inscription "Lord Have Mercy Upon Us." Often, inmates were unable to acquire fresh water and food, much less receive the help of friends. Still, at night, persons managed to escape, either fleeing to the countryside or returning home before daybreak with provisions. During an outbreak in Florence, the gold beater Alessandro Conti, in a frenzied effort to safeguard his son, lowered him one night from a household window. Of London's Great Plague, Daniel Defoe recounted the "running of distempered people about in the streets" at night, who were nearly impossible for officials to curb.[7]

No less common were homosexuals. By the sixteenth century or earlier, European cities including Florence, Venice, and Geneva contained homosexual networks, with London, Paris, and Amsterdam all following suit by the 1700s. In many localities, sodomy was a capital offense, which it became in England at the urging of Henry VIII. In London, more than twenty homosexual brothels, known as "molly-houses," were raided in 1726. At Margaret Clap's house, with "beds in every room," thirty or forty men were said to assemble each evening. Wherever the location, night was widely favored as the safest time for sexual encounters. In Tuscany, *la notte* was a popular metaphor for sodomy. The Florentine court chiefly responsible for the prosecution of homosexuals in the late Middle Ages was titled the Officials of the Night. In Paris, public gardens were favorite sites, where clumps of shrubs and trees provided shelter on moonlit evenings. On a summer night in 1723, the abbé de la Vieuxville informed a fellow stroller in the Tuileries, "I see you here every evening. If you want to, come with me under the yew trees, for there's no staying here because the moonlight is too bright and there are too many people around." Less often, nighttime for homosexuals posed risks of its own. In Florence, Jacopo di Niccolò Panuzzi, amid the gathering darkness of evening, offered money to a young male for the commission of "shameful gestures," only to discover that the "youth" was a constable.[8]

II

Their shortliv'd jubilee the creatures keep,
Which but endures, whilst tyrant-man does sleep.

ANNE FINCH, 1713[9]

Religious and political minorities, the diseased and disabled, and homosexuals—all were wayfarers instead of permanent denizens of the nocturnal world. Rather than laying claim to darkness, each sought, as the French saying went, to make "a hole in the night"—or, as a Spanish rabbi remarked, "to hide from the world." Their scattered numbers only enhanced their anonymity. Quite different was the larger body of people for whom nighttime spawned an alternate existence, a separate realm rather than just a passing refuge.[10]

Many evenings, few looked forward to sunset more eagerly than did the indigent and dispossessed. Along with unskilled laborers and struggling peasants, the preindustrial countryside teemed with vagrants and beggars, many of them refugees from regional wars and economic dislocation. Predominantly male and single, they streamed to cities, where poverty, according to conservative estimates, swelled during years of economic crisis to between 20 and 30 percent of municipal populations. Having scant opportunities for employment, these unfortunates, in Daniel Defoe's words, comprised "the miserable, that really pinch and suffer want."[11]

At night, indigent men and women grew bold. Darkness freed untold numbers from the control of their betters, including, for some, the oversight of masters. "They lie close in their dens and holes all the day, and at night range the country for their prey," fumed a contemporary. Anxious superiors likened the movements of the lower classes to those of owls, wolves, and other nocturnal creatures—"wicked night birds," groused a commentator. "They are like the beasts that creep forth in the night," declared Solomon Stoddard of Massachusetts. Such comparisons attested to both their prowess and their prevalence at night. Paintings by artists as disparate as Leonaert Bramer, David Teniers the Younger, and Johann Konrad Seekatz reveal not only the nighttime camps of the poor but also their favored haunts for camaraderie and drink. "Those who appear," observed

Johann Konrad Seekatz, *Gypsies Before a Campfire*, eighteenth century.

Oliver Goldsmith in 1759, "no longer now wear their daily mask, nor attempt to hide their lewdness or their misery."[12]

Impatient of patriarchal authority, the young were also drawn to evening hours—apprentices, students, and other adolescents whose subordination was more often the consequence of age than class. For adults, the young were a persistent concern. The years between seventeen and twenty-seven, declared the sixteenth-century scholar Roger Ascham, were "the most dangerous of all in a man's life." Moralists warned of their restless temperaments and the need for close control. Apprenticeship, undertaken by young males of modest origins, offered training over a period of years in a craft or trade while supplying moral supervision both on the job and off. Across Europe, the institution was a popular means of socializing adolescents, as well as a cheap source of labor. Although large numbers failed to complete their training, London alone by the early seventeenth century contained upwards of twenty-five thousand apprentices, roughly 12 percent of its population. Not only were they supposed to reside in their masters' households, but there was little free time except for meals and, at most, a midday rest.[13]

Under a master's thumb by day, many fled their domination at night. "Lying-out" was the term reserved for dependents that remained abroad much of the evening, often in defiance of a household curfew. "They can't bear the orders, the restraints, the seasonable hours, whereto their *parents* or *master*s would have them obliged," a contemporary observed in 1705. The self-styled "masters of the night," adolescents provoked fear among urban denizens throughout the early modern world. Just as Cotton Mather condemned "knotts of riotous young men" in Boston, including his own son Increase ("Cressy"), so in Germany, a Protestant synod protested, "Decent people can no longer be sure of anything and must fear the most shameful insults, even physical attacks." Of London, Sir William Davenant declared in 1673, "Our city fam'd for government, is by / These nightly riots and disorders, grown / Less safe then galleys, where revolted slaves / Inchain their officers."[14]

So, too, for bound laborers, night brought uncommon opportunity. So pervasive was servitude in Europe that even poor households sometimes possessed a single maid. Eighteenth-century Paris contained forty thousand domestics, with London having at least as many. Like apprentices, servants were predominantly young, generally from fifteen to thirty years of age. Although they often changed jobs, servitude, unlike apprenticeship, rarely represented a stepping-stone to propertied independence. Working conditions were demanding. By definition, servants were subject to the will of their masters, and to their verbal and physical abuse. Maidservants fell prey to sexual exploitation. Worse were the lives of indentured servants in the American colonies, whose terms averaged from three to five years. If banished from Britain as convicts, they labored for seven years. Still, the lot of colonial servants was superior to that of African slaves, whose miserable material existence, especially on Southern plantations, was compounded by strenuous labor and savage discipline.[15]

And, yet, once evening's tasks were done, masters were hard-pressed to curtail their laborers' jaunts. The General Court of Massachusetts in 1675 condemned the "evil of inferiours absenting themselves out of the families whereunto they belong in the night." Sarah Cowper complained bitterly of "impudent wretches who go where they will." In Scotland, a vicar reported, "A farmer must often rise from bed at 3 or 4 o'clock, in a winter's morning to admit his servants, who have been junketing all night."[16] Equally peripatetic were slaves. "Both sexes are frequently travelling all night," remarked a white resident of Barbados, "going to or returning from a distant connection." A correspondent in the *Boston Evening-Post* railed against the "great disorders committed by Negroes, who are permitted by their imprudent masters, &c. to be out late at night." In short, as a North Carolina planter remarked, "night" was "their day."[17] Then, also, apprentices, servants, and slaves bent on escape were most likely to abscond after sunset, lurking by day in woods and marshes and navigating at night by the stars. In Germany, two ship's apprentices in March 1588, having fled their river vessel, escaped to Bonn "with help of the darkness of night," only to be discovered in the morning. Alerted a colonial newspaper advertisement for runaway servants, "It is supposed they will travel mostly in the night."[18]

In certain respects, the members of these four groups—adolescents, servants, slaves, and the poor—had little in common. Some resided on the social margins of early modern communities, while others were partially integrated. The lot of Carolina slaves varied immensely from that of lower-class whites, as did the prospects facing hardened vagrants compared to those of young servants. The groups themselves were fragmented by occupation, ethnicity, gender, and religion. Among slaves, important, too, were their identities as creoles or native Africans. Yet these groups frequently overlapped, and boundaries separating one from another were often blurred. Thus, for instance, apprentice riots in London were rumored to include "forlorn companions" and "masterless men." Most of all, these men and women, despite their diverse backgrounds, were alike in one fundamental respect. Rather than living in one world, they each resided in two. Days mired in misery and fear often gave way to nights of opportunity and promise. Alienated from daily reality, only in the evening could they work and play with their own kind by their own rules. Recalled a former North Carolina slave, "We hated to see da sun rise in slavery time cause it meant annudder hard day, but den we wus glad to see it go down." Or, as a New England minister wrote of the young, "Because they are *weary* of the *restraint*, which they have been under in the day time, wherefore when they get liberty, they are apt to run mad, like water, that has been pent all the day."[19]

If night posed myriad dangers, the lower orders were well equipped to navigate its darkness. Most were intimately familiar with their physical environs and versed in the mysteries of the natural world. Both servants and apprentices were regularly required to traverse their communities, running errands or retrieving their masters after dark. In colonial Virginia, upon a slave's overnight death in a meadow after visiting his wife on another plantation, his owner attributed the mishap to drunkenness, "for he must have known every foot of the way so well." Drink, too, for at least some individuals, must have eased nocturnal fears. So in Somerset, young James Lackington's father, on a gloomy night, "drank too large a quantity of ale to be much afraid of any thing." "Night knows no shame," went a popular saying, "or love and wine no fear."[20]

For the lower orders, theirs was a world in motion long past sunset. On mild evenings, friends and relations congregated in small clusters in the open-air past midnight. Laughter and camaraderie, stoked by ale, beer, or wine, animated their hours. "Every evening in every village," remarked Giovanni Gelsi of Italian peasants during the seventeenth century, "you'll see them dance into the night as they carouse together. Laughing in our faces, they all make merry." In Rome, laborers and paupers gathered by the Piazza Navona, while in Paris, parks like the Tuileries and the Luxembourg drew men and women. Jesuits in Bavaria described "night-time gatherings" as "rooted habits among peasants," and in Lisbon a visitor wrote that revelers "frisk, and dance, and tinkle their guitars from sunset to sunrise." A London resident complained of an "idle, drunken, dissolute set of miscreants and gamblers" that assembled in an open field each evening.[21] Homes, barns, and stables permitted cardplay and dice, stories and gossip, and derisive songs. Constables in Berkshire discovered one night six couples "dancing naked." Declared a seventeenth-century ballad:

Let the lazy great-ones of the town,
Drink night away
And sleep all day,
'Till gouty, gouty, they are grown:
Our daily works such vigour give,
That nightly sports we oft' revive;
And kiss our dames,
With stronger flames,
Than any prince alive.[22]

Slaves routinely fraternized on neighboring properties, especially spouses owned by different masters. "Amusements" included "legendary ballads" and "narratives of alternate dialogue and singing," according to the Richmond lawyer George Tucker—"the night is their own." A traveler to Virginia reported that the average slave, rather than retire to rest at day's end, "generally sets out from home, and walks six or seven miles in the night, be the weather ever so sultry, to a negroe dance, in which he performs with astonishing agility, and the most vigorous exertions." A common precaution, of West African origin, was a kettle or pot. Placed upside-down, it was meant to capture human voices and other sounds. Using traditional techniques to tell time by the moon and stars, slaves returned before dawn. Along with moonlight, burning candlewood provided illumination as well as warmth on cool evenings. "Dem old pine knots would burn for a long time and throw a fine bright light," a former slave observed.[23]

Of course, drinking houses, too, catered to the lower orders. Such favorites as Lille's Savage Man's Tavern or Eva's Whores and Thieve's Bar in Amsterdam left little to the imagination. The Darkened Room in Augsburg provided a refuge in the 1590s to a notorious gang of thieves. Worst, in the eyes of the upper classes, were alehouses that remained open through most of the evening. In England, many of these night-cellars, as they came to be called in the early 1700s, were squalid, ill-lit hovels. In contrast to other drinking houses, they were more affordable as well as less accessible to social superiors. Reeking of tobacco fumes, vomit, and urine, they attracted a steady stream of patrons eager to tipple away the small hours. So at the Three Daggers, a London alehouse, the cellar-man Joshua Travers drank with comrades until 6:00 A.M. "Here are discharged vollies of oaths and execrations, ribaldry and nonsense, blasphemy and obscenity," noted a London resident. Often, in Paris, late-night revelers refused to leave cabarets at closing time. "Most cabaretiers," complained authorities in 1760, "keep their houses open during the night, and receive people of every estate, and often give shelter to debauched women, soldiers, beggars and sometimes to thieves." In Strasbourg, so-called sleeping houses were faulted during the mid-1600s for "all kinds of wantonness, forbidden dancing, excessive drinking, eating, and carousing." So, too, in Virginia, the planter Landon Carter denounced the proliferation of "night shops" and their popularity among slaves and poor whites as receptacles for stolen goods. Not only did the shops dispense rum, but proprietors sold "to anybody any thing whatever." "At best," chided Carter, "they must steal what they sell."[24]

III

Darkness endows the small and ordinary ones among mankind with poetical power.

THOMAS HARDY, 1886[25]

"He that does ill hates the light," affirmed a Scottish proverb. Numerous folk, besides burglars, robbers, and other hardened rogues, exploited the evening darkness, often for illicit purposes. Petty criminals were far more numerous, if less feared. For poor families, social and legal constraints of all sorts eased. Indigent households buried their dead at night to escape paying parish dues, which had the added benefit of protecting gravesites from thieves, often needy themselves. Where grave robbers at night stole clothing and caskets, "resurrection men" unearthed entire bodies, freshly interred in churchyards, to sell for medical dissection.[26] Meanwhile, struggling mothers, after dark, abandoned newborns for whom they could ill afford to care. In London, the Royal Exchange became a favored location for castaways. Mothers in Paris attached tags to their infants, identifying their sex, birth date, and first name. By the beginning of the eighteenth century, approximately two thousand abandoned children were annually admitted to the foundling hospital in Paris, one of numerous such institutions throughout Catholic Europe. Provincial roads, too, received their share. On a dark winter evening in 1760, for example, a new mother, Jane Brewerton, placed her illegitimate daughter beside a byroad in the Yorkshire town of Chapell Allerton, waiting at a distance until a couple discovered the child.[27]

Impoverished souls too proud to beg by day dotted urban streets after sunset, desperate for bread. As the monk Woulter Jacobszoon described a nun in Amsterdam, "She went out at night when it was dark, because during the day she was ashamed, being respectable at heart."[28] Likewise, debtors and other fugitives, fearful of arrest, traveled freely. At night, wrote Thomas Dekker, "The banckrupt, the fellon, and all that owed any mony, and for feare of arrests, or justices warrants, had like so many snayles kept their houses over their heads all day before, began to creep out of their shels." Many a tenant, unable to make their rent, took moonlight flight, "moving house with as little noise as possible."[29] Darkness also offered the indigent an opportunity for squatting, if only overnight, in urban sheds and stables or in barns and other outbuildings in the country. Yeomen, claimed Dekker, from their fear of arson "dare not deny them." Squatters in parts of western England and Wales laid more permanent claims. A local custom of uncertain origins permitted one to occupy a piece of waste or common land by building a turf cottage overnight, generally known as a *caban unnos*. The work had to be completed between twilight and dawn, though friends and family were permitted to help.[30]

And there were opportunities at night for sorcery. On both sides of the Atlantic, members of the poor and dispossessed resorted to magic, especially as private charity in communities declined and poverty rose. "Poverty," noted a sixteenth-century authority on witchcraft, "is often the source of many evils in persons who do not choose it voluntarily or endure it patiently." By night, those on the economic margins eagerly participated in a "supernatural economy," pinning their hopes on magical charms believed to help locate buried gold and silver. The spells used by Hans Heinrich Richter, a disabled blacksmith in eighteenth-century Prussia, had both Christian and pagan roots. The best time for treasure hunting fell after midnight, with some evenings preferred to others depending on the moon's phase. Silence was critical. As a defense against demons, it was customary to draw one or more circles at the supposed spot. More alarming to authorities, malevolent spirits might be invoked to assist in unearthing the treasure. An English statute in 1542 threatened hunters with the death penalty for "invocacions and conjurations of sprites" to "get knowledge for their own lucre in what place treasure of golde and silver shulde or mought be founde."[31]

For some desperate sorts, sorcery offered a means of punishing their persecutors—or smiting neighbors who had turned a blind eye to one's misfortune. When a farmer in Worcestershire, one night, apprehended an elderly woman, her arms filled with stolen wood, she immediately fell upon her knees and prayed with uplifted hands that "he might never more

John Quidor, *The Money Diggers*, 1832.

be warm, nor ever know the warmth of a fire." Other practitioners pierced wax images with thorns or called directly upon Satan's assistance. Slaves, by resorting to magic, sought to escape their oppression. In Kentucky, Henry Bibb, having "great faith in conjuration and witchcraft," learned to make a magical concoction from an older slave. After heating a mixture of fresh cow manure, red pepper, and "white people's hair," he ground the substance into a fine powder, which he sprinkled at night about his master's chamber—all for the purpose, Bibb later wrote, of preventing "him from ever abusing me in any way." Still more ambitious was a plan hatched by the German servant Johannes Butzbasch. Too scared to abscond from his master on foot, he instead considered visiting "an old hag," hoping he might receive a "black cow upon which he could escape through the air."[32]

Sorcery was employed at all hours, but its power was thought most potent when spirits roamed. Common belief held that some curses and spells worked solely at night, making wary neighbors all the more suspicious of single women found abroad after dark. It was not unusual in colonial New England for women to be warned that their "nightwalking" could fuel suspicions of witchcraft. Seventeen-year-old Lydia Nichols, questioned during the Salem witch hunt in 1692 "how she darst lie out a nights in the woods alone," replied that "she was not a fraid of any thing" for "she had sold her selfe boddy & soull to the old boy." In 1665 a Connecticut colonist named John Brown was alleged, late one night inside a neighbor's home, to have drawn a satanic symbol for his brother. According to a witness, "He went to the doore & called his brother out to looke upon ye stars, then hee told him he [Satan] was there in ye stars, then he comes in & burnt his paper & sd if he had not burnt ye paper, the divell would have come presently."[33]

None of these nocturnal pursuits, however—neither black magic nor other misdeeds—ever attracted the large numbers given to pilfering. Servants, slaves, apprentices, laborers, husbandmen, all engaged in petty theft. "They steal every thing they can lay their hands on," exclaimed Arthur Young of the Irish poor. Of Italian peasants, a poem, "De Natura Rusticorum," railed: "At night they make their way, as the owls, / and they steal as robbers." In eighteenth-century Paris, laborers, apprentices, and journeymen committed two-thirds of petty thefts.[34] Along with theft at urban worksites, pilfering by domestic servants was rife. Samuel Pepys one evening discovered half the wine in his cellar missing, which he attributed to midnight frolics among his servants—"after we were in bed," he groused. Servile larceny prompted Parliament in 1713 to enact a draconian law rendering a capital offense, without benefit of clergy, the theft of goods valued at more than forty shillings from a dwelling.[35]

In rural regions, crops and livestock made tempting targets. Vulnerable, too, were beehives, fishponds, and the week's wash. "Never let your linen hang out after dark," advised a writer. Despite surveillance by landowners, fields were too large and nights too dark. In 1709, items stolen by Agnes Park from neighbors in the Scottish parish of Cathcart included peas and beans, bowkail, straw, and malt from a brewhouse. A visitor to Ireland discovered, "Turnips are stolen by car loads, and two acres of wheat pluckt off in a night." For rural families without land, stolen grass supplied fodder for livestock. Sometimes, too, cattle were grazed overnight in neighboring pastures. Closes were breached to rob cows of their milk—the Virginia planter Landon Carter complained that his slave Criss encouraged her children to "milk my cows in the night." Perhaps most prized was wood, dead or alive, for cooking in summer and in winter for heat. In addition to fallen branches from storms, green limbs were "brumped" from trees, and estate fences stripped of their rails. "Gates will be cut in pieces, and conveyed in many places as fast as built; trees as big as a man's body, and that would require ten men to move, gone in a night," reported Young.[36]

Most goods appear to have been purloined for domestic consumption, but at least a portion resurfaced in local markets. In 1664, for example, a Norfolk court charged three women with the overnight theft of green peas from a neighbor, allegedly having the intention of feeding them to their pigs and selling the rest. In America, slaves and free blacks both engaged in a lively traffic, selling to families and small traders stolen provisions along with those from personal plots. A Moravian visitor to Virginia, discovering blacks one evening "roaming everywhere," deemed the colony "full of thieves." George Washington blamed the overnight loss of his sheep on slaves with dogs. "It is astonishing to see the command under which their dogs are." Of free blacks, a resident of Maryland declared, "It is well known that these free negroes are stealing poultry and fruit in the season in the night, to sell in the market in the towns and cities."[37]

In the countryside, poaching drew added numbers afield—tenants, husbandmen, and servants, armed with snares, nets, and guns. Some, claiming no trade, were vagrants. In 1599, Sir Edward Coke described poachers in Staffordshire as "verie dissolute, riotous and unruly persons, common nightwalkers and stealers of deare." Not only was hunting forbidden in aristocratic deer parks but also, more often than not, in royal forests. Standard prey included rabbits and hares, partridges, pheasants, and deer. Certain types of nightfishing were also illegal, though widely practiced. Game laws were far less stringent in colonial America than in Europe, although Virginia and the Carolinas enacted legislation prohibiting fire-hunting, a nocturnal technique of Indian origin by which hunters used torchlight to blind their quarry. Besides the risks of fire, cattle and horses were sometimes mistaken for deer.[38]

For households in rural England, poaching was a favorite pastime and, often, a valued source of income. Proclaimed a popular ballad, "The Lincolnshire Poacher": "When I was bound apprentice, in famous Lincolnsheer, / Full well I served my master for more than seven year, / Till I took up poaching, as you shall quickly hear: / Oh! 'tis my delight of a shiny night, in the season of the year." Certainly, no youths were better trained in woodcraft: mastering shifts in weather and phases of the moon as well as learning the scents and habits of both gamekeepers and game. "Parents take care to instruct their children," observed a contemporary. Years later, a retired poacher recalled of his boyhood, "We knew every inch of the countryside and darkness was our friend."[39]

As often nighttime was for smugglers. Common throughout the Continent, smuggling reached epidemic proportions in the British Isles in the eighteenth century. With the imposition of import duties on such commodities as brandy, tobacco, and tea, the contraband trade involved thousands. Smugglers unloaded goods, usually at night, all along the British seashore, though the southern coastline acquired the greatest notoriety. The Isle of Man and the Channel Islands served as staging grounds offshore. Through an inland nexus of drop points and distributors, much of the contraband ultimately found its way to cities. Reported a London newspaper in 1738, "The present dark nights being very favourable for the smugglers designs, the gentlemen in that employ have made a diligent use of them, and have run a large quantity of tea and other rich goods in town." As the adolescent son of a Berkshire horse trader, Joseph Jewell worked for an innkeeper, whose house served as "a resort for smugglers." "My master followed smuggling on his own account," Jewell wrote in his autobiography, "so that I frequently had to ride out nights with tea, spirits etc. I used to carry a whip with about 2 pound weight of lead run into the large end of it, made for the purpose of defence if I should meet with excise officers." To disguise his "goods," he wore a "long, loose, great coat."[40]

In turn, a lively export trade of illegal wool arose, popularly known as "owling" because of smugglers' penchant for nighttime—just as spirits shipped to the coasts of Sussex and Kent were dubbed "moonshine." It was along the same shore that large, at times violent bands of smugglers, like the Hawkhurst gang in the 1740s, operated, to the alarm of government authorities. Less troubled were local inhabitants, who generally welcomed the cheaper merchandise. Parson Woodforde, for one, received periodic supplies of gin at night, left on his doorstep by the village blacksmith, himself nicknamed Moonshine. "Busy all the morning almost in bottling two tubs of gin, that came by Moonshine this morn' very early,"

Woodforde wrote in his diary. Jewell, on one of his many "night rides," traveled fifteen miles to deliver contraband goods to an elderly woman. So little fear did smugglers inspire that burglars adopted that disguise in 1782 upon entering the Suffolk town of Orford. As a consequence, "no notice was taken of them," and the thieves successfully broke into several homes toward nightfall. Elsewhere, lest villagers dare to interfere, smugglers occasionally masqueraded as ghosts or spread rumors of haunted caves. "Ghosts, warlocks, and witches were the best and cheapest guards against vagrants strolling about at night," a veteran smuggler later reflected.[41]

The vast majority of smugglers came from humble backgrounds. Like Woodforde's connection, most were bit players, relying upon the trade to augment their meager incomes. Endemic smuggling in France was dominated by day-laborers and peasants, many of them women and children. On a December night in 1775, three hundred people, mostly peasants, assembled on the Brittany coast to take delivery of a shipment of tobacco. Armed with pistols and clubs, they blacked their faces to counter the moonlight.[42]

Economic necessity begot most nocturnal license. With subsistence a never-ending struggle, impoverished households naturally turned to poaching, smuggling, or scavenging food and fuel. "All the common people are thieves and beggars," wrote Tobias Smollett, "and I believe this is always the case with people who are extremely indigent and miserable." Crime could also be a matter of dignity and self-worth—the ability of men and women to feed and shelter their families while keeping the wolf from the door. Or, as the struggling schoolmaster John Cannon put it, the right for any "poor devil" not to be "piss against." Before robbing a London coach in 1752, John Wilks informed a friend, "I owe my landlord rent, and you must go with me to rob coaches to pay it, and we shall be made men of in a night or two's time." Similarly, the robber Daniel Drummond tried to enlist the aid of a Leeds laborer, swearing that "if they would but get as much money, as would carry them up to London, they might live like men." Theft helped to mend the psychological damage of being an apprentice, servant, or slave—taking back by night what was extracted by day. Reported an estate steward in the late seventeenth century, "All people break and steal away the fences and prey upon us as if a landlord were a common enemy." Many years later, in the English village of Bowers Row, the reported credo among poachers was, "He robs us all day, we'll rob him all night." Despite the risks of detection, some poachers kept deer antlers as trophies of their "exploits." In East Sussex, Thomas Bishe bragged to friends in 1641 that "he would have two braces of buckes and two of does out of Sir Richard Weston's ground yearely. And he had killed fower deere in one night there."[43]

Finally, as an *avocat* of the Parlement de Paris reflected, "Night oftens lends its veil to mercenary loves." Unlike poaching, pilfering, and smuggling, which normally supplemented livings, prostitution represented a major source of income for many impoverished women between the ages of fifteen and thirty. In the fifteenth and sixteenth centuries, it gradually increased as more and more women found themselves forced from customary crafts and trades. A census in 1526 reported that nearly one-tenth of Venice's fifty-five thousand residents were nightwalkers. Every metropolis and numerous provincial cities and towns contained sizable numbers, some quartered in brothels while most populated streets and drinking houses. A visitor to Norwich in 1681 reported, "This town swarms with alehouses, and every one of them they tell is alsoe a bawdy house." Already by the late seventeenth century, Boston and Philadelphia were beset by prostitutes, while of New York City in 1744, a friend informed Dr. Alexander Hamilton that the Battery after dark "was a good way for a stranger to fit himself with a courtezan." London, by that time, according to a conservative estimate contained three thousand nightwalkers. A correspondent to the *Public Advertiser* reported that it was "next to impossible" to go anywhere in the city in the evening "without meeting with some gross insult from them, or being presented with scenes of the most abominable obscenity."[44]

For needy young women with scant training, alternatives to prostitution were few, limited mostly to toiling as seamstresses or servants. Although many were victimized by violence and venereal disease, prostitutes found a rare measure of autonomy in a trade that defied patriarchal authority. "Freedom is the most precious gem a courtesan possesses and contains within itself everything she desires," observes a courtesan in Francesco Pona's *La Lucerna* (1630). No longer was one "subject to the tyranny of husband or parents." More vulnerable than most women, prostitutes were also more independent, especially nightwalkers, who operated outside a brothel's strictures. Controlling their own bodies and labor, they were foul-mouthed, boisterous, and outspoken—in short, "insolent." "A whore is not a woman," commented a writer, "as being obliged to relinquish all those frailties that render the sex weak and contemptible."[45]

To gauge from trials conducted at London's Old Bailey, prostitutes were prone to violence. While some received protection from male "bullies," most seem to have been on their own. Not only did they steal coins and watches from clients too drunk or tired to care, but they also resorted to brute force—either stabbing victims or pinning their arms while emptying their pockets. "They opened my breeches, and took my money out," testified John Catlin in 1743 against two women, one of whom had first "clapped her arms" around his chest. Joseph Lasebee, robbed by two prostitutes in an alley, was forcibly detained by one as the other fled. "She d——d me, and would not let me go: it struck such a terror upon me, I did not know whether she would cut my throat."[46]

Often, too, violence erupted at night in exhibitions of bravado by gangs of young men. Capitals and provincial towns, cities from Padua to New York, all suffered, to varying degrees, nocturnal tumults led by males flexing their muscles, their numbers far in excess of the aristocratic libertines out and about. Apprentices and laborers, their spirits leavened by youth, dominated bands, joined some evenings by servants and, in the colonies, by slaves and free blacks. Fairly typical was the early-eighteenth-century complaint of the Leipzig city council: "Late in the evening many apprentices, boys, maids and such unmarried folk are found idly in the streets, where they practice many improper things," shouting and "running about." In the French city of Laval, disturbances during the eighteenth century occurred in different neighborhoods "almost every night." *Coureurs de nuit* (night ramblers), they were called. In Italian cities, such gangs were known as *nottolónes*. Residents of Coventry, fretted an official in 1605, "are afraide almost to lye in their owne howses in safety" due to "lewde youthes." Remonstrances spoke of "nightly riots and disorders," and "tumultuous companies of men, children and negroes." In the Pyrenean village of Limoux, a dozen youths were said to assemble "in one particular house, where they decide what disturbance they will create each night."[47]

For maximum impact, noise, the louder the better, was a critical element. Angry curses, obscene ballads, and random gunshots proclaimed the sovereignty of youth at night, daring respectable households to contest their reign. German youths grew infamous for yodeling (*Jauchzen*), while in Denmark running amok through towns (*grassatgang*) was a favorite ritual. Even in a small Swiss village, a person complained in 1703, "The young unmarried fellows rush around the lanes emitting horrible yells and yodels, whistling and shouting." Often, horns, trumpets, and other musical instruments magnified the cacophony, as did town bells, which slumbering citizens sometimes mistook for fire alarms. In Philadelphia, "great numbers of Negroes & others" each night sat about the courthouse, with milk pails for drums. Bolder still was the reaction of slaves on a Jamaican sugar plantation after the accidental drowning of the overseer's nephew. In his diary, Thomas Thistlewood, the overseer, recorded, "Last night between 8 and 9 o'clock heard a shell blow on the river, and afterwards in the night, two guns fired, with a loud huzza after each, on the river against our negroe's houses, for joy that my kinsman is dead I imagine. Strange impudence."[48]

Vandalism often followed. Dwellings received the brunt of the damage—walls splattered with mud and excrement, brass knockers torn from their hinges, and windows shattered by stones. A dead cat might be hung on the front door. Street lanterns were especially vulnerable. Besides the destructive delight that could be derived from broken glass, the faint glow of lamps threatened a band's anonymity. Manchester youths on a March night in 1752 stole numerous doorknockers only after first destroying "a great number of lamps in most of the principal streets." Soon after the installation of overhead lamps in Paris in 1667, an ordinance threatened to punish "pages, lackeys, and all other persons of bad life and disturbers of public peace and security who would break any lanterns." Alternatively, when a Laval merchant left his house to investigate a street disturbance, a youth urged his compatriots to "shoot anyone who has a candle."[49]

Nor was the countryside exempt. Rural homes fell prey to nocturnal assaults, as did orchards, barns, and small outbuildings. In one seventeenth-century village, a set of youths routinely visited a farmer's well-kept yard "to discharge their bellies." Pranks included masquerading as werewolves and fixing candles onto the backs of animals to give the appearance of ghosts. Worse, fishponds might be poisoned, trees uprooted, and ricks of hay set ablaze. In "The Legend of Sleepy Hollow," Washington Irving's rustic character Brom Bones and his gang of "rough riders" vandalize Ichabod Crane's schoolhouse one night "so that the poor schoolmaster began to think all the witches in the country held their meetings there."[50]

As tests of daring and physical strength, gangs occasionally battled one another in the streets, proudly displaying their wounds the next morning. Night was their proving ground. The sudden sighting of a band from a neighboring parish or village invariably mobilized youths. On Guernsey, ministers complained in 1633 of young men running "in great companies from parish to parish and place to place, as a consequence of which there often occur various assaults, excesses and debauchery." In 1673, a small group of Northamptonshire servants, returning one spring night with fresh beer, was badly beaten by rival villagers with stakes. "Mr. Baxter's man," reported Thomas Isham of Lamport, "has had his skull laid bare in several places and almost fractured."[51]

Passersby also fell victim to bloodshed. One night in 1513, a company of Munich adolescents resolved "to beat to death the first man they met in the street." After sparing a poor soul with just one arm, they fell upon a servant of the Duke of Wirtenberg in a "test of courage." Students in Padua "take a barbarous liberty in the evenings," John Evelyn discovered. His party was forced to arm themselves with pistols to "defend" their doors. Most persons understandably gave wide berth to marauding bands. Pepys, in fear of apprentices "abroad in the fields," made certain, early one evening, to reach home by dark.[52]

Usually, gangs displayed greater discrimination. Favorite targets included travelers and other outsiders. "It was not safe for any stranger, much lesse for an Englishman," Fynes Moryson found in Hamburg, "to walke abroade after dinner, when the common people are generally heated with drinke." Adolescent girls made easy prey, with most attacks limited to jostling and tousled hair, acts charged with sexuality. Aggravated assaults, however, were not unknown. In Dijon during the fifteenth century, artisans and laborers grew notorious for gang rapes. As many as twenty assaults occurred each year, with perhaps one-half of the city's adult male population having participated as adolescents. In The Hague, David Beck and a married couple, strolling at night, were beset by six or more servants, who, mistaking the woman for a prostitute, tried to tear her away for themselves. Attacks upon servant girls were frequent occurrences in London, whereas a young woman in seventeenth-century Massachusetts had a lantern stripped from her hands before being molested by a "company of rude boys," of whom one repeatedly "put his hand under" her "apron & spake filthey beastly words." Deflowering young women, at its heart, savagely mocked the established order sworn to upholding their good name before marriage—an ever-graver affront when men of marginal status were the assailants.[53]

At risk each night were the pillars themselves of that order, including merchants, shopkeepers, and local officials. Night exposed society's fault lines. "There is no insult that I have not received," a salt-tax collector in Limoux bewailed. In the rural community of Ötelfingen, the treasurer, having incurred "the Night Boy's revenge," had his fence torn down and eight cords of wood scattered on the ground. Clerics of all habits found themselves bedeviled by bands. "Like looking for Easter eggs," was how Swiss laborers in 1529 described plans for driving "trashy priests" from "their hiding places." Few targets were spared, no matter how sacred. A small band of adolescents in 1718 invaded a Norfolk church just after midnight. Besides ringing the bells, drinking strong beer, and vandalizing pews, they built a fire in the belfry for cooking beefsteaks. In Dijon, armed bands—*malvivantz*—were blamed for breaking the windows of "persons of quality," including "Messieurs du Parlement." Married men made equally tempting targets. Paragons of middle-class propriety, they incited cries of "Go to bed! Go to bed!" when caught on public streets in a French village. Shouted an angry youth, "I will not listen to you. You are married. On to sleep with your wife."[54]

Less often did slaves or free blacks, risking worse retribution, resort to violence. Assaults on whites were few, though there was striking exceptions. A law passed in Massachusetts in 1703 referred to the "great disorders, insolencies, and burglaries" committed at night by "Indians, negro and molatto servants and slaves." In Northumberland County, Virginia, a slave named Dick in 1752 took a broad axe to the head of his sleeping master. Less than two years later, in Bridgetown, Barbados, following an "abundance of mischief" for "some time past," four blacks knocked down, bruised, and cut "a white man, passing quietly along one night." Nicholas

Cresswell, walking one evening with a friend in Barbados, received "a shower of stones from a Mangeneel grove by some Negroes." Years later, a black man in Boston, upon exchanging insults with several white gentlemen, muttered as he walked away, "If it was night, and I had a good cudgel in my hand, how would I make them rascals run." Instead, in the broad light of day, he was arrested and punished for his impudence.[55]

In much of the early modern world, one finds the lower orders in *de facto* control of the nocturnal landscape, putting to flight passersby in their paths. Theirs were not the traditional "weapons of the weak," such as feigning illness and footdragging, employed during the day to circumvent the established order. Nor were they play-acting, as celebrants sometimes did at ritualistic festivities like Carnival.[56] Determined in their purpose, bands aggressively laid claim to the hours of darkness. Francis Place, the "radical tailor of Charing Cross," recalled how he and fellow apprentices would "go to Temple Bar in the evening, set up a shouting and clear the pavement between that and Fleet Market of all the persons there." Of one escapade, a contemporary described assaulting "every one we met," breaking lamps, kicking "strumpets," and abusing the watch. The slightest challenge to the young's supremacy invited violence—"knocking down all" who dared "to reprove" them, a person wrote of London apprentices. Students in Padua ranged at will. A visitor observed, "None dare stir abroad after it grows dark for fear of scholars and others who walk up and down most part of the night, with carbines and pistols, 20 or 30 in a company, everyone habited in dark cloaths." In the colonial city of Charleston, South Carolina, even slaves and free blacks roamed freely some evenings, prompting a grand jury to condemn the riotous behavior of slaves in city streets "at all times in the night." In urban neighborhoods, where the young and the poor were most concentrated, their power was greatest. But neither did small communities escape violence. When a master tailor in Limoux left the safety of his home to investigate noise from the street, he was met by stones. "You scoundrel," a youth scolded him, "how dare you venture out against so large a gang! I thumb my nose at you and the whole town."[57]

So menacing were the young and dispossessed and so great were their numbers that only the hardiest members of the nightwatch dared to challenge their supremacy, especially when lives were not imperiled. Guards in

Laval, according to eighteenth-century reports, frequently retreated in order "to avoid greater danger." In Boston, when three watchmen came across a young band at 2:00 A.M., they desisted from apprehending them after being threatened with a sword—"one of the watchmen being very much affrightened cryed out Murder, the other two having no assistance quitted the young men and they made off." Outmanned and underarmed, watchmen were themselves favorite targets. Far from restoring public order, they were frequently assaulted, or "scoured," as gangs boasted. A band of Coventry youths, having "scattered the watchmen," repaired to "alehouses by way of triumphe." No braver was the watch in London's St James's Park, "over-run" with prostitutes. "What can half a dozen men, that are half starved with cold and hunger, do with forty or fifty abandoned wretches, whose trade makes them desperate?" asked a newspaper correspondent in 1765.[58]

Some areas, such as London's Black Boy Alley, authorities avoided at all costs, fearing a shower of brickbats and bottles. Where lamps hung by day, they were knocked down by night. Yet more perilous were night-cellars, which Sir John Fielding declared "a terror to the watchmen." Of one cellar, the watch complained, "We are afraid to enter at any time upon any occasion, for if we do, the candles are all put out, and the constables are severely beaten."[59] Rural officers fared little better. In southern England, smugglers brazenly assaulted dragoons. "Often times these are attacked in the night with such numbers," related Defoe, "that they dare not resist, or if they do, they are wounded and beaten, and sometimes kill'd." In Spain, remarked a visitor, peasants who trembled "at the bayonet in the face of day" grew "bold with the knife in the hour of darkness."[60]

Not that every city, town, and village resounded at night with the triumphant cries of the lower orders. Many evenings found the typical laborer prostrate in bed, hoping for rest in preparation for another punishing day. Otherwise, drinking pints, courting, and raiding orchards always drew far greater numbers than exhibitions of mayhem and violence. In all likelihood, the midnight experience in 1600 of a servant and two friends in Essex, who, after a wedding, repaired to a neighbor's wheat field to snare rabbits, was much more common. Similarly, of a Sunday evening, the Buckinghamshire farmworker Joseph Mayett recalled, "I set off down to

William Hogarth, *The Idle 'Prentice Betrayed by a Prostitute* (pl. 9 of *Industry and Idleness*), 1747. The raucous interior of a night-cellar, which many watchmen wisely avoided, unlike those in the engraving. In addition to Tom Idle's exchange of stolen merchandise, there are images of a brawl, a soldier urinating against a rear wall, and a corpse being dumped into the cellar, the victim of Tom's villainy.

the town where I met with a girl that had worked for my master in the haytime and stayed with her until nearly midnight when I left her in order to return home, but meeting with two more of my companions in vice we presently agreed to go and rob a pear tree." That accomplished, Mayett returned to the orchard several nights later, only to flee after the arrival of other thieves.[61]

Despite the multiracial cast of some colonial bands, there was no unified counterculture at night. Dominating the landscape instead was a cluster of overlapping subcultures, some more cohesive than others. Certainly, few groups anywhere could match, in longevity or internal discipline, the formal youth groups that in France had a hand in fostering nocturnal disturbances; or, for that matter, the "night-kingdoms" of West Indian slaves, replete with monarchs, regiments, and flags. In 1805, an investigation uncovered a slave conspiracy in Trinidad plotted by several "kings," each with his own courtiers and army.[62] Instead, most nocturnal gangs, grounded in casual associations, possessed neither distinctive ranks nor their own ceremonies. Unlike guilds, for example, there was no established hierarchy, uniform membership, or fixed code of behavior. This was only natural in light of the values they epitomized of personal autonomy and self-assertion. On the other hand, members shared common bonds of friendship. Vagabonds, roaming in small groups, typically referred to one another as "brethren" and "walk-fellows," with some swearing "by their soul" never to betray a comrade. So strong was the "fraternall affection" uniting London apprentices, claimed a writer in 1647, that they instinctively followed the credo, "Knock him down, he wrongs a prentice." And in Paris, when a young band of servants on a winter night in 1749 spied the city watch marching three soldiers to jail, one of the domestics exclaimed, "We've got to jump those bastards; we can't let them haul off three good boys." A nearby coachman, ready to join the fray, was barely restrained by his bourgeois master. Members of the lower orders shared familiar songs and slang as well as customary haunts and meeting places, which they routinely frequented at night, employing their mastery of the nocturnal terrain. A London newspaper spoke, for example, of "the dialect of the night-cellar." Not only did reliance on "cant" strengthen social ties, but it also concealed conversations from one's betters.[63]

Most of all, these diverse subcultures shared common adversaries and a familiar vision of life, freedom from the constraints of the visible world and domineering masters of all sorts (adults, parents, employers, and owners)—a mentality that night reinforced and intensified by creating a coherent experience very different from daily life. According to an Italian proverb, "The dogs of Casaserro in the daytime, they are ready to kill one another, and in the night time, they go out a robbing together."[64]

IV

. . . In night all creatures sleep;
Only the malcontent, that 'gainst his fate
Repines and quarrels. . . .

JOHN MARSTON, ca. 1600[65]

Such, then, was the alternate realm inhabited by substantial segments of the early modern population on both sides of the Atlantic Ocean. One can only speculate on the broader consequences this nocturnal universe had for the character of daily life, including whether its impact had any positive value from the perspective of the established order. It is after all true that some youth groups contributed to social control, disciplining adulterers, abusive husbands, and cuckolds for violating common morality. Often occurring at night, *charivaris* in France, *mattinata* in Italy, and "skimmington rides" in England subjected errant neighbors to "rough music," mockery, and on occasion, physical abuse. Such traditional rituals helped to reaffirm the sanctity of marriage, which the young themselves expected one day to embrace. For the same reason, bachelors were known to battle adolescent bands from rival communities in order to protect the virginity of local maidens. And, too, gangs of apprentices sometimes razed houses of prostitution, prompting Charles II to inquire incredulously, "Why do they go to them then?"[66]

Still, did these bands represent moral watchdogs or, more often perhaps, wolves in sheeps' clothing? For there remains a strong possibility that such outbursts served as a frequent pretext for mischief, as the historian Daniel Fabre has remarked in noting the contradiction of "achieving order through disorder." An early eighteenth-century poem, "The Libertine's Choice," suggested as much in recounting the drunken antics of the young when attacking brothels: "When thus well freighted with the chearful juice, / We'd sally forth and give our selves a loose, / Break brothel windows, scowre the crazy watch, / And with fresh mischiefs crown the nights debauch." *Charivaris*, despite their conservative purpose, were condemned, beginning in the sixteenth century, by civil and religious leaders. Too often, from the authorities' point of view, these "nocturnal assemblies" degenerated into riots. "Frequently there are brawls," Felix Platter observed in France.[67] Further, the incidence of such popular rituals, however an expression of communal values, paled in comparison to the number of times bands voiced slogans and perpetrated violence diametrically opposed to the prevailing social order.

So, also, in the political realm, the threat of nighttime violence enforced conformity. In English and American cities, especially during the eighteenth century, street crowds celebrated military triumphs as well as more radical causes by compelling households to place lit candles in their windows—those that did not thus signal their solidarity risked having their homes pelted with rocks. Of anti-Irish mobs on a summer evening in London in 1736, an onlooker reported, "Late that night assembled many hundred disturbers of the peace, proclaiming thro' the streets a law of their own making, viz. *that every Englishman should put out lights in their windows*; and then the cry run, *Down with the Irish*." Whatever the source of agitation, the "mob," rather than guardians of the law, controlled the streets after dark.[68]

Perhaps, in the eyes of authorities, nighttime served the well-known function of a safety valve, a concept familiar to the age. Resigned to the human capacity for sin, proponents favored channeling mortal appetites in ways least harmful to the established order—hence the cathartic value of holidays for letting off steam. Argued a petitioner defending a Feast of Fools before the Paris Faculty of Theology in 1444: "Such a diversion is necessary, because folly, which is our second nature and seems inherent to man, can thus express itself at least once a year. Wine barrels will burst if one does not occasionally release the plug to give them some air."[69] Customary in rural Britain were evening feasts held by farmers for laborers at the end of the yearly harvest. These "harvest suppers" were renown for generous offerings of food, drink, and good fellowship. According to Henry Bourne, "At this the servant and his master are alike, and every thing is done with an equal freedom." But, of course, such occasions, considered all together, were fleeting respites whose provisional nature underscored the necessity to resume anew one's normal life. As Henry Fielding noted in 1751, "The diversions of the people have been limited and restrained to certain seasons." After Carnival followed the spartan regimen of Lent. Of harvest suppers, the Wiltshire poet Stephen Duck remarked,

"The next morning soon reveals the cheat, / When the same toils we must again repeat."[70]

Night, by contrast, was neither a set piece of ritual license nor a temporary escape from reality. Instead, it represented an alternate reality for a substantial segment of the preindustrial population, a realm of its own that, at a minimum, implicitly challenged the institutions of the workaday world. As a resident of Maryland said of slaves, "Though you have them slaves all the day, they are not so in the night." Nor were night's excesses limited just to the hours of darkness. Aftershocks from an evening's merriment reverberated past dawn. "The next morning," noted a writer of the typical journeyman mechanic, "he is both too ill and too lazy for work." William West, an apprentice to a London cutler, returning home from "bouts of revelry," typically stank of drink and would "swear and curse and throw his tools away." Stolen livestock and crops, besotted servants, weary slaves, broken fences and windows, not to mention assorted cuts, scrapes, and bruises, numbered among the inventory of damages that darkness bequeathed, lending force to the Elizabethan saying, "Midnight feastings are great wasters, / Servants' riots undo masters."[71]

Superiors frequently expressed exasperation over their dependents' revels. Complaints echoed across the Atlantic of "wicked" and "impudent" inferiors, as "bold" and "saucy" as they were "thievish." One Leeds master, out of desperation, lashed his servant to a bed. Others took to locking doors with padlocks. John Clare, while a gardener's apprentice, was confined each night to an outbuilding to prevent him from stealing fruit.[72] Nevertheless, inferiors regularly outwitted their masters, usually waiting until families had retired to bed. Many domestics had access to keys. Clare escaped out a window, stealing "every opportunity" to visit a nearby village for his "midnight revels." Moreover, if laborers found their tenure too restrictive, they could elect in the future to serve another master, as many evidently did, "running from place to place," fumed a critic. Upon hearing a friend bemoan his punishment for lying out all night, Richard Wilkinson retorted, "What need of that? There [are] more masters than parish churches."[73]

Slaves, of course, lacked that opportunity; still, they faced few obstacles at night if bent on escaping their quarters, which on plantations stood apart from the residences of owners and overseers. There was little that a master could do. Landon Carter, who generally resigned himself to their rambles, placed his slave Jimmy under surveillance one evening only because earlier protestations of lameness had kept him from working. "They that cannot work for me," groused Carter, "cannot without great deceit walk 2 or 3 miles in the night." George Washington, while president, attributed "the fatigue and drowsiness" of his slaves to "night-walking, and other practices which unfit them for the duties of the day." An absentee planter, Washington expressed alarm over the extent of theft by his slaves, for which he blamed the nighttime "frolicking" of negligent overseers. Not until the nineteenth century would masters systematically spread ghost tales among slaves to deter their travels, with overseers impersonating spirits by donning white sheets.[74]

The prevalence of nocturnal revelry also alarmed authorities. Whatever cathartic value nighttime once possessed increasingly diminished over time. Unlike isolated acts of crime, violence by roving bands raised fears of social disorder, especially when leading citizens were targeted for abuse—the affront to established authority exceeded only by their sense of personal injury. Some officials, to impose order, resorted to curfews not unlike medieval restrictions. Large towns and small enacted injunctions, with the young and dispossessed singled out for sanctions. During periodic rioting in the sixteenth and seventeenth centuries, London officials vainly tried to impose curfews on apprentices. In the city of Bratislava, officials during the early eighteenth century threatened paupers, Jews, and other "disorderly people" at night with military conscription. Meanwhile, American colonies up and down the eastern seaboard mandated that servants, slaves, free blacks, Indians, and adolescents all retire early to their homes, usually by nine o'clock.[75]

Rather than performing the function of a safety valve, nocturnal license helped to pave the way instead for greater disorder. Not only did nighttime suggest an alternate way of life, but organized violence among the lower classes most often erupted after dark. For reasons habitual as well tactical, obscurity was their preferred stage. In Britain, apprentices, hedge-breakers, Spitalfields weavers, and Jacobins all drew on a long-standing tradition of nocturnal revelry and resistance, as did vandals of turnpikes and dikes. The Waltham Blacks, boasted a member in 1723, "could raise 2,000 men in a night's time." Often, darkness was central to prolonged hours of preparation in remote locations. In order to drill with the United Irishmen, a secret society pledged, beginning in the mid-1790s, to home rule, the adolescent John "Michael" Martin made off from home once his parents fell asleep. "The meetings," he later recalled, "were generally appointed at different places each night—sometimes near my father's; and frequently many miles off."[76]

Almost everywhere, arsonists struck at night, from incendiaries in Chesapeake tobacco fields to bands of *mordbrenner* in Central Europe. The vicar of a Hampshire village lamented in 1729, "As oft as night returns we are all under the dreadful apprehension of having our houses & barns fired."[77] In 1712, upwards of thirty slaves in New York City ignited a building and then killed a handful of whites drawn to fight the blaze. Time and again, slave insurrections were set for the dead of night—for example, conspiracies in Barbados (1675 and 1816), Stono in South Carolina (1739), Tacky's Revolt in Jamaica (1760), and the Virginia rebellions of Gabriel Prosser (1800) and Nat Turner (1832). Most plots involved nights of clandestine meetings to map strategy, with messengers crossing miles of terrain in the dark or, in the West Indies, beating drums or blowing conch shells to summon conspirators. Often, midnight became the bleeding edge of early-morning violence. On the eve of the American Revolution, such was the close association between slaves and nocturnal resistance that some Loyalists dreamed of enlisting black support against their Whig enemies. A Maryland Tory reputedly declared, "If I had a few more white people to join me, I could get all the negroes in the county to back us, and they would do more good in the night than the white people could in the day."[78]

Besides secrecy and surprise, darkness afforded insurgents other familiar advantages. In England, for instance, fenland commoners in 1653 routed at midnight a military guard appointed to protect drainage works in Norfolk. Unfamiliar with the local terrain, the soldiers put up a weak defense, having "lost themselves in the night." Even the distant rumble of advancing cavalry, the Luddites knew, could better be heard in the still darkness. Magic, too, occasionally played a supporting role. Conspirators in the New York uprising of 1712 believed that a supernatural powder would make them invincible. During the nights leading up to an abortive slave rebellion on Antigua in 1736, an obeahman administered a ritual oath to conspirators. In southern Ireland, agrarian rebels known as White Boys, whose nighttime musters attracted hundreds of followers, even called themselves "fairies," as much to bolster morale as to intimidate their adversaries. Years later, for the same reasons, peasant rioters in France, dressed in white robes, adopted the name *Demoiselles*, "white fairies of the past." Because, for the lower orders, night represented their day, it also became their chosen field of battle for insurgencies large and small. Luddites, having drilled in darkness for many evenings, proclaimed in the cropper's song, "Night by night, when all is still, / And the moon is hid behind the hill, / We forward march to do our will / With hatchet, pike and gun!"[79]

PART FOUR

PRIVATE WORLDS

PRELUDE

Half our dayes wee passe in the shadowe of the earth, and the brother of death exacteth a third part of our lives.

SIR THOMAS BROWNE, n.d.[1]

"WHAT," ASKED JOHN MILTON, "hath night to do with sleep?" Surprisingly little, perhaps, at the inception of the human race. Contrary to common belief, our earliest ancestors may not have instinctively slept after dark. The custom of reserving nighttime for rest, some psychologists now surmise, evolved gradually among prehistoric peoples. Only with the passage of time did these first generations learn to sleep away the dangers of darkness by resting in caves, sheltered from foraging predators. Sleep made nighttime seem both shorter and safer. Rather than night, according to the Talmud, having been created for sleep, self-preservation may have required that sleep be reserved for night. "Man slept through the dark hours," Stanley Coren has remarked, "because it was too inefficient and too dangerous to do anything else." Intense physiological activity during intervals of dreaming might have served the purpose of a sentinel, readying the body to respond quickly to imminent peril. Irregular heart rates and respiration, muscular twitches, and eye movements, all may have permitted potential prey to awaken prepared for battle or flight.[2]

Whether "diurnal man" evolved slowly or emerged, instead, practically overnight, genetically configured from day's first dawn, certainly by the early modern era nocturnal repose had become inseparable from life's natural order. Despite the high level of human activity after dark, never was there any doubt that sleep remained best suited for evening hours.

"We must follow the course of nature," affirmed Thomas Cogan, a Manchester physician, "to wake in the day, and sleepe in the night." Thus in the imaginary world of the *Leigerdumaynians*, where none stirred but at night, reigned thieves, usurers, and knaves. "They hate the sun," related the Elizabethan satirist Joseph Hall, "and love the moone."[3]

Few characteristics of sleep in past ages have received examination since Samuel Johnson complained in 1753 that "so liberal and impartial a benefactor" should "meet with so few historians." More even than the subject of night itself, sleep has long eluded historical attention. "Our entire history," lamented the eighteenth-century scholar Georg Christoph Lichtenberg, "is only the history of waking men." Sleep in preindustrial communities remains largely unstudied, for only the subject of dreams has drawn sustained scrutiny.[4] Historical indifference has stemmed partly from a seeming shortage of sources, in particular our misguided notion that contemporaries rarely reflected upon a state of existence at once common yet hidden from the waking world. In truth, however, buried within such disparate evidence as diaries, medical books, imaginative literature, and legal depositions are regular references to sleep, often lamentably terse but nonetheless revealing. Far from being ignored, the subject frequently absorbed people's thoughts.

And, too, the relative tranquillity of modern slumber has dulled perceptions of sleep's past importance. Much like the Scottish cleric Robert Wodrow, historians appear to have concluded that "sleep can scarce be justly reconed part of our life." Lacking the drama and intensity of life's waking hours, sleep has suffered from its association with indolence and inactivity. Whereas our daily lives are animated, volatile, and highly differentiated, sleep seems, by contrast, passive, monotonous, and uneventful—qualities scarcely designed to spark the interest of historians dedicated to charting change across time, the faster-paced the better. "I cannot see how sleeping can offend any one," contends Porco in *The Universal Passion* (1737), an attitude that could easily explain our current ignorance.[5]

CHAPTER TEN

ORDINANCES OF THE BEDCHAMBER: RITUALS

I

There is not any one thing in the constitution of animals which is more to be wonder'd at than sleep.

WEEKLY REGISTER, OR, UNIVERSAL JOURNAL, SEPT. 22, 1738[1]

AMONG LEARNED AUTHORITIES, a night's sound slumber was thought critical not only for withered spirits but also for bodily health. Most medical opinion by the late Middle Ages still embraced the Aristotelian belief that the impetus for sleep originated in the abdomen by means of a process called *concoction.* Once food has been digested in the stomach, Thomas Cogan explained in *The Haven of Health* (1588), fumes ascend to the head "where through coldnesse of the braine, they being congealed, doe stop the conduites and waies of the senses, and so procure sleepe." Not only did nighttime invite repose "by its moisture, silence and darkness," but those properties were thought enormously well suited to concoction.[2] Among sleep's other salutary effects, according to William Vaughan in 1607, it "strengthenth all the spirits," "comforteth the body," "taketh away sorrow," and "asswageth furie of the mind." Noted an Italian adage, "Bed is a medicine."[3] A parallel belief was that by retiring early, one could best reap the benefits of slumber. "By going early to asleep and early from it, we rise refreshed, lively and active," claimed the author of *An Easy Way to Prolong Life* (1775). How widespread this notion was may be seen in such proverbs as "Go to bed with the lamb and rise with the lark," and, well before it was adopted by Benjamin Franklin, "Early to bed and early to rise makes a man healthy, wealthy, and wise."[4]

Less clear, in retrospect, was the time of night intended by the injunction "early to bed," a judgment, perhaps, that truly rested in the heavy-lidded eyes of the beholder. Did popular convention favor sunset or some later hour as a time for repose? Another proverb affirmed, "One hour's sleep before midnight is worth three after," suggesting that going to bed "early" may have borne an altogether different meaning from retiring at the onset of darkness.[5] And while contemporaries routinely lauded sleep's contributions to personal health, they even more frequently scorned excessive slumber. Sleep's purpose, emphasized the author of *The Whole Duty of Man* (1691), is to restore "our frail bodies" to "make us more profitable" spiritually and materially, "not more idle." Imbued by a strong work ethic, Puritans in England and America often railed against what Richard Baxter called "unnecessary sluggishness," but so, too, did myriad others who were increasingly time-conscious by the sixteenth century. Most condemned immoderate slumber for its sinful association with idleness and sloth, but it was also thought dangerous to personal health. Apart from a heightened propensity for lechery, ill consequences included damaged digestion, undernourished blood, and troubled spirits. "Much slep ingendereth diseases and payne, / It dulles the wyt and hurteth the brayne," claimed *The Schoole of Vertue* in 1557. Far better, remarked an author, "to redeem as much time from sleeping as our health will permit, and not profusely waste it in that state of darkness so nearly resembling death." It was "to *redeem* more *time*" that in 1680 the English Puritan Ralph Thoresby, determined to rise every morning by five o'clock, devised an early alarm clock. "So much precious time," he regretted, having already been slept away.[6]

What, in the eyes of moralists and physicians, was the proper amount of sleep? Several authorities, like the Tudor physician Andrew Boorde, believed that sleep needed to be taken as the "complexcyon of man" required. One author singled out porters, laborers, carvers, and sailors as exceptions deserving more than his standard recommendation of eight hours.[7] Some prescribed seasonal adjustments, such as sleeping eight hours in the summer and nine hours during long winter evenings. In a distinct minority, Jeremy Taylor, onetime chaplain to Charles I (1600–1649), prescribed a nightly regimen of only three hours.[8] More commonly, writers, not just in Britain but throughout the Continent, urged from six to eight hours in bed, unless special circumstances such as illness, melancholy, or just a large supper mandated more. Fundamental to most of this spillage of ink was the conviction that not more than one quarter to one third of every twenty-four hours should be allotted to nightly repose.[9]

At least that is what writers on the subject of sleep reasoned. Although medical books were widely reprinted (Thomas Elyot's *Castel of Helthe*, appearing in 1539, went through more than a dozen editions in the sixteenth century), it is difficult to gauge their influence. Whether these opinions shaped popular mores or instead reflected them, as seems likely, common aphorisms expressed similar attitudes toward sleep's proper length. The adage "Six hours' sleep for a man, seven for a woman, and eight for a fool" had numerous variations. Different in substance but alike in tone was "Nature requires five, *custom takes seven* [my italics], laziness nine, and wickedness eleven." The physician Guglielmo Gratarolo, in *A Direction for the Health of Magistrates and Studentes* (1574), pointedly distinguished slumber of eight hours duration according to "common custome" from more prolonged sleep in "ancient time" as Hippocrates had advised.[10]

To be certain, some laborers retired early, exhausted from the day's toil, especially in rural areas during summer months. In the winter, frigid temperatures occasionally hastened families to bed. The schoolmaster David Beck one January evening retired prematurely, "not being able to do anything because of the cold."[11] And at least a few individuals went to bed to conserve fuel and light. Instructs a character in the Restoration comedy *The Projectors* (1665), "Eat little, drink less, and sleep much, to save fire and candle-light."[12] Still, few adults beneath the higher ranks could afford to sleep more than six to eight hours, much less the entire night, for both work and sociability claimed precious hours of their own.

Diaries, though weighted toward the upper classes, not only suggest as much but also indicate that the standard bedtime fell between nine and ten o'clock. "This family goes to bed between 9 and 10," noted Dame Sarah Cowper, a rule that likely applied to other social ranks. "Breeches-off time" was the customary term for nine o'clock in parts of Germany, whereas a seventeenth-century English proverb instructed, "To sup at six and go to bed at ten, will make a man live ten times ten." Consider, wrote a London resident in 1729, "the life of a careful honest man who is industrious all day at his trade . . . spends the evening in innocent mirth with his family, or perhaps with his neighbors or brother tradesmen; sometimes sits an hour or two at an alehouse, and from thence goes to bed by 10 and is at work by 5 or 6." An inscription over the parlor of a Danish pastor read: "Stay til nine you are my friend, til ten, that is alright, but if you stay til 11, you are my enemy."[13]

Of course, not only did large numbers of people routinely remain awake past ten o'clock, but personal curfews, whatever the hour, proved elastic. Although the writer Thomas Tusser advised, "In winter at nine, and in summer at ten," seasonal variations appear to have been minor. More important, as in other traditional cultures, bedtime often depended less upon a fixed timetable than upon the existence of things to do. Samuel Pepys, whose late hours alternated between temptations of the flesh and the burdens of government, kept a particularly erratic schedule. Others, too, worked or socialized past their normal bedtimes, in rural as well as urban settings. "Always go to bed at or before ten o'clock when it can be done," wrote the Sussex shopkeeper Thomas Turner. Although he tried to allow himself between seven and eight hours of slumber, Turner's duties as a parish officer and his thirst for drink, among other "emergent" occasions, sometimes delayed his rest. One December evening after a vestry meeting, he stumbled "home about 3:20 [A.M.] not very sober. Oh, liquor," he moaned, "what extravagances does it make us commit!"[14]

II

O Lord, now that the darke night is come, which is a signe of horror, death, and woe; and that I am to lie and sleepe on my bedde, which is an image of the grave wherein my body after this life is like to rest; let thy holy spirit so guarde, protect, direct, and comfort mee, that neither terrours of conscience, assaultes of Sathan, suggestions to sinne, fleshly concupiscence, idle slothfulnesse, nor tearefull dreames, may trouble mee.

W. F., 1609[15]

In 1764, readers of the *London Chronicle* learned that "an extraordinary sleeper" near the French village of Mons for fifteen years had slept each day from three in the morning until eight or nine at night. Such mysteries of sleep, including instances of narcolepsy and sleepwalking, received lengthy exploration both in literary works and newspapers. Whether in *Macbeth*, *Henry V*, or *Julius Caesar*, many of Shakespeare's works patently appealed to a popular preoccupation with sleep. And not just dreams, long a source of fascination in their own right. Oliver Goldsmith recounted in the pages of the *Westminster Magazine* the story of Cyrillo Padovano, a pious Paduan, who stole from a convent and plundered a cemetery while walking in his sleep—undoing in his slumber "all the good actions for which he had been celebrated by day." In his journal, James Boswell, who thought sleep "one of the most unaccountable and marvellous" wonders of nature, recorded that he and another attorney once conducted a brief conversation while both were asleep in their beds.[16]

For the most part, these curiosities represented aberrations born in the shadowlands separating sleep from wakefulness. Vastly more relevant to most people was the quality of their own repose. "To sleep soundly is a treasure," proclaimed an Italian adage. Nicholas Breton deemed poor slumber, by contrast, one of the greatest "miseries in the life of man." After all, explained a French author, "Sleep and waking being the hinges on which all the others of our life do hang, if there be any irregularity in these, confusion and disorder must needs be expected in all the rest." Such was its importance that sleep inspired a typology more nuanced than that routinely employed today. The widely used expressions "dog," "cat," or "hare" sleep referred to slumber that was not only light but anxious. "He is so wary," wrote the cleric Thomas Fuller, "that he sleeps like a hare, with his eyes open." "Ye sleep like a dog in a mill," declared a Scottish saying.[17] More desirable was "dead" or "deep" sleep, what Boswell described as "absolute, unfeeling, and unconscious." Most coveted, still, was sleep both deep and continuous, or "soft" and "calm" as it was sometimes described. "Quiet sleep," emphasized an early text, "although it is short, bears more usefulness," a link confirmed by modern research emphasizing that whether or not individuals feel rested in the morning chiefly depends upon the number of times they awaken during the night.[18]

Families went to enormous lengths to ensure both the tranquillity and the safety of their slumber. As bedtime neared, households followed painstaking rituals. Such habitual if not compulsive behavior no doubt helped to alleviate anxieties as persons surrendered themselves to the vulnerability of sleep. "We are unable to think of, much more to provide for, our own security," noted an eighteenth-century poet. Even a cosmopolitan figure of the Enlightenment like Boswell wrote of "gloomy" nights when he was "frightened to lie down and sink into helplessness and forgetfulness." With Satan and his disciples at large—"an enemy," fretted Cowper, "who is alwaies awake"—moral dangers were many. A seventeenth-century devotion likened the devil at night to a lion pacing back and forth outside a sheepfold. Mental and physical exhaustion weakened personal defenses against intemperate passions, including the wickedness of "self-pollution." A soft bed, writers warned, helped to fuel sensual thoughts, whether one was awake or asleep. The twelfth-century theologian Alan of Lille urged Christians "to restrain stirrings of the flesh and the attacks of the devil which are the most to be feared and avoided in the darkness of this world."[19]

No less perilous were threats to life and limb. Before bed, doors and shutters were double-checked. The writer George Herbert affirmed, "Many go to bed in health, and there are found dead." Such was the alarming fate of the Hegen family in Knezta, Franken, whose members all mysteriously perished while asleep on Christmas Eve in 1558—Hans, his wife, their three sons, and a maidservant. The day before, each had been "fresh, healthy, and in good spirits." When discovered, the bodies still possessed their "natural coloring" and did not betray any injuries or wounds. From the murder of Ishbosheth to the loss of Samson's locks, men throughout

Ein sehr abscheülich vnnd aber gantz warhafftigs wunderwerck vnd geschicht/im eingang diß lauffendē 1558. Jars/im Franckenland geschehen/vñ freylich vns allen zur besondern warnung dermassen ergangen.

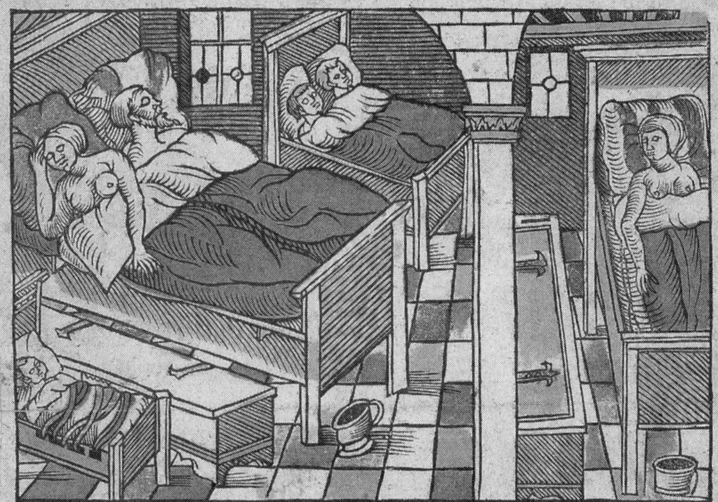

AM Heyligen Christabent diß anfahenden gegenwertigen 1558. Jars/ist Hans Hegen ein Heckers man zu Knetzka im Franckenlande/ zů angehender Nacht/ mit sampt seiner Ehewirtin/dreyen schönen Knaben/so jr baider aygne Söne gewesen vnd einer Dienstmayd/frisch/gesundt vnd wolgemůt zu beth an sein růhe gegangen/ vnnd hat sich nyder gelegt vnd geschlaffen. Aber auff volgenden morgen/ hat man sie samentlich vnd sonderlich (dieweyl sie auß des Herren vnerforschlichen gewalt alle sechs vrplützlich vnnd gähling verstorben) todt gefunden/ vnnd haben gleichwol jre natürliche farben vnnd gewonliche gestalt gehabt/darob allermenigklich ein abschewlich erschrecken/vnd die gröst verwunderung eingenommen vnd empfangen.

¶ Johannis am 8. cap. Warlich/warlich ich sage euch/ So jemandt mein wort wirdt halten/der wirdt den Todt nit sehen ewigklich. Johañis am 11. cap. Ich bin die aufferstehung vnd das leben/ Wer an mich glaubet/ der wirdt leben ob er gleich sturbe: Vnd wer da lebet vñ glaubet an mich/der wirdt nymmermehr sterbē.

¶ Gedruckt zů Nürnberg durch Georg Merckel/Wonhafft auff dem Newen baw/ bey der Kalckhüten. Anno 1558.

Georg Merckel, *The Curious Death of the Hegen Family, Christmas Eve, 1558*, sixteenth century.

history had fallen victim while asleep to their enemies, a late sixteenth-century writer reminded his readers; just as easily he could have included the grotesque demise of Sisera and the beheading of Holofernes.[20]

In preparation for sleep, families engaged in "hunts" of furniture and bedding for both fleas (*pulex irritans*) and bedbugs (*cimex lectularius*), which had arrived in Britain by the sixteenth century. Lice (*pediculus humanus*) needed to be combed from hair and picked from clothing and skin. The French expression "dirty like a comb" (*sale comme un peigne*) may have originated from this nightly task. Bugs were everywhere, especially given the proximity of dogs and livestock. To keep gnats at bay, families in the fen country of East Anglia hung lumps of cow dung at the foot of their beds, whereas John Locke advised placing the leaves of kidney beans about a bed to avert insect bites.[21]

Sheets could never be damp from washing ("dirt is better than death," observed John Byng), and in frigid weather, beds required warming with copper pans of coals or, in modest dwellings, with hot stones wrapped in rags.[22] Temperatures dipped all the more quickly once hearths were banked to keep smoldering embers alive without setting homes ablaze. "In the evening," advised the *Domostroi*, "you should again go all around the house, to look it over and to sniff out where the fires have not been banked." Some households recited verses in order to charm hearths. "Sleep my fire, like a mouse in a nest," urged a Latvian verse; whereas English families, according to John Aubrey, marked a cross in the ashes before praying. In addition, most lights were snuffed. "Every night we go to bed, we have nothing but combustibles under us and about us," warned a writer in reference to the frame houses of urban denizens.[23]

Not only windows but also chamber doors were shut to "keepe out the evil aire of the night." If homes boasted curtains, they needed to be drawn to block drafts and stave off rheumatic diseases attributed to sleeping in moonlight. Pepys, to keep from catching a cold, tried to tie his hands inside his bed. To shield heads, nightcaps were customary. "Nothing is more wholesome than to have the head well covered from the dampness of the night air," proclaimed Boswell.[24] Nightdress, for middle- and upper-class families, introduced by the sixteenth century, consisted of simple garments, mostly chemises and smocks. Women cleansed their faces of cosmetics, prompting a Spaniard to jest, "Why, after they have practiced to deceive during the day do they wish to spend the night clean?" The lower classes donned coarse "night-gear," slept unclad in "naked" beds, or remained in "day-clothes," either to save the expense of blankets or to rise quickly in the morning. The Westmorland servant Margaret Rowlandson "did not put off her clothes, being to rise early next morning to wash." On the colonial frontier, a young George Washington wrote of sleeping in his clothes "like a Negro."[25]

Within well-to-do households, feet at bedtime might be washed, beds beaten and stirred, and chamber pots set, all by servants. Laurence Sterne referred to these and other servile duties as "ordinances of the bedchamber." Of a lad in training, Pepys wrote, "I had the boy up tonight for his sister to teach him to put me to bed," which included singing or reading to his master with the aid of a "night-light," commonly a squat candle or rushlight in a perforated holder. Few persons, admittedly, went to the lengths of Henry VIII, whose bed each night was "arrayed" by ten attendants with pillows, linen sheets, and fine blankets—only after the bottom mattress had been stabbed with a dagger to guard against an assassin.[26]

To calm attacks of anxiety, individuals at bedtime swallowed medicine, which in France was called a *dormitoire*. Laudanum, a solution made from opium and diluted alcohol, was a popular potion among the propertied classes. The Sussex merchant Samuel Jeake, for a soporific, placed leaves from the poisonous plant nightshade on his forehead and temples. Tiny bags of aniseed bound to each nostril or rags spread with camomile, bread, and vinegar tied to the soles of the feet—"as hot as you can suffer"—were also believed to encourage sleep.[27] Alcohol served a dual purpose: it spurred slumber and numbed the flesh on frigid nights. Germans, said Fynes Moryson, refused to "suffer any man to goe to bed" sober. Habitual before bedtime was a *Schlafdrincke* (sleeping drink). "How many men and women go to bed drunk?" a London newspaper asked rhetorically.[28]

On the other hand, to avoid an upset stomach, common wisdom discouraged heavy suppers. Game and beef were risky at best, and sleep should not follow too quickly afterwards. As Stephen Bradwell insisted, "Let it be two houres at the soonest after supper." Even by the second half of the eighteenth century, when social elites began to ridicule such "vulgar errors," many persons clung to timeworn conventions. The diarist Sylas Neville, for instance, skipped eating meat at night, whereas Thomas Turner avoided supper altogether every Wednesday evening. "Light suppers make clean sheets," counseled an English proverb.[29] Moreover, to promote proper digestion, medical authorities urged, as Hippocrates once had, that sleep be taken on the right side of the body after first retiring—at least until the "meat" from supper "descended from the mouth of the stomach." Then, explained an early sixteenth-century scholar, it "may approche the lyver, whiche is to the stomake, as fyre under the pot, & by hym is digested." To prevent nightmares and apoplexy, among other maladies, sleeping on one's back was always unwise. "Many thereby, are made starke ded in their sleepe," attested the English physician William Bullein.[30]

The family patriarch bore a responsibility at bedtime for setting minds at rest by conducting prayers. The fabled "lock" of every night, these afforded pious thoughts during sleep. By the sixteenth century, evening devotions had become commonplace. Many households, including servants, assembled with clasped hands. Family prayers could either be a substitute for or a supplement to personal devotions. Only because he had drunk "so much wine" one Sunday did Pepys neglect reading verses to his household—"for fear of being perceived by my servants in what case I was." A young East Anglian servant, Isaac Archer, noted that "it was the custome of our lads to pray together," though he himself was occasionally excluded. "Because my speech was stammering," he explained in his diary, "they said God would not heare mee."[31]

Protestant and Catholic verses shared distinctive features. Along with giving thanks for spiritual guidance, requesting peaceful sleep, and asking forgiveness for moral failings, most devotions appealed for divine protection from nocturnal harm. The well-known verse "Now I lay me down to sleep, / I pray the Lord my soul to keep" dates from the Middle Ages. Some prayers spoke formulaically of "works of darkness" or "enemies both bodily and ghostly,"[32] but, often, they contained more graphic expressions of nocturnal fears. A seventeenth-century verse sought deliverance "from sudden death, fire and theeves, stormes, tempests, and all affrightments."[33] Rural households in France were known to keep holy water near beds, lest death suddenly strike. According to an ancient prayer, "Sacred water I take. If sudden death takes me, may it be my last sacrament." In Anjou, a pail of water left overnight in a kitchen supposedly allowed one's soul, after death, to cleanse itself.[34]

In addition, less affluent households invoked magic when preparing for sleep. Besides potions to prevent bedwetting and spells to speed slumber, families recited charms to avert nightmares. "No ill dreams shall vex his bed, Hell's dark land he ne'er shall tread," comforted an early Welsh verse. In much of Europe, turning over one's shoes each evening by the

Matthias Stom, *Old Woman Praying*, seventeenth century.

foot of the bed was considered a deterrent. In her diary, Cowper, ever the staunch Anglican, relates her servant's clandestine efforts, through this stratagem, to ease her mistress's stomach cramps. Insisting that "there was nothing in the feat," Cowper forbade her servant's assistance, believing that it was the work of the devil and that she "wou'd not be beholden to him for any benefit whatsoever." Notably, Cowper observed that, upon refusing such aid, she was "hugely laughed att by some" for her ignorance.[35]

III

Let the bedsted be large and long and no higher than a man may easily fall into it.

THOMAS COGAN, 1588[36]

The centrality of sleep to the lives of preindustrial folk is underscored by the importance they attached to their beds, typically the most expensive articles of family furniture. Between the fifteenth and seventeenth centuries, European beds evolved from straw pallets on earthen floors to wooden frames complete with pillows, sheets, blankets, coverlets, and "flock" mattresses, filled with rags and stray pieces of wool. William Harrison in 1557 recalled of his youth, "Our fathers, yea, and we ourselves also, have lien full oft upon straw pallets, on rough mats covered only with a sheet, under coverlets made of dagswain or hapharlots . . . and a good round log under their heads, instead of a bolster." "Pillows," he noted, "were thought meet only for women in childbed." In Harrison's view, bedding was one of the "things" most "marvelously altered in England." Well-to-do homes by the mid-sixteenth century contained elevated bedsteads with canopies, feather mattresses, and heavy curtains to ward off drafts, insects, and inquisitive eyes. So large was the interior space that wealthy Tuscans referred to each bedstead as a "room." Bedclothes included linen sheets, wool blankets, and quilts.[37]

The growth in superior beds mirrored other innovations in domestic comfort and convenience in the sixteenth century. In addition to chimneys, which helped to conserve heat from hearths while dispersing smoke, improvements included partitioned rooms, facilitating the specialization of household space, and glass windows, resulting in greater warmth and enhanced light. The adoption of these and other refinements in the domestic environment would be hastened, beginning in the late seventeenth century, by a major revolution in mass consumption, making household comforts increasingly available to broad segments of the population on both sides of the North Atlantic. But of all these material advancements, none, perhaps, were more popular or more widely enjoyed than improvements in bedding. Beds were among the first items bequeathed in wills to favored heirs as well as the first possessions purchased by newlyweds. In

Anon., *Tobias and Sara*, ca. 1530. The Old Testament couple sleep contentedly under the sumptuous covers of an elevated bedstead more representative of a wealthy sixteenth-century household. Note the pillows, heavy drapes, and slippers, as well as the nightcaps to protect their heads from the night air. In lieu of a chamber pot, a "close-stool," a small box-shaped privy, appears to sit in an alcove behind the bed.

modest homes, beds sometimes represented over one-third the value of all domestic assets. Although humble families often made their own frames, a bed was usually the piece of furniture first acquired upon entering the "world of goods." In 1598 a German visitor was surprised to find English beds "covered with tapestry, even those of farmers." Only half in jest, one historian of material culture has quipped that the early modern era might be rechristened the Age of the Bed.[38]

Families invested heavily in beds not only as a mark of social prestige but also for their physical comfort. A bed, of course, served many functions over the course of a lifetime. It was where most persons were conceived and born, convalesced from illness, made love, and died. "The near approach a bed may show of human bliss to human woe," wrote Isaac de Benserade. No other role, however, matched the bed's everyday importance in facilitating sleep. "Because nothing," remarked the sixteenth-century Dutch physician Levinus Lemnius, "is holesomer than sounde and quiet sleepe," a person needed "to take his full ease and sleepe in a soft bedde." Declared another, "Let the bed bee soft, well shaken, and made rising up toward the feete." Elevation was essential, Stephen Bradwell explained in 1625. "The nearer the earth, the more deadly is the air; and the immediate stroke of the cold ground is very dangerous." A raised bed frame also permitted storage of a "truckle" or "trundle" bed underneath during the day.[39]

Much of the population beneath the middling orders, however, still suffered from tattered blankets and coarse mattresses, with many families hard put to afford those essentials. In Gloucestershire during the late seventeenth century, most estate inventories left by householders worth less than £50 (weavers, small farmers, poorer artisans) contained mattresses and bedsteads but not sheets. Bereft of any comforts was a weaver in Hastings visited by John Taylor the Water-Poet: "No lodging but the floor, / No stool to sit, no lock upon the door, / No straw to make us litter in the night."[40] In Scotland and Ireland, entire families slept upon earthen floors strewn with rushes, straw, and heather. Not only was the cost of bedsteads prohibitive, but they occupied valuable space in cramped dwellings. Of the "better sort of cabins," a visitor to Ireland found in the late 1600s, "there is generally one flock bed, seldom more, feathers being too costly; this serves the man and his wife, the rest all lie on straw, some

William Hogarth, *The Idle 'Prentice Returned from Sea and in a Garret with a Prostitute* (pl. 7 of *Industry and Idleness*), 1747. A bed shared by Tom Idle and a prostitute features sheets and a blanket, but the wooden bedstead has collapsed amid the squalor of their rat-infested garret.

with one sheet and blanket, others only their clothes and blanket to cover them. The cabins have seldom any floor but the earth." As the acerbic writer Ned Ward ridiculed, "The *beds* are upon such a firm foundation, that nothing but an *earthquake* can move them."[41]

Little better were quarters for servants, unless allowed to sleep with a member of their master's family. "As for servants," Harrison wrote of the early sixteenth century, "if they had any sheete above them, it was well, for seldom had they any under their bodies, to keep them from the pricking straws that ran oft through the canvas of the pallet and rased their hardened hides." Even by the 1700s, the most fortunate domestics in France received only narrow cots to support their straw mattresses; whereas a London servant, Mary Clifford, before being beaten to death in 1767, often was forced to lie in her master's cellar, "sometimes" having a "bit of a sack" and a "bit of a blanket" for bedding. Pepys also forced his "little girle" servant to lie in the cellar, after she was beaten one evening. Apprentices and journeymen reclined wherever space permitted, including on the floor of their masters' shops. More fortunate were journeymen bakers in Paris, who slept in empty flour sacks on top of warm ovens.[42]

Beggars and vagrants fared the worst of all. The urban poor slept in doorways fronting public streets or, if lucky, atop or beneath wooden platforms ("bulks") abutting shop windows—"bulkers," these indigents were nicknamed in England. The fifteenth-century French poet François Villon wrote of "outcasts under butchers' stalls." In 1732, the London Court of Common Council observed that "divers poor vagrant children are suffered to skulk in the night-time, and lie upon bulks, stalls, and other places in the publick street." Some years hence, youths were found sleeping within hollow trees in Hyde Park. Hayracks, stables, and barns afforded "nests" for rural vagabonds, such as the thirty men, women, and children found "naked in straw" in a barn near Tewkesbury in 1636. "To lie at the sign of the star" (*coucher a l'enseigne de l'estoile*) was a French expression for the fate of countless paupers. Alternatively, many of the "poorer sort," in such far-flung locations as Naples and Philadelphia, took refuge at night inside caves.[43]

Inadequate bedding meant that families in the lower ranks routinely slept two, three, or more to a mattress, with overnight visitors included. Sharing not only the same room but also the same covers conserved resources and generated welcome warmth during frigid nights. An Italian proverb urged, "In a narrow bed, get thee in the middle."[44] Probably most parents slept apart from children other than infants, although entire households of European peasants, numbering up to five or six persons, occasionally shared the same bed. There was little evident dissatisfaction. "Do you not remember those big beds in which everyone slept together without difficulty," queries a dialogue of Noël Du Fail, a sixteenth-century storyteller. In poor households, as the French historian Jean-Louis Flandrin has pointed out, the communal bed enjoyed a special aura. Often the only meeting-place for families apart from meals, it was a critical source of domestic cohesion.[45]

"To pig" was a common British expression for sleeping with one or more bedfellows, with designated positions for family members according to age and gender. Of Irish households, an early nineteenth-century observer recorded, "They lie down decently and in order, the eldest daughter next the wall farthest from the door, then all the sisters according to their ages, next the mother, father and sons in succession, and then the strangers, whether the travelling pedlar or tailor or beggar." Males, by lying closest to the door, secured the household before retiring. More important, female members of the family were insulated from both invited guests and unexpected intruders. Forced to sleep overnight at the home of an acquaintance, Jacques-Louis Ménétra slept on one side of the bed, with his host in the middle, and the host's wife next to the wall.[46]

Peasant families at night brought farm animals under their roofs, still a customary practice in traditional societies today. Besides providing protection from predators and thieves, boarding beasts generated greater warmth, notwithstanding the "nastiness of theire excrements." In eighteenth-century Wales, "every edifice" reportedly represented a "Noah's Ark"—among other reasons, Welsh peasants believed that cows yielded better milk if allowed to view a fire. And they were easier at night to milk indoors. Often, stock were confined within homes to adjoining biers, though pigs were known to roam freely. In Scotland and parts of northern Europe, curtained beds were built into walls, in part to allow animals additional room. According to a visitor to the Hebrides in the 1780s, the urine from cows was regularly collected in tubs and discarded, but the dung was removed just once a year.[47]

IV

The bed is the best rendezvous of mankind.

SIR THOMAS OVERBURY, 1614[48]

Even well-to-do individuals, when separated from home, occasionally shared beds overnight. Proper behavior required that bedfellows adhere to well-understood conventions, especially among strangers. New norms of civility in Western society extended to slumber. A "good careful bedfellow" was expected to lie still, keep to himself, and not pull away the blankets; and "when ze have talkyd what ze wyll," to "byd" your sleepmate "gode nyght." Among the bons mots contained in a French phrase book compiled for English travelers: "You are an ill bed-fellow," "You pull all the bed cloathes," and "You do nothing but kick about." Few protected their prerogatives as zealously as Philippe d'Orléans, the only brother of Louis XIV. Confided his wife, the Duchess, to a friend: "When His Grace slept in my bed I had to lie so close to the edge that I sometimes fell out of bed in my sleep, for His Grace did not like to be touched, and if perchance I happened to stretch a foot in my sleep and to touch him, he would wake me up and scold me for half an hour."[49] By the eighteenth century, communal sleep inspired widespread disdain among the gentle classes, likely spawning the contemptuous term "bed-faggot." In no other sphere of preindustrial life did a mounting appreciation for personal privacy among the upper ranks of society manifest itself more plainly. Many religious leaders added their voice, condemning the morality of families in common beds.[50]

Yet, often, even in middle-class households, bedfellows were thought a blessing. Sleeping beside a familiar soul, whether a family member, a fellow servant, or a friend brought advantages beyond enjoying another's warmth or saving the cost of an extra bed. It also provided a sense of security. On especially foreboding nights, friends and relations, to allay common fears, slept under the same covers. Boswell, seized by "gloomy terrors" as night approached, importuned a friend to share his bed since he "durst not stay" by himself. Another evening, after conversing about apparitions ("I was afraid that ghosts might be able to return to earth"), he again was tempted to join a companion. So fearful of the devil was the Pennsylvanian Isaac Heller that "many times rather than lay alone" he "got up & gone to bed with black persons" on the farm where he labored.[51]

Doubly appealing were the close bonds of affection between bedmates, fostered by hours of intimate conversation. Some persons, of course, rapidly succumbed to exhaustion. Richard Baxter thought workers in the evening "so toiled and wearied with hard labour" that they could "scarce open their eyes from sleeping," and a London beer porter attested in 1758, "Our business is very laborious, so that we soon fall asleep after we get to bed."[52] But most members of preindustrial households probably did not drift quickly to sleep. Whereas the current time for lapsing to sleep averages from ten to fifteen minutes, the normal period three hundred years ago may have been notably longer. During a recent study designed to simulate sleeping conditions at night before the advent of artificial lighting, subjects remained awake for two hours after entering their beds. Much more typical in the past, probably, was the regimen followed by a dutiful daughter in *The Manners of the Age* (1733): "In bed by eight—her blessing ask'd, at seven; in her first sleep at nine." Elizabeth Drinker observed, "I retire about 11 o'clock, and seldom or ever, I may almost say never, am asleep till after midnight."[53]

However long this final phase of wakefulness, communal sleep afforded persons a trusted comrade in whom to confide on a level of intimacy rare for daytime relationships. "Most men," wrote an essayist, "follow nature no longer than they are in their night-gowns," whereas "all the busy part of the day they act in characters." Conviviality among bedmates may help to explain the enigmatic expression "blanket fair," which in Sheffield, among other parts of England, signified retiring to bed.[54] Some bedfellows rarely bared their souls or ever displayed a "humour to discourse," as a Dorsetshire falconer complained in explaining his own bedtime penchant for reading. But most relationships appear to have been tightly knit, with each typically referring to another as his "bedfellow" or "companion," caring for him when sick, and sharing his secrets. Unable to attend school, the sixteenth-century apprentice Simon Forman "lerned by nighte" lessons from his bedmate Henry, who went to "free scole" during the day. In the Restoration tale *The Princess Cloria* (1661), the male character Locrinus expresses surprise that the politician Hercrombrotus spoke "with such loving and familiar language, as if that night I should have been his bed-fellow." Solitary sleepers, by contrast, may have felt a keen personal loss, including persons of privilege. At seventy-one years of age, Lady Newport astounded her friend Sarah Cowper by coveting a parrot with which to converse alone in bed.[55]

Lying side by side in the dark, bedfellows proved more willing to transgress social mores. Male servants consigned to the same bed might engage in homosexual relations. Similarly, when male and female dependents in small households shared beds, illegitimate births often followed.[56] Communal sleeping could even subvert relations between master and servant. However hierarchical and uncaring household relationships could be during the day, bedtime brought a frequent shift in tempers. In *The English Rogue* (1671), a mistress who usually shares her bed with a maidservant is "very free in all" her "discourse," acquainting the servant "with all passages" involving her "sweet-hearts." Less polite is the bedtime "match at farting" between mistress and maid described in the Restoration melody

"She Went to Bed in the Dark." Female domestics, when sleeping with their mistresses, afforded protection at night from abusive husbands. In short, as Thomas Yalden's "Hymn To Darkness" allowed, "Though light distinction makes, thou giv'st equality." The authors of a conduct book thought it necessary to remind bedfellows to defer to their superiors: "Any tyme that you schall lye with any man that is better than you, spyre hym what syde of the bedd that most best will ples hym." Madame de Liancourt admonished her granddaughter never to share her bed with servants, which would be "contrary to the respect they owe you, and goes against cleanliness and decency."[57]

Most altered in bed were bonds between husband and wife. Rarely was the potential so promising for physical and emotional intimacy. As in their daily behavior, some men remained insensitive—abusive, selfish, and deaf to their wives' entreaties. Sylvia in *The Atheist* (1684) condemns the typical husband as "heavy and useless, comes faint and loth to bed, turns him about, grunts, snores." Still, less fortunate was Mary Arthur, of Massachusetts, who in 1754 was "kick't" by her husband out of bed with such violence that a lodger elsewhere in the house feared a passing earthquake.[58] But often, having been apart much of the day, couples found time abed for quiet conversation, games, and sexual pleasure. Pillow talk included events of the day or yet more pressing matters. In "The Second Nun's Tale" of Chaucer's *Canterbury Tales*, the maiden Cecilia says to her husband, "O my sweet husband, well beloved and true, I have a secret to impart to you." Lord Wariston "discoursed a long tyme" with his wife about a biblical verse, whereas Pepys derived "great pleasure talking and discoursing" in bed. Boswell, an unfaithful spouse, like Pepys, grew depressed when away from his "good bed" and "dear wife."[59]

As tired souls reclined, laid low were traditional distinctions between wives and husbands, resulting in moments of rare autonomy for women within the patriarchal household. Sexual boundaries were redrawn. Lying abed in the dark encouraged wives to express concerns unsuited to other hours. "Women know their time to work their craft," claimed Joshua Swetman in 1702, "for in the night, they will work a man like wax." Flattery and wit were fabled artifices, as was withholding sexual relations, or, as husbands lamented, coming "cold" to bed. "Absolutely avoid discord in the bedroom," an authority counseled men, so that a "pleasurable occasion

Anon., *A Boulster Lecture*, seventeenth century.

for lifting cares" did not become "yet another vexation." *The Fifteen Joys of Marriage* (n.d.), a misogynist work from the late Middle Ages, recounts at length tactics wives reportedly used to manipulate their husbands at ease.[60] Least pleasant was a scolding widely known as a "curtain" or "boulster" lecture. "It is a resource which belongs to the rights of women," proclaims Miss Plimlimmon in *The Welch Heiress* (1795). An obscure diary kept by John Eliot of Connecticut contains a vivid account of the authority some wives wielded. "These curtain lectures," he wrote of his wife, "very frequent, severe & long (every other night almost to the keeping both awake great part of the night & sometimes every night or night after night) with the most vile & scurrilous language . . . raking up the old stories about a first & second wife, first & second children etc." Besides upbraiding Eliot for his past marriages and spurning his bedtime advances, sometimes his wife insisted that he sleep in another room, as did the wife of John Richards, a Dorsetshire gentleman, banished to the dining room or the cellar.[61]

Mortal violence against husbands, although rare, was likeliest in bed. Short of being poisoned, never were men so vulnerable to aggrieved wives.

An abused housewife in York warned her loutish spouse "that she could kill him in bed at night if she wanted." In Germany, Margaretha Craft of Hallbach slew her second husband in bed with an axe "shortly after their union," later covering with manure his severed remains in the cellar. In 1737, a Connecticut husband—perchance while snoring—received from his wife a shovel of hot embers in his gaping mouth, whereas in Derby, the girlfriend of a journeyman stocking-maker named Samuel Smith took a knife to his penis as he lay asleep in the dark. She protested that "he had courted her for several years, and had often promised to mary her, but always deceived her." Only after losing a "great quantity of blood" and "his pain increasing" did Smith "apprehend what was amiss."[62]

CHAPTER ELEVEN

UNRAVELING THE KNITTED SLEEVE: DISTURBANCES

I

Happy are those who can get rid of their problems when sleeping.

GUILLAUME BOUCHET, 1584–1598[1]

IMPLICIT IN MODERN conceptions of sleep before the Industrial Revolution remains the wistful belief that our forebears enjoyed tranquil slumber, if often little else, in their meager lives. Notwithstanding the everyday woes of preindustrial existence, most families, we like to think, at least rested contentedly until dawn. Evening silence coupled with overpowering darkness contributed to unusually peaceful repose, as did the fatigue ordinary men and women suffered from their labors. A leading modern authority on sleep, reliving this "more primitive pattern" when camping outdoors, recently rhapsodized, "With the stars as our only night-light, we are rocked in the welcoming arms of Mother Nature back to the dreamy sleep of the ancients. It's little wonder we wake the next morning feeling so refreshed and alive."[2]

Our nostalgia lies deeply rooted in Western literature. With the explosive expansion during the sixteenth century in imaginative writing in England and much of continental Europe, the peacefulness of sleep became a favorite topic for all forms of literary adulation, especially verse drama and poetry. Samuel Johnson later claimed that because poets required "respite from thought," they were naturally "well affected to sleep," which not only bestowed "rest, but frequently" led "them to happier regions." Life's daily miseries made beds appear all the more oases of serenity—"the onelie giver of tranquility" for poets, hailed the German physician Christof Wirsung.[3] Writers typically celebrated sleep as a sanctuary that locked "sences from their cares." Macbeth, in a famous passage, speaks of "sleep that knits up the ravell'd sleave of care." "Oh sleep! Thou only cordial," exclaimed William Mountfort, "for injured and disorder'd souls!"[4] Scant surprise that writers regularly likened slumber to the gentle embrace of death—"la mort petite," according to the French Jesuit Louis Richeome. "So like it, that I dare not trust it without my prayers," observed Sir Thomas Browne.[5]

Nor were sleep's blessings reserved just for persons of privilege. What Edmund Spenser called "the forgetfulness of slepe" was, like death, peculiarly egalitarian. At a time when distinction, rank, and preferment ordinarily reigned in Western societies, slumber made "the wretched equal with the blest." Sir Philip Sidney called sleep "the poor man's wealth, the prisoner's release, / The indifferent judge between the high and low." For Sancho Panza in *Don Quixote* (1605), sleep was "the balancing weight that levels the shepherd with the king, and the simple with the wise."[6] A corollary to this assumption, rooted in the medieval concept of the "sleep of the just," was the belief that the soundest slumber, in fact, belonged to those with simple minds and callused hands, society's laboring classes. A French poet wrote of "sweet sleep" that restores "with rest the weary limbs of work-men overprest." Felled by fatigue, simple rustics brought to their beds none of the anxiety that plagued the slumber of wealthy and powerful men. In *Henry V*, Shakespeare wrote that none "laid in bed majestical, / Can sleep so soundly as the wretched slave, / Who with a body fill'd and vacant mind / Gets him to rest."[7]

Sleep, to be sure, granted weary men and women of all ranks some measure of relief from daily cares as well as an interval of hard-won rest. Rare was the early modern family that did not shoulder its share of tribulations both petty and severe. Sleep's principal contribution was not merely physiological but psychological. Thus, according to East Anglian slang, falling asleep was to "forget the world." If only because "its pleasures are purely negative," surmised Sarah Cowper, "sleep may be reckon'd one of the blessings of life." "When our spirits are exhausted," she noted, "we wish for sleep as old men for death, only because we are tired with our present condition" (in fact, Cowper complained that her husband, Sir William, commonly went to bed early to escape her presence). Even for night owls, slumber provided an occasional haven. Having survived yet another "drunken delirium," James Boswell stole "into bed" to avoid his wife's wrath—"I say into," he later confided, "because it was truly a refuge."[8]

Also possible is that the solace persons derived from sleep varied in inverse proportion to their quality of life, with those farther down the social ladder, such as servants and slaves, most looking forward to bed. A French priest noted, "The Prince hath no advantage over his subjects, when they are both asleep." In bed, kings forswore their crowns, bishops their miters, and masters their servants. "Sleep hab no Massa," affirmed a Jamaican slave proverb. Set against the drudgery of their waking hours, retiring to bed for most laborers, if only on a thin mattress of straw, must have been welcome indeed, all the more since few claimed furniture of any greater comfort. "How dead sleep our people sleeps," complained Samuel Pepys after trying to rouse his servants one night. When, on another evening, his wife failed by ringing a bell to summon her wash-maids, Pepys vowed to obtain a yet bigger bell.[9]

But did slumber ordinarily offer individuals a genuine asylum? Did most, in an era before sleeping pills, body pillows, and earplugs, enjoy the reasonable expectation of undisturbed rest? If one defining characteristic of sleep is the barrier it erects between the conscious mind and the outside world, another is that sleep's defenses are easily breached. Unlike sleep-like states resulting from anesthesia, coma, or hibernation, sleep itself is interrupted with relative ease. The Elizabethan Thomas Nashe wrote of "our thoughts troubled and vexed when they are retired from labour to ease," and Cowper, in her diary, noted that "even sleep it self" was "not altogether free from uneasiness."[10]

II

Let no lamenting cryes, nor dolefull teares,
Be heard all night within nor yet without.

EDMUND SPENSER, 1595[11]

Notwithstanding idyllic stereotypes of repose in simpler times, early modern slumber was highly vulnerable to intermittent disruption, much more so, in all likelihood, than is sleep today. Past descriptions contained such adjectives as "restless," "troubled," and "frighted." A seventeenth-century religious devotion spoke of "terrors, sights, noises, dreames and paines, which afflict manie men" at rest. "Our sleepe," the writer Francis Quarles remarked, "is oft accompanied with frights, / Distracting night dreames and dangers of the night." Early diaries, in some instances, are riddled with complaints of inadequate rest. For Peter Oliver, the "best nights rest for a period beyond the reach of memory" meant "not awaking once from going to bed." Among the "plagues" visited upon a lodger in the colony of Delaware were a "male bedfellow," a "very restless one," the "stink of the candle-snuff," "buggs," "musquittoes," the "grunting & groaning of a person asleep in the next room," and the "mewing of a cat" that had to be turned out twice![12]

Sickness, among all social ranks, took the greatest toll. Not only do strokes and acute heart attacks strike more frequently at night, but symptoms of other ailments tend to worsen: cluster headaches, congestive heart failure, heartburn, gout, gallbladder attacks, and toothaches, as well as both peptic and gastric ulcers.[13] Victims of respiratory tract illnesses sometimes hung "spitting sheets" by their beds, if not for greater convenience then to inspect their sputum for blood. Bedding rife with house mites triggered asthma, as did lying prone. So severe was the asthma afflicting Elizabeth Freke's husband that for more than two months he slept in a chair, with watchers forced to hold his head upright. Of course, communal sleeping only helped to spread infectious diseases. "Crowding the sick and the healthy together in one bed," reported a Scottish rector, was one reason for the prevalence of consumption in his Highlands parish.[14]

Making illness more onerous is that sensitivity to pain intensifies at night. Cowper, who like many diarists recorded vivid accounts of her noc-

William Hogarth, *Francis Matthew Schutz in His Bed*, late 1750s.

turnal woes, had no doubt that her back pain worsened "in the night season," as did a toothache one evening before plucking out the "stump." Similarly tormented, the Massachusetts minister Ebenezer Parkman smeared a mixture of cow manure and hog fat on his face at night. "Despicable as it seems," he averred, "it gave me relief." Without the range of medications and procedures available today, physical maladies caused prolonged loss of rest or, at best, sleep that rarely went unbroken. Hence the Welsh maxim, "Apart will keep disease and sleep," or as Thomas Legg, the author of *Low-Life or One Half of the World Knows Not How the Other Half Live . . .* (1750), described Londoners between 1:00 and 2:00 A.M., "Sick and lame people meditating and languishing on their several disorders, and praying for day-light."[15]

Illness magnified anxiety and depression, insidious sources of disturbed sleep in their own right. "Waking, by reason of their continual cares, fears, [and] sorrows is a symptom that much crucifies melancholy men," Robert Burton wrote in *The Anatomy of Melancholy* (1621). Sleeplessness was among the most common symptoms reported by mentally disturbed patients of the seventeenth-century healer Richard Napier. Of some two thousand men and women seen over several decades, just over four hundred (20 percent) complained of insomnia. All manner of unpleasant feelings, from sorrow to anger, disrupted rest. Burdened by debt, the struggling farmer Ulrich Bräker bewailed all his "sour sweat and so many sleepless nights." Because of anxiety, the Scottish parson George Ridpath once complained that he had enjoyed "scarce half my ordinary sleep for 9 or 10 days." "If bodily disease abates," lamented Cowper, "pain of the mind succeeds" to "break my rest in the night."[16]

If, as early writers contended, the affluent suffered broken sleep because of mental stress, diverse psychological disorders, not least depression, afflicted the lower classes. Likely, those with the fewest resources to cope with life's problems remained most "wakensome," or vulnerable to insomnia. Of the urban poor, an observer remarked, "They sleep, but they feel their sleep interrupted by the cold, the filth, the screams and infants' cries, and by a thousand other anxieties."[17] The immersion every evening of poor households into ill-lit obscurity could only have deepened gloom and unease, particularly in wintertime, *la mauvaise saison*. Well before the clinical diagnosis of Seasonal Affective Disorder, or SAD, whereby depression in northern climates has been linked to abnormal levels of the brain hormone melatonin due to a paucity of light, observers sensed a connection between depression and darkness. "A grosse, darke, gloomish, stinking ayre, is very contrarie," noted the sixteenth-century French physician André Du Laurens. For the medical scientist Benjamin Rush, depression was one reason physical illnesses seemed worse at night to sufferers. "How often," he declared, "do the peevish complaints of the night in sickness give way to the composing rays of the light of the morning!"[18]

Of all mortal emotions, fear most often broke sleep. Among mammals generally, those with the safest sleeping quarters, usually predators, enjoy the most satisfying slumber, while animals at greater risk from their enemies experience lighter sleep. Men and women in early modern communities were no exception. "The secure man sleeps soundly," remarked Sir Thomas Overbury. People's apprehensions intensified at night for very good reasons, including peaking adrenal hormones between 4:00 and 8:00 A.M., coupled with the loneliness of early morning hours. "Solitude, the night and fear makes all my danger double to appear," wrote Henry Nevil Payne. Georg Christoph Lichtenberg reflected, "I have gone to bed at night quite untroubled about certain things and then started to worry fearfully about them at about four in the morning, so that I often lay tossing and turning for several hours, only to grow indifferent or optimistic again at nine or even earlier."[19]

Not all fears were unfounded. Genuine perils loomed, thereby keeping persons more on edge, some sleeping "with one eye open" and "fists clenched," according to a French saying. Dudley Ryder tossed in his London bed all evening after leaving his sword downstairs where thieves could steal it. Strange sounds invariably mobilized families from bed. In The Hague, David Beck, hearing "commotion and noises" in the middle of the night, jumped naked out of bed with his bedmate, one armed with a knife, the other with an iron spade, only to discover a set of playful cats.[20] Popular dread of demons kept some persons awake. A diary kept by the Connecticut colonist Hannah Heaton, from adolescence to old age, recounts

Henry Fuseli, *The Nightmare*, 1781.

nocturnal battles with Satan, resulting in frequent loss of rest. Of one night, she recorded, "I thot I felt the devil twitch my cloaths, I jump up and run in fild with terror and o how did I look at the winders in the night to see if Christ was not coming to judgment." "Many cannot sleep for witches and fascinations, which are too familiar in some places," declared Burton.[21]

Even once sleep ensued, there was always the danger of nightmares, viewed by many not as unpleasant dreams but as attempts by evil spirits to suffocate their prey. In West Cornwall, "nag-ridden" was the common term for victims of nightmares. As late as 1730, a written guide urged servants to repair quickly at night when summoned since "many a life has been lost by the night-mare, for want of momentary assistance; and a person who has just power to ring the bell, may be suffocated, whilst a maid stays to rub her eyes, light her candle, or adjust her cap." Perhaps because of the frequency of crib deaths among infants, children were thought at special risk. Boasts a witch in Ben Jonson's *The Masque of Queenes* (1609), "When the childe was a-sleepe / At night, I suck'd the breath."[22]

III

He that dwells in a rotten ruinous house dares scarce sleep in a tempestuous night.

THOMAS ADAMS, 1629[23]

Environmental annoyances aggravated mental and physical woes. With few exceptions, sleeping quarters were ill suited to peaceful repose. Most urban dwellings abutted streets, and buildings were badly insulated, even those whose residents could afford shutters and glass windows.[24] Not only did poor vision at night make auditory nerves more sensitive, but once asleep, hearing represented one's principal link to the external world.[25] All of this would have mattered less had cities and towns, many nights, not been so noisy, whether from brawling drunkards, toiling craftsmen, or country folk arriving after midnight with produce. Passing bells signaled the death of neighbors. The aural landscape of urban areas amplified these noises thanks to their timbered dwellings. Of evenings in a provincial town, the 1673 play *Epsom-Wells* bore witness: "There are such vile noises all night"; while of Paris, Boileau complained, "What noise is this, good God!

What doleful cries / Assaults my ears and keep unshut my eyes?" A resident thought London in 1700 a place "where repose and silence dare scarce shew their heads in the darkest night."[26] If the most frightening sound was a clanging fire bell, with "that peculiar, hurried, monotonous alarm,"[27] urban denizens reserved their sharpest annoyance for the nightwatch. Many residents never grew habituated to their cries. An exception was Elizabeth Drinker, who observed in 1794, "I never was much disturb'd by common noises in the night, as many are, if they were such as I could account for, and not exceeding loud." Sometimes, her sleep suffered too, as Drinker discovered one evening upon hearing "screaming in the street, howling of dogs, and a thumping as I thought in our house," all of which was later followed "by the cry of fire." "Did not sleep," she recorded in her diary, "an hour all night."[28]

More cloistered were evenings in the countryside, with dispersed populations, wide-open fields, and far less bustle. "Half its inhabitants wished us at the devil," grumbled William Beckford when his companion coughed one night upon entering a remote Spanish town. If not human voices, sleep nonetheless remained vulnerable to other branches of the animal kingdom, from frogs and katydids to barking dogs, lovesick cats, and needy livestock, not all of which grew familiar with time. In the dairy region of East Anglia, "bull's noon" was a common expression for midnight, the hour when bullocks, in full throat, bellowed for their mates. And vice-versa. Complained a Somerset diarist, "Up rather early, a disagreeable cow running and roaring under our window disturbed us much. Our cow makes too much noise, she must be sent to the bull."[29]

Within some homes, most notoriously those with wooden frames fixed in the earth, such was the tumult created by rats and mice that walls and rafters seemed on the verge of collapse. "We might have rested," a traveler in Scotland remarked in 1677, "had not the mice rendezvoused over our faces." Ill-constructed houses generated their own cacophony, owing to shrinking timber, loose boards, drafty doors, broken windows, and open chimneys. All of which inclement weather made worse. Not only did keyholes whistle, but hinges and bolts gave way, and roofs leaked. "Tiles and thatch are things that storms and tempests have a natural antipathy to," observed George Woodward of East Hendred. Not surprisingly, once awakened in a storm's midst, families refused to re-enter their beds until wind and rain had subsided. In 1703, Thomas Naish, his wife, and the maid all arose during a "violent storm of wind" about 2:00 A.M., "not being able to lye a bed for the violence of the noise, ratling of the tyles, and for fear that my house would fall down upon me. I went down into [the] parlour for prayers."[30]

Frigid temperatures assaulted sleep during the winter, all the more since Western Europe and northern North America experienced a "Little Ice Age" in the sixteenth, seventeenth, and eighteenth centuries. Growing seasons were abbreviated, winters unusually raw, and the Thames froze on eighteen occasions. Most mammals, including human beings, appear to sleep best while temperatures hover between 70 and 85 degrees Fahrenheit, with 77 degrees optimum. Temperatures much below a person's thermal comfort zone lead to wakefulness and fragmented sleep, as early modern families, huddled in homes with no insulation from either the ground or the weather, readily understood. So frigid were conditions one January in Massachusetts, according to Cotton Mather, that sap froze as it seeped from the bare ends of burning logs. Even in otherwise comfortable lodgings during winter, inkhorns, water basins, and chamber pots sometimes froze overnight. To the London readers of *Lloyd's Evening Post*, "Dillenius" railed in 1767: "I have often been kept awake for hours by the coldness of my legs and feet. I have loaded myself with cloaths to no purpose. I have had my bed heated till I could scarce bear the touch. Thus baffled, night after night have I shivered through the winter." "The cold almost too much for me at going to bed," remarked Parson James Woodforde. Once there, many must have been loath the following morning to leave their blankets.[31]

Unless, of course, insects feasted first. Bedding afforded notorious homes to lice, fleas, and bedbugs, the unholy trinity of early modern entomology. Compounding the irritation, in all likelihood, is that the sensitivity of human skin peaks towards 11:00 P.M., as does one's propensity to itching. British sleepers did not have to endure all the pests to which Europeans in warmer climes like Italy were subjected, including tarantulas and scorpions. Nor did they have to contend with the voracious mosquitoes for which England's colonies in North America most summers were infamous; worse, the Virginia servant John Harrower found a snake one night under his pillow. It is nonetheless telling that people in Britain often referred to

Gerrit van Honthorst, *The Flea Hunt*, 1621.

bedtime pests in martial terms—for example, "troops," "detachments," "a compleat regiment," and "whole armies" of bugs. Legg in *Low-Life* wrote of "poor people who have been in bed some time, . . . groping about for their tinder-boxes, that they may strike a light in order to go a bugg-hunting." The street ballad "How Five and Twenty Shillings were Expended in a Week" mentions "a three farthing rushlight every night, to catch the bugs and fleas." Naturally, hunters had to weigh the cost of artificial lighting; so the caution, "To waste a candle and find a flea."[32]

Less often did beds themselves disrupt slumber, at least among the propertied classes. Despite the heavy sums invested, the thickness and composition of mattresses may have mattered less than was imagined—unless, ironically, their softness awakened sleepers by restricting their movements. Some persons complained of hard beds and featherless pillows, but those criticisms often emanated from travelers forced to rest in unfamiliar settings. Though but a "poor man," so demanding were the requirements of John Byng, the future Viscount Torrington, that he found good bedding (the "first comfort of life") wanting "in almost every house" he "ever enter'd." Never did he sleep in another bed like his own, "smooth, deeply mattress'd, and 6 feet wide." Cultural prejudices mattered most. Attested Montaigne, "You make a Germane sicke, if you lay him upon a matteras, as you distemper an Italian upon a fetherbed, and a French man to lay him in a bed without curtaines." In 1646, while in Switzerland, John Evelyn bewailed having to sleep on a "bed stuff'd with leaves, which made such a crackling, & did so prick my skin through the tick." Among the Swiss upper classes, however, mattresses filled with beech leaves were greatly preferred to those made from straw.[33] Unfortunately, portions of the preindustrial population confined to the meanest quarters left behind few firsthand impressions of their bedding. Notwithstanding John Locke's contention that sound slumber "matters not whether it be on a soft bed, or the hard boards," sleeping on a thin mattress, much less a rigid surface, must have been all the more uncomfortable for emaciated human frames with minimal bodyfat for padding.[34]

Even a well-constructed mattress could not always comfort multiple bedmates. "Packed like herrings," David Beck described a night in 1624 between two other sleepers. Entitled "One Sleeps Better than Two," a French song complained: "One coughs, one talks; one's cold, one's hot; / One wanting to sleep and the other one not." Worst were the gyrations of unaccustomed bedmates. Forced to lie one evening with a friend in his chamber, Pepys "could hardly get any sleep all night, the bed being ill-made and he a bad bedfellow." Similarly, the Scottish-American physician Andrew Hamilton, trying to sleep one night in Delaware, shared a room with two bedfellows, one of whom, an "Irish teague," constantly tossed and turned while "bawling out, 'O sweet Jesus!' "[35]

In moist night air, chamber pots reeked. "So barbarous a stink" engulfed two women sharing an inn room that they first "accused each other for some time," only to discover a latrine at the head of their beds. The Restoration melody "Aminta One Night had Occasion to Piss" describes in Rabelaisian detail a conversation between two companions when both awaken to use the chamber pot, concluding with one scolding the other, "That tempest broke out from behind ye; / And though it was decently kept from my eyes, / The troubled air offends my nose." As a chambermaid informed a traveler when asked about the chamber pot and privy, "If you see them not you shall smell them well enough."[36] Embarrassing accidents often ensued, with pots overturned and broken. Riskier still was reliance on a urinal, often in the shape of a small flask.[37] Alternatives, particularly for the lower classes, included urinating outside the front door or, more commonly, in the fireplace. Protested Thomas Tusser, "Some make the chimnie chamber pot to smel lyke filthy sinke." Lacking a pot, Pepys "shit in the chimney" twice one night, whereas the Yorkshire laborer Abram Ingham used his "clogg" [shoe] to "make water in." If all else failed, an Italian adage instructed, "You may piss a bed, and say you sweated."[38]

IV

How is it possible to be well, where one is kill'd for want of sleep?

COLLEY CIBBER AND SIR JOHN VANBRUGH, 1728[39]

In affluent households, perfume-burners became popular to disguise septic smells, and privies could always be secreted from bedchambers. Cosimo, Duke of Tuscany, appears to have placed his close-stool, a portable toilet, inside a servant's chamber.[40] But, then, in this, as in many respects, the lower orders were peculiarly disadvantaged in their sleep. If noxious aromas more commonly afflicted their quarters, so, too, did discordant noises, cold temperatures, and voracious pests. Plainly, lower-class households lay more exposed to unwanted intrusions. In Paris, due to the high cost of obtaining quiet quarters, Boileau remarked, "Sleep like other things is sold, / And you must purchase your repose with gold."[41] Feverish individuals, capable of affording two beds, could "find great luxury in rising, when they awake in a hot bed, and going into the cool one," advised Benjamin Franklin. And should a spouse's illness or pregnancy prove unsettling, a husband like Pepys could always retire to another room. In fact, by the eighteenth century, aristocratic couples in France typically kept separate chambers. Neither did indigent families enjoy curtained beds to block drafts or the option exercised by a gentleman in colonial North Carolina who, tormented by bugs, exchanged beds with his servant.[42]

Perhaps for the laboring population, as poets and playwrights often claimed, fatigue and clear consciences alleviated the hardships incurred at bedtime. The Virginia tutor Philip Fithian studied many evenings to the point of exhaustion to render his sleep "sound & unbroken" and immune to "cursed bugs."[43] But probably more realistic than most pieces of verse, if less well known, was a passage from *The Complaints of Poverty* (1742) by Nicholas James:

> *And when, to gather strength and still his woes,*
> *He seeks his last redress in soft repose,*
> *The tatter'd blanket, erst the fleas' retreat,*
> *Denies his shiv'ring limbs sufficient heat;*
> *Teaz'd with the sqwalling babes nocturnal cries,*
> *He restless on the dusty pillow lies.*

Similarly, George Herbert wrote in 1657 of "manie" who "worke hard all day, and when night comes, their paines increase, for want of food or rest." The author of *L'État de Servitude* (1711) complained, "In an attic with no door and no lock, / Open to cold air all winter long, / In a filthy and vile sort of garret, / A rotten mattress is laid out on the ground."[44]

Sleep, the poor man's wealth, the prisoner's release? Not, it would seem, in any conventional sense, except for allowing a sometimes troubled respite from what was likely an even more onerous day. If most people in bed did not experience prolonged bouts of wakefulness, merely a series of "brief arousals" of at most several minutes apiece, unknown even to the sleeper, could impose an enormous burden on the mind and body in terms of physical repair.[45] Far from enjoying blissful repose, ordinary men and women likely suffered some degree of sleep deprivation, feeling as weary upon rising at dawn as when retiring at bedtime. All the more arduous as a consequence were their waking hours, especially when sleep debts were allowed to accumulate from one day to the next and superiors remained unsympathetic. Returning to his London quarters one evening to find his "man" asleep, William Byrd II delivered a prompt beating, as did the Yorkshire yeoman Adam Eyre to a maidservant for her "sloathfulnesse." Late hours of merriment, some nights, could only have compounded the fatigue of apprentices, servants, and slaves.[46]

If complaints are to be believed, the work of laborers was erratic and their behavior lethargic—"deadened slowness" was one description of rural labor. "At noon he must have his sleeping time," groused Bishop Pilkington of the typical laborer in the late 1500s. While previous historians

Thomas Rowlandson, *Haymakers at Rest*, 1798.

have explained such behavior as the product of a preindustrial work ethic, greater allowance must be made for the chronic fatigue that probably afflicted much of the early modern population. Indeed, napping during the day appears to have been common, with sleep less confined to nocturnal hours than it is in most Western societies today.[47] No doubt exhaustion occasioned other symptoms of sleep deprivation, including losses in motivation and physical well-being as well as increased irritability and social friction. "Whether due to sleeping on a bed fouler than a rubbish heap, or not being able to cover oneself," a Bolognese curate observed of insomnia among the poor, "who can explain how much harm is done?"[48]

CHAPTER TWELVE

SLEEP WE HAVE LOST: RHYTHMS AND REVELATIONS

I

For the waking there is one common world only; but when asleep, each man turns to his own private world.

HERACLITUS, ca. 500 B.C.[1]

"I AM AWAKE, but 'tis not time to rise, neither have I yet slept enough. . . . I am awake, yet not in paine, anguish or feare, as thousands are." So went a seventeenth-century religious meditation intended for the dead of night. As if illness, foul weather, and fleas were not enough, there was yet another, even more familiar source of broken sleep in preindustrial societies, though few contemporaries regarded it in that light. So routine was this nightly interruption that it provoked little comment at the time. Neither has it attracted scrutiny from historians, much less systematic investigation. But as a vital commonplace of an earlier age, country-folk yet knew about it in the early twentieth century.[2] Some probably still do today.

Until the close of the early modern era, Western Europeans on most evenings experienced two major intervals of sleep bridged by up to an hour or more of quiet wakefulness. In the absence of fuller descriptions, fragments in several languages in sources ranging from depositions and diaries to imaginative literature give clues to the essential features of this puzzling pattern of repose. The initial interval of slumber was usually referred to as "first sleep," or, less often, "first nap" or "dead sleep."[3] In

French, the term was *premier sommeil* or *premier somme*,[4] in Italian, *primo sonno* or *primo sono*,[5] and in Latin, *primo somno* or *concubia nocte*.[6] The succeeding interval of sleep was called "second" or "morning" sleep, whereas the intervening period of wakefulness bore no name, other than the generic term "watch" or "watching." Alternatively, two texts refer to the time of "first waking."[7]

Both phases of sleep lasted roughly the same length of time, with individuals waking sometime after midnight before returning to rest. Not everyone, of course, slept according to the same timetable. The later at night that persons went to bed, the later they stirred after their initial sleep; or, if they retired past midnight, they might not awaken at all until dawn. Thus in "The Squire's Tale" in *The Canterbury Tales*, Canacee slept "soon after evening fell" and subsequently awakened in the early morning following "her first sleep"; in turn, her companions, staying up much later, "lay asleep till it was fully prime" (daylight). William Baldwin's satire *Beware the Cat* recounts a quarrel between the protagonist, "newly come unto bed," and two roommates who "had already slept" their "first sleep."[8]

Men and women referred to both intervals as if the prospect of awakening in the middle of the night was common knowledge that required no elaboration. "At mid-night when thou wak'st from sleepe," described the Stuart poet George Wither; while in the view of John Locke, "That all men sleep by intervals" was a normal feature of life, extending as well to much of brute creation.[9] For the thirteenth-century Catalan philosopher Ramón Lull, *primo somno* stretched from mid-evening to early morning, whereas William Harrison in his *Description of England* (1557) referred to "the dull or dead of the night, which is midnight, when men be in their first or dead sleep."[10]

Customary usage confirms that "first sleep" constituted a distinct period of time followed by an interval of wakefulness. Typically, descriptions recounted that an aroused individual had "had," "taken," or "gotten" his or her "first sleep." An early seventeenth-century Scottish legal deposition referred to Jon Cokburne, a weaver, "haveing gottin his first sleip and awaiking furth thairof," while Noel Taillepied's *A Treatise Of Ghosts* (1588) alluded more directly to "about midnight when a man wakes from his first sleep." "So I tooke my first sleepe," states the protagonist in the play *Endimion* (1591), "which was short and quiet"; and the servant Club in

George Farquhar's *Love and a Bottle* (1698) declares, "I believe 'tis past midnight, for I have gotten my first sleep." "I am more watchful," states Rampino in *The Unfortunate Lovers* (1643) "than / A sick constable after his first sleep / On a cold bench."[11]

Although in some descriptions a neighbor's quarrel or a barking dog woke people prematurely from their initial sleep, the vast weight of surviving evidence indicates that awakening naturally was routine, not the consequence of disturbed or fitful slumber. Medical books, in fact, from the fifteenth to eighteenth centuries frequently advised sleepers, for better digestion and more tranquil repose, to lie on their right side during "the fyrste slepe" and "after the fyrste slepe turne on the lefte side."[12] And even though the French historian Emmanuel Le Roy Ladurie investigated no further, his study of fourteenth-century Montaillou notes that "the hour of the first sleep" was a customary division of night, as was "the hour halfway through the first sleep." Indeed, though not used as frequently as expressions like "candle-lighting," the "dead of night," or "cock-crow," the term "first sleep" remained a common temporal division until the late eighteenth century. As described in *La Démonolâtrie* (1595) by Nicolas Rémy, "Comes dusk, followed by nightfall, dark night, then the moment of first sleep and finally the dead of night."[13]

At first glance, it is tempting to view this pattern of broken sleep as a cultural relic rooted in early Christian experience. Ever since St. Benedict in the sixth century required that monks rise after midnight for the recital of verses and psalms ("At night we will rise to confess to Him"), this like other regulations of the Benedictine order spread to growing numbers of Frankish and German monasteries. By the High Middle Ages, the Catholic Church actively encouraged early morning prayer among Christians as a means of appealing to God during the still hours of darkness. "Night vigils," Alan of Lille declared in the twelfth century, "were not instituted without reason, for by them it is signified that we must rise in the middle of the night to sing the night office, so that the night may not pass without divine praise." Best known for this regimen was St. John of the Cross, author of *The Dark Night of the Soul* (ca. 1588), though in England voices within both the Catholic and Anglican churches still prescribed late-night vigils in the seventeenth century. Where the Puritan divine Richard Baxter thought it "a foppery and abuse of God and ourselves, to think that the breaking of our sleep is a thing that itself pleaseth God," more widespread was the conviction expressed by the author of *Mid-Night Thoughts* (1682) that the "regenerate man finds no time so fit to raise his soul to Heaven, as when he awakes at mid-night."[14]

Although Christian teachings undoubtedly popularized the imperative of early morning prayer, the Church itself was not responsible for introducing segmented sleep. However much it "colonized" the period of wakefulness between intervals of slumber, references to "first sleep" antedate Christianity's early years of growth. Not only did such figures outside the Church as Pausanias and Plutarch invoke the term in their writings, so, too, did early classical writers, including Livy in his history of Rome, Virgil in the *Aeneid*, both composed in the first century B.C., and Homer in the *Odyssey*, written in either the late eighth or early seventh century B.C. And while the Old Testament contains no direct references to first sleep, there are several suggestive passages, including Judges 16:3, in which Samson arises at midnight to pull down the city gate of Gaza.[15] Conversely, as recently as the twentieth century some non-Western cultures with religious beliefs other than Christianity still exhibited a segmented pattern of sleep remarkably similar to that of preindustrial Europeans. In Africa, anthropologists found villages of the Tiv, Chagga, and G/wi, for example, to be surprisingly alive after midnight with newly roused adults and children. Of the Tiv, subsistence farmers in central Nigeria, a study in 1969 recorded, "At night, they wake when they will and talk with anyone else awake in the hut." The Tiv even employed the terms "first sleep" and "second sleep" as traditional intervals of time.[16]

Thus the basic puzzle remains—how to explain this curious anomaly or, in truth, the more genuine mystery of seamless sleep that we experience today. There is every reason to believe that segmented sleep, such as many wild animals exhibit, had long been the natural pattern of our slumber before the modern age, with a provenance as old as humankind. As suggested by recent experiments at the National Institute of Mental Health in Bethesda, Maryland, the explanation likely rests in the darkness that enveloped premodern families. In attempting to recreate conditions of "prehistoric" sleep, Dr. Thomas Wehr and his colleagues found that human subjects, deprived of artificial light at night over a span of several weeks, eventually exhibited a pattern of broken slumber—one practically identical to that of preindustrial households. Without artificial light for up to fourteen hours each night, Wehr's subjects first lay awake in bed for two hours, slept for four, awakened again for two or three hours of quiet rest and reflection, and fell back asleep for four hours before finally awakening for good. Significantly, the intervening period of "non-anxious wakefulness" possessed "an endocrinology all its own," with visibly heightened levels of prolactin, a pituitary hormone best-known for stimulating lactation in nursing mothers and for permitting chickens to brood contentedly atop eggs for long stretches of time. In fact, Wehr has likened this period of wakefulness to something approaching an altered state of consciousness not unlike meditation.[17]

On the enormous physiological impact of modern lighting—or, in turn, its absence—on sleep, there is wide agreement. "Every time we turn on a light," remarks the chronobiologist Charles A. Czeisler, "we are inadvertently taking a drug that affects how we will sleep," with changes in levels of the brain hormone melatonin and in body temperature being among the most apparent consequences. Preindustrial peoples, the subjects in Wehr's experiments, and non-Western societies still experiencing broken slumber are all linked by a lack of artificial lighting, which in the early modern world fell hardest on the lower and middle classes.[18] Interestingly, allusions to segmented sleep are most evident in materials written or dictated by all but the wealthiest segments of society and sparse among the ample mounds of personal papers left by the upper classes—especially, beginning in the late seventeenth century, when both artificial lighting and the vogue of "late hours" grew increasingly prevalent among affluent households. The prolific diarists Pepys and Boswell, by their own admission, seldom woke in the middle of the night. Both, if not conspicuously wealthy themselves, circulated within the upper echelons of London society, patronizing genteel nightspots and homes. Complained Richard Steele in 1710, "Who would not wonder at this perverted relish of those who are reckoned the most polite part of mankind, that prefer sea-coals and candles to the sun, and exchange so many cheerful morning hours for the pleasures of midnight revels and debauches?"[19]

II

It is of no small benefit on finding oneself in bed in the dark to go over again in the imagination the main outlines of the forms previously studied, or of other noteworthy things conceived by ingenious speculation.

LEONARDO DA VINCI, n.d.[20]

After midnight, preindustrial households usually began to stir. Many of those who left their beds merely needed to urinate. The physician Andrew Boorde advised, "Whan you do wake of your fyrste slepe make water if you fele your bladder charged." An English visitor to Ireland around 1700 "wonder'd mightily to heare people walking to the fire place in the middle of the house to piss there in the ashes," something he was "forced to doe too for want of a chambrepot."[21] Some persons, however, after arising, took the opportunity to smoke tobacco, check the time, or tend a fire. Thomas Jubb, an impoverished Leeds clothier, rising around midnight, "went into Cow Lane & hearing ye clock strike twelve" returned "home & went to bed again." The diarist Robert Sanderson, who on one occasion was awoken prematurely "on my first sleepe" by his dog, arose other nights to sit and smoke a pipe, once after first checking upon his ill wife. Counseled an early English ballad, "Old Robin of Portingale": "And at the wakening of your first sleepe / You shall have a hott drinke made, / And at the wakening of your next sleepe / Your sorrowes will have a slake." Some varieties of medicine, physicians advised, might be taken during this interval, including potions for indigestion, sores, and smallpox.[22]

For others, work awaited. The Bath doctor Tobias Venner urged, "Students that must of necessity watch and study by night, that they do it not till after their first sleep," when they would be "in some measure refreshed." According to a former bedfellow, Seth Ward, while Bishop of Salisbury, frequently "after his first sleep," for purposes of private study, would "rise, light, and after burning out his candle, return to bed before day." Such, too, was the regimen of Aimar de Ranonet, president of the parliament of Paris. The seventeenth-century farmer Henry Best of Elmswell made a point to rise "sometimes att midnight" to prevent the destruction of his fields by roving cattle.[23] In addition to tending children, women left their beds to perform myriad chores. The servant Jane Allison got up one night between midnight and 2:00 A.M. to brew a batch of malt for her Westmorland master. "Often at midnight, from our bed we rise," bewailed Mary Collier in "The Woman's Labour." Of female peasants, *Piers Plowman* declared, "They themselves also suffer much hunger, / And woe in wintertime, and waking up nights / To rise on the bedside, to rock the cradle, / Also to card and comb wool, to patch and to wash, / To rub flax and reel yarn and peel rushes." Suffice to say, domestic duties knew no bounds.[24]

And some hardy souls, if rested, remained awake. Thomas Ken, the Bishop of Bath and Wells, reputedly "rose generally very early, and never took a second sleep." In Smollett's *The Adventures of Peregrine Pickle* (1751), a physician counsels the protagonist "to rise immediately after his first sleep, and exercise himself in a morning-walk."[25] Equally invigorating was Benjamin Franklin's habit of taking cold air baths, which he considered an improvement over the vogue of bathing in cold water as a "tonic." While in London, he rose "early almost every morning" and sat naked in his chamber either reading or writing for up to an hour. "If I return to bed afterwards . . . as sometimes happens," he explained to an acquaintance, "I make a supplement to my night's rest, of one or two hours of the most pleasing sleep that can be imagined."[26]

For the poor, awakening in the dead of night brought opportunities of a different sort. At no other time of the night was there such a secluded interval in which to commit petty crimes: filching from dockyards and other urban workplaces, or, in the countryside, pilfering firewood, poaching, and robbing orchards. Perhaps a Scottish court exaggerated in claiming "that it is a known artifice in thieves to go to bed at night and rise in the morning in presence of others" to conceal "actions committed by them in the night time," but plainly an undercurrent of illegal activity reverberated through the early morning hours. In 1727, Gilbert Lambert, a laborer in Great Drisfield, summoned a friend, Thomas Nicholson, "out of his bed" around midnight, desiring him to help drive "a parcel of sheep" that were later found to be stolen. "Some wake," affirmed George Herbert, "to plot or act mischiefe"—or more serious offenses. Reverend Anthony Horneck condemned "high-way-men and thieves" that "rise at midnight to rob and murder men!" Examples are easily found. Of Luke Atkinson, charged with an early morning murder in the North Riding of Yorkshire, his wife admitted "that it was not the first time he had got up at nights and left her in bed to go to other folks houses." And in 1697, young Jane Rowth's mother, "after shee had gott her first sleep, . . . was gotten up out of bedd, and [was] smoaking a pipe at the fire side" when two male companions "called on her mother at the little window, and bad her make ready & come away" according to plans all three had hatched the preceding morning. Although nine-year-old Jane was told by her mother to "lye still, and shee would come againe in the morning," the mother's dead body was found a day or two later.[27]

Is it possible that persons rose to practice magic? One does not need to believe in witches' sabbaths to accept surviving descriptions of sorcery, some involving small groups of kindred spirits. Witchcraft prosecutions, such as those in Rémy's *Démonolâtrie* and Francesco Maria Guazzo's *Compendium Maleficarum* (1608), contain intriguing reports of women who left the sides of their slumbering husbands, allegedly to attend gatherings late at night. Pretending to be in a deep sleep, a charcoal burner of Ferrar, for example, claimed to have witnessed his wife rise from bed and "immediately vanish" upon anointing herself from a "hidden vase." In Lorraine, an admitted "witch" confessed to having put her husband under a spell to prevent, during her absence, his awakening: "She had many times tweaked his ear after having with her right hand anointed it with the same ointment which she used upon herself when she wished to be transported to the Sabot." And in the Dutch village of Oostbruck, a widow, her manservant testified, routinely went to the stables, once she thought her servants asleep, in order to practice black magic.[28]

None were more familiar than the Church with sinister forces in the dead of night. "Can men break their sleep to mind the works of darkness, and shall we not break ours," asked Reverend Horneck, "for doing things, which become the children of light?" With equal fervor, the late sixteenth-century Bishop of Portugal, Amador Arrais, stressed the need for nocturnal vigilance: "Not only do princes, captains, philosophers, poets, and heads of families stay awake and arise during the night . . . but also thieves and brigands do so, . . . and should we not abhor sleep that is the ally of vice? Should we not awaken to guard against cutthroats who remain awake to murder us?" Certainly, there was no shortage of prayers intended to be recited "when you awake in the night" or "at our first waking," a time not to be confused with either dawn or "our uprising," for which wholly separate devotions were prescribed. Prayers reminded vigilant men and women of God's glory, Satan's corruption, and the need to combat "fiery darts of the Devil," "arrows of temptation," and "noisome lusts."[29] Anecdotal evidence suggests that many persons took advantage of early morning hours for prayer. William Cowper's set of three poems "Watching Unto God in the Night Season" recounts his devotions in the middle of the night. A parent instructed his daughter that "the most profitable hour for you and us might be in the middle of the night after going to sleep, after digesting the meat, when the labors of the world are cast off . . . and no one will look at you except for God." The author of *Mid-Night Thoughts* "grew to such habit of nightly meditations (at his first waking) as prov'd more pleasant then sleep."[30]

Most people, upon awakening, probably never left their beds, or not for long. Besides praying, they conversed with a bedfellow or inquired after the well-being of a child or spouse. Lying with her daughter Sara, Mary Sykes, "after theire first sleepe," upon "heareing" Sara "quakeing and holding her hands together" asked her daughter "what she ailed."[31] Sexual intimacy often ensued between couples. According to one wife, it was her husband's "custom when he waketh to feele after me & than he layeth hym to slepe againe." Joked Louis-Sébastien Mercier of the midnight clatter of Parisian carriages, "The tradesman wakes out of his first sleep at the sound of them, and turns to his wife, by no means unwilling." According to ancient Jewish belief, copulating "in the middle of the night" prevented husbands from hearing "human voices" and thinking of "different women."[32]

Significantly, for our understanding of early modern demography, segmented sleep probably enhanced a couple's ability to conceive children, since reproductive fertility ordinarily benefits from rest. In fact, the sixteenth-century French physician Laurent Joubert concluded that early-morning intercourse enabled plowmen, artisans, and other laborers to beget numerous children. Because exhaustion prevented workers from copulating upon first going to bed, intercourse occurred "after the first sleep" when "they have more enjoyment" and "do it better." "Immediately thereafter," Joubert counseled those eager to conceive, "get back to sleep again, if possible, or if not, at least to remain in bed and relax while talk-

Jan Saenredam, *Night*, seventeenth century.

ing together joyfully." The physician Thomas Cogan similarly advised that intercourse occur not "before sleepe, but after the meate is digested, a little before morning, and afterwarde to sleepe a while."[33]

Perhaps even more commonly, persons used this shrouded interval of solitude to immerse themselves in contemplation—to ponder events of the preceding day and to prepare for the arrival of dawn. Never, during the day or night, were distractions so few and privacy so great, especially in crowded households. "As I lay in bed sleepless, I was ever meditating upon something," remarked the Italian scholar Girolamo Cardano. Thomas Jefferson before bed routinely read works of moral philosophy "whereon to ruminate in the intervals of sleep." For the moralist Francis Quarles, darkness, no less than silence, encouraged internal reflection. In order "to take the best advantage of thy selfe (especially in matters where the fancy is most imploy'd)," he recommended:

> Let the end of thy first sleep raise thee from thy repose: then hath thy body the best temper; then hath thy soule the least incumbrance; then no noyse shall disturbe thine ear; no object shall divert thine eye.[34]

Naturally, midnight reflections sometimes proved painful. A character in the Jacobean comedy *Everie Woman in Her Humor* (1609) "everie night after his first sleepe" wrote "lovesicke sonnets, rayling against left handed fortune his foe." For better or worse, this interval was yet another reason for night's far-flung reputation as the "mother of counsel."[35] The seventeenth-century merchant James Bovey, reputedly from age fourteen, kept a "candle burning by him all night, with pen, inke, and paper, to write downe thoughts as they came into his head." Meanwhile, a German lawyer, beside his bed, attached a black marble table on which to record his reflections. Indeed, by the mid-eighteenth century, in order to better preserve midnight ruminations, methods were devised to "write in the dark, as straight as by day or candle-light," according to a report in 1748. Twenty years later, after first obtaining a patent, a London tradesman, Christopher Pinchbeck, Jr., advertised his "Nocturnal Remembrancer," an enclosed tablet of parchment with a horizontal aperture for a guideline whereby "philosophers, statesmen, poets, divines, and every person of genius, business or reflection, may secure all those happy, often much regretted, and never to be recovered flights or thoughts, which so frequently occur in the course of a meditating, wakeful night."[36]

Still, one should not be misled by Georgian ingenuity. For every active intellect following first sleep, there were others initially neither asleep nor awake. The French called this ambiguous interval of semi-consciousness *dorveille*, which the English termed "twixt sleepe and wake." Unless preceded by an unsettling dream, the moments immediately following first sleep were often characterized by two features: confused thoughts that wandered "at will" coupled with pronounced feelings of contentment.[37] "My heart is free and light," wrote William Cowper. In his evocative description of awakening from "midnight slumber" in "The Haunted Mind," Nathaniel Hawthorne insisted, "If you could choose an hour of wakefulness out of the whole night, it would be this.... You have found an intermediate space, where the business of life does not intrude; where the passing moment lingers, and becomes truly the present." Less sanguine about "our solitary hours" when "waking in the night or early in the morning" was the Hammersmith minister John Wade, who complained in 1692 of men's "unsettled independent thoughts," "vain unprofitable musing," and "devising mischief upon their beds."[38]

III

> *The prisoner, loaded with the fetters of despotism, sits far from his dungeon, and accuses his tyrant before assembled worlds. The odious inequality amongst men has, in a manner, ceased.*
>
> LOUIS-SÉBASTIEN MERCIER, 1788[39]

Often, persons emerged from their first sleep to ponder a kaleidoscope of partially crystallized images, slightly blurred but otherwise vivid tableaus born of their dreams—what Tertullian rightly labeled the "business of sleep." So in an early English story, the Emperor Dolfinus receives during "his first slepe" a prophetic vision, and Canacee in "The Squire's Tale," after she "slept her first sleep," awakens in the warm glow of a dream—"for on her heart so great a gladness broke." Of a March night in 1676, the mystic Jane Lead recorded, "In my first sleep, in the night time, many magical workings and ideas were presented to me." Less happily, Oliver Heywood—"at my first sleep"—had a "terrible dream" in which his son "was fallen to the study of magick or the black art." And in *Ram Alley* (1611), Sir Oliver speaks of the hours before cock-crow "when maids awak'd from their first sleep, / Deceiv'd with dreams begin to weep."[40]

As in previous eras, dreams played a profound role in early modern life, every bit as revealing, according to popular sentiment, of prospects ahead as of times past. Of their disparate origins, the Stuart poet Francis Hubert wrote:

Dreames are the daughters of the silent night,
Begot on divers mothers, most, most vaine;
Some bred by dayes-discourse, or dayes-delight,
Some from the stomacke fuming to the braine.

Some from complexion; sanguine constitutions
Will dreame of maskes, playes, revels, melody:
Some of dead bones, and gastly apparitions,
Which are the true effects of melancholly.

And some are merely forg'd to private ends,
And (without doubt) some are propheticke to,
Which gracious God out of his goodnesse sends,
To warne us what to shun, or what to doe.[41]

Well before the literate classes in the late eighteenth century ridiculed dream interpretation among "the vulgar," critics like Sir Thomas Browne condemned the "fictions and falshoods" born at night. For Thomas Nashe, a dream was nothing else but a "bubbling scum or froth of the fancy."[42] Even skeptics, however, acknowledged a widespread fascination with visions. The author Thomas Tryon wrote in 1689 that an "abundance of ignorant people (foolish women, and men as weak) have in all times, and do frequently at this day make many ridiculous & superstitious observations from their dreams." The *Weekly Register* in 1732 observed, "There is a certain set of people in the world, who place the greatest faith imaginable in their dreams."[43] Critics, too, sometimes proved ambivalent in their denunciations. Browne, for one, conceded that dreams could enable persons to "more sensibly understand" themselves; and the Massachusetts patriarch John Winthrop, while professing that dreams merited "no credit nor regard," reverently recorded in his journal a colonist's vision of divine intervention.[44]

That "the English nation has ever been famous for dreaming," as "Somnifer" observed in 1767, was reflected in the surging sales of dream-books (chapbooks, sections of fortune books, or compendiums) devoted to interpreting different varieties of visions, often with remarkable specificity. Selling in the mid-eighteenth century for prices of only one to six pence, dream-books had long been widely accessible as alternatives to local cunning-men. Several thick collections existed, including the only surviving ancient guide to nocturnal visions, *The Interpretation of Dreams*, written in the second century by Artemidorus of Ephesus. During the sixteenth century, it attracted such an eager following that translations appeared in Italian, French, German, Latin, and English. By 1740, the English text alone had spawned twenty-four editions. Homegrown competitors, published in London, included Thomas Hill's *The Most Pleasuante Arte of the Interpretacion of Dreames*. . . , with early editions in 1571 and 1576, and *Nocturnal Revels: or, a Universal Dream-Book*. . . , first published in 1706. With topics from "acquaintance" to "writing" arranged alphabetically, *Nocturnal Revels* previewed several hundred dreams, weighing each for its hidden portent, including, for example, that "to dream you see white hens upon a dunghill, signifies disgrace by some false accusation."[45]

The general public valued not only the oracular quality of dreams but also the deeper understanding they permitted of one's body and soul. Some visions, in the view of physicians, lay rooted in physical health, as Aristotle and Hippocrates once claimed. Asserted the sixteenth-century French surgeon Ambroise Paré, "Those who abound with phlegm, dream of floods, snows, showers, and inundations, and falling from high places." More fortunate were "those whose bodies abound in blood," who "dream of marriages, dances, embracings of women, feasts, jests, laughter, or orchards and gardens."[46] Other dreams, according to common belief, threw a shaft of light on the inner core of a person's character. Well before the Romantic philosophers of the nineteenth century and, later, Sigmund Freud, Europeans prized dreams for their personal insights, including what they revealed of one's relationship with God. "The wise man," the essayist Owen Feltham wrote in 1628, "learnes to know himselfe as well by the nights blacke mantle, as the searching beames of day." Between the two, night was the superior instructor, for "in sleepe, wee have the naked and naturall thoughts of our soules." For Tryon, who denied their prophetic qualities, dreams "not only shew the present state of each man's soul . . . but also what our dispositions, complexions, and inclinations are waking."[47]

Some revelations were unwelcome. The Puritan cleric Ralph Josselin reported in his diary: "They say dreames declare a mans temperament, this night I dreamd I was wondrous passion with a man that wrongd mee and my child insomuch as I was shamed of my selfe, god in mercy keepe mee from that evill." The Anglican Archbishop William Laud was much troubled by a dream in which he "reconciled to the Church of Rome," as was Samuel Sewall after dreaming that "stairs going to heaven" led nowhere.[48]

Oppressive rituals and rules that made daily life more arduous less often applied in the boundless freedom of dreams. Hence the proverb "The dogge dreameth of bread, of rauging in the fields, & of hunting." According to the Marquis de Caraccioli in 1762, the soul is finally able to "see, talk, and listen. . . . We gain a new world when we sleep." Those persons forced to adopt a foreign language by day could dream at night in their native tongues; others in their visions freely swore oaths or enjoyed erotic fantasies. Leering husbands, spouses suspected, committed adultery without once leaving their sides. Such visions Pepys cherished all the more dearly during the height of London's Great Plague. After dreaming of a liaison with Lady Castlemaine ("the best that ever was dreamed"—"all the dalliance I desired with her"), Pepys reflected: "What a happy thing it would be, if when we are in our graves . . . we could dream, and dream but such dreams as this." "Then," he added, "we should not need to be so fearful of death as we are this plague-time." So suspicious of his visions was Pepys's wife that she took to feeling his penis while he slept for signs of an erection. By contrast, John Cannon had "a wonderful dream," full of "different turns & postures," only to discover, at the end, that his paramour was his own spouse.[49]

One can only guess how many visions escaped mention by diarists.

Jacob Jordaens, *The Dream, or The Apparition by Night*, seventeenth century.

Most dreams likely appeared too routine to record. Laud set down in his journals but thirty-two dreams from 1623 to 1643, whereas Josselin described a total of thirty-three during the entire period from 1644 to 1683.[50] In his autobiography, Cardano explained, "I have no desire to dwell upon the insignificant features of dreams," choosing instead to relate "those important aspects of dreams which seem to be the most vivid and determining." Unfortunately, what Cardano dismissed as unimportant—"What would be the use?" he wondered—may have been more revealing than less pedestrian visions. In addition, he informed his readers that he did "not wish to relate" numerous "amazing dreams" that were "strange beyond belief." Thus, he excluded dreams either too commonplace or too sensational. An eighteenth-century Virginia planter, in his own diary, declined to "set down" an "ugly dream" lest, he feared, "these pages fall into bad hands." Little wonder that even Freud, the most famous modern advocate of dream interpretation, expressed pessimism over being able to penetrate the visions of historical figures.[51]

Still, general impressions are possible, based upon a range of visions recorded by individuals. Most dreams, it seems clear, were fairly ordinary, mirroring day-to-day concerns. A visitor to North Wales dreamed of "eternally climbing over rocks," while a scholar dreamed of books both lost and found.[52] Despite one historian's assertion that dreams before the nineteenth century dealt largely with symbols of heaven and hell, diverse images crowded visions—profane as well as sacred. Even in clerics' dreams, spiritual themes did not predominate. Samuel Sewall dreamed in 1686 that Christ personally visited Boston, lodging overnight at "Father Hull's." Yet, as Thomas Jolly acknowledged, "Sometimes my dreams are holy and things hang together therein, but my dreams are ordinarily vain, God knows."[53]

Numerous dreams were unpleasant. Many of those recorded in diaries reflected feelings of anxiety, sadness, or anger. "There are more bad dreams than good," rued Margaret Cavendish.[54] While the frequency of negative emotions is not unusual, compared to analyses of twentieth-century visions, more revealing are the specific sources of unease among diarists. Some dreamers had special fears, such as falling prey to financial distress, lawsuits, political chicanery, or even military attack. Sewall, for example, twice dreamed of French invasions of Boston.[55] More elementary concerns, however, dominated. Physical ills loomed large, especially, it seems, the fear of rotting teeth (a persistent source of anxiety even today). In one vision, Laud lost nearly all of his teeth after contracting scurvy.[56] Other agonies ranged from catching fire (not just in hell but asleep in bed) to being mauled by mad dogs (rabid animals were no small concern). Elizabeth Drinker dreamed of her son choking on a rind of roast pork.[57] A common fear was violence by another's hand. Poisoning frightened many, as did grislier deaths. Elias Ashmole dreamed that his father, in escaping from prison, besides suffering a blow to his head, had "his right thigh cut off near the groin." And Boswell, during a visit to Edinburgh, envisioned a "poor wretch lying naked on a dunghill in London, and a blackguard ruffian taking his skin off with a knife in the way an ox is flayed."[58] Evil spirits abounded, both in visions of hell and familiar settings. The Methodist

Benjamin Lakin recorded a dream of having been forced one night to elude demons when returning home from a religious service.[59]

Death was inescapable. Among others, Josselin, Sewall, Parson Woodforde, and William Byrd II all dreamed of their deaths. John Dee's vision in 1582 foretold his disembowelment as well as death, and the Cambridge Alderman Samuel Newton in 1708 dreamed of digging his own grave. Josselin and Sewall both dreamed of the loss of their wives and children, and Boswell of the passing of his daughter and his father (on three separate occasions), with whom his relations were often strained.[60] Other visions contained miscarriages and deaths by plague. Newton dreamed in 1695 of a "great many persons" carrying corpses. An entry in Laud's diary recalled, "I dreamed of the burial of I know not whom, and I stood by the grave. I awakened sad."[61]

Among more pleasant dreams, visits with dead or distant loved ones were prevalent, no small comfort in times of high mortality. The author of *Mid-Night Thoughts* wrote of "frequent conversations with dead friends when we sleep." A Venetian rabbi, Leon Modena, recorded one such reunion with a revered teacher and another with his mother. "Very soon, you will be with me," she informed him. Lady Wentworth, on the other hand, dreamed of her distant son. "Thees three nights," she wrote him in 1710, "I have been much happyer then in the days, for I have dreamt I have been with you." In parts of the Alps, large numbers believed in the existence of the *Nachtschar*, "night phantoms" that returned from the dead in the dreams of shamans. Just a few holy men, such as the Bavarian herdsman Chonrad Stoeckhlin of Oberstdorf, were thought to possess the mysterious ability, when asleep, to join the phantoms' feasts. At these, according to Stoeckhlin and other shamans, there was dancing and joyous music. In the Americas, some slaves, in their visions, flew home to West Africa. Of a trip under the aegis of a "good spirit," a New England slave recounted, "At length we arrived at the African coast and came in sight of the Niger. . . . The shades of night seemed to break away, and all at once he gave me a fair view of Deauyah, my native town."[62]

If, as playwrights and poets romanticized, sleep soothed the weary and oppressed, their principal relief likely came from dreams. Although at times unpleasant, the mere act of dreaming was testament to the independence of souls. As a French writer reflected in 1665, sleep's ability to

Jean-Honoré Fragonard, *The Beggar's Dream*, ca. 1769. An aging pauper dreams of a happier time as a young man with a family.

refresh the "body and mind" was less important than "the liberty" it gave to "the soul." While sleep itself often proved unsatisfying, visions represented not only a road to self-awareness but a well-traveled route of escape from daily suffering. The allure of dreams may have grown after the Middle Ages when for many years the Catholic Church held fast to a doctrine that only monarchs and ecclesiastics likely experienced meaningful visions. A character in one of Jean de La Fontaine's fables averred, "Fate's woven me no life of golden thread, / Nor are there sumptuous hangings by my bed: / My nights are worth no less, their dreams as deep: / Felicities still glorify my sleep."[63]

No doubt for some indigent people, as the satirist William King remarked, "Night repeats the labours of the day." But other persons derived solace from their visions. "The bed generally produces dreams, and so gives that happiness," wrote an eighteenth-century newspaper correspondent, "which nothing else cou'd procure." If the sick dreamed of health, so did unrequited lovers of wedded bliss and the poor of sudden wealth. In Norfolk, a popular folktale told how a peddler from the village of Swaffham thrice dreamt that "joyfull newse" awaited him on London Bridge. After the long journey, he stood patiently on the bridge until a shopkeeper, happening by, asked "if he was such a fool to take a jorney on such a silly errand." What's more—the story went—the shopkeeper related his own dream from the preceding night in which he discovered a vast treasure buried behind a peddler's house in Swaffham. What, the shopkeeper wondered, could be more foolish? Thanking him for his words, the peddler returned home only, of course, to unearth the treasure from his own backyard.[64]

Less frequently, dreams afforded humble men and women opportunities for combating evil and avenging past wrongs. The theologian Synesius of Cyrene, as early as the fifth century, lauded the inability of tyrants to censor their subjects' visions. Dreams, as George Steiner has remarked, "can be the last refuge of freedom and the hearth of resistance." During the early modern era, this occurred most famously among peasants in the Italian region of Friuli who belonged to a fertility cult. Known as *benandanti*, they battled witches in their dreams in order to protect crops and livestock. Explained the cult member Battista Moduco, "I go invisibly in spirit and the body remains behind; we go forth in the service of Christ, and the witches of the devil, we fight with each other, we with bundles of fennel and they with sorghum stalks."[65] An English ballad, "The Poet's Dream," complained that laws "burthen'd the poor till they made them groan." "When I awakened from my dream," describes the ballad, "methoughts the world turn'd upside down." During the English Civil War, the Digger leader William Everard cited a divine vision in support of his own radicalism. A dream, in fact, led the Diggers to select St. George's Hill in Surrey for their egalitarian commune.[66]

A few aggrieved souls even acted out violent visions in their sleep—a propensity confirmed in modern psychiatric research. A Spanish treatise in the mid-fifteenth century spoke of murderous sleepwalkers—"as is well-known, has happened in England." In France, a schoolboy's quarrel with a companion so poisoned his dreams that he rose when at rest to stab his sleeping nemesis with a dagger. A Scottish apprentice, Mansie Wauch, nearly pummeled his wife one night, dreaming that she was, in fact, his master attempting to drag him from a playhouse. "Even in my sleep," Wauch later reflected, "it appears that I like free-will"—demonstrably more in his dreams than in his waking hours.[67]

The impact of dreams in preindustrial communities never became as enduring as it has long been in many non-Western societies. Not only do dreams in some African cultures still provide a critical source of guidance, but they also constitute alternate realms of reality with distinctive social structures. Among the Alorese in the East Indies, entire households are awakened once or several times each night by family members anxious to communicate fresh visions.[68] All the same, early modern communities attached great weight to dreams. Numerous people practiced the "art of procuring pleasant dreams," whether by reading before bed, avoiding heavy meals, or by placing a piece of cake beneath one's pillow. No friend to superstition, Franklin devoted an entire essay to the subject of sanguine dreams, advising, among other measures, moderate meals and fresh air. Country maidens reportedly resorted to charms in order to glimpse their future husbands. One sixteenth-century spell, reprinted in an English chapbook, required the girl to place an onion beneath her pillow before reciting a short verse. Whereupon, "lying on thy back, with thy arms abroad, go to sleep as soon as you can, and in your first sleep you shall dream of him."[69] Such was their currency that the contents of visions often bore repeating within households, between neighbors, and in letters and diaries. In the late summer of 1745, Ebenezer Parkman recorded, "A story has got about of a dream of Mrs. Billings, and which I took the freedom to enquire into and which she confirmed." "There are still many," voiced a critc in 1776, "who are frequently tormenting themselves and their neighbours with their ridiculous dreams." Nearly thirty years later, a man's dream of an impending earthquake in Germantown, Pennsylvania, sent several residents in whom he confided scampering for safety.[70]

From this distance, the influence that dreams had upon individuals and their personal relationships is difficult to imagine. Reverberations could last from fleeting minutes to, in rare instances, entire lifetimes. In the wake of dreams, diarists wrote of feeling "stured up," "perplex'd," and "much afflicted." Margaret Baxter's dreams of murders and fires, according to her husband Richard, "workt half as dangerously on her as realities." "There are many whose waking thoughts are wholly employed on their

Henry Fuseli, *Midnight*, 1765. Two men conversing in their beds (perhaps after their first sleep), with one plainly startled, likely from a dream or nightmare.

sleeping ones," observed a contributor to the *Spectator* in 1712. Friendships might be severed, romances kindled, and spirits either lifted or depressed. A dream prompted the decision of the Virginia colonist John Rolfe to marry the Indian maiden Pocahontas. In 1738 George II was so disturbed by a vision of his deceased wife that, in the dead of night, he went by coach to Westminster Abbey to visit her coffin.[71] Some persons, by drawing religious inspiration from dreams, found their lives enriched. Although Hannah Heaton in Connecticut labeled visions a "foundation of sand," she, like many others, believed that they could "do good when they drive or lead the soul to god & his word." Similarly, a Lancashire doctor opined that it was "below a Christian to be too superstitious and inquisitive" about dreams, yet he also believed in "extraordinary dreams in extraordinary cases."[72]

So influential were visions, so vast was the "prerogative of sleep" that frontiers grew blurred between the waking and invisible worlds. Events in visions occasionally appeared genuine days afterward. An Aberdeen minister, after viewing an unusual spectacle outside his window, later could not remember "whither he dreamed it or seemed to see it in reality." Claimed a correspondent to the *Sussex Weekly Advertiser*, "How many dreams do we daily hear related, and with such consequence and plausibility, that the relater himself believes he was awake." At the Old Bailey in 1783, Richard Deavill defended his theft of four iron bars by claiming the owner's consent. That it came in a dream appears, to Deavill, to have been an afterthought, or so he claimed. More remarkable is that a credulous jury found him not guilty of the crime.[73]

Had preindustrial families not stirred until dawn, remaining instead asleep, many visions of self-revelation, solace, and spirituality would have perished by the bedside—some lost in the throes of sleep, others dissipated by the distractions of a new day—"flitting with returning light," wrote the poet John Whaley. "Like a morning dream," affirmed John Dryden's *Oedipus* (1679), "vanish'd in the business of the day."[74] Instead, the habit of awakening in the middle of the night, after one's first sleep, allowed many to absorb fresh visions before returning to unconsciousness. Unless distracted by noise, sickness, or some other discomfort, their mood was probably relaxed and their concentration complete. In fact, the force of some visions—their impact intensified by elevated levels of the hormone prolactin—might have kept nighttime vexations at bay. After the moment of awakening, there also would have been ample time for a dream to "acquire its structure" from the initial "chaos of disjointed images." It is probably not coincidental that Boswell, whose sleep was rarely broken, just as rarely "had a recollection" of dreams when he woke each morning. In contrast, the earnest author of *The New Art of Thriving* (1706), felt compelled to warn readers against pondering their visions:

> What a 'shame is it to spend half ones lifetime in dreams and slumbers; leave your bed therefore when first sleep hath left you, lest custom render your body sluggish, or (which is worse) *your mind a cage of unclean thoughts* [my italics].[75]

Nearly two hundred years ago, a European psychologist, Sigismund Ehrenreich Graf von Redern, deduced that persons "rudely awakened" from their "first sleep" had the "same feeling" as if they had been "interrupted at a very serious task." Clinical experiments at the National Institute of Mental Health confirm that subjects who experienced two stages of slumber were in rapid eye movement (REM) sleep just before they awakened around midnight, with REM being the stage of sleep directly connected to dreaming. What's more, Thomas Wehr has found, "transitions to wakefulness are most likely to occur from REM periods that are especially intense," typically accompanied by "particularly vivid dreams" distinguished by their "narrative quality," which many of the subjects in his experiment contemplated in the darkness.[76]

So in the drama *Gallathea*, before an audience that included Queen Elizabeth on New Year's night in 1592, the character Eurota remarked, "My sleeps broken and full of dreams." Affirmed Nicholas Breton, around one o'clock the "spirits of the studious start out of their dreames." Hannah Heaton awoke in the night from a dream bearing news of an angel from God. "Good part of the night," she jotted in her diary, "I watcht for fear I should forget this lovely dream." And in Lancashire, Richard Kay reflected, "I have dreamed dreams that when I have awoke out of them they have, even in the dark and silent night, brought me upon my knees and deeply humbled me."[77]

COCK-CROW

I

Ghosts and witches, at present, rarely make their appearance. A better philosophy has laid those spirits, and rendered our churchyards far less dreadful.

GENTLEMAN'S MAGAZINE, 1755[1]

BEGINNING IN THE eighteenth century, nighttime in cities and towns changed dramatically. "THE REIGN OF THE NIGHT is finally going to end," proclaimed a Parisian in 1746. No previous time in Western history experienced such a sustained assault upon the nocturnal realm as did the period from 1730 to 1830. Not only did people stay up later, but, more importantly, growing numbers after dark ventured outdoors in search of pleasure and profit. Evening strolls became a popular pastime in their own right, both solitary walks and public promenades to showcase one's wealth. "I greatly love to walk out on a moon light night," Elizabeth Drinker commented at the turn of the century. Where curfew bells yet tolled, in small and large communities, their plaintive knell paid homage to a bygone age. In the remote Scottish town of Elgin, a passing visitor observed in 1790, "The curfew still tolls, but it seems rather a signal to light than put out the candle." Even the term "night season," denoting the distinctiveness of nocturnal hours, gradually faded from everyday speech.[2]

It would be difficult to exaggerate the importance of this remarkable transformation in urban life. Especially for the middle classes, hours once dominated by darkness became more familiar. The public spaces that people shared were larger and more crowded. Just as coaches and pedestrians filled major avenues, so did squares and plazas become hubs of commotion and activity. Time and again, observers commented on the liveliness of city streets at night. Of the *Pont Neuf* across the Seine, a visitor to Paris reported in 1777, "All through the night, without ceasing, pedestrians are wending their way over it." In Naples, Robert Semple found the main street "thronged" with people past sunset. "Life awake at all hours of the night," a person observed of London in 1801. Early American cities experienced expanded traffic of their own. "There is hardly any one," remarked a letter in the *Boston Newsletter*, "who is not obliged to be frequently abroad in an evening, either on the calls of friendship, humanity, business, or pleasure." A visitor in 1796 found Philadelphia's streets after dark full of "commotion."[3]

The origins of this nocturnal revolution were diverse. Certainly, it owed much to the rapid spread of scientific rationalism during the early stages of the Enlightenment. By the first years of the eighteenth century, learned men and women on both sides of the Atlantic increasingly rejected the preindustrial worldview of centuries past. Coupled with advances in literacy, mounting clerical hostility, and the growth of capitalism, Enlightenment beliefs steadily led to the "disenchantment" of the Western world, as Max Weber famously postulated. Among the propertied classes, reason and skepticism triumphed over magic and superstition. On the Continent, witchcraft prosecutions almost everywhere subsided by the late 1600s, as they did in colonial America. The final trial in England occurred in 1712, with Parliament formally repealing its statute against witchcraft twenty-four years later. Observed the *Public Advertiser* in 1762, "We experience every day, that as science and learning increases, the vulgar notions of spirits, apparitions, witches and demons, decrease and die of themselves."[4]

True, false alarms still arose from time to time. During the eighteenth century, London, Bristol, and Dublin all experienced well-publicized encounters with "evil spirits." The infrequency of such incidents contributed to their sensationalism. Best known was London's Cock Lane Ghost in 1762, which, after an investigation led by Samuel Johnson, proved to be an elaborate hoax. By 1788, a newspaper could report, "Not a single building in all London is perhaps now to be heard of, which bears the repute of being an haunted house." London had given up the ghost. About the same time, a Scottish minister affirmed that "ghosts, goblins, witches, and fairies have relinquished the land."[5]

With the decline in magical beliefs, nighttime for most urban households became less menacing. Like the natural world generally, darkness lost much of its aura of terror and mystery. Formerly a source of fear within educated circles, night even became, for some observers, an object of awe and admiration. The very air at night, once thought perilous, now appeared sweet and refreshing. Celestial spectacles such as comets inspired rapture rather than dread, as unprecedented numbers delighted in using telescopes. Artists, travelers, and poets all celebrated night's beauty and grandeur. Visiting the Continent in 1787, a London bookseller exulted, "The evening was still & tranquil & the sky perfectly serene, enriched with millions of stars shining in perfect beauty." Similarly, a traveler in France opined, "Nothing could be more delightful than this journeying by moonlight, in a serene night." A growing number of essayists dilated upon night's "peculiar beauties." No praise was too effusive. "Transcendentally beautiful," proclaimed a writer in 1795. Indeed, claimed "Valverdi" in the *Literary Magazine*, "Day, with the resplendent sun flaming along the glowing heavens, in all the pomp of splendour, is inferior in touching beauty to the milder glories of night—soft, but not insipid; glorious, but not glaring; beautiful, but yet sublime."[6]

If nighttime appeared less sinister, it also became, during the eighteenth century, more profitable. More and more, darkness fell subject to consumerism and nascent industrialization, both fueled by a commercial revolution sweeping Britain and much of the Continent. Improved road and river systems along with innovations in communications spurred expanding markets at home and abroad. Within northwestern Europe, a rising middle class in urban areas, swollen in size and wealth, contributed in the 1700s to a wave of domestic consumption. Craftsmen, shopkeepers, and clerks set their sights on purchasing luxury goods in addition to basic necessities. In many cities and towns, bustling shops, markets, and arcades stayed open well past nightfall. "All the shops are open till ten o'clock at night, and exceedingly well lighted," remarked a visitor to London in 1789. At a fair in The Hague, shopkeepers displayed their wares past midnight, relying upon moonlight and lamps. The Palais-Royal was Paris's principal center for evening consumers. "Just picture a beautiful square palace," wrote a traveler, "and beneath it arcades, where in countless shops glitter treasures from all the world"—all "wonderfully displayed and illuminated by bright, dazzling lights, of many colors." Night, declared the commercial classes, was open for business.[7]

Meanwhile, early manufacturers, with heavy capital investments in mills and machinery, achieved gains in productivity from operating around the clock. In the Midlands, Sir Richard Arkwight's cotton mills, a passer-by wrote in 1790, "never leave off working." "When they are lighted up, on a dark night," he marveled, they "look most luminously beautiful." And, too, a growing number of iron foundries blazed, sending smoke and flashes of light across the sky. At the famed site of Coalbrookdale in Shropshire, a visitor commented, "The fires from the furnaces were bursting forth in the darkness."[8] Not least, commerce increasingly coursed through the evening hours, as goods flowed to inland markets and farmers brought livestock and produce to cities. Wagons and carriages crisscrossed the countryside, as did, by the mid-1700s, postal riders and mail-coaches. Lying at an inn overnight in the Kent town of Sittingbourne, James Essex complained in 1773, "Much disturbed all night by the chaises and coaches which were going from thence or coming in at all hours."[9]

It bears noting that trade, coupled with urban sprawl and advances in

Philip James de Loutherbourg, *Coalbrookdale by Night*, 1801.

military technology, rapidly rendered urban walls obsolete. Originally designed to repel one's foes, these immense fortifications proved an impediment to commerce, particularly at night once gates were shut. By the end of the eighteenth century, most cities and towns across Europe had either abandoned or demolished their walls. Of Bordeaux's ramparts, a contemporary reflected in 1715, "They are a relic of the past, overtaken by the expansion of the faubourgs and hampering the development of the port, and condemned by economic necessity and the growth of the town as much as new strides in the art of war." Where walls yet remained, they often served as little more than promenades for pedestrians and carriages. In Paris, where more than half of its outer wall still stood in the eighteenth century, coaches could be seen along the ramparts.[10]

Of parallel importance was the leisured affluence of urban households. Assemblies, pleasure gardens, masquerades, gaming, and theatres, now more than ever, adorned the evening hours of the beau monde. "Fashionable hours" only drew later. In London, a critic wrote in 1779, "The nightly entertainments, which used to begin at six in the evening, are now begun at eight or nine." York and Bath became famed for assemblies, with numerous provincial towns, from Scarborough to Tunbridge Wells, following suit. Elsewhere in Europe, genteel amusements, if anything, reflected greater opulence. In Naples, gatherings did not break up before five in the morning. Declared a German journal in 1786, "The pleasures of the evening and night . . . are the ruling fashion in every large city, where luxury and the need for entertainment constantly increase." Even on the Isle of Man, there were frequent card-parties and assemblies in the town of Douglas. And in America, which experienced its own surge of prosperity in the 1700s, a southerner boasted, "We have constant assemblys & many other amusements."[11]

Where aristocrats once claimed such gatherings to themselves, well-to-do bourgeois families eagerly emulated their betters. New wealth and dreams of gentility altered traditional haunts and habits. A London newspaper noted in 1733, "Traders, instead of amusing themselves of an ev'ning as we did over a pipe and a dish of coffee, are running to the play, the opera, or the ridotto." The following year, "people of all ranks" reportedly flocked to Dublin theaters, while in Venice a visitor in 1739 discovered that masquerades were the "favorite pleasure both of the grandees and the commonalty." In fact, to judge from upper-class complaints, mounting numbers of upstarts gained entrance to aristocratic diversions. Because many of these—playhouses, assemblies, and pleasure gardens—were commercial in nature, access was difficult to restrict. Playhouse audiences in London became largely middle-class. Excluded from private parties, bourgeois families in Frankfurt am Main held "assemblies of the same kind among themselves." Immensely popular, too, were clubs, of which there was an explosion in England and colonial America. Serving a variety of interests and occupations, these afforded members a private setting for fellowship and drink, with many clubs reserving taverns and coffeehouses for meetings. Most famous was the Lunar Society of Birmingham, whose founders in the late 1760s included Erasmus Darwin, James Watt, and Josiah Wedgwood. Devoted to scientific progress, the Society acquired its name, ironically, from holding its monthly meetings when the moon was full and travel safest.[12]

II

> *Were the whole body of lewd offenders attack'd at once, in the street, and out of the street; were all the publick houses that entertain them obliged to shut them out; all noted brothels, bawdy-houses and night-houses shut up, and well guarded, the streets and dark retreats thoroughly scour'd, and well lighted; and all disorderly persons taken up and punish'd, as the law directs . . . vice would be even harras'd out of the town.*
>
> *BRITISH JOURNAL*, SEPT. 12, 1730[13]

There was, then, all the more reason, with the rise of wealthy leisure classes, for growing public alarm over the nocturnal disorder long plaguing cities and towns. If evil spirits fled urban haunts during the eighteenth century, theft, vandalism, and violence remained persistent dangers. Crime seemed to spread on both sides of the Atlantic. Population growth, large-scale unemployment, and rising food prices contributed among the lower orders to widespread hardship, particularly in Europe. Although homicide rates actually declined in England over the 1700s, property crime was rampant. The poor "starve, and freeze, and rot among themselves," wrote Henry Fielding, "but they beg, steal and rob among their betters." A newspaper warned, "The common people, especially the inhabitants of London, are more abandoned than their fore-fathers." Whether or not perceptions of mounting crime were always correct, at stake, in the view of civic functionaries, was the sovereignty of the public arena. Who at night should rule: thieves, prostitutes, and other urban riffraff, or, instead, their natural superiors, including members of the burgeoning middle class? "What insolences people are exposed to in the evening, and at night, even in so public a place as the Strand," the social reformer Jonas Hanway moaned in 1754. In French cities, it was commonly complained that *coureurs de nuit* "insult and maltreat" citizens "who are obliged to be abroad in the streets during the night about their affairs." Urban centers from Geneva to Philadelphia feared rising lawlessness, but arguably none experienced the profound anxiety that gripped London. So crime-ridden was the capital and its environs that in 1774 even the prime minister, Lord Frederick North, was robbed. On top of everything else, the anti-Catholic Gordon Riots rocked London in 1780, resulting in nearly three hundred deaths, and the city suffered an epidemic of theft and violence during the decade following the American Revolution. "We can neither travel abroad, nor sleep at home in our beds," exclaimed a resident in 1785.[14]

Authorities in London and other beleaguered cities took a variety of steps to impose greater discipline. Most of these measures were designed to pacify public spaces, already the focus of efforts to improve sanitation and paved streets. The late hours kept by alehouses became a favorite target for government regulation. A newspaper in 1785 urged that night-houses be closed altogether—"the actual receptacles of all the male and female villains who prey nightly on the public, and disturb its peace."[15]

Of greater importance, however, were two more sweeping offensives, which in many cities proceeded on parallel paths. The first called for improvements in public illumination. A widespread symbol of progress during the eighteenth century, light had enormous potential as a weapon of social control. In 1736, London received nearly five thousand oil lamps, to be lit at all hours of the night during every season of the year. The preamble to Parliament's act for "better enlightening the streets" cited London's "frequent murders, robberies, burglaries," and other "felonies" in the "night season." Advances in urban lighting, fueled in cities on both sides of the Atlantic by oil from the whaling trade, gained momentum over the century. "What man has so little experience to ignore that crimes are almost always committed by night," pleaded Geneva petitioners in 1775 for better lighting. The introduction in London of Argand oil lamps in the mid-1780s featured a radically redesigned wick that burned at higher temperatures. That innovation, coupled with a new glass cylinder enclosing the lamp's flame, produced a notably brighter light.[16]

Still more significant, as the eighteenth century gave way to the nineteenth, was the introduction of street lamps that burned coal gas. After an initial display along London's Pall Mall in early 1807, the *Times* exclaimed, "There is nothing so important to the British realm, since that of navigation." Indeed, the light emitted from a lone gas mantle was ten to twelve times as strong as that from a candle or an old-fashioned oil lamp. As lamps spread throughout the principal arteries of the city, frosted glass became necessary to soften the glare. By 1823, nearly forty thousand lamps lit more than two hundred miles of London's streets. Many British cities and towns quickly followed in London's path, as did foreign cities like Paris, Berlin, and Baltimore. Such was the burgeoning popularity of gas lighting, the *Liverpool Mercury* proclaimed that "daylight" would soon "prevail in our streets and shops all night round." Gas, affirmed Sidney Parker in Jane Austen's *Sandition* (1817), "was doing more for the prevention of crime than any single body in England since the days of Alfred the Great."[17]

Equally important to public safety was the reformation of law enforcement. As the *London Chronicle* asserted in 1758, "Light and a watch are the greatest enemies to villains." Over the course of the eighteenth century, nightwatches grew in size and competence. With the creation of separate forces for firefighting, watchmen concentrated instead upon combating crime. Paris, in fact, already relied upon a force of trained police, the *garde*, as did several other European cities. Less enthusiastic were English localities, which traditionally opposed reliance on authoritarian forces. Critics of a parliamentary bill reforming Bristol's watch in 1755 complained of the heightened power that constables and watchmen would enjoy to apprehend nightwalkers, by which "the liberty of the best citizens may be endangered." No less emphatic, a writer in the *Public Advertiser* protested the creation of night patrols, on the order of the French police, "to shock us at every corner."[18]

All the same, public sentiment slowly shifted in the face of rising

Thomas Rowlandson, *A Peep at the Gas Lights in Pall-Mall*, 1809. Among other comments, a prostitute declares, "If this light is not put a stop to—we must give up our business. We may as well shut up shop." To which a pedestrian responds, "True, my dear: not a dark corner for love or money."

crime, and London gradually revamped its watch. An early proponent of a "regularly established police" for London wrote in 1762, "Our houses would be secure from fire, and our persons from the attack of robbers; idle 'prentices would not be suffered to scour the streets, nor the daring strumpet to delude the unwary." First in Westminster, then elsewhere, patrols grew more regimented, more numerous, and more aggressive, ultimately culminating in the creation in 1829 of the Metropolitan Police, followed several years later by parliamentary authorization for provincial police. The foremost proponent of the Metropolitan Police, Home Secretary Sir Robert Peel, wrote the prime minister, "I want to teach people that liberty does not consist in having your house robbed by organized gangs of thieves, and in leaving the principal streets of London in the nightly possession of drunken whores and vagabonds."[19]

During the nineteenth century, gas lighting and professional police transformed nocturnal life on both sides of the Atlantic. By blurring the boundaries between day and night, they altered the pace and scope of people's lives. Ironically, in some areas afflicted by industrial pollution, nights grew brighter just as smoke and soot darkened streets by day. More than ever, there was greater freedom of movement at night, temporally and spatially, in cities and towns. And with larger numbers of pedestrians, streets and squares appeared safer. Already, a visitor to London in 1829 reported:

> Thousands of lamps, in long chains of fire, stretch away to enormous distances. The display of the shops, lighted up with peculiar brillancy, and filled with valuable merchandise, which to decoy the customer, are rendered oftentimes more brillant by the reflection of numerous mirrors, is most striking in effect. The streets are thronged with people, and thousands of elegant equipages roll along to the appointed dinner-hour party, or to listen to the strains of Pasta. The night-watch, too, is going on, headed by some modern Dogberry. Two and two they set out for their beat from the Parish watch-house, well coated, lanterned, and cudgelled; big with their brief authority, and full of ferocious determination to keep the King's peace.

A resident of New York echoed in 1853, "The facilities for going abroad in the evening have been greatly increased, and in many streets it is as safe and agreeable to walk out in the evening as by daylight." Then, too, domestic lighting became both brighter and safer. Declining reliance upon candles, coupled with less flammable building materials, dramatically reduced the number of urban fires, thereby encouraging families, even more, to illuminate their homes in the evening.[20]

Whether lives were consistently enriched by pushing back the darkness is less evident. Besides emitting a nauseating smell, coal gas was a growing source of pollution. Critics complained that the light was too harsh. Shift labor expanded in factories, as did industrial surveillance by owners. If night became more accessible, it also became less private, on the job and off. Not only could the human eye now see a farther distance, but there were infinitely more eyes in public by which to be observed, including, first and foremost, those belonging to the police. Urban centers became policed communities, insofar as authorities grew better equipped to enforce their will. All persons faced greater scrutiny at night, occasionally with embarrassing consequences. In a minor cause célèbre in 1825, a London barrister, George Price, was charged with indecent exposure after urinating near a streetlamp in Maiden Lane—though such behavior in the darkness of night had been customary. By necessity, personal conduct in public grew more repressed. Drunkeness, brawling, all forms of rowdiness fell prey to social oversight. Sexual liaisons, even romantic gestures, needed to be more circumspect, as did control of one's bodily impulses. "All these mysteries," wrote a French poet of illicit behavior, "have for witnesses, the street lights from the bad corners."[21]

Advances in lighting and professional police created a tension between public safety and personal privacy. No one framed the conflict as elegantly as Ralph Waldo Emerson, who observed, "As gas-light is found to be the best nocturnal police, so the universe protects itself by pitiless publicity." Often, in English cities, not only did police departments maintain street lights, but the lamps themselves became known as "police lamps." Even domestic interiors, owing to improved lighting, grew more visible to passersby, some of whom took evening strolls just to scrutinize their neighbors. With little exaggeration, the author of *Berlin Becomes a Metropolis* remarked in 1868, "Since the invention of gas light, our evening life has experienced an indescribable intensification, our pulse has accelerated, nervous excitation has been heightened; we have had to change our appearance, our behaviour and our customs, because they had to be accommodated to a different light."[22]

As did patterns of sleep, which became more compressed as persons lengthened their days. Equally important, sleep for increasing numbers became seamless. Beginning in the late seventeenth century, divided slumber gradually grew less common in cities and towns, first among propertied households, then, more slowly, among other social ranks due to later bedtimes and improved illumination. Heightened exposure to artificial lighting, both at home and abroad, altered circadian rhythms as old as man himself. By the mid-1800s, only people unable to afford adequate lighting, in all likelihood, still experienced segmented sleep, particularly if forced to retire at an early hour. The working-class author of *The Great Unwashed*, for example, remarked in 1868 that laborers who had "to turn out early in the morning" were "already in their first sleep" at night when the streets of his town were "still in a state of comparative bustle." Altered, too, was the relative importance of nocturnal dreams. No longer did most sleepers experience an interval of wakefulness in which to ponder visions in the dead of night. With the transition to a new pattern of slumber, at once consolidated and more compressed, increasing numbers lost touch with their dreams and, as a consequence, a traditional avenue to their deepest emotions. It is no small irony that, by turning night into day, modern technology has helped to obstruct our oldest path to the human psyche. That, very likely, has been the greatest loss, to paraphrase an early poet, of having been "disannulled of our first sleep, and cheated of our dreams and fantasies."[23]

III

Now we want electric lamps brutally to cut and strip away with their thousand points of light your mysterious, sickening, alluring shadows!

FILIPPO TOMMASO MARINETTI, 1912[24]

At least a few major cities resisted improvements in artificial illumination. In Rome, Pope Gregory XVI (1765–1846), in an odd twist of logic, forbade street lamps lest the populace use their light to foment rebellion. Opposition to lighting was also pronounced in Cologne, which in 1801 a visitor pronounced "at least two centuries behind the rest of Germany in the improvement of arts and sciences." The *Kölnische Zeitung* in 1819 printed a litany of arguments, including the conviction that lamps interfered "with the divine plan of the world" preordaining "darkness during the night time." In England, to save money, such provincial centers as Sheffield, Leicester, and Norwich, as late as the 1820s, still reserved street lighting for "dark nights."[25] Even in cities with gas, not all streets fared the same. Central boulevards stood the best chance of receiving lamps, as did shopping districts and neighborhoods of the propertied classes. Artificial illumination became both a symbol and a determinant of urban differentiation. Numerous back lanes, side streets, and alleys remained bereft of public lighting. Of his childhood in Berlin, a writer recalled, "A step into the side streets, and you felt set back by centuries." For their part, the lower orders found themselves in ill-lit warrens segregated from major thoroughfares and wealthier residential areas. Whereas their forbears had once roamed cities and towns at will, exerting nocturnal authority over a vast domain, the indigent were increasingly confined to zones of darkness riddled by extensive crime, as captured by Gustave Doré in his prints of London slums. "Beyond the bounds of civilization," a well-to-do resident of New York City observed of impoverished neighborhoods at mid-century.[26]

Notably, when urban disorders occasionally flared, among the first casualties were street lamps. Contrary to papal fears, light was a friend of the established order. For tactical and symbolic reasons, these weapons of government surveillance fell prey to destruction from Milan to Goteborg. Set in Paris during the upheavals of 1830, Victor Hugo's famous novel *Les Misérables* (1862) contains a chapter entitled "The Street Urchin an Enemy of Light," depicting the lantern-smashing techniques of the orphan Gavroche in bourgeois neighborhoods. "Along with the réverbères," stated an account of the first night of the July Revolution, "all other symbols of the treacherous king's authority were destroyed." Similarly, during the Revolution of 1848 in Vienna, an observer recalled, "Many people, mostly of the lower classes, had assembled on the Glacis, smashing the gas lanterns, destroying the lantern poles. . . . Out of the pipes came the gas and produced gigantic red columns of fire."[27]

However spectacular, this was not the final gasp of resistance to modern lighting. For much of the nineteenth century, darkness found welcome sanctuary in the countryside, which still contained large pockets of rural fundamentalism inimical to enhanced trade, transportation, and communications. There, the forces of modernization were temporarily checked or forced, at least, to adapt to rural ways. Labor discipline in a Lancashire cotton mill during the 1830s entailed parading the effigy of a ghost across the shop floor at night to deter child workers from sleeping. For artificial illumination, village households continued to rely upon tallow candles, rushlights, and oil lamps. Thus did the West Yorkshire village of Pudsey escape the "vulgar intrusion" of "busy-bodies," boasted a resident in 1887. "There is no gas, no street lamps, and very little light shown from the dwellings." The European countryside, still mysterious and unpredictable, remained a world of fairies and fireside tales, poaching, and midnight pranks. "There was no gas in the streets then," recalled a Staffordshire tex-

Eine Nacht-Scene vom 13. auf den 14. März 1848 in der Nähe der k. k. Stallungen.

Anon., *Lantern Smashing in Vienna, 1848*, 1849.

tile worker in 1892. "This dispeller of mischief and ghosts had not then come into the available resources of civilization."[28]

Toward the turn of the century, gas, then electricity, along with other marvels of modernity, inexorably transformed rustic communities. By World War I, if not sooner, country villages comprised an unmarked grave for many vestiges of traditional life. So in his small classic, *Change in the Village* (1912), the Surrey wheelwright George Sturt described how "braying" motorcars, "new road-lamps," and "lit-up villa windows" breached the "quiet depths of darkness." For the time being, Sturt also wrote of his "first sleep," though that too would pass.[29]

Today we inhabit a nonstop culture characterized by widespread electric lighting both within and outside homes and businesses. Never before, in our everyday lives, have we been more dependent upon artificial illumination, arguably the greatest symbol of modern progress. Besides boasting all-night television and radio, twenty-four-hour service stations and supermarkets, evening has become the primary time of employment for a

Europe at Night, W. Sullivan, n.d.

growing segment of the Western workforce, not to mention millions of moonlighters. Darkness represents the largest remaining frontier for commercial expansion. Thomas Edison's dictum "Put an undeveloped human being into an environment where there is artificial light and he will improve" has carried the night as well as the day. No shortage of metropolitan areas in Europe and North America currently bill themselves as "twenty-four-hour" cities. Not surprisingly, sleep, too, has fallen prey to the hurried pace and busy schedules of modern life. In the United States today, perhaps 30 percent of adults average six or fewer hours of rest a night, with that portion rising as more persons stretch their waking hours. Disdaining sleep as a waste of time, many adolescents find their slumber harmed by television, computers, and other sources of sensory stimulation. Meanwhile, the United States military, seeking a battlefield advantage, has begun investigating ways to keep soldiers awake for periods of up to seven days.[30]

In John Dryden's comedy *Amphitryon* (1690), the ancient deity Mercury demands of Night, "What art thou good for . . . but only for love and fornication?" In view of our present trajectory of technological change, we might well pose the same question today. Increasingly, rather than render nighttime more accessible, we are instead risking its gradual elimination. Already, the heavens, our age-old source of awe and wonder, have been obscured by the glare of outdoor lighting. Only in remote spots can one still glimpse the grandeur of the Milky Way. Entire constellations have disappeared from sight, replaced by a blank sky. Conversely, the fanciful world of our dreams has grown more distant with the loss of segmented sleep and, with it, a better understanding of our inner selves. Certainly, it is not difficult to imagine a time when night, for all practical purposes, will have become day—truly a twenty-four/seven society in which traditional phases of time, from morning to midnight, have lost their original identities.[31] The Russian government has even attempted to launch an experimental "space mirror" designed to transform night into twilight in selected locations with the aid of reflected light from the sun.[32]

The residual beauty of the night sky, alternating cycles of darkness and light, and regular respites from the daily round of sights and sounds—all will be impaired by enhanced illumination. Ecological systems, with their own patterns of nocturnal life, will suffer immeasurably. With darkness diminished, opportunities for privacy, intimacy, and self-reflection will grow more scarce. Should that luminous day arrive, we stand to lose a vital element of our humanity—one as precious as it is timeless. That, in the depths of a dark night, should be a bracing prospect for any spent soul to contemplate.

NOTES

(A fuller set of citations may be found at www.wwnorton.com.)

ABBREVIATIONS

Add. Mss.	Additional Manuscripts, British Library, London
AHR	*American Historical Review*
Assi 45	Northern Assize Circuit Depositions, Public Record Office, London
Bargellini, "Vita Notturna"	Piero Bargellini, "La Vita Notturna," in *Vita Privata a Firenze nei Secoli XIV e XV* (Florence, 1966), 75–89
BC	*British Chronicle* (London)
Beattie, *Crime*	J. M. Beattie, *Crime and the Courts in England, 1600–1800* (Princeton, N.J., 1986)
Beck, *Diary*	David Beck, *Spiegel van Mijn Leven; een Haags Daboek uit 1624,* ed. Sv. E. Veldhijsen (Hilversum, 1993)
Best, *Books*	Donald Woodward, ed., *The Farming and Memorandum Books of Henry Best of Elmswell, 1642* (London, 1984)
BL	British Library, London
Bodl.	Bodleian Library, Oxford
Bourne, *Antiquitates Vulgares*	Henry Bourne, *Antiquitates Vulgares; or, the Antiquities of the Common People* . . . (Newcastle, Eng., 1725)
Bräker, *Life*	Ulrich Bräker, *The Life Story and Real Adventures of the Poor Man of Toggenburg,* trans. Derek Bowman (Edinburgh, 1970)
Brand 1777	John Brand, *Observations on Popular Antiquities* . . . (New Castle upon Tyne, 1777)
Brand 1848	John Brand et al., *Observations on the Popular Antiquities of Great Britain* . . . , 3 vols. (London, 1848)
Breton, *Works*	Alexander B. Grosart, ed., *The Works in Verse and Prose of Nicholas Breton* . . . , 2 vols. (1879; rpt. edn., New York, 1966)
Burke, *Popular Culture*	Peter Burke, *Popular Culture in Early Modern Europe* (London, 1978)
Burt, *Letters*	Edward Burt, *Letters from a Gentleman in the North of Scotland to His Friend in London* . . . , 2 vols. (London, 1754)

Cannon, Diary — Memoirs of the Birth, Education, Life, and Death of Mr. John Cannon, 1684–1742, Somerset Archaeological and Natural History Society, Taunton, England

Carter, *Diary* — Jack P. Greene, ed., *The Diary of Colonel Landon Carter of Sabine Hall, 1752–1778*, 2 vols. (Charlottesville, Va., 1965)

Clegg, *Diary* — Vanessa S. Doe, ed., *The Diary of James Clegg of Chapel en le Frith, 1708–1755*, 2 vols. (Matlock, Eng., 1978)

Cohens, *Italy* — Elizabeth Storr Cohen and Thomas V. Cohen, *Daily Life in Renaissance Italy* (Westport, Ct., 2001)

Cole, *Diary* — Francis Griffin Stokes, ed., *The Blecheley Diary of the Rev. William Cole . . . 1765–67* (London, 1931)

Cowper, Diary — Diary of Dame Sarah Cowper, Hertfordshire County Record Office, Hertford, England

Crusius, *Nocte* — Jacobus Andreas Crusius, *De Nocte et Nocturnis Officiis, Tam Sacris, Quam Prophanis, Lucubrationes Historico-Philologico-Juridicae* (Bremen, 1660)

Defoe, *Tour* — Daniel Defoe, *A Tour thro' the Whole Island of Great Britian . . .* , 2 vols. (1724–1726; rpt. edn., London, 1968)

Dekker, *Writings* — Thomas Dekker, *The Wonderful Year [Etc] and Selected Writings*, ed. E. D. Pendry (Cambridge, Mass., 1968)

Dietz, *Surgeon* — Master Johann Dietz, *Surgeon in the Army of the Great Elector and Barber to the Royal Court: From the Old Manuscripts in the Royal Library in Berlin*, trans. B. Miall (London, 1923)

Drinker, *Diary* — Elaine Forman Crane et al., eds., *The Diary of Elizabeth Drinker*, 3 vols. (Boston, 1991)

DUR — *Daily Universal Register* (London)

Dyer, Diary — Diary of William Dyer, 2 vols., Bristol Central Library, Bristol

East Anglian Diaries — Matthew Storey, ed., *Two East Anglian Diaries, 1641–1729: Isaac Archer and William Coe* (Woodbridge, Eng., 1994)

ECR — George Francis Dow, ed., *Records and Files of the Quarterly Courts of Essex County, Massachusetts*, 8 vols. (Salem, Mass., 1911–1921)

Evelyn, *Diary* — Esmond Samuel De Beer, ed., *The Diary of John Evelyn*, 6 vols. (Oxford, 1951)

F. Platter, *Journal* — Seán Jennett, ed. and trans., *Beloved Son Felix: The Journal of Felix Platter, a Medical Student in Montpellier in the Sixteenth Century* (London, 1962)

Falkus, "Lighting" — Malcolm Falkus, "Lighting in the Dark Ages of English Economic History: Town Streets before the Industrial Revolution," in D. C. Coleman and A. H. John, eds., *Trade, Government, and Economy in Pre-Industrial England: Essays Presented to F. J. Fisher* (London, 1976), 248–273

Flaherty, *Privacy* — David H. Flaherty, *Privacy in Colonial New England* (Charlottesville, Va., 1972)

FLEMT — David I. Kertzer and Marzio Barbagli, eds., *Family Life in Early Modern Times*, Vol. 1 of *The History of the European Family* (New Haven, 2001)

G and LDA — *Gazetteer and London Daily Advertiser*

G and NDA — *Gazetteer and New Daily Advertiser* (London)

Garnert, *Lampan* — Jan Garnert, *Anden i Lampan: Etnologiska Perspektiv på ljus Och Mörker* (Stockholm, 1993)

GM — *Gentleman's Magazine* (London)

Griffiths, *Youth* — Paul Griffiths, *Youth and Authority: Formative Experiences in England, 1560–1640* (Oxford, 1987)

Grose, *Dictionary* — Francis Grose, *A Classical Dictionary of the Vulgar Tongue* (London, 1785)

Harrison, *Description* — William Harrison, *The Description of England*, ed. Georges Edelen (Ithaca, N.Y., 1968)

Heywood, *Diaries* — J. Horsfull Turner, ed., *The Rev. Oliver Heywood, B.A., 1630–1702; His Autobiography, Diaries, Anecdote and Event Books . . .*, 4 vols. (Brighouse, Eng., 1882)

HMM and GA — *Harrop's Manchester Mercury and General Advertiser*

HPL II — Georges Duby, ed., *Revelations of the Medieval World*, trans. Arthur Goldhammer, Vol. 2 of Philippe Ariès and George Duby, eds., *History of Private Life* (Cambridge, Mass., 1988)

HPL III — Roger Chartier, ed., *Passions of the Renaissance*, trans. Arthur Goldhammer, Vol. 3 of Philippe Ariès and Georges Duby, eds., *History of Private Life* (Cambridge, Mass., 1989)

HWW III — Natalie Zemon Davis and Arlette Farge, eds., *Renaissance and Enlightened Paradoxes*, Vol. 3 of Georges Duby and Michelle Perrot, eds., *A History of Women in the West* (Cambridge, Mass., 1993)

Isham, *Diary* — Norman Marlow, ed., *The Diary of Thomas Isham of Lamport (1658–81) . . .* (Farnborough, Eng., 1971)

Janekovick-Römer, "Dubrovniks" — Zdenka Janekovick-Römer, "'Post Tertiam Campanam': Das Nachtleben Dubrovniks im Mittelalter," *Historische Anthropologie* 3 (1995), 100–111

JIH — *Journal of Interdisciplinary History*

Josselin, *Diary* — Alan Macfarlane, ed., *The Diary of Ralph Josselin* (London, 1976)

JRAI — John Cameron and John Imrie, eds., *The Justiciary Records of Argyll and the Isles, 1664–1742*, 2 vols. (Edinburgh, 1949, 1969)

JSH — *Journal of Social History*

JUH — *Journal of Urban History*

Jütte, *Poverty* — Robert Jütte, *Poverty and Deviance in Early Modern Europe* (Cambridge, 1994)

Kay, *Diary* — W. Brockbank and F. Kenworthy, eds., *The Diary of Richard Kay, 1716–51 of Baldingstone, Neary Bury: A Lancashire Doctor* (Manchester, 1968)

Koslofsky, "Court Culture" — Craig Koslofsky, "Court Culture and Street Lighting in Seventeenth-Century Europe," *Journal of Urban History* 28 (2002), 743–768

Lavater, *Spirites* — Lewes Lavater, *Of Ghostes and Spirites Walking by Nyght, 1572*, ed. John Wilson Dover and May Yardley (1572; rpt. ed., Oxford, 1929)

LC — *London Chronicle*

LDA — *London Daily Advertiser*

Lean, *Collectanea* — Vincent Stuckey Lean, *Lean's Collectanea . . .*, 4 vols. (Bristol, 1902–1904)

Legg, *Low-Life* — Thomas Legg, *Low-life or One Half of the World, Knows not How the Other Half Live . . .* (London, 1750)

Le Loyer, *Specters* Pierre Le Loyer, *A Treatise of Specters of Straunge Sights, Visions, and Apparitions*... (London, 1605)

LEP *Lloyd's Evening Post* (London)

LE-P *London Evening-Post*

Lewis, Diary Diary of John Lewis, 1718–1760, Bodleian Library, Oxford, MS. Eng. misc. f. 10

LM *Leeds Mercury*

Lottin, *Chavatte* Alain Lottin, *Chavatte, Ouvrier Lillois: Un Contemporain de Louis XIV* (Paris, 1979)

Lowe, *Diary* W. L. Sachse, ed., *The Diary of Roger Lowe* (New Haven, 1938)

Matthiessen, *Natten* Hugo Matthiessen, *Natten: Stuier I Gammelt Byliv* ([Copenhagen], 1914)

Ménétra, *Journal* Jacques-Louis Ménétra, *Journal of My Life*, ed. Daniel Roche, trans. Arthur Goldhammer (New York, 1986)

Moryson, *Itinerary* Fynes Moryson, *An Itinerary Containing His Ten Yeeres Travell*..., 4 vols. (Glasgow, 1907)

Moryson, *Unpublished Itinerary* Charles Hughes, ed., *Shakespeare's Europe: A Survey of the Condition of Europe at the End of the 16th Century, being Unpublished Chapters of Fynes Moryson's Itinerary (1617)*... (New York, 1967)

Muchembled, *Violence* Robert Muchembled, *La Violence au Village: Sociabilitié et Comportements Populaires en Artois du XVe au XVIIe Siècle* (Turnhout, France, 1989)

Nashe, *Works* Ronald B. McKerrow, ed., *The Works of Thomas Nashe*, 5 vols. (Oxford, 1958)

NHCR I Charles J. Hoadly, ed., *Records of the Colony and Plantation of New Haven, 1638–1649* (Hartford, Ct., 1857)

NHCR II Charles J. Hoadley, ed., *Records of the Colony or Jurisdiction of New Haven, 1653 to the Union* (1663) (Hartford, Ct., 1858)

NHTR Franklin Bowditch Dexter and Zara Jones Powers, eds., *New Haven Town Records*, 3 vols. (New Haven, 1917–1962)

NYWJ *New York Weekly Journal*

O'Dea, *Lighting* William T. O'Dea, *The Social History of Lighting* (London, 1958)

OBP *The Proceedings on the King's Commissions of the Peace, Oyer and Terminer, and Gaol Delivery for the City of London; and also Gaol Delivery for the County of Middlesex, Held at Justice-Hall in the Old Bailey*

ODNB *Oxford Dictionary of National Biography* (Oxford, 2004)

OED *Oxford English Dictionary*, 1st edn. (Oxford, 1888–1928)

PA *Public Advertiser* (London)

Parkman, *Diary* Francis G. Walett, ed., *The Diary of Ebenezer Parkman 1703–1782* (Worcester, Mass., 1974)

Paroimiographia *Paroimiographia: Proverbs, or, Old Savves & Adages, in English (or the Saxon toung) Italian, French, and Spanish, whereunto the British, for Their Great Antiquity and Weight are Added*... (London, 1659)

Patten, *Diary* *The Diary of Matthew Patten of Bedford, N. H.* (Concord, N. H., 1903)

Pepys, *Diary* Samuel Pepys, *The Diary of Samuel Pepys*, ed. Robert Latham and William Matthews, 11 vols. (Berkeley, Calif., 1970–1983)

PG *Pennsylvania Gazette* (Philadelphia)

Pinkerton, *Travels*	John Pinkerton, ed., *A General Collection of the Best and Most Interesting Voyages and Travels in all Parts of the World . . .* , 17 vols. (London, 1808–1814)
Pitou, "Coureurs de Nuit"	Frédérique Pitou, "Jeunesse et Désorde Social: Les Coureurs de Nuit á Laval au XVIIIe Siècle," *Revue d'Histoire Moderne et Contemporaine* 47 (2000), 69–92
PL	*Public Ledger* (London)
PL 27	Palatinate of Lancaster Depositions, Public Record Office, London
Pounds, *Culture*	Norman John Greville Pounds, *The Culture of the English People: Iron Age to the Industrial Revolution* (Cambridge, 1994)
Pounds, *Home*	Norman John Greville Pounds, *Hearth & Home: A History of Material Culture* (Bloomington, Ind., 1989)
PP	*Past and Present*
RB	William Chappell and J. W. Ebsworth, eds., *The Roxburghe Ballads*, 9 vols. (1871–1899; rpt. edn., New York, 1966)
Remarks 1717	Remarks on Severall Parts of Flanders, Brabant, France, and Italy in the Yeare 1717, Boldleian Library, Oxford
Ripae, *Nocturno Tempore*	Polydori Ripae, *Tractatus de Nocturno Tempore: In quo Absoluta Criminalium Praxis, Canonicaeq; Materiae, Beneficiorum Praecipuè Continentur. Contractus Etiam, Seruitutes, Judicia Civilia, Vltimae Voluntates ad Susceptam Prouinciam Obseruantur* (Venice, 1602)
Roche, *Consumption*	Daniel Roche, *A History of Everyday Things: The Birth of Consumption in France, 1600–1800*, trans. Brian Pearce (Cambridge, 2000)
Ruff, *Violence*	Julius R. Ruff, *Violence in Early Modern Europe, 1500–1800* (Cambridge, 2001)
Ryder, *Diary*	William Matthews, ed., *The Diary of Dudley Ryder, 1715–1716* (London, 1939)
SAI	William Shaw Mason, comp., *A Statistical Account, or Parochial Survey of Ireland, Drawn Up from the Communications of the Clergy*, 3 vols. (Dublin, 1814–1819)
Sanderson, Diary	Robert Sanderson Diary, St. John's College, Cambridge
Sanger, *Journal*	Lois K. Stabler, ed., *Very Poor and of a Lo Make: The Journal of Abner Sanger* (Portsmouth, N. H., 1986)
SAS	Sir John Sinclair, ed., *The Statistical Account of Scotland: Drawn up from the Communications of the Ministers of the Different Parishes*, 21 vols. (Edinburgh, 1791–1799)
Schindler, "Youthful Culture"	Norbert Schindler, "Guardians of Disorder: Rituals of Youthful Culture at the Dawn of the Modern Age," in Giovanni Levi and Jean-Claude Schmitt, eds., *A History of Young People in the West* (Cambridge, Mass., 1997), 240–282
Schindler, *Rebellion*	Norbert Schindler, *Rebellion, Community and Custom in Early Modern Germany*, trans. Pamela E. Selwyn (Cambridge, 2002)
Scott, *Witchcraft*	Reginald Scott, *The Discoverie of Witchcraft* (Carbondale, Ill., 1964)
Select Trials	*Select Trials at the Sessions-House in the Old-Bailey* (1742; rpt. edn., New York, 1985)
Sewall, *Diary*	Milton Halsey Thomas, ed., *The Diary of Samuel Sewall, 1674–1729*, 2 vols. (New York, 1973)
SH	*Social History*

SJC — *St. James Chronicle* (London)
SWA or LJ — *Sussex Weekly-Advertiser: or, Lewes Journal*
Swift, *Journal* — Jonathan Swift, *Journal to Stella*, ed. Harold Williams (Oxford, 1948)
SWP — Paul Boyer and Stephen Nissenbaum, eds., *The Salem Witchcraft Papers: Verbatim Transcripts of the Legal Documents of the Salem Witchcraft Outbreak of 1692*, 3 vols. (New York, 1977)

T. Platter, *Journal* — Seán Jennett, ed. and trans., *Journal of a Younger Brother: The Life of Thomas Platter as a Medical Student in Montpellier at the Close of the Sixteenth Century* (London, 1963)
Taillepied, *Ghosts* — Noël Taillepied, *A Treatise of Ghosts . . .*, trans. Montague Summers (1933; rpt. edn., Ann Arbor, Mich., 1971)
Thomas, *Religion and the Decline of Magic* — Keith Thomas, *Religion and the Decline of Magic: Studies in Popular Beliefs in Sixteenth and Seventeenth Century England* (London, 1971)
Thoresby, *Diary* — Joseph Hunter, ed., *The Diary of Ralph Thoresby*, 2 vols. (London, 1830)
Tilley, *Proverbs in England* — Morris Palmer Tilley, ed., *A Dictionary of the Proverbs in England in the Sixteenth and Seventeenth Centuries . . .* (Ann Arbor, Mich., 1966)
Torriano, *Proverbi* — Giovanni Torriano, *Piazza Universale Di Proverbi Italiani: or, a Common Place of Italian Proverbs* (London, 1666)
Torrington, *Diaries* — John Byng, 5th Viscount Torrington, *The Torrington Diaries . . .*, ed. C. Bryan Andrews, 4 vols. (New York, 1935)
Turner, *Diary* — David Vaisey, ed., *The Diary of Thomas Turner 1754–1765* (Oxford, 1985)

UM — *Universal Magazine*
US and WJ — *Universal Spectator, and Weekly Journal* (London)

Verdon, *Night* — Jean Verdon, *Night in the Middle Ages*, trans. George Holoch (Notre Dame, Ind., 2002)
VG — *Virginia Gazette* (Williamsburg)

Watts, *Works* — George Burder, comp., *The Works of the Reverend and Learned Isaac Watts . . .*, 6 vols. (London, 1810)
Weinsberg, *Diary* — K. Höhlbaum et al., eds., *Das Buch Weinsberg, Kölner Denkwürdigkeiten aus dem 16. Jahrhundert*, 5 vols. (Leipzig-Bonn, 1886–1926)
Wilson, *English Proverbs* — F. P. Wilson, ed., *The Oxford Dictionary of English Proverbs* (Oxford, 1970)
WJ — *Weekly Journal* (London)
WMQ — *William and Mary Quarterly*
Wood, *Life* — Andrew Clark, comp., *The Life and Times of Anthony Wood, Antiquary, of Oxford, 1632–1695 . . .*, 5 vols. (Oxford, 1891–1900)
Woodforde, *Diary* — John E. Beresford, ed., *The Diary of a Country Parson*, 5 vols. (London, 1924–1931)
WR or UJ — *Weekly Register, or, Universal Journal* (London)

York Depositions — *Depositions from the Castle of York, Relating to Offences Committed in the Northern Counties in the Seventeenth Century* (London, 1861)

PREFACE

1. Tryon, *Wisdom's Dictates: Or, Aphorisms & Rules*... (London, 1691), 68.
2. Middleton, *A Mad World*, ... (London, 1608); Rousseau, *Emile: or On Education*, trans. Allan Bloom (New York, 1979), 133. Among the first in modern memory to note the lack of historical attention to night was George Steiner, who in 1978 observed, "To an extent often unnoticed by social historians, the great mass of mankind passed a major portion of its life in the varying shades of opacity between sundown and morning" (*A Reader* [New York, 1984], 351). Indeed, the subject of nighttime continues to be ignored in historical studies on all levels, from surveys of Western culture to academic monographs. Among the best accounts, despite its age and obscurity, is Matthiessen, *Natten*. Other early explorations included Maurice Bouteloup, "Le Travail de Nuit dans la Boulangerie" (Ph.D. diss., Université de Paris, 1909); A. Voisin, "Notes sur la Vie Urbaine au XV. Siècle: Dijon la Nuit," *Annales de Bourgogne* 9 (1937), 265–279; Bargellini, "Vita Notturna." More recently, scholars have begun to probe selected aspects of nocturnal life, though night in its totality, in the form of a broad social or cultural history, has remained unexplored. See Elisabeth Pavan, "Recherches sur la Nuit Vénitienne à la Fin du Moyen Age," *Journal of Medieval History* 7 (1981), 339–356; Peter Reinhart Gleichmann, "Nacht und Zivilisation," in Martin Caethge and Wolfgang Essbach, eds., *Soziologie: Entdeckungen im Alltäghchen* (Frankfurt, 1983), 174–194; Silvia Mantini, "Per un'Immagine Della Notte fra Tercento e Quattrocento," *Archivio Storico Italino* 4 (1985), 565–594; Wolfgang Schivelbusch, *Disenchanted Night: The Industrialization of Light in the Nineteenth Century*, trans. Angela Davies (Berkeley, Calif., 1988); Corinne Walker, "Esquisse Pour une Histoire de la Vie Nocturne: Genéve au XVIIIe Siècle, *Revue du Vieux Genève* 19 (1989), 73–85; Piero Camporesi, *Bread of Dreams: Food and Fantasy in Early Modern Europe*, trans. David Gentilcore (Chicago, 1989), 92–102; Robert Muchembled, "La Violence et la Nuit sous l'Ancien Régime," *Ethnologie Francaise* 21 (1991), 237–242; Mario Sbriccoli, ed., *La Notte: Ordine, Sicurezza e Disciplinamento in Età Moderna* (Florence, 1991); Janekovick-Römer, "Dubrovniks"; Joachim Schlör, *Nights in the Big City: Paris, Berlin, London 1840–1930*, trans. Pierre Gottfried Imhof and Dafydd Rees Roberts (London, 1998); Paul Griffiths "Meanings of Nightwalking in Early Modern England," *Seventeenth Century* 13 (1998), 212–238; Bryan D. Palmer, *Cultures of Darkness: Night Travels in the Histories of Transgression* (New York, 2000); Pitou, "Coureurs de Nuit"; Schindler, "Youthful Culture"; Verdon, *Night*; Schindler, *Rebellion*; Koslofsky, "Court Culture."
3. G. C. Faber, ed., *The Poetical Works of John Gay*... (London, 1926), 204; Edward Ward, *The Rambling Rakes, or, London Libertines* (London, 1700), 58; Christopher Sten, "'When the Candle Went Out': The Nighttime World of Huck Finn," *Studies in American Fiction* 9 (1981), 49. Of "season," the Bible famously declares, "To everything there is a season, and a time to every purpose under the heaven" (*Ecclesiastes* III, 1).
4. Michael McGrath, ed. and trans., *Cinnine Amhiaoibh Ui Shuileabháin: The Diary of Humphrey O'Sullivan*, 4 vols. (London, 1936–1937); Émile Guillaumin, *The Life of a Simple Man*, ed. Eugen Weber, trans. Margaret Crosland (Hanover, N. H., 1983); Thomas Hardy, *Tess of the d'Urbervilles: A Pure Woman* (1891; rpt. edn., London, 1993), 18.
5. Eugen Weber, *Peasants into Frenchmen: The Modernization of Rural France, 1870–1914* (Stanford, Calif., 1976), 419.

SHUTTING-IN

1. Fletcher and Francis Beaumont, *Fifty Comedies and Tragedies* (London, 1679), 217.
2. Lorus Johnson Milne and Margery Joan Milne, *The World of Night* (New York, 1956), 22; Thomas Hardy, *The Return of the Native* (1880; rpt. edn., London, 1993), 19; Nov. 5, 1830, Michael McGrath, ed., *Cinnine Amhiaoibh Ui Shuileabháin: The Diary of Humphrey O'Sullivan* (London, 1936), II, 355–356; John Florio, comp., *Queen Anna's New World of Words, or Dictionarie of the Italian and English Tongues* (London, 1611), 79. Cries of the screech owl were traditionally thought to foretell death. Gilbert White, *The Natural History and Antiquities of Selborne* (London, 1994), 142–143; Brand 1848, III, 209–210.
3. Shakespeare, *The Merchant of Venice*, V, 1, 124, and *Measure for Measure*, IV, 1, 56–57.

PART ONE

PRELUDE

1. Daniel Boorstin, *The Discoverers* (New York, 1983), 26.
2. Edmund Burke, *A Philosophical Enquiry into the Origins of Our Ideas of the Sublime and Beautiful* (1757; rpt. edn., New York, 1971), 272–281; John Locke, *An Essay Concerning Human Understanding*, ed. Peter H. Nidditch (Oxford, 1975), 397–398.
3. Juliette Favez-Boutonier, *L'Angoisse* (Paris, 1945), 134–150.
4. *The Iliad*, trans. Robert Fitzgerald (New York, 1992), 338; Kevin Coyne, *A Day in the Night of America* (New York, 1992), 35; Richard Cavendish, *The Powers of Evil in Western Religion, Magic, and Folk Belief* (New York, 1975), 88–89; Geoffrey Parrinder, *Witchcraft: European and African* (London, 1970), 123–124; Norman Cohn, *Europe's Inner Demons: An Enquiry Inspired by the Great Witch-Hunt* (New York, 1975), 206–207.
5. Psalms 23:4; John 1:5; Matthew 27:45; Cavendish, *Powers of Evil*, 87–91; Ernst Cassirer, *The Philosophy of Symbolic Forms*, trans. Ralph Manheim (New Haven, 1964), 98–99.
6. Alan Macfarlane, *Witchcraft in Tudor and Stuart England: A Regional and Comparative Study* (London, 1970), 212; Lucy Mair, *Witchcraft* (New York, 1969), 42–43; B. Malinowski, "The Natives of Mailu: Preliminary Results of the Robert Mond Research Work in British New Guinea," in *Transactions and Proceedings of the Royal Society of South Australia* 39 (1915), 647–648; Parrinder, *Witchcraft*, 134–146; John Middleton and E. H. Winter, eds., *Witchcraft and Sorcery in East Africa* (London, 1969), passim.
7. Rolfe Humphries, trans., *The Satires of Juvenal* (Bloomington, Ind., 1966), 43–44; Mark J. Bouman, "Luxury and Control: The Urbanity of Street Lighting in Nineteenth-Century Cities," *JUH* 14 (1987), 9; Hazel Rossotti, *Fire* (Oxford, 1993), 59; O'Dea, *Lighting*, 14–16, 220.
8. Richard M. Dorson, ed., *America Begins: Early American Writing* (Bloomington, Ind., 1971), 280, 282; Theodore M. Andersson, "The Discovery of Darkness in Northern Literature," in Robert B. Burlin and Edward B. Irving, Jr., eds., *Old English Studies in Honour of John C. Pope* (Toronto, 1974), 9–12.

CHAPTER ONE

1. Nashe, *Works*, I, 345.
2. J. P. Arival, *The Historie of this Iron Age: Wherein is Set Down the True State of Europe as It Was in the Year 1500 . . .*, trans. B. Harris (London, 1659), 2; George Herbert, *Jaculum Prudentium: or Outlandish Proverbs . . .* (London, 1651), 70; "Quid Tunc," *SJC*, Aug. 29, 1767; Honoré de Balzac, *The Human Comedy* (New York, 1893), II, 6; William G. Naphy and Penny Roberts, eds., *Fear in Early Modern Society* (Manchester, 1997).
3. Richard Steele, *The Husbandmans Calling . . .* (London, 1670), 270; Shakespeare, *Henry V*, IV, 0, 4; Shakespeare, *The Rape of Lucrece*, 764–767; Anthony J. Lewis, "The Dog, Lion, and Wolf in Shakespeare's Descriptions of Night," *Modern Language Review* 66 (1971), 1–11; Anthony Harris, *Night's Black Agents: Witchcraft and Magic in Seventeenth-Century English Drama* (Manchester, 1980); Jean-Marie Maguin, *La Nuit dans le Théâtre de Shakespeare et de ses Prédécesseurs*, 2 vols. (Lille, 1980).
4. John Hayward, *Hell's Everlasting Flames Avoided . . .* (London, 1712), 30; Shakespeare, *Love's Labour's Lost*, IV, 3, 252; Thomas Granger, *The Light of the World . . .* (London, 1616), 29; Piero Camporesi, *The Fear of Hell: Images of Damnation and Salvation in Early Modern Europe*, trans. Lucinda Byatt (University Park, Pa., 1991), 42; Nashe, *Works*, I, 346; John Dryden and Nathaniel Lee, *Oedipus* (London, 1679), 27; Jean Delumeau, *La Peur en Occident, XIVe-XVIIIe Siècles: Une Cité Assiégée* (Paris, 1978), 97; Robert Muchembled, "La Violence et la Nuit sous l'Ancien Régime," *Ethnologie Francaise* 21 (1991), 241.
5. Anthony Synnott, "The Eye and the I: A Sociology of Sight," *International Journal of Politics, Culture and Society* 5 (1992), 619, 618; Constance Classen, *Worlds of Sense: Exploring the Senses in History and Across Cultures* (New York, 1993), 58.
6. Maria Bogucka, "Gesture, Ritual, and Social Order in Sixteenth- to Eighteenth-century Poland," in Jan Bremmer and Herman Roodenburg, eds., *A Cultural History of Gesture* (Ithaca, N.Y., 1992), 191.
7. See, for example, *US* and *WJ*, July 9, 1737.
8. Thomson, *The Seasons*, ed. James Sambrook (Oxford, 1981), 192.
9. Mill, *A Nights Search: Discovering the Nature and Condition of all Sorts of Night Walkers . . .* (London, 1639); *Herberts Devotions . . .* (London, 1657), 231; Mark Warr, "Dangerous Situations: Social Context and Fear of Victimization," *Social Forces* 68 (1990), 892–894.
10. R. B., "A Serious Address to the Common Council of the City of London," *G and NDA*, July 16, 1768; Thomas Middleton, *The Wisdome of Solomon Paraphrased* (London, 1597); July 18, 1709, Cowper, Diary. See also Henry Chettle, *Piers Plainnes Seauen Yeres Prentiship* (London, 1595); Shakespeare, *Julius Caesar*, II, 1, 77.
11. Lavater, *Spirites*, 10.
12. Richard Jackson, June 7, 1656, *York Depositions*, 74; Heywood, *Diaries*, III, 187.
13. Mar. 3, 1727, "The Diary of George Booth," *Journal of the Chester and North Wales Architectural Archaeogical and Historic Society*, New Ser., 28 (1928), 38; *Perpetual and Natural Prognostications . . .* (London, 1591), 27; T. F. Thiselton-Dyer, *Old English Social Life as Told by the Parish Registers* (1898; rpt. edn., New York, 1972), 233; Heywood, *Diaries*, II, 218; Sara Schechner Genuth, *Comets, Popular Culture, and the Birth of Modern Cosmology* (Princeton, 1997).
14. 1719, Lewis, Diary, 25; June 5, 1742, "Diary of Rev. Jacob Eliot," *Historical Magazine and Notes and Queries . . .*, 2nd Ser., 5 (1869), 34.
15. May 21, 1668, Pepys, *Diary*, 208; Walter L. Strauss, ed., *The German Single-Leaf Woodcut, 1550–1600* (New York, 1975), III, 968–969; T. Platter, *Journal*, 217; Heywood, *Diaries*,

II, 232; Steven Ozment, *Three Behaim Boys Growing up in Early Modern Germany: A Chronicle of Their Lives* (New Haven, 1990), 52.

16. M. de Fontenelle, *Conversations on the Plurality of Worlds*, trans. H.A. Hargreaves (Berkeley, Calif., 1990), 130; Charles Stevens and John Liebault, *Maison Rustique, or, the Countrey Farme*, trans. Richard Surflet (London, 1616), 30; Thomas B. Forbes, "By What Disease or Casualty: The Changing Face of Death in London," *Journal of the History of Medicine and Allied Sciences* 31 (1976), 408; Thomas, *Religion and the Decline of Magic*, 296–297.
17. Niccols, *A Winter Night's Vision* . . . (London, 1610), 831; Francis T. Havergal, comp., *Herefordshire Words & Phrases* . . . (Walsall, Eng., 1887), 13; Francois Joseph Pahud de Valangin, *A Treatise on Diet, or the Management of Human Life*... (London, 1768), 275; High Court of Justiciary, Small Papers, Main Series, JC 26/42–43, passim, Scottish Record Office, Edinburgh; JRAI, passim.
18. Laurent Joubert, *The Second Part of the Popular Errors*, trans. Gregory David de Rocher (Tuscaloosa, Ala., 1995), 280–282. For a similar critique, see *The Second Lash of Alazonomastix*... (London, 1655), 234.
19. Owen Feltham, *Resolves, a Duple Century* (1628; rpt. ed., Amsterdam, 1975), 211. See also Denham, *The Sophy* (London, 1642), 20.
20. Camporesi, *Fear of Hell*, 13; Thomas Dekker, *The Gull's Hornbook*, ed. R.B. McKerrow (New York, 1971), 23; Jan. 12, 1706, Cowper, Diary; Caufurd Tait Ramage, *Ramage in South Italy* . . . , ed. Edith Clay (London, 1965), 6; J. Churton Collins, ed., *The Plays & Poems of Robert Greene* (Oxford, 1905), II, 249; Angelo Celli, *The History of Malaria in the Roman Campagna from Ancient Times*, ed. Anna Celli-Fraentzel (London, 1933), 130–154.
21. Anglicus, *On the Properties of Things*, trans. John Trevisa (Oxford, 1975), I, 540; Thomas Amory, *Daily Devotion Assisted and Recommended, in Four Sermons*... (London, 1772), 15.
22. Leon Kreitzman, *The 24 Hour Society* (London, 1999), 90–91; Solomon R. Benatar, "Fatal Asthma," *New England Journal of Medicine* 314 (1986), 426–427; Sharon A. Sharp, "Biological Rhythms and the Timing of Death," *Omega* 12 (1981–1982), 17.
23. Hanway, *Domestic Happiness... Calculated to Render Servants in General Virtuous and Happy* . . . (London, 1786), 101; Mary J. Dobson, *Contours of Death and Disease in Early Modern England* (New York, 1997), 247, 252; Pounds, *Culture*, 239, 245–246.
24. Anna Brzozowska-Krajka, *Polish Traditional Folklore: The Magic of Time* (Boulder, Colo, 1998), 115.
25. Francis B. Gummere, "On the Symbolic Use of the Colors Black and White in Germanic Tradition," *Haverford College Studies* 1 (1889), 116; John Fletcher, *The Nightwalker, or the Little Theife* (London, 1640); Daniel Defoe, *A System of Magick*... (London, 1727), 380–381; Normal Cohn, *Europe's Inner Demons: An Enquiry Inspired by the Great Witch-Hunt* (New York, 1975), 66.
26. C. Scott Dixon, *The Reformation and Rural Society: The Parishes of Brandenburg-Ansbach-Kulmbach, 1528–1603* (Cambridge, 1996), 191; Thomas, *Religion and the Decline of Magic*, 472, 473–477; Nashe, *Works*, I, 346; George C. Schoolfield, *The German Lyric of the Baroque in English Translation* (New York, 1966), 199.
27. Nashe, *Works*, I, 346, 348; Bella Millett and Jocelyn Wogan-Browne, *Medieval English Prose for Women: Selections from the Katherine Group and Ancrene Wisse* (Oxford, 1990), 91; Jacob Bauthumley, *The Light and Dark Sides of God*... (London, 1650), 29.
28. Hale, *A Collection of Modern Relations of Matter of Fact, Concerning Witches & Witchcraft*... (London, 1693), 16, 12–13; Thomas, *Religion and the Decline of Magic*, 472.
29. SAS, XIII, 652; Le Loyer, *Specters*, fo. 78; July 1, 1712, Donald F. Bond, ed., *The Spectator*, (Oxford, 1965), III, 572; *Essex People, 1750–1900: From Their Diaries, Memoirs and Letters* (Chelmsford, Eng., 1972), 32.

30. Brand 1777, II, 430–431; *A View of London and Westminster: or, the Town Spy, etc.* (London, 1725), 1–2; Robert Holland, comp., *A Glossary of Words Used in the County of Chester* (1886; rpt. ed., Vaduz, Liecht, 1965), 182; Brand 1848, II, 507–512; Minor White Latham, *The Elizabethan Fairies: The Fairies of Folklore and the Fairies of Shakespeare* (1930; rpt. edn., New York, 1972), 219–262.
31. Georgina F. Jackson, comp., *Shropshire Word-Book* . . . (London, 1879), 117; Samuel Butler, *Hudibras, the First Part* (London, 1663), 19.
32. Mr. Pratt, *Gleanings through Wales, Holland, and Westphalia* (London, 1798), 142, 136; T. Campbell, *Philosophical Survey of the South of Ireland* . . . (London, 1777), 280; *Archaeologia: or Miscellaneous Tracts Relating to Antiquity* (London, 1814), 144; R. D. Heslop, comp., *Northumberland Words* . . . (London, 1892), I, 257; Brand 1777, II, 359.
33. A. J. Gurevich, *Categories of Medieval Culture*, trans. G. L. Campbell (London, 1985), 107–108; Lewis, Diary, 17; Thomas, *Religion and the Decline of Magic*, 587–606.
34. Thomas Alfred Spalding, *Elizabethan Demonology* . . . (London, 1880), 54; *WJ*, Nov. 5, 1726; John Holloway, ed., *The Oxford Book of Local Verses* (Oxford, 1987), 215–216; Cannon, Diary, 134; Jean Claude Schmitt, *Ghosts in the Middle Ages: The Living and the Dead in Medieval Society* (Chicago, 1998), 185; Nov. 29, 1667, Pepys, *Diary*, VIII, 553; Brand 1777, II, 430.
35. John Carr, *The Stranger in Ireland: or, a Tour in the Southern and Western Parts of that Country in the Year 1805* (1806; rpt. edn., Shannon, Ire., 1970), 264–265; Anne Plumptre, *A Narrative of a Three Years' Residence in France* . . . (London, 1810), III, 179; *Craftsman* (London), May 20, 1732; Dietz, *Surgeon*, 166–167; Pierre Goubert, *The Ancien Régime: French Society 1600–1750*, trans. Steve Cox (London, 1973), 280; Caroline Frances Oates, "Trials of Werewolves in the Franche-Comte in the Early Modern Period" (Ph.D. diss., Univ. of London, 1993); Le Loyer, *Specters*, fo. 101.
36. Scott, *Witchcraft*, 29; Geert Mak, *Amsterdam*, trans. Philipp Blom (Cambridge, Mass., 2000), 48; E. S. De Beer, ed., *The Correspondence of John Locke* (Oxford, 1976), 421–422; Francis Grose, *A Provincial Glossary* (1787; rpt. edn., Menston, Eng., 1968), 17.
37. Saint Basil, *Exegetic Homilies*, trans. Sister Agnes Clarke Way (Washington, D.C., 1963), 26; Ellery Leonard, trans., *Beowulf* (New York, 1939), 8, 5; Martha Grace Duncan, "In Slime and Darkness: The Metaphor of Filth in Criminal Justice," *Tulane Law Review* 68 (1994), 725–801; James Sharpe, *Instruments of Darkness: Witchcraft in England, 1550–1750* (New York, 1996), 15; Cavendish, *Powers of Evil*, 87, 96–97; Cohn, *Europe's Inner Demons*, 207–210.
38. Muchembled, "La Nuit sous l'Ancien Régime," 239–241; Schmitt, *Ghosts in the Middle Ages*, 177; Thomas, *Religion and the Decline of Magic*, 455; Harris, *Night's Black Agents*, 25–26, 33; Nancy Caciola, "Wraiths, Revenants and Ritual in Medieval Culture," *PP* 152 (1996), 3–45; Pierre Jonin, "L'Espace et le Temps de la Nuit dans les Romans de Chrétien de Troyes," *Mélanges de Langue et de Littérature Médiévals Offerts à Alice Planche* 48 (1984), 235–246.
39. Cohn, *Europe's Inner Demons*, 71–74, 97, 100–101; Lynn A. Martin, *Alcohol, Sex, and Gender in Late Medieval and Early Modern Europe* (New York, 2001), 79; Thomas, *Religion and the Decline of Magic*, 454–456.
40. G.R. Quaife, *Wanton Wenches and Wayward Wives: Peasants and Illicit Sex in Early Seventeenth Century England* (London, 1979), 31; S. Taylor, "Daily Life—and Death—in 17th Century Lamplugh," *Transactions of the Cumberland & Westmorland Antiquarian & Archaeological Society*, New Ser. 44 (1945), 138–141; Thomas, *Religion and the Decline of Magic*, 455–461, 498–499.
41. Cohn, *Inner Demons*, 105; *VG*, Aug. 19, 1737; Christina Larner, *Enemies of God: The Witch-Hunt in Scotland* (Baltimore, 1981), 22–25; Robin Briggs, "Witchcraft and Popular

Mentality in Lorraine, 1580–1630," in Brian Vickers, ed., *Occult and Scientific Mentalities in the Renaissance* (Cambridge, 1984), 346–347; Thomas, *Religion and the Decline of Magic*, 560–569.

42. Jon Butler, "Magic, Astrology, and the Early American Religious Heritage, 1600–1760," *AHR* 84 (1979), 322.
43. Scott, *Witchcraft*, 25; Taillepied, *Ghosts*, 94.
44. Wilson, *English Proverbs*, 203.
45. Mrs. Bray, *Traditions, Legends, Superstitions, and Sketches of Devonshire* . . . (London, 1838), I, 168–169; Kingsley Palmer, *The Folklore of Somerset* (Totowa, N.J., 1976), 23; Taillepied, *Ghosts*, 29, 30. See also Nashe, *Works*, I, 358; Brand 1848, III, 52.
46. *SAS*, IX, 748; Cohens, *Italy*, 150–151; Roy Porter, "The People's Health in Georgian England," in Tim Harris, ed., *Popular Culture in England, c.1500–1850* (New York, 1995), 139–142; P.E.H. Hair, "Accidental Death and Suicide in Shropshire, 1780–1809," *Transactions of the Shropshire Archaeological Society* 59 (1969), 63–75; Robert Campbell, "Philosophy and the Accident," in Roger Cooter and Bill Luckin, eds., *Accidents in History: Injuries, Fatalities, and Social Relations* (Amsterdam, 1997), 19–32.
47. Apr. 16, 1769, Diary of Sir John Parnell, 1769–1783, 57, British Library of Political and Economic Science, London School of Economics; Christopher Hibbert, *The English: A Social History* (London, 1988), 348–349.
48. Watts, *Works*, II, 189; Marsilia Ficino, *Three Books on Life*, ed. and trans. Carol V. Kaske and John R. Clark (Binghampton, N.Y., 1989), 127; Stanley Coren, *Sleep Thieves: An Eye-Opening Exploration into the Science and Mysteries of Sleep* (New York, 1996), 97, 185; Lydia Dotto, *Losing Sleep: How Your Sleeping Habits Affect Your Life* (New York, 1990), 53.
49. *VG*, Jan. 5, 1739; Dec. 15, 1744, C. E. Whiting, ed., *Two Yorkshire Diaries: The Diary of Arthur Jessop and Ralph Ward's Journal* (Gateshead on Tyne, Eng., 1952), 95; 1721, Dec. 26, 1713, Oct. 26, 1698, *East Anglian Diaries*, 251, 236, 208; Heywood, *Diaries*, II, 302.
50. *The True-Born English-man* . . . (London, 1708), 16; *New England Weekly Journal* (Boston), July 6, 1736; Penry Williams, *The Later Tudors: England, 1547–1603* (Oxford, 1995), 216; Thomas, *Religion and the Decline of Magic*, 17–19; Ruff, *Violence*, 126.
51. John D. Palmer, *The Living Clock: The Orchestrator of Biological Rhythms* (New York, 2002), 32–34.
52. Edward Burghall, *Providence Improved* (London, 1889), 155, 157, 159; *WJ*, Aug. 14, 1725; Helen Simpson, ed. and trans., *The Waiting City: Paris 1782–88* . . . (Philadelphia, 1933), 227; Clifford Morsley, *News from the English Countryside: 1750–1850* (London, 1979), 143.
53. Defoe, *Tour*, I, 308; *PG*, Nov. 1, 1733; Dobson, *Death and Disease*, 245.
54. J. W. Goethe, *Italian Journey, 1786–1788* (New York, 1968), 347; P.E.H. Hair, "Deaths from Violence in Britain: A Tentative Secular Survey," *Population Studies* 25 (1971), 5–24.
55. Peter Borsay, *The English Urban Renaissance: Culture and Society in the Provincial Town 1660–1770* (Oxford, 1989), 3–11; Christopher R. Friedrichs, *The Early Modern City, 1450–1750* (London, 1995), 20–21.
56. Raffaella Sarti, *Europe at Home: Family and Material Culture, 1500–1800*, trans. Allan Cameron (New Haven, 2002), 109–111.
57. Aug. 16, 1693, Michael Hunter and Annabel Gregory, eds., *An Astrological Diary of the Seventeenth Century: Samuel Jeake of Rye, 1652–1699* (Oxford, 1988), 224; Elborg Forster, ed. and trans., *A Woman's Life in the Court of the Sun King: Letters of Liselotte von der Pfalz, 1652–1722* (Baltimore, 1984), 246; *Some Bedfordshire Diaries* (Streatley, Eng., 1960), 8.
58. June 30, 1766, Diary of Mr. Tracy and Mr. Dentand, 1766, Bodl., 14; John Spranger, *A Proposal or Plan for an Act of Parliament for the Better Paving, Lighting, and Cleaning the Streets* . . . (London, 1754); Paul Zumthor, *Daily Life in Rembrandt's Holland* (New York, 1963),

23–24; Walter King, "How High Is Too High? Disposing of Dung in Seventeenth-Century Prescot," *Sixteenth Century Journal* 23 (1992), 446–447; James Clifford, "Some Aspects of London Life in the Mid-18th Century," in Paul Fritz and David Williams, eds., *City & Society in the 18th Century* (Toronto, 1973), 19–38; Sarti, *Europe at Home*, trans. Cameron, 110–114.

59. Martin Lister, *A Journey to Paris in the Year 1698* (London, 1699), 24; Marcelin Defourneaux, *Daily Life in Spain: The Golden Age*, trans. Newton Branch (New York, 1971), 63; G. M. Trevelyan, *English Social History, a Survey of Six Centuries: Chaucer to Queen Victoria* (New York, 1965), 438; G. E. Rodmell, ed., "An Englishman's Impressions of France in 1775," *Durham University Journal* (1967), 85; Joseph Palmer, *A Four Months Tour through France* (London, 1776), II, 58–60; Bargellini, "Vita Notturna," 80; A. H. de Oliveira, *Daily Life in Portugal in the Late Middle Ages* (Madison, Wisc., 1971), 101–102, 141.
60. Mar. 17, 1709, Sewall, *Diary*, II, 616; Thomas Pennant, *The Journey from Chester to London* (London, 1782), 166; June 30, 1666, Pepys, *Diary*, VII, 188; *WJ*, Jan. 2, 1725; James K. Hosmer, ed., *Winthrop's Journal: "History of New England," 1630–1649* (New York, 1908), II, 355.
61. Burton E. Stevenson, *The Home Book of Proverbs, Maxims and Familiar Phrases* (New York, 1948), 1686; Cotton Mather, *Frontiers Well-Defended: An Essay, to Direct the Frontiers of a Countrey Exposed unto the Incursions of a Barbarous Enemy* (Boston, 1707), 14; Oct. 19, 1691, Sewall, *Diary*, I, 283; Vito Fumagalli, *Landscapes of Fear: Perceptions of Nature and the City in the Middle Ages* (Cambridge, 1994), 136–148.
62. *A General Collection of Discourses of the Virtuosi of France, upon Question of All Sorts of Philosophy, and other Natural Knowledge* . . . , trans. G. Havers (London, 1664), 204.

CHAPTER TWO

1. Jean Delumeau, *La Peur en Occident, XIVe–XVIIIe Siècles: Une Cité Assiégée* (Paris, 1978), 90.
2. P. M. Mitchell, trans., *Selected Essays of Ludvig Holberg* (Westport, Ct., 1976), 51; John Worlidge, *Systema Agriculturae; The Mystery of Husbandry Discovered* . . . (1675; rpt. edn., Los Angeles, 1970), 220; Lawrence Wright, *Warm and Snug: The History of the Bed* (London, 1962), 120.
3. Sara Tilghman Nalle, *Mad for God: Bartolomé Sánchez, the Secret Messiah of Cardenete* (Charlottesville, Va., 2001), 129; Samuel Rowlands, *The Night-Raven* (London, 1620); *The Ordinary of Newgate, His Account of the Behaviour, Confession, and Dying Words, of the Malefactors Who were Executed at Tyburn*, Nov. 7, 1750, 10.
4. Marjorie Keniston McIntosh, *Controlling Misbehavior in England, 1370–1600* (Cambridge, 1998), 66–67; Jütte, *Poverty*, 163; F. Alteri, *Dizionario Italiano ed Inglese* . . . (London, 1726); Paul Griffiths, "Meanings of Nightwalking in Early Modern England," *Seventeenth Century* 13 (1998), 213, 216–217.
5. *OBP*, Jan. 15–18, 1748, 54; *Midnight the Signal: In Sixteen Letters to a Lady of Quality* (n.p., 1779), I, 9, passim; John Crowne, *Henry the Sixth, the First Part* . . . (London, 1681), 18; Griffiths, "Nightwalking," 217–238.
6. *OBP*, May 17, 1727, 6.
7. For an introduction to the large literature on early modern crime, see J. A. Sharpe, *Crime in Early Modern England, 1550–1750* (London, 1984); Joanna Innes and John Styles, "The Crime Wave: Recent Writings on Crime and Criminal Justice in Eighteenth-Century England," *Journal of British Studies* 25 (1986), 380–435; Ruff, *Violence*.
8. Kyd, *The Spanish Tragedie* (London, 1592); Watts, *Works*, II, 190.

9. Hadrianus Junius, *The Nomenclator*... (London, 1585), 425; *The Works of Monsieur Boileau* (London, 1712), I, 199; Heywood, *Diaries*, II, 286; *OBP*, Sept. 7, 1737, 163; S. Pole, "Crime, Society and Law Enforcement in Hanoverian Somerset" (Ph.D. diss., Cambridge Univ., 1983), 302–303; Julius Ralph Ruff, "Crime, Justice, and Public Order in France, 1696–1788: the Senechausee of Libourne" (Ph.D. diss., Univ. of North Carolina at Chapel Hill, 1979), 238; *Select Trials*, II, 234; Beattie, *Crime*, 167–192.
10. Sept.8, 1666, Aug. 21, 1665, Pepys, *Diary*, VII, 282; VI, 200; *OBP*, Sept. 6–11, 1738, 146; M. Dorothy George, *London Life in the 18th Century* (New York, 1965), 10–11; Beattie, *Crime*, 148–154.
11. Jeremy Black, *British Abroad: The Grand Tour in the Eighteenth Century* (New York, 1992), 177; Joseph Jacobs, ed., *Epistolae Ho-Elianeae: The Familiary Letters of James Howell*... (London, 1900), 45; *DUR*, Dec. 26, 1788; Marcelin Defourneaux, *Daily Life in Spain: The Golden Age*, trans. Newton Branch (New York, 1971), 68; Moryson, *Itinerary*, I, 141.
12. *An Effectual Scheme for the Immediate Preventing of Street Robberies, and Suppressing All Other Disorders of the Night*... (London, 1731) 65; Colm Lennon, *Richard Stanyhurst the Dubliner, 1547–1618* (Blackrock, Ire., 1981), 148; Beattie, *Crime*, 180–181; J. A. Sharpe, *Crime in Seventeenth-Century England: A County Study* (Cambridge, 1983), 103.
13. Richard Head, *The Canting Academy; or Villanies Discovered* . . . (London, 1674), 69; Thomas Evans, Feb. 8, 1773, Assi 45/31/1/78; Ann Maury, *Memoirs of a Huguenot Family ...from the Original Autobiography of Rev. James Fontaine*... (New York, 1852), 303; Beattie, *Crime*, 152–161; Alan Macfarlane, *The Justice and the Mare's Ale: Law and Disorder in Seventeenth-Century England* (Oxford, 1981), 136–140; James A. Sharpe, "Criminal Organization in Rural England 1550–1750," in G. Ortalli, ed., *Bande Armate, Banditti, Banditismo* (Rome, 1986), 125–140.
14. William Lithgow, *The Totall Discourse of the Rare Adventures & Painefull Peregrinations*... (Glasgow, 1906), 310; Ruff, *Violence*, 31, 64–65, 217–239; Pierre Goubert, *The Ancien Régime: French Society 1600–1750*, trans. Steve Cox (London, 1973), 104; Uwe Danker, "Bandits and the State: Robbers and the Authorities in the Holy Roman Empire in the Late Seventeenth and Early Eighteenth Centuries," in Richard J. Evans, ed., *The German Underworld: Deviants and Outcasts in German History* (London, 1988), 75–107.
15. *OBP*, Jan. 17–20, 1750, 30, Dec. 7–12, 1743, 82, Jan. 12, 1733, 45; B., *Discolliminium: or a Most Obedient Reply to a Late Book*... (London, 1650).
16. William Keatinge Clay, ed., *Private Prayers, Put Forth by Authority during the Reign of Queen Elizabeth* (Cambridge, 1851), 444; Sir Edward Coke, *The Third Part of the Institutes of the Laws of England*... (1628; rpt. edn., New York, 1979), 63; Sir William Blackstone, *Commentaries on the Laws of England*, ed. William Draper Lewis (Phildadelphia, 1902), IV, 1615; Beattie, *Crime*, 163–165.
17. Head, *Canting Academy*, 179; Eric Partridge, ed., *A Dictionary of the Underworld* (Ware, Eng., 1989), 43, 469; John Poulter, *The Discoveries of John Poulter* (London, 1753), 43; Jan. 30, 1665, Pepys, *Diary*, VI, 25.
18. *OBP*, Jan. 16, 1734, 55; Beattie, *Crime*, 163; *WJ*, July 20, 1728.
19. July 11, 1664, Pepys, *Diary*, V, 201; *Hanging Not Punishment Enough, for Murtherers, Highway Men, and House-Breakers* (London, 1701), 6.
20. *OBP*, Dec. 10–13, 1707; *Select Trials*, I, 306; Michel Porret, *Le Crime et ses Circonstances: De l'Esprit de l'Arbitraire au Siècle des Lumières selon les Réquisitoires des Procureurs Genève* (Geneva, 1995), 258; Beattie, *Crime*, 164–165.
21. Mill, *A Nights Search: Discovering the Nature and Condition of all Sorts of Night-Walkers*... (London, 1639); Awnsham Churchill, comp., *A Collection of Voyages and Travels*... (London, 1746), VI, 726; Beattie, *Crime*, 161–167; Sharpe, *Seventeenth-Century Crime*, 107; *A*

New Journey to France (London, 1715), 85; Henry Swinburne, *Travels Through Spain, in the Years 1775 and 1776...* (London, 1779), I, 348–350.

22. John L. McMullan, *The Canting Crew: London's Criminal Underworld, 1550–1700* (New Brunswick, N.J., 1984), 162; *A Warning for House-Keepers...* (London, 1676), 4; Heywood, *Diaries*, III, 206; Cynthia B. Herrup, *The Common Peace: Participation and the Criminal Law in Seventeenth-Century England* (Cambridge, 1987), 27, 30–31, 170–171; Ruff, *Violence*, 221–224; George Huppert, *After the Black Death: A Social History of Early Modern Europe* (Bloomington, Ind., 1986), 107–109.
23. Florike Egmond, *Underworlds: Organized Crime in the Netherlands 1650–1800* (Cambridge, 1993), 33, 188–191; Schindler, *Rebellion*, 222; Ruff, *Violence*, 221; Albrecht Keller, ed., *A Hangman's Diary: Being the Journal of Master Franz Schmidt, Public Executioner of Nuremberg, 1573–1617*, trans. C. V. Calvert and A. W. Gruner (Montclair, N.J., 1973), 130.
24. Elisabeth Crouzet-Pavan, "Potere Politico e Spazio Sociale: It Controllo Della Notte a Venezia nei Secoli XIII–XV," in Mario Sbriccoli, ed., *La Notte: Ordine, Sicurezza e Disciplinamento in Età Moderna* (Florence, 1991), 48; Daniel Defoe, *Street-Robberies Consider'd* ... (1728; rpt. edn., Stockton, N.J., 1973), 68; Alan Williams, *The Police of Paris, 1718–1789* (Baton Rouge, 1979), 287.
25. Dekker, *Writings*, 193; *The Confession &c. of Thomas Mount...* (Portsmouth, N.H., [1791?]), 19; *Select Trials*, II, 236; Charles Dorrington, Feb. 10, 1764, Assi 45/27/2/125; *OBP*, Jan. 15–19, 1742, 31, Sept. 6, 1732, 188; *Select Trials*, I, 303.
26. John Nelson, Aug. 25, 1738, Assi 45/21/3/126.
27. *OBP*, May 15–17, 1746, 149.
28. *OBP*, June 28–July 2, 1744, 159, Apr. 25–30, 1750, 68, July 11–14, 1750, 87; Macfarlane, *Justice and the Mare's Ale*, 132; *OBP*, Dec. 5–10, 1744, 7, Dec. 5–10, 1744, 142.
29. *OBP*, Oct. 17–19, 1744, 257, Aug. 30, 1727, 4.
30. Lavater, *Spirites*, 22; Jeannine Blackwell and Susanne Zantop, eds., *Bitter Healing: German Women Writers from 1700 to 1830: An Anthology* (Lincoln, Neb., 1990), 60; Brand 1848, II, 314; Danker, "Bandits," 88. See also Taillepied, *Ghosts*, 31.
31. Crusius, *Nocte*, ch. 11.9; Keller, ed., *Hangman's Diary*, trans. Calvert and Gruner, 110; Brand 1848, I, 312, III, 278–279; Marjorie Rowling, *The Folklore of the Lake District* (Totowa, N.J., 1976), 26; Matthiessen, *Natten*, 94–95. See also Bargellini, "Vita Notturna," 84; John McManners, *Church and Society in Eighteenth-Century France* (Oxford, 1999), II, 232.
32. Karl Wegert, *Popular Culture, Crime, and Social Control in 18th Century Württemberg* (Stuttgart, 1994), 101; Keller, ed., *Hangman's Diary*, trans. Calvert and Gruner, 112–113; Brand 1848, I, 312; *Times* (London), July 3, 1790.
33. Torriano, *Proverbi*, 171.
34. Pinkerton, *Travels*, II, 565; Elisabeth Crouzet-Pavan, *Venice Triumphant: The Horizons of a Myth*, trans. Lydia G. Cochrane (Baltimore, 2002), 161; Ruff, *Violence*, 120–121.
35. Alessandro Falassi, *Folklore by the Fireside: Text and Context of the Tuscan Veglia* (Austin, 1980), 6; J. Mitchell and M.D.R. Leys, *A History of London Life* (London, 1958), 73; Claude Fouret, "Douai au XVIe Siècle: Une Sociabilté de l'Agression," *Revue d'Histoire Moderne et Contemporaine* 34 (1987), 9–10; Robert Muchembled, "La Violence et la Nuit sous l'Ancien Régime," *Ethnologie Francaise* 21 (1991), 237; Rudy Chaulet, "La Violence en Castille au XVIIe Siècle," *Crime, Histoire & Sociâetâes* 1 (1997), 14–16. See also Barbara A. Hanawalt, "Violent Death in Fourteenth- and Early Fifteenth-Century England," *Comparative Studies in Society and History* 18 (1976), 305, 319.
36. J. R. Hale, ed., *The Travel Journal of Antonio de Beatis...*, trans. J. R. Hale and J.M.A. Lindon (London, 1979), 82; James Casey, *The Kingdom of Valencia in the Seventeenth Century*

(Cambridge, 1979), 212; Moryson, *Unpublished Itinerary*, 463, 163; Cleone Knox, *The Diary of a Young Lady of Fashion in the Year 1764–1765* (New York, 1926), 220; Ménétra, *Journal*, 86; S. Johnson, *London: A Poem*... (London, 1739), 17; James Hervey, *Meditations and Contemplations* (New York, 1848), II, 33; J.S. Cockburn, "Patterns of Violence in English Society: Homicide in Kent, 1560–1985," *PP* 103 (1991), 86; Matthiessen, *Natten*, 141.

37. Dec. 21, 1494, Luca Landucci, ed., *A Florentine Diary from 1450 to 1516*..., trans. Alice De Rosen Jervis (1927; rpt. edn., Freeport, N.Y., 1971), 77; Remarks 1717, 238, 241; Ruff, *Violence*, 75–76; Jonathan Walker, "*Bravi* and Venetian Nobles, C. 1550–1650," *Studi Veneziani* 36 (1998), 85–113.
38. Aug. 18, 1692, Wood, *Life*, V, 398; G. C. Faber, *The Poetical Works of John Gay*... (London, 1926), 81; Robert Shoemaker, "Male Honour and the Decline of Public Violence in Eighteenth-Century London," *SH* 26 (2001), 190–208.
39. *The Rules of Civility* (London, 1685), 114–115, passim; Norbert Elias, *The Civilizing Process: The Development of Manners*..., trans. Edmond Jephcott, 2 vols. (New York, 1978–1982); Ruff, *Violence*, 7–8; Penelope Corfield, "Walking the City Streets: The Urban Odyssey in Eighteenth-Century England," *JUH* 16 (1990), 132–174; Jan Bremmer and Herman Roodenburg, eds., *A Cultural History of Gesture* (Ithaca, N.Y., 1992), passim.
40. Sir Thomas Overbury, *His Wife* (London, 1622); Feb. 8, 1660, Pepys, *Diary*, I, 46; Schindler, "Youthful Culture," 275; Thomas Bell, May 2, 1666, *York Depositions*, 142; *WJ*, Mar. 23, 1723.
41. Richard A. Page and Martin K. Moss, "Environmental Influences on Aggression: The Effects of Darkness and Proximity of Victim," *Journal of Applied Social Psychology* 6 (1976), 126–133.
42. Francis Lenton, *Characterismi: or, Lentons Leasures*... (London, 1631); Robert E. Thayer, *The Origin of Everyday Moods: Managing Energy, Tension, and Stress* (New York, 1996), passim.
43. Carolyn Pouncy, ed., *The "Domostroi": Rules for Russian Households in the Time of Ivan the Terrible* (Ithaca, N.Y., 1994), 81; Arne Jansson, *From Swords to Sorrow: Homicide and Suicide in Early Modern Stockholm* (Stockholm, 1998), 125.
44. F. G. Emmison, ed., *Elizabethan Life: Disorder; Mainly from Essex Sessions and Assize Records* (Chelmsford, Eng., 1970), 206; Matthiessen, *Natten*, 133; Ruff, *Violence*, 126; Muchembled, *Violence*, 31–32.
45. Francis Henderson, June 11, 1777, Assi 45/33/1/14a; *Plain Advice to Hard-Drinkers*... (London, 1796), 10; Pieter Spierenburg, "Knife Fighting and Popular Codes of Honor in Early Modern Amsterdam," in Pieter Spierenburg, ed., *Men and Violence: Gender, Honor, and Rituals in Modern Europe and America* (Columbus, Ohio, 1998), 109; Julius R. Ruff, *Crime, Justice and Public Order in Old Regime France: The Sénéchaussées of Libourne and Bazas, 1696–1789* (London, 1984), 80–81.
46. Dietz, *Surgeon*, 194; Johnson, *London*, 17; Muchembled, *Violence*, 32; Beattie, *Crime*, 93; Schindler, *Rebellion*, 215–216.
47. Matthiessen, *Natten*, 96.
48. "Palladio," *Middlesex Journal, or, Chronicle of Liberty* (London), July 30, 1769; Shakespeare, *Othello*, I, 1, 75; William Davenant, *The Wits* (London, 1636); Thomas, *Religion and the Decline of Magic*, 15; Johan Goudsblom, *Fire and Civilization* (London, 1992), 144–145.
49. James Gabriel Fyfe, ed., *Scottish Diaries and Memoirs, 1550–1746* (Stirling, Scot., 1928), 259; Samuel H. Baron, ed. and trans., *The Travels of Olearius in Seventeenth Century Russia* (Stanford, Calif., 1967), 112; Penny Roberts, "Agencies Human and Divine: Fire in

French Cities, 1520–1720," in William G. Naphy and Penny Roberts, eds., *Fear in Early Modern Society* (Manchester, 1997), 9.

50. Stephen Porter, "Fires in Stratford-upon-Avon in the Sixteenth & Seventeenth Centuries," *Warwickshire History* 3 (1976), 103, passim.

51. Thomas, *Religion and the Decline of Magic*, 333; Mar. 16, 1701, Cowper, Diary; Matthiessen, *Natten*, 121–122.

52. Sir Richard Blackmore, *Prince Arthur* (London, 1695), 190; E. L. Jones et al., *A Gazetteer of English Urban Fire Disasters, 1500–1900* (Norwich, 1984).

53. Roy Porter, *London, a Social History* (Cambridge, Mass., 1995), 85; Sept. 4, 1666, Evelyn, *Diary*, III, 454; Neil Hanson, *The Great Fire of London: In that Apocalyptic Year* (Hoboken, N.J., 2002).

54. *NYWJ*, Sept. 26, 1737; *SJC*, Aug. 4, 1785; Roberts, "Fire in French Cities," 9–27.

55. Mar. 30, 1760, "Stow, and John Gate's Diary," *Worcester Society of Antiquity Proceedings* (1898), 270; Carl Bridenbaugh, *Cities in the Wilderness: The First Century of Urban Life in America, 1625–1742* (Oxford, 1971), 55–63, 206–213, 364–372; Carl Bridenbaugh, *Cities in Revolt: Urban Life in America, 1743–1776* (Oxford, 1971), 18, 100–105, 292–294.

56. Ludwig Holberg, *Moral Reflections & Epistles*, ed. P. M. Mitchell (Norvik, Eng., 1991), 169; "The Diary of George Booth," *Journal of the Chester and North Wales Architectural Archaeological and Historic Society*, New Ser., 28 (1928), 40; Enid Porter, *Cambridgeshire Customs and Folklore* (New York, 1969), 205.

57. John Bancroft, *The Tragedy of Sertonius* (London, 1679), 20. See also Benjamin Keach, *Spiritual Melody* (London, 1691), 28; Rowlands, *Night Raven.*

58. Benjamin Franklin, *Writings*, ed. J. A. Leo Lemay, ed., (New York, 1987), 220–221; "Philanthropos," *LEP*, Jan. 25, 1763; Carl Bridenbaugh, *Vexed and Troubled Englishmen, 1590–1642* (New York, 1967), 144; *The Life and Errors of John Dunton...* (London, 1818), II, 606.

59. *Paroimiographia* (English), 5; Thomas Tusser, *Five Hundred Pointes of Good Husbandrie*, eds. V. Payne and J. Sidney (London, 1878), 179; Jan. 13, 1669, Josselin, *Diary*, 545; Nov. 3, 1710, Raymond A. Anselment, ed., *The Remembrances of Elizabeth Freke, 1671–1714* (London, 2001), 270; Mar. 22, 1683, J. E. Foster, ed., *The Diary of Samuel Newton* (Cambridge, 1890), 84; *PG*, Feb. 18, 1729.

60. Hugh Platte, *The Jewell House of Art and Nature . . .* (1594; rpt. edn., Amsterdam, 1979), 50.

61. July 20, 1709, Sewall, *Diary*, II, 622; George Lyman Kittredge, *The Old Farmer and His Almanack . . .* (Cambridge, Mass., ca. 1904), 147; *DUR*, July 11, 1787.

62. Marybeth Carlson, "Domestic Service in a Changing City Economy: Rotterdam, 1680–1780" (Ph.D. diss., Univ. of Wisconsin, 1993), 157–158; Wilson, *English Proverbs*, 167.

63. *Grub Street Journal* (London), May 16, 1734.

64. *PA*, July 15, 1763; *William Langland's Piers Plowman: The C Version*, trans. George Economou (Philadelphia, 1996), 25; Christopher R. Friedrichs, *The Early Modern City, 1450-1750* (London, 1995), 276–277.

65. William Hector, ed., *Selections from the Judicial Records of Renfrewshire . . .* (Paisley, Scot., 1876), 239; Bernard Capp, "Arson, Threats of Arson, and Incivility in Early Modern England," in Peter Burke et al., eds., *Civil Histories: Essays Presented to Sir Keith Thomas* (Oxford, 2000), 197–213; Matthiessen, *Natten*, 121.

66. Goudsblom, *Fire and Civilization*, 158; Roberts, "Fire in French Cities," 22; *Country Journal: or the Craftsman* (London), June 24, 1738.

67. *SJC*, May 25, 1769; Frank McLynn, *Crime and Punishment in Eighteenth-Century England* (London, 1989), 85; Ruff, "Crime, Justice, and Public Order," 262; *BC*, May 20, 1761.

68. Augustus Jessopp, ed., *The Autobiography of the Hon. Roger North* (London, 1887), 41; *WJ*, Aug. 15, 1724; *Effectual Scheme*, 69–70.
69. Bob Scribner, "The Mordbrenner Fear in Sixteenth-Century Germany: Political Paranoia or the Revenge of the Outcast?," in Evans, ed., *German Underworld*, 29–56; Penny Roberts, "Arson, Conspiracy and Rumor in Early Modern Europe," *Continuity and Change* 12 (1997), 9–29.
70. Jacqueline Simpson, *The Folklore of Sussex* (London, 1973), 135–136; Capp, "Arson," 204; Thomas D. Morris, *Southern Slavery and the Law, 1619–1860* (Chapel Hill, N.C., 1996), 330–332.
71. Weinsberg, *Diary*, I, 125; *SJC*, Nov. 4, 1769; Thomas, *Religion and the Decline of Magic*, 531–533.
72. Grose, *Dictionary*; 6 Anne c.31; *PG*, Apr. 30, 1730. See also *Effectual Scheme*, 69; Michael Kunze, *Highroad to the Stake: A Tale of Witchcraft*, trans. William E. Yuill (Chicago, 1987), 147.
73. Nashe, *Works*, I, 386.
74. Rudolph Braun, *Industrialisation and Everyday Life*, trans. Sarah Hanbury Tenison (Cambridge, 1990), 84.

PART TWO

PRELUDE

1. James M. Houston, ed., *The Mind on Fire: An Anthology of the Writings of Blaise Pascal* (Porland, Ore., 1989), 165.
2. [Foxton], *The Night-Piece: A Poem* (London, 1719), 10. For the institutions of daily life, see, for example, Pounds, *Culture*, 255–301; Cohens, *Italy*, 51–52, 116–125; David H. Flaherty, "Crime and Social Control in Provincial Massachusetts," *Historical Journal* 24 (1981), 339–360.
3. Ken Krabbenhoft, trans., *The Poems of St. John of the Cross* (New York, 1999), 19; James Scholefield, ed., *The Works of James Pilkington, B. D., Lord Bishop of Durham* (London, 1842), 340; Verdon, *Night*, 199–215; Paulette Choné, *L'Atelier Des Nuits: Histoire et Signification du Nocturne dans l'Art d'Occident* (Nancy, France, 1992), 146–150; John M. Staudenmaier, "Denying the Holy Dark: The Englightenment Ideal and the European Mystical Tradition," in Leo Marx and Bruce Mazlish, eds., *Progress: Fact or Illusion* (Ann Arbor, Mich., 1996), 184–185.
4. Daniello Bartoli, *La Ricreazione del Savio* (Parma, 1992), 191–192; John Northbrooke, *A Treatise wherein Dicing, Dauncing, Vaine Playes or Enterluds with Other Idle Pastimes . . .* (London, 1577), 20; John Clayton, *Friendly Advice to the Poor . . .* (Manchester, 1755), 38.
5. Piero Camporesi, *Exotic Brew: The Art of Living in the Age of Enlightenment* (Malden, Mass., 1994), 13.
6. Thomas Amory, *Daily Devotion Assisted and Recommended . . .* (London, 1772), 20; George Economou, trans., *William Langland's Piers Plowman: The C Version* (Philadelphia, 1996), 188; Cotton Mather, *Meat Out of the Eater* (Boston, 1703), 129; Keith Thomas, *Man and the Natural World: A History of the Modern Sensibility* (New York, 1983), 40.

CHAPTER THREE

1. Moryson, *Unpublished Itinerary*, 350.
2. Lean, *Lean's Collectanea*, I, 352; Gerhard Dohrn-van Rossum, *History of the Hour: Clocks and Modern Temporal Orders*, trans. Thomas Dunlap (Chicago, 1996), 204; Remarks 1717, 160; Sigridin Maurice and Klaus Maurice, "Counting the Hours in Community Life of the 16th Century," in Klaus Maurice and Otto Mayr, eds., *The Clockwork Universe: German Clocks and Automata, 1550–1650* (New York, 1980), 148.
3. T. P. Wiseman, *Remus: A Roman Myth* (Cambridge, 1995), 125; James D. Tracy, ed., *City Walls: The Urban Enceinte in Global Perspective* (Cambridge, 2000); R. A. Butlin, "Land and People, c. 1600," in T. W. Moody et al., eds., *Early Modern Ireland, 1534–1691* (Oxford, 1991), 160–161; Remarks 1717, 160; Matthiessen, *Natten*, 18; Ripae, *Nocturno Tempore*, ch. 19.
4. Adam Walker, *Ideas . . . in a Late Excursion through Flanders, Germany, France, and Italy* (London, 1790), 69; Verdon, *Night*, 81; *Batavia: or the Hollander Displayed . . .* (Amsterdam, 1675), 50; Alexander Cowan, *Urban Europe, 1500–1700* (London, 1998), 138–142.
5. John Chamberlayne, *Magna Britannia Notitia: or, the Present State of Great Britain . . .* (London, 1723), I, 255; Cowan, *Urban Europe*, 39–40.
6. Anglicus, *On the Properties of Things*, trans. John Trevisa (Oxford, 1975), I, 539; Christopher R. Friedrichs, *The Early Modern City, 1450–1750* (London, 1995), 23.
7. Corinne Walker, "Esquisse Pour une Histoire de la Vie Nocturne: Genéve au XVIIIe Siècle," *Revue du Vieux Genève* 19 (1989), 74; Moryson, *Itinerary*, I, 41; Remarks 1717, 101–104; Gerhard Tanzer, *Spectacle Müssen Seyn: Die Freizeit der Wiener im 18. Jahrhundert* (Vienna, 1992), 55.
8. *OED*, s.v. "curfew"; Raphael Holinshed, *Holinshed's Chronicles of England, Scotland, and Ireland*, ed. Charles Lethbridge (1807; rpt. edn., New York, 1965), II, 9.
9. Toulin Smith, ed., *English Gilds: The Original Ordinances of More than One Hundred Early English Gilds . . .* (1870; rpt. edn., London, 1963), 194; Falkus, "Lighting," 249–251; William M. Bowsky, "The Medieval Commune and Internal Violence: Police Power and Public Safety in Siena, 1287–1355," *AHR* 73 (1967), 6; A. Voisin, "Notes sur la Vie Urbaine au XV. Siècle: Dijon la Nuit," *Annales de Bourgogne* 9 (1937), 267.
10. Matthiessen, *Natten*, 21–22; Gerald Strauss, *Nuremberg in the Sixteenth Century: City Politics and Life Between Middle Ages and Modern Times* (Bloomington, Ind., 1976), 190–191; J. R. Hale, "Violence in the Late Middle Ages: A Background," in Lauro Martines, ed., *Violence and Civil Disorder in Italian Cities, 1200–1500* (Berkeley, Calif., 1972), 23; Verdon, *Night*, 81; Journal of Sir John Finch, 1675–1682, Historical Manuscripts Commission, *Report on the Manuscripts of Allan Finch, Esq. . . .* (London, 1913), I, 69.
11. Paul Griffiths, "Meanings of Nightwalking in Early Modern England," *Seventeenth Century* 13 (1998), 224–225; *The Lawes of the Market* (1595; rpt. edn., Amsterdam, 1974); Falkus, "Lighting," 250–251, passim.
12. W. O. Hassall, comp., *How They Lived: An Anthology of Original Accounts Written Before 1485* (Oxford, 1962), 207; Griffiths "Nightwalking," 218, passim; Marjorie Keniston McIntosh, *Controlling Misbehavior in England, 1370–1600* (Cambridge, 1998), 66–67; Bronislaw Geremek, *The Margins of Society in Late Medieval Paris*, trans. Jean Birrell (Cambridge, 1987), 126, 217; Moryson, *Itinerary*, I, 196; Walker, "Genève," 75; T. Platter, *Journal*, 204; Christopher Black, *Early Modern Italy: A Social History* (London, 2001), 102.
13. Benjamin Ravid, "The Venetian Government and the Jews," in Robert C. Davis and Benjamin Ravid, eds., *The Jews of Early Modern Venice* (Baltimore, 2001), 8, 21; Orest and Patricia Ranum, comps., *The Century of Louis XIV* (New York, 1972), 168; Black, *Early*

Modern Italy, 154–156; R.I. Moore, *The Formation of a Persecuting Society: Power and Deviance in Western Europe, 950–1250* (Oxford, 1987), 87.

14. Dekker, *Lanthorne and Candle-Light* (London, 1608); Kathryn Norberg, *Rich and Poor in Grenoble, 1600–1814* (Berkeley, Calif., 1985), 44; Griffiths, "Nightwalking," passim; Robert B. Shoemaker, *Prosecution and Punishment: Petty Crime and the Law in London and Rural Middlesex, c. 1660–1725* (Cambridge, 1991), 179–181; Luigi Cajan and Silva Saba, "La Notte Devota: Luci e Ombre Delle Quarantore," in Mario Sbriccoli, ed., *La Notte: Ordine, Sicurezza e Disciplinamento in Età Moderna* (Florence, 1991), 74.
15. 13 Edward I c.4; Sir Andrew Balfour, *Letters Written to a Friend* (Edinburgh, 1700), 86; Bartholomäus Sastrow et al., *Social Germany in Luther's Time: Being the Memoirs of Bartholomew Sastrow*, trans. H.A.L. Fisher (Westminster, Eng., 1902), 172; Moryson, *Unpublished Itinerary*, 405, 163; Ruth Pike, "Crime and Punishment in Sixteenth-Century Spain," *Journal of European Economic History* 5 (1976), 695; Andrew Trout, *City on the Seine: Paris in the Time of Richelieu and Louis XIV* (New York, 1996), 173–174, 217.
16. A. R. Myers, ed., *English Historical Documents, 1327–1485* (London, 1969), 1073; David Chambers and Trevor Dean, *Clean Hands and Rough Justice: An Investigating Magistrate in Renaissance Italy* (Ann Arbor, Mich., 1997), 100; Elisabeth Pavan, "Recherches sur la Nuit Vénitienne à la Fin du Moyen Age," *Journal of Medieval History* 7 (1981), 354–355.
17. Verdon, *Night*, 75; Pavan, "Nuit Vénitienne," 353.
18. E. S. De Beer, "The Early History of London Street-Lighting," *History* 25 (1941), 311–324; Falkus, "Lighting," 251–254; O'Dea, *Lighting*, 94; Paul Zumthor, *Daily Life in Rembrandt's Holland* (New York, 1963), 20.
19. Angelo Raine, ed., *York Civic Records* (Wakefield, Eng., 1942), III, 110; Falkus, "Lighting," 251–254; J. H. Thomas, *Town Government in the Sixteenth Century* . . . (London, [1933]), 56–57; Carl Bridenbaugh, *Vexed and Troubled Englishmen, 1590–1642* (New York, 1967), 153–154.
20. Charles Knight, *London* (London, 1841), I, 104; De Beer, "London Street-Lighting," 311–324; Matthiessen, *Natten*, 26.
21. Jean Shirley, trans., *A Parisian Journal, 1405–1449* (Oxford, 1968), 51; Thoresby, *Diary*, I, 190; Matthiessen, *Natten*, 24, 118; David Cressy, *Bonfires and Bells: National Memory and the Protestant Calendar in Elizabethan and Stuart England* (London, 1989), 74; Bargellini, "Vita Notturna," 79.
22. James S. Amelang, ed., *A Journal of the Plague Year: The Diary of the Barcelona Tanner Miquel Parets, 1651* (New York, 1991), 86; Koslofsky, "Court Culture," 746; Lord Herbert, ed., *Henry, Elizabeth and George (1738–80): Letters and Diaires of Henry, Tenth Earl of Pembroke and His Circle* (London, 1939), 371; Luca Landucci, ed., *A Florentine Diary from 1450 to 1516*, trans. Alice De Rosen Jervis (London, 1927), 161, 29; May 29, 1666, Pepys, *Diary*, VII, 136; Cressy, *Bonfires and Bells*, 85–92.
23. A. W. Verity, ed., *Milton's Samson Agonistes* (Cambridge, 1966), 7; Phillip Stubbes, *Anatomy of the Abuses in England* . . . , ed. Frederick J. Furnivall (London, 1877), I, 342; Dec. 6, 1764, Frederick A. Pottle, ed., *Boswell on the Grand Tour: Germany and Switzerland, 1764* (New York, 1953), 243; Eamon Duffy, *The Stripping of the Altars: Traditional Religion in England, c.1400–c.1580* (New Haven, 1992), 407, 419. See also Moryson, *Itinerary*, I, 167, 235, 310.
24. Schindler, *Rebellion*, 196; Remarks 1717, 69; John McManners, *Church and Society in Eighteenth-Century France* (Oxford, 1999), II, 219.
25. John Ray, *Observations Topographical, Moral, & Physiological* . . . (London, 1673), 317; Moryson, *Unpublished Itinerary*, 448; J. W. Goethe, *Italian Journey, 1786–1788* (New York, 1968), 344; Schindler, *Rebellion*, 195–201; Roche, *Consumption*, 116–118.
26. Apr. 16, 1708, Cowper, Diary; Stewart E. Fraser, ed., *Ludwig Holberg's Memoirs* . . . (Lei-

den, 1970), 115; "Decription of the City of Rome," *Town and Country Magazine* 24 (1792), 260; Henry Swinburne, *Travels in the Two Sicilies*... (London, 1783), II, 72–73; Cohens, *Italy*, 156–157; Sara T. Nalle, *God in La Mancha: Religious Reform and the People of Cuenca, 1500–1650* (Baltimore, 1992), 154–156.

27. J. M. Beattie, *Policing in London, 1660–1750: Urban Crime and the Limits of Terror* (Oxford, 2001), 172; Edward MacLysaght, *Irish Life in the Seventeenth Century* (New York, 1969), 197; Eugène Defrance, *Histoire de l'Éclairage des Rues de Paris* (Paris, 1904), 36; Falkus, "Lighting," 254–264; Lettie S. Multhauf, "The Light of Lamp-Lanterns: Street Lighting in 17th-Century Amsterdam," *Technology and Culture* 26 (1985), 236–252; Ruff, *Violence*, 3; Cohens, *Italy*, 116–117; Jonathan Irvine Israel, *The Dutch Republic: Its Rise, Greatness, and Fall, 1477–1806* (New York, 1995), 681–682; Voisin, "Dijon la Nuit," 278.

28. J. P. Marana, *Lettre Sicilienne* (1700; rpt. edn., Paris, 1883), 50–51; Martin Lister, *A Journey to Paris in the Year 1698*, ed. Raymond Phineas Stearns (Urbana, Ill., 1967), 25; John Beckman, *A History of Inventions, Discoveries, and Origins*, trans. William Johnston (London, 1846), 180–182; Koslofsky, "Court Culture," 748–752; Defrance, *Histoire de l'Éclairage*, 35–38; Leon Bernard, *The Emerging City: Paris in the Age of Louis XIV* (Durham, N.C., 1970), 162–166; Falkus, "Lighting," 254–260; Peter Borsay, *The English Urban Renaissance: Culture and Society in the Provincial Town, 1660–1770* (Oxford, 1989), 72–74.

29. *SJC*, Oct. 25, 1783; De Beer, "Street-Lighting," 317–320; Beckman, *Discoveries*, trans. Johnston, 180; Matthiessen, *Natten*, 26.

30. John Scott, *A Visit to Paris in 1814*... (London, 1815), 40; Defrance, *Histoire de l'Éclairage*, 47; G. E. Rodmell, ed., "An Englishman's Impressions of France in 1775," *Durham University Journal* (1967), 78. See also Maurice Déribéré and Paulette Déribéré, *Préhistoire et Histoire de la Lumière* (Paris, 1979), 117.

31. Koslofsky, "Court Culture," 759; Corinne Walker, "Du Plaisir à la Nécessité: l'Apparition de la Lumière dans les Rues de Genève à la Fin du XVIIIe Siècle," in François Walter, ed., *Vivre et Imaginer la Ville XVIIIe–XIXe Siècles* (Geneva, 1988), 107; Henry Hibbert, *Syntagma Theologcum*... (London, 1662), 31; Beattie, *Policing*, 170.

32. Smollet, *Humphry Clinker*... (New York, 1983), 113.

33. R. G. Bury, trans., *Plato in Twelve Volumes* (Cambridge, Mass., 1963), XI, 69; Crusius, *Nocte*, ch. 5.5.

34. 13 Edward I c.4; Beckman, *Discoveries*, trans. Johnston, 188; Joachim Schlör, *Nights in the Big City: Paris, Berlin, London 1840–1930*, trans. Pierre Gottfried Imhof and Dafydd Rees Roberts (London, 1998), 73.

35. Moryson, *Unpublished Itinerary*, 365–366; Clare Williams, ed., *Thomas Platter's Travels in England, 1599* (London, 1937), 174; Raine, ed., *York Civic Records*, V, 102; Bowsky, "Medieval Commune," 9–10; Alan Williams, *The Police of Paris, 1718–1789* (Baton Rouge, 1979), 67.

36. Carl Bridenbaugh, *Cities in the Wilderness: The First Century of Urban Life in America, 1625–1742* (Oxford, 1971), 64–67.

37. Beckman, *Discoveries*, trans. Johnston, 189; Schlör, *Nights in the Big City*, trans. Imhof and Roberts, 74; Duke of Ormond, "Whereas by the good and wholsome lawes of this realm... night-watches should be kept..." (Dublin, 1677); Ruff, *Violence*, 92; M. De La Lande, *Voyage en Italie*... (Paris, 1786), 154.

38. *Memoirs of François-René Vicomte de Chateaubriand*, trans. Alexander Teixera de Mattos (New York, 1902), IV, 27; William Young, *The History of Dulwich College... with a Life of the Founder, Edward Alleyn, and an Accurate Transcript of His Diary, 1617–1622* (London, 1889), II, 356; A.F.J. Brown, *Essex People, 1750–1900* (Chelmsford, Eng., 1972), 40; Robert C. Davis, *Shipbuilders of the Venetian Arsenal: Workers and Workplace in the Preindustrial City* (Baltimore, 1991), 157.

39. Mr. Ozell, trans., *M. Misson's Memoirs and Observations in His Travels over England* (London, 1719), 358–359; Beattie, *Policing*, 169–197; Williams, *Police of Paris*, 67; e-mail of Nov. 16, 2003, from Paul Griffiths; Frank McLynn, *Crime and Punishment in Eighteenth-Century England* (London, 1989).
40. *NHCR* I, 33; Beattie, *Policing*, 181; Matthiessen, *Natten*, 52; Thomas Forester, ed., *Norway and Its Scenery . . . the Journal of a Tour by Edward Price . . .* (London, 1853), 181–182; Pinkerton, *Travels*, I, 265; John Carr, *A Northern Summer or Travels Round the Baltic . . .* (Hartford, Ct., 1806), 129; *An Accurate Description of the United Netherlands . . .* (London, 1691), 65; Bridenbaugh, *Cities in the Wilderness*, 64–67.
41. Robert Poole, *A Journey from London to France . . .* (London, 1741), 10; Moryson, *Itinerary*, I, 18, 413; Moryson, *Unpublished Itinerary*, 365–366, 385; Sir Richard Carnac Temple and Lavina Mary Anstey, eds., *The Travels of Peter Mundy in Europe and Asia, 1608–1667* (London, 1914), IV, 169; Mr. Nugent, *The Grand Tour, or, a Journey through the Netherlands, Germany, Italy and France . . .* (London, 1756), I, 87; *A Tour through Holland, etc.* (London, 1788), 80–81; John Barnes, *A Tour throughout the Whole of France . . .* (London, 1815), 6; *NHCR* I, 485; Matthiessen, *Natten*, 13, 31–32; Theodor Hampe, *Crime and Punishment in Germany . . .*, trans. Malcolm Letts (London, 1929), 7–8.
42. Thomas Dekker, *Villanies Discovered by Lanthorne and Candle-Light . . .* (London, 1616); Walter George Bell, *Unknown London* (London, 1966), 213; Félix-L. Tavernier, *La Vie Quotidienne a Marseille de Louis XIV à Louis-Philippe* (Paris, 1973), 96, Hana Urbancová, "Nightwatchmen's Songs as a Component of the Traditional Musical Culture," *Studies*, 48 (2000), 14; John F. Curwen, *Kirkbie-Kendall . . .* (Kendall, Eng., 1900), 116. See also Einar Utzon Frank, ed., *De Danske Vaegtervers* (Copenhagen, 1932).
43. Matthiessen, *Natten*, 48; Moryson, *Unpublished Itinerary*, 350.
44. Samuel Rowlands, *Heavens Glory, Seeke It* (London, 1628); Henry Alexander, trans., *Four Plays by Holberg . . .* (Princeton, N.J., 1946), 170; "Insomnis," *PA*, Oct. 8, 1767; Colm Lennon, *Richard Stanyhurst the Dubliner, 1547–1618* (Blackrock, Ire., 1981), 147.
45. *Second Report of the Record Commissioners of the City of Boston, Containing the Boston Records 1634–1660 . . .* (Boston, 1877), 151; Louis-Sébastien Mercier, *The Picture of Paris Before & After the Revolution* (New York, 1930), 132; Pounds, *Culture*, 132–134; Bridenbaugh, *Cities in the Wilderness*, 374; Schindler, *Rebellion*, 218; Jacques Rossiaud, "Prostitution, Youth, and Society in the Towns of Southeastern France in the Fifteenth Century," in Robert Forster and Orest Ranum, eds., *Deviants and the Abandoned in French Society: Selections from the Annales Economies, Sociétés, Civilisations*, trans. Elborg Forster and Patricia Ranum (Baltimore, 1978), 45 n.85; Matthiessen, *Natten*, 115, 117.
46. Awnsham Churchill, comp., *A Collection of Voyages and Travels . . .* (London, 1745), I, 147; Sept. 11, 1663, Pepys, *Diary*, IV, 304.
47. Thomas Pennington, *Continental Excursions . . .* (London, 1809), I, 242; Fabian Philipps, *Regale Necessarium: or the Legality, Reason and Necessity of the Rights and Priviledges Justly Claimed by the Kings Servants . . .* (London, 1671), 580; William Edward Hartpole Lecky, *A History of England in the Eighteenth Century* (New York, 1892), II, 106–107; Edward Ward, *Nuptial Dialogues and Debates . . .* (London, 1723), 258; Shoemaker, *Prosecution and Punishment*, 264–265.
48. N. M. Karamzin, *Letters of a Russian Traveler: 1789–1790 . . .*, trans. Florence Jonas (New York, 1957), 305.
49. *The Midnight-Ramble; or, the Adventures of Two Noble Females . . .* (London, 1754), 20; Sept. 19, 1771, Basil Cozens-Hardy, ed., *The Diary of Sylas Neville, 1767–1788* (London, 1950), 117; Matthiessen, *Natten*, 23.
50. *New England Courant* (Boston), Nov. 16, 1724. For an excellent discussion of law enforcement in London, see Beattie, *Policing*, 77–225.

51. Walter Rye, ed., *Extracts from the Court Books of the City of Norwich, 1666–1688* (Norwich, 1905), 140–141; *OBP*, May 1, 1717, 5; *A Report of the Record Commissioners of the City of Boston, Containing the Boston Records from 1660 to 1701* (Boston, 1895), 8; *The Way to be Wiser . . .* (London, 1705), 28; Urbancová, "Nightwatchmen's Songs," 6; Beattie, *Policing*, 172–174.
52. *The Humourist: Being Essays Upon Several Subjects . . .* (London, 1724), II, 88; Dekker, *Writings*, 107; Shakespeare, *Much Ado About Nothing*, III, 3, 56–57.
53. Thomas Brennan, *Public Drinking and Popular Culture in Eighteenth-Century Paris* (Princeton, N.J., 1988), 304; Legg, *Low-Life*, 15; Edward Phillips, *The Mysteries of Love & Eloquence . . .* (London, 1658), 101; *ECR*, VI, 439–440; Matthiessen, *Natten*, 41, 46; Walker, "Genève," 76; Keith Wrightson, "Two Concepts of Order: Justices, Constables and Jurymen in Seventeenth-Century England," in John Brewer and John Styles, eds., *An Ungovernable People: The English and Their Law in the Seventeenth and Eighteenth Centuries* (London, 1980), 21–46, passim.
54. *Augusta Triumphans: or, the Way to Make London the Most Flourishing City in the Universe . . .* (London, 1728), 47; Richard Mowery Andrews, *Law, Magistracy, and Crime in Old Regime Paris, 1735–1789* (Cambridge, 1994), 521; Margaret J. Hoad, *Portsmouth Record Series: Borough Sessions Papers, 1653–1688* (London, 1971), 50; Janekovick-Römer, "Dubrovniks," 107; Matthiessen, *Natten*, 137–139; Schindler, *Rebellion*, 218–219; De La Lande, *Voyage en Italie*, 122.
55. Herbert, *Jaculum Prudentium: or Outlandish Proverbs . . .* (London, 1651), 54.
56. Jean Carbonnier, *Flexible Droit: Textes Pour une Sociologie de Droit sans Rigueur* (Paris, 1976), 46–51.
57. S. P. Scott, ed. and trans., *The Civil Law: Including the Twelve Tables . . .* (New York, 1973), I, 58; Crusius, *Nocte*, ch. 7.3, 7 passim, 13.6, 15.3; Ripae, *Noctunro Tempore*, passim; Nina Gockerell, "Telling Time without a Clock," in Maurice and Mayr, eds., *Clockwork Universe*, 137.
58. Matthew Hale, *Historia Placitorum Coronae: The History of the Pleas of the Crown* (1736; rpt. edn., London, 1971), I, 547; David H. Flaherty, *Privacy in Colonial New England* (Charlottesville, Va., 1972), 88; Matthew Bacon and Henry Gwillim, *A New Abridgement of the Law* (London, 1807), II, 346.
59. Legg, *Low-Life*, 101.
60. Ripae, *Nocturno Tempore*, ch. 91.11; *DUR*, Dec. 23, 1785; Tommaso Astarita, *Village Justice: Community, Family, and Popular Culture in Early Modern Italy* (Baltimore, 1999), 153–154; Patricia H. Labalme, "Sodomy and Venetian Justice in the Renaissance," *Legal History Review* 52 (1984), 221–222; Samuel Cohn, "Criminality and the State in Renaissance Florence, 1344–1466," *JSH* 14 (1980), 222; Guido Ruggiero, *Violence in Early Renaissance Venice* (New Brunswick, N.J., 1980), 6, 19; Matthiessen, *Natten*, 137; Aug. 17, 1497, Landucci, ed., *Florentine Diary*, trans. Jervis, 125–126.
61. Bowsky, "Medieval Commune," 4; Ripae, *Nocturno Tempore*, ch. 24:3, passim; *JRAI*, I and II, passim; High Court of Justiciary, Small Papers, Main Series, JC 26/42–43, passim, Scottish Record Office, Edinburgh; Julius R. Ruff, *Crime, Justice and Public Order in Old Regime France: The Sénéchaussées of Libourne and Bazas, 1696–1789* (London, 1984), 115; Matthiessen, *Natten*, 129.
62. Beattie, *Crime*, 148; Ian W. Archer, *The Pursuit of Stability: Social Relations in Elizabethan London* (Cambridge, 1991), 247; Ian Cameron, *Crime and Repression in the Auvergne and the Guyenne, 1720–1790* (Cambridge, 1981), 155–156; Edgar J. McManus, *Law and Liberty in Early New England: Criminal Justice and Due Process, 1620–1692* (Amherst, Mass., 1993), 30–31.
63. "Justus Sed Humanus," *London Magazine*, April 1766, 204; Sir William Blackstone,

Commentaries on the Laws of England, ed. William Draper Lewis (Phildadelphia, 1902), IV, 1579; Scott, ed. and trans., *Civil Law*, 59; Katherine Fischer Drew, trans., *The Lombard Laws* (Philadelphia, 1973), 58; F.R.P. Akehurst, ed., *The Coutumes de Beauvaisis of Philippe de Beaumanoir* (Philadelphia, 1992), 429–430; Ripae, *Nocturno Tempore*, ch. 24; Crusius, *Nocte*, ch. 11.5–8; Samuel E. Thorne, ed., *Bracton on the Laws and Customs of England* (Cambridge, Mass., 1968), II, 408; Porret, *Crime et ses Circonstances*, 288–289.

64. Lottin, *Chavatte*, 356; *JRAI*, II, 488; Blackstone, *Commentaries*, ed. Lewis, IV, 1618.
65. *An Effectual Scheme for the Immediate Preventing of Street Robberies, and Suppressing All Other Disorders of the Night* ... (London, 1731), 62; Edmond-Jean-François Barbier, *Journal d'un Bourgeois de Paris sous le Règne de Louis XV* (Paris, 1963), 169; Matthiessen, *Natten*, 12; Jeffry Kaplow, *The Names of Kings: The Parisian Laboring Poor in the Eighteenth Century* (New York, 1972), 22–23.

CHAPTER FOUR

1. Apr. 6, 1745, Parkman, *Diary*, 114.
2. Bräker, *Life*, 67; John Milton, *Complete Prose Works* (New Haven, 1953), I, 228; Nina Gockerell, "Telling Time without a Clock," in Klaus Maurice and Otto Mayr, eds., *The Clockwork Universe: German Clocks and Automata, 1550–1650* (New York, 1980), 131–143.
3. Giambattista Basile, *The Pentamerone* . . . , ed. and trans. Stith Thompson (1932; rpt. edn., Westport, Ct., 1979), I, 297; Randle Cotgrave, *A Dictionarie of the French and English Tongues* (London, 1611), Muchembled, *Violence*, 53; Thomas Hardy, *The Woodlanders* (1887; rpt. edn., London, 1991), 99–100; Gockerell, "Telling Time," 134–136.
4. Phineas Fletcher, *The Purple Island, or the Isle of Man* (n.p., 1633), 46; Wilson J. Litchfield, *The Litchfield Family in America* (Southbridge, Mass., 1906), V, 344; Sept. 30, 1774, Patten, *Diary*, 330, 385.
5. Henry Swinburne, *Travels in the Two Siciliies* ... (London, 1783), II, 269; William Sewell, *A Large Dictionary English and Dutch* (Amsterdam, 1708), 79; Shakespeare, *Macbeth*, I, 5, 51.
6. "Fantasticks," Breton, *Works*, II, 15.
7. Oct. 23, 1676, Sewall, *Diary*, I, 28; May 10, 1776, Andrew Oliver, ed., *The Journal of Samuel Curwen, Loyalist* (Cambridge, Mass., 1972), 156; Philippe Contamine, "Peasant Hearth to Papal Palace: The Fourteenth and Fifteenth Centuries," in *HPL* II, 499; W. Carew Hazlitt, ed., *English Proverbs and Proverbial Phrases* ... (London, 1882), 291.
8. Barbara A. Hanawalt, *The Ties That Bound: Peasant Families in Medieval England* (New York, 1986), 44; Sir Edward Coke, *The Reports* ... (London, 1658), 453; Burt, *Letters*, II, 206.
9. *OBP*, Apr. 29–May 1, 1747, 152, May 14, 1741, 12, July 15–17, 1767, 244; David Ogborne, *The Merry Midnight Mistake, or Comfortable Conclusion* (Chelmsford, Eng., 1765), 34; Timothy J. Casey, ed., *Jean Paul: A Reader*, trans. Erika Casey (Baltimore, 1992), 338; *FLEMT*, xi–xii.
10. Pounds, *Home*, 184–186; Hanawalt, *Ties That Bound*, 38; *A Warning for House-Keepers* ... (n.p., 1676), 4.
11. Pinkerton, *Travels*, I, 517; John E. Crowley, *The Invention of Comfort: Sensibilities & Design in Early Modern Britain & Early America* (Baltimore, 2001), 36–44, 62–69; Pounds, *Culture*, 118–120.
12. Edward Clarke, *Letters Concerning the Spanish Nation* ... (London, 1763), 344; June 20, 1766, Diary of Mr. Tracy and Mr. Dentand, Bodl.; John Fielding, *Thieving Detected* ... (London, 1777), 9; Monsieur du Sorbiere, *A Voyage to England* ... (London, 1709), 11.
13. Paolo Da Certaldo, *Libro di Buoni Costumi*, ed. Alfredo Schiaffini (Florence, 1945), 30;

Nov. 12, Oct. 21, 1666, Pepys, *Diary*, VII, 367, 336; Ann Feddon, Apr. 20, 1751, Assi 45/24/3/42; John Cooper, Dec. 13, 1765, Assi 45/28/2/137; Contamine, "Peasant Hearth to Papal Palace," 502; Eugen Weber, "Fairies and Hard Facts: The Reality of Folktales," *Journal of the History of Ideas* 42 (1981), 101–102.

14. Dec. 13, 1672, Isham, *Diary*, 175; John Worlidge, *Systema Agriculturae; The Mystery of Husbandry Discovered . . .* (1675; rpt. edn., Los Angeles, 1970), 221; *London Gazette*, Oct. 1, 1694; John Houghton, *A Collection for Improvement of Husbandry and Trade*, July 20, 1694; William Hamlet, *The Plan and Description of a Machine . . . against Fire and House-breaking* (Birmingham, 1786).
15. C. G. Crump, ed., *The History of the Life of Thomas Ellwood* (New York, 1900), 7; *An Account of a Most Barbarous Murther and Robbery . . . 25th of October, 1704* (London, 1704/1705); *OED*, s.v. "bedstaff"; Francis Bamford, ed., *A Royalist's Notebook: The Commonplace Book of Sir John Oglander* (New York, 1971), 55; Ruff, *Violence*, 49.
16. Mar. 21, 1763, Frederick A. Pottle, ed., *Boswell's London Journal, 1762–1763* (New York, 1950), 224; Leonard R. N. Ashley, ed., *A Narrative of the Life of Mrs. Charlotte Charke . . .* (1755; rpt. edn., Gainesville, Fla., 1969), 45; J. S. Cockburn, "Patterns of Violence in English Society: Homicide in Kent, 1560–1985," *PP* 130 (1991), 86–87.
17. Thoresby, *Diary*, I, 345; George Murray, Jan. 10, 1778, Assi 45/33/2/150; Oct. 25, 1704, A. H. Quint, "Journal of the Reverend John Pike," *Massachusetts Historical Society Proceedings*, 1st Ser., 14 (1875–1876), 139; *The Province and Court Records of Maine* (Portland, Maine, 1958), IV, 341.
18. *OED*, s.v. "bandog"; Harrison, *Description*, 339–348; Thomas Kirk and Ralph Thoresby, *Tours in Scotland, 1677 & 1681*, ed. P. Hume Brown (Edinburgh, 1892), 27; *OBP*, Apr. 9–11, 1746, 118; Keith Thomas, *Man and the Natural World* (New York, 1983), 101–104; Mrs. Reginald Heber, *The Life of Reginald Heber . . .* (New York, 1830), I, 217; George Sand, *Story of My Life . . .*, ed. Thelma Jurgrau (Albany, 1991), 631.
19. Augustin Gallo, *Secrets de la Vraye Agriculture . . .* (Paris, 1572), 204; Harrison, *Description*, 343; Daniel Defoe, *Street-Robberies Consider'd . . .*, (1728; rpt. edn. Stockton, N.J., 1973), 68; M. Conradus Heresbachius, comp., *Foure Bookes of Husbandry*, trans. Barnabe Googe, (London, 1577), fo. 154–156; Charles Stevens and John Liebrault, *Maison Rustique, or, the Countrey Farme*, trans. Richard Surflet (London, 1616), 120–122; Worlidge, *Systema Agriculturae*, 162, 222; *Times*, Jan. 16, 1790.
20. Campion, *The Discription of a Maske* (London, 1607).
21. Aug. 2, 1708, Cowper, Diary; Thomas, *Religion and the Decline of Magic*, passim, esp. 493–497.
22. George Peele, *The Old Wives Tale*, ed. Patricia Binnie (Manchester, 1980), 42 n. 104; Edward Young, *Night Thoughts*, ed. Stephen Cornford (Cambridge, 1989), 121; Casey, ed., *Jean Paul*, trans. Casey, 338; R. Sherlock, *The Practical Christian . . .* (London, 1699), 322; Taillepied, *Ghosts*, 169.
23. W. M., *Hesperi-neso-graphia: or, a Description of the Western Isle . . .* (London, 1716), 8; Thomas, *Religion and the Decline of Magic*, 496–497; Robert Muchembled, "Popular Culture," in Robert Muchembled et al., *Popular Culture* (Danbury, Ct., 1994), 11.
24. *SAS*, V, 335; C. Scott Dixon, *The Reformation and Rural Society: The Parishes of Brandenburg-Ansbach-Kulmbach, 1528–1603* (Cambridge, 1996), 183, 180–181, 194–195; George Saintsbury, ed., *The Works of John Dryden* (Edinburgh, 1884), IX, 443; Thomas, *Religion and the Decline of Magic*, 222–231; Burke, *Popular Culture*, passim.
25. *OED*, s.v. "night-spell"; Minor White Latham, *The Elizabethan Fairies: The Fairies of Folklore and the Fairies of Shakespeare* (1930; rpt. edn., New York, 1972), 38; Ralph Merrifield, *The Archaeology of Ritual and Magic* (London, 1987), 137–158.
26. Scott, *Witchcraft*, 27; Catherine Maloney, "A Witch-Bottle from Dukes Place,

Aldgate," *Transactions of the London & Middlesex Archaeological Society* 31 (1980), 157–159; John Demos, *Remarkable Providences: Readings on Early American History* (Boston, 1991), 437–438; Merrifield, *Archaeology*, 159–178.

27. Roderick A. McDonald, *The Economy and Material Culture of Slaves: Goods and Chattels on the Sugar Plantations of Jamaica and Louisiana* (Baton Rouge, 1993), 40; Carla Mulford et al., eds., *Early American Writings* (New York, 2002), 508.
28. Anna Brzozowska-Krajka, *Polish Traditional Folklore: The Magic of Time* (Boulder, Colo, 1998), 122; Matthiessen, *Natten*, 100; Anonymous, Travel Diary, 1795, Chetham's Library, Manchester, Eng.; *OED*, s.v. "mezuzah."
29. Sewall, *Diary*, I, 400; David D. Hall, "The Mental World of Samuel Sewall," in David Hall et al., eds., *Saints & Revolutionaries: Essays on Early American History* (New York, 1984), 80; Brand 1848, II, 73, III, 20–21; Kingsley Palmer, *The Folklore of Somerset* (Totowa, N.J., 1976), 45; Mrs. Gutch, *County Folk-Lore: Examples of Printed Folk-Lore Concerning the East Riding of Yorkshire* (London, 1912), 64; Karl Wegert, *Popular Culture, Crime, and Social Control in 18th Century Württemberg* (Stuttgart, 1994), 71.
30. Trenchard, *The Natural History of Superstition* (London, 1709), 24; Thomas, *Religion and the Decline of Magic*, 636–637, 647–648.
31. *UM*, May, 1751, 220.
32. Henry Bull, comp., *Christian Prayers and Holy Meditations . . .* (Cambridge, 1842), 75.
33. *BC*, July 1, 1761; Brand 1848, III, 180–182, 228; Brzozowska-Krajka, *Polish Folklore*, 67, 204; R.W. Scribner, *Popular Culture and Popular Movements in Reformation Germany* (London, 1987), 32; Mrs. M. MacLeod Banks, *British Calendar Customs: Scotland* (London, 1941), III, 112, 116–117; e-mail of Jan. 29, 2002 from David Bromwich, Somerset Archaeological and Natural History Society, Taunton, Eng.; Muchembled, "Popular Culture," 24.
34. Dec. 7, 1758, Dyer, Diary; June 3, 1662, Pepys, *Diary*, III, 101; Ian Cameron, *Crime and Repression in the Auvergne and the Guyenne, 1720–1790* (Cambridge, 1981), 127.
35. Eugen Weber, *Peasants into Frenchmen: The Modernization of Rural France, 1870–1914* (Stanford, Calif., 1976), 161; Pounds, *Culture*, 109–117; Roche, *Consumption*, 125–130; Raffaella Sarti, *Europe at Home: Family and Material Culture, 1500–1800*, trans. Allan Cameron (New Haven, 2002), 92–93.
36. William Carr, ed., *The Dialect of Craven, in the West-Riding of the County of York* (London, 1828), I, 30; Joseph Lawson, *Letters to the Young on Progress in Pudsey during the Last Sixty Years* (Stanningley, Eng., 1887), 23; Annik Pardailhe Galabrun, *The Birth of Intimacy: Privacy and Domestic Life in Early Modern Paris*, trans. Jocelyn Phelps (Philadelphia, 1991), 120.
37. Pounds, *Culture*, 110–112; Roche, *Consumption*, 130–131; Tobias George Smollett, *Travels through France and Italy*, ed. Frank Felsentein (Oxford, 1979), 209.
38. John Earl Perceval, *The English Travels of Sir John Percival and William Byrd II*, ed. Mark R. Wenger (Columbia, Mo., 1989), 137; Defoe, *Tour*, II, 676; Mr. Ozell, trans., *M. Misson's Memoirs and Observations in His Travels over England* (London, 1719), 37–39; Celia Fiennes, *The Illustrated Journeys of Celia Fiennes, 1685–c.1712* (London, 1982), 147, 161; Joan Thirsk, *The Agrarian History of England and Wales* (London, 1967), IV, 453.
39. Caroline Davidson, *A Woman's Work is Never Done: A History of Housework in the British Isles, 1650–1950* (London, 1982), 73–75; *SAS*, V, 424, XII, 297, 747; *SAI*, I, 4, 198; James Ayres, *Domestic Interiors: The British Tradition, 1500–1850* (New Haven, 2003), 16.
40. *SAS*, XVIII, 480; Edward Ward, *A Journey to Scotland . . .* (London, 1699), 9; Thirsk, *Agrarian History*, IV, 453; Davidson, *Woman's Work*, 81–87; E. Veryard, *An Account of Divers Choice Remarks . . . in a Journey . . .* (London, 1701), 19; Paul Zumthor, *Daily Life in Rembrandt's Holland* (New York, 1963), 45–46, 302.

41. Robert W. Malcolmson, *Life and Labour in England, 1700–1780* (New York, 1981), 46–47; Davidson, *Woman's Work*, 76–77; Carl Bridenbaugh, *Vexed and Troubled Englishmen, 1590–1642* (New York, 1967), 99.
42. Llewellynn Jewitt, ed., *The Life of William Hutton . . .* (London, 1872), 160; Davidson, *Woman's Work*, 101.
43. Pounds, *Culture*, 120; A. Alvarez, *Night: Night Life, Night Language, Sleep, and Dreams* (New York, 1995), 6.
44. Anne Elizabeth Baker, comp., *Glossary of Northamptonshire Words and Phrases* (London, 1854), I, 89; Wilson, *English Proverbs*, 377.
45. Joan Wildeblood and Peter Brinson, *The Polite World: A Guide to English Manners and Deportment from the Thirteenth to the Nineteenth Century* (London, 1965), 84; Witold Rybczynski, *Home: A Short History of an Idea* (New York, 1986), 138; O'Dea, *Lighting*, 217. The sum of 28,000 livres was roughly equivalent to £900. W. S. Lewis et al., eds., *Horace Walpole's Correspondence with Hannah More . . .* (New Haven, 1961), 80. For the cost of candles in England, see Lord Beveridge et al., *Prices and Wages in England: From the Twelfth to the Nineteenth Century* (London, 1939), I, passim.
46. Eric Sloane, *Seasons of America Past* (New York, 1958), 107; Shakespeare, *Cybleline*, I, 6, 110–111; O'Dea, *Lighting*, 35–37, 43; Crowley, *Comfort*, 112–115; Davidson, *Woman's Work*, 104–105, 110; R. D. Oliver Heslop, comp., *Northumberland Words . . .* (London, 1894), II, 666; S. K. Tillyard, *Aristocrats: Caroline, Emily, Louisa, and Sarah Lennox, 1740–1832* (New York, 1994), 202.
47. Nov. 1, 1794, Dec. 25, 1799, Woodforde, *Diary*, IV, 150, V, 231.
48. 8 Anne c.9; Sarti, *Europe at Home*, trans. Cameron, 105.
49. Cobbett, *Cottage Economy . . .* (1926; rpt. edn., New York, 1970), 144; *SAS*, V, 335; Gilbert White, *The Natural History and Antiquities of Selborne . . .* (1789; rpt. edn., Menston, Eng., 1972), 197–199; John Caspall, *Making Fire and Light in the Home Pre-1820* (Woodbridge, Eng., 1987), 171–179.
50. "A Dissertation on the Instruments that Communicate Light," *UM*, May, 1749, 229; Max J. Okenfuss, ed., *The Travel Diary of Peter Tolstoi, a Muscovite in Early Modern Europe* (DeKalb, Ill., 1987), 304; Oct. 8, 1773, Frederick A. Pottle and Charles H. Bennett, eds., *Boswell's Journal of a Tour to the Hebrides with Samuel Johnson, L.L.D., 1773* (New York, 1961), 281; Pinkerton, *Travels*, I, 766, III, 587; O'Dea, *Lighting*, 40–41; Crowley, *Comfort*, 111–113; Davidson, *Woman's Work*, 106, 109; Maurice Vaussard, *Daily Life in Eighteenth Century Italy*, trans. Michael Heron (New York, 1963), 194.
51. Caspall, *Making Fire and Light*, 176; Journal of James Robertson, 1767, 91–92, Manuscripts, National Library of Scotland, Edinburgh; "16th Century Lighting in Sweden," *Rushlight* 15 (1949), 4; *Rushlight* 39 (1973), 8; Jean Kathryn Berger, "The Daily Life of the Household in Medieval Novgorod (Russia)" (Ph.D. diss., Univ. of Minnesota, 1998), 92–94; Davidson, *Woman's Work*, 107–108; James Brome, *Travels over England, Scotland and Wales* (London, 1700), 99, 218; Perceval, *English Travels*, ed. Wenger, 139; Burt, *Letters*, II, 127–128; Ménétra, *Journal*, 32.
52. Everett Emerson, ed., *Letters from New England: The Massachusetts Bay Colony, 1629–1638* (Amherst, Mass., 1976), 36; Thomas Coulson, "The Story of Domestic Lighting," *Journal of the Franklin Institute* 256 (1953), 207–208; Caspall, *Fire and Light*, 262.
53. Tilley, *Proverbs in England*, 144; June 6, 1712, Louis B. Wright and Marion Tinling, eds., *The Secret Diary of William Byrd of Westover, 1709–1712* (Richmond, 1941), 540.
54. Garnert, *Lampan*, 104–105, 278–279; Magnús Gíslason, *Kvällsvaka: En Isländsk Kulturtradition Belyst Genom Studier i Bondebefolkningens Vardagsliv . . .* (Uppsala, 1977), 144, 149; Jonathan Swift, *Directions to Servants: and Miscellaneous Pieces, 1733–1742*, ed. Herbert John Davis (Oxford, 1959), 20.

55. George Washington Greene, ed., *The Works of Joseph Addison* (Philadelphia, 1883), I, 314; O'Dea, *Lighting*, 2; *Domestic Management* . . . (London, n.d.), 22, 48.
56. J. J. Evans, ed., *Welsh Proverbs: A Selection, with English Translations* (Llandysul, Wales, 1965), 31; Jean-Jacques Rousseau, *Emile: or On Education*, trans. Allan Bloom (New York, 1979), 133; Craufurd Tait Ramage, *Ramage in South Italy* . . . , ed. Edith Clay (London, 1965), 150; Garnert, *Lampan*, 76–77; Robert Cleaver, *A Godly Forme of Houshold Government* (London, 1621); Tour of Sotterley Plantation, Md., Oct. 11, 1992.
57. Alice Morse Earle, *Customs and Fashions in Old New England* (1893; rpt. edn., Detroit, 1968), 127; Henry Davidoff, *World Treasury of Proverbs* . . . (New York, 1946), 81; *UM*, May, 1751, 220; Peter Thornton, *The Italian Renaissance Interior, 1400–1600* (New York, 1991), 276; Moryson, *Itinerary*, IV, 201–202.
58. Cotgrave, *Dictionarie*.
59. Ruff, *Violence*, 76; Rétif de la Brétonne, *My Father's Life*, trans. Richard Veasey (Gloucester, Eng., 1986), 6; Rudolf Dekker, *Childhood, Memory and Autobiography in Holland: From the Golden Age to Romanticism* (New York, 2000), 33.
60. Apr. 30, 1645, Josselin, *Diary*, 39; May 18, 1668, Pepys, *Diary*, IX, 204.
61. James Gregory, Nov. 26, 1773, Assi 45/31/2; Sept. 6, 11, 1794, June 6, 1795, Drinker, *Diary*, I, 590, 592, 689; Dec. 2, 1766 and Feb. 8, 1767, Cole, *Diary*, 161, 184.
62. Vittore Branca, ed., *Mercanti Scrittori: Ricordi Nella Firenze Tra Medioevo e Rinascimento* (Milan, 1986), 379; Mar. 31, 1771, Carter, *Diary*, I, 554–555; Dec. 15, 1780, Apr. 14, 1781, Apr. 13, 1785, Dec. 28, 1794, Mar. 14, 17, 1795, Woodforde, *Diary*, I, 298, 307, II, 184, IV, 163, 182, 183.
63. Pinkerton, *Travels*, II, 94; May 20, 1786, Diary of Dr. Samuel Adams, 1758–1819, New York Public Library, and passim; June 7, 1745, Kay, *Diary*, 97, and passim.
64. Laurel Thatcher Ulrich, "Martha Ballard and Her Girls: Women's Work in Eighteenth-Century Maine," in Stephen Innes, ed., *Work and Labor in Early America* (Chapel Hill, N.C., 1988), 70; D. B. Horn and Mary Ransome, eds., *English Historical Documents, 1714–1783* (New York, 1957), 671–672; Apr. 10, 1785, Oct. 1, 1804, "Mrs. Ballard's Diary," in Charles E. Nash, *The History of Augusta, Maine* (Augusta, Maine, 1904), 237, 421, and passim; *PL*, Oct. 22, 1765; Laurel Thatcher Ulrich, *A Midwife's Tale: The Life of Martha Ballard, Based on Her Diary, 1785–1812* (New York, 1990), 203; Anthony F. Aveni, *Empires of Time: Calendars, Clocks, and Cultures* (New York, 1989), 35.
65. Apr. 1, 1657, Josselin, *Diary*, 395; Apr. 14, 1768, Woodforde, *Diary*, I, 74.
66. Abel Boyer, *Dictionaire Royal* . . . (Amsterdam, 1719); Marvin Lowenthal, trans., *The Memoirs of Glückel of Hameln* (n.p., 1932), 120; Frank D. Prager, ed., *The Autobiography of John Fitch* (Philadelphia, 1976), 41; Mary J. Dobson, *Contours of Death and Disease in Early Modern England* (New York, 1997), 274–276.
67. *Paroimiographia* (English), 8; Apr. 6, 1669, *East Anglian Diaries*, 119; Benjamin Franklin, *Writings*, ed. J. A. Leo Lemay (New York, 1987), 221; Thoresby, *Diary*, I, 7.
68. Smith, *De Republica Anglorum*, ed. Mary Dewar (Cambridge, 1982), 107; *OBP*, passim; Brettone, *Father's Life*, trans. Veasey, 119; Henry Brisker, Apr. 9, 1766, Assi 45/28/2/124; Elizabeth S. Cohen, "Honor and Gender in the Streets of Early Modern Rome," *JIH* 22 (1992), 614.
69. Dec. 13, 1672, Isham, *Diary*, 175; Henry Preston, Assi 45/14/1/135; *OBP*, Apr. 24–27, 1745, 137.
70. *OBP*, May 10, 1722, 7; *Select Trials*, I, 305.
71. *ECR*, VIII, 101; *OBP*, Oct. 16–21, 1728, Apr. 15, 1724, 4–5, Apr. 8–14, 1752, 131.
72. Jean-Louis Flandrin, *Families in Former Times: Kinship, Household and Sexuality*, trans. Richard Southern (Cambridge, 1979), 44; Oct. 5, 1725, Sanderson, Diary, 80–81; *OBP*, Jan. 16–18, 1745, 62–63; Samuel H. Baron, ed. and trans., *The Travels of Olearius in*

Seventeenth-Century Russia (Stanford, Calif., 1967), 150. See also A. Voisin, "Notes sur la Vie Urbaine au XV. Siécle: Dijon la Nuit," *Annales de Bourgogne* 9 (1937), 276.

73. Bonaventure Des Périers, *Cymbalum Mundi: Four Very Ancient Joyous and Facetious Poetic Dialogues* (New York, 1965), 66. See also *OBP*, May 2–5, 1739, 86; *Select Trials*, III, 336; *The Authentick Tryals at large of John Swan and Elizabeth Jeffryes* . . . (London, 1752), 10, 11.

CHAPTER FIVE

1. Davenant, *The Platonick Lovers* (London, 1636).
2. Aug. 28, 1624, Beck, *Diary*, 159–160; Nov. 27, 1683, Heywood, Diaries, II, 341; Sandford Fleming, *Children & Puritanism* (New York, 1969), 148.
3. Suzanne Chantal, *La Vie Quotidienne au Portugal, après le Tremblement de Terre de Lisbonne de 1755* (Paris, 1962), 245.
4. Dec. 24, 1647, *Yorkshire Diaries & Autobiographies in the Seventeenth and Eighteenth Centuries* (Durham, Eng., 1886), 81–82; Jan. 5, 1763, Frederick A. Pottle, ed., *Boswell's London Journal, 1762–1763* (New York, 1950), 125; Aug. 7–31, 1732, Clegg, *Diary*, I, 151–152.
5. Samuel Briggs, *The Essays, Humor, and Poems of Nathaniel Ames, Father and Son, of Dedham, Massachusetts, from Their Almanacks, 1726–1775* (Cleveland, 1891), 67; May 21, 1707, Cowper, Diary; Robert W. Malcolmson, *Life and Labour in England, 1700–1780* (New York, 1981), 95–96; Burke, *Popular Culture*; Robert Muchembled, *Popular Culture and Elite Culture in France, 1400–1750*, trans. Lydia Cochrane (Baton Rouge, 1985), 1–107.
6. Rousseau, *Emile: or On Education*, trans. Allan Bloom (New York, 1979), 63.
7. Bacon, *Essays* (Oxford, 1930), 3; Le Loyer, *Specters*, fo. 105; Lucretius, *On the Nature of Things: De Rerum Nautra*, ed. and trans. Anthony M. Esolen (Baltimore, 1995), 93; Leon Battista Alberti, *The Family in Renaissance Florence*, trans. Renée Neu Watkins (Columbia, S.C., 1969), 63.
8. Bacon, *Essays*, 3; Scott, *Witchcraft*, 139; Herman W. Roodenburg, "The Autobiography of Isabella de Moerloose: Sex, Childrearing, and Popular Belief in Seventeenth Century Holland," *JSH* 18 (1985), 522, 521, 523–524; Rudolf Dekker, *Childhood, Memory and Autobiography in Holland: From the Golden Age to Romanticism* (New York 2000), 28, 81–84; Mark Motley, *Becoming a French Aristocrat: The Education of the Court Nobility, 1580–1715* (Princeton, N.J., 1990), 48–49.
9. H. C. Barnard, trans., *Fénelon on Education* (Cambridge, 1966), 8; Pinkerton, *Travels*, II, 757; Timothy J. Casey, ed., *Jean Paul: A Reader*, trans. Erika Casey (Baltimore, 1992), 339; Olwen Hufton, "Women, Work, and Family," in *HWW* III, 40; Linda A. Pollock, "Parent-Child Relations," in *FLEMT*, 197.
10. Thomas Bewick, *A Memoir of Thomas Bewick*, ed. Iain Bain (London, 1975), 16.
11. *Dialogues on the Passions, Habits, and Affections Peculiar to Children* . . . (London, 1748), 40; William Hazlitt and Elbridge Colby, eds., *The Life of Thomas Holcroft* (New York, 1968), I, 14–15. See also *Hibernicus; or Memoirs of an Irishman* . . . (Pittsburgh, 1828).
12. Rousseau, *Emile*, trans. Bloom, 137; Mollie Harris, *A Kind of Magic* (London, 1969), 104–105; Restif de la Bretonne, *Monsieur Nicolas; or, the Human Heart Laid Bare* (London, 1966), 29; *Autobiography of John Younger, Shoemaker, St. Boswells* (Kelso, Eng., 1881), 45; Mrs. Laura M., Oct. 7, 14, 1938, "Game Songs and Rhymes," American Life Histories: Manuscripts from the Federal Writers' Project, 1936–1940, Manuscripts Division, Library of Congress, Washington, D.C.; Percy B. Green, *A History of Nursery Rhymes* (1899; rpt. edn., Detroit, 1968), 78–80.
13. Thomas Balston, *The Life of Jonathan Martin* . . . (London, 1945), 3. See also, for example, Joseph Bougerel, *Vie de Pierre Gassendi* . . . (1737; rpt. edn., Geneva, 1970), 3.

14. Torriano, *Proverbi*, 171.
15. Mar. 7, 1787, Diary of Dr. Samuel Adams, Diary, 1758–1819, New York Public Library; Jan. 4, 1705, Cowper, Diary.
16. Griffiths, *Youth*, 135; Robert Morgan, *My Lamp Still Burns* (Llandysul, Wales, 1981), 64; Bräker, *Life*, 57–58, 63, 67; Ménétra, *Journal*, 24; Valentin Jamerey-Duval, *Memoires: Enfance et Éducation d'un Paysan au XVIIIe Siècle*, ed. Jean Marie Goulemot (Paris, 1981), 114; Pounds, *Culture*, 273–274, 409.
17. Joachim Schlör, *Nights in the Big City: Paris, Berlin, London 1840–1930*, trans. Pierre Gottfried Imhof and Dafydd Rees Roberts (London, 1998), 57; Alberti, *Family in Renaissance Florence*, trans. Watkins, 107.
18. *PG*, Feb. 11, 1789.
19. *OED*, s.v. "cat's eye"; T. Row, "Hints for Constructing Glasses to Shew Objects in the Night," *GM*, 1777, 59; Lorus Johnson Milne and Margery Joan Milne, *The World of Night* (New York, 1956), 8–9; Faber Birren, *The Power of Color . . .* (Secaucus, N.J., 1997), 228–229. See also C. E. Roybet, ed., *Les Serées de Guillaume Bouchet Sieur de Brocourt* (Paris, 1874), III, 238–239.
20. John Caspall, *Making Fire and Light in the Home Pre-1820* (Woodbridge, Eng., 1987), 223–227; O'Dea, *Lighting*, 70–76.
21. Nov. 15, 1729, Sanderson, Diary, 30; *OBP*, Apr. 4, 1733, 119; Thomas Wright, *The Homes of Other Days: A History of Domestic Manners and Sentiments in England*. . . (New York, 1871), 460.
22. Eric Partridge, *A Dictionary of the Underworld . . .* (New York, 1950), 448; Eugène Defrance, *Histoire de l'Éclairage des Rues de Paris* (Paris, 1904), 30–33; Christopher Hibbert, *Venice: The Biography of a City* (New York, 1989), 166; Jeremy D. Popkin, ed., *Panorama of Paris: Selections from Le Tableau de Paris, Louis-Sébastien Mercier* (University Park, Pa., 1999), 132.
23. Defoe, *Second Thoughts Are Best*. . . (London, 1729), 15; G. C. Faber, ed., *The Poetical Works of John Gay*. . . (London, 1926), 81; Popkin, ed., *Panorama of Paris*, 132; *The Novels and Miscellaneous Works of Daniel Defoe* (London, 1885), 515.
24. *OBP*, Oct. 4, 1719, 5.
25. Donald E. Crawford, ed., *Journals of Sir John Lauder* (Edinburgh, 1900), 120; Harry Ross-Lewin, *With "The Thirty-Second" in the Peninsular and other Campaigns*, ed. John Wardell (Dublin, 1904), 146.
26. Torriano, *Proverbi*, 89; Shakespeare, *Venus and Adonis*, 825–826. Then, also, localities steadily restricted the use of flambeaux. Because of the threat of fire from open flames, cities by the late seventeenth century instead began to encourage reliance on lanterns. Stockholm in 1725 reserved torches for the royal family. Matthiessen, *Natten*, 28.
27. Tilley, *Proverbs in England*, 471; Anne Elizabeth Baker, comp. *Glossary of Northamptonshire Words and Phrases . . .* (London, 1854), 95; G. F. Northall, comp., *A Warwickshire Word-Book*. . . (1896; rpt. edn., Vaduz, Liecht, 1965), 167; J. W. Goethe, *Italian Journey, 1786–1788* (New York, 1968), 325; *OED*, s.v. "night-sun."
28. Victor Hugo Paltsits, "Journal of Benjamin Mifflin on a Tour from Philadelphia to Delaware and Maryland, July 26 to Aug. 14, 1762," *Bulletin of the New York Public Library* 39 (1935), 438; Mary Yates, Dec. 11, 1764, Assi 45/28/1/16.
29. William Dickinson, comp., *A Glossary of Words and Phrases Pertaining to the Dialect of Cumberland* (London, 1878), 103; *OBP*, Sept. 15–18, 1762, 164; *Street Lighting Manual: Prepared by the Street and Highway Lighting Committee of the Edison Electric Institute* (New York, 1969), 63–64; Milne and Milne, *World of Night*, 10.
30. Robert Bator, *Masterworks of Children's Literature, 1740–1836: The Middle Period* (New York,

1983), 254; "A.B.," *SJC*, Sept. 13, 1764; Margaret Spufford, *Small Books and Pleasant Histories: Popular Fiction and Its Readership in Seventeenth-Century England* (Athens, Ga., 1981), 2; Michael O'Malley, "Time, Work and Task Orientation: A Critique of American Historiography," *Time & Society* 1 (1992), 350.

31. Bradford Torrey, ed. *The Writings of Henry David Thoreau* (Boston, 1906), II, 372; Nov. 21, 1786, Woodforde, *Diary*, II, 284; Edward Browne, *Journal of a Visit to Paris in the Year 1664*, ed. Geoffrey Keynes (London, 1923), 22; Feb. 28, 1664, Pepys, *Diary*, V, 68, I–IX, passim; Swift, *Journal*, I, 356, passim; Nov. 9, 1792, Dorothy Heighes Woodforde, ed., *Woodforde Papers and Diaries* (London, 1932), 80.
32. *OBP*, Dec. 8, 1742, 16; *OED*, s.v. "shepherd's lamp"; John Clare, *Cottage Tales*, ed. Eric Robinson et al. (Manchester, 1993), 88; Baker, comp., *Northamptonshire Glossary*, III, 225; H. J. Deverson, ed., *Journey into Night* (New York, 1966), 138; *OBP*, May 30–31, 1745.
33. *Universal Magazine of Knowledge and Pleasure* 12 (Jan. 1753), 3; *OED*, s.v. "Milky Way," "Walsingham," "Watling-street"; Eveline Camilla Gurdon, *Suffolk* (London, 1893), 166; "Impressions of a Night Sky Unaffected by Light Pollution," International Dark-Sky Association, Information Sheet #111, Web: www.darksky.org.
34. Torrey, ed., *Thoreau Writings*, II, 383.
35. June 24, 1801, Drinker, *Diary*, II, 1422; M. McGrath, ed., *Cinnine Amhiaoibh Ui Shuileabháin: The Diary of Humphrey O'Sullivan* (London, 1936–1937), I–IV, passim; Peter Barber, "Journal of a Traveller in Scotland, 1795–1796," *Scottish Historical Review* 36 (1957), 43.
36. Mansie Wauch, *The Life of Mansie Wauch, Tailor in Dalkeith* (Edinburgh, 1827), 85; *ECR*, VIII, 387; William H. Cope, ed., *A Glossary of Hampshire Words and Phrases* (1883; rpt. edn., Vaduz, Liecht., 1965), 23; Walter W. Skeat, ed., *A Collection of English Words* . . . (London, 1874), 57, 87, 93; Baker, comp., *Northamptonshire Words and Phrases*, II, 119; Frederic Thomas Elsworthy, comp., *The West Somerset Word-Book* . . . (1886; rpt. edn., Vaduz, Liecht., 1965), 575; Jan. 18, 1666, Pepys, *Diary*, VII, 18; Giuseppe Marco Antonio Baretti, *A Dictionary, Spanish and English* . . . (London, 1794); *OBP*, Apr. 24–May 1, 1754, 183.
37. Jan. 23, 1786, Woodforde, *Diary*, II, 226; William Hazlitt, *Notes of a Journey through France and Italy* (London, 1826), 179.
38. Diary of Robert Moody, 1660–1663, Bodl., Rawlinson Coll. D.84; Crawford, ed., *Lauder Journals*, 177; George P. Rawick, ed., *The American Slave: A Composite Autobiography* (Wesport, Ct., 1972) XIII, 109. See also Oct. 9, 1662, Pepys, *Diary*, III, 217; Oct. 1, 1794, Woodforde, *Diary*, IV, 138; Barber, "Traveller," 49.
39. William Cobbett, *Rural Rides in Surrey, Kent, and Other Counties* (London, 1948), II, 139; Winslow C. Watson, ed., *Men and Times of the Revolution; or, Memoirs of Elkanah Watson, Including Journals of Travels* (New York, 1856), 59. See also Thomas Hardy, *The Woodlanders* (1887; rpt. edn., London, 1991), 12.
40. George Edward Dartnell and Edward Hungerford Goddard, comps., *A Glossary of Words Used in the County of Wiltshire* (London, 1893), 192; *Autobiography of the Rev. Dr. Alexander Carlyle, Minister of Inveresk* . . . (Edinburgh, 1860), 125–126; Barber, "Traveller," 48.
41. Burton E. Stevenson, ed., *The Home Book of Proverbs, Maxims and Familiar Phrases* (New York, 1948), 168; Walter W. Skeat, ed., *Five Reprinted Glossaries* . . . (London, 1879), 95; Bernard J. Hibbitts, "Making Sense of Metaphors: Visuality, Aurality and the Reconfiguration of American Legal Discourse," *Cardozo Law Review* 16 (1994), 229–356; Donald M. Lowe, *History of Bourgeois Perception* (Brighton, Eng., 1982), 6–8.
42. Shakespeare, *A Midsummer Night's Dream*, III, 2; Bruce R. Smith, *The Acoustic World of Early Modern England: Attending to the O-Factor* (Chicago, 1999), 58–59.

43. John M. Hull, *Touching the Rock: An Experience of Blindness* (New York, 1990), 166, 83; Julian Jaynes, *The Origin of Consciousness in the Breakdown of the Bicameral Mind* (Boston, 1977), 96–97.
44. Barber, "Traveller," 39; Diary of Rev. William Bennet, 1785, Bodl., Eng. Misc. f. 54, fo. 74; E. P. Thompson, *Customs in Common* (New York, 1991), 362; Joshua Lucock Wilkinson, *The Wanderer . . . through France, Germany and Italy in 1791 and 1793* (London, 1798), I, 58; Jasper Danckaerts, *Journal of a Voyage to New York and a Tour in Several of the American Colonies in 1679–80*, ed. and trans. Henry C. Murphy (New York, 1867), 125.
45. Sept. 20, 1791, Walter Johnson, ed., *Gilbert White's Journals* (1931; rpt. edn., New York, 1970), 394; Milne and Milne, *World of Night*, 13–14, 94; Claire Murphy and William Cain, "Odor Identification: The Blind are Better," *Physiology & Behavior* 37 (1986), 177–180. Memories of pungent scents stay with us long after we have forgotten most visual scenes. J. Douglas Porteous, *Landscapes of the Mind: Worlds of Sense and Metaphor* (Toronto, 1990), 34–36.
46. W. Carew Hazlitt, ed., *English Proverbs and Proverbial Phrases . . .* (London, 1882), 94; Edward Ward, *The London Spy* (1709; rpt. edn., New York, 1985), 40; Barber, "Traveller," 39; M. Betham-Edwards, ed., *The Autobiography of Arthur Young* (1898; rpt. edn., New York, 1967), 194. See also Sept. 15, 1779, Andrew Oliver, ed., *The Journal of Samuel Curwen, Loyalist* (Cambridge, Mass., 1972), 560.
47. *OED*, s.v. "blind road"; Sept. 16, 1795, "Dr. Pierce's Manuscript Journal," *Massachusetts Historical Society Proceedings*, 2nd Ser., 3 (1886–1887), 52; Laurel Thatcher Ulrich, *A Midwife's Tale: The Life of Martha Ballard, Based on Her Diary, 1785–1812* (New York, 1990), 202; Hull, *Touching the Rock*, 103.
48. Faber, ed., *Gay Works*, 83.
49. Descartes, *Selected Philosophical Writings*, trans. John Cottingham et al. (Cambridge, 1988), 58; Harry Porter, *The Pleasant History of the Two Angry Women of Abington* (n.p., 1599); Oct. 2, 1724, Parkman, *Diary*, 6.
50. Cecil Aspinall-Oglander, ed., *Admiral's Wife: Being the Life and Letters of the Hon. Mrs. Edward Boscawen from 1719 to 1761* (London, 1940), 235; Monique Savoy, *Lumiéres sur la Ville: Introduction et Promotion de l'Electricité en Suisse: L'Éclairage Lausannois, 1881–1921* (Lausanne, 1988), 50.
51. L'Estrange, *Fables of Aesop and Other Eminent Mythologists: With Morals and Reflections* (London, 1699), I, 103.
52. Torrey, ed., *Thoreau Writings*, III, 340.
53. *Farley's Bristol Journal*, Feb. 18, 1769; Ward, *London Spy*, III, 48–49; Aileen Riberio, *Dress in Eighteenth-Century Europe, 1715–1789* (New Haven, 2002), 85.
54. *OBP*, July 9–11, 1740, 174; Joseph Lawson, *Letters to the Young on Progress in Pudsey during the Last Sixty Years* (Stanningley, Eng., 1887), 33; Torriano, *Proverbi*, 170.
55. Hadrianus Junius, *The Nomenclator . . .* (London, 1585), 160–161; *OED*, s.v. "great-coat"; John Owen, *Travels into Different Parts of Europe, in the Years 1791 and 1792 . . .* (London, 1796), II, 81; Tobias Smollett, *The Life and Adventures of Sir Launcelot Greaves* (London, 1762), 239; Daniel Defoe, *The Life of . . . Robinson Crusoe* (London, 1729), 180; Henry Swinburne, *Travels in the Two Sicilies . . .* (London, 1783), II, 308; Jonas Hanway, *An Historical Account of the British Trade over the Caspian Sea . . .* (London, 1753), II, 336; Riberio, *Dress*, 22–24, 30–31, 87.
56. W. Hooper, ed., *Letters of Baron Bielfeld . . .* (London, 1768), IV, 166; *OED*, s.v. "night-kerchief," "mob"; Tilley, *Proverbs in England*, 296; John Owen, *Travels into Different Parts of Europe, in the Years 1791 and 1792 . . .* (London, 1796), II, 81; Apr. 24, 25, 1665, Pepys, *Diary*, VI, 89; F. Pomey and A. Lovell, *Indiculus Universalis; or, the Universe in Epitome . . .* (London, 1679), 68; Riberio, *Dress*, 49.

57. Thomas Burke, *English Night-Life: From Norman Curfew to Present Black-Out* (New York, 1971), 54; Andrew Henderson, ed., *Scottish Proverbs* (Edinburgh, 1832), 69; *OBP*, Oct. 4, 1719, 6; Cohens, *Italy*, 49.
58. Torrington, *Diaries*, III, 290.
59. Nov. 28, 1785, Woodforde, *Diary*, II, 216; James Peller Malcolm, *Anecdotes of the Manners and Customs of London during the Eighteenth Century* . . . (London, 1810), I, 145. See also July 30, 1755, Parkman, *Diary*, 293.
60. *LC*, Aug. 18, 1785.
61. Varro, *On the Latin Language*, trans. Roland G. Kent (Cambridge, Mass., 1957), I, 177–179; Censorinus, *De Die Natale*, trans. William Maude (New York, 1900), 40; Henry Hibbert, *Syntagma Theologicum* . . . (London, 1662), 30.
62. Augustin Gallo, *Secrets de la Vraye Agriculture* . . . (Paris, 1572), 213; Leonard Lawrence, *A Small Treatise betwixt Arnalte and Lucenda* (London, 1639), 7; Nina Gockerell, "Telling Time without a Clock," in Klaus Maurice and Otto Mayr, eds., *The Clockwork Universe: German Clocks and Automata, 1550–1650* (New York, 1980), 137. This chronology is constructed from reading numerous primary sources.
63. Ralph Knevet, *Rhodon and Iris* . . . (London, 1631); *OED*, s.v. "hen and chickens," "seven stars"; Weinsberg, *Diary*, I, 59; Gockerell, "Telling Time," 137.
64. Barber, "Traveller," 42; Crusius, *Nocte*, ch. 3.12; Shakespeare, *Hamlet*, I, 2, 198; *The Rape of Lucrece*, 113–119.
65. *OBP*, Oct. 12, 1737, 205; M. D'Archenholz, *A Picture of England* . . . (London, 1789), II, 79; Ménétra, *Journal*, 195–196.
66. *SWP*, I, 99; Shakespeare, *Hamlet*, I, 1, 143; Bourne, *Antiquitates Vulgares*, 38; Alan Gailey, "The Bonfire in North Irish Tradition," *Folklore* 88 (1977), 18; Crusius, *Nocte*, ch. 3.36.
67. William Howitt, *The Boy's Country Book* (London, n.d.), 196; Bourne, *Antiquitates Vulgares*, 87, 84, passim; Francis Grose, *A Provincial Glossary* (1787; rpt. ed., Menston, Eng., 1968), 3, 2. See also James Dawson Burn, *The Autobiography of a Beggar Boy*, ed. David Vincent (London, 1978), 67; Bartholomäus Sastrow et al., *Social Germany in Luther's Time: Being the Memoirs of Bartholomew Sastrow*, trans. H.A.L. Fisher (Westminster, Eng., 1902), 291.
68. Lynn Doyle, *An Ulster Childhood* (London, 1926), 61; Charles Jackson, ed., *The Diary of Abraham De la Pryme, the Yorkshire Antiquary* (Durham, Eng., 1870), 39. See also *Life and Struggles of William Lovett* . . . (London, 1876), 11.
69. *OBP*, Jan. 16–20, 1752, 48; Matthiessen, *Natten*, 63; Oct. 27, 1771, Basil Cozens-Hardy, ed., *The Diary of Sylas Neville, 1767–1788* (London, 1950), 132; Richard Cobb, *Paris and Its Provinces, 1792–1802* (New York, 1975), 45; Paul Zumthor, *Daily Life in Rembrandt's Holland* (New York, 1963), 249; James Lackington, *Memoirs of the First Forty-Five Years* . . . (London, 1792), 34.
70. June 23, 1745, Lewis, Diary, 184; "Journal of P. Oliver, 1776–1810," Egerton Mss. 2672, I, fo. 68, BL; Diary of John Leake, 1713, Rawlinson Mss., D. 428, fo. 37, Bodl.; F. Platter, *Journal*, 36.
71. Taillepied, *Ghosts*, 78; Moryson, *Itinerary*, IV, 294; *Early Prose and Poetical Works of John Taylor the Water Poet (1580–1653)* (London, 1888), 156; *Letters from Minorca* . . . (Dublin, 1782), 213; Matthiessen, *Natten*, 24.
72. Clare Williams, ed., *Thomas Platter's Travels in England, 1599* (London, 1937), 150; Sept. 19, 1662, Pepys, *Diary*, III, 201; Paolo Da Certaldo, *Libro di Buoni Costumi*, ed. Alfredo Schiaffini (Florence, 1945), 14; *OBP*, Oct. 17–19, 1749, 163; Mrs. Grant, *Essays on the Superstitions of the Highlanders of Scotland* . . . (New York, [1831?]), I, 121; Jackson, ed., *De la Pryme Diary*, 71; Schindler, *Rebellion*, 215.
73. Yves-Marie Bercé, *History of Peasant Revolts: The Social Origins of Rebellion in Early Modern*

France, trans. Amanda Whitmore (Ithaca, N.Y., 1990), 278; Diary of James Scudamore, ca. 1710, Hereford City Library, Eng.; Feb. 13, 14, 1667, Pepys, *Diary*, VIII, 60, 62; Lawrence F. Stone, *The Family, Sex and Marriage in England, 1500–1800* (New York, 1977), 94.

74. Nov. 18, 1762, Frederick A. Pottle, ed., *Boswell's London Journal, 1762–1763* (New York, 1950), 43. See also Dec. 17, 1769, Woodforde, *Diary*, I, 95.
75. Brian Hill, *Observations and Remarks in a Journey through Sicily and Calabria* (London, 1792), 49; Journal of Twisden Bradbourn, 1693–1967, 1698, 103, Miscellaneous English Manuscripts c. 206, Bodl. "The aspersion of Holy Water," wrote Noël Taillepied, is "a sure protection against the malice and attacks of evil spirits" (*Ghosts*, 174).
76. Grose, *Provincial Glossary*, 70; R. D. Oliver Heslop, comp., *Northumberland Words* . . . (London, 1894), I, 204; Brand 1848, III, 15; Muchembled, *Popular Culture*, trans. Cochrane, 84–85; Enid Porter, *Cambridgeshire Customs and Folklore* (New York, 1969), 62; Paul-Yves Sébillot, *Le Folklore de la Bretagne* . . . (Paris, 1968), II, 132; Jean Delumeau, *La Peur en Occident, XIVe-XVIIIe Siècles: Une Cité Assiégée* (Paris, 1978), 92; William Dillon Piersen, *Black Yankees: The Development of an Afro-American Subculture in Eighteenth-Century New England* (Amherst, Mass., 1988), 85.
77. Faber, ed., *Gay Works*, 81; Rousseau, *Emile*, trans. Bloom, 148; John Burnap, July 10, 1766, Assi 45/28/2/97c. See also Thomas Hardy, *The Trumpet-Major* . . . (1912; rpt. edn., New York, 1984), 274.
78. Remarks 1717, 175; Watson, ed., *Men and Times*, 115; Bernard Mandeville, *An Enquiry into the Causes of the Frequent Executions at Tyburn*, ed. Malvin R. Zirker, Jr. (Los Angeles, 1964), 10; Muchembled, *Violence*, 65, 120–121.
79. Schindler, *Rebellion*, 223; Muchembled, *Violence*, 120–123, 259; William Mowfitt, Aug. 14, 1647, Assi 45/2/1/229; T. Platter, *Journal*, 197; Pinkerton, *Travels*, I, 224; Milly Harrison and O.M. Royston, comps., *How They Lived* . . . (Oxford, 1965), II, 253; *OBP*, May 2–5, 1739, 73; Rousseau, *Emile*, trans. Bloom, 138.
80. Anna Brzozowska-Krajka, *Polish Traditional Folklore: The Magic of Time* (Boulder, Colo., 1998), 63; Sébillot, *Folklore de la Bretagne*, II, 162; *Autobiography of the Blessed Mother Anne of Saint Bartholomew* (St. Louis, 1916), 15; Casey, ed., *Jean Paul*, trans. Casey, 339; F. Platter, *Journal*, 104.
81. Abel Boyer, *Dictionaire Royal* . . . (Amsterdam, 1719); Paul Monroe, *Thomas Platter and the Educational Renaissance of the Sixteenth Century* (New York, 1904), 161, 107; Dietz, *Surgeon*, 110–111. See also Stephen Bradwell, *A Watch-Man for the Pest* . . . (London, 1625), 39.
82. Llewellynn Jewitt, ed., *The Life of William Hutton* . . . (London, 1872), 159; Bräker, *Life*, 58; David Pulsifer, ed., *Records of the Colony of New Plymouth in New England* (Boston, 1861), XI, 106; Dec. 13, 1765, Frank Brady and Frederick A. Pottle, eds., *Boswell on the Grand Tour: Italy, Corsica, and France, 1765–1766* (New York, 1955), 232.
83. Feb. 7, 1704, Cowper, Diary.
84. Jan. 29, 1735, Clegg, *Diary*, I, 217; June 14, 1757, Turner, *Diary*, 100.
85. *SWP*, II, 560–561; Oct. 28, 1833, McGrath, ed., *O'Sullivan Diary*, III, 247.

PART THREE

PRELUDE

1. L. E. Kastner, ed., *The Poetical Works of William Drummond of Hawthornden* . . . (New York, 1968), I, 46.
2. Flaherty, *Privacy*, 94; David Levine and Keith Wrightson, *The Making of an Industrial Society: Whickham, 1560–1765* (Oxford, 1991), 280.

3. Penry Williams, *The Later Tudors: England, 1547–1603* (Oxford, 1995), 515; G. R. Quaife, *Wanton Wenches and Wayward Wives: Peasants and Illicit Sex in Early Seventeenth Century England* (London, 1979), 180–181.
4. Gottfried Von Bulow, ed., "Diary of the Journey of Philip Julius, Duke of Stettin-Pomerania, through England in the Year 1602," *Transactions of the Royal Historical Society*, New Ser., 6 (1892), 65.
5. Oct. 16, 1773, Frederick A. Pottle and Charles H. Bennett, eds. *Boswell's Journal of a Tour to the Hebrides with Samuel Johnson, LL.D., 1773* (New York, 1961), 312; *A View of London and Westminster* . . . (London, 1725), 5–6.
6. Mar. 27, 1782, Sanger, *Diary*, 409; Yves Castan, "Politics and Private Life," in *HPL* III, 49; Lorna Weatherill, *Consumer Behavior and Material Culture in Britain, 1660–1760* (London, 1988), 76–77, 80, 88, 168.
7. "B," *Westminster Magazine* 8 (1780), 16. See also Georg Christoph Lichtenberg, *Aphorisms*, ed. R. J. Hollingdale (London, 1990), 44–45; Lena Cowen Orlin, ed., *Elizabethan Households: An Anthology* (Washington, D.C., 1995), 119–120; *SAS*, II, 311.
8. Norman Egbert McClure, ed., *The Letters of John Chamberlain* (Philadelphia, 1939), I, 283; May 17, 1709, PL 27/2; *OBP*, Apr. 28–May 3, 1742, 77; *SAS*, II, 311; Levine and Wrightson, *Making of an Industrial Society*, 281; Roger Thompson, "'Holy Watchfulness' and Communal Conformism: The Functions of Defamation in Early New England Communities," *New England Quarterly* 56 (1983), 513.
9. John Aubrey, *Miscellanies upon Various Subjects* (London, 1857), 215; *British Magazine*, 2 (1747), 441; Alexandre Wolowski, *La Vie Quotidienne en Pologne au XVIIe Siècle* (Paris, 1972), 184; Breton, *Works*, II, 11.
10. Kathleen Elizabeth Stuart, "The Boundaries of Honor: 'Dishonorable People' in Augsburg, 1500–1800" (Ph.D. diss., Yale Univ., 1993), 26, 38–40; Jütte, *Poverty*, 164; Ruth Mellinkoff, *Outcasts: Signs of Otherness in Northern European Art of the Late Middle Ages* (Berkeley, Calif., 1993), 43–47, 184–190; Raffaella Sarti, *Europe at Home: Family and Material Culture, 1500–1800*, trans. Allan Cameron (New Haven, 2002), 207–211.
11. *Weekly Rehearsal* (Boston), Apr. 24, 1732; Schindler, *Rebellion*, 288–289; Mellinkoff, *Outcasts*, 188–193.
12. *OED*, s.v. "privacy," "private" (also "privy" and "privity"); *The Bastard* (London, 1652), 71; *Herbert's Devotions* . . . (London, 1657), 217; Flaherty, *Privacy*, 1–13; Ronald Huebert, "Privacy: The Early Social History of a Word," *Sewanee Review*, 105 (1997), 21–38.
13. Frederick J. Furnivall, ed., *Philip Stubbes's Anatomy of the Abuses in England in Shakespeare's Youth, A.D. 1583* (London, 1877), I, 329; Natalie Zemon Davis, *Society and Culture in Early Modern France* (Stanford, Calif., 1975), 97–123; Maria José del Rio, "Carnival, the World Upside Down," in Robert Muchembled et al., *Popular Culture* (Danbury, Ct., 1994), 83–84.
14. Harrison, *Description*, 36; David Cressy, *Bonfires and Bells: National Memory and the Protestant Calendar in Elizabethan and Stuart England* (London, 1989), passim; Griffiths, *Youth*, 156–158; Burke, *Popular Culture*, 194–196.
15. Richard Lassels, *An Italian Voyage* . . . (London, 1698), II, 118; Iain Cameron, *Crime and Repression in the Auvergne and the Guyenne, 1720–1790* (Cambridge, 1981), 197–198; David Chambers and Trevor Dean, *Clean Hands and Rough Justice: An Investigating Magistrate in Renaissance Italy* (Ann Arbor, Mich., 1997), 20. See also Donald E. Crawford, ed., *Journals of Sir John Lauder* (Edinburgh, 1900), 118; Schindler, *Rebellion*, 200–201.
16. *The Works of Mr. Thomas Brown in Prose and Verse* . . . (London, 1708), III, 114; *The Poems of the Late Christopher Smart* . . . (London, 1790), II, 9; Charles Gildon, *The Post-Boy Rob'd of His Mail* . . . (London, 1692), 147; Mr. Dibdin, *The Lamplighter* ([London, 1790?]); Kenneth J. Gergen et al., "Deviance in the Dark," *Psychology Today* 7 (1973), 129–130.

17. Alastair Fowler, ed., *The New Oxford Book of Seventeenth Century Verse* (Oxford, 1991), 416; Bernard Bailyn, "The Boundaries of History: The Old World and the New," in *The Dedication of the Casperen Building* . . . (Providence, 1992), 36; *The London Jilt: or, the Politick Whore* . . . (London, 1683), Pt. II, 156; Aphra Behn, *Five Plays* . . . , ed. Maureen Duffy (London, 1990), 35; Dionysius, "Contemplations by Moonlight," *European Magazine* 34 (1798), 307.
18. Rétif de la Bretonne, *Les Nuits de Paris, ou le Spectateur-Nocturne*, eds. Jean Varloot and Michel Delon (Paris, 1986), 38; Edward Young, *Night Thoughts*, ed. Stephen Cornfield (Cambridge, 1989), 122; Bernard Le Bovier de Fontenelle, *Conversations on the Plurality of Worlds*, trans. H. A. Hargreaves (Berkeley, Calif., 1990), 10; J. W. Goethe, *Italian Journey, 1786–1788* (New York, 1968), 182; Lewis, Diary, 161.

CHAPTER SIX

1. Mill, *A Nights Search: Discovering the Nature and Condition of all Sorts of Night-Walkers* . . . (London, 1639).
2. John 9:4; *Paroimiographia* (Spanish), 22; Georgina F. Jackson, comp., *Shropshire Word-Book* . . . (London, 1879), 38; Grose, *Dictionary*.
3. Gerhard Dohrn-van Rossum, *History of the Hour: Clocks and Modern Temporal Orders*, trans. Thomas Dunlap (Chicago, 1996), 293, 235, 246; Torriano, *Proverbi*, 171; Verdon, *Night*, 110–112; Monica Chojnacka and Merry E. Wiesner-Hanks, eds., *Ages of Woman, Ages of Man: Sources in European Social History, 1400–1750* (London, 2002), 159; Wilson, *English Proverbs*, 122; Henri Hauser, *Ouvriers du Temps Passé XVe–XVIe Siècles* (Paris, 1927), 82–83.
4. Dohrn-van Rossum, *History of the Hour*, trans. Dunlap, 311–312, 294; G. C. Coulton, ed., *Life in the Middle Ages* (Cambridge, 1929), 99; Hauser, *Ouvriers*, 82–85; Silvia Mantini, "Per Un'Immagine Della Notte," *Archivio Storico Italino* 4 (1985), 578–579; Maurice Bouteloup, "Le Travail de Nuit dans la Boulangerie" (Ph.D. diss., Université de Paris, 1909), 2.
5. Jan. 13, 1573, I. H. Van Eeghen, ed., *Dagboek Van Broeder Wouter Jacobsz (Gaultherus Jacobi Masius Prior Van Stein: Amsterdam, 1572–1578, En Montfoort, 1578–1579)* (Gronningen, Neth., 1959), I, 134; R.H. Tawney and Eileen Power, eds., *Tudor Economic Documents: Being Select Documents Illustrating the Economic and Social History of Tudor England* (London, 1953), I, 342; Pierre Goubert, *The French Peasantry in the Seventeenth Century*, trans. Ian Patterson (Cambridge, 1986), 100; Helen Simpson, ed. and trans., *The Waiting City: Paris 1782–88* . . . (Philadelphia, 1933), 75.
6. Anthony Horneck, *The Happy Ascetick, or, the Best Exercise* ([London], 1680), 409; Torriano, *Proverbi*, 104; Erskine Beveridge, comp., and J. D. Westwood, ed., *Fegusson's Scottish Proverbs from the Original Print of 1641* . . . (Edinburgh, 1924), 266.
7. Burkitt, *The Poor Man's Help* . . . (London, 1694), 16.
8. Thompson, "Time, Work-Discipline, and Industrial Capitalism," *PP* 38 (1967), 73, 56–97, passim.
9. "John Dane's Narrative," *New England Historical and Geneological Register* 8 (1854), 150; *ECR*, II, 150; Ménétra, *Journal*, 32–33; *OBP*, Sept. 7, 1722.
10. Wilson, *English Proverbs*, 169; Thomas Dekker, *The Seven Deadly Sinnes of London*, ed. H.F.B. Brett-Smith, ed. (New York, 1922), 30; *OBP*, Feb. 2–Mar. 2, 1765, 120; John Clayton, *Friendly Advice to the Poor* . . . (Manchester, 1755), 37; Franco Sacchetti, *Tales from Sacchetti*, trans. Mary G. Steegmann (1908; rpt. edn., Westport, Ct., 1978), 231.
11. Gaetano Zompini, *Le Arti Che Vanno per Via Nella Città di Venezia* (Venice, 1785), plate 15, passim; Max J. Okenfuss, trans., *The Travel Diary of Peter Tolstoi: A Muscovite in Early Mod-*

ern Europe (DeKalb, Ill., 1987), 301; Marybeth Carlson, "Domestic Service in a Changing City Economy: Rotterdam, 1680–1780" (Ph.D. diss., Univ. of Wisconsin, 1993), 158; Tim Meldrum, *Domestic Service and Gender, 1660–1750: Life and Work in the London Household* (Harlow, Eng., 2000), 150–51; *OBP*, Oct. 12, 1726, 3; Thompson, "Time, Work-Discipline," 60; Legg, *Low-Life*, 10; Restif de la Bretonne, *Oeuvres* (Geneva, 1971), II, 148–149.

12. Mar. 25, 1661, Pepys, *Diary*, II, 60; J. W. Goethe, *Italian Journey, 1786–1788* (New York, 1968), Part II, 315; *OED*, s.v. "bunter."
13. Beveridge, comp., and Westwood, ed., *Scottish Proverbs*, 25; Jan. 18, 1624, Beck, *Diary*, 34; *A General Description of All Trades . . .* (London, 1747), 204, passim; John Collinges, *The Weaver Pocket-Book, or, Weaving Spiritualized . . .* (n.p., 1695), 87; William Howitt, *The Boy's Country Book* (London, n.d.), 12–13.
14. Dec. 24, 1660, Pepys, *Diary*, I, 322; Joan Wake and Deborah Champion Webster, eds., *The Letters of Daniel Eaton to the Third Earl of Cardigan, 1725–1732* (Kettering, Eng., 1971), 72; R. Campbell, *The London Tradesman; Being a Compendius View of All the Trades, Professions, Arts, both Liberal and Mechanic now Practised in the Cities of London and Westminster* (London, 1747), passim; *Description of Trades*, passim.
15. Steven L. Kaplan, *The Bakers of Paris and the Bread Question, 1700–1775* (Durham, N.C., 1996), 227, passim; Bouteloup, "Travail de Nuit," 3–5; *Description of Trades*, 10–11.
16. Campbell, *London Tradesman*, 264, 332; *OBP*, Jan. 17, 1728, Apr. 24–27, 1745, 104; Apr. 2, 8, 1777, Clement Young Sturge, ed., *Leaves from the Past: The Diary of John Allen, Sometime Brewer of Wapping (1757–1808) . . .* (Bristol, 1905), 30, 34.
17. Celia Fiennes, *The Illustrated Journeys of Celia Fiennes, 1685–c.1712*, ed. Christopher Morris (London, 1982), 70; "Speculations," *PA*, July 15, 1763; *The Memoirs of Charles-Lewis Baron de Pollnitz . . .* (London, 1739), I, 410; Bouteloup, "Travail de Nuit," 2; *The Lawes of the Market* (London, 1595).
18. T. Platter, *Journal*, 46; Woodward, ed., *Books*, 108; Goubert, *French Peasantry*, trans. Patterson, 140; John Webster, *The Displaying of Supposed Witchcraft . . .* (London, 1677), 299.
19. Edward Halle, *The Union of the Two Noble and Illustrious Families of Lancastre & Yorke . . .* (n.p., 1548), fo. xli; Sigrid Maurice and Klaus Maurice, "Counting the Hours in Community Life of the 16th and 17th Centuries," in Klaus Maurice and Otto Mayr, eds., *The Clockwork Universe: German Clocks and Automata, 1550–1650* (New York, 1980), 149; Moryson, *Itinerary*, I, 22–23; Pinkerton, *Travels*, I, 329.
20. Margaret Killip, *The Folklore of the Isle of Man* (Totowa, N.J., 1976), 170; Garnet, *Lampen*, 102, 278; Schindler, *Rebellion*, 194, James Orchard Halliwell, *A Dictionary of Archaic and Provincial Words . . .* (London, 1865), II, 924; Robert Greene, *A Quip for an Upstart Courtier* (1594; rpt. edn., Gainesville, Fla., 1954); George Latimer Apperson, *English Proverbs and Proverbial Phrases: A Historical Dictionary* (London, 1929), 78; Paul Mantoux, *The Industrial Revolution in the Eighteenth Century: An Outline of the Beginnings of the Modern Factory System in England* (London, 1952), 77; *LE-P*, Nov. 6, 1760.
21. Marjorie McIntosh, "The Diversity of Social Capital in English Communities, 1300–1640 (with a Glance at Modern Nigeria)," *JIH* 26 (1995), 471; Carol F. Karlsen, *The Devil in the Shape of a Woman: Witchcraft in Colonial New England* (New York, 1984), 171; Thomas Tusser, *Five Hundred Pointes of Good Husbandrie*, eds. V. Payne and Sidney J. Herrtage (London, 1878), 162; Raffaella Sarti, *Europe at Home: Family and Material Culture, 1500–1800*, trans. Allan Cameron (New Haven, 2002), 190–191.
22. Wilson, *English Proverbs*, 909; *RB*, III, Pt. 1, 302–303; Laurel Thatcher Ulrich, *A Midwife's Tale: The Life of Martha Ballard, Based on Her Diary, 1785–1812* (New York, 1990), 210;

Stephen Duck, *The Thresher's Labour (1736)* and Mary Collier, *The Woman's Labour (1739)* (rpt. edn., Los Angeles, 1985), 15; *Province and Court Records of Maine* (Portland, Maine, 1928), I, 140; Caroline Davidson, *A Woman's Work is Never Done: A History of Housework in the British Isles, 1650–1950* (London, 1982), 15.

23. Nov. 20, 1660, Pepys, *Diary*, I, 297; Mary Stower, Dec. 15, 1727, Assi 45/18/15/84; *OBP*, Apr. 28–May 4, 1756, 179; Davidson, *Woman's Work*, 136–152.
24. Collier, *Woman's Labour*, 16; Helen and Keith Kelsall, *Scottish Lifestyle 300 Years Ago: New Light on Edinburgh and Border Families* (Edinburgh, 1986), 97; Timothy J. Casey, ed., *Jean Paul: A Reader*, trans. Erika Casey (Baltimore, 1992), 339; *SAS*, XIV, 320, XV, 125; Richard Harvey, "The Work and Mentalité of Lower Orders Elizabethan Women," *Exemplaria* 5 (1993), 418–419.
25. *OBP*, Dec. 3, 1729, 6; "Extract of a Letter from Edinburgh, dated June 27," *SJC*, July 6, 1769; Catherine Parker, Jan. 7, 1773, Assi 45/31/1/55; *OBP*, Dec. 7–12, 1763, 2.
26. Grose, *Dictionary*; Tusser, *Good Husbandrie*, ed. Payne and Herrtage, 58; July 7, 1663, Pepys, *Diary*, IV, 220; Ferdinando Bottarelli, *The New Italian, English and French Pocket-Dictionary* . . . (London, 1777), III; Gerald Strauss, *Nuremberg in the Sixteenth Century: City Politics and Life Between Middle Ages and Modern Times* (Bloomington, Ind., 1976), 192; James Clifford, "Some Aspects of London Life in the Mid-18th Century," in Paul Fritz and David Williams, eds., *City & Society in the 18th Century* (Toronto, 1973), 23–34; Burt, *Letters*, I, 25; Susan B. Hanley, "Urban Sanitation in Preindustrial Japan," *JIH* 18 (1987), 1–26.
27. Donald Lupton, *London and the Countrey Carbonadoed and Quartered into Severall Characters* (1632; rpt. edn. Amsterdam, 1977), 94–96; Kathleen Elizabeth Stuart, "The Boundaries of Honor: 'Dishonorable People' in Augsburg, 1500–1800 (Ph.D. diss., Yale Univ., 1993), 171–175; Mar. 5–7, 1799, Drinker, *Diary*, II, 1142–1143; Clifford, "London Life," 27.
28. Daniel Defoe, *A Journal of the Plague Year* . . . (1722; rpt. edn., London, 1927), 223, 233, passim; James S. Amelang, *A Journal of the Plague Year: The Diary of the Barcelona Tanner Miguel Parets, 1651* (New York, 1991), 82; *OED*, s.v. "vespillon"; F. Altieri, *Dizionario Italiano ed. Inglese* . . . (London, 1726), I; *A Report of the Record Commissioners of the City of Boston, Containing the Selectmen's Minutes from 1764 to* 1768 (Boston, 1889), 12; Aug. 15, 20, 1665, Pepys, *Diary*, VI, 192, 199; Michael Kunze, *Highroad to the Stake: A Tale of Witchcraft*, trans. William E. Yuill (Chicago, 1987), 163.
29. *The Ecologues and Georgics of Virgil*, trans. C. Day Lewis (Garden City, N.Y., 1964), 105.
30. Oct. 21, 1807, Diary of Hiram Harwood (typescript), Bennington Historical Society, Bennington, Vt.; *A Journal for the Years 1739–1803 by Samuel Lane of Stratham New Hampshire*, ed. Charles J. Hanson (Concord, N.H., 1937), 29; "Mus Rusticus," SJC, Apr. 27, 1773; Crusius, *Nocte*, ch. 4.25; Lucius Junius Moderatus Columella, *On Agriculture and Trees*, trans. E. S. Forster and Edward H. Heffner (Cambridge, Mass., 1955), III, 57.
31. Nov. 4, 1777, Sanger, *Journal*, 165, passim; *SAS*, XVII, 597; July 1, 1767, Cole, *Diary*, 236; May 7, 1665, James M. Rosenheim, ed., *The Notebook of Robert Doughty, 1662–1665* (Aberystwyth, Wales, 1989), 54.
32. Aug. 27, 1691, H. J. Morehouse and C. A. Hulbert, eds., *Extracts from the Diary of the Rev. Robert Meeke* (London, 1874), 43; Awnsham Churchill, comp., *A Collection of Voyages and Travels* . . . (London, 1746), VI, 729; Journal of James Robertson, 1767, 118, Manuscripts, National Library of Scotland, Edinburgh; William W. Hagen, *Ordinary Prussians: Brandenburg, Junkers and Villagers (1500–1840)* (Cambridge, 2002), 120.
33. John Brown, Mar. 19, 1777, Assi 45/33/10c; Augustin Gallo, *Secrets de la Vraye Agriculture* . . . (Paris, 1572), 16; Tusser, *Good Husbandrie*, ed. Payne and Herrtage, 177; Charles Stevens and John Liebault, comps., *Maison Rustique, or, the Countrey Farme*, trans. Richard Surflet (London, 1616), 22.

34. Apr. 25, 1698, Diary of John Richards, 52, Dorset Record Office, Bournemouth, Eng.; Best, *Books*, 124; Feb. 27, 1692, Sewall, *Diary*, I, 288; Patten, *Diary*, 190; July 26, 1749, Parkman, *Diary*, 199; Aug. 21, 1782, Sanger, *Journal*, 432; Cole, *Diary*, 90.
35. Halliwell, *Archaic and Provincial Words*, I, 149; Giacomo Agostinetti, *Cento e Dieci Ricordi Che Formano[il] Bvon Fattor di Villa* (Venice, 1717), 230; Feb. 23, 1764, Carter, *Diary*, I, 257, passim, II, passim; Aug. 14, 1672, Isham, *Diary*, 139; "Henry Vagg," *B. Chron.*, June 28, 1788; Howitt, *Country Book*, 71; Henry Fielding, *The History of the Adventures of Joseph Andrews* (New York, 1950), 158; *Yorkshire Diaries & Autobiographies in the Seventeenth and Eighteenth Centuries* (Durham, Eng., 1886), 106; Best, *Books*, 145.
36. Stevens and Liebault, comps., *Maison Rustique*, trans. Surflet, 24–26; Leonard Digges and Thomas Digges, *A Prognostication Everlastinge*... (London, 1605), fo. 6; Piero Camporesi, *The Anatomy of the Senses: Natural Symbols in Medieval and Early Modern Italy* (Cambridge, 1994), 196–197.
37. Best, *Books*, 152; Nov. 7, 1774, Feb. 5, 1776, Mar. 13, 1779, Sanger, *Journal*, 13, 86, 236; James Kelly, *A Complete Collection of Scottish Proverbs* . . . (London, 1818), 212; Jasper Charlton, *The Ladies Astronomy and Chronology* . . . (London, 1735), 35; "Charles Ley," *SWA or LJ*, Dec. 10, 1770; "On the Harvest Moon," *SJC*, Sept. 1, 1774.
38. *SAS*, XVII, 557; Robert Southey, *Journal of a Tour in Scotland*, ed. C.H. Hertford (London, 1929), 113–114; P. Brydone, *A Tour through Sicily and Malta*... (London, 1773), 220; Patten, *Diary*, passim; *SAS*, XIII, 602.
39. Jonas Hanway, *An Historical Account of the British Trade over the Caspian Sea*... (London, 1753), II, 216; "A Visit to Rome in 1736," *GM* 39 (1853), 264; Gallo, *Secrets de la Vraye Agriculture*, 370, 204; Moryson, *Unpublished Itinerary*, 355; Pinkerton, *Travels*, VI, 370; Samuel Deane, *The New England Farmer*... (Worcester, Mass., 1790), 327.
40. *NYWJ*, May 4, 1741; John Lough, *France Observed in the Seventeenth Century by British Travellers* (Stocksfield, Eng., 1984), 44; Cohens, *Italy*, 168, 268–269. See also William Langland, *Piers Plowman: The C Version*, trans. George Economou (Philadelphia, 1996), 43.
41. Hester Lynch Piozzi, *Observations and Reflections Made in the Course of a Journey through France, Italy, and Germany*, ed. Herbert Barrows (Ann Arbor, Mich., 1967), 103–104; Joseph Palmer, *A Four Months Tour through France* (London, 1776), II, 13; Jan. 28, 1708, Cowper, Diary; Jeremy D. Popkin, ed., *Panorama of Paris: Selections from Le Tableau de Paris, Louis-Sébastien Mercier* (University Park, Pa., 1999), 96; *NYWJ*, Aug. 20, 1750; Richard Cobb, *Paris and Its Provinces, 1792–1802* (New York, 1975), 18–19, 26–27.
42. *Paroimiographia* (French), 21; Columella, *On Agriculture and Trees*, trans. Forster and Heffner, III, 123; Josiah Tucker, *Instructions for Travellers, 1757* (New York, n.d.), 243; Patricia James, ed., *The Travel Diaries of Thomas Robert Malthus* (London, 1966), 73; G. E. Fussell and K. R. Fussell, *The English Countrywoman: A Farmhouse Social History,* A.D. *1500–1900* (New York, 1971), 38, 69–70.
43. Feb. 9, 12, 1767, Woodforde, *Diary*, I, 62; Rétif de la Brétonne, *My Father's Life*, trans. Richard Veasey (Gloucester, Eng., 1986), 162; Apr. 8, 1777, Sanger, *Journal*, 139, passim; *Markham's Farewell to Husbandry*.... (London, 1620), 146.
44. Philip D. Morgan, *Slave Counterpoint: Black Culture in the Eighteenth-Century Chesapeake and Lowcountry* (Chapel Hill, N.C., 1998), 153, 168, 191, 195.
45. Taylor, *A Preter-Pluperfect*... (n.p., 1643), 1.
46. Verdon, *Night*, 113–114; "Mus Rusticus," *SJC*, Apr. 27, 1773; Jeffry Kaplow, *France on the Eve of Revolution: A Book of Readings* (New York, 1971), 145; *OBP*, Apr. 17–20, 1765, 174; Frank Cundall, ed., *Lady Nugent's Journal: Jamaica One Hundred and Thirty-eight Years Ago* (London, 1939), 86; Michael Sonenscher, "Work and Wages in Paris in the Eighteenth Century," in Maxine Berg et al., eds., *Manufacture in Town and Country before the Factory* (Cambridge, 1983), 167.

47. Bouteloup, "Travail de Nuit," 3; Lydia Dotto, *Losing Sleep: How Your Sleeping Habits Affect Your Life* (New York, 1990), 226, 229; Kaplan, *Bakers of Paris*, 264–265.
48. *SAS*, IX, 480.
49. *OBP*, Aug. 28, 1728; Peter Linebaugh, *The London Hanged: Crime and Civil Society in the Eighteenth Century* (Cambridge, 1992), 377; Robert C. Davis, *Shipbuilders of the Venetian Arsenal: Workers and Workplace in the Preindustrial City* (Baltimore, 1991), 160–161; Beattie, *Crime*, 175–178. See also Kaplan, *Bakers of Paris*, 244.
50. Merry E. Wiesner, *Working Women in Renaissance Germany* (New Brunswick, N.J., 1986), 94; "Dane's Narrative," 150; *ECR*, II, 373.
51. Bräker, *Life*, 76, 56; Thompson, "Time, Work-Discipline," 77; Paul Monroe, ed., *Thomas Platter and the Educational Renaissance of the Sixteenth Century* (New York, 1904), 155–156. See also Émile Guillaumin, *The Life of a Simple Man*, ed. Eugen Weber, trans. Margaret Crosland (Hanover, N.H., 1983), 74.
52. Evangeline W. and Charles M. Andrews, eds., *Journal of a Lady of Quality; Being the Narrative of a Journey from Scotland to the West Indies, North Carolina, and Portugal, in the Years 1774 to 1776* (New Haven, 1923), 108; Morgan, *Slave Counterpoint*, 138, 140, 251–253, 358–376, passim; Roderick A. McDonald, *The Economy and Material Culture of Slaves: Goods and Chattels on the Sugar Plantations of Jamaica and Louisiana* (Baton Rouge, 1993), 47.
53. Piero Camporesi, *Bread of Dreams: Food and Fantasy in Early Modern Europe*, trans. David Gentilcore (Chicago, 1989), 96; June 15, 1760, Drinker, *Diary*, I, 66; *SAS*, XI, 110; William Moraley, *The Infortunate: or, the Voyage and Adventures of William Moraley . . .* (Newcastle, Eng., 1743), 51; George Lyman Kittredge, *The Old Farmer and His Almanack . . .* (New York, 1967), 172–173; Roger D. Abrahams, *Singing the Master: The Emergence of African American Culture in the Plantation South* (New York, 1982), 81.
54. J. J. Evans, ed., *Welsh Proverbs . . .* (Llandysul, Wales, 1965), 23; Tilley, *Proverbs in England*, 753.
55. Abel Boyer, *Dictionaire Royal . . .* (Amsterdam, 1719); Mr. Ozell, trans., *M. Misson's Memoirs and Observations in His Travels over England* (London, 1719), 332; Suzanne Tardieu, *La Vie Domestique dans le Mâconnais Rural Préindustriel* (Paris, 1964), 154–161; Verdon, *Night*, 117–123; Hans Medick, "Village Spinning Bees: Sexual Culture and Free Time among Rural Youth in Early Modern Germany," in Hans Medick and David Warren Sabean, eds., *Interest and Emotion: Essays on the Study of Family and Kinship* (Cambridge, 1984), 317–339; Stephen P. Frank, "'Simple Folk, Savage Customs?' Youth, Sociability, and the Dynamics of Culture in Rural Russia, 1856–1914," *JSH* 25 (1992), 716, 711–737, passim; Alessandro Falassi, *Folklore by the Fireside: Text and Context of the Tuscan Veglia* (Austin, 1980), 3, 248, passim; Dec. 16, 1783, Lady T. Lewis, ed., *Journals and Correspondence of Miss Berry* (London, 1865), I, 53; Darryl Ogier, "Night Revels and Werewolfery in Calvinist Guernsey," *Folklore* 109 (1998), 54–56; Magnús Gíslason, *Kvällsvaka: En Isländsk Kulturtradition Belyst Genom Studier i Bondebefolkningens Vardagsliv och Miljö Under Senare Hälften av 1800-Talet och Början av 1900-Talet* (Uppsala, 1977); James H. Delargy, "The Gaelic Story-Teller, with Some Notes on Gaelic Folk-Tales," *Proceedings of the British Academy* 31 (1945), 191–192; *SAS*, VI, 482–483; Mrs. Grant, *Essays on the Superstitions of the Highlanders of Scotland . . .* (New York, [1831?]), I, 103; Hugh Evans, *The Gorse Glen* (Liverpool, 1948), 146.
56. Leona C. Gabel, ed., *Memoirs of a Renaissance Pope: The Commentaries of Pius II, an Abridgement*, trans. Florence A. Gragg (New York, 1962), 35; G. E. Mingay, "Rural England in the Industrial Age," in G. E. Mingay, ed., *The Victorian Countryside* (London, 1981), I, 14.
57. Robert Bell, *A Description of the Conditions and Manners . . . of the Peasantry of Ireland . . .* (London, 1804), 20.

58. Medick, "Spinning Bees," 322–323; Jakob Stutz, *Siebenmal Sieben Jahre aus Meinem Leben: Als Beitrag zur Näheren Kenntnis des Volkes* (Frauenfeld, Switz., 1983), 66–67; James Macpherson, *The Poems of Ossian* (Edinburgh, 1805), II, 341; *SAI*, I, 318.
59. Daniello Bartoli, *La Ricreazione del Savio* (Parma, 1992), 336; Burke, *Popular Culture*, 105–106; Bernard J. Hibbitts, "Making Sense of Metaphors: Visuality, Aurality and the Reconfiguration of American Legal Discourse," *Cardozo Law Review* 16 (1994), 343–344; Crusius, *Nocte*, ch. 6.3; Takashi Tomita, *Yoru no Shinrijutsu: Hiru Kara Yoru e no Kåodåo, Korkoro no Henka o* (Tokyo, 1986), 24–25; Henrie Glassie, *Passing the Time in Ballymenone: Culture and History of an Ulster Community* (Philadelphia, 1982), 40–41, 74, 105; Mircea Eliade, *Myth and Reality* (London, 1964), 10; Raffaele Pettazzoni, *Essays on the History of Religions* (Leiden, 1954), 13–14.
60. Moses Heap, "My Life and Times, or an Old Man's Memories, Illustrated with Numerous Anecdotes and Quaint Sayings," 3, District Central Library, Rawtenstall, Eng.; Bourne, *Antiquitates Vulgares*, 76; Garnert, *Lampan*, 114.
61. Brétonne, *My Father's Life*, trans. Veasey, 111; Eric Robinson et al., eds., *The Early Poems of John Clare, 1804–1822* (Oxford, 1989), II, 126; *SAS*, XVII, 518; Roger Chartier, "Leisure and Sociability: Reading Aloud in Early Modern Europe," in Susan Zimmerman and Ronald F. E. Weissman, eds., *Urban Life in the Renaissance* (Newark, Del., 1989), 112.
62. William Howitt, *The Rural Life of England* (1844; rpt. edn., Shannon, Ire., 1972), 238; Pierre-Jakez Hélias, *The Horse of Pride: Life in a Breton Village*, trans. June Guicharnaud (New Haven, 1978), 73–74; George Peele, *The Old Wive's Tale* (London, 1595).
63. Jean-Louis Flandrin, *Families in Former Times: Kinship, Household and Sexuality*, trans. Richard Southern (Cambridge, 1979), 108–109.
64. Breton, *Works*, II, 10; Medick, "Spinning Bees," 334; *Paroimiographia* (Italian), 7; Schindler, "Youthful Culture," 257.
65. Medick, "Spinning Bees," 334; Martine Segalen, *Love and Power in the Peasant Family: Rural France in the Nineteenth Century*, trans. Sarah Matthews (Chicago, 1983), 126; Madeline Jeay, ed., *Les Évangiles des Quenouilles . . .* (Paris, 1985), passim; Verdon, *Night*, 121–122; Rozsika Parker, *The Subversive Stitch: Embroidery and the Making of the Feminine* (London, 1984), 98.
66. Rudolph M. Bell, *How to Do It: Guides to Good Living for Renaissance Italians* (Chicago, 1999), 249; Medick, "Spinning Bees," 333, 331; Lyndal Roper, *The Holy Household: Women and Morals in Reformation Augsburg* (Oxford, 1989), 179.
67. *SAS*, VIII, 417; Bell, *Peasantry of Ireland*, 20–21; Harvey Mitchell, "The World between the Literate and Oral Traditions in Eighteenth-Century France: Ecclesiastical Instructions and Popular Mentalities," in Roseann Runte, ed., *Studies in Eighteenth-Century Culture: Volume 8* (Madison, Wisc., 1979), 55; Jean-Michel Boehler, *La Paysannerie de la Plaine d'Alsace* (Strasbourg, 1995), II, 1963.

CHAPTER SEVEN

1. Mercier, *The Night Cap* (Philadelphia, 1788), 4.
2. *RB*, I, 87; Sean Shesgreen, *Hogarth and the Times-of-the-Day Tradition* (Ithaca, N.Y., 1983), 47.
3. Jan. 10, 1694, *East Anglian Diaries*, 207, passim; John Holloway, ed., *The Oxford Book of Local Verses* (Oxford, 1987), 15; Keith Thomas, "Work and Leisure in Pre-Industrial Society," *PP* 29 (1964), 50–62; Peter Burke, "The Invention of Leisure in Early Modern Europe," *PP* 146 (1995), 136–151; Joan-Lluis Marfany, "The Invention of Leisure in Early Modern Europe: Comment," *PP* 156 (1997), 174–192.

4. John Aubrey, *Aubrey's Natural History of Wiltshire* (1847; rpt. edn., New York, 1969), 11; Edward Shorter, *The Making of the Modern Family* (New York, 1975), 76.
5. Sept. 10, 1758, Woodforde, *Diary*, IV, 226, passim; July 26, 1761, Mar. 7, 1758; Turner, *Diary*, 232, 141, passim; *ECR*, passim.
6. Jan. 14, Mar. 14, Nov. 10, 15, 1624, Beck, *Diary*, 32, 61, 203, 206, passim; Jeroen Blaak, "Autobiographical Reading and Writing: The Diary of David Beck (1624)," in Rudolph Dekker, ed., *Egodocuments and History: Autobiographical Writing in Its Social Context since the Middle Ages* (Hilversum, 2002), 61–87.
7. Jan. 23, 1662, June 5, 1661, Pepys, *Diary*, III, 17, II, 115, passim.
8. Clare Williams, trans., *Thomas Platter's Travels in England, 1599* (London, 1937), 189; Keith Wrightson, "Alehouses, Order and Reformation in Rural England, 1590–1660," in Eileen and Stephen Yeo, eds., *Popular Culture and Class Conflict, 1590–1914: Explorations in the History of Labour and Leisure* (Sussex, Eng., 1981), 10, passim; Burke, *Popular Culture*, 110; Peter Clark, *The English Alehouse: A Social History* (London, 1983), passim; Thomas Brennan, *Public Drinking and Popular Culture in Eighteenth-Century Paris* (Princeton, N.J., 1988); B. Ann Tlusty, *Bacchus and Civic Order: The Culture of Drink in Early Modern Germany* (Charlottesville, Va., 2001).
9. Monsieur Sorbiere, *A Voyage to England* . . . (London, 1709), 62; *LC*, June 6, 1761; William W. Hagen, "Village Life in East-Elbian Germany and Poland, 1400–1800: Subjections, Self-Defence, Survival," in Tom Scott, ed., *The Peasantries of Europe: From the Fourteenth to the Eighteenth Centuries* (Harlow, Eng., 1998), 146; Wrightson, "Alehouses," 2; Thomas, *Religion and the Decline of Magic*, 19; Hans-Joachim Voth, *Time and Work in England 1750–1830* (Oxford, 2000), 80–81; Brennan, *Public Drinking*, 160–171; Tlusty, *Bacchus*, 150, 158, 187, passim.
10. *OED*, s.v. "kidney"; Daniel Defoe, *The True-Born English-Man* . . . (London, 1708), 15; L. H. Butterfield et al. eds., *Diary and Autobiography of John Adams* (Cambridge, Mass., 1961), I, 214; *RB*, I, 414; *LC*, Jan. 23, 1762, 76; A. M., *The Reformed Gentleman* . . . (London, 1693), 49; *LE-P*, June 23, 1763; Yves-Marie Bercé, *History of Peasant Revolts: The Social Origins of Rebellion in Early Modern France*, trans. Amanda Whitmore (Ithaca, N.Y., 1990), 59.
11. *The Works of Mr. Thomas Brown in Prose and Verse* . . . (London, 1708), 3; May 30, 1760, Butterfield et al., eds., *Adams Diary and Autobiography*, I, 130; John Addy, *Sin and Society in the Seventeenth Century* (London, 1989), 141; A. Lynn Martin, *Alcohol, Sex, and Gender in Late Medieval and Early Modern Europe* (New York, 2001), 89–91; *RB*, VII, 231; Richard Rawlidge, *A Monster Late Found Out* . . . (London, 1628), 6.
12. *A Curtaine Lecture* (London, 1638), 7.
13. David Herlihy, *Cities and Society in Medieval Italy* (London, 1980), 136; Jeffrey R. Watt, "The Impact of the Reformation and Counter-Reformation," in *FLEMT*, 147–150; Edward Muir, *Ritual in Early Modern Europe* (Cambridge, 1997), 135.
14. Jan. 6, 1761, Butterfield et al., eds., *Adams Diary and Autobiography*, I, 195; Sara Mendelson and Particia Crawford, *Women in Early Modern England, 1550–1720* (Oxford, 1998), 119.
15. Shakespeare, *The Rape of Lucrece*, 674; Ménétra, *Journal*, 37–38, 168. See also Jack Ayres, ed., *Paupers and Pig Killers: The Diary of William Holland: A Somerset Parson, 1799–1818* (Gloucester, Eng., 1984), 19.
16. David P. French, comp., *Minor English Poets, 1660–1780* (New York, 1967), III, 318; *Paroimiographia* (British), 4; John S. Farmer, ed., *Merry Songs and Ballads Prior to the Year A.D. 1800* (New York, 1964), IV, 6; *Lusts Dominion; or, the Lascivious Queen* (London, 1657); John Lough, *France Observed in the Seventeenth Century by British Travellers* (Boston, 1985),

119; "A New and Accurate Description of the City of Rome . . . ," *Town and Country Magazine* 24 (1792), 261; *ECR*, IX, 29.

17. Maurice Andrieux, *Daily Life in Venice in the Time of Casanova*, trans. Mary Fitton (London, 1972), 128; Shakespeare, *Romeo and Juliet*, II, 2, 165; Hannah Richards, n.d., Suffolk Court Files #874, Suffolk County Court House, Boston; J. Douglas Porteous, *Landscapes of the Mind: Worlds of Sense and Metaphor* (Toronto, 1990), 7; Takashi Tomita, *Yoru no Shinrijutsu: Hiru Kara Yoru e no Kåodåo, Korkoro no Henka o* (Tokyo, 1986), 13; Darrell L. Butler and Paul M. Biner, "Preferred Lighting Levels: Variability Among Settings, Behaviors, and Individuals," *Environment and Behavior* 19 (1987), 696, 702, 709, 710.

18. Grose, *Dictionary*; Robert Abbot, *The Young Mans Warning-Piece* . . . (London, 1657), 35 (taken from Job 24:15); F. Platter, *Journal*, 80; Samuel Rowlands, *The Night-Raven* (London, 1620); Wendy Doniger, *The Bedtrick: Tales of Sex and Masquerade* (Chicago, 2000), passim; Joanne Bailey, *Unquiet Lives: Marriage and Marriage Breakdown in England, 1660–1800* (Cambridge, 2003), 140–167.

19. Aug. 18, June 2, 1668, Nov. 8, 1665, Apr. 9, 1667, Pepys, *Diary*, IX, 282, 221, VI, 294, VIII, 159, passim; Lawrence Stone, *The Family, Sex and Marriage in England 1500–1800* (New York, 1977), 552–561.

20. Frederick J. Furnivall, ed., *Phillip Stubbes's Anatomy of the Abuses in England in Shakespeare's Youth A.D. 1583* (London, 1877), I, 149; David Cressy, *Birth, Marriage & Death: Ritual, Religion, and the Life-Cycle in Tudor and Stuart England* (Oxford, 1997), 352; Moryson, *Unpublished Itinerary*, 380.

21. Brand 1848, II, 229; Clodagh Tait, *Death, Burial and Commemoration in Ireland, 1550–1650* (New York, 2002), 34–35; Cressy, *Birth, Marriage & Death*, 427; Margo Todd, *The Culture of Protestantism in Early Modern Scotland* (New Haven, 2002), 212–213; Edward MacLysaght, *Irish Life in the Seventeenth Century* (1950; rpt. edn., New York, 1970), 318.

22. Darryl Ogier, "Night Revels and Werewolfery in Calvinist Guernsey," *Folklore* 109 (1998), 54; Jean-Louis Flandrin, *Families in Former Times: Kinship, Household and Sexuality*, trans. Richard Southern (Cambridge, 1979), 108–109; John McManners, *Church and Society in Eighteenth-Century France* (Oxford, 1999), II, 203; Steven Ozment, *Flesh and Spirit: Private Life in Early Modern Germany* (New York, 1999), 208.

23. Farmer, ed., *Songs and Ballads*, II, 82; Gloria L. Main, *Peoples of a Spacious Land: Families and Cultures in Colonial New England* (Cambridge, Mass., 2001), 7; C. Scott Dixon, *The Reformation and Rural Society: The Parishes of Brandenburg-Ansbach-Kulmbach, 1528–1603* (Cambridge, 1996), 112, 128; Griffiths, *Youth*, 258; *Paroimiographia* (British), 25; Thomas Willard Robisheaux, "The Origins of Rural Wealth and Poverty in Hohenlohe, 1470–1680" (Ph.D. diss., Univ. of Virginia, 1981), 170; Sara Tilghman Nalle, *God in La Mancha: Religious Reform and the People of Cuenca, 1500–1650* (Baltimore, 1985), 28–29; Schindler, "Youthful Culture," 256.

24. Aug. 19, 1794, Drinker, *Diary*, I, 584; *The Roving Maids of Aberdeen's Garland* ([Edinburgh?], 1776); Feb. 10, 1873, William Plomer, ed., *Kilvert's Diary: Selections from the Diary of the Rev. Francis Kilvert* . . . (London, 1971), II. 322. See also Charles Woodmason, *The Carolina Backcountry on the Eve of the Revolution* . . . , ed. Richard J. Hooker (Chapel Hill, N.C., 1953), 100.

25. Roger Lonsdale, *The New Book of Eighteenth-Century Verse* (Oxford, 1984), 405; George Parfitt and Ralph Houlbrooke, eds., *The Courtship Narrative of Leonard Wheatcroft, Derbyshire Yeoman* (Reading, Eng., 1986), 52; Émile Guillaumin, *The Life of a Simple Man*, ed. Eugen Weber, trans. Margaret Crosland (Hanover, N.H., 1983), 41, 43–44.

26. Lochwd, *Ymddiddan Rhwng Mab a Merch, Y'nghylch Myned I Garu yn y Gwely* (n.p., [1800s]), 4.

27. *A Tour in Ireland in 1775* (London, 1776), 103–104; Ernest W. Marwick, *The Folklore of Orkney and Shetland* (Totowa, N.J., 1975), 86; Rosalind Mitchison and Leah Lenman, *Sexuality and Social Control: Scotland, 1660–1780* (Oxford, 1989), 180; *A Tour in Ireland in 1775* (London, 1776), 103. For early America, including not just New England but also New Jersey and Pennsylvania, see Richard Godbeer, *Sexual Revolution in Early America* (Baltimore, 2002), 246–255; Laurel Thatcher Ulrich and Lois K. Stabler, "'Girling of it' in Eighteenth-Century New Hampshire," *Annual Proceedings*, Dublin Seminar for New England Folklife (1985), 24–36; "John Hunt's Diary," *New Jersey Historical Society Proceedings* 53 (1935), 111, 112, 122; John Robert Shaw, *An Autobiography of Thirty Years, 1777–1807*, ed. Oressa M. Teagarden and Jeanne L. Crabtree (Columbus, Ohio, 1992), 108; Bernard Chevignard, "*Les Voyageurs Europeens et la Pratique du 'Bondelage' (Bundling) en Nouvelle-Angleterre a la Fin du XVIIIe Siècle*," in *L'Amerique et l'Europe: Réalities et Représentations* (Aix-en-Provence, 1986), 75–87.
28. May 5, 1663, William L. Sachse, ed., *The Diary of Roger Lowe of Ashton-in-Makerfield, Lancashire, 1663–74* (New Haven, 1938), 20, passim; *Reports of Special Assistant Poor Law Commissioners on the Employment of Women and Children in Agriculture* (1843; rpt. edn., New York, 1968), 365; Griffiths, *Youth*, 259–261; Apr. 5, 18, 1765, Turner, *Diary*, 318, 320; Parfitt and Houlbrooke, eds., *Courtship*, 53, passim.
29. *Tour in Ireland*, 103–104; Rudolf Braun, *Industrialization and Everyday Life*, trans. Sarah Hanbury Tension (Cambridge, 1990), 44; J.-L. Flandrin, "Repression and Change in the Sexual Life of Young People in Medieval and Early Modern Times," in Robert Wheaton and Tamara K. Hareven, eds., *Family and Sexuality in French History* (Philadelphia, 1980), 34–35.
30. Enid Porter, *Cambridgeshire Customs and Folklore* (New York, 1969), 5; *Les Nuits d'Épreuve des Villageoises Allemandes . . .* (Paris, 1861), 8.
31. Cannon, Diary, 137.
32. Howard C. Rice, Jr., and Anne S. K. Brown, trans. and eds., *The American Campaigns of Rochambeau's Army 1780, 1781, 1782, 1783* (Princeton, N.J., 1972), I, 245; Michael Drake, *Population and Society in Norway 1735–1865* (Cambridge, 1969), 144; Henry Reed Stiles, *Bundling: Its Origin, Progress and Decline in America* (1871; rpt. edn., New York, 1974), 33; Stone, *Family, Sex and Marriage*, 606.
33. Moryson, *Unpublished Itinerary*, 385; Hugh Jones, *O Gerddi Newyddion* (n.p., [1783?]), 3; Rice, Jr., and Brown, trans. and eds., *Rochambeau's Army*, I, 32, 169; Drake, *Population*, 144; Christine D. Worobec, *Peasant Russia: Family and Community in the Post-Emancipation Period* (Princeton, N.J., 1991), 138–139; Flandrin, "Repression," 36.
34. Lochwd, *Ymddiddan Rhwng Mab a Merch*, 4; Stiles, *Bundling*, 96, 29–30; Flandrin, "Repression," 36; Dana Doten, *The Art of Bundling: Being an Inquiry into the Nature & Origins of that Curious but Universal Folk-Custom . . .* (Weston, Vt., 1938), 156; History and Journal of Charles Joseph de Losse de Bayac, 1763–1783, I, Manuscripts Department, Alderman Library, University of Virginia, Charlottesville; Jack Larkin, *The Reshaping of Everyday Life, 1790–1840* (New York, 1988), 193–195, 199; Martine Segalen, *Historical Anthropology of the Family*, trans. J. C. Whitehouse and Sarah Matthews (Cambridge, 1986), 130–131.
35. Flandrin, "Repression," 35–36; John R. Gillis, *For Better, For Worse: British Marriages, 1600 to the Present* (New York, 1985), 30–31; Moryson, *Unpublished Itinerary*, 385.
36. *Jollie's Sketch of Cumberland Manners and Customs . . .* (1811; rpt. edn., Beckermet, Eng., 1974), 40; Bernard Capp, *English Almanacs, 1500–1800: Astrology and the Popular Press* (Ithaca, N.Y., 1979), 122.
37. Feb. 8, 1779, Sanger, *Journal*, 29; Farmer, ed., *Songs and Ballads*, IV, 220–222.
38. Bräker, *Life*, 96; Rice, Jr., and Brown, trans. and eds., *Rochambeau's Army*, I, 245; Baker,

Folklore and Customs of Rural England, 139; *Les Nuits d'Épreuve*, 9; Sara F. Matthews Grieco, "The Body, Appearance, and Sexuality," in *HWW* III, 69; Stone, *Family*, 607; Gillis, *British Marriages*, 30; Shorter, *Family*, 103.

39. Cereta, *Collected Letters of a Renaissance Feminist*, ed. Diana Maury Robin (Chicago, 1997), 34.
40. Leo P. McCauley, S. J. and Anthony A. Stephenson, trans., *The Works of Saint Cyril of Jerusalem* (Washington, D.C., 1969), I, 188; *Another Collection of Philosophical Conferences of the French Virtuosi of France . . .*, trans. G. Havers and J. Davies (London, 1665), 316–317; Daniello Bartoli, *La Ricreazione del Savio* (Parma, 1992), 192–193.
41. Burton E. Stevenson, *The Home Book of Proverbs, Maxims and Familiar Phrases* (New York, 1948), 1686; Lucien Febvre, *Life in Renaissance France*, ed. and trans. Marion Rothstein (Cambridge, Mass., 1977), 34–36; *ODNB*, s.v. "Elizabeth Carter" and "John Scott"; Cecile M. Jagodzinski, *Privacy and Print: Reading and Writing in Seventeenth-Century England* (Charlottesville, Va., 1999), 13; Raffaella Sarti, *Europe at Home: Family and Material Culture, 1500–1800*, trans. Allan Cameron (New Haven, 2002), 138–139.
42. William Davenant, *The Works . . .* (London, 1673); Roger Chartier, "The Practical Impact of Writing," in *HPL* III, 111–124.
43. J. R. Hale, *Machiavelli and Renaissance Italy* (London, 1972), 112; Chartier, "Writing," 124–157; Jagodzinski, *Privacy and Print*, 2–6; Anthony Grafton, "The Humanist as Reader," in Guglielmo Cavallo and Roger Chartier, *A History of Reading in the West*, trans. Lydia G. Cochrane (Amherst, Mass., 1999), 179–181.
44. May 19, 1667, Pepys, *Diary*, VIII, 223, X, 34–39; Nov. 4, 1624, Beck, *Diary*, 199–200, passim; Canon, Diary, 41, 56; Blaak, "Reading and Writing," 64–76, 83–87.
45. Apr. 27, 1706, Cowper, *Diary*, passim; Jagodzinski, *Privacy and Print*, 20, 25–43; François Lebrun, "The Two Reformations: Communal Devotion and Personal Piety" and Chartier, "Writing," in *HPL* III, 96–104, 130–134.
46. Yehonatan Eibeshitz, *Yearot Devash* (Jerusalem, 2000), 371; Rabbi Aviel, ed. *Mishnah Berurah: Laws Concerning Miscellaneous Blessings, the Minchah Service, the Ma'ariv Service and Evening Conduct . . .* (Jerusalem, 1989), 413; Salo Wittmayer Baron, *The Jewish Community: Its History and Structure to the American Revolution* (Westport, Ct., 1972), II, 169, 176, III, 163.
47. Thomas Wright, *Autobiography . . . 1736–1797* (London, 1864), 24; Steven Ozment, *Three Behaim Boys Growing Up in Early Modern Germany: A Chronicle of Their Lives* (New Haven, 1990), 103; Alexander Teixeira de Mattos, trans., *The Memoirs of François René Vicomte de Chateaubriand . . .* (New York, 1902), I, 54.
48. Dec. 31, 1666, Pepys, *Diary*, VII, 426, X, 174–176, passim; Apr. 26, 1740, Kay, *Diary*, 34.
49. Tilley, *Proverbs in England*, 79; Jan. 2, 1624, Beck, *Diary*, 27–28, passim; Cereta, *Letters*, ed. Robin, 101, 31–32, passim; Lorraine Reams, "Night Thoughts: The Waking of the Soul: The Nocturnal Contemplations of Love, Death, and the Divine in the Eighteenth-Century and Nineteenth-Century French Epistolary Novel and *Roman-Mémoire*" (Ph.D. diss., Univ. of North Carolina or Chapel Hill, 2000), 138; William Riley Parker, *Milton: A Biography* (Oxford, 1968), I, 578, II, 710; Blaak, "Reading and Writing," 79–87; Chartier, "Writing," Madeleine Foisil, "The Literature of Intimacy," and Jean Marie Goulemont, "Literary Practices: Publicizing the Private," in *HPL* III, 115–117, 157–159, 327–332, 380–383.
50. Henry Halford Vaughan, ed., *Welsh Proverbs with English Translations* (1889; rpt. edn., Detroit, 1969), 94; Michael J. Mikos, ed., *Polish Renaissance Literature: An Anthology* (Columbus, Ohio, 1995), 168; *RB*, I, 84.

CHAPTER EIGHT

1. Shakespeare, *Antony and Cleopatra*, III, 13, 184–187.
2. Verdon, *Night*, 127–131; Pierre Jonin, "L'Espace et le Temps de la Nuit dans les Romans de Chrètiens de Troyes," *Mélanges de Langue et de Littérature Médiévales Offerts à Alice Planche* 48 (1984), 242–246; Gary Cross, *A Social History of Leisure Since 1600* (State College, Pa., 1990), 17–18.
3. Edward Ward, *The London Spy* (1709; rpt. edn., New York, 1985), 43; Koslofsky, "Court Culture," 745–748; Thomas D'Urfey, *The Two Queens of Brentford* (London, 1721); *Another Collection of Philosophical Conferences of the French Virtuosi* . . . , trans. G. Havers and J. Davies (London, 1665), 419; Schindler, *Rebellion*, 194–195.
4. Diary of Robert Moody, 1660–1663, Rawlinson Coll. D. 84, Bodl.; Marie-Claude Canova-Green, *Benserade Ballets pour Louis XIV* (Paris, 1997), 93–160.
5. Ben Sedgley, *Observations on Mr. Fielding's Enquiry into the Causes of the Late Increase of Robbers* . . . (London, 1751), 8; "A Short Account, by Way of Journal, of What I Observed Most Remarkable in My Travels . . . ," June 2, 1697, Historical Manuscripts Commission., 8th *Report*, Part 1 (1881), 99–100; Marcelin Defourneaux, *Daily Life in Spain: The Golden Age*, trans. Newton Branch (New York, 1971), 70–71; Koslofsky, "Court Culture," 745–748; Thomas Burke, *English Night-Life: From Norman Curfew to Present Black-Out* (New York, 1971), 11–22.
6. Tobias George Smollet, *Humphry Clinker*, ed. James L. Thorson (New York, 1983), I, 87; P. Brydone, *A Tour through Sicily and Malta* . . . (London, 1773), II, 87–90; Remarks 1717, 56; Sedgley, *Observations*, 8; *The Memoirs of Charles-Lewis, Baron de Pollnitz* . . . (London, 1739), I, 222; Burke, *Night-Life*, 23–70, passim.
7. *US and WJ*, Feb. 28, 1730; Vanessa Harding, *The Dead and the Living in Paris and London, 1500–1670* (Cambridge, 2002), 197, passim; Craig M. Koslofsky, *The Reformation of the Dead: Death and Ritual in Early Modern Germany, 1450–1700* (New York, 2000), 138, 133–152, passim; Clare Gittings, *Death, Burial and the Individual in Early Modern England* (London, 1984), 188–200.
8. Richards, *The Tragedy of Messallina* (London, 1640).
9. Walter R. Davis, ed., *The Works of Thomas Campion* . . . (New York, 1967), 147; Terry Castle, "The Culture of Travesty: Sexuality and Masquerade in Eighteenth-Century England," in G. S. Rousseau and Roy Porter, eds., *Sexual Underworlds of the Englightenment* (Manchester, 1987), 158; Terry Castle, *Masquerade and Civilization: The Carnivalesque in Eighteenth-Century English Culture and Fiction* (Stanford, Calif., 1986).
10. *The Rich Cabinet* . . . (London, 1616), fo. 20; Sara Mendelson, "The Civility of Women in Seventeenth-Century England," in Peter Burke et al., eds., *Civil Histories: Essays Presented to Sir Keith Thomas* (Oxford, 2000), 114; Stephen J. Greenblatt, *Renaissance Self-Fashioning: From More to Shakespeare* (Chicago, 1980).
11. Castle, *Masquerade*, 25, 1–109, passim; Castle, "Culture of Travesty," 166–167; *HMM and GA*, Jan. 28, 1755.
12. Castle, *Masquerade*, 73, 1–109, passim; "W.Z.," *GM* 41 (1771), 404; *WJ*, May 16, 1724; *Occasional Poems, Very Seasonable and Proper for the Present Times* . . . (London, 1726), 5; Amanda Vickery, *The Gentleman's Daughter: Women's Lives in Georgian England* (New Haven, 1998), 243.
13. Castle, *Masquerade*, 73, 1–109, passim; Nancy Lyman Roelker, ed. and trans., *The Paris of Henry of Navarre, as Seen by Pierre de l'Estoile: Selections from His Mémoires-Journaux* (Cambridge, Mass., 1958), 58; Bulstrode Whitelock, *The Third Charge* . . . (London, 1723), 21.
14. Henry Alexander, trans., *Four Plays by Holberg* (Princeton, N.J., 1946), 171.
15. Goffe, *The Raging Turk* (London, 1631).

16. Alexander Hamilton, *Gentleman's Progress: The Itinerarium of Dr. Alexander Hamilton, 1744*, ed. Carl Bridenbaugh (Chapel Hill, N.C., 1948), 177; *PG*, Dec. 23, 1762.
17. Douglas Grant, ed., *The Poetical Works of Charles Churchill* (Oxford, 1956), 52, 55; John S. Farmer, ed., *Merry Songs and Ballads prior to the Year A.D. 1800* (New York, 1964), III, 67; Anna Bryson, *From Courtesy to Civility: Changing Codes of Conduct in Early Modern England* (Oxford, 1998), 245, 246–275, passim.
18. May 31, 1706, Cowper, Diary; *The Works of Mr. Thomas Brown in Prose and Verse . . .* (London, 1708), III, 3; S. Johnson, *London: A Poem . . .* (London, 1739), 17; *US* and *WJ*, Apr. 11, 1730; Bryson, *Courtesy to Civility*, 248–249; Vickery, *Daughter*, 213–214; G.J. Barker-Benfield, *The Culture of Sensibility: Sex and Society in Eighteenth-Century Britain* (Chicago, 1992), 50–51.
19. Elborg Forster, ed. and trans., *A Woman's Life in the Court of the Sun King: Letters of Liselotte von der Pfalz, 1652–1722* (Baltimore, 1984), 219; M. Dreux du Radier, *Essai Historique, Critique, Philologuique, Politique, Moral, Litteraire et Galant, sur les Lanternes . . .* (Paris, 1755), 92–96; Jeffry Kaplow, *The Names of Kings: The Parisian Laboring Poor in the Eighteenth Century* (New York, 1972), 106.
20. Oct. 10, 1764, Frederick A. Pottle, ed., *Boswell on the Grand Tour: Germany and Switzerland, 1764* (New York, 1953), 135; June 4, 1763, Frederick A. Pottle, ed., *Boswell's London Journal, 1762–1763* (New York, 1950), 272–273, 264 n.1, passim; Craig Harline and Eddy Put, *A Bishop's Tale: Matthias Hovius Among His Flock in Seventeenth-Century Flanders* (New Haven, 2000), 253–254; John Owen, *Travels into Different Parts of Europe, in the Years 1791 and 1792 . . .* (London, 1796), II, 85.
21. Sara Mendelson and Patricia Crawford, *Women in Early Modern England, 1550–1720* (Oxford, 1998), 109; Jerome Nadelhaft, "The Englishwoman's Sexual Civil War: Feminist Attitudes towards Men, Women, and Marriage, 1650–1740," *Journal of the History of Ideas* 43 (1982), 573, 576; Linda Pollock, "'Teach Her to Live under Obedience': The Making of Women in the Upper Ranks of Early Modern England," *Continuity and Change* 4 (1989), 231–258.
22. *Westward for Smelts. Or, the Water-man's Fare of Mad-Merry Western Wenches . . .* (London, 1620), 24; Giovannia Boccaccio, *The Corbaccio*, ed. and trans. Anthony K. Cassell (Urbana, Ill., 1975), 28; George Chapman, *An Humerous Dayes Myrth* (London, 1599), 9; Feb. 14, 1668, Pepys, *Diary*, IX, 71; April 1683, Wood, *Life*, 42; Jeffrey Merrick and Bryant T. Ragan, Jr., eds., *Homosexuality in Early Modern France: A Documentary Collection* (New York, 2001), 38; Piero Camporesi, *Exotic Brew: The Art of Living in the Age of Enlightenment* (Malden, Mass., 1994), 12.
23. Thomas D'Urfey, *Squire Oldsapp: or, the Night-Adventures* (London, 1679), 29; Dec. 27, 1775, Charles Ryskamp and Frederick A. Pottle, eds., *Boswell: The Ominous Years, 1774–1776* (New York, 1963), 206, passim; Cecil Aspinall-Oglander, *Admiral's Widow: Being the Life and Letters of the Hon. Mrs. Edward Boscawen from 1761 to 1805* (London, 1942), 88–89; July 13, 1716, William Matthews, ed., *The Diary of Dudley Ryder, 1715–1716* (London, 1939), 274, passim; June 5, 1763, Pottle, ed., *Boswell's London Journal*, 273.
24. "A City Night-piece in Winter," *Walker's Hibernian Magazine* 9 (1779), 272; *OBP*, Apr. 28, 1731, 16–17; "The Watchman's Description of Covent Garden at Two o'Clock in the Morning," *Weekly Amusement* (London), May 5, 1764.
25. "X.Y.," *LM*, Jan. 26, 1773; Graham Greene, *Lord Rochester's Monkey, Being the Life of John Wilmot, Second Earl of Rochester* (London, 1974), 106; Oct. 23, 26, 1668, Feb. 3, 1664, Pepys, *Diary*, IX, 335–336, 338–339, V, 37; "The Connoisseur," *HMM and GA*, Mar. 18, 1755; Bryson, *Courtesy to Civility*, 250, 254–255; James Grantham Turner, *Libertines and Radicals in Early Modern London: Sexuality, Politics, and Literary Culture, 1630–1685* (Cambridge, 2002), 226–227.

26. Harold Love, ed., *The Works of John Wilmot, Earl of Rochester* (Oxford, 1999), 45; Guy Chapman, ed., *The Travel-Diaries of William Beckford of Fonthill* (Cambridge, 1928), II, 55; Robert Shoemaker, "Male Honour and the Decline of Public Violence in Eighteenth-Century London," *SH* 26 (2001), 200; Bryson, *Courtesy to Civility*, 249; Barker-Benfield, *Sensibility*, 47; May 3, 1709, Cowper, Diary; Julius R. Ruff, *Crime, Justice and Public Order in Old Regime France: The Sénéchaussées of Libourne and Bazas, 1696–1789* (London, 1984), 91.
27. Thornton Shirley Graves, "Some Pre-Mohock Clansmen," *Studies in Philology* 20 (1923), 395–421; Grose, *Dictionary*; Moryson, *Unpublished Itinerary*, 463; Helen Langdon, *Caravaggio: A Life* (New York, 1999), 133, 312–314.
28. Graves, "Pre-Mohock Clansmen," 399, 395–421, passim; Bryson, *Courtesy to Civility*, 249; May 30, 1668, Pepys, *Diary*, IX, 218–219; *The Town-Rakes: or, the Frolicks of the Mohocks or Hawkubites* (London, 1712); Swift, *Journal*, II, 524–525, 508–515, passim; Mar. 20, 1712, Cowper, Diary; Daniel Statt, "The Case of the Mohocks: Rake Violence in Augustan London," *SH* 20 (1995), 179–199.
29. Shakespeare, *1 Henry IV*, I, 2, 137–139, 159; Verdon, *Night*, 46; *US and WJ*, Apr. 11, 1730; *A Pleasant and Delightful Story of King Henry the VIII, and a Cobler* (n.p., [1670?]); Theophilius Cibber, *The Lives of the Poets of Great Britain and Ireland* (1753; rpt. edn., Hildesheim, Ger., 1968), II, 289; Roelker, ed. and trans., *Paris of Henry of Navarre*, 52, 47, 77; Edouard Fournier, *Les Lanternes: Histoire de l'Ancien Éclairage de Paris* (Paris, 1854), 15; Matthiessen, *Natten*, 134, 132; Benjamin Silliman, *A Journal of Travels in England, Holland, and Scotland . . .* (New Haven, 1820), I, 179; Frederic J. Baumgartner, *France in the Sixteenth Century* (New York, 1995), 222.

CHAPTER NINE

1. Shakespeare, *King John*, I, 1, 172.
2. Thomas Dekker, *The Seven Deadly Sinnes of London*, ed. H.F.B. Brett-Smith (1606; rpt. edn., New York, 1922), 31; Eric Robinson et al., eds., *The Early Poems of John Clare, 1804–1822* (Oxford, 1989), II, 197; Douglas Grant, ed., *The Poetical Works of Charles Churchill* (Oxford, 1956), 58; E. P. Thompson, "Eighteenth-Century English Society: Class Struggle without Class?," *SH* 3 (1978), 158; Mihaly Csikszentmihalyi and Eugene Rochberg-Halton, *The Meaning of Things: Domestic Symbols and the Self* (Cambridge, 1981), 16–52, passim.
3. May 23, 1693, May 25, 1686, Wood, *Life*, V, 423, 187; E.S. De Beer, ed., *Diary of Mary, Countess Cowper* (London, 1864), I, 19; Legg, *Low-Life*, 93.
4. Franco Mormando, *The Preacher's Demons: Bernardino of Sienna and the Social Underworld of Early Renaissance Italy* (Chicago, 1999), 85; Nov. 27, 28, 1625, [Andrés De La Vega], *Memorias de Sevilla, 1600–1678*, ed. Francisco Morales Padrón (Córdoba, 1981), 50; Thomas V. Cohen, "The Case of the Mysterious Coil of Rope: Street Life and Jewish Persona in Rome in the Middle of the Sixteenth Century," *Sixteenth Century Journal* 19 (1988), 209–221; Elliot Horowitz, "The Eve of the Circumcision: A Chapter in the History of Jewish Nightlife," *JSH* 23 (1989), 48; Anna Foa, *The Jews of Europe after the Black Death*, trans. Andrea Grover (Berkeley, Calif., 2000), 143.
5. M[aster] Elias Schad, "True Account of an Anabaptist Meeting at Night in a Forest and a Debate Held There with Them," *Mennonite Quarterly Review* 58 (1984), 292–295; E. Veryard, *An Account of Divers Choice Remarks . . . Taken in a Journey . . .* (London, 1701), 75; Famiano Strada, *De Bello Belgio: The History of the Low-Countrey Warres*, trans. Sir

Robert Stapylton (London, [1650?]), 61–62; Henry Hibbert, *Syntagma Theologicum* . . . (London, 1662), 252; Natalie Zemon Davis, *Society and Culture in Early Modern France* (Stanford, Calif., 1975), 214.

6. Jan. 20, 1640, Joseph Alfred Bradney, ed., *The Diary of Walter Powell of Llantilo Crosseny in the County of Monmouth, Gentleman: 1603–1654* (Bristol, 1907), 25; Henry Fishwick, ed., *The Note Book of the Rev. Thomas Jolly* A.D. *1671–1693* (Manchester, 1894), 54, passim; David Cressy, *Agnes Bowker's Cat: Travesties and Transgressions in Tudor and Stuart England* (Oxford, 2001), 116–137; Heywood, *Diaries*, I, passim.
7. F. P. Wilson, *The Plague in Shakespeare's London* (Oxford, 1957), 61; Giula Calvi, *Histories of a Plague Year: The Social and the Imaginary in Baroque Florence*, trans. Dario Biocca and Bryant T. Ragan, Jr. (Berkeley, Calif., 1989), 90–91; Daniel Defoe, *A Journal of the Plague Year* . . . (1722; rpt. edn., London, 1928), 233, passim; Walter George Bell, *The Great Plague in London in 1665* (1924; rpt. edn., London, 1979), 210.
8. Angeline Goreau, "'Last Night's Rambles': Restoration Literature and the War Between the Sexes," in Alan Bold, ed., *The Sexual Dimension in Literature* (London, 1983), 51; *OBP*, Apr. 20, 1726, 6; Michael Rocke, *Forbidden Friendships: Homosexuality and Male Culture in Renaissance Florence* (New York, 1996), 151–152, 154–155; Jeffrey Merrick and Bryant T. Ragan, Jr., eds., *Homosexuality in Early Modern France: A Documentary Collection* (New York, 2001), 59.
9. Katherine M. Rogers, ed., *Selected Poems of Anne Finch, Countess of Winchilsea* (New York, 1979), 157.
10. *Paroimiographia* (French), 28; Richard L. Kagan and Abigail Dyer, eds. and trans., *Inquisitorial Inquiries: Brief Lives of Secret Jews and Other Heretics* (Baltimore, 2004), 97.
11. Joyce M. Ellis, *The Georgian Town, 1680–1840* (New York, 2001), 74; Jütte, *Poverty*, 52–59, 146–149; Olwen H. Hufton, *The Poor of Eighteenth-Century France, 1750–1789* (Oxford, 1974).
12. *An Effectual Scheme for the Immediate Preventing of Street Robberies, and Suppressing All Other Disorders of the Night* . . . (London, 1731), 33; Schindler, "Youthful Culture," 271; Solomon Stoddard, *Three Sermons Lately Preach'd at Boston* . . . (Boston, 1717), 104; Arthur Friedman, ed., *Collected Works of Oliver Goldsmith* (Oxford, 1966), 431.
13. Susan Brigden, "Youth and the English Reformation," *PP* 95 (1982), 38, 44; Griffiths, *Youth*, 36, passim; Gary Cross, *A Social History of Leisure Since 1600* (State College, Pa., 1990), 15.
14. *Nicetas: or, Temptations to Sin* . . . (Boston, 1705), 35; Schindler, "Youthful Culture," 243, 278; June 5, 1713, *Diary of Cotton Mather* (New York, [1957?]), I, 216; William Davenant, *The Works* . . . (London, 1673).
15. David Garrioch, *The Making of Revolutionary Paris* (Berkeley, Calif., 2002), 36; Tim Meldrum, *Domestic Service and Gender, 1660–1750: Life and Work in the London Household* (Harlow, Eng., 2000), 34–67, 92–110; Bridget Hill, *Servants: English Domestics in the Eighteenth Century* (Oxford, 1996), 101, 105–106; Griffiths, *Youth*, 314–321; Anne Kussmaul, *Servants in Husbandry in Early Modern England* (Cambridge, 1981); Cissie Fairchilds, *Domestic Enemies: Servants & Their Masters in Old Regime France* (Baltimore, 1984); Richard S. Dunn, "Servants and Slaves: The Recruitment and Employment of Labor," in Jack P. Greene and J. R. Pole, eds., *Colonial British America: Essays in the New History of the Early Modern Era* (Baltimore, 1984), 157–194; Philip D. Morgan, *Slave Counterpoint: Black Culture in the Eighteenth-Century Chesapeake and Lowcountry* (Chapel Hill, N.C., 1998).
16. Nathaniel B. Shurtleff, ed., *Records of the Governor and Company of the Massachusetts Bay in New England* (Boston, 1854), V, 62; Aug. 27, 1705, Cowper, Diary; SAS, XIV, 397.
17. Hillary Beckles, *Black Rebellion in Barbados: The Struggle Against Slavery, 1627–1838*

(Bridgetown, Barbados, 1987), 70; David A. Copeland, *Colonial American Newspapers: Character and Content* (Newark, Del., 1997), 134; Sarah McCulloh Lemmon, ed., *The Pettigrew Papers* (Raleigh, N.C., 1971), I, 398; Morgan, *Slave Counterpoint*, 524–526, passim.

18. Weinsberg, *Diary*, IV, 11; *PG*, Aug. 2, 1750; Peter H. Wood, *Black Majority: Negroes in Colonial South Carolina from 1670 through the Stono Rebellion* (New York, 1974), 257.

19. Tim Harris, "Perceptions of the Crowd in Later Stuart London," in J. F. Merritt, ed., *Imagining Early Modern London: Perceptions and Portrayals of the City from Stow to Strype, 1598–1720* (Cambridge, 2001), 251; George P. Rawick, ed., *The American Slave: A Composite Autobiography* (Westport, Ct., 1972), XV, 365; Samuel Phillips, *Advice to a Child . . .* (Boston, 1729), 49, passim.

20. Feb. 3, 1772, Carter, *Diary*, II, 648; James Lackington, *Memoirs of the First Forty-Five Years . . .* (London, 1792), 35; Edward Ward, *The Rambling Rakes, or, London Libertines* (London, 1700), 9; Meldrum, *Domestic Service*, 168–169.

21. Piero Camporesi, *The Land of Hunger* (Cambridge, Mass., 1996), 132; Louis Châtellier, *The Religion of the Poor: Rural Missions in Europe and the Formation of Modern Catholicism, c.1500–c.1800*, trans. Brian Pearce (Cambridge, 1997), 171; Guy Chapman, ed., *The Travel-Diaries of William Beckford of Fonthill* (Cambridge, 1928), II, 54; "An Inhabitant of Bloomsbury," *PA*, Aug. 8, 1770; Bronislaw Geremek, *Poverty: A History* (Oxford, 1994), 215; Jeffry Kaplow, *The Names of Kings: The Parisian Laboring Poor in the Eighteenth Century* (New York, 1972), 108.

22. John Bruce, ed., *Diary of John Manningham . . .* (1868; rpt. edn., New York, 1968), 83; *The Vocal Miscellany: A Collection of Above Four Hundred Celebrated Songs . . .* (London, 1734), 120.

23. Willie Lee Rose, ed., *A Documentary History of Slavery in North America* (New York, 1976), 19; J.F.D. Smyth, *A Tour in the United States of America* (London, 1784), I, 46; Roger D. Abrahams, *Singing the Master: The Emergence of African American Culture in the Plantation South* (New York, 1982), 5; Mark M. Smith, "Time, Slavery and Plantation Capitalism in the Ante-Bellum American South," *PP* 150 (1996), 160.

24. Lottin, *Chavatte*, 141; Pieter Spierenburg, "Knife Fighting and Popular Codes of Honor in Early Modern Amsterdam," in Pieter Spierenburg, ed., *Men and Violence: Gender, Honor, and Rituals in Modern Europe and America* (Columbus, Ohio, 1998), 108; Ann Tlusty, "The Devil's Altar: The Tavern and Society in Early Modern Augsburg (Germany)" (Ph. D. diss., Univ. of Maryland, 1994), 184; *OBP*, Sept. 11, 1735, 110; *The Countryman's Guide to London or, Villainy Detected . . .* (London, 1775), 78; Thomas Brennan, *Public Drinking and Popular Culture in Eighteenth-Century Paris* (Princeton, N.J., 1988), 282–283, passim; Merry E. Wiesner, *Working Women in Renaissance Germany* (New Brunswick, N.J., 1986), 133–134; Daniel Roche, *The People of Paris: An Essay in Popular Culture in the 18th Century*, trans. Marie Evans (Leamington Spa, Eng., 1987), 255; Feb. 3, 1772, Carter, *Diary*, II, 649.

25. Hardy, *The Life and Death of the Mayor of Casterbridge: A Story of a Man of Character* (New York, 1984), 307.

26. Erskine Beveridge, comp., and J. D. Westwood, ed., *Fergusson's Scottish Proverbs . . .* (Edinburgh, 1924), 39; Legg, *Low-Life*, 21; Bargellini, "Vita Notturna," 83; F. Platter, *Journal*, 89–90; Fernando de Rojas, *The Celestina: A Novel in Dialogue*, trans. Lesley Byrd Simpson (Berkeley, Calif., 1971), 81; Ernest A. Gray, ed., *The Diary of a Surgeon in the Year 1751–1752* (New York, 1937), 74–75; *WJ*, Mar. 20, 1725.

27. Laura Gowing, "'The Freedom of the Streets': Women and Social Space, 1560–1640," in Mark S. R. Jenner and Paul Griffiths, eds., *Londinopolis: Essays in the Cultural and Social History of Early Modern London* (Manchester, 2000), 143; Linda A. Pollock, "Parent-Child Relations," in *FLEMT*, 215–217; Alan Williams, *The Police of Paris, 1718–1789*

(Baton Rouge, 1979), 196; Jane Brewerton, Feb. 29, 1760, Assi 45/26/4/6.

28. Jan. 23, 1574, I. H. Van Eeghen, ed., *Dagboek Van Broeder Wouter Jacobsz (Gaultherus Jacobi Masius Prior Van Stein: Amsterdam, 1572–1578, En Montfoort, 1578–1579)* (Gronningen, Neth., 1959), 359.
29. Thomas Dekker, *The Seven Deadly Sinnes of London*, ed. H.F.B. Brett-Smith (New York, 1922), 41; Nicolas-Edme Restif de la Bretonne, *Les Nuits de Paris or the Nocturnal Spectator* (New York, 1964), 68; *Select Trials*, II, 11; Legg, *Low-Life*, 100; Wilson, *English Proverbs*, 542; *OED*, s.v. "flitting."
30. Dekker, *Writings*, 230; Richard Head, *The Canting Academy; or Villanies Discovered . . .* (London, 1674), 37, 40; Roger B. Manning, *Village Revolts: Social Protest and Popular Disturbances in England, 1509–1640* (Oxford, 1988), 173; Gilbert Slater, *The English Peasantry and the Enclosure of Common Fields* (1907; rpt. edn., New York, 1968), 119–120; Hugh Evans, *The Gorse Glen*, trans. E. Morgan Humphreys (Liverpool, 1948), 70.
31. Carol F. Karlsen, *The Devil in the Shape of a Woman: Witchcraft in Colonial New England* (New York, 1987), 159; Alan Taylor, "The Early Republic's Supernatural Economy: Treasure Seeking in the American Northeast, 1780–1830," *American Quarterly* 38 (1986), 6–34 (I want to thank Alan Taylor for providing me with a copy of his article); William W. Hagen, *Ordinary Prussians: Brandenburg, Junkers and Villagers, 1500–1840* (Cambridge, 2002), 479; W. R. Jones, "'Hill-Diggers' and 'Hell-Raisers': Treasure Hunting and the Supernatural in Old and New England," in Peter Benes, ed., *Wonders of the Invisible World: 1600–1900* (Boston, 1995), 97–106. See also Benjamin Franklin, *Writings*, ed. J. A. Leo Lemay (New York, 1987), 113–115.
32. *PA*, Jan. 3, 1786; Rose, ed., *Slavery*, 460; Malcolm Letts, "Johannes Butzbach, a Wandering Scholar of the Fifteenth Century," *English Historical Review* 32 (1917), 31; Thomas, *Relgion and the Decline of Magic*, 506–523; H. C. Erik Midelfort, "Were There Really Witches," in Robert M. Kingdon, ed., *Transition and Revolution: Problems and Issues of European Renaissance and Reformation History* (Minneapolis, 1974), 198–199; David Thomas Konig, *Law and Society in Puritan Massachusetts: Essex County, 1629–1692* (Chapel Hill, N.C., 1979), 145–179, passim.
33. Karlsen, *Shape of a Woman*, 140; *SWP*, II, 413; *NHTR*, II, 130–131.
34. Pinkerton, *Travels*, III, 316; *Carmina Medii Aevi* (Torino, 1961), 35; Jütte, *Poverty*, 152–153. See also *Letters from Barbary, France, Spain, Portugal . . .* (London, 1788), II, 113.
35. June 2, 1663, Pepys, *Diary*, IV, 171; Beattie, *Crime*, 173–175. See also Best, *Books*, 35.
36. *Domestic Management, or the Art of Conducting a Family; with Instructions to Servants in General* (London, 1740), 59; Pinkerton, *Travels*, III, 316; Mar. 22, 1770, Carter, *Diary*, I, 372; John Greaves Nall, ed., *Etymological and Comparative Glossary of the Dialect of East Anglia* (London, 1866), 521; William Hector, ed., *Selections from the Judicial Records of Renfrewshire . . .* (Paisley, Scot., 1876), 203–204.
37. Newton D. Mereness, ed., *Travels in the American Colonies, 1690–1783* (New York, 1916), 592, 606–607; John C. Fitzpatrick, ed., *The Writings of George Washington* (Washington, D.C., 1939), XXXII, 264; Richard Parkinson, *The Experienced Farmer's Tour in America* (London, 1805), 446–447; James M. Rosenheim, ed., *The Notebook of Robert Doughty, 1662–1665* (Norfolk, 1989), 39; Morgan, *Slave Counterpoint*, passim.
38. Manning, *Village Revolts*, 296, 284–305, passim; Rachel N. Klein, "Ordering the Backcountry: The South Carolina Regulation," *WMQ*, 3rd Ser., 38 (1981), 671–672.
39. Robert Bell, *Early Ballads . . .* (London, 1889), 436–437; David Davies, *The Case of Labourers in Husbandry . . .* (Dublin, 1796), 77; Spike Mays, *Reuben's Corner* (London, 1969), 197; Frank McLynn, *Crime and Punishment in Eighteenth-Century England* (London, 1989), 172–197. See also *Walker's Hibernian Magazine*, April 1792, 296.
40. *LEP*, Oct. 5, 1738; Arthur Walter Slater, ed., *Autobiographical Memoir of Joseph Jewell,*

1763–1846 (London, 1964), 134; Cal Winslow, "Sussex Smugglers," in Douglas Hay et al., eds., *Albion's Fatal Tree: Crime and Society in Eighteenth-Century England* (New York, 1975), 119–166; Hufton, *Poor of Eighteenth-Century France*, 284–305.

41. Defoe, *Tour*, I, 123; *OED*, s.v. "owler"; McLynn, *Crime and Punishment*, 177; Burton E. Stevenson, *The Home Book of Proverbs, Maxims and Familiar Phrases* (New York, 1948), 1623; Eric Partridge, ed., *A Dictionary of the Underworld* . . . (New York, 1950),449; Dec. 13, 1794, Woodforde, *Diary*, IV, 160, passim; Slater, ed., *Jewell Memoir*, 135; "Extract of a Letter from Orford," *LC*, March 23, 1782; John Kelso Hunter, *The Retrospect of an Artist's Life: Memorials of West Countrymen and Manners of the Past Half Century* (Kilmarnock, Scot., 1912), 42.

42. T.J.A. Le Goff and D.M.G. Sutherland, "The Revolution and the Rural Community in Eighteenth-Century Brittany," *PP* 62 (1974), 100; Jütte, *Poverty*, 153–156. In contrast to smuggling, "wrecking," whereby shipwrecked vessels were pillaged by coastal inhabitants, was not, exclusively, a nocturnal crime. Despite occasional allegations that false lights at night were displayed ashore to lure ships aground, the evidence for this is scanty. Otherwise, plunderers looted wrecks as soon as they could, whatever the hour. See "An Act for Enforcing the Laws Against Persons Who Shall Steal or Detain Shipwrecked Goods . . . ," 26 George II c.19; W. H. Porter, *A Fenman's Story* (London, 1965), 129; John G. Rule, "Wrecking and Coastal Plunder," in Hay et al., eds., *Albion's Fatal Tree*, 180–181.

43. Tobias Smollett, *Travels through France and Italy* (Oxford, 1979), 215; Cannon, Diary, 183; *OBP*, Sept. 18, 1752, 244; Richard Jefferson, Oct. 16, 1734, Assi 45/20/1/9; D. R. Hainsworth, *Stewards, Lords, and People: The Estate Steward and His World in Later Stuart England* (Cambridge, 1992), 208–209; Jim Bullock, *Bowers Row: Recollections of a Mining Village* (Wakefield, Eng., 1976), 163; Douglas Hay, "Poaching and the Game Laws on Canock Chase," in Hay et al., eds., *Albion's Fatal Tree*, 201–202; Manning, *Village Revolts*, 293; Douglas Hay "War, Dearth and Theft in the Eighteenth Century: The Record of the English Courts," *PP* 95 (1982), 117–160. As E. P. Thompson put it, "The same man who touches his forelock to the squire by day—and who goes down to history as an example of deference—may kill his sheep, snare his pheasants or poison his dogs at night" (*Customs in Common: Studies in Traditional Popular Culture* [New York, 1991], 66).

44. Robert M. Isherwood, *Farce and Fantasy: Popular Entertainment in Eighteenth-Century Paris* (New York, 1986), 208; Roger Thompson, *Unfit for Modest Ears: A Study of Pornographic, Obscene and Bawdy Works Written or Published in England in the Second Half of the Seventeenth Century* (Totowa, N.J., 1979), 59; Alexander Hamilton, *Gentleman's Progress: The Itinerarium of Dr. Alexander Hamilton, 1744*, ed. Carl Bridenbaugh (Chapel Hill, N.C., 1948), 46; "T.S.C.P.," *PA*, Nov. 13, 1767; Kathryn Norberg, "Prostitutes," in *HWW* III, 459–474.

45. Helen Langdon, *Caravaggio: A Life* (New York, 1999), 144; Ferrante Pallavicino, *The Whores Rhetorick* . . . (London, 1683), 144; *OBP*, passim; Norberg, "Prostitutes," 462, 472–474.

46. *OBP*, Dec. 7–12, 1743, 13, Dec. 9–11, 1747, 15; J. M. Beattie, "The Criminality of Women in Eighteenth-Century England," *JSH* 8 (1975), 90.

47. Koslofsky, "Court Culture," 759; Fréderique Pitou, "Jeunesse et Désordre Social: Les 'Coureurs de Nuit' à Laval au XVIIIe Siècle," *Revue d'Histoire Moderne et Contemporaine* 47 (2000), 69; Ferdinando Bottarelli, *The New Italian, English and French Pocket-Dictionary* . . . (London, 1795), I; S.A.H. Burne, ed., *The Staffordshire Quarter Sessions Rolls, 1581–[1606]* (Kendall, Eng., 1940), V, 238; *PA*, July 30, 1762; Davenant, *Works*; *The Acts and Resolves, Public and Private, of the Province of Massachusetts Bay* (Boston, 1881), III, 647; Daniel Fabre, "Families: Privacy versus Custom," in *HPL* III, 546–561.

48. Schindler, *Rebellion*, 210; Matthiessen, *Natten*, 137; Rudolf Braun, *Industrialization and Everyday Life*, trans. Sarah Hanbury Tension (Cambridge, 1990), 84; *Minutes of the Common Council of the City of Philadelphia, 1704–1776* (Philadelphia, 1847), 405; J. R. Ward, "A Planter and His Slaves in Eighteenth-Century Jamaica," in T. C. Smout, ed., *The Search for Wealth and Stability: Essays in Economic and Social History Presented to M. W. Flinn* (London, 1979), 19.
49. *HMM and GA*, Mar. 10, 1752; Koslofsky, "Court Culture," 760; Pitou, "Coureurs de Nuit," 72, 82–84; Elisabeth Crouzet-Pavan, "Potere Politico e Spazio Sociale," in Mario Sbriccoli, ed., *La Notte: Ordine, Sicurezza e Disciplinamento in Età Moderna* (Florence, 1991), 61; Maurice Andrieux, *Daily Life in Venice in the Time of Casanova*, trans. Mary Fitton (London, 1972), 29; Elizabeth S. Cohen, "Honor and Gender in the Streets of Early Rome," *JIH* 22 (1992), 597–625; Matthiessen, *Natten*, 129; Schindler, "Youthful Culture," 258–260; Auguste Philippe Herlaut, "L'Èclairage des Rues à Paris à la Fin du XVIIe Siècle et au XVIIIe Siècles," *Mémoire de la Société de l'Histoire de Paris et de l'Ile-de-France* 43 (1916), 221–222, 226.
50. Iona Opie and Moira Tatem, eds., *A Dictionary of Superstitions* (Oxford, 1989), 142; Washington Irving, *History, Tales and Sketches*, ed. James W. Tuttleton (New York, 1983), 1071–1072; Darryl Ogier, "Night Revels and Werewolfery in Calvinist Guernsey," *Folklore* 109 (1998), 56–57; Lavater, *Spirites*, 21–22; A.Voisin, "Notes sur la Vie Urbaine au XV. Siècle: Dijon la Nuit," *Annales de Bourgogne* 9 (1937), 271.
51. D. M. Ogier, *Reformation and Society in Guernsey* (Rochester, N.Y., 1996), 137; Apr. 30, 1673, Isham, *Diary*, 207; Pavan, "*Nuit Vénitienne*," 345; Muchembled, *Violence*, 124.
52. Schindler, "Youthful Culture," 275; Evelyn, *Diary*, II, 472; Mar. 25, 1668, Pepys, *Diary*, IX, 133.
53. Moryson, *Itinerary*, IV, 373; Hannah Miurk[?], Feb. 28, 1677, Suffolk Court Files #1549, Suffolk County Court House, Boston; Janekovick-Römer, "Dubrovniks," 103; Koslofsky, "Court Culture," 755; Jacques Rossiaud, "Prostitution, Youth, and Society," in Robert Forster and Orest Ranum, eds., *Deviants and the Abandoned in French Society: Selections from the Annales Economies, Sociétés, Civilisations*, trans. Elborg Forster and Patricia Ranum (Baltimore, 1978), 12–13; Aug. 16, 1624, Beck, *Diary*, 152; T. Platter, *Journal*, 249; George Huppert, *After the Black Death: A Social History of Early Modern Europe* (Bloomington, Ind., 1986), 38.
54. Fabre, "Families," 547; Schindler, "Youthful Culture," 261; Dec. 26, 1718, Lewis, Diary; James R. Farr, *Hands of Honor: Artisans and Their World in Dijon, 1550–1650* (Ithaca, N.Y., 1988), 211; Muchembled, *Violence*, 124; Pitou, "Coureurs de Nuit," 73–74. See also Nov. 20, 1680, Heywood, *Diary*, I, 276.
55. Eli Faber, "The Evil That Men Do: Crime and Transgression in Colonial Massachusetts" (Ph.D. diss., Columbia Univ., 1974), 168; *VG*, Aug. 28, 1752; *Boston Gazette*, Jan. 8, 1754; Sept. 6, 1774, *The Journal of Nicholas Cresswell* (New York, 1924), 35; *NYWJ*, May 22, 1738; Morgan, *Slave Counterpoint*, 394–398.
56. James C. Scott, "Everyday Forms of Peasant Resistance," in James C. Scott and Benedict J. Kerkvliet, eds., *Everyday Forms of Peasant Resistance in South-east Asia* (London, 1986), 6. This is not to deny that celebrations of Carnival stometimes produced unforeseen disorder, especially after nightfall. See Davis, *Society and Culture*, 103–104, 117–119, 122–123; Mikhail Baktin, *Rabelais and His World*, trans. Helene Iswoldky (Cambridge, Mass., 1968).
57. M. Dorothy George, *London Life in the XVIIIth Century* (London, 1925), 280; Joe Thompson, *The Life and Adventures . . .* (London, 1788), I, 93; "Advice to Apprentices," *Walker's Hibernian Magazine* (1791), 151; Awnsham Churchill, comp., *A Collection of Voyages and Travels . . .* (London, 1746), VI, 542; Philip D. Morgan, "Black Life in Eighteenth-

Century Charleston," *Perspectives in American History*, New Ser., 1 (1984), 324–325; Fabre, "Families," 550, 548.

58. Pitou, "Coureurs de Nuit," 88; *A Report of the Record Commissioners of the City of Boston, Containing the Selectmen's Minutes from 1764 to 1768* (Boston, 1889), 100; *OED*, s.v. "scour"; Burne, ed., *Staffordshire Quarter Sessions*, V, 238. See also Matthiessen, *Natten*, 137–139; "John Blunt," *G and NDA*, Oct. 31, 1765.
59. George, *London Life*, 400 n. 101; *OBP*, Sept. 7, 1737, 187, 190.
60. Defoe, *Tour*, I, 123; Robert Semple, *Observations on a Journey through Spain and Italy to Naples*... (London, 1807), II, 218.
61. F. G. Emmison, *Elizabethan Life: Disorder* (Chelmsford, Eng., 1970), 245; Ann Kussmaul, ed., *The Autobiography of Joseph Mayett of Quainton (1783–1839)* (London, 1979), 14–15.
62. V. S. Naipaul, *The Loss of El Dorado: A History* (London, 1969), 251–257; Davis, *Society and Culture*, 97–123; Bernard Capp, "English Youth Groups and 'The Pinder of Wakefield,'" *PP* 76 (1977), 128–129; Giffiths, *Youth*, 169–175; Janekovick-Römer, "Dubrovniks," 110; Ilana Krausman Ben-Amos, *Adolescence and Youth in Early Modern England* (New Haven, 1994), 176–177. For the concept of "overlapping sub-cultures," see Bob Scribner, "Is a History of Popular Culture Possible?," *History of European Ideas* 10 (1989), 184–185; David Underdown, "Regional Cultures? Local Variations in Popular Culture during the Early Modern Period," in Tim Harris, ed., *Popular Culture in England, c. 1500–1800* (New York, 1995), 29.
63. Jütte, *Poverty*, 180–185; Schindler, *Rebellion*, 275; *The Honour of London Apprentices: Exemplified, in a Brief Historicall Narration* (London, 1647); Richard Mowery Andrews, *Law, Magistracy, and Crime in Old Regime Paris, 1735–1789* (Cambridge, 1994), 521–535; "A Constant Correspondent," *PA*, Apr. 22, 1763; Dekker, *Writings*, 187–191; Schindler, "Youthful Culture," 248–249; A. L. Beier, *Masterless Men: The Vagrancy Problem in England, 1560–1640* (London, 1985), 125–126.
64. Torriano, *Proverbi Italiani*, 34; Robert W. Malcolmson, *Popular Recreations in English Society, 1700–1850* (Cambridge, 1973), 75.
65. Marston, *The Malcontent*, ed. M. L. Wine (Lincoln, Neb., 1964), 64.
66. Griffiths, *Youth*, 151–152; Davis, *Society and Culture*, 104–123; Fabre, "Families," 533–556, passim; Thompson, *Customs in Common*, 467–533; Burke, *Popular Culture*, 199–201.
67. Fabre, "Families," 555–566; *The Libertine's Choice*... (London, 1704), 14–15; F. Platter, *Journal*, 172; Schindler, "Youthful Culture," 252–253; Giffiths, *Youth*, 397.
68. *American Weekly Mercury* (Philadelphia), Oct. 21, 1736; John Brewer, *Party Ideology and Popular Politics at the Accession of George III* (Cambridge, 1976), 186–188; Stanley H. Palmer, *Police and Protest in England and Ireland, 1780–1850* (Cambridge, 1988), 129–130.
69. Jean Delumeau, *Sin and Fear: The Emergence of a Western Guilt Culture, 13th–18th Centuries*, trans. Eric Nicholson (New York, 1990), 128; Muchembled, *Violence*, 241; Malcolmson, *Recreations*, 60–61, 75–76, 81–84; Burke, *Popular Culture*, 190, 201–203.
70. Bourne, *Antiquitates Vulgares*, 229–230; Henry Fielding, *An Enquiry into the Causes of the Late Increase of Robbers and Related Writings*, ed. Malvin R. Zirker (Middletown, Ct., 1988), 81; Stephen Duck, *Poems on Several Occasions* (London, 1736), 27.
71. Parkinson, *Farmer's Tour*, 440; *G and NDA*, Sept. 15, 1767; Paul S. Seaver, "Declining Status in an Aspiring Age: The Problem of the Gentle Apprentice in Seventeenth-Century London," in Bonnelyn Young Kunze and Dwight D. Brautigam, eds., *Court, Country and Culture: Essays on Early Modern British History in Honor of Perez Zagorin* (Rochester, N.Y., 1992), 139–140; Dekker, *Writings*, 173.
72. Oct. 13, 1703, May 20, 21, 1704, Jan. 27, 1707, Cowper, Diary; Oct. 15, 1780, Nov. 25,

1782, Woodforde, *Diary*, I, 293, II, 45; Carter, *Diary*, I, 359; Henry Wakefield, Aug. 4, 1729, Assi 45/18/7/1; Eric Robinson, ed., *John Clare's Autobiographical Writings* (Oxford, 1983), 62.

73. Robinson, ed., *Clare's Autobiographical Writings*, 167; *OBP*, Oct. 16, 1723, 7; May 24, 1711, Cowper, Diary; Marybeth Carlson, "Domestic Service in a Changing City Economy: Rotterdam, 1680–1780" (Ph.D. diss., Univ. of Wisconsin, 1993), 132; Fairchilds, *Domestic Enemies*, 209; Patricia S. Seleski, "The Women of the Laboring Poor: Love, Work and Poverty in London, 1750–1820" (Ph.D. diss., Stanford Univ., 1989), 89.

74. Jan., 24, 1770, Carter, *Diary*, I, 348; Fitzpatrick, ed., *Washington Writings*, XXXII, 246, XXXIII, 369, 444; Gladys-Marie Fry, *Night Riders in Black Folk History* (Knoxville, Tenn., 1975), 60–73; Morgan, *Slave Counterpoint*, 524–526.

75. Griffiths, *Youth*, 78; Manning, *Village Revolts*, 72–73, 97, 197, 207; Mihoko Suzuki, "The London Apprentice Riots of the 1590s and the Fiction of Thomas Deloney," *Criticism* 38 (1996), 181–182; Matthiessen, *Natten*, 139; Thomas Willard Robisheaux, *Rural Society and the Search for Order in Early Modern Germany* (Cambridge, 1989), 119; Koslofsky, "Court Culture," 759; Martina Orosová, "Bratislavskí Zobráci V 18. Storocí," *Slovenska Archivistika* 34 (1999), 95; Faber, "Evil That Men Do," 169–171; William M. Wiecek, "The Statutory Law of Slavery and Race in the Thirteen Mainland Colonies of British America," *WMQ*, 3rd Ser., 34 (1977), 272; Carl Bridenbaugh, *Cities in the Wilderness: The First Century of Urban Life in America, 1625–1742* (Oxford, 1971), 219.

76. *WJ*, Apr. 20, 1723; *Life of Michael Martin, Who Was Executed for Highway Robbery, December 20, 1821* (Boston, 1821), 6–7; Keith Lindley, *Fenland Riots and the English Revolution* (London, 1982), passim; Manning, *Village Revolts*, 217–218; *G and NDA*, Aug. 24, Sept. 9, 13, 1769; J. R. Dinwiddy, "The 'Black Lamp' in Yorkshire, 1801–1802," *PP* 64 (1974), 118–119; Assi 45/25/2/30; *Whitehall Evening-Post* (London), Aug. 3, 1749; Andrew Barrett and Christopher Harrison, eds., *Crime and Punishment in England: A Sourcebook* (London, 1999), 169–170.

77. E. P. Thompson, "The Crime of Anonymity," in Hay et al., eds., *Albion's Fatal Tree*, 278; Thomas D. Morris, *Southern Slavery and the Law, 1619–1860* (Chapel Hill, N.C., 1996), 330–332; Bob Scribner, "The Mordbrenner Fear," in Richard J. Evans, ed., *The German Underworld: Deviants and Outcasts in German History* (London, 1988), 29–56; Penny Roberts, "Arson, Conspiracy and Rumor in Early Modern Europe," *Continuity and Change* 12 (1997), 9–29; André Abbiateci, "Arsonists in Eighteenth-Century France: An Essay in the Typology of Crime," in Forster and Ranum, eds., *Deviants and the Abandoned*, trans. Forster and Ranum, 157–179; Bernard Capp, "Arson, Threats of Arson, and Incivility in Early Modern England," in Peter Burke et al., eds., *Civil Histories: Essays Presented to Sir Keith Thomas* (Oxford, 2000), 199–200.

78. Morgan, *Slave Counterpoint*, 309; Kenneth Scott, "The Slave Insurrection in New York," *New York Historical Quarterly* 45 (1961), 43–74; Rose, ed., *Slavery*, 99–101, 104, 109–113; Michael Craton, *Testing the Chains: Resistance to Slavery in the British West Indies* (Ithaca, N.Y., 1982), passim; Wood, *Black Majority*, 308–326; James Sidbury, *Ploughshares into Swords: Race, Rebellion, and Identity in Gabriel's Virginia, 1730–1810* (New York, 1997); David Barry Gaspar, *Bondmen & Rebels: A Study of Master-Slave Relations in Antigua* (Baltimore, 1985), 222; Elsa V. Goveia, *Slave Society in the British Leeward Islands at the End of the Eighteenth Century* (Westport, Ct., 1980), 184; Beckles, *Black Rebellion*, passim; Gwendolyn Midlo Hall, *Africans in Colonial Louisiana: The Development of Afro-Creole Culture in the Eighteenth Century* (Baton Rouge, 1992), 354–355.

79. Lindley, *Fenland Riots*, 179; E. P. Thompson, *The Making of the English Working Class* (New York, 1964), 559, 565; Gaspar, *Bondmen & Rebels*, 246–247; Craton, *Testing the Chains*, 122–123; Scott, "Slave Insurrection in New York," 47; James S. Donnelly Jr., "The

Whiteboy Movement, 1761–5," *Irish Historical Studies* 21 (1978), 23; Peter Sahlins, *Forest Rites: The War of the Demoiselles in Nineteenth-Century France* (Cambridge, Mass., 1994), 42–47.

PART FOUR

PRELUDE

1. Geoffrey Keynes, ed., *The Works of Sir Thomas Browne* (London, 1931), III, 230.
2. Alastair Fowler, ed., *The New Oxford Book of Seventeenth Century Verse* (Oxford, 1991), 416; Stanley Coren, *Sleep Thieves: An Eye-Opening Exploration into the Science and Mysteries of Sleep* (New York, 1996), 9; "Why Did the Caveman Sleep? (Not Just Because He Was Tired)," *Psychology Today* 16 (March 1982), 30; Burton E. Stevenson, ed., *The Home Book of Proverbs, Maxims and Familiar Phrases* (New York, 1948), 1685; Carol M. Worthman and Melissa K. Melby, "Toward a Comparative Ecology of Human Sleep," in Mary A. Carskadon, ed., *Adolescent Sleep Patterns: Biological, Social and Psychological Influences* (Cambridge, 2002), 102–103.
3. Thomas Cogan, *The Haven of Health* (London, 1588), 233; [Joseph Hall], *The Discovery of a New World* (Amsterdam, 1969), 219–244.
4. *The Adventurer*, Mar. 20, 1753, 229; Craig Tomlinson, "G. C. Lichtenberg: Dreams, Jokes, and the Unconscious in Eighteenth-Century Germany," *Journal of the American Psychoanalytic Association* 40 (1992), 781. Other than Francis Bacon, who projected a history of sleep, most ardent in highlighting the importance of historical research has been George Steiner. Studies of sleep, Steiner has argued, "would be as essential, if not more so, to our grasp of the evolution of mores and sensibilities as are the histories of dress, of eating, of child-care, of mental and physical infirmity, which social historians and the *historiens des mentalités* are at last providing for us" *No Passion Spent: Essays 1978–1996* [London, 1996], 211–212). More recently, Daniel Roche has implored, "Let us dream of a social history of sleep" (*Consumption*, 182). Historical accounts of dreams have included Peter Burke, "L'Histoire Sociale des Rêves," *Annales Economies, Sociétés, Civilisations* 28 (1973), 329–342; Richard L. Kagan, *Lucrecia's Dreams: Politics and Prophecy in Sixteenth-Century Spain* (Berkeley, Calif., 1990); Steven F. Kruger, *Dreaming in the Middle Ages* (Cambridge, 1992); Carole Susan Fungaroli, "Landscapes of Life: Dreams in Eighteenth-Century British Fiction and Contemporary Dream Theory" (Ph.D. diss., Univ. of Virginia., 1994); S.R.F. Price, "The Future of Dreams: From Freud to Artemidorous," *PP* 113 (1986), 3–37; Manfred Weidhorn, *Dreams in Seventeenth-Century English Literature* (The Hague, 1970); David Shulman and Guy G. Stroumsa, eds. *Dream Cultures: Explorations in the Comparative History of Dreaming* (New York, 1999); Mechal Sobel, *Teach Me Dreams: The Search for Self in the Revolutionary Era* (Princeton, N.J., 2000). Attitudes toward sleep, from the ancient world to the twentieth century, are chronicled in Jaume Rosselló Mir et al., "Una Aproximacion Historica al Estudio Cientifico de Sueño: El Periodo Intuitivo el Pre-Cientifico," *Revista de Historia de la Psicologia* 12 (1991), 133–142. For a brief survey of sleep in the Middle Ages, see Verdon, *Night*, 203–217; and for an examination of key medical texts touching on sleep during the early modern era, see Karl H. Dannenfeldt, "Sleep: Theory and Practice in the Late Renaissance," *Journal of the History of Medicine* 41 (1986), 415–441. More recently, Phillipe Martin has analyzed the attitudes of Catholic authors toward sleep during the eighteenth century. "Corps en Repos ou Corps en Danger?

Le Sommeil dans les Livres de Piété (Seconde Moitré du XVIIIe Siècle)," *Revue d'Histoire et de Philosophie Religieuses* 80 (2000), 255.

5. Wodrow, *Analecta: or, Materials for a History of Remarkable Providences* . . . , ed. Matthew Leishman (Edinburgh, 1843), III, 496; James Miller, *The Universal Passion* (London, 1737), 46.

CHAPTER TEN

1. *WR or UJ*, Sept. 22, 1738
2. Cogan, *The Haven of Health* (London, 1588), 232–233; Karl H. Dannenfeldt, "Sleep: Theory and Practice in the Late Renaissance," *Journal of the History of Medicine* 41 (1986), 422–424.
3. Vaughan, *Naturall and Artificial Directions for Health*. . . (London, 1607), 53; Henry Davidoff, ed., *World Treasury of Proverbs*. . . (New York, 1946), 25; Dannenfeldt, "Renaissance Sleep," 7–12.
4. John Trusler, *An Easy Way to Prolong Life*. . . (London, 1775), 11; F.K. Robinson, comp., *A Glossary of Words Used in the Neighbourhood of Whitby* (London, 1876), 55; Tilley, *Proverbs in England*, 36.
5. Wilson, *English Proverbs*, 389.
6. *The Whole Duty of Man* . . . (London, 1691), 188–189; Stephen Innes, *Creating the Commonwealth: The Economic Culture of Puritan New England* (New York, 1995), 124; *The Schoole of Vertue, and Booke of Good Nourture*. . . (London, 1557); *An Essay on Particular Advice to the Young Gentry* . . . (London, 1711), 170; David Hackett Fischer, *Albion's Seed: Four British Folkways in America* (New York, 1989), 160–161.
7. Andrew Boorde, *A Compendyous Regyment or a Dyetary of Health*. . . (London, 1547); Levinus Lemnius, *Touchstone of Complexions*. . ., trans. T. Newton (London, 1576), 57.
8. Robert Macnish, *The Philosophy of Sleep*, ed. Daniel N. Robinson (Washington, D.C., 1977), 279; Boorde, *Compendyous Regyment*; Lawrence Wright, *Warm and Snug: The History of the Bed* (London, 1962), 195.
9. William Bullein, *A Newe Boke of Phisicke Called y Goveriment of Health*. . . (London, 1559), 91; Boorde, *Compendyous Regyment*; Tobias Venner, *Via Recta ad Vitam Longam* . . . (London, 1637), 279–280; *Directions and Observations Relative to Food, Exercise and Sleep* (London, 1772), 22; Dannenfeldt, "Renaissance Sleep," 430.
10. Wilson, *English Proverbs*, 738; Torriano, *Proverbi*, 76; Wright, *Warm and Snug*, 194; Gratarolus, *A Direction for the Health of Magistrates and Studentes* (London, 1574); Sir Thomas Elyot, *The Castel of Helthe* (New York, 1937), iii; Dannenfeldt, "Renaissance Sleep," *JHM*, 420.
11. Jan. 29, 1624, Beck, *Diary*, 39.
12. John Wilson, *The Projectors* (London, 1665), 45.
13. Nov. 27, 1705, Cowper, Diary; Schindler, *Rebellion*, 216; Lean, *Collectanea*, I, 503; Wright, *Warm and Snug*, 117; Matthiessen, *Natten*, 8–9.
14. Eric Sloane, *The Seasons of America Past* (New York, 1958), 26; Feb. 8, 1756, Dec. 26, 1763, Turner, *Diary*, 26–27, 283; Carol M. Worthman and Melissa K. Melby, "Toward a Comparative Developmental Ecology of Human Sleep," in Mary A. Carskadon, ed., *Adolescent Sleep Patterns: Biological, Social, and Psychological Influences* (Cambridge, 2002), 79.
15. W. F., *The Schoole of Good Manners* (London, 1609).
16. "Letter of M. Brady," *LC*, July 31, 1764; Arthur Friedman, ed., *Collected Works of Oliver*

Goldsmith (Oxford, 1966), II, 214–218; James Boswell, *The Hypochondriack*, ed. Margery Bailey (Stanford, Calif., 1928), II, 110; George Steiner, *No Passion Spent: Essays, 1978–1996* (London, 1996), 211–212; Simon B. Chandler, "Shakespeare and Sleep," *Bulletin of the History of Medicine* 29 (1955), 255–260.

17. Torriano, *Proverbi*, 77; "Wits Private Wealth," in Breton, Works, II, 9; *Another Collection of Philosophical Conferences of the French Virtuosi* . . . , trans. G. Havers and J. Davies (London, 1665), 419; Richard Oliver Heslop, comp., *Northumberland Words* . . . (1892; rpt. edn., Vaduz, Liecht., 1965), I, 248, II, 659; Alexander Hislop, comp., *The Proverbs of Scotland* (Edinburgh, 1870), 346.
18. William Rowley, *All's Lost By Lust* (London, 1633); Thomas Shadwell, *The Amorous Bigotte* (London, 1690), 43; *The Dramatic Works of Sir William D'Avenant* (New York, 1964), 146; Boswell, *Hypochondriack*, ed. Bailey, II, 112; Erik Eckholm, "Exploring the Forces of Sleep," *New York Times Magazine*, Apr. 17, 1988, 32.
19. James Hervey, *Meditations and Contemplations* . . . (London, 1752), II, 42; Boswell, *Hypochondriack*, ed. Bailey, II, 110; N. Caussin, *The Christian Diary* (London, 1652), 35; June 2, 1706, Cowper, Diary; Alan of Lille, *The Art of Preaching*, trans. G.R. Evans (Kalamazoo, Mich., 1981), 135. For Freud's influential discussion of "neurotic ceremonials" pertaining to sleep, see his "Obsessive Actions and Religious Practices," in James Strachey, ed., *The Standard Edition of the Complete Psychological Works of Sigmund Freud* (London, 1975), IX, 117–118; Barry Schwartz, "Notes on the Sociology of Sleep," *Sociological Quarterly* 11 (1970), 494–495.
20. *Herbert's Devotions* . . . (London, 1657), 237; Walter L. Straus, ed., *The German Single-Leaf Woodcut, 1550–1600: A Pictorial Catalogue* (New York, 1975), II, 739; Stephen Bateman, *A Christall Glasse of Christian Reformation* . . . (London, 1569).
21. Eugen Weber, *My France: Politics, Culture, Myth* (Cambridge, Mass., 1991), 85; Thomas Moffett, *The History of Four-Footed Beasts and Serpents* . . . (London, 1658), II, 956–957; July 16, 1678, John Lough, ed., *Locke's Travels in France, 1675–1679* (Cambridge, 1953), 207; John Southall, *A Treatise of Buggs* . . . (London, 1730); J.F.D. Shrewsbury, *The Plague of the Philistines and Other Medical-Historical Essays* (London, 1964), 146–161.
22. July 16, 1784, Torrington, *Diaries*, I, 174; James P. Horn, *Adapting to a New World: English Society in the Seventeenth-Century Chesapeake* (Chapel Hill, N.C., 1994), 318–319. The day before arriving home from a journey, Sylas Neville dispatched a note requesting that his housekeeper and her daughter sleep that night in his bed to "season" it (Basil Cozens-Hardy, ed., *The Diary of Sylas Neville, 1767–1788* [London, 1950], 162).
23. Carolyn Pouncy, ed., *The "Domostroi": Rules for Russian Households in the Time of Ivan the Terrible* (Ithaca, N.Y., 1994), 170; Anna Brzozowska-Krajka, *Polish Traditional Folklore: The Magic of Time* (Boulder, Colo, 1998), 119; *PA*, Mar. 20, 1764.
24. Steven Bradwell, *A Watch-man for the Pest* . . . (London, 1625), 39; Oct. 20, 1763, Frederick A. Pottle, ed., *Boswell in Holland 1763–1764* (New York, 1952), 49–50; Venner, *Via Recta*, 275; Israel Spach, *Theses Medicae de Somno et Vigilia* . . . (Strasburg, 1597).
25. Jon Cowans, ed., *Early Modern Spain: A Documentary History* (Philadelphia, 2003), 121; Alan Macfarlane, *The Justice and the Mare's Ale: Law and Disorder in Seventeenth-Century England* (Oxford, 1981), 56; John C. Fitzpatrick, ed., *The Writings of George Washington* . . . (Washington, D.C., 1931), I, 17. Information is sparse about sleeping garments, but see C. Willett and Phillis Cunnington, *The History of Underclothes* (London, 1951), 41–43, 52, 61; Almut Junker, *Zur Geschichte der Unterwäsche 1700–1960: eine Ausstellung des Historischen Museums Frankfurt, 28 April bis 28 August 1988* (Frankfurt, 1988), 10–78; Norbert Elias, *The Civilizing Process: The Development of Manners* . . . , trans. Edmund Jephcott (New York, 1978), I, 164–165. For the absence of clothing among sleepers, see

Edmond Cottinet, "La Nudité au Lit Selon Cathos et l'Histoire," *Le Moliériste* (April 1883), 20–25 (June 1883) 86–89; Dannednfeldt, "Renaissance Sleep," 426.

26. Randle Cotgrave, *A Dictionaire of the French and English Tongues* (London, 1611); Laurence Sterne, *The Life & Opinions of Tristam Shandy, Gentleman* (New York, 1950), 568; Sept. 22, 1660, Pepy, *Diary*, I, 251; Alison Weir, *Henry VIII: The King and His Court* (New York, 2001), 84.
27. *The Queens Closet Opened* . . . (London, 1661), 60–61, 101–102; Aug. 11, 1678, Michael Hunter and Annabel Gregory, eds., *An Astrological Diary of the Seventeenth Century: Samuel Jeake of Rye, 1652–1699* (Oxford, 1988), 140; Christof Wirsung, *Praxis Medicinae Universalis; or a Generall Practise of Phisicke* . . . (London, 1598), 618.
28. Moryson, *Itinerary*, IV, 44; "T.C.," *PL*, Dec. 5, 1765. In the *Celestina: A Novel in Dialogue* by Fernando de Rojas, trans. Lesley Byrd Simpson (Berkeley, Calif., 1971), the protagonist says of wine, "There's no better warming pan on a winter's night. If I drink three little jugs like this when I go to bed I don't feel the cold all night long" (104).
29. Bradwell, *Watch-man*, 38; "W.," *LC*, Oct. 9, 1763; Henry G. Bohn, *A Hand-book of Proverbs* . . . (London, 1855), 28; May 25, 1767, Cozens-Hardy, ed., *Neville Diary*, 8; Feb. 29, 1756, Turner, *Diary*, 32.
30. Thomas Elyot, *The Castel of Helthe* (London, 1539), fo. 46; Governal, *In this Tretyse that Is Cleped Governayle of Helthe* (New York, 1969); Bullein, *Goveriment of Health*, 90.
31. Sept. 29, 1661, Pepys, *Diary*, II, 186; *East Anglian Diaries*, 51; Thomas, *Religion and the Decline of Magic*, 113–128; François Lebrun, "The Two Reformations: Communal Devotion and Personal Piety," in *HPL* III, 96–97. References to the "lock" of the night may be found in Owen Feltham, *Resolves* (London, 1628), 406; Oct. 2, 1704, Cowper, Diary; Andrew Henderson, ed., *Scottish Proverbs* (Edinburgh, 1832), 48.
32. John Bartlett, *Familiar Quotations* . . . , ed. Emily Morison Beck et al. (Boston, 1980), 320; *Whole Duty of Man*, 388; Thomas Becon, *The Early Works* . . . , ed. John Ayre (Cambridge, 1843), 403.
33. *Thankfull Remembrances of Gods Wonderful Deliverances* . . . (n.p., 1628). See also July 18, 1709, Cowper, Diary. Well-known is the venerable Cornish prayer, "From ghoulies and ghosties and long-leggety beasties and things that go bump in the night, Good Lord, deliver us!" (Bartlett, *Familiar Quotations*, ed. Beck et al., 921).
34. Martine Segalen, *Love and Power in the Peasant Family: Rural France in the Nineteenth Century*, trans. Sarah Matthews (Chicago, 1983, 124–125; Phillipe Martin, "Corps en Repos ou Corps en Danger? Le Sommeil dans les Livres de Piété (Second Moitié du XVIIIe Siècle)," *Revue d'Histoire et de Philosophie Religieuses* 80 (2000), 253.
35. Gwyn Jones, comp., *The Oxford Book of Welsh Verse in English* (Oxford, 1977), 78; July 15, 1705, Cowper, Diary; Gervase Markham, *Countrey Contentments* . . . (London, 1615), 31; William Lilly, *A Groatsworth of Wit for a Penny; or, the Interpretation of Dreams* (London, [1750?]), 18.
36. Cogan, *Haven of Health*, 235.
37. Harrison, *Description*, 200–201; Raffaella Sarti, *Europe at Home: Family and Material Culture, 1500–1800*, trans. Allan Cameron (New Haven, 2002), 120; John E. Crowley, *The Invention of Comfort: Sensibilities & Design in Early Modern Britain & Early America* (Baltimore, 2001), 73–76; Anne Fillon, "Comme on Fait son Lit, on se Couche 300 Ans d'Histoire du Lit Villageois," in *Populatiens et Cultures* . . . *Etudes Réunies en l'Honneur de François Lebrun* (Rennes, 1989), 153–161.
38. Stephanie Grauman Wolf, *As Various as Their Land: The Everyday Lives of Eighteenth-Century Americans* (New York, 1993), 66; Carole Shammas, "The Domestic Environment in Early Modern England and America," *JSH* 14 (1990), 169, 158; Dannenfeldt,

"Renaissance Sleep," 426 n. 31; Crowley, *Comfort*, passim; F. G. Emmison, *Elizabethan Life: Home, Work & Land* (Chelmsford, Eng., 1976), 12–15; Roche, *Consumption*, 182–185.

39. Bartlett, *Familiar Quotations*, ed. Beck et al., 290; Lemnius, *Touchstone of Complexions*, trans. Newton, 73; Cogan, *Haven of Health*, 235; Bradwell, *Watch-man*, 39.
40. Alan Everitt, "Farm Labourers," in Joan Thirsk, ed., *The Agrarian History of England and Wales, IV, 1500–1640* (London, 1967), 449; Horn, *Adapting to a New World*, 310–311, 324–325.
41. A. Browning, ed., *English Historical Documents, 1660–1714* (New York, 1953), 729; [Ward], *A Trip to Ireland . . .* (n.p., 1699), 5.
42. Harrison, *Description*, 201; *OBP*, Sept. 9–16, 1767, 259; Feb. 19, 1665, Pepys, *Diary*, VI, 39; Cissie Fairchilds, *Domestic Enemies: Servants & Their Masters in Old Regime France* (Baltimore, 1984), 39; Steven L. Kaplan, *The Bakers of Paris and the Bread Question, 1700–1775* (Durham, N.C., 1996), 259. A servant in colonial Maryland complained, "What rest we can get is to rap ourselves up in a blanket and ly upon the ground" (Elizabeth Sprigs to John Sprigs, Sept. 22, 1756, in Merrill Jensen, ed., *English Historical Documents: American Colonial Documents to 1776* [New York, 1955], 489), which was also the fate of most early American slaves. Although some quarters contained "boarded beds," more often slaves slept upon the ground amid straw, rags, or, if fortunate, a few coarse blankets (Morgan, *Slave Counterpoint*, 114).
43. *OED*, s.v. "bulkers"; John Heron Lepper, *The Testaments of François Villon* (New York, 1926), 12; Order of Nov. 28, 1732, London Court of Common Council, BL; Menna Prestwich, *Cranfield: Politics and Profits Under the Early Stuarts* (Oxford, 1966), 529; *Paroimiographia* (French), 18; H. S. Bennett, *Life on the English Manor: A Study of Peasant Conditions, 1150–1400* (Cambridge, 1967), 233; Richard Parkinson, ed., *The Private Journal and Literary Remains of John Byrom* (Manchester, 1854), I, Part 2, 407.
44. *RB*, VI, 220; Torriano, *Proverbi*, 127.
45. Alain Collomp, "Families: Habitations and Cohabitations," in *HPL* III, 507; Flandrin, *Families*, trans. Southern, 98–99; Flaherty, *Privacy*, 76–79.
46. Constantia Maxwell, *Country and Town in Ireland under the Georges* (London, 1940), 123; Ménétra, *Journal*, 137; Flandrin, *Families*, trans. Southern, 100. For the expression "to pig," see *OED*; Journal of Twisden Bradbourn, 1693–1694, 1698, 19, Miscellaneous English Manuscripts c. 206, Bodl.; Edward Peacock, comp., *A Glossary of Words Used in the Wapentakes of Manley and Corringham, Lincolnshire* (Vaduz, Liecht., 1965), 191.
47. John Dunton, *Teague Land, or a Merry Ramble to the Wild Irish: Letters from Ireland, 1698*, ed. Edward MacLysaght (Blackrock, Ire., 1982), 21; Howard William Troyer, *Five Travel Scripts Commonly Attributed to Edward Ward* (New York, 1933), 5, 6; Maxwell, *Ireland*, 125; Patricia James, ed., *The Travel Diaries of Thomas Robert Malthus* (London, 1966), 188; Pinkerton, *Travels*, III, 667.
48. James E. Savage, ed., *The "Conceited Newes" of Sir Thomas Overbury and His Friends* (Gainesville, Fla., 1968), 260.
49. Elias, *Civilizing Process*, trans. Jephcott, I, 160–163; Abel Boyer, *The Compleat French-Master . . .* (London, 1699), 6; Elborg Forster, ed. and trans., *A Woman's Life in the Court of the Sun King: Letters of Liselotte von der Pfalz, 1652–1722* (Baltimore, 1984), 149.
50. John Greaves Nall, ed., *An Etymological and Comparative Glossary of the Dialect and Provincialism of East Anglia* (London, 1866), 512; Elias, *Civilizing Process*, trans. Jephcott, I, 166–168.
51. May 4, 1763, Frederick A. Pottle, ed., *Boswell's London Journal, 1762–1763* (New York, 1950), 253; June 14, 1765, Frank Brady and Frederick A. Pottle, eds., *Boswell on the Grand Tour: Italy, Corsica, and France, 1765–1766* (New York, 1955), 253; Isaac Heller, *The*

Life and Confession of Isaac Heller . . . (Liberty, Ind., 1836). See also Mary Nicholson, Feb. 28, 1768, Assi 45/29/1/169; Mar. 23, 1669, Pepys, *Diary*, IX, 495.

52. Milly Harrison and O. M. Royston, comps., *How They Lived* (Oxford, 1965), II, 235; *OBP*, Sept. 13–16, 1758, 291.
53. Thomas Newcomb, *The Manners of the Age* . . . (London, 1733), 454; June 22, 1799, Drinker, *Diary*, II, 1180; Thomas A. Wehr, "The Impact of Changes in Nightlength (Scotoperiod) on Human Sleep," in F. W. Turek and P. C. Zee, eds., *Neurobiology of Sleep and Circadian Rhythms* (New York, 1999), 263–285.
54. *LDA*, June 10, 1751; Sidney Oldall Addy, comp., *A Supplement to the Sheffield Glossary* (Vaduz, Liecht., 1965), 19; Kenneth J. Gergen et al., "Deviance in the Dark," *Psychology Today* 7 (October 1973), 130.
55. Richard Bovet, *Pandaemonium* (Totowa, N.J., 1975), 118; James Orchard Halliwell, ed., *The Autobiography and Personal Diary of Dr. Simon Forman* . . . (London, 1849), 8–9; *The Princess Cloria: or, the Royal Romance* (London, 1661), 530; Dec. 15, 1710, Cowper, Diary.
56. Helmut Puff, *Sodomy in Reformation Germany and Switzerland, 1400–1600* (Chicago, 2003), 77–78; *OBP*, Sept. 10–16, 1755, 309; G. R. Quaife, *Wanton Wenches and Wayward Wives: Peasants and Illicit Sex in Early Seventeenth-Century England* (London, 1979), 73; Michael Rocke, *Forbidden Friendships: Homosexuality and Male Culture in Renaissance Florence* (New York, 1996), 156.
57. *The English Rogue* . . . (London, 1671), Part III, 31; David P. French, comp., *Minor English Poets, 1660–1780* (New York, 1967), III, 318; Elias, *Civilizing Process*, trans. Jephcott, I, 161; Maza, *Servants and Masters*, 184.
58. J. C. Ghosh, ed., *The Works of Thomas Otway: Plays, Poems, and Love-Letters* (Oxford, 1968), II, 340; Joanna Brooker, Nov. 21, 1754, Suffolk Court Files #129733b, Suffolk County Court House, Boston.
59. Geoffrey Chaucer, *Canterbury Tales* (Avon, Ct., 1974), 440–441; George Morison Paul, ed., *Diary of Sir Archibald Johnston of Wariston* (Edinburgh, 1911), 56; Jan. 1, 1663, Pepys, *Diary*, IV, 2; Nov. 29, 1776, Charles McC. Weiss and Frederick A. Pottle, eds., *Boswell in Extremes, 1776–1778* (New York, 1970), 62; Dec. 28, 1780, Joseph W. Reed and Frederick A. Pottle, eds., *Boswell: Laird of Auchinleck, 1778–1782* (New York, 1977), 281.
60. Joshua Swetman, *The Arraignment of Lewd, Idle, Froward* [sic], *and Unconstant Women* . . . (London, 1702), 43–44; May 11, 1731, Clegg, *Diary*, I, 118; Rudolph M. Bell, *How to Do It: Guides to Good Living for Renaissance Italians* (Chicago, 1999), 232; *The Fifteen Joys of Marriage*, trans. Elisabeth Abbott (London, 1959), 22–24, 72–84.
61. Edward Jerningham, *The Welch Heiress* (London, 1795), 70; Diary of John Eliot, 1768, 3, passim, Connecticut Historical Society, Hartford; July 21, 1700, Diary of John Richards, Dorsetshire Record Office, Dorchester. See also *Autobiography of the Rev. Dr Alexander Carlyle, Minister of Inveresk* . . . (Edinburgh, 1860), 545.
62. P.J.P. Goldberg, *Women in England, c. 1275–1525: Documentary Sources* (Manchester, 1995), 142; Ulinka Rublack, *The Crimes of Women in Early Modern Germany* (Oxford, 1999), 227; *Boston Post-Boy*, Aug. 17, 1752; *NYWJ*, Dec. 12, 1737.

CHAPTER ELEVEN

1. C. E. Roybet, ed., *Les Serees de Guillaume Bouchet Sieur de Brocourt* (Paris, 1874), III, 154.
2. William C. Dement, *The Promise of Sleep* (New York, 1999), 101.
3. *Adventurer* 39, Mar. 20, 1753, 228; Christof Wirsung, *Praxis Medicinae Universalis; or a Generall Practise of Phisicke* . . . (London, 1598), 618.

4. T. D. Gent, *Collin's Walk through London and Westminster* . . . (London, 1690), 43; Shakespeare, *Macbeth*, II, 2, 35; William Mountfort, *The Injur'd Lovers* . . . (London, 1688), 49.
5. Sylvain Matton, "Le Rêve Dans les «Secrètes Sciences»: Spirituels, Kabbalistes Chrétiens et Alchimistes," *Revue des Sciences Humaines* 83 (1988), 160; *Adventurer* 39, Mar. 20, 1753, 229. Of course, in Greek mythology "sleep" (*hypnos*) and "death" (*thantos*) were considered twin sons of "night."
6. J.C. Smith and E. De Selincourt, eds., *Spenser: Poetical Works* (London, 1969), 606; Burton E. Stevenson, ed., *The Home Book of Proverbs, Maxims and Familiar Phrases* (New York, 1948), 2134; Philip Sidney, *Astrophel and Stella* . . . (London, 1591); Miguel de Cervantes Saavedra, *The Adventures of Don Quixote*, trans. J. M. Cohen (Baltimore, 1965), 906.
7. Joshua Sylvester, trans., *Du Bartas: His Divine Weekes and Workes* (London, 1621), 465; Shakespeare, *King Henry V*, IV, 1, 264–267; Verdon, *Night*, 203–206. The belief that "the sleep of a labouring man is sweet" is found in *Ecclesiastes* V, 12.
8. George Laurence Gomme, ed., *The Gentleman's Magazine Library: Being a Classified Collection of the Chief Contents of the Gentleman's Magazine from 1731 to 1868: Popular Superstitions* (London, 1884), 122; July 22, Feb. 13, 1712, Cowper, Diary; Oct. 4, 1776, Charles McC. Weiss and Frederick A. Pottle, eds., *Boswell in Extremes, 1776–1778* (New York, 1970), 39.
9. Jean-François Senault, *Man Become Guilty, or the Corruption of Nature by Sinne*, trans. Henry Earle of Monmouth (London, 1650), 243; Philip D. Morgan, "British Encounters with Africans and African Americans, circa 1600–1780," in Bernard Bailyn and Philip D. Morgan, eds., *Strangers within the Realm: Cultural Margins of the First British Empire* (Chapel Hill, N.C., 1991), 206; Nov. 16, 1664, Oct. 6, 1663, Pepys, *Diary*, V, 322, IV, 325.
10. Nashe, *Works*, I, 355; July 22, 1712, Oct. 12, 1703, Cowper, Diary; Dement, *Promise of Sleep*, 17.
11. Spenser, *Amoretti and Epithalamion* (1595; rpt. edn., Amsterdam, 1969).
12. *Herbert's Devotions* . . . (London, 1657), 1; Alexander B. Grosart, ed., *The Complete Works in Prose and Verse of Francis Quarles* (New York, 1967), II, 206; Apr. 4, 1782, Journal of Peter Oliver, Egerton Manuscripts, BL; Benjamin Mifflin, "Journal of a Journey from Philadelphia to the Cedar Swamps & Back, 1764," *Pennsylvania Magazine of History and Biography* 52 (1928), 130–131.
13. Kenneth Jon Rose, *The Body in Time* (New York, 1989), 87–88; Jane Wegscheider Hyman, *The Light Book: How Natural and Artificial Light Affect Our Health, Mood and Behavior* (Los Angeles, 1990), 140–141; Gay Gaer Luce, *Body Time* (London, 1973), 151, 178.
14. November 21, 1662, Pepys, *Diary*, III, 262; May 25, 1709, Cowper, Diary; *OED*, s.v. "spitting"; *SAS*, XI, 124–125; Jan. 1, Feb. 21, 1706, Raymond A. Anselment, ed., *The Remembrances of Elizabeth Freke, 1671–1714* (Cambridge, 2001), 84; Hyman, *Light Book*, 140–141; Mary J. Dobson, *Contours of Death and Disease in Early Modern England* (Cambridge, 1997), 242, 252–253; Carol M. Worthman and Melissa K. Melby, "Toward a Comparative Developmental Ecology of Human Sleep," in Mary A. Carskadon, ed., *Adolescent Sleep Patterns: Biological, Social, and Psychological Influences* (Cambridge, 2002), 74.
15. Charles Severn, ed., *Diary of the Rev. John Ward* . . . (London, 1839), 199; Sept. 24, 1703, Oct. 18, 1715, Cowper, Diary; Suellen Hoy, *Chasing Dirt: The American Pursuit of Cleanliness* (Oxford, 1995), 5; Henry Vaughan, *Welsh Proverbs with English Translations* (Felinfach, Wales, 1889), 85; Legg, *Low-Life*, 9.
16. Burton, *The Anatomy of Melancholy* (New York, 1938), 597; Bräker, *Life*, 82; Nov. 28, 1759, James Balfour Paul, ed., *Diary of George Ridpath* . . . *1755–1761* (Edinburgh, 1922), 288; Oct. 1, 1703, Cowper, Diary; Michael MacDonald, *Mystical Bedlam: Madness, Anxiety, and Healing in Seventeenth-Century England* (Cambridge, 1981), 245.

17. Piero Camporesi, *Bread of Dreams: Food and Fantasy in Early Modern Europe*, trans. David Gentilcore (Chicago, 1989), 64; John Wilson, *The Projectors* (London, 1665), 18; Lydia Dotto, *Losing Sleep: How Your Sleep Habits Affect Your Life* (New York, 1990), 157.
18. M. Andreas Laurentius, *A Discourse of the Preservation of the Sight* . . . , trans. Richard Surphlet (London, 1938), 104, 96; Dagobert D. Runes, ed., *The Selected Writings of Benjamin Rush* (New York, 1974), 200; Hyman, *Light Book*, 87, 96–97, passim.
19. Thomas Overbury, *The "Conceited Newes" of Sir Thomas Overbury and His Friends*, ed. James E. Savage (1616; rpt. edn., Gainesville, Fla., 1968), 262; Henry Nevil Payne, *The Siege of Constantinople* (London, 1675), 51; Georg Christoph Lichtenberg, *Aphorisms*, trans. R. J. Hollingdale (London, 1990), 83–84; Luce, *Body Time*, 204–210.
20. Stevenson, ed., *Proverbs*, 2132; Henry Bachelin, *Le Serviteur* (Paris, 1918), 216; Nov. 6, 1715, William Matthews, ed., *The Diary of Dudley Ryder, 1715–1716* (London, 1939), 105; May 20, 1624, Beck, *Diary*, 99. See also Jan. 30, 1665, Pepys, *Diary*, VI, 25.
21. Heaton, "Experiences or Spiritual Exercises" (typescript), 4, North Haven Historical Society, North Haven, Ct.; Burton, *Anatomy of Melancholy*, 465; Barbara E. Lacey, "The World of Hannah Heaton: The Autobiography of an Eighteenth-Century Connecticut Farm Woman," *WMQ*, 3rd Ser., 45 (1988), 284–285.
22. M. A. Courtney and Thomas Q. Couch, eds., *Glossary of Words in Use in Cornwall* (London, 1880), 39; *OED*, s.v. "nightmare"; Edward Phillips, *The Chamber-Maid* . . . (London, 1730), 57; *The Works of Benjamin Jonson* (London, 1616), 951.
23. Joseph Angus and J. C. Ryle, eds., *The Works of Thomas Adams* . . . (Edinburgh, 1861), II, 29.
24. Charles P. Pollak, "The Effects of Noise on Sleep," in Thomas H. Fay, ed., *Noise and Health* (New York, 1991), 41–60.
25. Wilson, *English Proverbs*, 169; R. Murray Schafer, *The Tuning of the World* (Philadelphia, 1977), 59; Luce, *Body Time*, 141.
26. Thomas Shadwell, *Epsom-Wells* (London, 1672), 83; *The Works of Monsieur Boileau* (London, 1712), I, 193–194, 200–201; *The Works of Mr. Thomas Brown in Prose and Verse* . . . (London, 1708), III, 15; Bruce R. Smith, *The Acoustic World of Early Modern England: Attending to the O-Factor* (Chicago, 1999), 52–71. Of course, some early modern noises, Francis Bacon observed, aided sleep, including trickling water and soft singing. James Spedding et al., eds., *The Works of Francis Bacon* (London, 1859), II, 579–580.
27. Joseph Leech, *Rural Rides of the Bristol Churchgoer*, ed. Alan Sutton (Gloucester, Eng., 1982), 70; Mar. 16, 1706, Cowper, Diary.
28. Oct. 24, 1794, Oct. 19, 1796, Drinker, *Diary*, II, 610, 853.
29. William Beckford, *Dreams, Waking Thoughts and Incidents*, ed. Robert J. Gemmett (Rutherford, N.J., 1972), 165; Robert Forby, comp., *The Vocabulary of East Anglia* (Newton Abbot, Eng., 1970), I, 43; June, 15, 1800, Jack Ayres, ed., *Paupers and Pig Killers: The Diary of William Holland, a Somerset Parson* (Gloucester, Eng., 1984), 38.
30. P. Hume Brown, ed., *Tours in Scotland, 1677 & 1681* . . . (Edinburgh, 1892), 33; Donald Gibson, ed., *A Parson in the Vale of White Horse: George Woodward's Letters from East Hendred, 1753–1761* (Gloucester, Eng., 1982), 37; Nov. 26, 1703, Doreen Slatter, ed., *The Diary of Thomas Naish* (Devizes, Eng., 1965), 51; Pounds, *Culture*, 364–365; Smith, *Acoustic World*, 71–82.
31. Alice Morse Earle, *Customs and Fashions in Old New England* (1893; rpt edn., Detroit, 1968), 128; *LEP*, Jan. 12, 1767; Dec. 19, 1799, Woodforde, *Diary*, V, 230; Brian Fagan, *The Little Ice Age: How Climate Made History, 1300–1850* (New York, 2000), 113–147; Stanley Coren, *Sleep Thieves: An Eye-Opening Exploration into the Science and Mysteries of Sleep* (New York, 1996), 164.
32. Legg, *Low-Life*, 4; John Ashton, comp., *Modern Street Ballads* (New York, 1968), 51;

Stevenson, ed., *Proverbs*, 280; Lynne Lamberg, *Bodyrhythms: Chronobiology and Peak Performance* (New York, 1994), 111–112; Remarks 1717, 193–194; Aug. 3, 1774, Edward Miles Riley, ed., *The Journal of John Harrower: An Indentured Servant in the Colony of Virginia, 1773–1776* (Williamsburg, 1963), 52.

33. Torrington, *Diaries*, III, 317; Evelyn, *Diary*, II, 507; Robert Southey, *Journal of a Tour in Scotland* (1929; rpt edn. Edinburgh, 1972), 91–92.
34. John Locke, *The Works . . .* (London, 1963), IX, 23; Coren, *Sleep Thieves*, 160–161.
35. Apr. 4, 1624, Beck, *Diary*, 71; Lawrence Wright, *Warm and Snug: The History of the Bed* (London, 1962), 199–200; Oct. 22, 1660, Pepys, *Diary*, I, 271; Carl Bridenbaugh, ed., *Gentleman's Progress: The Itinerarium of Dr. Alexander Hamilton* (Chapel Hill, N.C., 1948), 195; F.P. Pankhurst and J. A. Horne, "The Influence of Bed Partners on Movement during Sleep," *Sleep* 17 (1994), 308–315.
36. A. Aspinall, ed., *Lady Bessborough and Her Family Circle* (London, 1940), 111–112; John S. Farmer, ed., *Merry Songs and Ballads Prior to the Year A.D. 1800* (New York, 1964), I, 202–203; Lawrence Wright, *Clean and Decent: The Fascinating History of the Bathroom & the Water Closet . . .* (New York, 1960), 78; Pounds, *Culture*, 366–367.
37. See, for example, Thomas Brewer, *The Merry Devill of Edmonton* (London, 1631), 44; *OED*, s.v. "urinal"; Mar. 27, 1706, Sewall, *Diary*, I, 543; Jonathan Swift, *Directions to Servants . . .* (Oxford, 1959), 61; Burt, *Letters*, II, 47.
38. James T. Henke, *Gutter Life and Language in the Early "Street" Literature of England: A Glossary of Terms and Topics Chiefly of the Sixteenth and Seventeenth Centuries* (West Cornwall, Ct., 1988), 51; Sept. 28, 1665, Pepys, *Diary*, VI, 244; John Greenwood, Mar. 9, 1771, Assi 45/30/1/70; *Paroimiographia* (Italian), 16.
39. Cibber and Vanbrugh, *The Provok'd Husband; or a Journey to London* (London, 1728), 76.
40. Peter Thornton, *The Italian Renaissance Interior 1400–1600* (New York, 1991), 248, 249–251, and *Seventeenth-Century Interior Decoration in England, France, and Holland* (New Haven, 1978), 324–326, 328.
41. *Boileau Works*, I, 201.
42. Benjamin Franklin, *Writings*, ed. J. A. Leo Lemay (New York, 1987), 1121–1122; Feb. 16, 17, 1668, Pepys, *Diary*, IX, 73, 75; Louis B. Wright and Marion Tinling, ed., *Quebec to Carolina in 1785–1786: Being the Travel Diary and Observations of Robert Hunter Jr. . . .* (San Marino, Calif., 1943), 278–279; Raffaella Sarti, *Europe at Home: Family and Material Culture, 1500–1800*, trans. Allan Cameron (New Haven, 2002), 122.
43. July 9, 1774, Philip Vickers Fithian, *Journal & Letters of Philip Vickers Fithian, 1773–1774: A Plantation Tutor of the Old Dominion*, ed. Hunter Dickinson Farish (Williamsburg, 1943), 178.
44. Nicholas James, *Poems on Several Occasions* (Truro, Eng., 1742), 13; *Herbert's Devotions*, 223; Sarah C. Maza, *Servants and Masters in Eighteenth-Century France: The Uses of Loyalty* (Princeton, N.J., 1983), 183 n. 61. The working-class author John Younger later derided "toddy-noodled writers of gentle novels" for "describing the happy ignorance of the snoring *peasantry* without any real knowledge of such people's matters" (*Autobiography of John Younger, Shoemaker, St. Boswells . . .* [Edinburgh, 1881], 133).
45. Pollak, "Effects of Noise," 43.
46. Apr. 13, 1719, William Byrd, *The London Diary (1717–1721) and Other Writings*, ed. Louis B. Wright and Marion Tinling (Oxford, 1958), 256; Oct. 9, 1647, *Yorkshire Diaries and Autobiographies in the Seventeenth and Eighteenth Centuries* (Durham, Eng., 1875), I, 67; Coren, *Sleep Thieves*, 72–74, 286. Little wonder that among the lower classes in early modern Europe the mythical "Land of Cockaigne" exerted broad appeal. In addition to other delights in this utopian paradise, men and women rested in "silken beds,"

and "he who sleeps most earns the most" (Piero Camporesi, *The Land of Hunger*, trans. Tania Croft-Murray [Cambridge, Mass., 1996], 160–164).

47. Mechal Sobel, *The World They Made Together: Black and White Values in Eighteenth-Century Virginia* (Princeton, N.J., 1987), 24; James Scholefield, ed., *The Works of James Pilkington, B. D., Lord Bishop of Durham* (New York, 1968), 446; E. P. Thompson, "Time, Work-Discipline, and Industrial Capitalism," *PP* 38 (1967), 56–97.
48. Camporesi, *Bread of Dreams*, 68–69; Coren, *Sleep Thieves*, passim.

CHAPTER TWELVE

1. Philip Wheelwright, *Heraclitus* (Princeton, N.J., 1959), 20.
2. *Herbert's Devotions . . .* (London, 1657), 236; Robert Louis Stevenson, *The Cevennes Journal: Notes on a Journey through the French Highlands*, ed. Gordon Golding (Edinburgh, 1978), 79–82.
3. For the term "first sleep," I have discovered eighty-three references within a total of seventy-two different sources from the period 1300–1800. See the text for examples. For references to "first nap" and "dead sleep," see A. Roger Ekirch, "Sleep We Have Lost: Pre-industrial Slumber in the British Isles," *AHR* 106 (2001), 364. The fewer references to segmented sleep I have found in early American sources suggests that this pattern, though present in North America, may have been less widespread than in Europe, for reasons ranging from differences in day/night ratios to the wider availability of artificial illumination in the colonies. Two sources—Benjamin Franklin, "Letter of the Drum," *PG*, Apr. 23, 1730, and Hudson Muse to Thomas Muse, Apr. 19, 1771, in "Original Letters," *WMQ* 2 (1894), 240—contain the expression "first nap." See also Ekirch, "Sleep We Have Lost," 364.
4. I have found twenty-one references to these terms within a total of nineteen sources from the seventeenth and eighteenth centuries (Ekirch, "Sleep We Have Lost," 364).
5. For "primo sonno" and "primo sono," the Opera del Vocabolario Italiano database of early Italian literature, furnished by the ItalNet consortium (Web: www.lib.uchicago.edu/efts/ARTFL/projects/OVI/), contains fifty-seven references within a total of thirty-two texts from just the fourteenth century.
6. For "primo somno" or some slight variation like "primus somnus" or "primi somni," for which I have discovered nineteen references within sixteen texts, half of the latter before the thirteenth century, see, for example, Ekirch, "Sleep We Have Lost," 364–365. For "concubia nocte," see D. P. Simpson, *Cassell's Latin Dictionary* (London, 1982), 128.
7. *Mid-Night Thoughts, Writ, as Some Think, by a London-Whigg, or a Westminster Tory . . .* (London, 1682), A 2, 17; William Keatinge Clay, ed., *Private Prayers, Put Forth by Authority during the Reign of Queen Elizabeth* (London, 1968), 440–441; *OED*, s.v. "watching."
8. Geoffrey Chaucer, *The Canterbury Tales* (Avon, Ct., 1974), 403; William Baldwin, *Beware the Cat*, ed. William Ringler, Jr., and Michael Flachmann (San Marino, Calif., 1988), 5.
9. George Wither, *Ivvenila* (London, 1633), 239; Locke, *An Essay Concerning Human Understanding* (London, 1690), 589. See also Francis Peck, *Desiderrata Curiosa . . .* (London, 1732), II, 33. For references to the "first sleep" of animals, see, for example, James Shirley, *The Constant Maid* (London, 1640); Samuel Jackson Pratt, *Harvest-Home . . .* (London, 1805), II, 457.
10. Raimundus Lullus, *Liber de Regionibus Sanitatis et Informitatis* (n.p., 1995), 107; Harrison, *Description*, 382. See also Crusius, *Nocte*, ch. 3.11.

11. *The Dramatic Works of Sir William D'Avenant* (New York, 1964), III, 75; J. Irvine Smith, ed, *Selected Justiciary Cases, 1624–1650* (Edinburgh, 1974), III, 642; Taillepied, *Ghosts*, 97–98; Richard Hurst, trans., *Endimion: An Excellent Fancy First Composed in French by Mounsieur Gombauld* (London, 1639), 74; Shirley Strum Kenny, ed., *The Works of George Farquhar* (Oxford, 1988), I, 100.
12. Governal, *In this Tretyse that Is Cleped Governaylę of Helthe* (New York, 1969); William Bullein, *A Newe Boke of Phisicke Called y Goveriment of Health . . .* (London, 1559), 90; Andrew Boorde, *A Compendyous Regyment or a Dyetary of Health . . .* (London, 1547); André Du Laurens, *A Discourse of the Preservation of the Sight . . .*, ed. Sanford V. Larkey, trans. Richard Surfleet ([London], 1938), 190.
13. Emmanuel Le Roy Ladurie, *Montaillou: The Promised Land of Error*, trans. Barbara Bray (New York, 1978), 277, 227; Nicolas Rémy, *La Démonolâtrie*, ed. Jean Boës (1595; rpt. edn., Lyons, n.d.), 125. See also Jean Duvernoy, ed., *Le Régistre d'Inquisition de Jacques Fournier, Évêque de Pamiers (1318–1325)* (Toulouse, 1965), I, 243.
14. Anthony C. Meisel and M. L. del Mastro, trans., *The Rule of St. Benedict* (Garden City, N.Y., 1975), 66; Alan of Lille, *The Art of Preaching*, trans. Gillian R. Evans (Kalamazoo, Mich., 1981), 136; Richard Baxter, *Practical Works . . .* (London, 1838), I, 339; *Mid-Night Thoughts*, 158–159; Abbot Gasquet, *English Monastic Life* (London, 1905), 111–112; C. H. Lawrence, *Medieval Monasticism: Forms of Religious Life in Western Europe in the Middle Ages* (London, 1984), 28–30; John M. Staudenmaier, S. J., "What Ever Happened to the Holy Dark in the West? The Enlightenment Ideal & the European Mystical Tradition," in Leo Marx and Bruce Mazlish, eds., *Progress: Fact or Illusion?* (Ann Arbor, Mich., 1996), 184.
15. *Livy with an English Translation in Fourteen Volumes*, trans. F. G. Moore (Cambridge, Mass., 1966), VI, 372–373; Virgil, *The Aeneid*, trans. Robert Fitzgerald (New York, 1992), 43; Pausanias, *Description of Greece*, trans. W.H.S. Jones and H. A. Ormerod (Cambridge, 1966), II, 311; Plutarch, *The Lives of the Noble Grecians and Romans*, trans. John Dryden (New York, 1979), 630, 1208; Allardyce Nicoll, ed., *Chapman's Homer: The Iliad, The Odyssey and the Lesser Homerica* (Princeton, N.J., 1967), II, 73.
16. Paul Bohannon, "Concepts of Time among the Tiv of Nigeria," *Southwestern Journal of Anthropology* 9 (1953), 253; Paul and Laura Bohannan, *Three Source Notebooks in Tiv Ethnography* (New Haven, 1958), 357; Bruno Gutmann, *The Tribal Teachings of the Chagga* (New Haven, 1932); George B. Silberbauer, *Hunter and Habitat in the Central Kalahari Desert* (Cambridge, 1981), 111.
17. Thomas A. Wehr, "A 'Clock for All Seasons' in the Human Brain," in R. M. Buijs et al., eds., *Hypothalamic Integration of Circadian Rhythms* (Amsterdam, 1996), 319–340; Thomas A. Wehr, "The Impact of Changes in Nightlength (Scotoperiod) on Human Sleep," in F. W. Turek and P. C. Zee, eds., *Neurobiology of Sleep and Circadian Rhythms* (New York, 1999), 263–285; Natalie Angier, "Modern Life Suppresses Ancient Body Rhythm," *New York Times*, Mar. 14, 1995; personal communications from Thomas Wehr, Dec. 23, 31, 1996.
18. Warren E. Leary, "Feeling Tired and Run Down? It Could be the Lights," *NYT*, Feb. 8, 1996; Charles A. Czeisler, "The Effect of Light on the Human Circadian Pacemaker," in Derek J. Chadwick and Kate Ackrill, eds., *Circadian Clocks and Their Adjustment* (Chichester, Eng., 1995), 254–302; William C. Dement, *The Promise of Sleep* (New York, 1999), 98–101. Wehr, to his credit, has speculated that other conditions in his experiments, apart from darkness, might have produced a bimodal pattern of sleep—such as boredom or the enforced rest of his subjects. "Further research will be necessary," he has written, "to determine whether, and to what extent, darkness

per se or factors associated with the dark condition" were "responsible for the differences that we observed in the subjects' sleep." (Thomas A. Wehr et al., "Conservation of Photoperiod-responsive Mechanisms in Humans," *American Journal of Physiology* 265 [1993], R855.) But plainly such factors did not normally prevail in the voluminous number of preindustrial allusions to first and second sleep. Rest in those instances was neither involuntary nor the consequence of monotonous surroundings.

19. Dec. 14, 1710, George Aitken, ed., *The Tatler* (1899; rpt. edn., New York, 1970), IV, 337, 339; Apr. 9, 1664, Pepys, *Diary*, V, 118; Mar. 19, 1776, Charles Ryskamp and Frederick A. Pottle, eds., *Boswell: The Ominous Years, 1774–1776* (New York, 1963), 276.
20. Edward MacCurdy, ed., *The Notebooks of Leonardo Da Vinci* (New York, 1938), II, 256–257.
21. Boorde, *Compendyous Regyment*, viii; John Dunton, *Teague Land, or A Merry Ramble to the Wild Irish: Letters from Ireland, 1698*, ed. Edward MacLysaght (Blackrock, Ire., 1982), 25.
22. Thomas Jubb, Nov. 17, 1740, Assi 45/22/1/102; Nov. 12, 1729, Nov. 30, 1726, Jan. 4, 1728, Robert Sanderson, Diary, St. John's College, Cambridge; Francis James Child, ed., *The English and Scottish Popular Ballads* (New York, 1965), II, 241; Robert Boyle, *Works* . . . (London, 1772), V, 341; Richard Wiseman, *Eight Chirurgical Treatises* . . . (London, 1705), 505; Lyne Walter, *An Essay towards a . . . Cure in the Small Pox* (London, 1714), 37.
23. Tobias Venner, *Via Recta ad Vitam Longam* . . . (London, 1637), 272; Walter Pope, *The Life of the Right Reverend Father in God Seth, Lord Bishop of Salisbury* . . . (London, 1697), 145; Best, *Books*, 124; Vosgien, *An Historical and Biographical Dictionary* . . . , trans. Catharine Collignon, (Cambridge, 1801), IV.
24. Jane Allison, Mar. 15, 1741, Assi 45/22/2/64B; Stephen Duck, *The Thresher's Labour* (Los Angeles, 1985), 16; A. R. Myers, ed., *English Historical Documents, 1327–1485* (London, 1969), 1190.
25. *Notes and Queries*, 2nd Ser., 5, no. 115 (Mar. 13, 1858), 207; Tobias Smollett, *Peregrine Pickle* (New York, 1967), II, 244.
26. Franklin, *Writings*, ed. J. A. Leo Lemay (New York, 1987), 835.
27. *JRAI*, II, 376; Thomas Nicholson, June 2, 1727, Assi 45/18/4/39–40; *Herbert's Devotions*, 237; Anthony Horneck, *The Happy Ascetick, or, the Best Exercise* ([London], 1680), 414; Mary Atkinson, Mar. 9, 1771, Assi 45/30/1/3; Jane Rowth, Apr. 11, 1697, Assi 45/17/2/93.
28. Nicolas Remy, *Demonolatry*, ed. Montague Summers and trans. E. A. Ashwin (Secaucus, N.J., 1974), 43–46; Francesco Maria Guazzo, *Compendium Maleficarum*, ed. Montague Summers and trans. E. A. Ashwin (Secaucus, N.J., 1974), 33–48.
29. Horneck, *Happy Ascetick*, 415; M. Lopes de Almeida, *Diálogos de D. Frei Amador Arrais* (Porto, 1974), 19; *The Whole Duty of Prayer* (London, 1657), 13; Richard and John Day, *A Booke of Christian Praiers* . . . (London, 1578), 440–441; R. Sherlock, *The Practical Christian: or, the Devout Penitent* . . . (London, 1699), 322–323; Frederick James Furnivall, ed., *Phillip Stubbes's Anatomy of the Abuses in England in Shakespere's Youth, A.D. 1583* (London, 1877), 221.
30. Cowper, *The Works* (London, 1836), IX, 45–50; Danielle Régnier-Bohler, "Imagining the Self," in *HPL* II, 357; *Mid-Night Thoughts*.
31. Dorothy Rhodes, Mar. 18, 1650, *York Depositions*, 28. See also Geoffroy de La Tour-Landry, *Book of the Knight of La Tour Landry* (London, 1906), fo. 3b.; Jan. 4, 1728, Sanderson, Diary.
32. *The Deceyte of Women* . . . (n.p., 1568); Helen Simpson, ed. and trans., *The Waiting City: Paris, 1782–88. Being an Abridgement of Louis-Sébastian Mercier's "Le Tableau de Paris"*

(Philadelphia, 1933), 76; Aviel Orenstein, ed., *Mishnah Berurah: Laws Concerning Miscellaneous Blessings, the Minchah Service, the Ma'ariv Service and Evening Conduct* . . . (Jerusalem, 1989), 435.

33. Laurent Joubert, *Popular Errors*, trans. Gregory David de Rocher (Tuscaloosa, Ala., 1989), 112–113; Thomas Cogan, *The Haven of Health* (London, 1588), 252. See also Boorde, *Compendyous Regyment;* Orenstein, ed., *Mishnah Berurah*, 441.
34. Cardano, *The Book of My Life* (New York, 1962), 82; Thomas Jefferson, *Writings*, ed. Merrill D. Peterson (New York, 1984), 1417; Francis Quarles, *Enchiridion* . . . (London, 1644), ch. 54.
35. *Everie Woman in Her Humor* (London, 1609); Wilson, *English Proverbs*, 566. See also July 12, 1702, Cowper, Diary; May 24, 1595, Richard Rogers and Samuel Ward, *Two Elizabethan Puritan Diaries*, ed. Marshall Mason Knappen (Gloucester, Mass., 1966), 105.
36. Oliver Lawson Dick, ed., *Aubrey's Brief Lives* (London, 1950), 131; Crusius, *Nocte*, ch. 1.5; *GM* 18 (1748), 108; *G and NDA*, Feb. 11, 1769; Rita Shenton, *Christopher Pinchbeck and His Family* (Ashford, Eng., 1976), 29.
37. Régnier-Bohler, "Imagining the Self," 390; Edmund Spenser, *The Works* . . . , ed. Edwin Greenlaw (Baltimore, 1947), II, 249; Richard Brome, *The Northern Lasse* (London, 1632); William Davenant, *The Platonick Lovers* (London, 1636); Cowper, *Works*, IX, 45.
38. Roy Harvey Pearce, ed., *Nathaniel Hawthorne: Tales and Sketches* . . . (New York, 1982), 200–201; John Wade, *Redemption of Time* . . . (London, 1692), 187. Worried by the potential for masturbation, another moralist cautioned that a sleeper "accustom himself to rise immediately after his first sleep" (S.A.D. Tissot, *Onanism: Or a Treatise upon the Disorders Produced by Masturbation* . . . [London, 1767], 122).
39. Mercier, *The Night Cap* (Philadelphia, 1788), 4.
40. Tertullian, *Apologetical Works*, trans. Rudolph Arbesmann et al. (New York, 1950), 288; Sidney J. H. Herrtage, ed., *Early English Versions of the Gesta Romanorum* (London, 1879), 207; Chaucer, *Canterbury Tales*, 403–404; Mar. 11, 1676, Jane Lead, *A Fountain of Gardens* . . . (London, 1697), 121; Jan. 6, 1677, Heywood, *Diaries*, I, 340; Peter Corbin and Douglas Sedge, eds., *Ram Alley* (Nottingham, 1981), 56.
41. Hubert, *Egypts Favourite. The History of Joseph* . . . (London, 1631). See also, for example, William Vaughan, *Naturall and Artificial Directions for Health* . . . (London, 1607), 55.
42. *Looker-On*, May 22, 1792, 234; Geoffrey Keynes, ed., *The Works of Sir Thomas Browne* (London, 1931), V, 185; Nashe, *Works*, I, 355.
43. Thomas Tryon, *A Treatise of Dreams & Visions* . . . (London, 1689), 9; *WR or UJ*, Dec. 30, 1732; Thomas, *Religion and the Decline of Magic*, 128–130.
44. Keynes, ed., *Browne Works*, V, 185; James K. Hosmer, ed., *Winthop's Journal: "History of New England," 1630–1649* (New York, 1908), I, 121.
45. "Somnifer," *PA*, Oct. 24, 1767; S.R.F. Price, "The Future of Dreams: From Freud to Artemidorous," *PP* 113 (1986), 31–32; Thomas Hill, *The Most Pleasaunt Arte of the Interpretation of Dremes* . . . (London, [1571]); *Nocturnal Revels: or, a General History of Dreams* . . . , 2 vols. (1706–1707).
46. Thomas Johnson, trans., *The Workes of that Famous Chirurgion Ambrose Parey* (London, 1649), 27; Ripa, *Nocturno Tempore*, ch. 9.27; Levinus Lemnius, *The Touchstone of Complexions* . . . , trans. T. Newton (London, 1576), 113–114.
47. Feltham, *Resolves* (London, 1628), 18, 163; Thomas Tryon, *Wisdom's Dictates: or, Aphorisms & Rules* . . . (London, 1691), 68.
48. Sept. 12, 1644, Josselin, *Diary*, 20; Mar. 8, 1626, *The Works of the Most Reverend Father in God, William Laud* . . . (Oxford, 1853), III, 201; July 31, 1675, Sewall, *Diary*, I, 12.
49. Lemnius, *Touchstone*, trans. Newton, 114; Phillipe Martin, "Corps en Repos ou Corps en Danger? Le Sommeil dans les Livres de Piété (Seconde Moitié du XVIIIe Siècle),"

Revue d'Histoire et de Philosophie Religieuses 80 (2000), 255; Aug. 15, 1665, Feb. 7, 1669, Pepys, *Diary*, VI, 191, IX, 439; Cannon, Diary, 344. The penis routinely becomes erect during a dream, regardless of its content; in fact, men on average experience "four to five erections a night (when they are asleep), each lasting from five to ten minutes" (Kenneth Jon Rose, *The Body in Time* [New York, 1989], 54, 95).

50. Charles Carlton, "The Dream Life of Archbishop Laud," *History Today* 36 (1986), 9–14; Alan Macfarlane, *The Family Life of Ralph Josselin, a Seventeenth-Century Clergyman* (Cambridge, 1970), 183–187.
51. Cardano, *Book of My Life*, 156, 161; July 24, 1751, James MacSparran, *A Letter Book and Abstract of Out Services, Written during the Years 1743–1751*, ed. Daniel Goodwin (Boston, 1899), 45; James Strachey, ed., *The Standard Edition of the Complete Psychological Works of Sigmund Freud* (London, 1975), XXI, 203.
52. Torrington, *Diaries*, I, 165; Aug. 2, 1589, Aug. 6, 1597, J. O. Halliwell, ed., *The Private Diary of Dr. John Dee* (London, 1842), 31, 59.
53. Jan. 2, 1686, Sewall, *Diary*, I, 91; Henry Fishwick, ed., *The Note Book of the Rev. Thomas Jolly, A.D. 1671–1693* (Manchester, 1894), 100; Jean Bousquet, *Les Thèmes du Rêve dans la Littérature Romantique* (Paris, 1964).
54. Lady Marchioness of Newcastle, *Orations of Divers Sorts* . . . (London, 1662), 300.
55. Apr. 4, 1706, Aug. 22, 1716, Sewall, *Diary*, I, 544, II, 829.
56. Sept. 4, 1625, *Laud Works*, III, 173; Oct. 17, 1588, Halliwell, ed., *Dee Diary*, 29; Mar. 20, 1701, Robert Wodrow, *Analecta: or, Materials for a History of Remarkable Providences* . . . , ed. Matthew Leishman (Edinburgh, 1842), I, 6; Feb. 17, 1802, Woodforde, *Diary*, V, 369.
57. Nov. 20, 1798, Drinker, *Diary*, II, 112. See, for example, Cardano, *Book of My Life*, 89; Wodrow, *Analecta*, II, 315, III, 339; July 15, 1738, Benjamin Hanbury, *An Enlarged Series of Extracts from the Diary, Meditations and Letters of Mr. Joseph Williams* (London, 1815), 131.
58. Jan. 7, 1648, C.H. Josten, ed., *Elias Ashmole (1617–1692)* . . . (Oxford, 1967), II, 467; Jan. 6, 1784, Irma Lustig and Frederick Albert Pottle, eds., *Boswell, The Applause of the Jury, 1782–1785* (New York, 1981), 175.
59. Feb. 10, 1799, William Warren Sweet, *Religion on the American Frontier, 1782–1840: The Methodists* . . . (Chicago, 1946), IV, 217–218.
60. June 30, 1654, Feb. 15, 1658, Josselin, *Diary*, 325, 419; June 16, 1689, Mar. 18, 1694, Feb. 13, 1705, Sewall, *Diary*, I, 219, 328, 518; May 28, 1789, Woodforde, *Diary*, III, 108; Dec. 2, 1720, William Byrd, *The London Diary (1717–1721) and Other Writings*, ed. Louis B. Wright and Marion Tinling (Oxford, 1958), 481; Oct. 12, 1582, Halliwell, ed., *Dee Diary*, 17; Jan. 29, 1708, J. E. Foster, ed., *The Diary of Samuel Newton* (Cambridge, 1890), 118; Aug. 27, Oct. 14, 1773, Frederick A. Pottle and Charles H. Bennett, eds., *Boswell's Journal of a Tour to the Hebrides with Samuel Johnson, LL.D., 1773* (New York, 1961), 87–88, 303–304; Feb. 3, 15, 1776, Ryskamp and Pottle, eds., *Ominous Years*, 230, 235.
61. May 30, 1695, Foster, ed., *Newton Diary*, 109; Dec. 21, 1626, *Laud Works*, III, 197; Carlton, "Dream Life of Laud," 13.
62. *Mid-Night Thoughts*, 34; Mark R. Cohen, ed. and trans., *The Autobiography of a Seventeenth-Century Venetian Rabbi: Leon Modena's Life of Judah* (Princeton, N.J., 1988), 94, 99; James J. Cartwright, *The Wentworth Papers, 1705–1739* (London, 1883), 148; Wolfgang Behringer, *Shaman of Oberstorf: Chonrad Stoeckhlin and the Phantoms of the Night*, trans. H. C. Erik Midelfort (Charlottesville, Va., 1998); Boyereau Brinch, *The Blind African Slave* . . . (St. Albans, Vt., 1810), 149–150; Michael Craton, *Testing the Chains: Resistance to Slavery in the British West Indies* (Ithaca, N.Y., 1982), 250.
63. *Another Collection of Philosophical Conferences of the French Virtuosi* . . . , trans. G. Havers and J. Davies (London, 1665), 3; Jean de La Fontaine, *Selected Fables*, ed. Maya Slater and

trans. Christopher Wood (Oxford, 1995), 283; Jacques Le Goff, *The Medieval Imagination*, trans. Arthur Goldhammer (Chicago, 1988), 234. See also Torriano, *Proverbi*, 261.

64. David P. French, comp., *Minor English Poets, 1660–1780; A Selection from Alexander Chalmers' The English Poets* (New York, 1967), II, 259; "Meditations on a Bed," *US and WJ*, Feb. 5, 1737; Enid Porter, *The Folklore of East Anglia* (Totowa, N.J., 1974), 126–127; David Simpson, *A Discourse on Dreams and Night Visions; with Numerous Examples Ancient and Modern* (Macclesfield, Eng., 1791), 61.

65. Hence the bluster of the Nazi Robert Ley: "The only person in Germany who still leads a private life is one who is asleep" (George Steiner, *No Passion Spent: Essays 1978–1996* [London, 1996], 211); Augustine FitzGerald, ed., *The Essays and Hymns of Synesius of Cyrene . . .* (London, 1930), 345; Carlo Ginzburg, *The Night Battles: Witchcraft & Agrarian Cults in the Sixteenth & Seventeenth Centuries*, trans. John and Anne Tedeschi (London, 1983).

66. *RB*, VII, 11–12; Thomas, *Religion and the Decline of Magic*, 148; Mercier, *Night Cap*, I, 4; Robert L. Van De Castle, *Our Dreaming Mind* (New York, 1994), 333–334.

67. For "sleep behavior disorder," see the communication from Jonathan Woolfson, Oct. 30, 1997, H-Albion; D. M. Moir, ed., *The Life of Mansie Wauch: Tailor in Dalkeith* (Edinburgh, 1828), 273–274; Dement, *Promise of Sleep*, 208–211.

68. Erika Bourguignon, "Dreams and Altered States of Consciousness in Anthropological Research," in Francis L. K. Hsu, ed., *Psychological Anthropology* (Cambridge, Mass., 1972), 403–434; Vilhelm Aubert and Harrison White, "Sleep: A Sociological Interpretation. I," *Acta Sociologica* 4 (1959), 48–49; Beryl Larry Bellman, *Village of Curers and Assassins: On the Production of Fala Kpelle Cosmological Categories* (The Hague, 1975), 165–178; Cora Du Bois, *The People of Alor: A Social-Psychological Study of an East Indian Island* (New York, 1961), I, 45–46.

69. John Ashton, ed., *Chap-Books of the Eighteenth Century* (New York, 1966), 85; Franklin, *Writings*, ed. Lemay, 118–122. See also Jan. 5, 1679, Josselin, *Diary*, 617.

70. Sept. 16, 1745, Parkman, *Diary*, 124; "On Dreams," *Pennsylvania Magazine, or American Monthly Museum*, 1776, 119–122; July 2, 1804, Drinker, *Diary*, III, 1753. See also Simpson, *Discourse on Dreams*, 59; John Robert Shaw, *An Autobiography of Thirty Years, 1777–1807*, ed. Oressa M. Teagarden and Jeanne L. Crabtree (Columbus, Ohio, 1992), 131.

71. Patricia Crawford, "Women's Dreams in Early Modern England," *History Workshop Journal* 49 (2000), 140; "Titus Trophonius," Oct. 4, 1712, Donald F. Bond, ed., *The Spectator* (Oxford, 1965), V, 293–294; Karen Ordahl Kupperman, *Indians and English: Facing Off in Early America* (Ithaca, N.Y., 2000), 128–129; Cartwright, ed., *Wentworth Papers*, 538; Thomas, *Religion and the Decline of Magic*, 130.

72. Lacey, "Hannah Heaton," 286; Aug. 20, 1737, Kay, *Diary*, 12, 39; Mechal Sobel, "The Revolution in Selves: Black and White Inner Aliens," in Ronald Hoffman et al., eds., *Through a Glass Darkly: Reflections on Personal Identity in Early America* (Chapel Hill, N.C., 1997), 180–200; David Hackett Fischer, *Albion's Seed: Four British Folkways in America* (New York, 1989), 519.

73. William Philips, *The Revengeful Queen* (London, 1698), 39; Jan. 1723, Wodrow, *Analecta*, ed. Leishman, III, 374; *SWA or LJ*, Sept. 3, 1770; *OBP*, June 4, 1783, 590.

74. John Whaley, *A Collection of Original Poems and Translations* (London, 1745), 257; John Dryden and Nathaniel Lee, *Oedipus* (London, 1679), 14.

75. Marcel Foucault, *Le Rêve: Études et Observations* (Paris, 1906), 169–170; Jan. 16, 1780, Joseph W. Reed and Frederick A. Pottle, eds., *Boswell: Laird of Auchinleck, 1778–1782* (New York, 1977), 169; *The New Art of Thriving; or, the Way to Get and Keep Money . . .* (Edinburgh, 1706); Van De Castle, *Dreaming Mind*, 466.

76. Jean Anthelme Brillat-Savarin, *The Physiology of Taste, or, Meditations on Transcendental*

Gastronomy, trans. M.F.K. Fisher (New York, 1949), 222; Wehr, "Clock for All Seasons," 338; Wehr, "Changes in Nightlength," 269–273; Personal communications from Wehr, Dec. 23, 31, 1996; Carter A. Daniel, ed., *The Plays of John Lyly* (Lewisburg, Pa., 1988), 123; Breton, *Works*, II, 12; Barbara E. Lacey, ed., *The World of Hannah Heaton: The Diary of an Eighteenth-Century New England Farm Woman* (DeKalb, Ill., 2003), 83; Aug. 20, 1737, Kay, *Diary*, 12, 39. Although less likely to be recalled and internalized, dream activity, of course, also occurred during "morning" or "second sleep" (Ekirch, "Sleep We Have Lost," 382).

COCK-CROW

1. *GM* 25 (1755), 57.
2. M. De Valois d'Orville, *Les Nouvelles Lanternes* (Paris, 1746), 4; May 10, 1797, Drinker, *Diary*, II, 916; R.L.W., *Journal of a Tour from London to Elgin Made About 1790 . . .* (Edinburgh, 1897), 74; Hans-Joachim Voth, *Time and Work in England, 1750–1830* (Oxford, 2000), 67–69.
3. Elkan Nathan Adler, ed., *Jewish Travellers: A Treasury of Travelogues from 9 Centuries* (New York, 1966), 350; Robert Semple, *Observations on a Journey through Spain and Italy to Naples . . .* (London, 1808), II, 83; Humphrey Jennings, *Pandaemonium, 1660–1886: The Coming of the Machine as Seen by Contemporary Observers* (New York, 1985), 115; *Boston Newsletter*, Feb. 27, 1772; Duke de la Rochefoucault Liancourt, *Travels through the United States of North America . . .* (London, 1799), II, 380.
4. *PA*, July 15, 1762; Thomas, *Religion and the Decline of Magic*, 650–655; James Sharpe, *Instruments of Darkness: Witchcraft in England, 1550–1750* (New York, 1996), 229–230, 257–275, 290–293; Alan Macfarlane, *The Culture of Capitalism* (Oxford, 1987), 79–82, 100–101.
5. *DUR*, Sept. 4, 1788; *SAS*, XII, 244; "Your Constant Reader," and "A Bristol Conjuror," *BC*, Feb. 17, 1762; "Crito," *LEP*, Mar. 15, 1762; Jonathan Barry, "Piety and the Patient: Medicine and Religion in Eighteenth Century Bristol," in Roy Porter, ed., *Patients and Practitioners: Lay Perceptions of Medicine in Pre-Industrial Society* (Cambridge, 1985), 160–161.
6. Diary of James Robson, 1787, Add. Mss. 38837, fo. 9, BL; Winslow C. Watson, ed., *Men and Times of the Revolution; or, Memoirs of Elkanah Watson, Including Journals of Travels* (New York, 1856), 96; Bryan Edwards, "Description of a Nocturnal Sky, as Surveyed Nearly Beneath the Line," *Massachusetts Magazine* 7 (1795), 370; "Valverdi," *Literary Magazine* 7 (1807), 449; Macfarlane, *Culture of Capitalism*, 80–81, 102–103. For the popularity of telescopes, see, for example, Nov. 12, 1720, *The Family Memoirs of the Rev. William Stukeley, M.D. . . .* (London, 1882), I, 75; Sept. 30, 1756, J. B. Paul, ed., *Diary of George Ridpath* (Edinburgh, 1910), 92; June 22, 1806, Drinker, *Diary*, III, 1940.
7. M. D'Archenholz, *A Picture of England . . .* (London, 1789), I, 136; Nikolai Mikhailovich Karamzin, *Letters of a Russian Traveler, 1789–1790 . . .* (New York, 1957), 181, 268; Mr. Pratt, *Gleanings through Wales, Holland, and Westphalia* (London, 1798), 167; Peter Borsay, *The English Urban Renaissance: Culture and Society in the Provincial Town, 1660–1770* (Oxford, 1989), 22, 34.
8. Torrington, *Diaries*, II, 195, 196, I, 20; John Henry Manners, *Journal of a Tour through North and South Wales* (London, 1805), 64; Gary Cross, *A Social History of Leisure since 1600* (State College, Pa., 1990), 59.
9. James Essex, *Journal of a Tour through Part of Flanders and France in August 1773*, ed. W. M. Fawcett (Cambridge, 1888), 2.

10. Pierre Goubert, *The Ancien Régime: French Society, 1600–1750*, trans. Steve Cox (London, 1973), 223; William Edward Mead, *The Grand Tour in the Eighteenth Century* (New York, 1972), 222, 359; Christopher Friedrichs, *The Early Modern City, 1450–1750* (London, 1995), 25.
11. *Midnight the Signal: In Sixteen Letters to a Lady of Quality* (London, 1779), I, 147, passim; Koslofsky, "Court Culture," 744; Barbara DeWolfe Howe, *Discoveries of America: Personal Accounts of British Emigrants to North America during the Revolutionary Era* (Cambridge, 1997), 217; Pinkerton, *Travels*, II, 790.
12. *US and WJ*, Oct. 13, 1733; *A Humorous Description of the Manners and Fashions of Dublin* (Dublin, 1734), 5; *The Memoirs of Charles-Lewis, Baron de Pollnitz* . . . (London, 1739), I, 411; Robert Anderson, *The Works of John Moore, M.D.* . . . (Edinburgh, 1820), 171; Roy Porter, *The Creation of the Modern World: The Untold Story of the British Enlightenment* (New York, 2000), 435–436; Peter Clark, *British Clubs and Societies, 1580–1800: The Origins of an Associational World* (Oxford, 2000).
13. *British Journal*, Sept. 12, 1730.
14. Henry Fielding, *An Enquiry into the Causes of the Late Increase of Robbers and Related Writings*, ed. Malvin R. Zirker (Middletown, Ct., 1988), 231; *LC*, Sept. 9, 1758, Mar. 19, 1785; J. Hanway, *Letter to Mr. John Spranger* . . . (London, 1754), 34; Frederique Pitou, "Jeunesse et Désordre Social: Les 'Coureurs de Nuit' à Laval au XVIIIe Siècle," *Revue d'Histoire Moderne et Contemporaine* 47 (2000), 70; *G & NDA*, Nov. 27, 1767; Horace Walpole, *Correspondence with Sir Horace Mann*, ed. W. S. Lewis et al. (New Haven, 1967), VIII, 47; Bruce Lenman and Geoffrey Parker, "The State, the Community and the Criminal Law in Early Modern Europe," in V.A.C. Gatrell et al., eds., *Crime and the Law: The Social History of Crime in Western Europe since 1500* (London, 1980), 38; J. Paul De Castro, *The Gordon Riots* (London, 1926); Carl Bridenbaugh, *Cities in Revolt: Urban Life in America, 1743–1776* (Oxford, 1971), 300–303.
15. *DUR*, Nov. 30, 1785; Borsay, *Urban Renaissance*, passim; Peter Clark, *The English Alehouse: A Social History* (London, 1983), 256–259.
16. 9 George II. c.20; "Mémoire sur Necessité d'Éclairer la Ville, Présenté par Quelques Citoyens au Conseil," Jan. 26, 1775, Archives Geneve, Geneva; J. M. Beattie, *Policing and Punishment in London, 1660–1750: Urban Crime and the Limits of Terror* (Oxford, 2001), 221–223; Wolfgang Schivelbusch, *Disenchanted Night: The Industrialization of Light in the Nineteenth Century*, trans. Angela Davies (Berkeley, Calif., 1988), 9–14.
17. *Times*, May 14, 1807; "F. W.," *LM*, Jan. 6, 1815; Jane Austen, *Sandition* (Boston, 1975), 221; O'Dea, *Lighting*, 98; Pounds, *Home*, 388; Brian T. Robson, *Urban Growth: An Approach* (London, 1973), 178–183; John A. Jakle, *City Lights: Illuminating the American Night* (Baltimore, 2001), 26–37.
18. *LC*, Jan. 17, 1758; "Case of the Petitioners against the Bill, for Establishing a Nightly-Watch within the City of Bristol," 1755, BL; *PA*, July 15, 1785; Alan Williams, *The Police of Paris, 1718–1789* (Baton Rouge, 1979), 71; Ruff, *Violence*, 88–91.
19. *BC*, Aug. 11, 1762; David Philips and Robert D. Storch, *Policing Provincial England, 1829–1856: The Politics of Reform* (London, 1999), 63; Beattie, *Crime*, 67–72; Elaine A. Reynolds, *Before the Bobbies: The Night Watch and Police Reform in Metropolitan London, 1720–1830* (Stanford, Calif., 1998); Stanley H. Palmer, *Police and Protest in England and Ireland, 1780–1850* (Cambridge, 1988), passim; David Philips, "'A New Engine of Power and Authority': The Institutionalization of Law-Enforcement in England 1780–1830," in Gatrell et al., eds., *Crime and the Law*, 155–189; James F. Richardson, *Urban Police in the United States* (Port Washington, N.Y., 1974), 19–28.
20. "Night Hawk," *Mechanics Free Press* (Philadelphia), Nov. 7, 1829; Louis Bader, "Gas Illumination in New York City, 1823–1863" (Ph.D. diss., New York Univ., 1970), 334;

Mary Lee Mann, ed., *A Yankee Jeffersonian: Selections from the Diary and Letters of William Lee of Massachusetts* (Cambridge, Mass., 1958), 37; Pounds, *Home*, 388; Johan Goudsblom, *Fire and Civilization* (London, 1992), 150, 176–178. For the salutary impact of street lighting, in general, on crime, see Jane Jacobs, *The Death and Life of Great American Cities* (New York, 1961), 41–42; Kate Painter, "Designing Out Crime—Lighting, Safety and the Urban Realm," in Andrew Lovatt et al., eds., *The 24-Hour City . . .* (Manchester, 1994), 133–138.

21. Maurice Rollinat, *Oeuvres* (Paris, 1972), II, 282. Allan Silver, "The Demand for Order in Civil Society: A Review of Some Themes in the History of Urban Crime, Police and Riot," in D. Bordua, ed., *The Police: Six Sociological Essays* (New York, 1967), 1–24; Anna Clark, *Women's Silence, Men's Violence: Sexual Assault in England, 1770–1845* (New York, 1987), 118.
22. Ralph Waldo Emerson, *Essays & Lectures*, ed. Joel Porte (New York, 1983), 1067; Joachim Schlör, *Nights in the Big City: Paris, Berlin, London 1840–1930*, trans. Pierre Gottfried Imhof and Dafydd Rees Roberts (London, 1998), 287; Mark J. Bouman, "The 'Good Lamp Is the Best Police' Metaphor and Ideologies of the Nineteenth-Century Urban Landscape," *American Studies* 32 (1991), 66.
23. The Journeyman Engineer, *The Great Unwashed* (London, 1869), 199; A. H. Bullen, ed., *The Works of Thomas Middleton* (1885; rpt. edn., New York, 1964), VIII, 14; A. Roger Ekirch, "Sleep We Have Lost: Pre-industrial Slumber in the British Isles," *AHR* 106 (2001), 383–385; Thomas A. Wehr, "A 'Clock for All Seasons' in the Human Brain," in R. M. Buijs et al., eds., *Hypothalamic Integration of Circadian Rhythms* (Amsterdam, 1996), 319–340; Thomas A. Wehr, "The Impact of Changes in Nightlength (Scotoperiod) on Human Sleep," in F.W. Turek and P.C. Zee, eds., *Neurobiology of Sleep and Circadian Rhythms* (New York, 1999), 263–285; P. Lippmann, "Dreams and Psychoanalysis: A Love-Hate Story," *Psychoanlytic Psychology* 17 (2000), 627–650. Of dreams, Roger Bastide has written: "In our Western civilization, . . . the bridges between the diurnal and nocturnal halves of man have been cut. Of course, people can always be found—and not only in the lower classes of society—who consult dream books, or who at least examine their dreams and assign to them a role in their lives. But such vital functions of the dream remain personal and never become institutionalized. On the contrary, far from constituting regularized norms of conduct they are considered aberrant; they are classed as 'superstitions'; sometimes it is even suggested that people who look for significance or direction in dreams are not entirely all there" ("The Sociology of the Dream," in Gustave Von Grunebaum, *The Dream and Human Societies* [Berkeley, Calif., 1966], 200–201).
24. R. W. Flint, ed., *Marinetti: Selected Writings*, trans. R. W. Flint and Arthur A. Coppotelli (New York, 1979), 56.
25. Frederic J. Baumgartner, *A History of Papal Elections* (New York, 2003), 191; Rev. Dr. Render, *A Tour through Germany . . .* (London, 1801), II, 37. Although the year is wrongly given as 1816, the *Zeitung* article, "Arguments against Light," is translated in M. Luckiesh, *Artificial Light: Its Influence upon Civilization* (New York, 1920), 157–158.
26. Schlör, *Nights in the Big City*, trans. Imhof and Roberts, 66; Christian Augustus Gottlief Goede, *A Foreigner's Opinion of England . . .*, trans. Thomas Horne (Boston, 1822), 47; Richard L. Bushman, *The Refinement of America: Persons, Houses, Cities* (New York, 1992), 365; Garnert, *Lampan*, 126; Schindler, *Rebellion*, 221; Eugen Weber, *France Fin de Siècle* (Cambridge, Mass., 1986), 54.
27. Victor Hugo, *Les Misérables*, trans. Isabel F. Hapgood (New York, 1887), II, Pt. 1, 313–316; Schivelbusch, *Disenchanted Night*, 105, 97–114, passim; Wolfgang Schivelbusch, "The Policing of Street Lighting," *Yale French Studies* 73 (1987), 73, 61–74, pas-

sim; Eugène Defrance, *Histoire de l'Éclairage des Rues de Paris* (Paris, 1904), 104–106; Garnert, *Lampan*, 123–129.

28. Joseph Lawson, *Letters to the Young on Progress in Pudsey during the Last Sixty Years* (Stanningley, Eng., 1887), 33; [Charles Shaw], *When I Was a Child* (1903; rpt. edn., Firle, Eng., 1977), 37; Silvia Mantini, "Notte in Città, Notte in Campagna tra Medioevo ed Età Moderna," in Mario Sbriccoli, ed., *La Notte: Ordine, Sicurezza e Disciplinamento in Età Moderna* (Florence, 1991), 42; Pounds, *Culture*, 420–423; James Obelkevich, *Religion and Rural Society: South Lindsey, 1825–1875* (Oxford, 1976), passim; Judith Develin, *The Superstitious Mind: French Peasants and the Supernatural in the Nineteenth Century* (New Haven, 1987).
29. George Sturt, *Change in the Village* (1912; rpt. edn., Harmondsworth, Eng., 1984), 121, 8.
30. Dagobert D. Runes, *The Diary and Sundry Observations of Thomas Alva Edison* (New York, 1948), 232; Ekirch, "Sleep We have Lost," 383–385; Patricia Edmonds, "In Jampacked Days, Sleep Time is the First to Go," *USA Today*, April 10, 1995; Andree Brooks, "For Teen-Agers, Too Much to Do, Too Little Time for Sleep," *New York Times*, Oct. 31, 1996; Amanda Onion, "The No-Doze Soldier: Military Seeking Radical Ways of Stumping Need for Sleep," Dec. 18, 2002, Web: www.abcNEWS.com. For explorations of nighttime in modern life, see Murray Melbin, *Night as Frontier: Colonizing the World after Dark* (New York, 1987); Kevin Coyne, *A Day in the Night of America* (New York, 1992); A. Alvarez, *Night: Night Life, Night Language, Sleep, and Dreams* (New York, 1995); Christopher Dewdney, *Acquainted with the Night: Excursions through the World after Dark* (New York, 2004).
31. Montague Summers, ed., *Dryden: The Dramatic Works* (1932; rpt. edn., New York, 1968), VI, 159; Arthur R. Upgren, "Night Blindness," *Amicus Journal* 17 (1996), 22–25; David L. Crawford, "Light Pollution—Theft of the Night," in Derek McNally, ed., *The Vanishing Universe: Adverse Environmental Impacts on Astronomy* (Cambridge, 1994), 27–33.
32. Warren E. Leary, "Russia's Space Mirror Bends Light of Sun into the Dark," *NYT, Times*, Feb. 5, 1993; "Russian Space Mirror Reflector Prototype Fails," *Boston Globe*, Feb.5, 1999.

INDEX

Page numbers in *italics* refer to illustrations